Prosocial Motives, Emotions, and Behavior

Prosocial Motives, Emotions, and Behavior

The Better Angels of Our Nature

Edited by Mario Mikulincer and Phillip R. Shaver

American Psychological Association • Washington, DC

First Printing August 2009
Second Printing December 2010

Published by
American Psychological Association
750 First Street, NE
Washington, DC 20002
www.apa.org

To order
APA Order Department
P.O. Box 92984
Washington, DC 20090-2984
Tel: (800) 374-2721; Direct: (202) 336-5510
Fax: (202) 336-5502; TDD/TTY: (202) 336-6123
Online: www.apa.org/books/
E-mail: order@apa.org

In the U.K., Europe, Africa, and the Middle East, copies may be ordered from
American Psychological Association
3 Henrietta Street
Covent Garden, London
WC2E 8LU England

Typeset in Goudy by Stephen McDougal, Mechanicsville, MD

Printer: United Book Press, Inc., Baltimore, MD
Cover Designer: Mercury Publishing Services, Rockville, MD
Technical/Production Editor: Kathryn Funk

Library of Congress Cataloging-in-Publication Data

Prosocial motives, emotions, and behavior : the better angels of our nature / edited by Mario Mikulincer and Phillip R. Shaver. — 1st ed.
p. cm.
Includes bibliographical references and index.
ISBN-13: 978-1-4338-0546-2
ISBN-10: 1-4338-0546-4
1. Helping behavior. 2. Altruism. 3. Empathy. I. Mikulincer, Mario. II. Shaver, Phillip R.

BF637.H4P76 2010
155.2'5—dc22 2009011240

British Library Cataloguing-in-Publication Data
A CIP record is available from the British Library.

Printed in the United States of America
First Edition

CONTENTS

CONTRIBUTORS

Christopher R. Agnew, PhD, Department of Psychology, Purdue University, West Lafayette, IN

Leslie Ashburn-Nardo, PhD, Department of Psychology, Indiana University–Purdue University Indianapolis

Daniel Bar-Tal, PhD, Department of Education, Tel-Aviv University, Tel-Aviv, Israel

C. Daniel Batson, PhD, Department of Psychology, University of Kansas, Lawrence

Lane Beckes, MA, Department of Psychology, University of Minnesota, Twin Cities

Yael Ben-David, MA, Department of Psychology, Tel-Aviv University, Tel-Aviv, Israel

Nancy L. Collins, PhD, Department of Psychology, University of California, Santa Barbara

John F. Dovidio, PhD, Department of Psychology, Yale University, New Haven, CT

Nancy Eisenberg, PhD, Department of Psychology, Arizona State University, Tempe

Brooke C. Feeney, PhD, Department of Psychology, Carnegie Mellon University, Pittsburgh, PA

Beverley Fehr, PhD, Department of Psychology, University of Winnipeg, Winnipeg, Manitoba, Canada

Frank D. Fincham, PhD, Family Institute, Florida State University, Tallahassee

Máire B. Ford, PhD, Department of Psychology, Loyola Marymount University, Los Angeles, CA

Samuel L. Gaertner, PhD, Department of Psychology, University of Delaware, Newark

Matthew T. Gailliot, PhD, Faculty of Social and Behavioral Sciences, University of Amsterdam, Amsterdam, The Netherlands

AnaMarie C. Guichard, PhD, Department of Psychology, California State University, Stanislaus

Samer Halabi, PhD, Department of Psychology, Zfat College, Zfat, Israel

Eran Halperin, PhD, Department of Psychology, Stanford University, Stanford, CA

Gal Harapz-Gorodeisky, PhD, Department of Education and Psychology, Open University, Raanana, Israel

Grit Hein, PhD, Center for Social Neuroscience and Neuroeconomics, University of Zürich, Zürich, Switzerland

Gilad Hirschberger, PhD, Department of Psychology, Bar-Ilan University, Ramat Gan, Israel

Salomon Israel, MA, Department of Psychology, Hebrew University, Jerusalem, Israel

James D. Johnson, PhD, Department of Psychology, University of North Carolina—Wilmington

Heidi S. Kane, MA, Department of Psychology, University of California, Santa Barbara

Johan C. Karremans, PhD, Behavioral Science Institute, Radboud University Nijmegen, Nijmegen, The Netherlands

Ariel Knafo, PhD, Department of Psychology, Hebrew University, Jerusalem, Israel

Mario Mikulincer, PhD, School of Psychology, Interdisciplinary Center, Herzliya, Israel

Arie Nadler, PhD, Department of Psychology, Tel-Aviv University, Tel-Aviv, Israel

Heather Orom, PhD, Karmanos Cancer Institute, Wayne State University, Detroit, MI

Adam R. Pearson, MA, Department of Psychology, Yale University, New Haven, CT

Louis A. Penner, PhD, Karmanos Cancer Institute, Wayne State University, Detroit, MI, and Research Center for Group Dynamics, University of Michigan, Ann Arbor

Caryl E. Rusbult, PhD, Department of Social Psychology, Free University, Amsterdam, The Netherlands

Tamar Saguy, MA, Department of Psychology, University of Connecticut, Storrs

Shalom H. Schwartz, PhD, Department of Psychology, Hebrew University, Jerusalem, Israel

Phillip R. Shaver, PhD, Department of Psychology, University of California, Davis

Moran Shemesh-Iron, MA, Department of Psychology, Bar-Ilan University, Ramat Gan, Israel

Nurit Shnabel, PhD, Department of Psychology, Yale University, New Haven, CT
Jeffry A. Simpson, PhD, Department of Psychology, University of Minnesota, Twin Cities
Tania Singer, PhD, Center for Social Neuroscience and Neuroeconomics, University of Zürich, Zürich, Switzerland
Eliane Sommerfeld, PhD, Department of Behavioral Sciences, Ariel University Center, Ariel, Israel
Rami Tolmacz, PhD, Department of Psychology, Bar-Ilan University, Ramat Gan, Israel
Paul A. M. Van Lange, PhD, Department of Social Psychology, Free University, Amsterdam, The Netherlands

PREFACE

In a world riddled with greed, crime, violence, and intergroup conflict, the need for a better understanding of prosocial feelings and actions is obvious. Within the social and behavioral sciences, and now within the brain sciences as well, there are several fascinating and empirically supported theoretical and methodological perspectives on prosocial behavior, but they rarely get drawn into a single constructively critical and potentially integrative conversation. Some writers, for example, have considered prosocial behavior from genetic, or evolutionary, vantage points by treating "selfish" genes and selfish human beings as equivalent. We know, however, that selfish (i.e., self-perpetuating) genes can sometimes multiply by promoting cooperation, love, and human kindness in situations in which these prosocial qualities foster survival and reproduction. Similarly, there have been many insight-provoking social–psychological experiments on helping behavior, but the findings are rarely used to craft beneficial interventions in the real world. There are many important findings in research on the development of pro- and antisocial motives and behavior during childhood, but they are not often mentioned in discussions of evolutionary psychology.

The time is therefore right for an open, creative conversation among experts on the variety of approaches to prosocial motives, emotions, and behavior, including the study of basic processes and the evaluation of promising interventions and prospects for social change. The timeliness and social relevance of theory and research related to empathy, compassion, and generous behavior led us to choose this topic as the theme of the inaugural Herzliya Symposium on Personality and Social Psychology. This annual symposium is intended to explore cutting-edge, socially significant topics with the help of a group of world-class researchers who are invited to come to the Interdisciplinary Center, Herzliya, Israel, engage in intense constructively critical but also collaborative discussions, and then create a book that can be shared with other members of the discipline as well as a broader group of interested readers. The present volume is the first in the Herzliya Series on Personality and Social Psychology.

The chapter authors generously and enthusiastically agreed to deliver lectures, participate in hours of discussion of the lectures, and then return home and prepare chapters based on the lectures and discussion. The Herzliya Symposium was cohosted by the two volume editors, and we worked, together with the chapter authors, to make the book as accessible, coherent, and clear as possible, so that it is suitable for researchers and application-oriented professionals, as well as for university classes and seminars at the graduate or upper-level undergraduate level. The book is well written throughout, so it should also be of interest to journalists and educated readers from diverse professions. The book provides a state-of-the-art review of the major theoretical perspectives on prosocial behavior; the basic psychological processes underlying such behavior; and recent research on core prosocial emotions and their roles in close relationships, groups, and intergroup relations.

We are extremely grateful to everyone who made the first Herzliya conference and the preparation of this book so stimulating and successful. We thank all of the speakers and chapter authors—an amazing group of scholars and admirable human beings. We are especially grateful to Professor Uriel Reichmann, president of the Interdisciplinary Center Herzlyia, who generously provided financial and staff support for an annual series of conferences on personality and social psychology. We thank the staff of the New School of Psychology in the Interdisciplinary Center Herzliya—Ziv Ravfogel and Tsachi Ein-Dor—who handled all of the arrangements for the conference, dealt effectively with the many onsite details, and coped masterfully with the inevitable glitches and emergencies. We would also like to acknowledge and thank the Fetzer Institute, which has made studies of compassionate love and human virtues possible. We thank Maureen Adams, senior acquisitions editor in the American Psychological Association Books Department, for seeing the value of this project from the beginning and being a generous, thoughtful, and supportive friend during the book's preparation. Finally, we thank Caroline Barnes, Ron Teeter, Kathryn Funk, and Steve Ingle for their careful copyediting and indexing, respectively.

Mario Mikulincer, PhD
Interdisciplinary Center, Herzliya, Israel

Phillip R. Shaver, PhD
University of California, Davis

Prosocial Motives, Emotions, and Behavior

INTRODUCTION

MARIO MIKULINCER AND PHILLIP R. SHAVER

When each day's news overflows with lurid reports of fraud, theft, rape, domestic violence, and war, it's easy to agree with philosopher Thomas Hobbes (1651/2008) that human beings, unless constrained by an all-powerful sovereign, are destined to live in "continual fear and danger of violent death" (p. 86), an existence that is "nasty, brutish, and short" (p. 86). Almost 2 centuries after Hobbes made that dismal claim, Charles Darwin's (1859) theory of evolution seemed to justify Alfred Lord Tennyson's (1850/1906) poetic image of "nature [including human nature], red in tooth and claw" (p. 72). In 1976, Richard Dawkins's influential book, *The Selfish Gene*, added—partly through readers' misperceptions—the idea that evolutionary theory and genetics imply that human beings and their genes are inherently selfish and hence conducive to Hobbes's imagined "war of all against all" (Hobbes, 1651/2008, p. vii).

In recent years, however, there has been an upsurge of interest in empathy, compassion, altruism, and forgiveness—laudable human capacities that Abraham Lincoln called "the better angels of our nature" in his 1861 call for national unity, a phrase used in a 2009 speech by Barack Obama on his way to being inaugurated as president. These better angels of our nature have been embraced by a new *positive psychology* (e.g., Seligman, 2002). And simultaneously, primatologists (e.g., De Waal, 1996, 2006) and evolutionary biologists (e.g., Richerson & Boyd, 2005; Sober & Wilson, 1998) have begun to emphasize the evolutionary roots of *prosocial behavior*—voluntary behavior enacted with the intention of benefiting others. It is increasingly clear that "selfish genes" can achieve their goal of self-replication by fostering generous prosocial behavior. Although the genes "selfishly" act to replicate themselves, they often do so by encouraging compassion, kindness, and cooperation.

This emphasis on positive, prosocial aspects of the human mind inspired us to create a comprehensive book on the psychology of prosocial behavior viewed from various levels of analysis, from the neural to the societal. We invited experts on the science of prosocial behavior to explain their ideas and research findings and encouraged them to trace the historical and theoretical background of their research and speculate about where it might lead in the future. Readers of this book will learn a great deal about prosocial motives and values; about emotions such as empathy and compassion; and about the diversity of empathic, generous, and loving behavior—along with the methods and measures used to study these issues. Readers will also learn about forces and processes that impede prosocial behavior.

The volume is organized into five parts. Part I, focusing on major theoretical perspectives, includes six chapters on social psychological, evolutionary, psychodynamic, personality, and neuroscience perspectives on prosocial motives, emotions, and behavior. Part II, focusing on basic processes underlying prosocial emotions and behavior, includes six chapters on genetic factors, developmental processes, self-regulatory mechanisms, power and self-esteem motives, existential anxieties and defenses, and basic values. Part III includes four chapters dealing with theory and research concerning core prosocial emotions (compassionate love, gratitude, forgiveness, and generosity), and Part IV includes three chapters on the role of prosocial motives, emotions, and behavior in close relationships, such as romantic relationships and marriages. Finally, Part V considers the role of prosocial feelings and behavior at the group and societal levels. It includes three chapters on harmonious intergroup relations, intergroup reconciliation following conflicts, and peace making.

In chapter 1, Daniel Batson, one of the most innovative and influential of the researchers who study empathy—or empathic concern, as he calls it—and its role in prosocial behavior, summarizes his provocative studies and innovative theoretical contributions to the understanding of empathy. He argues convincingly that empathy is a natural human capacity that contributes to prosocial behavior, one that cannot be explained away by selfish motives. He also shows that people have different or mixed reactions to their fellow human beings' suffering, and that some of these reactions, including empathic concern, motivate people to behave prosocially, whereas others, including what Batson calls *personal distress*, may not.

In chapter 2, expanding on Batson's claim that empathy is an evolved human capacity, Jeffry Simpson and Lane Beckes explain how the capacities for empathy and prosocial behavior might have evolved in humans. Explaining our exceptional degree of sociality and interdependence requires multiple midlevel evolutionary concepts: inclusive fitness, reciprocal altruism, group-level selection, and gene-culture coevolution. There is no other mammalian species with such large, complex, and highly interdependent groups that depend on an ability to imagine and empathize with each other's experiences. This ability is the subject of several of the other chapters in the volume.

In chapter 3, Louis Penner and Heather Orom summarize the extensive body of empirical evidence for a prosocial personality syndrome, or at least for multiple prosocial personality traits. These specific traits can be conceptualized in terms of two larger traits: Other-Oriented Empathy, characterized by social responsibility, empathic concern, perspective taking (i.e., cognitive empathy), and other-oriented moral reasoning; and Helpfulness, the tendency to engage in prosocial behavior without undue personal distress. The prosocial personality megatraits are stable over time; relate positively to real-world prosocial behavior, such as volunteering in the community; and interact with situational forces in theoretically predictable ways.

In chapter 4, Phillip Shaver, Mario Mikulincer, and Moran Shemesh-Iron use attachment theory as a basis for studying prosocial motives and behavior. The theory divides human motivation into several domains, such as attachment, exploration, caregiving, and sex, and considers the evolutionary function of the behavioral system that governs each domain. Emotions such as empathy, sympathy, and caring fall within the domain of the caregiving system. Shaver et al. explain the development of a Caregiving Behavioral System Scale, which measures "hyperactivated" and "deactivated" caregiving. The former pattern is associated, across different kinds of relationships, with personal distress and perceived deficits in emotion-regulation, self-regulation, and social skills. The second pattern, deactivated caregiving, is associated with reduced empathy, more negative appraisals of others, and motives to maintain independence and emotional distance.

In chapter 5, Rami Tolmacz reviews psychoanalytic explanations of concern for others. Whereas Freud and some of his earliest followers (e.g., Klein) considered concern for others to be secondary to, or an offshoot of, aggression, object relations and intersubjectivity theorists paid greater attention to children's innate capacity for empathy. Tolmacz shows how the more recent psychoanalytic theories can be combined with Buber's famous conceptualization of I–Thou relationships (between human subjects, as distinct from objects) and with Bowlby's attachment theory to analyze clinical cases in which a person treats either self or others as objects rather than subjects.

In chapter 6, Grit Hein and Tania Singer move to the neuroscientific level and consider how some of the distinctions made by the other chapter authors are manifested in the brain. They find different neural correlates of cognitive perspective taking, on the one hand, and empathy, or sharing another person's affective state, on the other. They also find correlations between scores on empathy questionnaires and empathy-related activation in anterior cingulate cortex and anterior insula, which will please users of self-report measures who often worry about response biases and invalid self-reports. It is interesting that specific patterns of brain activation are related to a person's affective ties to a suffering other, his or her appraisal of whether the other's suffering is justified, his or her prior experience with the kind of suffering being encountered, and the intensity of the other's pain. Many exciting ideas for future research are proposed in this chapter.

Part II begins with chapter 7 by Nancy Eisenberg, who, like Batson, is a pioneer in the study of prosocial behavior, especially its childhood and developmental origins. In this chapter, Eisenberg argues for distinguishing among different kinds of empathy-related reactions (e.g., empathy, sympathy, personal distress). She finds that sympathy may be preferable to empathy in situations in which empathy alone would cause physiological overarousal. She also shows that individual differences in self-regulation (including temperamental impulsivity and effortful control) play a role in sympathetic and altruistic behavior and that self-regulation accounts in part for associations among sympathy, moral judgment, and various forms of social and psychological maladjustment.

In chapter 8, Ariel Knafo and Salomon Israel review evidence from their own and other researchers' studies of the role of genes in prosocial behavior. They show that prosocial behavior is partially attributable to genes and that the heritability of prosocial behavior increases with age, perhaps because some of the skills involved, such as understanding other people's minds, take years to develop. Although there are relatively few behavior-genetic (e.g., twin) studies of prosocial behavior, Knafo and Israel have already moved to the level of molecular genetics to reveal some of the specific genes involved in human altruism. Their findings parallel results from genetic studies of other mammals.

In chapter 9, Matthew Gailliot offers a different perspective on self-regulation from the one developed by Eisenberg in chapter 7. Whereas Eisenberg focused on the role of individual differences in self-regulatory skills that protect a person from empathic overarousal and impulsivity, Gailliot emphasizes the discovery that self-regulation is impaired by previous self-regulatory exertion. This impairment occurs because glucose—the brain's source of energy—is 'burned' faster during self-regulation than it is replenished. Research on helping behavior reveals a similar pattern in which people are less helpful following previous self-regulatory effort. It is interesting that ingestion of glucose allows a person to continue helping even after self-regulatory depletion. This finding implies that resources, experiences, and skills that allow a person to store more glycogen, which gets converted into glucose when energy is needed, can make prosocial behavior more likely and more sustainable.

Continuing the analysis of factors that may interfere with successful helping behavior, Arie Nadler and Samer Halabi focus in chapter 10 on the fact that helping relations are often power relations between an agent who has more knowledge or resources and a recipient who is dependent on the agent's help. This can threaten the recipient's self-esteem, or in the case of one group or nation helping another, the recipient group's status. Nadler and Halabi's research on helping relations as power relations reveals some of the unintended consequences of social inequality for the willingness to provide or receive help. The outcome depends partly on how settled and accepted the status relations between the two parties are at the time help is offered. If the status relation is challenged, as in the case of feminists who no longer wanted men to hold doors open for them, what was initially considered helpful can be viewed as demeaning.

In chapter 11, Gilad Hirschberger considers another, perhaps even less expected, barrier to prosocial behavior—fear of death. He shows that requests for help that remind a person of mortality, such as being asked to sign an organ-donation agreement that will take effect upon one's death (when the organs will certainly no longer be needed), can be rejected because they arouse death anxiety. The same thing happens when a person encounters an apparently innocent other who has suffered serious bodily injury. Hirschberger reports a series of studies based on terror management theory, which explains the defenses, such as ethnocentrism and self-esteem enhancement, people use to avoid acknowledging their own mortality. In Hirschberger's studies, people's willingness to help was influenced by a combination of mortality salience (induced by a request for organs after death or by seeing a person in a wheelchair), values, and attributions of blame for an accident that caused bodily harm.

In chapter 12, Shalom Schwartz, a pioneer in the study of human values and social behavior, argues that basic values can motivate or inhibit prosocial behavior, both consciously and unconsciously. He explicates the cross-culturally universal structure of 10 basic values, which are organized around the two dimensions of self-enhancement/self-transcendence and conservatism/openness to experience, and he explains the implications of this structure for prosocial behavior. Schwartz reports a series of studies showing that benevolence, universalism, and conformity values motivate prosocial behavior, whereas power and achievement values interfere with it. He also comments on why benevolence and universalism, the most common motivators of prosocial behavior, are two of the three values considered most important to people in the 76 cultures that have been studied to date.

Part III of the volume begins with Beverley Fehr's chapter (chap. 13) on the prosocial emotion of compassionate love—a feeling or attitude toward others that includes caring, concern, tenderness, and a desire to understand, support, and help. In the first section of the chapter, she presents both experts' and laypeople's definitions of compassionate love. In the second section, she discusses the various contexts in which compassionate love may be experienced. She reviews key findings from a program of research on the predictors, correlates, and outcomes of compassionate love in various relational contexts. In the final section of the chapter, she offers suggestions for future research aimed at understanding the role of compassionate love in personal well-being and healthy interpersonal relationships.

In chapter 14, Mario Mikulincer and Phillip Shaver show that well-documented links between the emotion of gratitude and prosocial behavior depend to some extent on a person's sense of attachment security. More secure individuals have more uniformly positive experiences of gratitude and more easily transform positive feelings into prosocial actions. Less secure individuals have complex, mixed experiences of gratitude (tinged, for example, with feeling obligated or diminished by someone else's generous behavior). The link between gratitude and prosocial behavior can be strengthened or disrupted by priming a person with thoughts of a secure or an insecure relationship. Hence, "to an important extent, moral virtue depends on feeling loved, valued, supported, and cared for, both in the moment and over the years" (p. 280).

Johan Karremans and Paul Van Lange show in chapter 15 that forgiveness—a prosocial act and emotional state that is often described and recommended to injured parties as a conscious decision process—is influenced by situational circumstances and unconscious processes. People who are reminded, even only subtly, of the concepts of justice or helpfulness are more likely to be forgiving, as are those who are reminded of a close relationship or are induced to feel momentarily more powerful. They are also more likely to forgive an offense if they are encouraged to frame it as having happened a long time ago, rather than very recently. The authors' research on such influences causes them to believe that conscious forgiveness, and achieving a stable sense of forgiveness, is not just a conscious matter but often involves a conscious overlay on unconscious or unattended processes.

In chapter 16, Eliane Sommerfeld reports a series of studies designed to illuminate the subjective experience of another prosocial emotion or kind of action: generosity. She finds that generosity, like gratitude, can have both positive and negative aspects. On the positive side, a person who engages in a generous act may feel virtuous and pleased to be the recipient of another person's gratitude. On the negative side, the person may feel that the generous act was costly or should have been even more generous. Sommerfeld shows that measures of these four aspects of generosity are related to a host of other personality and attachment measures. It is interesting that negative aspects of generosity bear some resemblance to Freud's early ideas about "anal" personality traits, such as stinginess or miserliness.

At the beginning of Part IV, Caryl Rusbult and Christopher Agnew (chap. 17) provide another perspective, based on interdependence theory, on prosocial behavior in the context of close relationships. They show how and why partners in close relationships sometimes exhibit such behaviors as accommodation, forgiveness, and sacrifice and engage in relationship-enhancing cognitive maneuvers such as derogation of alternatives and maintenance of positive illusions. They explain how self-interested motives can be psychologically transformed into prorelationship motives and states, such as commitment and trust. They also review research on what they call mutual cyclical growth, the interdependence process whereby each person's prosocial motives and behaviors feed back on and influence the other's motives and behaviors.

In chapter 18, Frank Fincham considers feelings and acts of forgiveness within close relationships, emphasizing both their importance to relationship quality and the difficulty with which they are chosen. He provides an overview of the major theoretical and methodological approaches to the study of forgiveness in close relationships and describes the concurrent and longitudinal correlates of forgiveness among intimates. He considers such issues as communication processes related to forgiveness, victim versus transgressor perspectives on forgivable and unforgivable acts, and the sometimes "dark" side of forgiveness.

Nancy Collins, Máire Ford, AnaMarie Guichard, Heidi Kane, and Brooke Feeney explore in chapter 19 individual differences in the ability and willingness to provide responsive care to needy partners in close romantic or couple relationships. Adopting an attachment perspective, they analyze the personal and interpersonal factors that promote or interfere with effective caregiving, and describe the features (skills, personal resources, and motives) of sensitive and responsive caregiving. They present highlights from several of their probing studies that explored the interpersonal dynamics of caregiving in romantic couples and identify cognitive and emotional factors that enhance or interfere with responsive caregiving.

The final part of the volume considers prosocial behavior at the group and societal levels. In chapter 20, Jack Dovidio, James Johnson, Samuel Gaertner, Adam Pearson, Tamar Saguy, and Leslie Ashburn-Nardo consider the role of empathy, which has usually been studied in the context of personal relationships, in improving intergroup relations. They begin by briefly reviewing prior evidence for empathy as a common mediator in many practical interventions designed to reduce intergroup bias. They then describe a series of creative and revealing studies from their laboratories that examine factors that moderate (i.e., inhibit or facilitate) intergroup empathy. They explore how intergroup empathy directly affects intergroup attitudes and may have indirect effects by creating conditions for reciprocal prosocial action and increased trust between individuals and groups.

In chapter 21, Nurit Shnabel and Arie Nadler present a needs-based analysis of the process of reconciliation, explaining how the route to reconciliation is different for victims and perpetrators. Specifically, they argue that conflict threatens different psychological resources of victims and perpetrators, and that the threats contribute to maintenance of the conflict, whereas amelioration of the threats increases both parties' willingness to reconcile. Being a victim is associated with threat to one's status and power, whereas being a perpetrator threatens one's moral self-image and reputation in the wider community. To ameliorate these threats, victims need to be recognized as having rights for status and power, and perpetrators need be recognized as understood and accepted by the wider community. Negotiators can help to bring these threat-reducing perceptions to light. Shnabel and Nadler review recent experimental research on interpersonal and intergroup reconciliation that supports their needs-based model of reconciliation.

In the final chapter, chapter 22, Daniel Bar-Tal and Eran Halperin analyze intractable conflicts between groups and societies and the various psychological barriers that obstruct the peace process. After delineating and analyzing these barriers, Bar-Tal and Halperin consider ways of overcoming them, especially by illuminating future losses entailed by continuing a conflict. The authors provide many provocative ideas that should stimulate further theoretical development and empirical research.

As can be seen from these brief thumbnail sketches of the chapters, the authors endorse the idea that human beings have an innate capacity for prosocial motivation, emotion, and action, but they also show how often these prosocial forces can be blocked, inhibited, or overcome by more selfish, neurotic, or culturally engrained attitudes and values. This mixture of pro- and antisocial states within individuals is influenced by personality, past social experiences, social and cultural identities, and various contextual factors. To the same extent that it was unrealistic and overly simplistic to believe that humans and their genes are "selfish" and that human interactions are bound to be "red in tooth and claw" (Tennyson, 1850/1906, p. 72) it is overly simplistic to think that humans are largely and usually motivated by prosocial feelings and forces. Both research and common sense lead to the conclusion that human motives and emotions are complex and multivalent, and that social conditions can powerfully influence the degree to which human behavior is empathic, generous, and kind or vindictive, destructive, and cruel. Social scientists have made considerable progress in recent years in understanding what tips the balance for good or evil. We hope this book, a compendium of recent theory and research, contributes to the science of prosocial behavior and the social creation of a better world. Our goals will be achieved if the chapter authors' highly stimulating and rewarding lectures and discussions get communicated to readers in ways that promote the contributors' deeply held prosocial values.

REFERENCES

Darwin, C. (1859). *On the origin of species by means of natural selection.* London: John Murray.

Dawkins, R. (1976). *The selfish gene*. New York: Oxford University Press.

de Waal, F. B. M. (1996). *Good natured: The origins of right and wrong in humans and other animals*. Cambridge, MA: Harvard University Press.

de Waal, F. B. M. (2006). *Primates and philosophers: How morality evolved*. Princeton, NJ: Princeton University Press.

Hobbes, T. (2008). *Leviathan*. Charleston, SC: Forgotten Books. (Original work published 1651)

Richerson, P. J., & Boyd, R. (2005). *Not by genes alone: How culture transformed human evolution*. Chicago: University of Chicago Press.

Seligman, M. E. P. (2002). *Authentic happiness: Using the new positive psychology to realize your potential for lasting fulfillment*. New York: Simon & Schuster.

Sober, E., & Wilson, D. S. (1998). *Unto others: The evolution and psychology of unselfish behavior*. Cambridge, MA: Harvard University Press.

Tennyson, A. L. (1906). *In memoriam*. New York: Silver, Burdett and Company. (Original poem published 1850)

I

THEORETICAL PERSPECTIVES

1

EMPATHY-INDUCED ALTRUISTIC MOTIVATION

C. DANIEL BATSON

About 30 years ago, I began conducting research on the motivational repertoire of humans. Specifically, I was interested in motivation for helping. I wanted to know whether when we help others, our motivation is always and exclusively self-interested—universal egoism—or whether we are capable of being altruistically motivated as well.

To be honest, I started with a clear bias. I thought altruism was a myth. In the words of the wise and witty Duke de La Rouchefoucauld: "The most disinterested love is, after all, but a kind of bargain, in which the dear love of our own selves always proposes to be the gainer some way or other" (1691, Maxim 82). Bernard Mandeville (1714/1732) put it even more graphically:

> There is no merit in saving an innocent babe ready to drop into the fire. The action is neither good nor bad, and what benefit soever the infant received, we only obliged our selves, for to have seen it fall, and not strove to hinder it, would have caused a pain, which self-preservation compelled us to prevent. (p. 42)

Like La Rouchefoucauld and Mandeville, I assumed that everything we humans do, no matter how beneficial to others, is really directed toward the ultimate goal of one or more forms of self-benefit. But over the years, I have come to believe that this assumption is wrong.

What caused me to lose my faith in universal egoism was a series of experiments that colleagues and I conducted to test the *empathy–altruism hypothesis*—the hypothesis that empathic concern produces altruistic motive. Before I discuss that line of research, let me state explicitly what I mean by altruism. Depending on how altruism is defined, the question of its existence can be either profound or trivial. I hope my definition does not make the question trivial.

DEFINING ALTRUISM AND EGOISM

By *altruism* I mean a motivational state with the ultimate goal of increasing another's welfare. Altruism is juxtaposed to *egoism*, a motivational state with the ultimate goal of increasing one's own welfare. I use the term *ultimate* here to refer to means–end relations, not to a metaphysical first or final cause. An *ultimate goal* is an end in itself. In contrast, an *instrumental goal* is a stepping stone on the way to reaching an ultimate goal. If a barrier to reaching an instrumental goal arises, then alternative routes to the ultimate goal will be sought. Should the ultimate goal be reached while bypassing the instrumental goal, the motivational force will disappear. If a goal is ultimate, it cannot be bypassed in this way (Lewin, 1938). Both instrumental and ultimate goals should be distinguished from unintended consequences, results of an action—foreseen or unforeseen—that are not the goal of the action. Each ultimate goal defines a distinct goal-directed motive. Hence, altruism and egoism are distinct motives, even though they can co-occur.

Altruism and egoism, as defined, have much in common. Each refers to a motivational state; each is concerned with the ultimate goal of this motivational state; and for each, the ultimate goal is to increase someone's welfare. These common features provide the context for highlighting the crucial difference: Whose welfare is the ultimate goal? Is it another person's or one's own?

The term *altruism* has been used in the following three other ways, from which the present conception should be distinguished:

1. *As helping behavior, not motivation.* Some scholars set aside the issue of motivation, simply equating altruism with helping behavior (i.e., with acting in a way that benefits another). This definition has been common among developmental psychologists. It has also been common among evolutionary biologists, who have defined altruism as behavior that reduces an organism's reproductive fitness—the potential to put its genes in the next generation—relative to the reproductive

fitness of one or more other organisms. Using this definition, evolutionary biologists can speak of altruism across a very broad phylogenetic spectrum, ranging from social insects to humans (e.g., Dawkins, 1976; Hamilton, 1964; Trivers, 1971). However, as Sober and Wilson (1998) pointed out, it is important to distinguish between evolutionary altruism and psychological altruism. *Evolutionary altruism* is behavior that reduces one's reproductive fitness. *Psychological altruism* is motivation with the ultimate goal of increasing another's welfare. Sober and Wilson emphasized that there is no necessary connection between these two concepts. Evolutionary altruism is neither necessary nor sufficient to produce psychological altruism. I hope it is clear that my interest is in psychological altruism.

2. *As acting morally*. A second use of the term *altruism* focuses on a specific set of helpful acts—those that meet some standard of goodness or morality. The link between altruism and morality appears to be based on the juxtaposition of each to self-interest. Self-interest is often equated with selfishness, which is in turn often considered the epitome of immorality. Altruism involves other-interest rather than self-interest. It may seem that if self-interest is not moral, and altruism is not self-interest, then altruism is moral, but this logic is flawed. Apart from whether self-interest should be equated with immorality—Rawls (1971) and many others have challenged this equation—to say that A (altruism) is not B (self-interest) and B is not C (moral) does not imply that A is C. Altruistic motivation as I have defined it can produce behavior that, depending on the moral standard applied, is moral, amoral, or immoral. Similarly, egoistic motivation can produce behavior that is moral, amoral, or immoral.
3. *As helping in order to gain internal rather than external rewards*. A third use of altruism does consider the motivation for benefiting others. But rather than treating altruistic motivation as an alternative to egoistic motivation, the third use reduces altruism to a special form of egoism. This use, quite common among contemporary psychologists, defines altruism in a way that includes benefiting another as a means to benefit oneself, as long as the self-benefits are internally rather than externally administered. According to this definition, if you help in order to gain a good feeling, to avoid guilt, or to reduce your aversive arousal caused by witnessing another's suffering, then your motivation is altruistic. By my definition, these ultimate goals simply define relatively subtle forms of egoism.

Why Worry About Motivation?

Having offered my definition of altruism, it is time to face a pragmatic question: As long as a person in need is helped, why worry about the nature of the underlying motivation? The answer depends on one's interest. If one is interested only in getting help for this person in this situation, the nature of the motivation may not matter. If, however, one is interested in knowing more generally when and where help can be expected, and how effective it is likely to be—perhaps with an eye to creating a more caring society, then understanding the underlying motivation is crucial. Behavior is highly variable. Occurrence of a particular behavior, including helping, depends on the strength of the motive or motives that might evoke that behavior, and on (a) the strength of competing motives, if any; (b) how the behavior relates to each of these motives; and (c) other behavioral options available in the situation at the time (see chap. 4, this volume). It also depends on whether the behavior promotes an instrumental or an ultimate goal. The more directly a behavior promotes an ultimate goal, and the more uniquely it does so among the behavioral options available, the more likely the behavior is to occur. Behavior that promotes an instrumental goal can easily change if the causal association between the instrumental and ultimate goal changes or if behavioral pathways to the ultimate goal arise that bypass the instrumental goal. Lewin (1951) argued that invariance (and explanatory stability) is found not in behavior or consequences but in the link of a given motive to its ultimate goal.

A Failed Philosophical Finesse

It is also time for a little philosophical brush clearing. One frequently heard argument against the existence of altruism attempts to rule out its existence on logical rather than empirical grounds. The argument goes as follows: Even if it were possible for a person to have another's welfare as an ultimate goal, such a person would be interested in attaining this goal and would experience pleasure on doing so; therefore, even this apparent altruism would actually be a product of egoism.

Philosophers have shown that this argument, which invokes the general principle of psychological hedonism, fails because it confuses two different meanings of self and two different forms of hedonism (see MacIntyre, 1967). Concerning self, the meaning at issue for altruism is not self as agent (Who has the goal?) but self—and other—as object (Whose welfare is the goal?). Concerning hedonism, there are strong and weak forms. The strong form of psychological hedonism asserts that attainment of personal pleasure is always the goal of human action. The weak form asserts only that goal attainment always brings pleasure. The weak form is not inconsistent with the possibility that an ultimate goal of some action is to benefit another.

Pleasure obtained can be a consequence of reaching this goal without being the goal. The strong form of psychological hedonism is inconsistent with the possibility of altruism. But to affirm the strong form is simply to assert that altruistic motivation does not exist, not that it logically cannot exist. This affirmation is about empirical claims that may or may not be true. One can accept the weak form of psychological hedonism, as I do, and still entertain the existence of a motivational state with the ultimate goal of increasing another's welfare (i.e., altruistic motivation).

THE RESEARCH PROBLEM

Given my definitions of altruism and egoism, helping another person—even at great cost to self—may be altruistically motivated, egoistically motivated, or both (see chap. 5, this volume, for a conceptually similar typology of prosocial behavior). To know which it is, a person must determine whether benefit to the other is (a) an ultimate goal and any self-benefits are unintended consequences (altruism) or (b) an instrumental means to reach the ultimate goal of benefiting oneself (egoism).

If helping benefits both a person in need and the helper, as it often does, how are we to know which is the ultimate goal? This puzzle has led many scientists to give up on the question of the existence of altruism, concluding that it cannot be answered empirically—often adding that motivation does not really matter anyway (e.g., de Waal, 2008). I think their surrender is premature. I think that we can empirically discern people's ultimate goals. Indeed, we do it all the time. We do it when we infer whether a student is really interested or only seeking a better grade (e.g., What happens to the student's interest after the grades are turned in?), why a friend chooses one job over another, and whether politicians mean what they say or are only after votes. We also do it when someone does us a favor or is kind.

The following four principles are important when attempting to discern a person's ultimate goal:

1. We cannot trust self-reports. People often do not know—or will not tell—their ultimate goals.
2. We do not observe goals or intentions directly; we infer them from behavior.
3. If we observe a behavior that has two potential ultimate goals, the true ultimate goal cannot be discerned. It is like having one equation with two unknowns.
4. However, if we change the situation so that this behavior is no longer the best route to one of these goals, and we still observe the behavior, then that goal is not ultimate. We can cross it off the list of possible ultimate goals.

These principles suggest a strategy to test for the existence of altruistic motivation for helping. First, we need to identify a likely source of altruistic motivation to help. Second, we need to identify plausible egoistic ultimate goals of motivation from this source. Third, we need to vary the situation so that either the altruistic goal or one or more of the egoistic goals can be better reached without having to help. Finally, we need to see whether this variation reduces helping. If it does, this goal may be ultimate. If it does not, we can cross this goal off the list.

THE EMPATHY–ALTRUISM HYPOTHESIS AND ITS EGOISTIC ALTERNATIVES

Over the past 30 years, other social psychologists and I have used this general strategy to address the question of the existence of altruism in humans. The likely source of altruistic motivation that we have considered is empathic concern. By *empathic concern* I mean an other-oriented emotional response elicited by and congruent with the perceived welfare of someone in need. Empathic concern is other-oriented in that it involves feeling *for* the other. It includes feelings of sympathy, compassion, tenderness, and the like. This other-oriented emotion has been named as a source, if not *the* source, of altruism by Thomas Aquinas, David Hume, Adam Smith, Charles Darwin, Herbert Spencer, William McDougall, and several contemporary psychologists. Empathic concern should not be confused with the cognitive ability to correctly perceive another person's internal state—sometimes referred to as *empathic accuracy* (Ickes, 1993)—or with feeling *as* another person feels—referred to as *empathy*, *emotional contagion*, or *affective resonance* (de Waal, 2008; Hatfield, Caccioppo, & Rapson, 1994; chap. 6, this volume).

Considerable evidence supports the idea that empathic concern motivates helping directed toward reducing the empathy-inducing need (for extensive reviews, see Batson, 1991; chap. 7, this volume). However, evidence of increased motivation to help reveals nothing about the nature of that motivation. Relieving the other person's need could be (a) an ultimate goal producing self-benefits as unintended consequences, (b) an instrumental goal on the way to the ultimate goal of gaining one or more self-benefits, or (c) both. That is, the motivation could be altruistic, egoistic, or both.

The *empathy–altruism hypothesis* claims that empathic concern felt for a person in need produces altruistic motivation to relieve that need. But three possible self-benefits of empathy-induced helping have been identified, producing three egoistic alternatives: (a) *aversive-arousal reduction*—reducing the empathic concern caused by witnessing another in need; (b) *punishment avoidance*—avoiding empathy-specific material, social, and self-punishments; and (c) *reward seeking*—gaining empathy-specific material, social, and self-rewards. Advocates of the empathy–altruism hypothesis do not deny that relieving the empathy-inducing need is likely to enable the helper to reduce aversive arousal, avoid punishments, and gain rewards. However, they claim that these benefits to self are not the ultimate goal of empathy-induced helping, only unintended consequences. Advocates of the egoistic alternatives disagree. They claim that one or more of these self-benefits is the ultimate goal of the motivation to help produced by empathic concern.

EXPERIMENTAL DESIGNS TO TEST THE EMPATHY–ALTRUISM HYPOTHESIS AGAINST THE EGOISTIC ALTERNATIVES

Pursuing the strategy outlined previously, colleagues and I have conducted a series of experiments to test the empathy–altruism hypothesis against one or more of these three egoistic alternatives. Typically, although not always, we provide research participants with an opportunity to help a person in need—for example, a chance to take electric shocks in the place of a same-sex peer who finds the shocks unusually uncomfortable, or a chance to spend time helping a young woman struggling to care for her younger brother and sister after her parents were killed in an auto accident. Participants are confronted with what they believe are real need situations and real opportunities to help, not hypothetical situations or scenarios. (To determine the nature of the motivation evoked by empathic concern, we must be certain that participants actually feel empathic concern, not imagine it.) We then manipulate both the level of empathic concern felt for the person in need and some cross-cutting variable that changes whether helping is the most effective means to reach (a) the altruistic ultimate goal of removing the other's need or (b) one or more of the possible egoistic ultimate goals. Table 1.1 lists the cross-cutting variables we have used. These variables do not change the goal(s); they change the attractiveness or availability of behavioral routes to the different goal(s). As a result, each variable listed in Table 1.1 allows us to make competing empirical predictions from the empathy–altruism hypothesis and at least one of the egoistic alternatives.

Because the three egoistic alternatives involve three quite different psychological processes, none of the proposed cross-cutting variables listed in Table 1.1 allows a clear test of the empathy–altruism hypothesis against all three. As a result, it is necessary either to conduct an experiment in which several cross-cutting variables are manipulated at once, which seems unwieldy and unwise, or to conduct a series of experiments in which the egoistic alternatives are tested one after another. Following the latter strategy, care must be taken when moving from testing one egoistic alternative to testing another. Experimental situations must remain comparable so that cumulative comparisons can be made. The best way to maintain comparability is to use the same need situations, the same techniques for manipulating empathy, and the same dependent measures, changing only the cross-cutting variables.

TABLE 1.1
Variables That Can Differentiate Altruistic and Egoistic Motives for Helping

		Egoistic motive		
Variable	Altruistic motive	Arousal reducing	Punishment avoiding	Reward seeking
Viability of escape: Can the goal be reached by escape without helping?	Escape not viable	Escape viable (from victim's distress)	Escape viable (from own shame, guilt)	Escape not viable
Necessity of one's help being effective: Must one's help be effective to reach the goal?	Necessary	Necessary	Not necessary (if ineffectiveness justified)	Not necessary (if ineffectiveness justified)
Acceptability of other helpers: Whose help can attain the goal?	Oneself; others	Oneself; others	Oneself; others	Only oneself
Need for rewards of helping: What is the effect of increased need for the rewards of helping?	No effect	No effect	No effect	Increased motivation
Salient cognitions: What cognitions are salient when deciding whether to help?	Victim's welfare; costs of helping	Unclear	Anticipated punishments; costs of helping	Anticipated rewards; costs of helping

Note. From "Prosocial motivation: Is it ever truly altruistic?" by C. D. Batson, 1987, in *Advances in experimental social psychology, 20,* p. 105. New York: Academic Press. Copyright 1987 by Elsevier. Adapted with permission.

It is also important to test any given alternative in multiple experiments using different need situations, different techniques for inducing empathic concern, and, if possible, different cross-cutting variables.

CURRENT STATUS OF THE EMPATHY–ALTRUISM HYPOTHESIS

Reports have been published of more than 30 experiments in which one of the cross-cutting variables in Table 1.1 has been manipulated and empathy for a person in need has been either manipulated, measured, or both (see Batson, 1991, for a review of over 20 experiments; Batson [in press] provides a more complete review). Cumulatively, these experiments have tested all of the competing predictions in Table 1.1. To cite but one example of research using each cross-cutting variable: (a) *viability of escape* was manipulated by Batson, Duncan, Ackerman, Buckley, and Birch (1981); (b) *necessity of one's help being effective* was manipulated by Batson and Weeks (1996); (c) *acceptability of other helpers* was manipulated by Batson et al. (1988; Study 1); (d) *need for rewards of helping* was manipulated by Batson et al. (1989); and (e) *salient cognitions* were measured by Batson et al. (1988, Study 5).

Overall, results of these experiments have consistently turned out as predicted by the empathy–altruism hypothesis; results have failed to support any of the egoistic alternatives. To the best of my knowledge, there is at present no plausible egoistic explanation of the cumulative evidence from these experiments. This evidence has led me to conclude—tentatively—that the empathy–altruism hypothesis is true, that is, that empathic concern produces altruistic motivation.

After reviewing the empathy–altruism research, as well as recent literature in sociology, economics, political science, and biology, Piliavin and Charng (1990) reached a similar conclusion:

> There appears to be a "paradigm shift" away from the earlier position that behavior that appears to be altruistic must, under closer scrutiny, be revealed as reflecting egoistic motives. Rather, theory and data now being advanced are more compatible with the view that true altruism—acting with the goal of benefiting another—does exist and is a part of human nature. (p. 27)

However, in apparent contradiction to this conclusion, Maner et al. (2002) claimed to provide evidence that once the effects of negative affect are removed, there is no longer a positive relation between empathic concern and motivation to help, altruistic or otherwise. But Maner et al. included only empathic emotions in their measure of negative affect (feeling sympathetic, compassionate, and soft-hearted, as well as sad, low-spirited, and heavy-hearted—sadness items that in response to the need situation they used likely tapped other-oriented sadness for the person in need). So, when controlling for negative affect, Maner et al. actually removed the effect of empathic concern. It is not very surprising, and also not very informative, to find that once the effect of empathic concern on helping is removed, there is no longer an effect of empathic concern on helping.

Today, almost 20 years later, Piliavin and Charng's (1990) conclusion still seems correct. Pending new evidence or a plausible new egoistic explanation of the existing evidence, the empathy–altruism hypothesis appears to be true.

THEORETICAL IMPLICATIONS OF EMPATHY-INDUCED ALTRUISTIC MOTIVATION

If the empathy–altruism hypothesis is true, the theoretical implications are wide ranging. *Universal egoism*—the assumption that all human behavior is motivated by self-interest—has long dominated not only psychology but other social and behavioral sciences as well (see Mansbridge, 1990). If empathic concern produces motivation with the ultimate goal of increasing another's welfare, then the assumption of universal egoism must be replaced by a more complex view that allows for altruism as well as egoism. Such a shift in our view of the human motivational repertoire requires, in turn, a revision of our assumptions about human nature and human potential. It implies that we humans are more social than we have thought. Other people can be more to us than sources of information, stimulation, gratification, and reward as we each seek our own welfare. We have the potential to care about them for their sakes, not simply for our own.

Perception of Self and Other When Feeling Empathic Concern

There are more specific theoretical implications as well. The strong support for the empathy–altruism hypothesis begs for a better understanding of the perception of self and other when we feel empathic concern. Several representations have been proposed. Concern for another's welfare is a product of (a) a sense of we-ness based on cognitive unit formation or identification with the other's situation (e.g., Hornstein, 1982); (b) the self expanding to incorporate aspects of the other (Aron & Aron, 1986); (c) seeing aspects of the self in the other (Cialdini, Brown, Lewis, Luce, & Neuberg, 1997); or (d) valuing the welfare of the other, who remains distinct from self (e.g., Batson, Eklund, Chermok, Hoyt, & Ortiz, 2007; Batson & Shaw, 1991).

Clearly, not all these proposals can be true, at least not at the same time. On the basis of research to date, it appears that neither empathic concern nor its effect on helping is a product of any of the various forms of self–other merging or overlap—we-ness, self-expansion, or self-projection (Batson, Sager, et al., 1997; Cialdini et al., 1997). Recent neuroimaging research also provides evidence that empathic concern involves self–other differentiation rather than merging (e.g., chap. 6, this volume; Jackson, Meltzoff, & Decety, 2005; Lamm, Batson, & Decety, 2007).

Evolutionary Origin of Empathic Concern

The support for the empathy–altruism hypothesis also forces us to face the question of the evolutionary origin of empathic concern (for an extensive discussion on evolutionary perspectives on prosocial behavior, see chap 2, this volume). What evolutionary function might this emotion serve? Speculating, I think the most plausible answer is that empathic concern evolved as part of the parental instinct among higher mammals, especially humans (also see de Waal, 1996; Zahn-Waxler & Radke-Yarrow, 1990). If mammalian parents were not intensely interested in the welfare of their very vulnerable progeny, these species would quickly die out. Humans have doubtless inherited key aspects of their parental instinct from ancestors they share with other higher mammalian species, but in humans this instinct has become considerably more flexible. The human parental instinct goes well beyond nursing, providing other kinds of food, protecting, and keeping the young close—the activities that characterize parental care in most other mammalian species. It includes inferences about the desires and feelings of the child (e.g., "Is that a hungry cry or a wet cry?" "She won't like the fireworks; they'll be too loud."). It also includes goal-directed motives and appraisal-based emotions (Scherer, 1984).

Antonio Damasio (1999, 2003) has pointed out that one of the virtues of relying on goal-directed motives and appraisal-based emotions to guide action—rather than on hard-wired, automatic responses to environmental cues (his *regulatory mechanisms*)—is that goal-directed motives and their associated emotions can be adaptive under a wide range of environmental conditions, circumstances, and events (for a similar view of caregiving behavior, see chap. 4, this volume). Such flexibility seems highly desirable when caring for human offspring because complex, novel situations abound.

To illustrate the flexibility that appraisal-based emotions introduce with an emotion quite different from empathic concern, consider anger. Aggressive responses occur in many species that likely do not experience anything like the emotion we would call *anger*. Among humans, however, aggressive responses are stimulated, tempered, and generalized by feelings of anger that are a product of complex cognitive appraisal of the situation, including appraisal of the intentions of others. Similarly, tender, empathic feelings permit more flexible and adaptive parental care, care that is not simply reflexive or reactive to distress cues but is directed toward the goal of enhancing the child's welfare in whatever way is needed in the particular situation. This flexibility includes anticipation of needs, even evolutionarily quite novel ones (e.g., the need to avoid sticking a pin in an electrical socket).

Of course, the human capacity for empathic concern extends well beyond one's own children. As long as there is no preexisting antipathy, people can feel empathic concern for a wide range of targets, including nonhumans (e.g., Batson, 1991; Batson, Lishner, Cook, & Sawyer, 2005). From an evolutionary perspective, this extension is usually attributed to cognitive generalization whereby one "adopts" the target, making it possible to evoke empathic concern and altruistic motivation when the target is in need (Batson, 1987). Such cognitive generalization may be facilitated by two factors: (a) human cognitive capacity (including symbolic thought) and (b) lack of evolutionary advantage in early human hunter–gatherer bands for strict limitation of empathic concern and parental nurturance to offspring. In these bands, those in need were often one's children or close kin, and survival of one's genes was tightly tied to the welfare even of those who were not close kin (Sober & Wilson, 1998). To the extent that the human nurturant impulse relies on appraisal-based other-oriented emotions such as empathic concern, it would be relatively easy to generalize. In contemporary society, the prospect of such generalization appears more plausible when one thinks of the emotional sensitivity and tender care typically provided by nannies and workers in day care centers to their young charges, by adoptive parents, and by pet owners.

Other Sources of Altruistic Motivation

Additionally, might there be sources of altruistic motivation other than empathic concern? Several have been proposed, including an altruistic personality (Oliner & Oliner, 1988; chap. 3, this volume), principled moral reasoning (Kohlberg, 1976), and internalized prosocial values (chap. 12, this volume). There is some evidence that each of these potential sources is associated with increased motivation to help, but as yet it is not clear that this motivation is altruistic. It may be, or it may be an instrumental means to the egoistic ultimate goals of (a) maintaining a positive self-concept or (b) avoiding guilt (Batson, 1991; Batson, Bolen, Cross, & Neuringer-Benefiel, 1986; chap. 7, this volume). More research is needed to explore these possibilities.

Practical Implications of Empathy-Induced Altruism

The empathy–altruism hypothesis also has wide-ranging practical implications. For example, it implies that people may at times wish to suppress or avoid feeling empathic concern. Aware of the extreme effort involved in helping or of the impossibility of helping effectively, caseworkers in the helping professions, nurses caring for terminal patients, and pedestrians confronted by homeless persons may try to avoid empathic concern to be spared the resulting altruistic motivation (Maslach, 1982; Shaw, Batson, & Todd, 1994; Stotland, Mathews, Sherman, Hansson, & Richardson, 1978). That is, there may be an egoistic motive to avoid altruistic motivation (for a discussion of ambivalent reactions to requests for help, see chap. 11, this volume).

More positively, empathic concern has been found to direct attention to the long-term welfare of those in need, producing more sensitive care (Sibicky, Schroeder, & Dovidio, 1995). Empathy-induced altruism has also been found to improve attitudes toward stigmatized outgroups. Empathy inductions have improved racial attitudes, as well as attitudes and action toward people with AIDS, homeless people, and even convicted murderers and drug dealers (Batson, Chang, Orr, & Rowland, 2002; Batson, Polycarpou, et al., 1997; Vescio, Sechrist, & Paolucci, 2003; chap. 20, this volume). Empathy-induced altruism also has been found to increase cooperation in a potentially competitive situation (a Prisoner's Dilemma)—even when one knows that the target of empathic concern has acted competitively toward oneself (Batson & Ahmad, 2001; Batson & Moran, 1999). In schools, empathy-based training has been used to increase mutual care among students (e.g., the Roots of Empathy project; Gordon, 2007). And, as Stephan and Finlay (1999) pointed out, the induction of empathic concern is often an explicit component of techniques used in conflict resolution workshops. Participants are encouraged to express their feelings, their hopes and fears, and to imagine the thoughts and feelings of those on the other side of the conflict (Kelman, 1990). These techniques affect perception of the other as in need and adoption of the other's perspective, two conditions that, in combination, have been used to produce empathic concern. (For a more extensive discussion of practical implications of empathy-induced altruism, see Batson, Ahmad, & Stocks, 2004.)

TWO OTHER FORMS OF PROSOCIAL MOTIVATION

Thinking more broadly, beyond the egoism–altruism debate that has been a focus of attention and contention for the past several decades, might there be other forms of prosocial motivation, forms in which the ultimate goal is neither to benefit self nor to benefit another individual? Two seem worthy of consideration: collectivism and principlism.

Collectivism

Collectivism is motivation to benefit a particular group as a whole. The ultimate goal is not one's own welfare or the welfare of specific others who are benefited; the ultimate goal is the welfare of the group. Dawes, van de Kragt, and Orbell (1988) put it succinctly: "Not me or thee but we" (p. 83). They suggested that collectivist motivation is a product of group identity (Turner, 1987).

As with altruism, what looks like collectivism may actually be a subtle form of egoism. Perhaps attention to group welfare is simply an expression of enlightened self-interest. Dawes, van de Kragt, and Orbell (1990) have conducted some research to address this question of the underlying motivation. More research is needed.

Principlism

Not only have most moral philosophers argued for the importance of a prosocial motive other than egoism, but most since Kant have also shunned altruism and collectivism. They reject appeals to altruism, especially empathy-induced altruism, because feelings of empathy, sympathy, and compassion are too fickle and too circumscribed. Empathic concern is not felt for everyone in need, at least not to the same degree. They reject appeals to collectivism because group interest is bound by the limits of the group; it not only permits but may even encourage doing harm to those outside the group. Given these problems with altruism and collectivism, moral philosophers have typically advocated prosocial motivation with an ultimate goal of upholding a universal and impartial moral principle, such as justice (Rawls, 1971). To add another "ism," I call this moral motivation *principlism.*

Is acting with an ultimate goal of upholding a moral principle really possible? When Kant (1788/1889) briefly shifted from his analysis of what ought to be to what is, he admitted that the concern we show for others that appears to be prompted by duty to principle may actually be prompted by self-love. Upholding moral principle may be only an instrumental goal pursued as a means to reach the social and self-rewards associated with being—or appearing—moral (or at least not immoral). If this is true, then principle-based motivation is actually egoistic. Once again, we need to know the nature of the motive (i.e., the ultimate goal). Experimental designs similar to those used to test the empathy–altruism hypothesis can help us find out.

ORCHESTRATING PROSOCIAL MOTIVES

Recognizing the existence of altruism, and possibly also collectivism and principlism, makes available more resources to those seeking to produce a more humane, caring society. Said crassly, there are more motivational buttons one can push. At the same time, this availability complicates matters. Different motives do not always work in harmony; they can undercut and compete with one another.

Well-intentioned appeals to self-interest can backfire by undermining other prosocial motives. Providing money or other incentives for showing concern may lead people to interpret their motivation as egoistic even when it is not (e.g., Batson, Coke, Jasnoski, & Hanson, 1978; Stukas, Snyder, &

Clary, 1999). In this way, the assumption that there is only one answer to the question of why people act for the common good—egoism—may become a self-fulfilling prophecy (Batson, Fultz, Schoenrade, & Paduano, 1987). It may create a self-perpetuating norm of self-interest (Miller, 1999).

Nor need altruism, collectivism, and principlism always work in harmony. They can conflict. For example, altruism can conflict with either collectivism or principlism. We humans may ignore the larger social good, or we may compromise our principles, not only to benefit ourselves but also to benefit others for whom we especially care, such as family and friends (Batson, Batson, et al., 1995; Batson, Klein, Highberger, & Shaw, 1995). And whereas there are clear social sanctions against unbridled self-interest, there are not clear sanctions against altruism. As a result, altruism can at times pose a greater threat to the common good than does egoism (Batson et al., 1999).

Different forms of prosocial motivation may also cooperate. Egoism, altruism, collectivism, and principlism each has strengths. Each also has weaknesses. The potential for the greatest good may come from strategies that orchestrate these motives so that the strengths of one can overcome weaknesses of another.

Strategies that combine appeals to either altruism or collectivism with appeals to principlism seem especially promising. For example, think about the principle of justice. It is universal and impartial, but motivation to uphold justice is easily co-opted and vulnerable to rationalization. We humans are quite good at justifying to ourselves, if not to others, why a situation that benefits us or those for whom we care does not violate our moral principles—why we have the right to a disproportionate share of the world's natural resources, why dumping our nuclear waste in someone else's backyard is fair, why attacks by our enemies are atrocities but attacks by our side are necessities. The abstractness and multiplicity of moral principles make it easy to convince ourselves that the relevant principles are those that just happen to serve our interests (Bandura, 1999; Batson & Thompson, 2001; Bersoff, 1999). Empathy-induced altruism and collectivism seem more robust, but they are limited in scope and produce partiality toward the interests of particular persons or groups. Perhaps if we can lead people to feel empathic concern for the victims of injustice, or to perceive themselves in a common group with them (Gaertner & Dovidio, 2000; also see chap. 20, this volume), then we can combine the unique strengths of two motives. Desire for justice may provide perspective and reason; empathy-induced altruism or collectivism may provide emotional fire and a force directed specifically toward seeing the victims' suffering end, preventing rationalization.

Something of this sort occurred, I believe, in a number of rescuers of Jews in Nazi Europe. A careful look at data collected by the Oliners and their colleagues (Oliner & Oliner, 1988) suggests that involvement in rescue activity frequently began with concern for a specific individual or individuals for whom compassion was felt—often someone known previously. This initial involvement subsequently led to further contacts and rescue activity, and to a concern for justice that extended well beyond the bounds of the initial empathic concern. Something of this sort also may lie at the heart of the nonviolent protest practiced by Gandhi and Martin Luther King. The sight on TV news of a small Black child being rolled down a street in Birmingham, Alabama, by water from a fire hose under the direction of local police, and the emotions this sight evoked, seemed to do more to arouse public opinion than did years of reasoned argument about civil rights.

Looking back, the evidence that empathic concern produces altruistic motivation has certainly changed the way I think about prosocial motives, emotion, and behavior. I suspect it has—or will—change the way you think about them as well.

REFERENCES

Aron, A., & Aron, E. N. (1986). *Love and the expansion of self: Understanding attraction and satisfaction.* Washington, DC: Hemisphere.

Bandura, A. (1999). Moral disengagement in the perpetration of inhumanities. *Personality and Social Psychology Review, 3,* 193–209.

Batson, C. D. (1987). Prosocial motivation: Is it ever truly altruistic? In L. Berkowitz (Ed.), *Advances in experimental social psychology* (Vol. 20, pp. 65–122). New York: Academic Press.

Batson, C. D. (1991). *The altruism question: Toward a social-psychological answer.* Hillsdale, NJ: Erlbaum.

Batson, C. D. (in press). *Altruism in humans.* New York: Oxford University Press.

Batson, C. D., & Ahmad, N. (2001). Empathy-induced altruism in a Prisoner's Dilemma II: What if the target of empathy has defected? *European Journal of Social Psychology, 31,* 25–36.

Batson, C. D., Ahmad, N., & Stocks, E. L. (2004). Benefits and liabilities of empathy-induced altruism. In A. G. Miller (Ed.), *The social psychology of good and evil* (pp. 359–385). New York: Guilford Press.

Batson, C. D., Ahmad, N., Yin, J., Bedell, S. J., Johnson, J. W., Templin, C. M., & Whiteside, A. (1999). Two threats to the common good: Self-interested egoism and empathy-induced altruism. *Personality and Social Psychology Bulletin, 25,* 3–16.

Batson, C. D., Batson, J. G., Griffitt, C. A., Barrientos, S., Brandt, J. R., Sprengelmeyer, P., & Bayly, M. J. (1989). Negative-state relief and the empathy–altruism hypothesis. *Journal of Personality and Social Psychology, 56,* 922–933.

Batson, C. D., Batson, J. G., Todd, R. M., Brummett, B. H., Shaw, L. L., & Aldeguer, C. M. R. (1995). Empathy and the collective good: Caring for one of the others in a social dilemma. *Journal of Personality and Social Psychology, 68,* 619–631.

Batson, C. D., Bolen, M. H., Cross, J. A., & Neuringer-Benefiel, H. E. (1986). Where is the altruism in the altruistic personality? *Journal of Personality and Social Psychology, 50,* 212–220.

Batson, C. D., Chang, J., Orr, R., & Rowland, J. (2002). Empathy, attitudes, and action: Can feeling for a member of a stigmatized group motivate one to help the group? *Personality and Social Psychology Bulletin, 28*, 1656–1666.

Batson, C. D., Coke, J. S., Jasnoski, M. L., & Hanson, M. (1978). Buying kindness: Effect of an extrinsic incentive for helping on perceived altruism. *Personality and Social Psychology Bulletin, 4*, 86–91.

Batson, C. D., Duncan, B., Ackerman, P., Buckley, T., & Birch, K. (1981). Is empathic emotion a source of altruistic motivation? *Journal of Personality and Social Psychology, 40*, 290–302.

Batson, C. D., Dyck, J. L., Brandt, J. R., Batson, J. G., Powell, A. L., McMaster, M. R., & Griffitt, C. (1988). Five studies testing two new egoistic alternatives to the empathy-altruism hypothesis. *Journal of Personality and Social Psychology, 55*, 52–77.

Batson, C. D., Eklund, J. H., Chermok, V. L., Hoyt, J. L., & Ortiz, B. G. (2007). An additional antecedent of empathic concern: Valuing the welfare of the person in need. *Journal of Personality and Social Psychology, 93*, 65–74.

Batson, C. D., Fultz, J., Schoenrade, P. A., & Paduano, A. (1987). Critical self-reflection and self-perceived altruism: When self-reward fails. *Journal of Personality and Social Psychology, 53*, 594–602.

Batson, C. D., Klein, T. R., Highberger, L., & Shaw, L. L. (1995). Immorality from empathy-induced altruism: When compassion and justice conflict. *Journal of Personality and Social Psychology, 68*, 1042–1054.

Batson, C. D., Lishner, D. A., Cook, J., & Sawyer, S. (2005). Similarity and nurturance: Two possible sources of empathy for strangers. *Basic and Applied Social Psychology, 27*, 15–25.

Batson, C. D., & Moran, T. (1999). Empathy-induced altruism in a Prisoner's Dilemma. *European Journal of Social Psychology, 29*, 909–924.

Batson, C. D., Polycarpou, M. P., Harmon-Jones, E., Imhoff, H. J., Mitchener, E. C., Bednar, L. L., et al. (1997). Empathy and attitudes: Can feeling for a member of a stigmatized group improve feelings toward the group? *Journal of Personality and Social Psychology, 72*, 105–118.

Batson, C. D., Sager, K., Garst, E., Kang, M., Rubchinsky, K., & Dawson, K. (1997). Is empathy-induced helping due to self-other merging? *Journal of Personality and Social Psychology, 73*, 495–509.

Batson, C. D., & Shaw, L. L. (1991). Evidence for altruism: Toward a pluralism of prosocial motives. *Psychological Inquiry, 2*, 107–122.

Batson, C. D., & Thompson, E. R. (2001). Why don't moral people act morally? Motivational considerations. *Current Directions in Psychological Science, 10*, 54–57.

Batson, C. D., & Weeks, J. L. (1996). Mood effects of unsuccessful helping: Another test of the empathy–altruism hypothesis. *Personality and Social Psychology Bulletin, 22*, 148–157.

Bersoff, D. M. (1999). Why good people sometimes do bad things: Motivated reasoning and unethical behavior. *Personality and Social Psychology Bulletin, 25*, 28–39.

Cialdini, R. B., Brown, S. L., Lewis, B. P., Luce, C., & Neuberg, S. L. (1997). Reinterpreting the empathy–altruism relationship: When one into one equals oneness. *Journal of Personality and Social Psychology*, *73*, 481–494.

Damasio, A. R. (1999). *The feeling of what happens: Body and emotion in the making of consciousness.* New York: Harcourt Brace.

Damasio, A. R. (2003). *Looking for Spinoza: Joy, sorrow, and the feeling brain.* Orlando, FL: Harcourt.

Dawes, R. M., van de Kragt, A. J. C., & Orbell, J. M. (1988). Not me or thee but we: The importance of group identity in eliciting cooperation in dilemma situations: Experimental manipulations. *Acta Psychologica*, *68*, 83–97.

Dawes, R. M., van de Kragt, A. J. C., & Orbell, J. M. (1990). Cooperation for the benefit of us—not me, or my conscience. In J. J. Mansbridge (Ed.), *Beyond self-interest* (pp. 97–110). Chicago: University of Chicago Press.

Dawkins, R. (1976). *The selfish gene.* New York: Oxford University Press.

de Waal, F. B. M. (1996). *Good natured: The origins of right and wrong in humans and other animals.* Cambridge, MA: Harvard University Press.

de Waal, F. B. M. (2008). Putting the altruism back into altruism: The evolution of empathy. *Annual Review of Psychology*, *59*, 279–300.

Gaertner, S. L., & Dovidio, J. F. (2000) *Reducing intergroup bias: The Common Ingroup Identity Model.* Philadelphia: Psychology Press.

Gordon, M. (2007). *Roots of empathy: Changing the world child by child.* Toronto, Canada: Thomas Allen.

Hamilton, W. D. (1964). The genetical evolution of social behavior (I, II). *Journal of Theoretical Biology*, *7*, 1–52.

Hatfield, E., Cacioppo, J. T., & Rapson, R. L. (1994). *Emotional contagion.* New York: Cambridge University Press.

Hornstein, H. A. (1982). Promotive tension: Theory and research. In V. Derlega & J. Grzelak (Eds.), *Cooperation and helping behavior: Theories and research* (pp. 229–248). New York: Academic Press.

Ickes, W. (1993). Empathic accuracy. *Journal of Personality*, *61*, 587–610.

Jackson, P. L., Meltzoff, A. N., & Decety, J. (2005). How do we perceive the pain of others?: A window into the neural processes involved in empathy. *NeuroImage*, *24*, 771–779.

Kant, I. (1889). *Kant's Critique of Practical Reason and other works on the theory of ethics* (4th ed.; T. K. Abbott, Trans.). New York: Longmans, Green & Co. (Original work published 1788)

Kelman, H. C. (1990). Interactive problem-solving: A social psychological approach to conflict resolution. In J. W. Burton & F. Dukes (Eds.), *Conflict: Readings in management and resolution* (pp. 199–215). New York: St. Martin's Press.

Kohlberg, L. (1976). Moral stages and moralization: The cognitive-developmental approach. In T. Lickona (Ed.), *Moral development and behavior: Theory, research, and social issues* (pp. 31–53). New York: Holt, Rinehart & Winston.

Lamm, C., Batson, C. D., & Decety, J. (2007). The neural substrate of human empathy: Effects of perspective-taking and cognitive appraisal. *Journal of Cognitive Neuroscience, 19,* 1–17.

La Rouchefoucauld, F., Duke de (1691). *Moral maxims and reflections, in four parts.* London: Gillyflower, Sare, & Everingham.

Lewin, K. (1938). The conceptual representation and measurement of psychological forces. *Contributions to psychological theory, 1*(4), 1–247.

Lewin, K. (1951). *Field theory in social science.* New York: Harper.

MacIntyre, A. (1967). Egoism and altruism. In P. Edwards (Ed.), *The encyclopedia of philosophy* (Vol. 2, pp. 462–466). New York: Macmillan.

Mandeville, B. (1732). *The fable of the bees: Or, private vices, public benefits.* London: J. Tonson. (Original work published 1714)

Maner, J. K., Luce, C. L., Neuberg, S. L., Cialdini, R. B., Brown, S., & Sagarin, B. J. (2002). The effects of perspective taking on helping: Still no evidence for altruism. *Personality and Social Psychology Bulletin, 28,* 1601–1610.

Mansbridge, J. J. (Ed.). (1990). *Beyond self-interest.* Chicago: University of Chicago Press.

Maslach, C. (1982). *Burnout: The cost of caring.* Englewood Cliffs, NJ: Prentice Hall.

Miller, D. T. (1999). The norm of self-interest. *American Psychologist, 54,* 1053–1060.

Oliner, S. P., & Oliner, P. M. (1988). *The altruistic personality: Rescuers of Jews in Nazi Europe.* New York: Free Press.

Piliavin, J. A., & Charng, H.-W. (1990). Altruism: A review of recent theory and research. *American Sociological Review, 16,* 27–65.

Rawls, J. (1971). *A theory of justice.* Cambridge, MA: Harvard University Press.

Scherer, K. R. (1984). On the nature and function of emotion: A component process approach. In K. R. Scherer & P. Ekman (Eds.), *Approaches to emotion* (pp. 293–317). Hillsdale, NJ: Erlbaum.

Shaw, L. L., Batson, C. D., & Todd, R. M. (1994). Empathy avoidance: Forestalling feeling for another in order to escape the motivational consequences. *Journal of Personality and Social Psychology, 67,* 879–887.

Sibicky, M. E., Schroeder, D. A., & Dovidio, J. F. (1995). Empathy and helping: Considering the consequences of intervention. *Basic and Applied Social Psychology, 16,* 435–453.

Sober, E., & Wilson, D. S. (1998). *Unto others: The evolution and psychology of unselfish behavior.* Cambridge, MA: Harvard University Press.

Stephan, W. G., & Finlay, K. (1999). The role of empathy in improving intergroup relations. *Journal of Social Issues, 55,* 729–743.

Stotland, E., Mathews, K. E., Sherman, S. E., Hansson, R. O., & Richardson, B. Z. (1978). *Empathy, fantasy, and helping.* Beverly Hills, CA: Sage.

Stukas, A. A., Snyder, M., & Clary, E. G. (1999). The effects of "mandatory volunteerism" on intentions to volunteer. *Psychological Science, 10,* 59–64.

Trivers, R. L. (1971). The evolution of reciprocal altruism. *The Quarterly Review of Biology*, *46*, 35–57.

Turner, J. C. (1987). *Rediscovering the social group: A self-categorization theory*. Oxford, England: Basil Blackwell.

Vescio, T. K., Sechrist, G. B., & Paolucci, M. P. (2003). Perspective taking and prejudice reduction: The mediational role of empathy arousal and situational attributions. *European Journal of Social Psychology*, *33*, 455–472.

Zahn-Waxler, C., & Radke-Yarrow, M. (1990). The origins of empathic concern. *Motivation and Emotion*, *14*, 107–130.

2

EVOLUTIONARY PERSPECTIVES ON PROSOCIAL BEHAVIOR

JEFFRY A. SIMPSON AND LANE BECKES

> It has often been assumed that animals were in the first place rendered social, and that they feel as a consequence uncomfortable when separated from each other, and comfortable whilst together; but it is a more probable view that these sensations were first developed, in order that those animals which would profit by living in society, should be induced to live together . . . for with those animals which were benefited by living in close association, the individuals which took the greatest pleasure in society would best escape various dangers; whilst those that cared least for their comrades and lived solitary would perish in greater numbers. (Darwin, 1871, p. 80)

As this quotation indicates, Charles Darwin believed that prosocial tendencies probably evolved via natural selection in many species. Indeed, one of the great misunderstandings in the life sciences is the notion that nature is merely "red in tooth and claw" (Tennyson, 1850/1906). Although organisms do compete for valuable and sometimes scarce resources, both against members of their own species and against members of other species, the majority of competition is neither direct nor violent (Trivers, 1985). Most competition occurs indirectly as organisms scramble to find, maintain, and control resources critical to their survival and reproduction. Over time, the most reproductively successful organisms—those leaving the most descendants across generations—evolve traits and behaviors that help them more efficiently and effectively identify, procure, and control the most valuable resources, which in turn are passed on to their progeny through genetic inheritance.

No one in the evolutionary sciences questions that many species, including *Homo sapiens*, are able and sometimes willing to act prosocially toward others, even total strangers. Humans are the most prosocial primate species and one of the most prosocial of all species, as indexed by the size and complexity of their societies. What is debatable is how and why stronger forms of prosociality (i.e., willingness to incur heavy costs or even death for the welfare of a group) were selected for during evolutionary history. The question of how and why strong prosociality might have evolved in humans is one of the most important ones within the evolutionary sciences today (Gangestad & Simpson, 2007).

The goal of this chapter is to review the major evolutionary theories that are most relevant to understanding whether, how, and why strong prosociality may have evolved via natural selection in humans. As we explain, more recent evolutionary theories and models have become increasingly open to the likelihood that prosociality evolved in humans.

The chapter is divided into four sections. In the first section, we describe the physical and social environments—particularly the most likely obstacles to survival and reproduction—that contemporary humans' ancestors probably had to confront and master during evolutionary history. We begin with this set of issues because one cannot understand how or why strong prosociality evolved without awareness of the primary physical and social conditions in which early humans lived. In the second section, we review major theoretical models relevant to the evolution of prosociality in humans, starting with Darwin's (1859) theory of natural selection and then working through inclusive fitness theory (Hamilton, 1964), reciprocal altruism theory (Trivers, 1971), group-selection models (Sloan Wilson & Sober, 1994), and more recent gene-culture coevolutionary models (e.g., Richerson & Boyd, 2005). In the third section, we review empirical work that has tested evolutionary theories or models of prosociality in humans. In the final section, we integrate the most significant theoretical and empirical work, identify gaps in the current understanding of how and why natural selection may have sculpted certain prosocial tendencies in humans, and suggest that multiple factors linked to different evolutionary theories and processes are all likely to have generated the "ultra" prosocial tendencies that humans often display (see Brewer & Brown, 1998).

STABLE FEATURES OF EVOLUTIONARY ENVIRONMENTS

To understand the distal factors that may be responsible for the development of prosocial tendencies in humans, one must look back to the most stable features of the environments in which humans probably evolved. During more than 98% of human evolutionary history, our ancestors lived as hunters and gatherers (Hill, 2002; Kelly, 1995), most likely in small, cooperative tribes or bands (Richerson & Boyd, 2005). Many people within a tribe or band were biologically related (Foley, 1992). Complete strangers were probably encountered infrequently, most often during either intertribal trading or war (Wright, 1994). Although some people migrated in and out of their original tribes or bands, most people probably lived in the same group their entire lives. Children were raised with considerable help from extended family members and most likely from the entire tribe or band, and older children, especially older siblings, assumed important roles in socializing and helping to rear younger children (Eibl-Eibesfeldt, 1989). Both genders participated in securing food, with men doing most of the hunting and women doing most of the gathering (Richerson & Boyd, 2005; Wood & Eagly, 2002). As a result, extensive cooperation with other tribe or band members—both kin and nonkin—was essential, particularly given the changing and precarious nature of the climate, competing tribes, and the food supply.

These conditions are ideal for reciprocal altruism to evolve (chap. 1, this volume; Cosmides & Tooby, 1992). Brewer and Caporeal (1990), in fact, suggested that active participation in cooperative groups probably was the primary "survival strategy" of early humans. Willingness to enter and maintain mutually cooperative, long-term alliances with others, therefore, may have been essential for survival, successful reproduction, and adequate parenting. Although some of these inferences are more speculative than others, the human mind most likely evolved to deal with problems that arose in physical and social environments containing these features.

EVOLUTIONARY THEORIES OF PROSOCIAL BEHAVIOR IN HUMANS

Several major theories are relevant to the evolution of prosocial behavior in human beings. In this section, we begin with an overview of natural selection theory, and then review several theories that, collectively, define the modern evolutionary perspective.

Natural Selection Theory

Darwin's (1859) theory of evolution by natural selection focused on the survival of the fittest and explained why, on the basis of the importance of differential reproduction across time, organisms often act in line with their self-centered interests. *Natural selection* is the process by which organisms in a species that possess traits or characteristics resulting in higher rates of survival and reproduction out-compete other organisms. Organisms that survive and successfully reproduce pass on these traits or characteristics to their offspring. Over time, traits that are most adaptive—that is, those that are differentially reproduced across many generations—increase in representation within a population, whereas those that are not eventually disappear. Through this process, some traits are naturally selected as organisms compete for resources.

Darwin's theory, however, left room for strong forms of prosociality and even altruism, particularly in humans, a species that was vulnerable to assorted dangers if individuals lived isolated from groups or collectives. Despite the fact that Darwin's theory of evolution was a remarkable intellectual accomplishment, it was incomplete and imprecise in several ways. To begin with, the theory was developed well before Mendel's pioneering work, which unlocked some of the secrets of genes and patterns of inheritance. Second, because Darwin did not conceive of genes as the principal units upon which natural selection operates, he could not explain why some organisms frequently engage in self-sacrificial or nonreproductive behavior. This enigma was solved by Hamilton (1964), who introduced and provided compelling evidence for inclusive fitness (i.e., the process by which differential gene replication drives evolution). Third, Darwin had only a dim understanding of how sexual recombination and genetic mutations provide the variation from which better adaptations and new species are selected. Fourth, like many theorists of his era, Darwin did not fully appreciate the extent to which specific adaptations are associated with both benefits and costs. What is most impressive about Darwin is that he envisioned, without the benefit of this subsequent knowledge, how natural selection is likely to have operated.

Inclusive Fitness Theory

Few significant theoretical advances occurred in the evolutionary sciences for nearly a century after Darwin published his second landmark book, *The Descent of Man*, in 1871. This state of affairs changed rapidly beginning in the mid-1960s. With the development of inclusive fitness theory, Hamilton (1964) introduced the notion of kin selection. By focusing on genes rather than on individual organisms as the primary units on which selection operates, Hamilton solved the biggest problem that eluded Darwin's grasp: In the struggle for reproductive fitness (i.e., an individual's ability to produce fertile and reproductively viable offspring at a rate higher than other organisms in the same species), why do some organisms forego reproduction to assist the reproductive efforts of their biological relatives?

Hamilton (1964) realized that an individual's total (inclusive) fitness depends on his or her own reproductive output (i.e., offspring) plus the total reproductive output of all kin who share some of the individual's genome. To the extent that genes are the units on which selection operates, and that individuals can facilitate the reproductive output of their biological relatives, there are situations in which it pays to sacrifice one's own reproductive output, including one's life, to facilitate the successful reproduction of close relatives. Unlike Darwin, Hamilton was able to calculate the degree to which pairs of individuals share novel genes. On average, parents share half their novel genes with their children, full siblings share half their genes with each other, grandparents share one quarter of their genes with their grandchildren, aunts and uncles share one quarter of their genes with their nieces and nephews, and first cousins share one eighth of their genes.

Armed with this knowledge, Hamilton discerned that self-sacrificial behavior should have been selected in situations in which the costs of engaging in an act were less than the benefits to be gained times the degree to which individuals were biologically related (that is, altruistic behavior should occur when $C < Br$, where C = costs, B = benefits, and r = the degree of relatedness; see Simpson, 1999). For example, although it would make sense to sacrifice one's own life to save at least two biological children (each of whom shares 50% of the parent's genes and has years of reproductive potential left), one would have to save many more nieces or nephews (who carry fewer genes) to achieve the same fitness benefits. Hamilton's intellectual breakthrough marked the dawn of modern theorizing in the evolutionary sciences.

Reciprocal Altruism Theory

In 1971, Trivers introduced the theory of reciprocal altruism, which explains why organisms that have inherently "selfish" genes should, at times, behave in a cooperative manner with certain nonkin. *Altruism* is defined as any "behavior that benefits another organism, not closely related, while being apparently detrimental to the organism performing the behavior, benefit and detrimental being defined in terms of contribution to inclusive fitness" (Trivers, 1971, p. 35). The theory suggests that recurrent situations may have arisen during evolutionary history in which nonkin who forged mutually beneficial long-term exchange relationships could have helped one another, facilitating each individual's survival and reproductive output. Trivers identified several special conditions under which selective reciprocal altruism should have enhanced an individual's inclusive fitness and, therefore, might have evolved.

According to Trivers (1971), reciprocal altruism is more likely to have evolved in species that (a) have longer life spans (which increases the probability that an individual will encounter others in altruistic situations), (b) have a higher dispersal rate (which increases the likelihood that an individual will interact repeatedly with the same people), (c) are more mutually dependent (which increases the probability that others could facilitate an individual's survival and successful reproduction), (d) have weak dominance hierarchies (i.e., social structures in which more people can potentially benefit from each other), (e) can benefit from aid in combat (whereby more individuals can assist one another during conflicts with outgroups), and (f) invest heavily in offspring and parental care (in terms of the quantity and the quality of resources directed to children). All of these conditions were met by human groups throughout most of their evolutionary history (Trivers, 1985).

Group Selection Theory

In 1994, Sloan Wilson and Sober reintroduced a model of group selection that revitalized interest in this topic. According to group selection perspectives, there may have been instances in which specific groups of people, rather than individuals, were the primary units of selection in evolutionary history. If certain groups were highly skillful, inventive, or productive across extended periods of time relative to other groups, the members of "successful" groups would have been more reproductively successful than members of less viable groups, on average. Because individuals in successful groups would have needed to be contributing and cohesive group members over time, greater prosociality directed toward all members of the group—including even nonkin—should have been selected for (for related analyses, see chap. 1, this volume; Sloan Wilson, 2002; Sloan Wilson & Sober, 1994). From an evolutionary standpoint, the probability that group selection occurred should have depended on several factors, including the severity of local environments requiring extensive cooperation within a group, the ability and willingness of group members to act self-sacrificially for the good of the group, and the nature and resourcefulness of competing outgroups.

According to Sloan Wilson and Sober's (1994) model, the probability that group selection evolved in certain cases hinges on three parameters: (a) the amount of personal costs associated with making sacrifices for the group, (b) the amount of personal benefits associated with doing so, and (c) the proportion of altruistic versus nonaltruistic members within the group. Simpson (1994) modeled these parameters to estimate the likelihood that group selection would have evolved. The results revealed that although there may have been isolated cases in which group selection emerged, they were probably atypical, aberrant, and unlikely. Specifically, the ratio of personal costs to benefits must have remained very low and the percentage of altruists within the group must have been quite high for extended periods of time to ensure that a group was stable enough to facilitate strong altruism. Although there may have been select cases in which group selection operated (e.g., the Hutterites in North America; see Sloan Wilson & Sober, 1994), these cases were probably rare.

Gene–Culture Coevolutionary Theories

Most recently, Richerson and Boyd (2005) proposed that group selection could have occurred through the joint operation of genetic and cultural evolution. To occur, group selection requires minimal within-group variation in a trait or characteristic critical to the reproductive fitness of individuals within a group, along with a great deal of between-group variation on that trait or characteristic. These conditions are rarely witnessed in primate species because of intergroup migration (Richerson & Boyd, 2005) and the absence of proper conditions (Simpson, 1994). Richerson and Boyd (2005) contended, however, that the evolution of culture may have created special conditions under which group selection could have emerged via gene-culture coevolutionary processes.

During the Pleistocene (1.8 million years ago to approximately 9600 B.C.E.; Lourens, Hilgen, Shackleton, Laskar, & Sloan Wilson, 2004), climate change may have been rapid enough for social learning to become very beneficial, an event that allowed our ancestors to develop novel abilities that supported rapid and diverse social learning. To the extent that social learning facilitated the rapid acquisition of adaptive skills, behaviors, and abilities, it could have been preferentially selected. These skills and abilities most likely spawned the development of cumulative culture, a phenomenon rarely seen in nonhuman societies (Richerson & Boyd, 2005). Not only are humans excellent social imitators but our imitative abilities are also far superior to even the most clever and social of other species, including chimpanzees (Whiten, Custance, Gomez, Teixidor, & Bard, 1996). Although Richerson and Boyd (2005) acknowledged that cultural and social learning occurs in species other than humans, they contended that cumulative knowledge and information is uniquely transmitted from generation to generation in human cultures, which are then built on by subsequent generations. No other species has such a complex cumulative cultural system.

Richerson and Boyd (2005) believed that this process operates through *cultural variants* (i.e., cultural knowledge, skills, and ideas), which are transmitted both between and across groups and also across generations, via social learning, and which are subject to selection pressures in the same general way that genes are. According to Richerson and Boyd, cultural variants that enhance survival and reproduction are more likely to continue within a culture due to selection-like processes, and they are also influenced by evolutionary forces such as genetic mutation and drift. However, cultural variants are also vulnerable to biased transmission in which certain variants become more successful because of their content (being easier to remember than that of other variants and thus more likely to be mimicked or used), their frequency (commonness within a population), and the people who model them (group leaders versus followers). For example, for difficult-to-attain knowledge, such as academic expertise, people must choose among many alternatives to decide what to learn. As a result, people may be prone to choose easier subjects, or subjects that are more common, because they are easier to learn or it is easier to find people from whom relevant skills can be learned.

Under the assumptions that cultures evolved and were adaptive for our ancestors, Richerson and Boyd (2005) proposed that cultural variants contain certain properties that make group selection much more likely to have evolved. If certain conditions were met during evolutionary history—if moralistic punishment was consistent and widespread within a group or culture, if pressures to conform to important group rules and norms were constant and strong, and if there was significant and sustained intergroup conflict—group selection could have evolved. More specifically, to the extent that important group rules and norms were consistently enforced by ingroup members, ingroup members remained motivated to conform "for the good of the group" to norms and rules, and sustained conflict existed between competing groups, within-group variability in terms of behaving in line with important ingroup norms and rules should have decreased and between-group variability should have increased. These factors could have created the necessary conditions for group selection to occur (see Richerson & Boyd, 2005). When these conditions coalesced, ancestral groups that encouraged self-sacrifice for the greater good of the group should have out-competed rival groups, and stronger forms of prosocial behavior toward ingroup members should have emerged.

Once this happened, genetic evolution may have been influenced by culture insofar as individuals who regularly behaved in ways that promoted the welfare of the group (e.g., recognizing ingroup members and distinguishing them from outgroup members, habitually conforming to basic group norms or rules, being willing to punish anyone who violated critical group norms or rules) became more reproductively successful (see also Haidt, 2007). This interaction between genetic and cultural evolution may have resulted in the evolution of what Richerson and Boyd (2005) called *tribal instincts*. These instincts encompass three attributes: (a) psychological predispositions (i.e., psychological mechanisms) that encouraged the enforcement of important group norms and rules; (b) psychological mechanisms that permitted easy and rapid discrimination between groups, especially ingroup versus outgroup members; and (c) emotional capabilities that permitted the experience and expression of certain complex social emotions, such as guilt and shame, which may have facilitated stronger forms of prosociality.

The Expansion of Prosociality in Evolutionary Theories

Over time, evolutionary theories have focused greater attention on the evolution of prosocial tendencies in humans. This trend, shown in Figure 2.1, can be depicted as a series of expanding circles, beginning with Darwin's (1859) theory of evolution by natural selection at the core.

Although Darwin was sympathetic to the idea that humans evolved to be highly prosocial, he focused on survival and reproduction at the level of the individual and could not fully explain how strong forms of prosociality

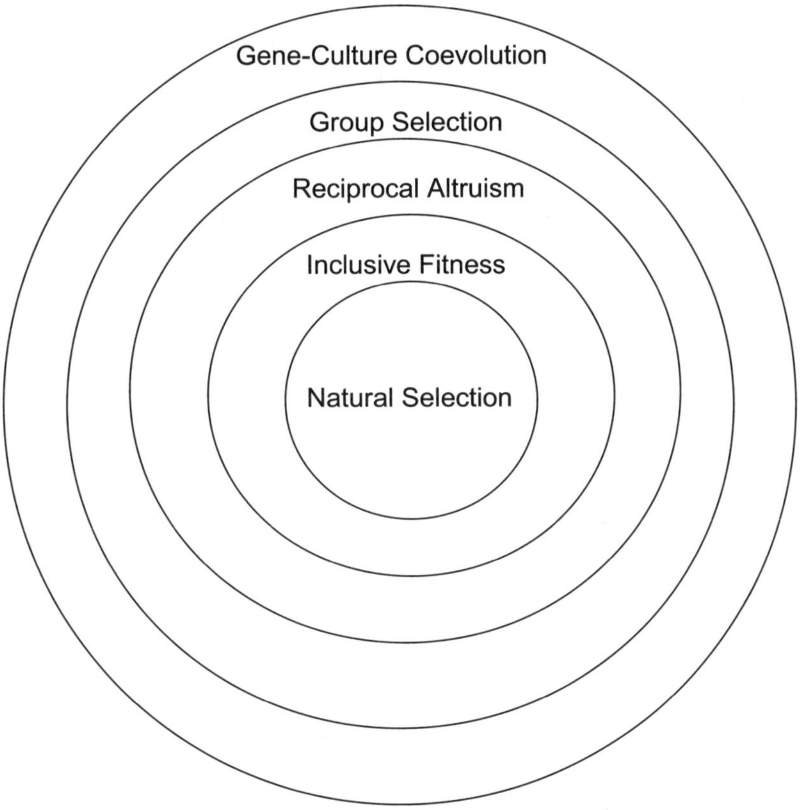

Figure 2.1. Major evolutionary theories relevant to prosociality in humans.

evolved in humans. Inclusive fitness theory (Hamilton, 1964) greatly expanded the evolutionary foundations of strong prosociality by documenting how and why organisms would have benefited by making sacrifices for biologically related relatives who carried a portion of their genes. Reciprocal altruism theory (Trivers, 1971) moved beyond a purely "gene-centered" perspective by indicating how and why long-term, mutually cooperative, and reciprocal exchanges with nonkin could also have evolved, especially in humans. Group selection models (e.g., Sloan Wilson & Sober, 1994) then directed attention to special cases in which strong prosociality in humans might have been amplified by the differential reproduction of individuals in highly cooperative, cohesive, and productive groups, compared with those in less cooperative, cohesive, and productive groups. Gene–environment coevolutionary models have substantially expanded the possible evolutionary foundations of strong prosociality in humans. These recent models have provided additional compelling reasons for how and why strong prosociality should have evolved. These most recent models were developed in response to both new theorizing (e.g., Boyd & Richerson, 1988; Brewer & Caporael, 1990) and anthropological evidence (e.g., Cronk, 1999; Kelly, 1995) suggesting the extremely interdependent, complex, and role-governed division of labor that characterizes existing hunter–gatherer tribes and, most likely, the majority of human groups during evolutionary history.

EMPIRICAL EVIDENCE FOR EVOLUTIONARY THEORIES OF PROSOCIAL BEHAVIOR

In this section, we review research that has tested evolutionary theories, models, or principles of prosociality in humans. Some of this work has tested gene-centered theories of evolution, particularly inclusive fitness theory. Other research inspired by coevolutionary models has investigated the conditions under which individuals are willing to display strong prosocial tendencies, including the willingness to punish cheaters for the good of a group at considerable cost to the self.

Inclusive Fitness Theory

Most of the research on gene-centered models of the evolution of prosociality in humans has tested predictions derived from inclusive fitness theory. Much of this work has investigated the conditions under which the degree of genetic relatedness between *helpers* and *recipients* of help is associated with how resources are distributed to close biological relatives, to more distant kin, and to nonbiologically related others.

According to inclusive fitness theory, people should be biased on average to distribute a larger percentage of assistance and resources to kin with whom they share more genes. For example, individuals ought to preferentially benefit persons with whom they share half their genes (e.g., full siblings), compared with more distantly related kin (e.g., half siblings, first cousins) or nonkin (e.g., good friends). Regardless of whether one examines financial estates (Judge, 1995), physical labor (Berte, 1988), or procuring food (e.g., fishing catches; Betzig & Turke, 1986), resources are almost always distributed preferentially to closer biological relatives. This nepotistic bias also extends to the willingness to endure pain for closer relatives. Fieldman, Plotkin, Dunbar, Robertson, and McFarland (described in Barrett, Dunbar, & Lycett, 2002) found that people are more willing to endure a painful physical task for longer periods of time if the money they will receive for doing so is given to closer biological relatives rather than more distant biological relatives or close friends. This willingness to endure greater pain for closer relatives does not depend on how much individuals like or spend time with their closer relatives; only the degree of genetic relatedness accounts for this effect. Moreover, when they asked how willing individuals would be to engage in risky behavior that would benefit other people,

Korchmaros and Kenny (2001) found that individuals are more willing to assume greater risks to help closer biological relatives, an effect that is only partially mediated by the degree of emotional closeness to closer relatives. Similar results have emerged when "empathic concern" (chap. 7, this volume) is treated as a mediating variable (Kruger, 2003).

Viewed together, these studies suggest that costly forms of assistance (altruism) are preferentially directed toward closer biological relatives and that these effects are not driven by greater psychological closeness, attachment, or connection with closer biological relatives. The degree of genetic relatedness appears to be the most parsimonious explanation of these effects.

Some of the most elegant tests of inclusive fitness theory have been conducted by Eugene Burnstein and his colleagues. Burnstein, Crandall, and Kitayama (1994), for example, performed several scenario studies in which they experimentally manipulated different sets of variables relevant to inclusive fitness theory, such as the benefits versus costs of helping a particular person, and the recipient's age, gender, and degree of kinship with the helper. In both the United States and Japan, the reported likelihood of giving assistance increases linearly with the degree of genetic relatedness between the helper and the recipient, especially when help might save the recipient's life. These findings support a central prediction based on inclusive fitness theory: The larger the ratio of benefits to costs of help to recipients, the more helpers should be biased to offer more help to closer biological relatives. The willingness to offer assistance also depends on the age of recipients, with the oldest and the youngest closer relatives—individuals who are most likely to be outcome dependent and least likely to reciprocate help—usually receiving more reported assistance than middle-aged closer relatives. By aiding the most vulnerable and outcome dependent, helpers might be "advertising" their benevolence and/or their ability to provide help and still remain resourceful (e.g., Grafen, 1990), either of which could lead to receiving fitness-enhancing benefits from other group members in the future.

Burnstein et al. (1994) also found that helpers are willing to give more assistance to healthy kin than to nonhealthy kin in life-or-death situations, whereas the reverse is true in everyday, nonthreatening situations. And when deciding how much to help members of different groups (e.g., kin groups versus nonkin groups), helpers strongly favor groups that are more likely to provide a better *reproductive return*, defined as the sum of the group members' degrees of genetic relatedness to the helper. Particularly in life-or-death situations, therefore, biological relatives tend to view themselves as a social unit that lives or dies together (Burnstein, 2005).

Reciprocal Altruism Theory

According to reciprocal altruism theory (Trivers, 1971), if two biologically unrelated individuals provide mutual benefits to one another that are greater than the costs each individual incurs by providing the benefits, both individuals ought to benefit through the economic principle of gains in trade. As a result, genes that led our ancestors to recognize and selectively enter mutually beneficial transactions with nonkin, such as long-term tit-for-tat exchanges with highly resourceful and trustworthy partners, could have been selected.

Axelrod (1984) established that tit-for-tat strategies, in which positive partner overtures are immediately rewarded and negative ones are immediately punished, tend to develop quickly and remain stable as long as interaction partners continue to make cooperative choices in two-person experimental games. All of the conditions necessary for the evolution of reciprocal altruism in humans—important benefits can be given to others, individuals have repeated interactions with the same people, individuals can remember to whom they have given benefits and from whom they have received benefits, and exchange decisions are based on the outcomes of earlier interactions with specific people—were probably present in evolutionary history.

Indeed, Hill (2002) documented "altruistic cooperation" in the Ache, a remote tribe that lives in the rugged mountains of Paraguay. Ache men and women spend approximately 10% of their foraging time engaged in activities that benefit biologically unrelated individuals in the tribe, often at noteworthy costs to themselves or their families. Furthermore, food sharing is based more on a person's current need than on his or her degree of genetic relatedness to the individual who secured the food if the needy person has assisted or shared with others in the past. These findings suggest that principles of equity and need rather than genetic relatedness alone govern food sharing decisions in the Ache. This makes sense when one considers the unpredictable and variable pattern of the Ache's food supply; sharing surplus food with cooperative and well-intentioned others is likely to be beneficial because currently needy individuals should be more likely to share food or other valuable resources when they have them in the future. Reciprocal altruism, therefore, may provide some measure of insurance against inevitable hardships and limited resources in the future.

Kurzban (2003) believed that the need for cooperative hunting could have been one of the major selection pressures that jump-started reciprocal altruism and strong prosociality in humans. Delayed exchanges of goods and resources may have been more common in evolutionary environments than simultaneous (immediate) exchanges, requiring that trust in others be carefully and judiciously placed. The successful use of a tit-for-tat strategy requires a willingness to trust partners and be cooperative on the first "move" (trial), after which decisions are based on whether partners have behaved cooperatively or noncooperatively on subsequent trials. Clutton-Brock and Parker (1995) proposed that spite—the inclination to punish or ostracize defecting or uncooperative individuals, even when such actions are costly to the self—may have evolved to "back up" prosocial orientations or expectations if partners reneged on important promises. And Tooby and Cosmides (1990, 1992) have conjectured that specialized cognitive abilities in humans (e.g., cheater detection, superior memory for faces) should have evolved to help individuals identify and envision new ways in which valuable resources could be exchanged, further fueling the evolution of reciprocal altruism in humans.

Gene–Culture Coevolutionary Theories

Gene–culture coevolutionary models (sometimes termed *multilevel selection models*) were formulated in response to the fact that gene-centered evolutionary models cannot fully explain the pervasiveness and depth of human altruism and prosociality. Establishing evidence for gene–culture coevolution requires convergent findings that meet the necessary conditions specified by theorists such as Richerson and Boyd (2005). If their model is correct, people should have evolved (a) strong tendencies to conform to important group rules and norms, (b) the clear ability to distinguish ingroup members from outgroup members, and (c) the propensity to punish persons who violate important group rules and norms.

These core propositions have been supported by classic research in social psychology as well as recent findings in the group decision-making area. The tendency for people to conform to group norms and pressures has been extensively documented (for a review, see Cialdini & Goldstein, 2004). The power and pervasiveness of group conformity effects was initially demonstrated by Sherif (1936) and Asch (1956). Asch's classic studies, for example, showed that individuals report blatantly incorrect evaluations of stimuli in easy judgment tasks in order to agree with group members who see things differently than they themselves do. However, social psychologists have only recently attempted to interpret conformity effects from the vantage point of evolutionary thinking (see, e.g., Griskevicius, Goldstein, Mortensen, Cialdini, & Kenrick, 2006).

Multitudes of studies have confirmed the powerful and almost automatic tendency for ingroup members to distinguish between and discriminate against outgroups (for a review, see Brewer & Brown, 1998). Tajfel and Turner's (1979) social identity theory and subsequent research, for instance, has demonstrated how easily and quickly people identify ingroup members, even when groups are based on arbitrary or meaningless attributes, and how willing they are to benefit ingroup members with valuable resources, often at the expense of outgroup members. Sherif, Harvey, White, Hood, and Sherif (1954/1961) revealed the powerful tendency of boys at a summer camp to immediately identify with their randomly assigned group and then to engage in hostile intergroup conflict with boys in another group, following only minimal provocation. Indeed, Brewer and Caporael (2006) have now recast some of the major principles of social identify theory within an evolutionary framework.

Other recent research supports the third component of Richerson and Boyd's (2005) model, the willingness of group members to engage in moralistic punishment. Humans are unique among species in their ability and willingness to display *strong reciprocity* (Fehr & Fischbacher, 2003). Strong reciprocity is witnessed when individuals take on the costs of rewarding or punishing others in situations in which cooperation is required to secure vital resources or good outcomes, even if "enforcers" receive no personal benefits or sometimes incur great costs. Unlike reciprocal altruism, which presumes that individuals should reward or punish others only if tangible benefits are likely to be received (Axelrod & Hamilton, 1981), strong reciprocity indicates that individuals are willing to enforce important social rules or norms to ensure that cheaters and noncooperators do not destroy cooperation and goodwill within groups. Laboratory studies using the ultimatum game have confirmed that individuals closely monitor and quickly punish those who behave unfairly (e.g., who cheat or fail to reciprocate cooperation) or who offer others unfair outcomes, even if providing sanctions harms their own rational self-interest (Fehr & Fischbacher, 2003). Research using intergenerational ultimatum games (i.e., games in which different players interact over time) has also confirmed that receiving advice from previous players increases altruistic punishments and rewards enacted by current players, and that players who receive advice usually achieve greater cooperation from other players across time.

What explains this clear willingness to make personal sacrifices in order to maintain cooperative norms and behavior within groups? The answer probably lies in how easily cooperation can disintegrate. Because a very small percentage of free riders or chronic cheaters can destroy cooperation in most groups, cooperative systems often fail unless a large majority of group members vigilantly monitor and sanction norm violaters, even if they have no personal stake or investment in a given interaction (Fehr & Schmidt, 1999). Individuals who regularly police and enforce important rules and norms, however, may also gain personal benefits through being seen as highly altruistic, which could enhance their reputation within a group (Alexander, 1987; Nowak & Sigmund, 1998) or signal that they are sufficiently resourceful to endure the costs of engaging in altruistic, self-sacrificial acts (Gintis, Smith, & Bowles, 2001).

Advocates of gene–culture coevolutionary models have questioned whether tit-for-tat strategies could have been responsible for the evolution of reciprocal altruism in humans. Even though the results of repeated two-person interaction studies indicate that tit-for-tat strategies can develop quickly and remain stable (Axelrod, 1984), these strategies become less stable in *n*-person Prisoner's Dilemma games unless virtually all group members cooperate on each experimental trial (Boyd & Richerson, 1988). Moreover, tit-for-tat paradigms typically stipulate that individuals cannot "leave the game" (exit) and that third parties cannot intervene unless they can personally benefit from rewarding fair players or punishing unfair ones. These conditions rarely exist in most real-world settings (see Boyd & Richerson, 1988; Richerson & Boyd, 2005).

In summary, gene–culture coevolutionary models contend that traditional purely gene-centered selection models do not and cannot fully account for the evolution and maintenance of strong reciprocity, whereas gene–culture coevolution theories can. These more recent models suggest that certain norms and institutions, such as sharing food, hunting and gathering, and serial monogamy, could have been maintained to benefit most members of a group to the extent that everyone monitored and was willing to sanction norm or rule violators. This propensity may have spawned widespread strong forms of prosociality, including altruism, in humans.

INTEGRATION AND CONCLUSIONS

According to Darwin, organisms that "profited" by living in society should have lived and worked together and doing so should have increased their reproductive and inclusive fitness. Early gene-centered models of evolution (e.g., inclusive fitness theory) focused on how and why strong forms of prosociality and altruism directed toward kin could have evolved. Indeed, research has begun to document the specific conditions under which individuals are willing to make major sacrifices for other people, often in line with the percentage of genes the helpers share with those in need. These effects are strongest, however, when closer biological relatives face life-or-death situations and immediate help may save their lives.

Later evolutionary theories, such as reciprocal altruism theory, showcased how and why individuals could also have experienced greater reproductive and inclusive fitness by entering certain long-term, mutually beneficial exchange relationships with nonrelatives who had skills, resources, or abilities that enhanced an individual's well-being. Particularly in harsh, difficult, or demanding environments in which resources were scare or difficult to secure, or competition for them was keen, preferences for selective reciprocal alliances are likely to have evolved to solve basic challenges of daily living.

The most recent approaches, particularly gene–environment coevolutionary models (e.g., Richerson & Boyd, 2005), have extended the possible evolutionary bases of prosociality in humans even further. These models outline how and why the emergence of complex, cumulative culture could have differentially increased the reproductive and inclusive fitness of individuals who were members of highly stable, cooperative, and productive groups or collectives. Richerson and Boyd (2005) believed that the three "tribal instincts" evolved in part to solve chronic problems associated with competition with other local groups and/or the benefits that were gained from residing in a group that enhanced the average group member's reproductive and/or inclusive fitness.

Darwin left intellectual room for all of these subsequent theories and models, each of which focuses on slightly different adaptive problems that our ancestors probably recurrently faced. Extreme forms of prosociality (e.g., saving someone's life) may have evolved to protect one's inclusive fitness when close relatives who had years of reproductive potential ahead of them required immediate assistance in order to live. More routine and mundane forms of prosociality (e.g., assisting or trading with nonrelatives on a regular basis) may have increased reproductive or inclusive fitness, especially when resources were limited, sporadic, or difficult to obtain, or when competition for them was intense. Other forms of prosociality (e.g., helping all members of one's group, even if a reciprocal alliance has not been established) might have further increased reproductive or inclusive fitness through the benefits of cumulative culture and living in a highly cohesive and productive group. Given the many daunting obstacles to survival, reproduction, good parenting, and good grandparenting that our ancestors faced (see Buss, 2005), humans should have evolved to take advantage of all opportunities that would have enhanced their inclusive fitness.

In conclusion, human society is difficult for evolutionary theories to fully explain. The degree of cooperative, prosocial behavior displayed within human groups and societies is rare within the animal kingdom. Only a few species, such as colonial invertebrates (e.g., corals) and social insects (e.g., *Hymenoptera*), develop societies and social structures that come anywhere close to rivaling the size and complexity of human groups and cultures. No other species has ever developed such large and complex societies that involve such an array of nongenetically related individuals (Richerson & Boyd, 1998). For species such as *Hymenoptera*, the puzzle of how prosocial "selfless" behavior could have evolved is easily solved by inclusive fitness theory, given that most organisms in a hive or colony are highly genetically related and sometimes genetically identical. To account for the extreme levels of prosociality witnessed in humans, one must draw on different evolutionary theories that address multiple levels of selection pressures.

Human prosociality is most likely the result of multiple selection pressures and multiple evolved mechanisms, all of which have pushed human evolution in an increasingly cooperative and prosocial direction relative to most other species. This premise—that multiple forces and selection pressures probably favored cooperation and caring during human evolutionary history—runs counter to the common misperception that evolution entails fierce direct competition and that nature is "red in tooth and claw." Each of the evolutionary theories we have reviewed indicates when, how, and why an individual's inclusive fitness could have been enhanced if he or she selectively acted in a cooperative and caring manner toward others in certain recurrent social contexts. Far from being competitive and antagonistic, our most reproductively successful ancestors may have been among the most cooperative and resourceful individuals within their groups.

REFERENCES

Alexander, R. D. (1987). *The biology of moral systems*. New York: Aldine de Gruyter.

Asch, S. E. (1956). Studies of independence and conformity: A minority of one against a unanimous majority. *Psychological Monographs, 70*(9).

Axelrod, R. (1984). *The evolution of cooperation*. New York: Basic Books.

Axelrod, R., & Hamilton, W. D. (1981, March 27). The evolution of cooperation. *Science, 211*, 1390–1396.

Barrett, L., Dunbar, R., & Lycett, J. (2002). *Human evolutionary psychology*. Princeton, NJ: Princeton University Press.

Berte, N. A. (1988). K'ekchi horticulture labor exchange: Productive and reproductive implications. In L. Betzig, M. Borgerhoff Mulder, & P. Turke (Eds.), *Human reproductive behavior: A Darwinian perspective* (pp. 83–96). Cambridge, England: Cambridge University Press.

Betzig, L., & Turke, P. (1986). Food sharing on Ifaluk. *Current Anthropology, 27*, 397–400.

Boyd, R., & Richerson, P. J. (1988). The evolution of reciprocity in sizable groups. *Journal of Theoretical Biology, 132*, 337–356.

Brewer, M. B., & Brown, R. J. (1998). Intergroup relations. In D. T. Gilbert, S. T. Fiske, & G. Lindzey (Eds.), *The handbook of social psychology* (Vol. 2; pp. 554–594). New York: McGraw-Hill.

Brewer, M. B., & Caporael, L. R. (1990). Selfish genes versus selfish people: Sociobiology as origin myth. *Motivation and Emotion, 14*, 237–243.

Brewer, M. B., & Caporael, L. R. (2006). An evolutionary perspective of social identity: Revisiting groups. In M. Schaller, J. A. Simpson, & D. T. Kenrick (Eds.), *Evolution and social psychology* (pp. 143–161). New York: Psychology Press.

Burnstein, E. (2005). Altruism and genetic relatedness. In D. Buss (Ed.), *The handbook of evolutionary psychology* (pp. 528–551). New York: Wiley.

Burnstein, E., Crandall, C., & Kitayama, S. (1994). Some neo-Darwinian decision rules for altruism: Weighting cues for inclusive fitness as a function of the biological importance of the decision. *Journal of Personality and Social Psychology, 67*, 773–789.

Buss, D. M. (Ed.). (2005). *The handbook of evolutionary psychology*. New York: Wiley.

Cialdini, R. B., & Goldstein, N. J. (2004). Social influence: Compliance and conformity. *Annual Review of Psychology*, 55, 591–621.

Clutton-Brock, T. H., & Parker, G. A. (1995, January 19). Punishment in animal societies. *Nature, 373*, 209–216.

Cosmides, L., & Tooby, J. (1992). Cognitive adaptations for social exchange. In J. Barkow, L. Cosmides, & J. Tooby (Eds.), *The adapted mind* (pp. 163–228). New York: Oxford University Press.

Cronk, L. (1999). *That complex whole: Culture and the evolution of human behavior.* New York: Westview.

Darwin, C. (1859). *On the origins of species*. London: John Murray.

Darwin, C. (1981). *The descent of man, and selection in relation to sex*. Princeton, NJ: Princeton University Press. (Original work published 1871)

Eibl-Eibesfeldt, I. (1989). *Human ethology*. New York: Aldine de Gruyter.

Fehr, E., & Fischbacher, U. (2003, October 23). The nature of human altruism. *Nature, 425*, 785–791.

Fehr, E., & Schmidt, K. M. (1999). A theory of fairness, competition and cooperation. *Quarterly Journal of Economics, 114*, 817–868.

Foley, R. (1992). Evolutionary ecology and fossil hominids. In E. Smith & B. Winterholder (Eds.), *Evolutionary ecology and human behavior* (pp. 29–64). New York: Aldine de Gruyter.

Gangestad, S. W., & Simpson, J. A. (Eds.). (2007). *The evolution of mind: Fundamental questions and controversies*. New York: Guilford Press.

Gintis, H., Smith, E. A., & Bowles, S. (2001). Costly signaling and cooperation. *Journal of Theoretical Biology, 213*, 103–119.

Grafen, A. (1990). Biological signals as handicaps. *Journal of Theoretical Biology, 144*, 517–546.

Griskevicius, V., Goldstein, N. J., Mortensen, C. R., Cialdini, R. B., & Kenrick, D. T. (2006). Going along versus going alone: When fundamental motives facilitate strategic (non)conformity. *Journal of Personality and Social Psychology, 91*, 281–294.

Haidt, J. (2007). The new synthesis in moral psychology. *Science, 316*, 998–1002.

Hamilton, W. D. (1964). The genetical evolution of social behavior. *Journal of Theoretical Biology, 7*, 1–52.

Hill, K. (2002). Altruistic cooperation during foraging by the Ache, and evolved human predisposition to cooperate. *Human Nature, 13*, 105–128.

Judge, D. S. (1995). American legacies and the variable life histories of women and men. *Human Nature, 6*, 291–324.

Kelly, R. L. (1995). *The foraging spectrum: Diversity in hunter-gatherer lifeways*. Washington, DC: Smithsonian Institution Press.

Korchmaros, J. D., & Kenny, D.A. (2001). Emotional closeness as a mediator of the effect of genetic relatedness on altruism. *Psychological Science, 12*, 262–265.

Kruger, D. J. (2003). Evolution and altruism: Combining psychological mediators with naturally selected tendencies. *Evolution and Human Behavior, 24*, 118–125.

Kurzban, R. (2003). Biological foundations of reciprocity. In E. Ostrom & J. Walker (Eds.), *Trust and reciprocity: Interdisciplinary lessons from experimental research* (pp. 105–127). New York: Russell Sage Foundation.

Lourens, L., Hilgen, F., Shackleton, N. J., Laskar, J., & Sloan Wilson, D. (2004). The neogene period. In F. Gradstein, J. Ogg, & A. G. Smith (Eds.), *A geologic time scale 2004*. Cambridge, England: Cambridge University Press.

Nowak, M. A., & Sigmund, K. (1998). Evolution of indirect reciprocity by imaging scoring. *Nature, 393*, 573–577.

Richerson, P. J., & Boyd, R. (1998). The evolution of human ultra-sociality. In I. Eibl-Eibisfeldt & F. Salter (Eds.), *Ideology, warfare, and indoctrinability* (pp. 71–95). New York: Berghahn Books.

Richerson, P. J., & Boyd, R. (2005). *Not by genes alone: How culture transformed human evolution*. Chicago: University of Chicago Press.

Sherif, M. (1936). *The psychology of social norms*. New York: Harper & Row.

Sherif, M., Harvey, O. J., White, B. J., Hood, W. R., & Sherif, C. W. (1954/1961). *Study of positive and negative intergroup attitudes between experimentally produced groups: Robbers Cave study*. Norman: University of Oklahoma.

Simpson, J. A. (1994). Adaptation and natural selection: A new look at some old ideas. *Behavioral and Brain Sciences, 17*, 634–636.

Simpson, J. A. (1999). Attachment theory in modern evolutionary perspective. In J. Cassidy & P. R. Shaver (Eds.), *Handbook of attachment: Theory, research, and clinical applications* (pp. 115–140). New York: Guilford Press.

Sloan Wilson, D. (2002). *Darwin's cathedral: Evolution, religion, and the nature of society*. Chicago, IL: University of Chicago Press.

Sloan Wilson, D., & Sober, E. (1994). Reintroducing group selection to the human behavioral sciences. *Behavioral and Brain Sciences, 17*, 585–608.

Tajfel, H., & Turner, J. C. (1979). An integrative theory of intergroup conflict. In W. G. Austin & S. Worchel (Eds.), *The social psychology of intergroup relations*. Monterey, CA: Brooks-Cole.

Tennyson, A. L. (1906). *In memorian*. New York: Silver Burdett Company. (Original poem published 1850).

Tooby, J., & Cosmides, L. (1990). On the universality of human nature and the uniqueness of the individual: The role of genetics and adaptation. *Journal of Personality, 58*, 17–68.

Tooby, J., & Cosmides, L. (1992). Psychological foundations of culture. In J. Barkow, L. Cosmides, & J. Tooby (Eds.), *The adapted mind* (pp. 19–136). New York: Oxford University Press.

Trivers, R. (1971). The evolution of reciprocal altruism. *Quarterly Review of Biology, 46*, 35–57.

Trivers, R. L. (1985). *Social evolution*. Menlo Park, CA: Benjamin/Cummings.

Whiten, A., Custance, D. M., Gomez, J. C., Teixidor, P., & Bard, K. A. (1996). Imitative learning of artificial fruit processing in children (*Homo sapiens*) and chimpanzees (*Pan troglodytes*). *Journal of Comparative Psychology*, 110, 3–14.

Wood, W., & Eagly, A. H. (2002). A cross-cultural analysis of the behavior of men and women: Implications for the origins of sex differences. *Psychological Bulletin, 128*, 699–727.

Wright, R. (1994). *The moral animal*. New York: Vintage.

3

ENDURING GOODNESS: A PERSON-BY-SITUATION PERSPECTIVE ON PROSOCIAL BEHAVIOR

LOUIS A. PENNER AND HEATHER OROM

Many laypeople believe that there are some individuals who consistently care about others and provide aid to them with little or no prompting. Further, they believe that these individuals' willingness to help is not motivated by selfish or self-centered desires to gain an interpersonal advantage over recipients of the help or as a way of making a favorable impression on others. Rather, these individuals' prosocial actions are believed to be due to a stable disposition that one might call "enduring goodness."

For a long time, however, social psychologists questioned whether personal dispositions were such important causes of prosocial actions. For example, many of the researchers who did the pioneering work on helping in emergencies (e.g., Latané & Darley, 1970) argued that prosocial actions such as helping a stranger are determined largely by characteristics of the situa-

Some of the research reported in this chapter was supported by a grant from the National Cancer Institute (5R01CA100027-03), on which the first author is a co-investigator. Terrance L. Albrecht is the principal investigator. Heather Orom is now in the Department of Health Behavior at the University of Buffalo, Buffalo, New York.

tion confronting potential helpers. That is, dispositions, if they even exist, were thought to play a relatively unimportant role in many prosocial actions. More recently, this strong situationist perspective has become less dominant in the study of prosocial behavior; as several chapters in this volume illustrate, a good number of researchers believe that dispositions play an important role in prosocial behavior (see chaps. 4, 7, 8, and 19). We share this perspective; however, as the chapter title suggests, we also believe that a full understanding of the causes of prosocial actions requires considering how person and situation interact to affect this class of behaviors.

To justify our (and others') interest in dispositions as causes of prosocial actions, we must find affirmative answers to four key questions. First, is there evidence of intraindividual consistency in prosocial actions across situations and across time? Second, is there evidence of reliable interindividual variability in prosocial responses among people who confront the same situation? Third, to what extent are both temporal/situational consistency and interindividual variability in prosocial action due to enduring personal dispositions? And fourth, can we identify these dispositions?

We begin the chapter by presenting our conceptualization of personal dispositions, and after this we present a brief history of theory and research on dispositional variables as causes of prosocial actions. Then, we discuss some of the personal attributes we believe are at the core of a prosocial personality orientation. In the next two sections, we examine how personal dispositions are associated with different kinds of helping. More precisely, we first consider dispositions and *macro level* prosocial actions—those that occur among strangers in the context of large formal and informal organizations (Penner, Dovidio, Schroeder, & Piliavin, 2005); second, we consider dispositions and *meso level* prosocial actions—helping that occurs in interpersonal dyads and other similar contexts (see chaps. 17–19, this volume). We close with a summary of the chapter and suggestions for future research directions.

RESEARCH ON DISPOSITIONS AND PROSOCIAL ACTIONS

We begin by noting that in this chapter we deliberately use the word *prosocial* rather than *altruistic*. *Prosocial action* is a generic term that encompasses any act intended to benefit another person or entity; the motivation responsible for that act is not considered. In contrast, *altruistic behavior* is a subset of prosocial behavior in which the sole motivation for the action is to improve another person's well-being, with there being no expectation of tangible or even intangible rewards. If we considered only altruistic personality tendencies, we would restrict ourselves to the dispositions associated with one specific kind of prosocial actions, which, although important and interesting, is probably not all that common. Further, if we claim that some disposition is linked to an altruistic action, then we need to demonstrate persuasively that the action is truly selfless and other oriented. As most readers know, this has not been an easy task (see, e.g., chap. 1, this volume, vs. Cialdini, Brown, Lewis, Luce, & Neuberg, 1997). Thus, we have opted to avoid claiming that either the dispositions or behaviors we study are due to altruism; to us, they are simply prosocial.

Our Conceptual Approach to Dispositions

For the most part, the dispositions of interest in this chapter are facets of personality. Our conceptualization of such dispositions reflects the two authors' different theoretical orientations to personality. Following Orom's more social–cognitive perspective (e.g., Orom & Cervone, 2009), we believe that a useful definition of dispositions should encompass psychological structures and processes that have the potential to cause behavior. Also, we do not presume that dispositions influence behavior regardless of context, but rather that dispositions are heuristics for grouping biopsychological structures and processes that unfold in subsets of individuals in similar ways, in similar contexts (chap. 4, this volume). In addition, consistent with Penner's (2002) approach to the prosocial personality orientation, we believe that a trait perspective on personality, although largely descriptive rather than explanatory, can substantially inform our understanding of how individuals function in the world and can lead the way to increased understanding of the structures and processes in the individual that are the proximal causes of behavior (see also chaps. 13 and 14, this volume).

Because dispositions such as attachment style and values are discussed elsewhere in this volume (e.g., chaps. 4, 14, and 19), we do not discuss how they are related to prosocial actions. Also, because of disagreements as to whether motives are dispositions as we have defined them, we do not discuss their role in prosocial actions. (However, readers interested in motives should see Omoto & Snyder, 1995; Penner, Midili, & Kegelmeyer, 1997; Rioux & Penner, 2001.)

Dispositions and Prosocial Behavior: A Brief Research History

The question of whether or not there are stable individual differences in prosocial tendencies is not a new one, and answers to this question have changed several times over the years. These changes are discussed and analyzed in the next few sections.

The Early Years

This brief history begins with Hartshorne and May's (1928) report on an investigation of whether there was consistency in children's "character." Hartshorne and May identified several situations in which the children might act honestly or dishonestly (e.g., lie, cheat) and assessed consistency across situations with respect to this aspect of the children's character. For example, did the same children behave honestly (or dishonestly) in both the classroom and on the playground? The correlations among behaviors related to honesty across situations were quite low. In subsequent studies, Hartshorne and May reported similar low correlations for cross-situational behaviors related to helpfulness and self-control (Rushton, 1981, disputed this conclusion, but he was one of the few researchers who took this position on Hartshorne and May's findings). Most personality theorists either ignored or dismissed Hartshorne and May's findings, perhaps because they contradicted trait theories of personality (e.g., Allport, 1937), which were extremely popular at the time. Thus, these early null findings regarding consistencies in prosocial behavior did not result in the immediate demise of dispositional approaches in psychology. However, in the 1960s, Hartshorne and May's findings were rediscovered and became part of the evidence for arguments that seriously questioned the role of dispositions in social behavior.

The major challenge to a dispositional approach to social behavior could be found in Walter Mischel's (1968) monograph, *Personality and Assessment*. In his book, Mischel reported on a large body of evidence that showed (a) low correlations (.30 or less) for behavioral consistency across situations, when either the same kinds of behaviors (e.g., being honest) or conceptually related behaviors (e.g., being helpful and honest) were examined, and (b) weak correlations (again, .30 or less) between self-reports of traits and observed behaviors that should be related to those dispositions. Mischel concluded from these findings that the "concept of personality traits as broad dispositions is thus untenable" (p. 140). Orom and Cervone (2009) have argued that Mischel's real goal in this critique was to point out the weaknesses of personality research that focused solely on inferring broad dispositions from behavioral signs and that personality researchers should instead seek to understand the "cognitive social learning" that shapes social behaviors. However, many researchers interpreted him as arguing that features of the situation were much stronger predictors of behavior than personality variables (i.e., the so-called situationist position). This position had widespread appeal to social and even some personality psychologists.

Research on prosocial behavior was especially influenced by the situationist zeitgeist. One reason was Latané and Darley's (1970) seminal work on bystander interventions in emergencies. Latané and Darley's model of the causes of bystander interventions clearly reflects a situationist approach to why bystanders do or do not help. However, they did examine the possibility that there were individual differences in bystanders' responses to emergencies. But like most other researchers at the time, they found no evidence that personality traits were systematically associated with prosocial behavior. Indeed, this research rarely produced correlations that even reached the modest .30 level Mischel had called the "personality coefficient" (Dovidio, Piliavin, Schroeder, & Penner, 2006).

Other researchers also challenged the dispositional approach to social behavior. For example, Nisbett (1980) believed that the "trait approach to the determination of social behavior . . . is largely wrong" (p. 110), and that laypeople's beliefs in the importance of traits as causes of social behavior were also largely wrong. In a review that focused specifically on personality and prosocial behaviors, Gergen, Gergen, and Meter (1972) identified studies that had found dispositional correlates of prosocial actions and examined the strength and replicability of these findings. Gergen et al.'s succinct and depressing conclusion was that the findings were a "quagmire of evanescent relationships among variables, conflicting findings and (very weak) correlations" (p. 110). Piliavin, Dovidio, Gaertner, and Clark (1981) took a similar position in their monograph on emergency interventions, concluding that "the search for the 'generalized helping personality' has been futile" (p. 184).

The Comeback

Despite the fact that dispositional approaches to social behavior were basically "on life support" in the 1970s and 1980s, they survived and rebounded. There are many reasons for the comeback of dispositional variables as explanations of prosocial behaviors, some of which we discuss here.

First, the simplistic version of the situationist position (i.e., situations, not dispositions, cause behavior; dispositions are largely irrelevant) was challenged on empirical, conceptual, and methodological grounds. The following were some of the more successful challenges: Bem and Allen's (1974) reconceptualization of when and why individual dispositions do and do not affect social behavior, which produced disposition-behavior correlation coefficients much greater than .30; Funder's (1987) conceptual arguments, which pointed out the logical fallacies of studies that purported to show that personality dispositions were largely illusory and did not predict social behavior; and Epstein's (1983) methodological criticisms of Mischel's approach to the prediction of social behavior. Epstein argued that Mischel had failed to consider measurement error as a primary cause of low estimates of transituational consistency and the poor predictive validity of self-report personality measures. Epstein pointed out that there is a considerable amount of measurement error when one uses a specific behavior measured at a single point in time as an indicator of a class or kind of behaviors. If one conducts multiple measurements, he said, the social behavior of interest will be measured much more reliably. As a result, one should find both substantial transituational consistency and good predictive validity for self-report personality measures. Epstein's data showed exactly these effects. Although Epstein's findings were challenged by Mischel and Peake (1982), his work did much to reinvigorate dispositional approaches to social behavior.

Interactionism

Perhaps the most cogent criticism of the original position of the situationists, however, is that they set up a false dichotomy by pitting person variables against situational variables. Critics of this position (e.g., Funder, 2008) return to Lewin's classic formulation B = f(P,E)—that is, behavior is a function of both the person and the situation—and use it to argue that one needs both classes of variables to predict social behavior. It is a mistake to argue that one class of variables is invariably a stronger or more influential cause of social behavior than the other. Social behavior is the product of reciprocal interactions between the characteristics of the person and the characteristics of the situation; researchers will understand much more about the causes of social behaviors by considering both classes of variables rather than only one of them (Funder, 2008; Graziano, Habashi, Sheese, & Tobin, 2007; Mischel, 2004).

As the preceding discussion suggests, the original situationist and dispositional perspectives have, to a large extent, merged, and there is more or less consensus that both classes of variables are necessary for an intelligent understanding of social behavior. Yet among some prosocial researchers, there is still skepticism about the value of studying dispositions and how they relate to prosocial thoughts, feelings, and actions. In the remainder of this chapter, we try to persuade the skeptics to reconsider their position.

PROSOCIAL DISPOSITIONS: A PROSOCIAL PERSONALITY ORIENTATION

In this section, we review research that attempts to identify the core elements of a *prosocial personality orientation*, which Penner and Finkelstein (1998) defined as "an enduring tendency to think about the welfare and rights of other people, to feel concern, and empathy, and to act in a way that benefits them" (p. 526). Specifically, we examine conceptual and empirical convergence among different attempts to define and measure a prosocial personality orientation. This section is not intended to be an exhaustive review of the literature on dispositions associated with prosocial behavior. Rather, we intend it to demonstrate that there is some substantial degree of agreement with regard to the core elements of a prosocial personality orientation.

We begin our discussion with the work of Penner and colleagues on the nature of a prosocial personality orientation (Penner, Fritzsche, Craiger, & Freifeld, 1995). They initially approached the question of what attributes make up a prosocial personality from an empirical perspective. Penner et al. (1995) did not believe there was one specific disposition or trait that would be associated with all prosocial behaviors. Rather, they suggested that there was a cluster of interrelated dispositions that collectively are related to prosocial thoughts, feelings, and behaviors. To identify these attributes, they did an exhaustive search of the literature and identified personality traits and related constructs that consistently correlated with prosocial behavior. These dispositions then had to meet two additional criteria: (a) there was a coherent theoretical explanation of why this attribute was associated with prosocial behavior, and (b) there were theory-based associations between this attribute and the others that had been identified. That is, Penner et al. (1995) sought to identify dispositions that could be reduced to a smaller number of theoretically meaningful underlying factors.

Initially, Penner et al. (1995) identified 10 dispositions and combined measures of these dispositions in one (very long) questionnaire. After considerable preliminary work that addressed both the reliability and validity of each measure and of the items it contained, a 56-item scale was derived that measured six dispositions: social responsibility, affective empathy, cognitive empathy, moral reasoning, past helpfulness, and egocentric personal distress in response to other people's distress. Factor analyses of the total scores on the measures led Penner et al. (1995) to a two-factor solution that has been replicated with a wide variety of different samples in the United States and Europe (Penner, 2002). The first factor was called Other-Oriented Empathy; it appears to represent prosocial feelings and thoughts. Measures of social responsibility, empathic concern, perspective taking (i.e., affective and cognitive empathy), and other-oriented moral reasoning had their primary loadings on this factor. People who score high on this factor are empathic and feel responsibility and concern for the welfare of others. The second factor is called Helpfulness and represents a tendency to engage in prosocial actions. Measures of past helping and of personal distress (from Davis's, 1980, empathy scale) loaded on this factor. High scorers on this factor report a history of being helpful and also report that they experience little egocentric distress in response to distress in others. The two factors typically correlate .40 or less.

Converging evidence indicates that the first factor represents the predisposition to have other-oriented thoughts and feelings and the second factor represents the tendency to act prosocially. For example, Penner et al. (1995) reported that whereas scores on the Other-Oriented Empathy factor correlated significantly with social desirability, scores on the Helpfulness factor did not. Our own and others' research (e.g., Graziano & Eisenberg, 1997; Graziano & Tobin, 2002) has suggested that this correlation does not represent a response bias that invalidates responses to items that load on the Other-Oriented Empathy factor. Rather, we believe that scores on the social desirability measure represent the need for social acceptance, which is more closely associated with prosocial thoughts and feelings than with prosocial behavioral tendencies.

Other research has identified unique correlates of each of the factors. The Other-Oriented Empathy factor correlates about .50 with the other-oriented agreeableness dimension of the Big Five, even when one controls for social desirability (Graziano et al., 2007; Penner et al., 1995). The Other-

Oriented Empathy factor also correlates strongly with a nurturant or communal interpersonal style (nurturance; Wiggins, 1991), that is, the tendency to be other oriented and to want to please and be accepted by others. By contrast, the Helpfulness factor correlates weakly or not at all with agreeableness and nurturance. However, there are moderate to strong positive correlations between Helpfulness and Wiggins's (1991) dimensions of agency (or dominance) and assertiveness. Helpfulness also consistently correlates positively with the predisposition to have a sense of self-efficacy or personal control (Penner et al., 1995).

A fair amount of theory and research on prosocial dispositions converges with Penner et al.'s (1995) empirically derived conceptualization of the prosocial personality orientation. Peterson and Seligman (2004), for example, argued that the three variables most commonly associated with altruism are empathy, moral judgment, and social responsibility. The dispositions that Eisenberg and colleagues (chap. 7, this volume; Eisenberg et al., 2002) found to be associated with prosocial thoughts and actions were quite similar to those identified by Penner et al. (1995; e.g., empathy, social responsibility). Furthermore, the pattern of intercorrelations among measures of these dispositions was largely the same as reported by Penner et al. (1995). Eisenberg et al. (2002) also found substantial consistency in self-reports and friends' reports of these dispositions over a 5-year period, indicating that prosocial orientations are temporally stable. This is consistent with Graziano and Eisenberg's (1997) review of the literature on the temporal stability of prosocial actions, in which they presented persuasive evidence for the consistency of prosocial responding across time and situations. They argued that such consistency is most reasonably attributed to "personality and/or sociocognitive functioning" (p. 810).

Other descriptions of the core elements of the prosocial personality are derived from comparisons of people who differed from one another in their willingness to help in real-world settings. For example, Bierhoff, Klein, and Kramp (1991) studied people who administered first aid to traffic accident victims and found that among the traits that differentiated them from nonhelpers were empathy, social responsibility, and locus of control. Heroic rescuers, specifically the "righteous gentiles" who rescued Jews from the holocaust, also had dispositional profiles similar to Penner et al.'s (1997) prosocial personality orientation. The most recent research on the rescuers was conducted by Midlarsky and her colleagues (Fagin-Jones & Midlarsky, 2007; Midlarsky, Jones, & Corley, 2005). Unlike earlier work on rescuers by Oliner and Oliner (1988), these rescuers had never been formally recognized for their behavior, but rather were identified by one of the people they had saved. Similar to the Oliners, Midlarsky et al. compared the rescuers with a group of demographically similar individuals who did not engage in any rescues. The personality characteristics that best discriminated between rescuers and nonrescuers were social responsibility, other-oriented moral reasoning, empathy, locus of control, autonomy, and risk taking (not surprisingly, given the dangers associated with the heroic rescues). S. Oliner's descriptions of personal attributes that distinguish holocaust rescuers from nonrescuers also identify several of the same characteristics we have been discussing: "[The rescuers] were definitely more empathic [than the nonrescuers]. . . [they] . . . had a strong sense of personal and social responsibility—a norm-based belief about how they should act" (as quoted in Hunt, 1990, p. 203); "As children, [the rescuers] were likely to have been disciplined by reasoning and taught to consider the consequences of their misbehavior" (Oliner, 2002, para. 24); and "[They] felt they could control events and shape their destinies . . . [and had a] stronger sense of personal efficacy" (Oliner & Oliner, 1988, p. 177).

There is substantial convergence among these independent investigations with regard to descriptions of prosocial individuals. Such people are predisposed to experience high levels of empathy in response to other's distress, feel responsibility for the welfare of others, and engage in other-oriented moral reasoning. These cognitive and affective responses are probably most likely to result in actual prosocial behavior among individuals who are also socially dominant and have a sense of self-efficacy or personal control. (For a different but quite compatible perspective on prosocial dispositions, see Graziano & Eisenberg, 1997, and Graziano et al.'s, 2007, discussions of the association between the Big-Five dimension of agreeableness and prosocial thoughts, feelings, and actions.)

As we conclude this section, we acknowledge the absence of a discussion of situational influences on prosocial actions. This does not mean we believe that situational influences on prosocial behavior are trivial; to the contrary, they are quite important. For example, both the Oliners (1988) and Midlarsky et al. (2005) identified situational factors associated with being a rescuer. Most of these are not surprising. For example, rescuers were substantially more likely to have been asked to help than nonrescuers. Rescuers also had interacted with Jews more, and had more Jewish friends and coworkers than the nonrescuers. Finally, probably because the rescues often involved hiding people, rescuers' dwellings typically had more rooms than those of nonrescuers. We discuss additional evidence for the importance of situational variables and how they interact with dispositions in the section on meso level prosocial behaviors.

DISPOSITIONS AND MACRO LEVEL PROSOCIAL ACTIONS

In this section, we examine the relation between dispositional variables and macro level helping; that is, helping that occurs within the context of groups and large organizations. We have chosen to begin with this level of helping, quite honestly, because it holds the greatest promise for positive findings for the dispositional approach to prosocial behavior. To explain why, we consider a very common kind of macro level prosocial behavior, volunteering.

Penner (2002) defined *volunteering* as "long-term, planned, prosocial behaviors that benefit strangers within an organizational context" (p. 448). We believe that three aspects of volunteering increase the potential for personal attributes to influence this prosocial behavior. The first is that volunteering usually involves long-term behaviors with multiple components and thus produces a reliable indicator of the class of behaviors of interest. As discussed earlier, reliability in outcome measures will increase the size of disposition–behavior associations. Second, the decision to volunteer is usually the result of thoughtful decision making. The more complex and elaborate the cognitive processes before an action, the more likely it should be that enduring social–cognitive processes and mechanisms (i.e., dispositions) will influence the person's decision. For example, there should be greater interindividual variability in volunteering decisions than in decisions in bystander emergency intervention situations, in which there is typically an immediate and pressing demand to make a decision about helping and strong, widely shared social norms regarding helping in these situations. And third, volunteers rarely know personally, have a preexisting relationship with, or in most instances, interact with the recipients of their aid. Volunteering is what Omoto and Snyder (1995) called "nonobligated helping." Because of this, volunteers are usually less likely than interpersonal helpers to experience influences such as their relationship with the recipient, the recipient's reactions to the situation, or the recipients' personal characteristics (Dovidio et al., 2006).

Of course, situational factors are associated with differences in volunteers' behavior. For example, many volunteers report that they first decided to volunteer because someone asked them to (Independent Sector, 2000), and the reputation and goals of the organization and the volunteer's relationship with the organization influence both how much time volunteers give and their tenure as a volunteer (Davis, Hall, & Meyer, 2003; Grube & Piliavin, 2000). And obviously, once people are active volunteers, their feelings, cognitions, and behaviors relevant to volunteering are going to be influenced by their relationships with other volunteers and any direct interactions they might have with the actual targets of their volunteer activities. Thus, like any other prosocial behavior, volunteering is the product of person–situation interactions. However, the situational forces that influence macro level helping probably allow for much more interindividual variability than is the case in short-term meso level helping.

In 1998, Penner and Finkelstein, studied the dispositional correlates of sustained volunteering among AIDS/HIV volunteers. Specifically, they assessed prosocial personality orientation, feelings about the organization, organizational commitment, and motives for volunteering. They then used these measures to predict how much time volunteers spent working for the AIDS/

HIV organization and the amount of contact volunteers had with an AIDS/HIV patient. These outcomes were obtained 5 and 10 months after the predictor variables were initially measured. Organizational commitment and prosocial motivations for helping predicted time spent volunteering at 5 and 10 months. However, in the context of this chapter the most important findings concern a prosocial personality orientation. Among the male volunteers, Other-Oriented Empathy predicted time spent volunteering and time spent with an AIDS/HIV patient 5 months after the initial assessment; it also predicted time spent with a patient at 10 months.

In 1999, Penner conducted a study in which readers of *USA Today*'s weekend supplement went online and anonymously completed his measure of prosocial personality orientation, provided demographic information, and indicated whether they had volunteered in the last year. If they had, volunteers answered questions about their length of tenure as a volunteer, the number of charities for which they volunteered, and the amount of time they spent in this activity (Penner, 2002). More than 1,100 people completed the online survey. Both the Other-Oriented Empathy and Helpfulness factors distinguished between people who had and had not volunteered in the past year. The two factors were also significantly associated with all three indices of volunteer activity—length of service, number of charities, and amount of time spent as a volunteer. Finally, Penner (2002) conducted hierarchical regression analyses in which the three outcome measures were regressed onto the respondents' demographic characteristics, followed by the two factors of the prosocial personality measure. In all three equations, Other-Oriented Empathy and/or Helpfulness added significantly to the explanation of variability in volunteering, even when demographic characteristics were controlled. Similar results have been obtained in a number of other studies of volunteering that used either Penner et al.'s (1997) measure or conceptually similar measures (e.g., Carlo, Okun, Knight, & de Guzman, 2005; Elshaug & Metzer, 2001; Finkelstein & Brannick, 2007; Pushkar, Reis, & Morros, 2002).

Finally, a longitudinal study of volunteerism by Atkins, Hart, and Donnelly (2005) speaks to the long-term impact of prosocial dispositions on volunteering. Specifically, Atkins et al. studied whether young children's personality attributes predicted their volunteering when they were adolescents. Parents in a national probability sample in the United States responded to a series of questions about their 6-year-old children. The responses were used to classify children as "resilient," "overcontrolled," or "undercontrolled." (The authors explicitly noted that their construct of resilience was conceptually related to Penner et al.'s [1995] prosocial personality orientation.) Eight and 10 years later, the now-adolescents reported whether they had volunteered in the previous 2 years. Atkins et al. found that at both time periods, those who had been characterized as resilient as children were more likely to be volunteers than were those who had been characterized as over- or undercontrolled. Significantly, this effect was not mediated by the things that usually predict volunteering, such as involvement in religious organizations and membership in other social organizations that provide opportunities for adolescent volunteering.

In summary, although some researchers have argued that dispositions play no role in volunteering (e.g., Wilson, 2000), there is rather strong and consistent evidence that differences in volunteering covary with differences in dispositions. These dispositions appear to be part of a prosocial personality orientation.

DISPOSITIONS AND MESO LEVEL PROSOCIAL ACTIONS

We now turn to the role of dispositional variables in meso level prosocial actions. Situational cues and related variables, such as social norms, are usually salient and potent in the helper–recipient dyads in which meso level kinds of prosocial behavior occur (Dovidio et al., 2006). Thus, although dispositional variables are clearly important in meso level helping, one would not expect to find many studies in which there are main effects for dispositional variables that are not somehow moderated by situational variables.

Graziano et al. (2007) provided an interesting and important illustration of such an interaction in meso level helping. They used two well-known paradigms from the prosocial research literature but added agreeableness as an independent variable. The first paradigm was taken from Burnstein, Crandall, and Kitayama's (1994) study on the effect of kinship on helping. Participants imagined situations in which they had the chance to help a friend, a relative, or a stranger by either (a) doing them a small favor or (b) saving their life from an imminent danger, and they estimated how likely it would be that they would help. Similar to Burnstein et al. (1994), Graziano et al. (2007) found that participants were most likely to say they would help when the recipient was a relative and was in imminent danger. However, there was also a significant three-way interaction among agreeableness, helper's relationship with the recipient, and kind of helping. When this interaction was decomposed, there were person by situation interactions of the type one would expect. For example, high- and low-agreeable participants did not differ in how much they would help siblings (or friends) when their lives were in danger, but when the helping involved doing a favor, high-agreeable people helped relatives and friends more than low-agreeable people.

In their second study, Graziano et al. (2007) replicated parts of Coke, Batson, and McDavis's (1978) bystander intervention paradigm, in which empathic responding was manipulated and amount of help offered was measured. Graziano et al. (2007) found a significant interaction between the empathy induction and agreeableness. In the high-empathy induction condition, high- and low-agreeable participants offered equal amounts of help, but in the low-empathy condition, high-agreeable participants offered significantly more help than did low-agreeable participants. Similar kinds of person by situation interactions have been found using other Batson paradigms (e.g., Bierhoff & Rohman, 2004; Otten, Penner, & Altabe, 1991).

In this section, we consider another way in which dispositional variables might affect meso level helping. We present data on how parents' dispositions might affect their empathic responses when their children are facing a potent stressor: invasive treatments for pediatric cancer. Pediatric patients and their parents often report that the pain and distress from such treatments are worse than the disease itself (Hedstrom, Haglund, Skolin, & von Essen, 2003). In our field study, we first measured parent and child traits; then on a treatment day (usually 3 to 4 weeks later), we assessed parents' negatively valenced (state anxiety and personal distress) and positively valenced (empathic concern) empathic responses just before their children received treatment, and we then videotaped parents and children in the treatment room. Parents, children, and nurses rated the children's pain, distress, or both while they were still in the treatment room; independent coders later used the video recordings to rate children's distress. The manner in which parents communicated with their children during treatment was also coded.

Parents' empathic responses just prior to their child's treatments were related to their child's pain and distress (Penner, Cline, & Albrecht, 2007). There was a significant positive association between parents' state anxiety before the procedures and parents' rating of their children's pain and distress during treatment; that is, the higher parents' state anxiety, the greater the children's pain and distress. However, there were significant negative correlations between parental empathic concern and nurses' ratings of child's pain, nurses' ratings of child's distress, and independent coders' ratings of child's distress; there was also a trend in this direction for children's own pain rating ($p < .08$). That is, the higher the parents' empathic concern, the less the children's pain/distress. Because child's age was significantly correlated with pain and distress; these correlations are actually partial correlations, with child's age partialed out.

Empathic concern was also associated with parents' communication patterns during treatment. Cline et al. (2006) developed a typology of parent communication patterns that can be used to classify parents on the basis of how they interact with their children during treatment sessions. One of these patterns was called "invalidation." It is characterized by communication that "denies, invalidates, and/or challenges the validity (merit, worth, or accuracy) of the child's experience" (p. 890). These parents may show anger and frustration and/or engage in name calling, ridicule, or criticism of their children. Cline et al. found that children of invalidating parents experienced significantly more pain and/or distress than did children of the parents with other types of communication patterns. Penner et al. (2007) found that invalidating parents also had significantly lower levels of pretreatment empathic concern than did parents with other communication patterns.

Thus, parents' pretreatment empathic responses seem to make a difference in how they and their children respond to the treatments. We now discuss dispositional variables associated with parents' empathic responses. The theoretical model that drove this research did not lead us to measure traits associated with a prosocial personality orientation. Rather, the dispositional measures in the study included personality traits that should be related to how the parents coped with the stresses of the pediatric cancer experience. Thus, we measured parent traits we thought would be negatively associated with adequate coping: trait anxiety, depression, and enduring emotions; we also measured traits we believed would be positively associated with coping: enduring positive emotions, resilience, and satisfaction with social support. Actually, we also measured dispositional empathy, but the abbreviated measure we used was not reliable.

Personality traits associated with enduring negative affect (trait anxiety, depression, and enduring negative emotions) were all significantly and positively associated with parents' state anxiety and personal distress before the procedures began. These associations were as strong as, or stronger than, the associations with two situational variables—children's age and the type of procedure the children were going to receive (either a port start, which involves inserting a needle into a port in the child's chest, or a lumbar puncture).

Neither child's age nor type of procedure was significantly related to parents' empathic concern, but there were significant positive associations between empathic concern and parents' enduring positive emotions and perceived level of social support ($rs > .40$, $ps < .01$). The correlation with parents' resilience, although also positive, was not significant. Thus, in this highly stressful situation, in which one might expect relative homogeneity in empathic responses across the parents, we found variability in parents' pretreatment empathic responses that could be accounted for by parents' dispositions.

Finally, we want to mention briefly that there were also significant associations between parents' empathic responses and their ratings of some of their children's attributes. We found, for example, that the higher the parents' ratings of the children's resilience, the higher the parents' pretreatment empathic concern (Penner et al., 2006), and the higher the parents' ratings of their children's problems with anxiety/depression and aggression, the greater the parents' pretreatment anxiety and personal distress. We recognize the method bias inherent in these data (parents filled out both measures) and the difficulty in arguing for a simple causal path from the children's dispositions to the parents' empathic responses, so these findings must remain tentative at this time. However, they suggest another, quite different, way in which dispositions may affect helpers' empathic responses in meso level helping among intimates. Specifically, if helpers believe they have accurate knowledge of a recipient's dispositions, this knowledge may influence helpers' estimates of how a recipient will be affected by the problem at hand (see chap. 19, this volume). These estimates, in turn, may influence helpers' thoughts, feelings, and actions in response to the need for help.

CONCLUSION

Our major conclusions about dispositions and prosocial actions can be summarized in answers to the four questions presented at the beginning of this chapter. First, there is substantial temporal stability and transituational consistency in prosocial thoughts, feelings, and actions. Second, there is reliable interindividual variability in prosocial responses among people who encounter the same situation. Third, enduring dispositions play important roles in both intraindividual consistency and interindividual variability in prosocial responses. And fourth, it is possible to identify the core elements of a prosocial personality orientation. Predispositions to respond empathically to others' distress, feel a sense of responsibility for others' welfare, and engage in other-oriented moral reasoning are associated with prosocial thoughts and feelings. Studies of both helpful and heroic individuals suggest that these thoughts and feelings are probably most likely to result in actual prosocial behavior among individuals who are also socially dominant and have a sense of self-efficacy or personal control.

However, significant questions about dispositions and prosocial behavior remain. One of the most important of these questions concerns the origins of enduring individual differences in prosocial dispositions. Answers to this question will come from understanding the complex reciprocal relationship between how genes express themselves and the influence of variability in environments (chap. 8, this volume). Another important question is how and under what circumstances the proximal affective and cognitive causes of prosocial behavior are activated. This will require researchers who study prosocial behavior to move beyond descriptions of the associations between dispositions and behavior and focus on identifying and understanding the feelings and cognitions that immediately precede prosocial responses. This should be done without arguing about people versus situations as causes of behavior because we cannot intelligently talk about one class of variables without considering its relation to the other. Ultimately it will be answers to these kinds of questions that clarify the true causes of enduring goodness.

REFERENCES

Allport, G. (1937). *Personality: A psychological interpretation*: New York: Holt.

Atkins, R., Hart, D., & Donnelly, T. M. (2005). The association of childhood personality type with volunteering during adolescence. *Merrill-Palmer Quarterly, 51*, 145–162.

Bem, D. J., & Allen, A. (1974). On predicting some of the people some of the time: The search for cross-situational consistencies in behavior. *Psychological Review, 81*, 506–520.

Bierhoff, H. W., Klein, R., & Kramp, P. (1991). Evidence for the altruistic personality from data on accident research. *Journal of Personality, 59*, 263–280.

Bierhoff, H., & Rohmann, E. (2004). Altruistic personality in the context of the empathy-altruism hypothesis. *European Journal of Personality, 18*, 351–365.

Burnstein, E., Crandall, C., & Kitayama, S. (1994). Some neo-Darwinian decision rules for altruism: Weighing cues for inclusive fitness as a function of the biological importance of the decision. *Journal of Personality and Social Psychology, 67*, 773–789.

Carlo, G., Okun, M. A., Knight, G. P., & de Guzman, M. R. T. (2005). The interplay of traits and motives on volunteering: Agreeableness, extraversion and prosocial value motivation. *Personality and Individual Differences, 38*, 1293–1305.

Cialdini, R. B., Brown, S. L., Lewis, B. P., Luce, C., & Neuberg, S. L. (1997). Reinterpreting the empathy–altruism relationship: When one into one equals oneness. *Journal of Personality and Social Psychology, 73*, 481–494.

Cline, R. J. W., Harper, F. W. K., Penner, L. A., Peterson, A. M., Taub, J. W., & Albrecht, T. L. (2006). Parent communication and child pain and distress during painful pediatric cancer treatments. *Social Science and Medicine, 63*, 883–898.

Coke, J., Batson, C., & McDavis, K. (1978). Empathic mediation of helping: A two-stage model. *Journal of Personality and Social Psychology, 36*, 752–766.

Davis, M. H. (1980). Measuring individual differences in empathy. *JSAS Catalog of Selected Documents in Psychology, 10*, 85.

Davis, M. H., Hall, J. A., & Meyer, M. (2003). The first year: Influences on the satisfaction, involvement, and persistence of new community volunteers. *Personality and Social Psychology Bulletin, 29*, 248–260.

Dovidio, J. F., Piliavin, J. A., Schroeder, D., & Penner, L. A. (2006). *The social psychology of prosocial behavior*. Mahwah, NJ: Erlbaum.

Eisenberg, N., Guthrie, I. K., Cumberland, A., Murphy, B. C., Shepard, S. A., Zhou, Q., & Carlo, G. (2002). Prosocial development in early adulthood: A longitudinal study. *Journal of Personality and Social Psychology, 82*, 993–1006.

Elshaug, C., & Metzer, J. (2001). Personality attributes of volunteers and paid workers engaged in similar occupational tasks. *Journal of Social Psychology, 141*, 752–763.

Epstein, S. (1983). Aggregation and beyond: Some basic issues on the prediction of behavior. *Journal of Personality, 51*, 360–392.

Fagin-Jones, S., & Midlarsky, E. (2007). Courageous altruism: Personal and situational correlates of rescue during the Holocaust. *The Journal of Positive Psychology, 2*, 136–147.

Finkelstein, M. A., & Brannick, M. T. (2007). Applying theories of institutional helping to informal volunteering: Motives, role identity, and prosocial personality. *Social Behavior and Personality, 35*, 101–114.

Funder, D. C. (1987). Errors and mistakes: Evaluating the accuracy of social judgment. *Psychological Bulletin, 101*, 75–90.

Funder, D. C. (2008). Personality, situations, and person-situation interactions. In L. A. Pervin, O. P. John, & R. W. Robins (Eds.), *Handbook of personality research* (3rd ed.). New York: Guilford Press.

Gergen, K. J., Gergen, M. M., & Meter, K. (1972). Individual orientations to prosocial behavior. *Journal of Social Issues, 8*, 105–130.

Graziano, W. G., & Eisenberg, N. (1997). Agreeableness and altruism. In S. Briggs, R. Hogan, & W. Jones (Eds.), *Handbook of personality* (pp. 725–895). New York: Academic Press.

Graziano, W. G., Habashi, M. M., Sheese, B. E., & Tobin, R. M. (2007). Agreeableness, empathy, and helping: A person × situation perspective. *Journal of Personality and Social Psychology, 93*, 583–599.

Graziano, W. G., & Tobin, R. M. (2002). Agreeableness: Dimension of personality or social desirability artifact? *Journal of Personality, 70*, 695–727.

Grube, J. A., & Piliavin, J. A. (2000). Role identity, organizational experiences and volunteer performance. *Personality and Social Psychology Bulletin, 26*, 1108–1119.

Hartshorne, H., & May, M. A. (1928). *Studies in the nature of character. Volume I: Studies in deceit.* New York: Macmillan.

Hedstrom, M., Haglund, K., Skolin, I., & von Essen, L. (2003). Distressing events for children and adolescents with cancer: Child, parent, and nurse perceptions. *Journal of Pediatric Oncology Nursing, 20*, 120–132.

Hunt, M. (1990). *The compassionate beast.* New York: William Morrow.

Independent Sector. (2002). *Giving and volunteering in the United States.* Washington, DC: Author.

Latané, B., & Darley, J. M. (1970). *The unresponsive bystander: Why doesn't he help?* New York: Appleton-Century-Crofts.

Midlarsky, E., Jones, S., & Corley, R. (2005). Personality correlates of heroic rescue during the holocaust. *Journal of Personality, 73*, 907–934.

Mischel, W. (1968). *Personality and assessment.* New York: Wiley.

Mischel, W. (2004) Toward an integrative science of the person. *Annual Review, 55*, 1–22.

Mischel, W., & Peake, P. K. (1982). Beyond deja vu in the search for cross-situational consistency. *Psychological Review, 90*, 394–402.

Nisbett, R. E. (1980). The trait construct in lay and professional psychology. In L. Festinger (Ed.), *Retrospections in social psychology* (pp. 109–130). New York: Oxford University Press.

Oliner, S. (2002, Winter). *Can love save the world?* Retrieved March 1, 2008, from http://www.yesmagazine.org/other/pop_print_article.asp?ID=482

Oliner, S., & Oliner, P. (1988). *The altruistic personality: Rescuers of Jews in Nazi Europe.* New York: Free Press.

Omoto, A. M., & Snyder, M. (1995). Sustained helping without obligation: Motivation, longevity of service, and perceived attitude change among AIDS volunteers. *Journal of Personality and Social Psychology, 68*, 671–686.

Orom, H., & Cervone, D. (2009). Personality dynamics meaning and idiosyncrasy: Assessing personality architecture and coherence idiosyncratically. *Journal of Research in Personality, 43,* 228–240.

Otten, C. A., Penner, L. A., & Altabe, M. N. (1991). An examination of therapists' and college students' willingness to help a psychologically distressed person. *Journal of Social and Clinical Psychology, 10,* 102–120.

Penner, L. A. (2002). The causes of sustained volunteerism: An interactionist perspective. *Journal of Social Issues, 58,* 447–468.

Penner, L. A., Cline, R. J. W., Albrecht, T. L., Harper, F. W. K., Peterson, A. M., Taub, J. M., et al. (2008). Parent's empathic responses and pain and distress in pediatric patients. *Basic and Applied Social Psychology, 30,* 102–114.

Penner, L. A., Dovidio, J. F., Schroeder, D. A., & Piliavin, J. A. (2005). Prosocial behavior: Multilevel perspectives. *Annual Review of Psychology, 56,* 365–392.

Penner, L. A., & Finkelstein, M. A. (1998). Dispositional and structural determinants of volunteerism. *Journal of Personality and Social Psychology, 74,* 525–537.

Penner, L. A., Fritzsche, B. A., Craiger, J. P., & Freifeld, T. R. (1995). Measuring the prosocial personality. In J. Butcher & C. D. Spielberger (Eds.), *Advances in personality assessment* (Vol. 10, pp. 147–163). Hillsdale, NJ: Erlbaum.

Penner, L. A., Midili, A. R., & Kegelmeyer, J. (1997). Beyond job attitudes: A personality and social psychology perspective on the causes of organizational citizenship behavior. *Human Performance, 10,* 111–132.

Peterson, C. & Seligman, M. E. P. (2004). *Character strengths and virtues: A handbook and classification.* Washington, DC: American Psychological Association and Oxford University Press.

Piliavin, J. A., Dovidio, J. F., Gaertner, S., & Clark, R. D. (1981). *Emergency intervention.* New York: Academic Press.

Pushkar, D., Reis, M., & Morros, M. (2002). Motivation, personality, and well-being in older volunteers. *International Journal of Aging and Human Development, 55,* 141–162.

Rioux, S., & Penner, L. A. (2001). The causes of organizational citizenship behavior: A motivational analysis. *Journal of Applied Psychology,* 86, 1306–1314.

Rushton, J. P. (1981). The altruistic personality. In J. Rushton & R. Sorrentino (Eds.), *Altruism and helping behavior* (pp. 251–266). Hillsdale, NJ: Erlbaum.

Wiggins, J. S. (1991). Agency and communion as conceptual coordinates for the understanding and measurement of interpersonal behavior. In W. M. Grove & D. Cicchetti (Eds.), *Thinking clearly about psychology. Volume 2: Personality and psychopathology* (pp. 89–113). Minneapolis: University of Minnesota Press.

Wilson, J. (2000). Volunteering. *Annual Review of Sociology, 26,* 215–240.

4

A BEHAVIORAL-SYSTEMS PERSPECTIVE ON PROSOCIAL BEHAVIOR

PHILLIP R. SHAVER, MARIO MIKULINCER, AND MORAN SHEMESH-IRON

Attachment theory (Bowlby, 1982)—the conceptual framework on which most of our own research is based (Mikulincer & Shaver, 2007)—shares themes and emphases with the research that Batson (chap. 1, this volume), Simpson and Beckes (chap. 2, this volume), and Penner and Orom (chap. 3, this volume) described in their chapters. Like Batson, Bowlby believed that human beings, when appropriately cared for as children, are naturally empathic and altruistic, at least toward family members and probably toward other human beings as well. Like Penner and Orom, Bowlby was interested in individual differences in social behavior, which he viewed as stemming from early social experiences, mostly in the family. Like Simpson and Beckes, Bowlby was interested in motivational systems in the brain, which he viewed as products of biological evolution. He was especially interested in the innate behavioral systems that ethologists such as Tinbergen and Lorenz had discussed, because the behavioral system construct seemed more amenable to empirical study than Freud's (1940/1949) conception of sexual and aggressive instincts, which Bowlby (1982) had studied while becoming a psychoanalyst but which seemed outmoded by subsequent research in cognitive and developmental psychology and primate ethology.

Bowlby (1982) and his collaborator Mary Ainsworth (e.g., Ainsworth, Blehar, Waters, & Wall, 1978) began their empirical research by focusing on what they called the *attachment behavioral system*, which they viewed as the source of emotional bonding between human infants and their primary caregivers. Attachment bonds were conceptualized as biologically adaptive processes because, by keeping children close to their protective caregivers, they increased the likelihood of the children's survival and, eventually, of their successful reproduction. Bowlby and Ainsworth said less about the other behavioral systems they postulated, such as exploration, caregiving, and sexual mating, but they viewed caregiving (discussed in terms of "sensitivity" and "responsiveness") as a product of an innate behavioral system (discussed in detail by George & Solomon, 2008). Parental caregivers' sensitivity and responsiveness to their young children's signals of fear, need, and dependence contributed to the children's survival, health, and eventual reproductive fitness.

Our own work began with applications of attachment theory to the study of adult close relationships and emotion regulation (e.g., Hazan & Shaver, 1987; Mikulincer, Florian, & Tolmacz, 1990). The heart of that work was a series of demonstrations that the individual-difference constructs developed by Ainsworth et al. (1978) in studies of mother–infant relationships—secure, anxious, and avoidant attachment—were also applicable to adolescent and adult romantic and marital relationships. Because Ainsworth et al. designed methods to measure individual differences in the quality of infants' attachment to parents, it was possible to translate the measures and measured constructs into terms applicable to adult relationships. For the most part, the hundreds of adult attachment studies conducted since 1987 have focused on correlates and consequences of attachment orientations, not on the other behavioral systems, although Kunce and Shaver (1994) made an early attempt to assess caregiving in the context of couple relationships (see chap. 19, this volume, for a related research program).

These days, we are attempting to map all of the behavioral systems and their consequences, beginning with caregiving. Conceived broadly, the function of the caregiving behavioral system is to respond to other human beings' needs for comfort, protection, support, and encouragement. If human beings are innately empathic and altruistic (chap. 1, this volume), it seems likely that their prosocial tendencies are rooted in the caregiving system. If we can measure individual differences in caregiving motives and strategies, this may provide one route to understanding the nature and causes of caregiving, which in turn may provide new insights into empathy, compassion, and altruism. In this chapter, we present our conceptualization of individual differences in the functioning of the caregiving behavioral system and report previously unpublished findings concerning the creation and validation of a self-report scale that measures dimensions of caregiving.

In the following section, we begin by explaining the behavioral system concept. We then focus on the caregiving behavioral system and show how individual differences in caregiving orientations can be measured with self-report scales like the ones used to measure attachment orientations. We describe the development of the Caregiving System Scale (CSS), which measures hyperactivation and deactivation of the caregiving system. We then show how these two processes relate to other measures of optimal and nonoptimal caregiving. We also examine the extent to which the new caregiving-strategy dimensions correlate with and differ from the previously studied dimensions of attachment anxiety and avoidance.

THE CONCEPT OF BEHAVIORAL SYSTEMS

Although Bowlby (1973, 1980, 1982) focused mainly on the formation of attachment bonds in childhood and the self-protective and affect-regulatory functions of seeking proximity to others in times of need, he also attempted to understand how evolution shaped other kinds of behavior (e.g., exploration, caregiving, affiliation, sexual mating). For this purpose, he borrowed from ethology the concept of *behavioral system*, a species-universal neural program that governs the choice, activation, and termination of behavioral sequences in ways that increase the likelihood of survival and reproductive success despite sometimes daunting environmental demands. Responding successfully to such demands (e.g., dealing with threats by relying on "stronger, wiser others"; exploring and learning how to cope with the environment; caring for dependent offspring) gradually contributed to the evolution of distinct but interrelated behavioral systems, each with a primary function and a set of motivated action strategies.

Each system was viewed by Bowlby (1982) as having a particular goal (e.g., attaining a sense of safety and security, relieving others' distress and promoting their safety and welfare, passing one's genes to the next generation by becoming pregnant or impregnating a partner). Each system includes a repertoire of interchangeable, functionally equivalent behaviors that constitute the primary strategy of the system for attaining its goal (e.g., attaining safety and security through proximity seeking, protecting or comforting another person, sexually attracting a mate). These behaviors are automatically activated by the particular stimuli or situations that make a particular goal salient (e.g., loud noises signaling danger, helping a distressed or needy person, meeting an attractive and available sex partner) and are deactivated or terminated by other stimuli or outcomes that signal the attainment of the desired goal state.

Because each behavioral system was designed or constructed by evolution to increase the likelihood of coping successfully with environmental demands, its optimal functioning is important for mental health, social adjustment, and quality of life. Consider the case of the attachment behavioral system. It is activated by perceived threats and dangers, which cause one person to seek proximity to another who is viewed as a "safe haven" or "secure base" (Bowlby, 1982, 1988). Successfully attaining proximity, protection, and emotional comfort results in feelings of security and positive mental representations of self and others. Bowlby considered the proper functioning of this behavioral system to be crucial for mental health, a positive self-image, and the formation and maintenance of warm and satisfying social relationships. Many empirical studies have provided strong evidence for these benefits of attachment security (for reviews, see Grossmann, Grossmann, & Waters, 2005; Mikulincer & Shaver, 2007).

Bowlby (1982) also assumed that behavioral systems undergo experience-based parameter adjustments that reflect a person's history of interactions with the physical and social environment. These interactions leave memory traces of times when a behavioral system was activated and either succeeded or failed in attaining its goal. Because the ability of a behavioral system to achieve its goal depends on actual transactions with the world, each system includes cognitive–behavioral mechanisms, such as monitoring and appraising the effectiveness of behaviors enacted in a particular context, that allow flexible, goal-corrected adjustment of the system's "programming" when necessary to put a person back on track for achieving important goals. Over time, after operating in a particular environment, a person's behavioral systems are shaped by actual experiences, which program their neural/behavioral capacities to fit environmental constrains and yield effective actions. Through this process, people learn to mold their behavioral systems to fit contextual demands and form reliable expectations about available access routes and barriers to goal attainment. These expectations, which Bowlby (1973) called internal working models of self and others, become part of a behavioral system's programming and are the basis of both stable individual differences and within-person continuity over time.

Changes in a behavioral system's programming can also include disengagement from the primary strategy following recurrent failures to attain the system's goal. These failures are a cause of considerable frustration and anguish, and they signal that the primary strategy should be replaced by alternative (secondary) strategies. Attachment theorists (e.g., Cassidy & Kobak, 1988; Mikulincer & Shaver, 2007) have emphasized two such secondary strategies: hyperactivation and deactivation. *Hyperactivating* strategies are "fight" (persist or protest) responses that intensify the primary strategy of a system in order to coerce another person to behave in accordance with the system's goals (e.g., to provide support, to accept one's help). They keep a behavioral system chronically activated until its set goal is achieved. These responses are learned in social environments that place a person on a partial reinforcement schedule for persistence (by providing sporadic but unpredictable goal attainment). Unfortunately, while sometimes successful in at least some situations, these responses heighten distress and increase worries about one's self-efficacy and value, and they lead to intrusive, controlling, or aggressive responses that create emotional difficulties and social maladjustment.

In contrast, *deactivating* strategies are "flight" (or avoidance) responses that require turning off a behavioral system so as to avoid the frustration and anguish of failed efforts to attain the system's goal. These responses are thought to develop in the presence of people and social environments that disapprove of or punish expressions of a system's primary strategy (e.g., proximity seeking, helping). In such contexts, people learn to expect better outcomes if the primary strategy is suppressed, and the behavioral system in question is deactivated despite not having completely attained its goal. The problem with these strategies is that they require a narrowing of interpersonal behavior (e.g., not being intimate, not providing care), result in frequent failure to achieve important goals, and deter a person from realizing that there are situations in which the system's primary strategy can be effective.

DEFINING THE CAREGIVING BEHAVIORAL SYSTEM

According to Bowlby (1982), humans are born with a capacity to develop caregiving behaviors aimed at providing protection and support to others who are either generally vulnerable and dependent or temporarily in need. Bowlby claimed that these caring behaviors, as they emerge in development, are organized by an evolved, adapted caregiving behavioral system. This system presumably emerged over the course of evolution because it increased the inclusive fitness of humans by making it more likely that children, siblings, and tribe members with whom a person shared genes would survive to reproductive age and succeed in producing and rearing offspring (Hamilton, 1964). According to this inclusive fitness logic, the proliferation of a particular person's genes depends not only on his or her own reproductive success (based on transmitting genes through sexual intercourse) but also on the extent to which people who share copies of the person's genes are able to survive and reproduce (see chap. 2, this volume).

Although the caregiving system presumably evolved primarily because it increased the viability of a person's own offspring and close relatives (George & Solomon, 2008), it may also have been more generally adapted to respond to the needs of other tribe members. Today, through educational elaboration (e.g., socializing children to view all human beings as members of a single human family or as "brothers and sisters"), the system can be extended to include genuine concern for anyone in need. Although most people probably care more, and more easily, for people to whom they are closely related, either psychologically or genetically, humans'caregiving motives and behaviors can be applied more widely to all suffering human beings and even to members of other species. Just as attachment-related motives can affect a broad array of social processes (Mikulincer & Shaver, 2007), caregiving motives can be applied more broadly than to one's immediate genetic relatives. In other words, compassion, loving kindness, and generosity can become general ways of reacting to other people.

Normative Parameters of the Caregiving System

According to attachment theorists, the goal of the caregiving system is to reduce other people's suffering, protect them from harm, and foster their growth and development (chap. 19, this volume; Collins & Feeney, 2000; Collins, Guichard, Ford, & Feeney, 2006; Mikulincer & Shaver, 2007). In other words, the caregiving system is designed to meet other people's needs for protection and support in times of danger or distress, which attachment researchers refer to as providing a safe haven, and to support others' exploration, autonomy, and growth when exploration is safe and desirable. (Bowlby and Ainsworth defined this aspect of caregiving as providing a secure base for exploration.) According to Collins et al. (chap. 19, this volume), the caregiving system is likely to be activated in one or both of two kinds of situations: (a) when another person has to cope with danger, stress, or discomfort and is either openly seeking help or would clearly benefit from it; and (b) when another person has an opportunity for exploration, learning, or mastery and either needs help in taking advantage of the opportunity or seems eager to talk about it or to be validated for having aspirations or achieving desired goals. In either case, once a person's caregiving system is activated (whether appropriately or not), he or she calls on a repertoire of behaviors aimed at restoring or supporting the other person's welfare. This repertoire includes showing interest in the other's problems or goals, affirming the other's competence and ability to deal with the situation, expressing love and affection, providing advice and instrumental aid as needed, not interfering with the person's own problem-solving efforts or exploratory activities, and admiring and applauding the person's successes (chap. 19, this volume; Feeney, 2004; Feeney & Collins, 2004).

A key element of the caregiving system's primary strategy is what Batson (1991; chap. 1, this volume) called empathic concern for another person's suffering, which often involves taking the person's perspective in order to help him or her reduce suffering or pursue growth. According to Collins et al. (2006), this empathic attitude includes sensitivity and responsiveness, the two aspects of parental caregiving emphasized by Bowlby (1982) and Ainsworth et al. (1978). *Sensitivity* includes attunement to, and accurate interpretation of, another person's signals of distress, worry, or need, and responding in harmony with the person's support-seeking behavior (George &

Solomon, 2008). *Responsiveness* includes generous intentions; validating the troubled person's needs and feelings; respecting his or her beliefs, attitudes, and values; and helping the person feel loved, understood, and cared for (Reis & Shaver, 1988).

When caregiving works properly, it benefits the person being cared for—by solving a problem, increasing the person's sense of safety and security, or bolstering the person's own coping abilities (Collins et al., 2006). Appropriate care also benefits the support provider, even though its primary goal is to benefit the other. It promotes an inner sense of what Erikson (1950/1993) called *generativity*—a feeling that one is more than an isolated self and is able to contribute significantly to others' welfare. The sense of generativity includes positive feelings about oneself as a person with admirable moral qualities and the ability to perform good deeds; strong feelings of self-efficacy (chap. 3, this volume); confidence in one's social skills; and heightened feelings of love and connection with others.

Individual Differences in Caregiving

Although we assume that everyone is born with the potential to become an effective caregiver, caregiving can be impaired by feelings, beliefs, and concerns that dampen or conflict with sensitivity and responsiveness (chap. 19, this volume). Optimal functioning of the caregiving system requires adaptive emotion-regulation strategies, which help caregivers deal effectively with the discomfort entailed by witnessing another person's distress. Deficient emotion regulation can cause a caregiver to feel overwhelmed by anxiety (of the kind Davis, 1983, and Batson, chap. 1, this volume, called *personal distress*); to slip into the role of another needy person rather than occupying the role of care provider; or to physically, cognitively, or emotionally distance oneself from the needy other in order to soothe one's own feelings, even if this requires abdicating the caregiving role. Optimal caregiving also requires effective self-regulation strategies. Addressing another person's problems often requires temporary suspension of one's own goals and plans. Moreover, one has to diagnose the other person's problem, develop a plan for assisting the person sensitively and effectively, and suppress interfering motives or behavioral tendencies that increase distance or interfere with the person's own coping efforts.

As with the other behavioral systems, dysfunctions of the caregiving system can trigger one of two nonoptimal (secondary) caregiving strategies: hyperactivation or deactivation of the caregiving system. Hyperactivated caregiving is intrusive, poorly timed, and effortful; it may be aimed at making oneself indispensable to a partner or applauding oneself for being competent or admirable as a caregiver. These goals can be achieved by exaggerating appraisals of others' needs, adopting a hypervigilant stance toward other people's imagined needs or troubles, forcing others to accept one's caregiving efforts, and focusing on others' needs to the neglect of one's own. On the other hand, strategies associated with caregiving-system deactivation involve insufficient empathy, withdrawal from caregiving, offering only half-hearted assistance, and insisting on maintaining emotional distance when the other person seeks care, consideration, closeness, and comforting (for related analyses of nonoptimal caregiving, see chaps. 5 and 6, this volume).

Assessing Individual Differences in Caregiving Strategies

A review of existing self-report measures of beliefs, attitudes, and feelings related to caregiving led us to conclude that no instrument had been explicitly designed to assess the two forms of nonoptimal caregiving that interest us: hyperactivated and deactivated caregiving. We did, however, gain important insights from examining existing scales. Davis's (1983) Interpersonal Reactivity Index includes an Empathic Concern subscale that assesses mainly the low end of the deactivated care dimension (e.g., "I often have tender, concerned feelings for people less fortunate than me") and a Personal Distress subscale that assesses the self-focused personal distress associated with hyperactivation (e.g., "Being in a tense emotional situation scares me"). Kunce and Shaver's (1994) questionnaire designed to measure caregiving within romantic relationships includes items that assess emotional distance from a suffering partner and lack of sensitivity to signals of need (e.g., "I sometimes push my partner away even though s/he seems to need me," "I sometimes miss the subtle signs that show how my partner is feeling"). Kunce and Shaver's measure also contains items assessing anxious, compulsive caregiving (e.g., "I tend to get overinvolved in my partner's problems and difficulties"). Despite such useful models, we wanted to create a new measure that, like the Experiences in Close Relationships Inventory (ECR; Brennan, Clark, & Shaver, 1998) used to measure insecure attachment, would be specifically designed to assess individual differences in hyperactivating and deactivating caregiving strategies. Here, we present data from the first stage of this research program—the construction of a self-report scale, the CSS, that assesses individual differences in hyperactivation and deactivation of the caregiving system.

ASSESSING HYPERACTIVATION AND DEACTIVATION OF THE CAREGIVING SYSTEM

In the first stage of scale development, we constructed a pool of 50 items that might assess either anxious hyperactivation or avoidant deactivation of the caregiving system. Our understanding of these two strategies was based partly on years of experience with the ECR Inventory, which measures hyperactivation and deactivation of the attachment system. In writing the new caregiving items, we attempted to capture the various cognitive, emotional, motivational, and behavioral aspects of hyperactivated and deactivated caregiving strategies reviewed earlier. For example, the 25 items designed to assess hyperactivation focused on the urgent need and exaggerated willingness to help others and on anxieties, insecurities, and worries about one's caregiving effectiveness. The 25 items designed to assess deactivation focused on uneasiness when helping others, attempts to avoid situations that call for caregiving, emotional distancing from people in need, and feelings of boredom or disengagement in caregiving situations. Some of the items were borrowed or adapted from existing caregiving scales (e.g., Feeney & Collins, 2004; Kunce & Shaver, 1994); others were constructed especially for the new scale.

The items do not refer to a specific relationship partner (e.g., one's child or romantic partner) but to anyone in need of help (see Table 4.1). Moreover, the instructions ask respondents to think about situations in which other people need help, without focusing on a specific person, and to rate (on a 7-point scale) the extent to which each item is or is not self-descriptive. In short, the CSS measures a person's global caregiving orientation rather than caregiving within a particular relationship, although the items could easily be adapted to assess relationship-specific caregiving strategies, as is sometimes done with the ECR measure of attachment insecurities.

Our initial 50-item scale was administered to a sample of 262 Israeli undergraduates (146 women and 116 men). Item and factor analyses indicated that the items did assess the two dimensions of caregiving: hyperactivating and deactivating strategies. On the basis of these analyses, we chose the 10 most representative items from each factor (i.e., the ones that loaded highest on the intended factor and lowest on the other factor), keeping in mind our goal of representing various elements or aspects of hyperactivation and deactivation. We then administered the new 20-item scale, in Hebrew, to 178 Israeli undergraduates (108 women and 70 men) and in English to 336 American undergraduates (263 women and 73 men) and conducted new factor analyses. In both samples, the analyses yielded the intended two factors, which accounted for more than 50% of the variance (see Table 4.1). The 10 deactivation items loaded higher than .50 on the first factor, and the 10 hyperactivation loaded higher than .50 on the second factor. Cronbach alphas for both scales were above .80 in both samples.

As intended, the correlation between the hyperactivation and deactivation scores was not significant ($r < .08$) in either the American or the Israeli sample. In other words, hyperactivation and deactivation are orthogonal strategies, and the two scales form a two-dimensional space in which different caregiving orientations can be represented. The region representing optimal caregiving is defined by low scores on hyperactivation and deactivation; the region of anxious hyperactivation is defined by high scores on hyperactivation and low scores on deactivation; the region of avoidant deac-

TABLE 4.1
Factor Loadings of CSS Items Following Varimax Rotation in Israeli and American Samples

Item	Factor 1 Israel	Factor 1 U.S.	Factor 2 Israel	Factor 2 U.S.
Deactivation items				
When I see people in distress, I don't feel comfortable jumping in to help. (1)	.63	.56		
I sometimes feel that helping others is a waste of time. (3)	.71	.59		
I often don't pay much attention to other people's discomfort or distress. (5)	.64	.66		
I don't invest a lot of energy trying to help others. (7)	.70	.74		
Thinking about helping others doesn't excite me very much. (9)	.82	.75		
I don't often feel an urge to help others. (11)	.67	.79		
I have no problem helping people who are troubled or distressed. (13)	.56	.54		
When I notice that someone seems to need help, I often prefer not to get involved. (15)	.56	.76		
It's hard for me to work up much interest in helping others. (17)	.77	.83		
I feel uncomfortable when I'm required to help others. (19)	.66	.69		
Hyperactivation items				
When helping people, I often worry that I won't be as good at it as other people are. (2)			.50	.57
When I'm unable to help a person who is in distress, I feel worthless. (4)			.59	.62
I feel bad when others don't want my help. (6)			.66	.55
I sometimes try to help others more than they actually want me to. (8)			.54	.56
When people don't want my help, I still sometimes feel compelled to help. (10)			.54	.54
I often get anxious when I think nobody needs my help. (12)			.59	.56
I often worry about not being successful when I try to help others who need me. (14)			.58	.71
When I decide to help someone, I worry that I won't be able to solve the problem or ease the person's distress. (16)			.63	.75
I sometimes worry that I try to help others more than they want me to. (18)			.69	.70
I sometimes feel that I intrude too much while trying to help others. (20)			.63	.61
Explained variance (%)	34.6	36.7	18.3	18.4
Cronbach alpha coefficients	.87	.88	.81	.82

Note. Numbers in parentheses are item numbers on the scale as it was administered. CSS = Caregiving System Scale. U.S. = United States.

tivation is defined by high scores on deactivation and low scores on hyperactivation; and the region of ambivalent or disorganized caregiving is defined by high scores on both dimensions.

In a new sample of 98 Israeli undergraduates, we administered the CSS twice in sessions separated by 4 months and found adequate test–retest reliability (.76 and .72, respectively, for the hyperactivation and deactivation scales). For another sample of 95 Israeli undergraduates, we asked two relatives, friends, or romantic partners (i.e., close relationship partners) of each participant to use the CSS items to describe the participant. Significant correlations were found between self-reports and partner reports regarding both the hyperactivation and deactivation dimensions of the caregiving system (*r*s ranged from .46 to .55), implying that the CSS measures, in part, behavioral tendencies that can be observed by relationship partners.

In an additional sample of 36 Israeli undergraduates, we conducted a two-session study to see whether CSS scores are related to people's open-ended accounts of their caregiving experiences. In the first session, participants completed the CSS; in the second session, they recalled three instances of helping a person in need and described what happened in each case. Two judges, blind to participants' scores on the CSS scale but familiar with our conception of caregiving hyperactivation and deactivation, read each participant's narratives and rated (on a 7-point scale) the extent to which signs of hyperactivation and deactivation appeared in each narrative. After averaging scores across narratives and judges for a particular participant, we correlated the scores with the participants' CSS scores. The correlations were statistically significant for both hyperactivation ($r = .51$) and deactivation ($r = .46$). Thus, a person's self-reports on the CSS are valid indicators of his or her caregiving orientation, at least as reflected in narratives about actual instances of providing care.

In five other samples of Israeli undergraduates, we examined the convergent validity of the two CSS scores. Participants completed the CSS together with preexisting self-report scales tapping various aspects of compassion and empathy (Davis's, 1983, Interpersonal Reactivity Index; Mehrabian & Epstein's, 1972, Emotional Empathy Scale; Sprecher & Fehr's, 2005, Compassionate Love Scale; Shiota, Keltner, & John's, 2006, Compassion Subscale of the Differential Positive Emotions Scale; and Penner's, 2002, measures of Other-Oriented Empathy and Helpfulness). In addition, participants read a vignette describing a person in need (similar to Batson, Fultz, & Schoenrade's, 1987, well-known story about Katie Banks) and rated how much they experienced empathy and personal distress while reading the vignette.

As expected, deactivation included cognitive and emotional distancing from others' suffering, as indicated by inverse correlations with perspective taking, empathic care, emotional empathy, Shiota et al.'s (2006) compassion subscale, compassionate love toward close others and all humanity,

TABLE 4.2
Pearson Correlations Between CSS Scores and Conceptually Related Constructs

Variable	CSS deactivation	CSS hyperactivaton
Interpersonal reactivity index[a]		
Perspective taking	−.32**	.08
Fantasizing	−.15	.35**
Empathic concern	−.57**	.09
Personal distress	−.13	.43**
Emotional empathy[b]	−.50**	.11
Compassionate love toward strangers[c]	−.41**	.12
Compassionate love toward close persons[c]	−.52**	.17
DPES compassion score[b]	−.54**	.11
Other-oriented empathy[c]	−.33**	.16
Helpfulness[c]	−.37**	−.32**
Empathic responses to story[d]	−.37**	.10
Personal distress responses to story[d]	.13	.36**
Communal orientation[d]	−.56**	.28**
Relational self-construal[d]	−.29**	.32**
Benevolence values[d]	−.38**	.07
Universalism values[d]	−.41**	.12
Cynicism[b]	.44**	.15
Esteem for humanity[e]	−.45**	−.08
Perceived self-efficacy as a caregiver[a]	.08	−.46**
Beliefs in others' deservingness of help[a]	−.30**	.04
Unmitigated communion[e]	−.16	.45**

Note. CSS = Caregiving System Scale. [a]Sample 1 (N = 178). [b]Sample 5 (N = 100). [c]Sample 3 (N = 120). [d]Sample 2 (N = 137). [e]Sample 4 (N = 118).
**p < .01.

other-oriented empathy, helpfulness/prosocial actions, and empathy-related emotions (see Table 4.2). The hyperactivation score was not associated with these measures of compassion and empathy, but it was significantly correlated with fantasizing and personal distress while witnessing others' suffering (see Table 4.2). That is, hyperactivation includes emotional overinvolvement with others' suffering (Batson's, 1991, personal distress), which is not necessarily transformed into empathy and compassion. This indicates that hyperactivated individuals are more concerned with their own distress than with that of the suffering other (chap. 19, this volume).

Participants also completed self-report measures relevant to our understanding of their attitudes toward needy others (see Table 4.2). Deactivation scores were associated with rejecting or denying personal responsibility for others' welfare (a low communal orientation; Mills & Clark, 1994), not using close relationships to define oneself (low relational self-construal; Cross, Bacon, & Morris, 2000), not valuing other people's safety or trying to improve other people's condition (low endorsement of benevolence and universalism values; Schwartz, 1992; chap. 12, this volume), cynical attitudes toward others (Moore, 1999), lack of esteem for humanity (Luke, Mayo, & Carnelley, 2004), and beliefs that others do not deserve help (Reizer & Mikulincer, 2007). As can be seen in Table 4.2, hyperactivation was associated with high scores on communal orientation and relational self-construal, and with a compulsion to help others even when they are not seeking assistance (high unmitigated communion; Fritz & Helgeson, 1998) and a lack of perceived self-efficacy in helping others (Reizer & Mikulincer, 2007).

In sum, deactivation is associated with somewhat cynical appraisals of others combined with lack of involvement in interdependent relationships and with denying or dismissing one's social responsibilities. In contrast, hyperactivation is not associated with a negative or a positive appraisal of others. Instead, it is organized around two themes: (a) the centrality of connectedness and interdependence in one's life, to the point that it inclines one toward unmitigated communion and excessive caregiving, and (b) negative views of oneself as a caregiver.

In our preliminary studies, we also considered the discriminant and construct validity of the two CSS scores. Participants completed the Crowne-Marlowe Social Desirability Scale (Crowne & Marlowe, 1964), the Big Five Inventory (John & Srivastava, 1999), the Behavioral Inhibition and Behavioral Activation Scales (BIS/BAS; Carver & White, 1994), and the ECR Inventory (Brennan et al., 1998). The two CSS scores were not significantly associated with biases related to the need for social approval, *r*s < .07, but they were correlated in theoretically expected ways with other personality constructs. Deactivation was associated with social avoidance and unpleasantness (low agreeableness) together with lack of interest in seeking rewards and or being excited (low BAS score) and lack of openness to new experiences and challenges (low openness to experience), with *r*s ranging from −.27 to −.48, all *p*s < .01. Deactivation was also positively associated with avoidant attachment, $r = .43$, $p < .01$. Hyperactivation was associated with emotional instability (neuroticism), sensitivity to threats (high BIS score), and attachment anxiety, with *r*s ranging from .29 to .46 and all *p*s < .01.

Fortunately, these correlations were only moderate in size, suggesting that the CSS dimensions are not simply redundant with attachment-style dimensions or with broad personality traits. We expected the CSS and ECR scales to be related because, theoretically, they both arise from child–parent attachment relationships. Previous studies (e.g., Kunce & Shaver, 1994) also found attachment and caregiving orientations to be related but not simply redundant, suggesting that although the two share a common origin, they—being parameters of two different behavioral systems, each with its own function (Bowlby, 1982)—should not be identical. In the study under discussion here, regression analyses indicated that although CSS scores were significantly associated with attachment dimensions, and with some of the Big Five personality traits and the BIS/BAS dimensions, they were nevertheless uniquely associated with measures of compassion, empathy, and caregiving.

That is, the CSS measures something unique to the caregiving system that is not measured by the ECR, Big Five trait measures, or the BIS/BAS scales.

Overall, our initial findings indicate that the new 20-item CSS is a reliable and valid measure of individual differences in the functioning of the caregiving system. Deactivation and hyperactivation scores are predictably associated with other measures related to compassion, empathy, and caregiving. Moreover, they are related in reasonable ways to more general personality variables and to attachment insecurities.

PREDICTING CAREGIVING BEHAVIORS

In a series of additional studies, we are examining the predictive validity of the CSS with respect to actual caregiving in different settings. Here, we briefly present data from three studies of parental caregiving, support provision within couple relationships, and engagement in volunteer activities.

Parental Caregiving

We asked 65 Israeli mothers of preschool children to complete the CSS, the ECR, and a measure of parenting stress (Loyd & Abidin's, 1985, Parenting Stress Index). The mothers and their children were then videotaped while the children attempted to solve increasingly difficult puzzles. Two independent judges, blind with respect to the mothers' CSS scores, rated the quality of support the mothers provided to their children. Hyperactivation but not deactivation was associated with parenting stress, $r(63) = .44$, $p < .01$, and judges rated the hyperactivating mothers as more distressed and less helpful when interacting with their children (*r*s of .32 and –.39, *p*s < .01). In addition, mothers scoring higher on deactivated caregiving were rated by judges as less warm and less helpful during the puzzle-solving task (*r*s of –.31 and –.37, *p*s < .01). Thus, both hyperactivation and deactivation of the caregiving system were associated with not being effectively helpful to one's child. The inadequate assistance stemmed from two different sources: coldness and distance in the case of deactivating mothers and distress in the case of hyperactivating mothers (see chap. 3, this volume, for other dispositions related to parental caregiving).

These associations remained significant even after controlling for attachment anxiety and avoidance, although the two attachment scores were related, respectively, to hyperactivated and deactivated caregiving and to parenting behaviors. That is, although the CSS scores were significantly associated with attachment insecurities, the caregiving scores still contributed uniquely to explaining maternal behavior beyond the previously studied contribution of attachment insecurity (e.g., Rholes, Simpson, & Blakely, 1995).

Support Provision in Couple Relationships

In a study of 100 young Israeli couples who had been dating for less than 5 months, one partner was randomly designated as the caregiver, and he or she completed the CSS, the ECR, and a scale assessing support provision in couple relationships (Kunce & Shaver's, 1994, Caregiving Scale). The other partner was then asked to disclose a personal problem, and the couple was videotaped while discussing this problem. Two independent judges who were blind to scores on the other measures rated the quality of support provided by the targeted caregiver (see chap. 19, this volume). We found that participants who scored higher on the CSS deactivation scale reported less responsiveness (lower scores on maintenance of proximity to a needy partner and sensitivity to the partner's signals and needs), with *r*s of –.45 and –.47, *p*s < .01, and more controlling care, $r(98) = .25$, $p < .01$. They were also coded by judges as less supportive toward their partner during the dyadic interaction task, $r(98) = -.32$, $p < .01$. Although hyperactivation was not significantly associated with reports of responsiveness, people who scored higher on the CSS hyperactivation scale reported more compulsive (i.e., intrusive) caregiving, $r(98) = .40$, $p < .01$, and were coded by judges as less supportive and more distressed during the dyadic interaction, *r*s of .36 and .43, *p*s < .01. Again, these associations were unique to the CSS and were not due to attachment insecurities, even though the CSS and ECR scales were correlated, as expected.

As in parental caregiving, support provision in couple relationships seems to be disrupted by either deactivation or hyperactivation of the caregiving system. Deactivation interferes with sensitive and responsive caregiving, and hyperactivation disrupts support provision by fostering overinvolvement with the partner's distress and insufficient sensitivity to the partner when providing assistance.

Volunteerism

In an attempt to examine the contribution of caregiving strategies to altruism in broader societal contexts, we asked a sample of 142 Israeli undergraduates to complete the CSS and two scales assessing engagement in volunteer charitable or altruistic activities. They completed a self-report scale designed by Gillath et al. (2005) to measure the number of altruistic activities a participant volunteered for and the time devoted to them (e.g., teaching reading, counseling troubled people, providing care to the sick). They also completed the Volunteer Functions Inventory (Clary et al., 1998), which measures the extent to which they volunteered for either self-oriented reasons (e.g., self-protection, career promotion, ego enhancement, achieving a sense of togetherness that soothes the self) or more altruistic reasons (e.g., other-focused values, achieving a more mature understanding of the world and oneself).

The CSS deactivation score was significantly associated with engaging in fewer volunteer activities and being involved for less altruistic reasons, *r*s of –.27 and –.39, *p*s < .01. The CSS hyperactivation score was not related significantly to engaging in volunteer activities, but it was associated with more egoistic reasons for volunteering, such as self-protection and self-enhancement, *r*s of .35 and .31, *p*s < .01. Overall, deactivation seems to interfere with altruistic volunteering, and hyperactivation, although not preventing volunteer behavior, seems to involve a more anxious, self-focused form of volunteering. In the latter case, volunteering is aimed partly at helping others and partly at helping oneself (for other dispositions related to volunteering, see chap. 3, this volume).

CONCLUSIONS

We have outlined the beginnings of a program of research on caregiving, which we believe is the prototype of empathic, altruistic, prosocial behavior. We view caregiving as the product of an innate behavioral system of the kind discussed by Bowlby (1969/1982) in his writings about attachment theory. In the same way that the functioning of the attachment behavioral system in adulthood has been illuminated by developing self-report measures of attachment anxiety and avoidance, we are beginning to illuminate the functioning of the caregiving behavioral system by exploring the correlates and implications of a new self-report measure of caregiving hyperactivation and deactivation. Our initial studies indicate that the two caregiving dimensions are related as expected to preexisting measures of empathy, compassion, and altruism, including observational measures of caregiving behavior.

We believe there is great potential in studying prosocial behavior within a larger theoretical framework. Attachment theory provides one such framework that has already yielded important insights about human social behavior. We look forward to extending its reach further in the domain of prosocial behavior.

REFERENCES

Ainsworth, M. D. S., Blehar, M. C., Waters, E., & Wall, S. (1978). *Patterns of attachment: Assessed in the Strange Situation and at home*. Hillsdale, NJ: Erlbaum.

Batson, C. D. (1991). *The altruism question: Toward a social-psychological answer*. Hillsdale, NJ: Erlbaum.

Batson, C. D., Fultz, J., & Schoenrade, P. A. (1987). Distress and empathy: Two qualitatively distinct vicarious emotions with different motivational consequences. *Journal of Personality*, *55*, 19–39.

Bowlby, J. (1973). *Attachment and loss: Vol. 2. Separation: Anxiety and anger.* New York: Basic Books.

Bowlby, J. (1980). *Attachment and loss: Vol. 3. Sadness and depression.* New York: Basic Books.

Bowlby, J. (1982). *Attachment and loss: Vol. 1. Attachment* (2nd ed.). New York: Basic Books. (Original work published 1969)

Bowlby, J. (1988). *A secure base: Clinical applications of attachment theory.* London: Routledge.

Brennan, K. A., Clark, C. L., & Shaver, P. R. (1998). Self-report measurement of adult attachment: An integrative overview. In J. A. Simpson & W. S. Rholes (Eds.), *Attachment theory and close relationships* (pp. 46–76). New York: Guilford Press.

Carver, C. S., & White, T. L. (1994). Behavioral inhibition, behavioral activation, and affective responses to impending reward and punishment: The BIS/BAS Scales. *Journal of Personality and Social Psychology, 67,* 319–333.

Cassidy, J., & Kobak, R. R. (1988). Avoidance and its relationship with other defensive processes. In J. Belsky & T. Nezworski (Eds.), *Clinical implications of attachment* (pp. 300–323). Hillsdale, NJ: Erlbaum.

Clary, E. G., Snyder, M., Ridge, R. D., Copeland, J., Stukas, A. A., Haugen, J., & Miene, P. (1998). Understanding and assessing the motivations of volunteers: A functional approach. *Journal of Personality and Social Psychology, 74,* 1516–1530.

Collins, N. L., & Feeney, B. C. (2000). A safe haven: An attachment theory perspective on support seeking and caregiving in intimate relationships. *Journal of Personality and Social Psychology, 78,* 1053–1073.

Collins, N. L., Guichard, A. C., Ford, M. B., & Feeney, B. C. (2006). Responding to need in intimate relationships: Normative processes and individual differences. In M. Mikulincer & G. S. Goodman (Eds.), *Dynamics of romantic love: Attachment, caregiving, and sex* (pp. 149–189). New York: Guilford Press.

Cross, S., Bacon, P. L., & Morris, M. L. (2000). The relational-interdependent self-construal and relationships. *Journal of Personality and Social Psychology, 78,* 791–808.

Crowne, D. P., & Marlowe, D. (1964). *The approval motive: Studies in evaluative dependence.* New York: Wiley.

Davis, M. H. (1983). Measuring individual differences in empathy: Evidence for a multidimensional approach. *Journal of Personality and Social Psychology, 44,* 113–126.

Erikson, E. H. (1993). *Childhood and society.* New York: Norton. (Original work published 1950)

Feeney, B. C. (2004). A secure base: Responsive support of goal strivings and exploration in adult intimate relationships. *Journal of Personality and Social Psychology, 87,* 631–648.

Feeney, B. C., & Collins, N. L. (2004). Interpersonal safe haven and secure base caregiving processes in adulthood. In W. S. Rholes & J. A. Simpson (Eds.),

Adult attachment: Theory, research, and clinical implications (pp. 300–338). New York: Guilford Press.

Freud, S. (1949). *An outline of psycho-analysis* (J. Strachey, Trans.). New York: Norton. (Original work published in 1940 in German)

Fritz, H., & Helgeson, V. S. (1998). Distinctions of unmitigated communion from communion: Self-neglect and over-involvement with others. *Journal of Personality and Social Psychology, 75*, 121–140.

George, C., & Solomon, J. (2008). The caregiving system: A behavioral systems approach to parenting. In J. Cassidy & P. R. Shaver (Eds.), *Handbook of attachment: Theory, research, and clinical applications* (2nd ed.). New York: Guilford Press.

Gillath, O., Shaver, P. R., Mikulincer, M., Nitzberg, R. A., Erez, A., & van IJzendoorn, M. H. (2005). Attachment, caregiving, and volunteering: Placing volunteerism in an attachment-theoretical framework. *Personal Relationships, 12*, 425–446.

Grossmann, K. E., Grossmann, K., & Waters, E. (Eds.). (2005). *Attachment from infancy to adulthood: The major longitudinal studies*. New York: Guilford Press.

Hamilton, W. D. (1964). The genetical evolution of social behavior: I and II. *Journal of Theoretical Biology, 7*, 1–52.

Hazan, C., & Shaver, P. R. (1987). Romantic love conceptualized as an attachment process. *Journal of Personality and Social Psychology, 52*, 511–524.

John, O. P., & Srivastava, S. (1999). The Big Five trait taxonomy: History, measurement, and theoretical perspectives. In O. P. John & L. A. Pervin (Eds.), *Handbook of personality: Theory and research* (2nd ed., pp. 102–138). New York: Guilford Press.

Kunce, L. J., & Shaver, P. R. (1994). An attachment-theoretical approach to caregiving in romantic relationships. In K. Bartholomew & D. Perlman (Eds.), *Advances in personal relationships* (Vol. 5, pp. 205–237). London: Kingsley.

Loyd, B. H., & Abidin, R. R. (1985). Revision of the Parenting Stress Index. *Journal of Pediatric Psychology, 10*, 169–177.

Luke, M. A., Maio, G. R., & Carnelley, K. B. (2004). Attachment models of the self and others: Relations with self-esteem, humanity-esteem, and parental treatment. *Personal Relationships, 11*, 281–303.

Mehrabian, A., & Epstein, N. (1972). A measure of emotional empathy. *Journal of Personality, 40*, 525–543.

Mikulincer, M., Florian, V., & Tolmacz, R. (1990). Attachment styles and fear of personal death: A case study of affect regulation. *Journal of Personality and Social Psychology, 58*, 273–280.

Mikulincer, M., & Shaver, P. R. (2007). *Attachment in adulthood: Structure, dynamics, and change*. New York: Guilford Press.

Mills, J., & Clark, M. S. (1994). Communal and exchange relationships: Controversies and research. In R. Erber & R. Gilmour (Eds.), *Theoretical frameworks for personal relationships* (pp. 29–42). Hillsdale, NJ: Erlbaum.

Moore, D. S. (1999). *The development and validation of the scale of interpersonal cynicism.* Unpublished doctoral dissertation, University of Tennessee, Knoxville.

Penner, L. A. (2002). Dispositional and organizational influences on sustained volunteerism: An interactionist perspective. *Journal of Social Issues, 58*, 447–467.

Reis, H. T., & Shaver, P. R. (1988). Intimacy as an interpersonal process. In S. Duck (Ed.), *Handbook of research in personal relationships* (pp. 367–389). London: Wiley.

Reizer, A., & Mikulincer, M. (2007). Assessing individual differences in working models of caregiving: The construction and validation of the mental representation of Caregiving Scale. *Journal of Individual Differences, 28*, 227–239.

Rholes, W. S., Simpson, J. A., & Blakely, B. S. (1995). Adult attachment styles and mothers' relationships with their young children. *Personal Relationships, 2*, 35–54.

Schwartz, S. H. (1992). Universals in the content and structure of values: Theory and empirical tests in 20 countries. In M. P. Zanna (Ed.), *Advances in experimental social psychology* (vol. 25; pp. 1–65). New York: Academic Press.

Shiota, M. N., Keltner, D., & John, O. P. (2006). Positive emotion dispositions differentially associated with Big Five personality and attachment style. *Journal of Positive Psychology, 1*, 61–71.

Sprecher, S., & Fehr, B. (2005). Compassionate love for close others and humanity. *Journal of Social and Personal Relationships, 22*, 629–651.

5

FORMS OF CONCERN: A PSYCHOANALYTIC PERSPECTIVE

RAMI TOLMACZ

Although the experience of concern for others is likely familiar to most people, it was not given much thought by early psychoanalytic theorists. As a psychological concept it was born late, appearing first in Winnicott's (1963) paper, "The Development of the Capacity for Concern." Although Winnicott regarded concern as a key concept, it was largely ignored or forgotten by other psychoanalysts and does not usually appear in dictionaries of psychoanalytic terms and concepts (e.g., De Mijolla, 2005). However, with the development of new approaches to psychoanalysis, the study of concern gained attention among intersubjective and relational psychoanalysts (e.g., Barbanel, 2006; Benjamin, 1988), who began to discuss the psychodynamic roots and forms of the sense of concern.

Whereas Freudian psychoanalysis focused on psychopathology and aggression, various psychoanalytic object relations theories (e.g., Winnicott, 1963) and intersubjective approaches to psychoanalysis (e.g., Benjamin, 1988), which came later, added a consideration of such positive issues as caring, sympathy, and compassion. This resulted in a number of distinctions between different forms of concern for others, which are characterized by the specific motives that generate them, the quality of emotions accompanying them, and the ego functions related to them.

In this chapter, I consider the history of the concept of concern in psychoanalysis as a complement to most of the other chapters in this volume, which stem from research by personality and social psychologists. I describe different forms of concern and explain how various psychoanalytic theorists have conceptualized them. Specifically, I discuss Winnicott's (1963) distinction between guilt-driven concern and joy-driven concern and Bowlby's (1980) distinction between sensitive caregiving and compulsive caregiving. I also explain how intersubjective approaches to psychoanalysis (e.g., Benjamin, 1988) conceptualize caring attitudes toward others and differentiate forms of concern based on the extent to which self and others are perceived as subjects or objects.

CONCERN IN THE DRIVE MODEL

Freud's (1920/1961a) psychoanalytic drive model characterized interpersonal relations in terms of the degree to which another person—a relationship partner—can further or prevent one's own need gratification. Genuine concern for the other played a limited role in the drive model and was often conceptualized as a defensive derivative of other drives, an indication of taking a parental stance toward others for whom one was not really a parent or an outcome of moral socialization (Benjamin, 1988). This approach, which reflects the focus of classical psychoanalysis on defenses and pathology, dealt more with the etiology of disorders than with the potential for human flourishing and optimal functioning. As Benjamin (1988) commented, "The hypothetical self presented by Hegel and Freud does not wish to recognize the other, does not perceive him as a person just like himself. He relinquishes omnipotence only when he has no other choice" (pp. 90–91). In addition, Freud's viewpoint regarding the importance of aggression as one of two drives underlying human behavior (the other being sex or libido) contributed to the relative neglect of concern.

In *Beyond the Pleasure Principle* (1920/1961a), Freud argued that

> men are not gentle creatures who want to be loved, and who at the most can defend themselves if they are attacked; they are, on the contrary, creatures among whose instinctual endowments is to be reckoned a powerful share of aggressiveness. As a result, their neighbor is for them not only a potential helper or sexual object, but also someone who tempts them to satisfy their aggressiveness on him, to exploit his capacity for work without compensation, to use him sexually without his consent, to seize his possessions, to humiliate him, to cause him pain, to torture and to kill him. *Homo homini lupus*. Who, in the face of all his experience of life and of history, will have the courage to dispute this assertion? (p. 53)

However, an exception to this emphasis was found in Freud's last theory of love. The main ideas were discussed in *Group Psychology and the Analysis of the Ego* (Freud, 1921/1961b), in which Freud expressed his understanding of the roots of concern. He claimed that

> the nucleus of what we mean by love naturally consists (and this is what is commonly called love, and what the poets sing of) in sexual love with sexual union as its aim. But we do not separate from this—what in any case has a share in the name 'love'—on the one hand, self love, and on the other, love for parents and children, friendship and love for humanity in general, and also devotion to concrete objects and to abstracts ideas. Our justification lies in the fact that psycho-analytic research has taught us that all these tendencies are an expression of the same instinctual impulses. (pp. 90–91)

Thus, according to Freud (1920/1961a, 1921/1961b), all love is a derivative of the sexual instincts. The nuclear case is sexual or romantic love, where the love object is a person of the opposite sex and the aim is sexual union. All other kinds of love, including familial love, friendship, compassionate love, and love of concrete objects and abstract entities, are formed by displacement of the original object or by inhibition or deflection of the original sexual aim (Santas, 1988).

In *Civilization and Its Discontents* (Freud, 1930/1961c), the last work in which Freud dealt with the concept of love, he discussed, among other things, a certain way in which love can find expression for a minority of people and which seems to be closely related to the sense of concern for others. These people make themselves independent of their object's acquiescence by displacing what they mainly value from being loved on to loving; they protect themselves against the loss of the object by directing their love not to a single object but to all persons alike; and they avoid the uncertainties and disappointments of sexual love by transforming the instinct into an evenly suspended, steadfast, affectionate feeling. Whereas this form of love seems to stem from a defense, later on in this book Freud adopted a much more inclusive conception, arguing that "civilization is a process in the service of Eros, whose purpose is to combine single human individuals, and after that families, then races, peoples and nations, into great unity, the unity of mankind" (p. 145). Thus, in Freud's broadest conception of love, concern can be viewed as a derivative of sexual love, whose defensive nature is sometimes recognizable, and it has the important function of bringing people together.

Although Klein (1937) agreed with Freudian metapsychology and with Freud's (1920/1961a) dual (eros/thanatos) theory of drives, her understanding of the origins of concern differed from his in giving an important role to the child's need to deal with his own aggression. In Kleinian theory, the emergence of the sense of concern parallels the emergence of guilt feelings and the resulting desire for reparation—both of them being products of the ongoing dialectic between love and hate and the development of the ability to distinguish between the self and the other, a stage that Klein called the *depressive position.* For Klein, reparation meant loving, and she viewed guilt as a powerful incentive for developing the capacity for empathy, caring, and compassion. In her view, the strength of guilt feelings and reparation urges is proportional to the strength of a child's aggressive drives. As Klein put it,

> for only when consideration has been given to the part that destructive impulses play in the interaction of hate and love, is it possible to show the ways in which feelings of love and tendencies to reparation develop in connection with aggressive impulses and in spite of them. (p. 57)

In discussing a child's emotional development, she claimed that

> his aggressive impulses give rise to strong feelings of guilt and to fear of the death of the loved person, all of which form part of feelings of love and reinforce and intensify them. . . . The child's early aggression stimulates the drive to restore and to make good, to put back into his mother the good things he had robbed her of in phantasy. (pp. 103–104)

In Klein's opinion, the drive to make people happy is related to a strong sense of responsibility, caring, and consideration, which she thought implies an ability to put ourselves in the other's place (i.e., to identify with the other) and is likely to be a way of coping with past suffering and frustrations. As shall become clear, the relationship that Klein noted between aggression, guilt, and concern for others greatly affected Winnicott's (1963) thinking about concern.

CONCERN IN OBJECT RELATIONS APPROACHES

The conceptualization of concern as a derivative of drives prevailed until the mid 20th century, when significant changes in psychoanalytic thought emerged and challenged classical theory (Greenberg & Mitchell, 1983). These changes included alternative conceptualizations of human nature and the abandonment of Freudian and Kleinian drive theories. The changes were proposed by early object-relations theorists, beginning with the pioneering work of Suttie (1935). Further contributions were made by theorists such as Bowlby (1973, 1979, 1980), Fairbairn (1954), and Winnicott (1963), and these contributions led to the notion that human beings primarily strive not to reduce sexual and aggressive drives but to find "objects" (relationship partners), assign meaning, test previous beliefs, and build new cognitive schemes. In this view, behaviors such as object seeking, attachment, curiosity, and exploration of one's surroundings, which previously were thought to be derived from sexual and aggressive drives, were portrayed as autonomous and primary.

Moreover, these object-relations and attachment theorists placed strong emphasis on human beings' basic yearning to form bonds with others and on a desire to be loved fully and unconditionally (Greenberg & Mitchell, 1983). They argued that alongside the thirst to receive warm treatment, humans naturally have concern for others. For example, Suttie (1935) asserted that

> the child wakes up to life with the germ of parenthood, [with] the impulse to "give" and to "respond" already in it. . . . The need to give continues as a dominant motive throughout life. . . . The feeling that our gifts (love) are not acceptable is as intolerable as the feeling that others' gifts are no longer obtainable. (p. 58)

Suttie stated that infants begin life with a generous disposition and that their need to give remains a dominant motivation throughout life. In his opinion, this need, like any other need, causes anxiety when it is frustrated. From the child's perspective, the relationship with mother is balanced, and the need to give is consequently just as vital as the need to receive. If a child senses that his or her gifts are being rejected, the child feels bad and unlovable.

Winnicott's Sense of Concern

This movement from traditional drive theory to an object-relations approach to conceptualizing human nature can also be seen in Winnicott's (1958, 1963, 1965) discussion of the sense of concern. Whereas originally Winnicott, like Klein, regarded the sense of concern as a derivative of guilt feelings (Abram, 1996), later Winnicott (1963) recognized the autonomous nature of concern and its importance in child development. He saw the capacity for concern as a matter of health, the result of good enough care, and an indication that the infant begins to be independent of the "auxiliary ego" provided by the mother. Winnicott (1963) assigned concern such a central role that he proposed the term *stage of concern* to describe one of the major developmental achievements. His proposals were later reinforced by observations of infant behavior, during which it emerged that children beyond the age of 1 or 2 years already comfort others (see chap. 7, this volume). An important milestone in children's development occurs when they respond to other people's unpleasant or painful experiences with a concerned response, such as patting the person comfortingly or gently rubbing a victim's wounds. These indications of concern are not limited to our species; some pets appear to be as upset as children by others' distress, hovering over them or placing their head in the suffering person's lap with what looks to be great concern. For example, one day a 3-month-old infant lemur, while climbing up an electric fence, received a jolt to her temple and fell to the ground in convulsions. The infant lemur was approached by her peers, who groomed her intensely for several minutes—a highly unusual behavior because infants rarely groom anyone. Three infants started a round-robin game among themselves near the dazed one, occasionally interrupting their play to take turns briefly grooming the victim (de Waal, 1996).

Winnicott (1963) proposed two forms of concern, each associated with a different developmental achievement and a different emotional state. Concern of the first type (concern as guilt) is a response to emerging feelings of guilt and anxiety experienced by an infant because of its "ruthless" behavior toward its mother. According to Winnicott, this kind of concern is the outcome of a developmental process by which the infant integrates two mental representations of the mother: the *object mother* and the *environment mother*. The former is the mother experienced by the infant in excited states; the latter is the mother experienced differently by the infant in a quiet and peaceful state. For the infant to develop a sense of concern, these two mothers must come together mentally. According to Winnicott, this capacity for concern is related to the infant's recognition that its mother is separate from the self and to feelings of guilt for hurting her. The infant experiences this as a result of ruthlessness toward mother. In other words, concern of this type comes about as an attempt to cope with guilt feelings, as Klein had earlier proposed.

The second kind of concern (concern as joy) is associated with a later developmental achievement. Here Winnicott (1965) provided a foundation for concern that stems from the child's joyful recognition that he or she and the caregiving figure can coexist, without compromising their existence as separate subjects. In this view of concern, Winnicott stressed the simultaneity of destruction, love, and survival, but this time without the need for reparation by the infant. The central emotion here is joy and not guilt. The infant feels grateful because he or she can destroy and love the object and the object survives. The realization that one can apply one's entire experiential repertoire in one's relationship with mother gives the infant a sense of integrity, which underlies the experience of joy and developing a sense of concern for the mother. In this merger of destructiveness and love proposed by Winnicott, love is strong enough to use destruction creatively, and thus guilt-based concern becomes unnecessary.

In differentiating these two kinds of concern, Winnicott (1965) distinguished between the need to be good enough to compensate for the bad and the freedom to experience unconditional love (Eigen, 1981). This distinction underlies Winnicott's view of concern as joy, in which "I love you" is not perceived as restitution for "I will destroy you" but instead can stand on its own. These two types of concern may be seen as points on an axis that represent a developmental continuum. At first, concern develops in the context of guilt, and at a later stage, which is dependent on the mother's reactions to the infant's expressions of aggression and concern, it becomes more autonomous and is associated with joy (Eigen, 1981). These two forms of concern can be seen across the life span, and their relative dominance depends on personality and the social circumstances to which they are exposed.

Bowlby's Conceptualization of the Caregiving Behavioral System

A more autonomous view of the sense of concern appears in Bowlby's (1980, 1982) conceptualization of the caregiving behavioral system (for a detailed account of Bowlby's ideas, see chap. 4, this volume). Bowlby (1988) assumed that for humans, as for other species, caregiving behavior is inborn to some degree and is primed to develop along certain lines when conditions permit. In addition to the inborn components, Bowlby (1988) proposed that this behavioral system is influenced by learned components—mainly through childhood social experiences. However, Bowlby did not go any further than this in describing the lines along which caregiving develops and the experiences that are relevant to it. In the absence of a comprehensive developmental model of caregiving, some researchers view it as a developmental product of early attachment experiences. They describe this viewpoint as a *model of assimilation* (e.g., Bretherton, 1985; Sroufe & Fleeson, 1986), arguing that we learn parental behavior from observing and experiencing our parents' behavior. According to this view, we learn to be caring toward others by noticing how we were cared for. George and Solomon (1996, 1999, 2008) argued that the caregiving behavioral system is first manifested in an infant's immature forms of care and affection—a parental way of relating, whether in real life or in play, toward other infants, animals, or dolls. These immature manifestations of care and affection may indicate that an experience of concern already exists at a young age. However, these manifestations of concern, according to George and Solomon, also depend on the care and affection received from caregivers.

Some of the fundamental elements of Bowlby's theory are similar to Suttie's (1935) ideas. One example of similarity is Suttie's assumption that there is a germ of parenthood in infants and Bowlby's assumption that aspects of the caregiving behavioral system are innate. However, despite the great similarity between the approaches of Bowlby and Suttie, a fundamental difference is discernible. Whereas Bowlby stressed the importance of the observable interaction between the infant and the caregiver (both substantively and in terms of the importance that he attributed to the development of an observational approach to research and clinical work), Suttie focused much more on various aspects of the infant's inner world and put more emphasis on experiential components.

Bowlby (1979) also distinguished between two forms of caregiving: sensitive caregiving and compulsive caregiving. In both, one may observe the needs of the other being catered to; however, it appears that the two forms of caregiving are activated by different motives. Sensitive caregiving is associated with a motive to care for the other, but without negating or ignoring oneself. In contrast, Bowlby claimed that an individual who is characterized by compulsive caregiving

> may engage in many close relationships but always in the role of giving care, never that of receiving it . . . [since he] has found that the only bond of affection available is one in which he must always be the care giver and the only care he can receive is the care he gives himself. . . . The typical childhood experience of such people is to have a mother who, due to depression or some other disability, was unable to care for the child but, instead, welcomed being cared for and perhaps also demanded help. (p. 207)

For such a child, compulsive caregiving may be a strategy to maintain proximity to a parent while suppressing attachment needs and behaviors. Concern of this kind is characterized by a tendency to focus on the welfare of the other while making radical sacrifices and denying or lacking regard for one's own feelings and needs, even the most basic (see chaps. 4 and 19, this volume).

This phenomenon led Barbanel (2006) to suggest a new diagnostic category: *caretaker personality disorder*. A person diagnosed with this disorder can be characterized as follows: (a) forms connections wherein he or she gives to others emotionally, physically, and psychologically, while avoiding gratification of self-needs; (b) is extremely vulnerable to guilt that is self and/or other induced; (c) manifests a pervasive and compulsive need to be needed; (d) represses the need for joy, pleasure, and intimacy; (e) is relentlessly overresponsible; (f) experiences emotional emptiness, loneliness, and physical exhaustion; (g) conceals past trauma and current crises by being other focused; (h) is counterdependent and appears independent, emotionally resilient, and self sustaining; (i) conceals fears of being alone, unloved, and abandoned; (j) has a profound sense of entitlement accompanied by (internalized) overreactions that include hypersensitivity to disappointment, withdrawal, bitterness, and rage; (k) avoids conflict, anger, and direct expression of displeasure to preserve contact with others; and (l) suffers from low self-esteem, usually rooted in repressed shame, guilt, embarrassment, and humiliation.

CONCERN AND INTERSUBJECTIVITY

During the last 2 decades of the 20th century, object-relations theorists' understanding of the sense of concern as a derivate of a person's mental representations of his or her relations with others was challenged by intersubjective theories that emphasized the representation of others as subjects rather than objects (e.g., Benjamin, 1988; Loewald, 1978; Ogden, 1990; Stern, 1985). In these theories, the sense of concern primarily depends on the extent to which a person perceives the object of concern as having a subjective world of his or her own. Failing to recognize or denying the existence of the other's subjective world (desubjectivisation of the other) accounts for the absence of concern in a variety of situations. For example, Ogden (1990) argued that only in the context of a sense of the other's subjectivity is he or she perceived to be a three-dimensional subject warranting empathy, caring, or guilt following harm.

The intersubjective approach relies to a large extent on Stern's (1985) research on mother–infant interactions, in which Stern concluded that infants strive from the start to separate themselves from others. He emphasized the development of infants' awareness of others as independent subjects and their ability to share subjective experiences. In his opinion, between the age of 7 and 9 months infants begin to become aware of the existence of "other minds" that can experience intentions and feelings. The term *intersubjectivity*, as Stern uses it, denotes the state of realizing that there are others who, like oneself, feel and think. Similar ideas were articulated by Loewald (1978): "The sense of needs and feelings being one's own, of being a subject, as distinguishable from an object, develops together with the sense of another's needs and feelings being *his* own. It is the same developmental step" (p. 34).

Buber's Dialogical Philosophy

Two major intersubjective approaches are relevant to the sense of concern. One approach is Buber's (1971) dialogical philosophy, and the other is relational psychoanalysis (e.g., Benjamin, 1988; Mitchell, 2000), which in recent decades has gained many adherents. Buber created his dialogical philosophy in response to a difficult spiritual challenge presented by the modern world. He thought that dissolution of traditional forms of social life, such as the tribe, clan, and family, and the emergence of a highly technological environment, engendered stress, alienation, powerlessness, loneliness, boredom, and a lack of meaning. He claimed that modernity causes people to experience themselves as subjects but others as objects that can help or hinder goal attainment. Buber called this kind of relating to others *I–It* relations. An alternative to this relationship pattern was the *I–Thou* relationship, which exists between two subjects. Here, one relates to the other as another subject, whose meaning is not dependent on being an object that hinders or advances one's own goals. In an I–Thou relationship, the self and other are equals with mutual needs and goals. The other is not a mere instrument or object. In Buber's opinion, the I–Thou pattern of relations is a prerequisite for developing concern and care.

Relational Psychoanalysis

With ideas similar to Buber's, and relying on clinical observations and research findings, relational psychoanalysts emphasize that infants develop a capacity for mutual recognition by which significant others are perceived not only as objects characterized by the functions they fulfill but also as subjects with internal worlds of their own. Moreover, the discovery of the other as a subject tends to elicit an instinctive reaction of interest and concern.

Benjamin (1988) argued that the need for mutual recognition is what unites the intersubjective theories. In her opinion, many theories fail to acknowledge the need for mutual recognition and instead see the evolving relationship between the infant and the mother as a subject–object relationship. The intersubjective approach is important because of its emphasis on the infant's need and ability to treat mother as a separate subjective reality. Without this process, concern for others is largely meaningless. In contrast to Lear (1998), who argued that we cannot love others and the world if it does not first present itself to us as worthy of our love, Benjamin contended that the infant, discovering the other as a subject, reacts to the other instinctively from a position of care and love.

Mitchell (2000), in his last book, suggested distinguishing between motivational aspects and relational aspects of human nature: "To define humans as relational is quite different from specifying object seeking as a specific drive" (p. 23). In Mitchell's opinion, from early childhood on, people seek interactions with other human minds, not to satisfy any specific need but because we are wired to respond visually to human faces, with our sense of smell to human scents, and with our hearing to human voices. In this way we seek mutual regulation and sharing with other people. In keeping with Mitchell's opinion, the human capacity for concern may not necessarily be a derivative of the drives proposed by classical psychoanalytic theory, of guilt or gratitude (Winnicott), or of a need for attachment (Bowlby) or companionship (Suttie); rather, this capacity may simply be part of our social nature as human beings.

There are two important differences between the relational approach and Buber's (1971) philosophy. Whereas Buber emphasized the influence of society, culture, and technology on the development of concern, relational psychoanalysis focuses on the microlevel, emphasizing early modes of relating developed in close relationships with caregivers. In addition, whereas in the two modes of relating proposed by Buber—I–It and I–Thou—the attitude toward self is as to a subject, relational psychoanalysts noted that just as a person can regard the other as an object or as a subject, a person can also regard himself or herself in these two modes (Benjamin, 1988).

Four Forms of Concern

According to relational psychoanalytic theory, the self and the other can both be experienced as subject and object. It follows that there are four forms of relationship: self–subject and other–subject, self–subject and other–object, self–object and other–subject, and self–object and other–object. Although the capacity to relate to self and other as subject or object is shared by most people, there are significant individual differences in the proclivity to adopt one of the four relationship patterns. Some of these differences are probably innate, but most are likely to stem from early relationships in which the capacity for mutual recognition was encouraged or discouraged.

I propose that the specific manner in which a person is inclined to perceive self and other has a significant effect on his or her ability to feel different forms of concern. In fact, by distinguishing among the four relationship patterns, relational psychoanalysis enables people to distinguish between two forms of concern. In one form, regard for self as a subject accompanies a caring attitude toward the other—a scenario that can be regarded as *good* concern (similar to what Batson, in chap. 1 of this volume, calls *empathic concern*). To the extent that a person has developed a capacity for mutual recognition, he or she will be capable of expressing a caring attitude toward the other without being alienated from his or her own feelings and needs. This situation allows for concern of the sensitive caregiving type (Bowlby, 1979, 1988) and concern as an expression of joy (Winnicott, 1965). This concern will make itself apparent both in response to the other's distress and in sharing the joy of the other's achievements (see chap. 19, this volume).

In the second form of concern, regard for self as an object accompanies a caring attitude toward the other—a scenario that can be regarded as *bad* concern. To the extent that mutual recognition did not develop properly, there will be an imbalance in one's attitudes toward self and other. This imbalance underlies concern of the compulsive caregiving type, in which people focus on the needs of others while having difficulty paying attention to their own legitimate needs (Bowlby, 1979; see also chap. 4, this volume).

Such people are characterized by high levels of anxiety, depression, fragile self-image, and feelings of unfairness. It is interesting to note that alongside their great concern for the other's distress, they may find it difficult to demonstrate a similar joyful involvement in the other's achievements. In fact, the other's achievements may increase the compulsive caregiver's anxiety and depression, both because the other's joy implies less need for care and because it increases the difference between the other's happiness and the self's discontent.

Another form of imbalance can interfere with what I call *good* concern. This happens when a concerned attitude toward oneself is accompanied by alienation from or obliviousness to the experiences and needs of the other, who is perceived mainly as a tool or means of satisfying one's own needs (see chaps. 1, 4, and 7, this volume). In such cases, a person may help someone else only if it has self-benefits (see chap. 1, this volume). In some cases, people who have difficulty perceiving the other's subjectivity while being intensely preoccupied by their own subjective world may qualify for a diagnosis of narcissistic personality disorder or antisocial disorder.

A CLINICAL EXAMPLE

These fairly abstract ideas become clearer if we consider an example of pathological (bad) concern, an example of the kind I called *self–object, other–subject*. David, a single man in his mid twenties, entered psychotherapy a couple of months after the death of his mother, whom he had nursed with ultimate devotion. In the first session following his return from a vacation overseas, he gave the following account.

Client: One evening I rested, went to sleep, in a very quiet place. I dreamt that I was a small child, and that I was in bed with a naked woman who took my hand and caressed her body with it and put my hand inside her vagina. I was shocked by this and tried to understand who this woman was and what I was doing there.

Therapist: Do you remember how you were feeling?

Client: It was a feeling that I was being used as an instrument. It was really frightening: The person was unfamiliar, and I was powerless. I thought about what's going on in my waking life with the woman I'm having a sexual relationship with. We have sex, but not full intercourse, and I mainly masturbate her and that's it. And she enjoys it. And that's enough for me. I mean, I make sure she feels good. I'm not saying I feel bad about it; I feel very good, but that's it. And it's really good for her, and very enjoyable for her, but I'm not included here. It's a by-product, my pleasure. I'm a tool for her. I'm a human vibrator. A vibrator that is more sensitive and gentler . . . yes, less mechanical, that's the difference. It's not two bodies that meet. It's a tool that meets with a body. And many times, I, in general, project this not only on the sexual relationship but in relationships at work; I'm a tool for—even here, I'm a tool for you. I am a client and you are a therapist but you are using me for your studies. And that's OK. I feel much better about it. It's clear to me that this is the way things are. I have nothing else.

Therapist: If you try to fantasize about living with someone, what is it like in your imagination?

Client: I really don't imagine it. I really can't. . . . It is more of a nightmare than a fantasy. As time goes by, I feel that I don't . . . even want to live with somebody. My fantasy is a two-room apartment, in old North Tel Aviv, with a neighborhood that resembles a kibbutz; to live there, to rent a nice apartment, to work at something a bit more creative and that earns more money, to travel abroad once a year, tour, that's it. That satisfies me and I really don't want anything more. I don't want to adopt, I don't want couplehood, or even a relationship with

> someone—maximum, I'm ready to have a dog. I'm not even sure about that. And to stay like this and continue on with my life, for as long as it lasts. And that's OK. It's terrific. I'm not responsible for anyone, I don't have to worry about anyone, nobody worries about me, nothing. I'm not old in terms of age, but it would suit me to live in protected housing, a center for senior citizens. Nice rooms, protected housing is on a high level now. Really nice, quiet, there's a doctor, nurse there, everything. You can go out for a walk, get up in the morning; I think that's really the good life. Really, it sounds funny, but really . . . that's it, nothing more. I have passed the stage, as far as I can see, of the race, with a desire for . . . that's it.

This clinical example illustrates what I call pathological (bad) concern, in which the self is perceived as an object and the other is perceived as a subject. These representations of the self and the other can result in what Bowlby (1979) called *compulsive caregiving* and can generate feelings of frustration, anger, resentment, and alienation.

CONCLUSIONS

In this chapter, I have explained how the concept of concern has evolved within psychoanalytic writings, from the classic drive model to recent relational psychoanalysis. I have also described different forms of concern, including Winnicott's (1963) distinction between guilt-driven concern and joy-driven concern, Bowlby's (1980) distinction between sensitive caregiving and compulsive caregiving, and my own conceptualization of four types of concern based on the extent to which self and others are perceived as subjects or objects. These distinctions indicate that the sense of concern is not a monolithic construct in psychoanalysis, and its various forms are influenced by multiple, and sometimes antagonistic, motives, wishes, fears, mental representations of the self and others, emotions, and action tendencies.

I close by noting the relation between the sense of security, as conceptualized in attachment theory, and the existence of a self–subject, other–subject relationship, which I have conceptualized here. The intersubjective approach emphasizes the importance of making an individual aware of the subjective world of the other, as a way of promoting experiences and expressions of concern. In contrast, Mikulincer and Shaver (2007) found that increasing an individual's sense of security promotes compassion and care. The fact that concern for others can be fostered in these two different ways raises the issue of the relation between them. It may be surmised that the individual's sense of security promotes a capacity to participate in a self–subject, other–subject relationship. However, it is possible that encountering the other as a subject promotes a sense of security, partly based on triggering an innate capacity for care or concern. Both attachment theory and intersubjective approaches to psychoanalysis postulate some kind of innate propensity to care (or innate caregiving behavioral system). The details of how this innate potential is or is not realized in a particular person's development still needs to be worked out. This is a task for many different kinds of psychologists—genetic, developmental, clinical, and social—as indicated by the breadth of the present volume.

REFERENCES

Abram, J. (1996). *The language of Winnicott*. London: Karnak.

Barbanel, L. (2006). *Removing the mask of kindness*. Northvale, NJ: Jason Aronson.

Benjamin, J. (1988). *The bonds of love*. New York: Pantheon Books.

Bowlby, J. (1973). *Attachment and loss: Vol. 2. Separation: Anxiety and anger*. New York: Basic Books.

Bowlby, J. (1979). *The making and breaking of affectional bonds*. London: Tavistock.

Bowlby, J. (1980). *Attachment and loss: Vol. 3. Sadness and depression*. New York: Basic Books.

Bowlby, J. (1982). *Attachment and loss: Vol. 1. Attachment* (2nd ed.). New York: Basic Books.

Bowlby, J. (1988). *A secure base: Clinical applications of attachment theory*. London: Routledge.

Bretherton, I. (1985). Attachment theory: Retrospect and prospect. In I. Bretherton & E. Waters (Eds.), *Growing in attachment theory and research. Monographs of the Society for Research in Child Development, 50*(1-2, Serial No. 209), 3–35.

Buber, M. (1971). *I and Thou*. New York: Simon & Schuster.

De Mijolla, A. (Ed.). (2005). *International dictionary of psychoanalysis*. New York: MacMillan.

De Waal, F. (1996). *Good natured: The origins of right and wrong in humans and other animals*. Cambridge, MA: Harvard University Press.

Eigen, M. (1981). The area of faith in Winnicott, Lacan, and Bion. *International Journal of Psychoanalysis, 62*, 413–433.

Fairbairn, W. R. D. (1954). *An object-relations theory of the personality*. New York: Basic Books.

Freud, S. (1961a). Beyond the pleasure principle. In J. Strachey (Ed.), *The standard edition of the complete psychological works of Sigmund Freud* (Vol. 18, pp. 3–64). London: Hogarth Press. (Original work published 1920)

Freud, S. (1961b). Group psychology and the analysis of the ego. In J. Strachey (Ed.), *The standard edition of the complete psychological works of Sigmund Freud* (Vol. 18, pp. 65–143). London: Hogarth Press. (Original work published 1921)

Freud, S. (1961c). Civilization and its discontents. In J. Strachey (Ed.), *The standard edition of the complete psychological works of Sigmund Freud* (Vol. 21, pp. 64–145). London: Hogarth Press. (Original work published 1930)

George, C., & Solomon, J. (1996). Representational models of relationships: Links between caregiving and attachment. *Infant Mental Health Journal, 17*, 198–216.

George, C., & Solomon, J. (1999). Attachment and caregiving: The caregiving behavioral system. In J. Cassidy & P. R. Shaver (Eds.), *Handbook of attachment: Theory, research, and clinical applications* (pp. 649–670). New York: Guilford Press.

George, C., & Solomon, J. (2008). The caregiving system: A behavioral systems approach to parenting. In J. Cassidy & P. R. Shaver (Eds.), *Handbook of attachment: Theory, research, and clinical applications* (2nd ed., pp. 833–856). New York: Guilford Press.

Greenberg, J. R., & Mitchell, S. A. (1983). *Object relations theories in psychoanalysis.* Cambridge, MA: Harvard University Press.

Klein, M. (1937). *Love, hate, and reparation.* London: Hogarth Press.

Lear, J. (1998). *Love and its place in nature: A philosophical interpretation of Freudian psychoanalysis.* New Haven, CT: Yale University Press.

Loewald, H. (1978). *Psychoanalysis and the history of the individual.* New Haven, CT: Yale University Press.

Mikulincer, M., & Shaver, P. R. (2007). *Attachment in adulthood: Structure, dynamics, and change.* New York: Guilford Press.

Mitchell, S. (2000). *Relationality: From attachment to intersubjectivity.* Hillsdale, NJ: Analytic Press.

Ogden, T. (1990). On potential space. In P. Giovacchini (Ed.), *Tactics and techniques in psychoanalytic therapy: The implications of Winnicott's contributions* (pp. 90–112). Northvale, NJ: Jason Aronson.

Santas, G. (1988). *Plato and Freud: Two theories of love.* Oxford, England: Basil Blackwell.

Sroufe, L., & Fleeson, J. (1986). Attachment and the construction of relationships. In W. Hartup & Z. Rubin (Eds.), *The nature and development of relationships* (pp. 51–71). Hillsdale, NJ: Erlbaum.

Stern, D. (1985). *The interpersonal world of the infant: A view from psychoanalysis and developmental psychology.* New York: Basic Books.

Suttie, I. (1935). *The origins of love and hate.* London: Free Association Books.

Winnicott, D. (1958). The depressive position in normal emotional development. In *Collected papers: Through pediatrics to psychoanalysis* (pp. 262–277). London: Tavistock.

Winnicott, D. (1963). The development of the capacity for concern. *Bulletin of the Menninger Clinic, 27*, 167–176.

Winnicott, D. (1965). Psychoanalysis and the sense of guilt. In *The maturational processes and the facilitating environment* (pp. 15–28). New York: International Universities Press.

6

NEUROSCIENCE MEETS SOCIAL PSYCHOLOGY: AN INTEGRATIVE APPROACH TO HUMAN EMPATHY AND PROSOCIAL BEHAVIOR

GRIT HEIN AND TANIA SINGER

From the moment we are born, we interact with our social environment. Long-term deprivation of social interaction causes uttermost despair and neural damage (Innocenti, 2007), supporting the notion that human beings are innately social. The question of how "people's thoughts, feelings, and behaviors are influenced by the actual, imagined, or implied presence of others" is the focus of research in social psychology (Allport, 1954. p. 5). The long and fruitful tradition of social psychological research has produced a variety of empirical approaches and models concerning prosocial motives, emotions, and behavior, as outlined in the other chapters of this book.

The field of neuroscience has only recently become interested in studying the affective and social brain. A new interdisciplinary field, social neuroscience, has emerged from a union of classical cognitive neuroscience and

---

We thank Daniel Batson for valuable comments on the manuscript. This work was supported by the University of Zürich and the Society in Science: The Branco Weiss Fellowship (G. H.).

social psychology. Recent neuroscientific research has addressed classical social psychological issues such as peoples' ability to understand other people's minds: their beliefs, intentions, and feelings. In this chapter, we review recent advances in neuroscience research that, in connection with social psychology findings, help to illuminate our understanding of prosocial behavior. The first part of the chapter summarizes the social neuroscience perspective on "understanding others" and describes some of the key research findings. The second part of the chapter discusses approaches and results related to the study of empathy and prosocial behavior in social and developmental psychology. The last part of the chapter provides a preliminary integration of the social neuroscience and social psychology perspectives and discusses implications for future research.

UNDERSTANDING OTHERS: A SOCIAL NEUROSCIENCE PERSPECTIVE

In the late 1990s, social neuroscience focused mainly on the investigation of basic social abilities (for a review and overviews, see Adolphs, 2003; Blakemore, Winston, & Frith, 2004; Ochsner & Lieberman, 2001). Several functional neuroimaging studies, for example, have investigated the neural correlates of attending, recognizing, and remembering socially relevant stimuli such as facial expressions of fear, attractive faces, indicators of trustworthiness, racial identity, and faces of fair and unfair players in a game (Hart et al., 2000; Morris et al., 1996; O'Doherty et al., 2003; Singer et al., 2004; Winston, Strange, O'Doherty, & Dolan, 2002).

Extending this line of research, social neuroscientists have begun to clarify the neural mechanisms underlying our ability to understand other people's beliefs and thoughts, an ability known as having a *theory of mind* (e.g., Premack & Woodruff, 1978), *mentalizing* (Frith & Frith, 2003), *mindreading* (Baron-Cohen, 1995), or *cognitive perspective taking*, and our ability to share other people's feelings, referred to as *empathy* (for a similar distinction between cognitive and affective aspects of reactions to other people, see chap. 1, this volume; Blair, 2005; de Vignemont & Singer, 2006; Decety & Lamm, 2007; Gallese, 2003; Keysers & Gazzola, 2007; Preston & de Waal, 2002; Singer, 2006). Even though mentalizing and empathizing are often used in concert when we try to understand other people's minds, preliminary evidence from studies of patients with marked social deficits, such as autism or psychopathy, has suggested that mentalizing and empathizing are two distinct abilities that rely on different neural circuitries (see also Blair, 2005; Singer, 2006). For example, patients with autistic spectrum disorders often have deficits in cognitive perspective taking, whereas psychopaths are very good at understanding other people's intentions and consequently at manipulating other people's behavior. In contrast to autistic patients, psychopaths lack empathy, which may be part of the reason for their antisocial behavior.

This dissociation points to an important difference between our ability to mentalize and our ability to empathize. Whereas both abilities play an important role in drawing inferences about other people's cognitive and emotional states, it has been suggested that empathy is not just a matter of cognition but also has motivational, emotional, and social aspects (for a similar argument, see de Vignemont & Singer, 2006). De Vignemont and Singer (2006) described empathy as follows: We *empathize* with others when we have (a) an affective state (b) that is isomorphic to another person's affective state and (c) was elicited by observing or imagining another person's affective state, and (d) when we know that the other person's affective state is the source of our own affective state.

Defining *empathy* as an affective state is important because it differentiates empathy from theory of mind, cognitive perspective taking, and mentalizing. The term *mentalizing* connotes a person's ability to cognitively represent the mental states of another, including his or her affective states, without necessarily becoming emotionally involved. The term *empathizing* connotes the capacity to share other people's feelings. Accordingly, when one empathizes with another person who is in pain, one feels the other person's pain in one's own body. In contrast, when one understands someone else's thoughts, one does not feel the other's thoughts in one's own body. There are no qualia attached to the representation of the other person's thoughts. This difference and its significance become clearer when psychopaths are considered: They do not have an impaired ability to understand other people's wishes, beliefs, intentions, and desires, but they seem to lack the embodied feeling of empathy, which allows nonpsychopaths to anticipate and appreciate others' suffering, thereby often preventing them from harming others. Thus, although psychopaths possess the ability to mentalize, they are not able to empathize (for a similar argument, see Blair, 2005).

Part b of de Vignemont and Singer's (2006) description of empathy is important in distinguishing empathy from sympathy or compassion (for a similar distinction, see chap. 7, this volume; Eisenberg & Miller, 1987). In all three cases, we feel vicariously for the other person. But when we empathize, we share the other person's feelings; when we sympathize or show compassion, we do not necessarily share the same feeling. For example, to use first-person language for a moment, when I empathize with a person who is sad, I feel sad myself. When I sympathize with or feel compassion for a sad person, I feel pity, love, or concern for the person but am not sad myself. Also, when I notice that someone is jealous or envious of me, I can sympathize with or show compassion toward that person, but I am not jealous or envious myself. Further, empathy is not necessarily linked to prosocial motivation—that is, a wish to maximize the other person's happiness or alleviate the other person's distress—whereas there is such a link from sympathy or compassion to prosocial motivation and actions or action tendencies. Empathy can be misused, for example, by a torturer who empathizes to find his victim's weakest point, but he is far from showing compassion for the suffering person.

Finally, de Vignemont and Singer's (2006) conception of empathy distinguishes between empathy and what might be called *emotional contagion*. The latter term refers to a reaction in which one shares an emotion with another person without realizing that the other person's emotion was the trigger. For example, babies start crying when they hear other babies crying, long before they develop a sense of a self as separate from others. Those reactions might be a precursor of the development of a capacity for empathy (see Sagi & Hoffman, 1976), but they are not considered empathic responses per se because the babies are not aware that they are vicariously feeling another person's distress.

This discussion emphasizes the difference between perspective taking—the cooler, more cognitive apprehension of others' emotions—and empathy, which is a warmer, more embodied sharing of emotions perceived in another person. From the neuroscientific perspective, this distinction is expected to be reflected in differences in the neural systems involved in cognitive perspective taking and empathic sharing of emotions.

Theory-of-Mind Studies

Neuroimaging studies of cognitive perspective taking are often referred to as *theory-of-mind experiments*. In most cases, they are conducted with healthy adults who are asked to understand the intentions, beliefs, and desires of a protagonist in a story or a cartoon (for a review, see Gallagher & Frith, 2003). Theory-of-mind studies have consistently revealed a neural network comprising the posterior superior temporal sulcus (STS), extending into the temporoparietal junctions (TPJ), the medial prefrontal cortex (mPFC), and sometimes the temporal poles (TP).

It is interesting that the mPFC is involved not only when people mentalize other people's thoughts, intentions, and beliefs but also when people reflect on their own states (Mitchell, Banaji, & Macrae, 2005a). Mitchell and colleagues (Mitchell et al., 2002, 2005b, 2006) recently conducted a series of experiments on mentalizing that revealed functional differences between judging the mental states of similar and dissimilar others. A more ventral part of the mPFC was recruited when participants made self-judgments or judgments about people whom they perceived as being similar to themselves with respect to appearance or political attitudes. By contrast, a more dorsal part of the mPFC showed enhanced activation—close to the activation found in the mentalizing studies cited previously—when participants judged the mental states of people perceived as being dissimilar to themselves. This suggests that we use two different strategies when inferring other people's mental states: With one strategy, we simulate the other person's states on the basis of knowledge we have about ourselves; with the other strategy, we infer the mental states of the other on the basis of more abstract knowledge about the world.

Studies of Empathy

Whereas theory-of-mind research focuses on complex inferences about abstract mental states such as other people's beliefs, another line of neuroscientific research focuses on our ability to understand other people's goals and intentions by neuronally simulating them. This line of research is based on the groundbreaking discovery of *mirror neurons* in monkey premotor cortex, which fire both when a monkey performs hand movements itself and when it merely observes another monkey or a human performing the same hand movements (Ferrari, Gallese, Rizzolatti, & Fogassi, 2003; Gallese, Fadiga, Fogassi, & Rizzolatti, 1996; Rizzolatti, Fadiga, Gallese, & Fogassi, 1996). Later on, a similar common coding of the perception and generation of motor actions was demonstrated in the human brain using imaging techniques such as positron emission tomography or functional magnetic resonance imaging (fMRI; for a review, see Grezes & Decety, 2001). In line with the monkey studies, the human studies revealed that the same circuitry was recruited when participants merely observed another person performing an action and when they performed the same action themselves.

The idea that perception–action links in the brain enable us to understand others, a claim that was originally established in the motor domain, has recently been expanded to feelings and sensations (Decety & Jackson, 2004; Decety & Lamm, 2006; de Vignemont & Singer, 2006; Gallese, 2003; Preston & de Waal, 2002). Indeed, fMRI studies in humans have provided evidence that such shared neural networks enable us to "share" pain, touch, or disgust with another person merely by perceiving or imagining the other person in a relevant situation, in the absence of any stimulation of our own body. For example, a study by Wicker et al. (2003) showed that viewing pictures of disgusted faces and smelling disgusting odors produced corresponding neural responses in viewers. Jabbi, Swart, and Keysers (2007) had participants watch video clips showing people sampling pleasant and unpleasant tastes and then experience the different tastes themselves. Both studies (Jabbi et al., 2007; Wicker et al., 2003) found neural activation in anterior insula cortex, a brain region involved in processing disgust and taste, among other sensations, when people passively watched disgust in another person and when they were disgusted themselves.

The majority of studies on empathic brain responses have been conducted in the domain of pain (Avenanti, Bueti, Galati, & Aglioti, 2005; Avenanti, Paluello, Bufalari, & Aglioti, 2006; Botvinick et al., 2005; Bufalari, Aprile, Avenanti, Di Russo, & Aglioti, 2007; Cheng et al., 2007; Gu & Han,

2007; Jackson, Brunet, Meltzoff, & Decety, 2006; Jackson, Meltzoff, & Decety, 2005; Lamm, Batson, & Decety, 2007; Moriguchi et al., 2007; Morrison, Lloyd, di Pellegrino, & Roberts, 2004; Morrison, Peelen, & Downing, 2007; Saarela et al., 2007; Singer et al., 2004, 2006). For example, in an early study, Singer et al. (2004) recruited couples and measured empathy in vivo by assessing brain activity in the female partner while painful stimulation was applied either to her own or to her partner's right hand via electrodes attached to the back of the hand. The male partner was seated next to the MRI scanner, and a mirror system allowed the female partner to see her own as well as her partner's hand lying on a tilted board in front of her. Before the experiment started, the couples were allowed to engage in social interaction to increase the feeling of being in a "real-life situation." Differently colored flashes of light on a screen behind the board pointed to either the male or the female partner's hand, indicating which of them would receive painful and which would receive nonpainful stimulation.

This procedure permitted the measurement of pain-related brain activation when pain was applied to the scanned participant (felt pain) or to her partner (empathy for pain). The results indicated that parts of the so-called pain matrix—bilateral anterior insula (AI), rostral anterior cingulate cortex (ACC), brainstem, and cerebellum—were activated when participants experienced pain themselves as well as when they saw a signal indicating that a loved one had experienced pain. These areas are involved in the processing of the affective component of pain—that is, the degree to which the subjectively felt pain is unpleasant. Thus, both the experience of one's own pain and the knowledge that a beloved partner is experiencing pain activate the same affective pain circuits, suggesting that if a beloved partner suffers pain, our brains also cause us to suffer a similar pain.

Activation in this network was also observed when participants saw an unknown but likeable person suffering pain (Singer et al., 2006) or watched videos showing body parts in potentially painful situations (Jackson et al., 2005, 2006), painful facial expressions (Lamm et al., 2007), or hands being pricked by needles (Morrison et al., 2004; for a review, see de Vignemont & Singer, 2006).

Analyses of empathic brain responses obtained while participants were observing other people suffering, be it their loved ones or people the participants liked (Singer et al., 2004, 2006), have revealed individual differences in activity in empathy-related pain-sensitive areas (ACC and AI). According to the results of Singer and associates, these differences covary with scores on the Empathic Concern Scale of the Interpersonal Reactivity Index (IRI; Davis, 1980) and the Balanced Emotional Empathy Scale (BEES; Mehrabian & Epstein, 1972). The higher participants scored on these questionnaires, the higher their activation in ACC and AI. It is interesting that Jabbi et al. (2007) observed similar correlations between IRI subscales and empathic brain responses in the AI among participants who had observed others tasting pleasant or unpleasant drinks associated with facial expressions of joy or disgust.

Empathic brain responses are positively correlated not only with trait measures of empathy but also with unpleasantness ratings given online after each trial of an empathy-inducing task (Jackson et al., 2005; Lamm et al., 2007; Saarela et al., 2007). Future research will have to clarify how these individual differences in empathic brain responses come about and whether they are able to explain individual differences in prosocial behavior, two lines of research that have not yet been sufficiently developed.

UNDERSTANDING OTHERS: A SOCIAL PSYCHOLOGY PERSPECTIVE

In social psychology, the term most commonly used in the context of understanding others' emotional states is *empathy*. Depending on the focus of research, different definitions of empathy have been offered. Hoffman (1981) proposed a relatively broad definition: "an affective response appropriate to someone else's situation rather than one's own" (p. 44). He considered empathy to be the result of a developmental sequence, beginning with babies crying when they hear another baby's cry and arriving, after considerable development, at a clear sense of others as distinct from the self. Perceived distress in the other can elicit *empathic distress* or *sympathetic distress*. The latter is the basis for altruistic motivation, which consists mainly of the urge to relieve one's own distress.

Eisenberg and her associates (see chap. 7, this volume) distinguished between empathy and sympathy. Eisenberg and Miller (1987) defined empathy as "an affective state that stems from the apprehension of another's emotional state or condition, and that is congruent with it" (p. 91) and sympathy as "an emotional response stemming from another's emotional state or condition that is not identical to the other's emotion, but consists of feelings of sorrow or concern for another's welfare" (p. 92). Empathy in its pure form is not other-oriented. With further cognitive processing it can turn into sympathy, personal distress, or a combination of both (Eisenberg, 2000). Prosocial behavior is negatively correlated with personal distress and positively associated with sympathy (Eisenberg & Miller, 1987). Sympathy can derive from empathy but also from cognitive perspective taking. In children, empathic responding is observed in the 2nd year of life (Zahn-Waxler, Radke-Yarrow, & King, 1979; Zahn-Waxler, Radke-Yarrow, Wagner, & Chapman, 1992). It correlates with parents' expressivity, mediated by the level of the child's effortful control (Valiente et al., 2004), and predicts measurable prosocial dispositions, which are stable across 5 years in early adulthood (see chap. 7, this volume; Eisenberg et al., 2002).

The term *empathic concern*, introduced by Batson (see review in chap. 1, this volume) is similar to Eisenberg's definition of sympathy. Empathic concern is defined as an other-oriented response congruent with the perceived distress experienced by another person (e.g., Batson, Turk, Shaw, & Klein, 1995). It is elicited by adopting the other's perspective and requires valuing the other's welfare (Batson, Eklund, Chermok, Hoyt, & Ortiz, 2007). In many cases, similarity between the individual and the person in need increases empathic concern but is neither a necessary nor a sufficient condition (Batson, Lishner, Cook, & Sawyer, 2005). Valuing the welfare of the other is also affected by similarity and remains stable even after situational empathy has declined (Batson et al., 1995).

In line with the results of Eisenberg and associates on children and young adults (e.g., Eisenberg, & Miller, 1987), the findings of Batson and colleagues support the assumption that feeling empathy for a person in need leads to increased helping, one kind of prosocial behavior (see chap. 1, this volume). Experiments have shown that most people are willing to receive uncomfortable electrical shocks themselves to help someone in need, even if the potential helpers are offered an "easy escape" that would not require helping. Only people who report a high level of personal distress instead of empathy prefer to escape rather than help (Batson, 1991).

What is the difference between someone who is empathic and helps, and someone who is distressed and opts to escape? One approach to answering this question is to identify personality traits that make up a *prosocial personality* (Penner, Fritzsche, Craiger, & Freifeld, 1995; see also chap. 3, this volume). Penner and associates have identified two major components of a prosocial personality. The first concerns prosocial thoughts and feelings, such as a sense of responsibility and a tendency to experience cognitive and affective empathy. A second factor concerns being helpful—that is, perceiving oneself as someone who is willing and able to help. Both factors are significantly associated with actual prosocial behavior, such as helping coworkers or volunteering in the community (e.g., Penner, 2002; Penner, Dovidio, Piliavin, & Schroeder, 2005).

Another framework for investigating individual differences in empathy and prosocial behavior is attachment theory, proposed originally by Bowlby (1982) and elaborated and experimentally tested by Mikulincer and Shaver (2007; see also chaps. 4 and 14, this volume). According to this theory, human beings are innately equipped with attachment and caregiving behavioral systems. The attachment system is especially apparent during the first years of life but has also proven to influence social interactions across the life span (Fraley & Shaver, 2000; Mikulincer & Shaver, 2007). Individual differences in attachment style can be measured along two orthogonal dimensions: attachment-related anxiety and avoidance (Brennan, Clark, & Shaver, 1998). Relatively low scores on these dimensions indicate attachment security, which has been associated with empathy in young children (2 to 3 years old; Kerstenbaum, Farber, & Sroufe, 1989; van der Mark, van IJzendoorn, & Bakermans-Kranenburg, 2002) and in adults (Mikulincer et al., 2001). Increasing security by experimental techniques such as implicit and explicit priming has been shown to affect compassion and altruistic behavior (Mikulincer, Shaver, Gillath, & Nitzberg, 2005), whereas attachment insecurity can interfere with the natural tendency to help others in need (Gillath, Shaver, & Mikulincer, 2005; Feeney & Collins, 2001; also see chap. 19, this volume).

Besides the influences of individual differences, the relation between empathy and actual prosocial behavior is influenced by social factors, such as whether the person in need is seen as a member of one's own or a different group (see chap. 20, this volume). There is a large body of evidence indicating strong favoritism toward members of one's group (e.g., Hewstone, Rubin, & Willis, 2002; Mullen, Brown, & Smith, 1992). Empathy is a better predictor of helping an ingroup member, probably because empathic concern is facilitated by familiarity and attachment, whereas prosocial behavior toward outgroup members is based on factors such as attraction (Sturmer, Snyder, & Omoto, 2005). Taking the perspective of an outgroup member (Finlay, & Stephan, 2000), however, or focusing on the person's feelings (Batson et al., 1997; Vescio, Sechrist, & Paolucci, 2003) reduces intergroup prejudice and bias (Dovidio et al., 2004).

UNDERSTANDING OTHERS IN NEUROSCIENCE AND SOCIAL PSYCHOLOGY: AN INTEGRATIVE PERSPECTIVE

In both disciplines, empathy is seen as central to our ability to understand another person's emotional states, but does empathy have the same meaning in social neuroscience and in social and developmental psychology? In some social psychological definitions, empathy is viewed as an affective response that is congruent with (see chap. 7, this volume) or appropriate for (Hoffman, 1981) another's emotion. Other definitions emphasize that empathy is related to adopting the other's perspective (e.g., chap. 1, this volume). Although affective empathic responses and perspective taking are often linked, the reviewed neuroscientific studies suggest a clear distinction between putting oneself into another's shoes (or mind: cognitive perspective taking) and sharing the other's affective state in an embodied manner (empathy). In social neuroscience, empathy is distinguished from cognitive perspective taking (Blair, 2005; Decety & Lamm, 2007; de Vignemont & Singer, 2006; Gallese, 2003; Keysers & Gazzola, 2007; Singer, 2006). This distinction is in line with early social psychological work, which also proposed a distinction between perspective taking and empathic concern (e.g., Coke, Batson, & McDavis, 1978).

Although, so far, empathy research has developed relatively independently in the two disciplines, there is consistency between measures of empathy in social psychology and neuroscience. This is reflected by covariation between scores on empathy questionnaires such as the IRI (Davis, 1980) and the BEES (Mehrabian & Epstein, 1972), on the one hand, and empathy-related activation of ACC and AI (Singer et al., 2004, 2006), on the other hand. Social neuroscience has taken only preliminary steps in investigating individual differences in empathy-related brain activity. But it is already clear that the neural empathy response is related to a participant's affective ties to the other person (Singer et al., 2004, 2006), the participant's appraisal of whether the other person's suffering is justified (Lamm et al., 2007), prior experience with the situation (Cheng et al., 2007), and the intensity of the inflicted pain (e.g., seeing a needle pricking vs. penetrating a muscle; Avenanti et al., 2006).

CONCLUSION

In the future, it would be worthwhile to investigate whether differences in prosocial personality traits (see chap. 3, this volume) or attachment styles (see chaps. 14 and 19, this volume) predict differences in activation of the brain network associated in social neuroscience studies of empathy. There is already evidence that attachment-style differences in ability to suppress emotionally painful thoughts modulate brain activity (Gillath, Bunge, Shaver, Wendelken, & Mikulincer, 2005).

Another focus for future research would be possible links between empathic brain responses, sympathy, and prosocial behavior. On the basis of current neuroscientific evidence, it is difficult to decide whether empathic brain responses reflect feeling *like* the other person, in the sense of simulating the other's feelings, or feeling *for* the other, in the sense of sympathy. One way to disentangle the two would be to correlate empathic brain responses with nuanced situational self-reports, as already done in social psychology (for example, in distinguishing between empathy and personal distress). Moreover, social and developmental psychologists have designed clever experimental paradigms to investigate the links between empathy or sympathy and prosocial behavior, and some of these could be adapted for neuroscience experiments.

Working from the other side of the disciplinary divide, social and developmental psychologists might be able to avoid some difficulties in previous empathy research by using neuroimaging methods. For example, in many behavioral empathy studies, participants are repeatedly asked to report their feelings. This can be problematic because it creates strong demand characteristics (Eisenberg & Lennon, 1983) and may induce social desirability biases. Neuroimaging methods should be beneficial in such cases because empathy and related phenomena can be investigated without such explicit instructions and self-observations (e.g., Singer et al., 2004, 2006). Moreover, neuroimaging methods can help to disentangle separate psychological processes, which may have similar behavioral correlates yet be importantly distinct. For example, emotionally empathizing with or cognitively taking the perspective of another person can lead to the same behavioral outcome, but if they have different neural correlates they can be more carefully distinguished. Another interesting contribution of neuroscience methods is the quantification of changes in empathic response over the life span and as a function of empathy training or other interventions. For example, assessing the neural plasticity in empathic responses in children of different ages would add to our understanding of developmental aspects of empathy, complementing the already existing behavioral data.

Last but not least, our brains do not exist in isolation, and their functioning should be modulated by the social factors and culture on the mesolevel of groups and the macrolevel of society (Penner et al., 2005; see also chap. 3, this volume). According to research in social psychology, ingroup and intergroup processes have strong effects on empathy and prosocial behavior (see chap. 20, this volume), but such effects have not yet been explored with neuroscientific methods. It would be interesting to investigate whether ingroup and intergroup effects modulate empathy-related brain activity, opening yet another broad avenue for future social neuroscience research.

Social neuroscience and social and developmental psychology have contributed different pieces to the large, complex puzzle of empathy and prosocial behavior. So far, social neuroscience has elucidated how emotional contagion and empathy are implemented in the human brain, but it has not yet explored how empathy, sympathy, and empathic concern affect prosocial behavior. Empathy research in social and developmental psychology starts there, providing knowledge and measures related to connections between mental processes, individual differences, and prosocial behavior. It will prove useful to have a more extensive dialogue between the different kinds of researchers.

In this chapter, we have reviewed findings related to empathy and prosocial behavior from social neuroscience and social and developmental psychology. In the young field of social neuroscience, empathy research has focused on identifying brain regions and mechanisms involved in empathy and perspective taking, which leaves a variety of open questions concerning the sources of individual differences in empathic brain responses, the development of the empathic brain, and the links between empathic brain responses and actual helping behavior. Social and developmental psychologists have acquired expertise in these domains. We are convinced that integrating and linking the social neuroscience and the social and developmental psychology of empathy and prosocial behavior would be fruitful for both fields and would improve our understanding of a very important domain of human experience and behavior.

REFERENCES

Adolphs, R. (2003). Cognitive neuroscience of human social behaviour. *Nature Reviews: Neuroscience, 4*, 165–178.

Allport, G. W. (1954). *The nature of prejudice*. Cambridge, MA: Addison Wesley.

Avenanti, A., Bueti, D., Galati, G., & Aglioti, S. (2005). Transcranial magnetic stimulation highlights the sensorimotor side of empathy for pain. *Nature Neuroscience*, 8, 955–960.

Avenanti, A., Paluello, I. M., Bufalari, I., & Aglioti, S. M. (2006). Stimulus-driven modulation of motor-evoked potentials during observation of others' pain. *Neuroimage, 32*, 316–324.

Baron-Cohen, S. (1995). *Mindblindness: An essay on autism and theory of mind*. Cambridge, MA: MIT Press.

Batson, C. D. (1991). *The altruism question: Toward a social-psychological answer*. Hillsdale, NJ: Erlbaum.

Batson, C. D., Eklund, J. H., Chermok, V.L., Hoyt, J. L., & Ortiz, B. G. (2007). An additional antecedent of empathic concern: Valuing the welfare of the person in need. *Journal of Personality and Social Research*, 93, 65–74.

Batson, C. D., Lishner, D. A., Cook, J., & Sawyer, S. (2005). Similarity and nurturance: Two possible sources of empathy for strangers. *Basic and Applied Social Psychology, 27*, 15–25.

Batson, C. D., Polycarpou, M. P., Harmon-Jones, E., Imhoff, H. J., Mitchener, E. C., Bednar, L. L., et al. (1997). Empathy and attitudes: Can feeling for a member of a stigmatized group improve feelings toward the group? *Journal of Personality and Social Psychology, 72*, 108–118.

Batson, C. D., Turk, C. L., Shaw, L. L., & Klein, T. R. (1995). Information function of empathic emotion: Learning that we value the other's welfare. *Journal of Personality and Social Psychology*, 68, 1042–1054.

Blair, R. J. (2005). Responding to the emotions of others: Dissociating forms of empathy through the study of typical and psychiatric populations. *Consciousness and Cognition, 14*, 698–718.

Blakemore, S. J., Winston, J., & Frith, U. (2004). Social cognitive neuroscience: Where are we heading? *Trends in Cognitive Sciences*, 8, 216–222.

Bowlby, J. (1982). *Attachment and loss. Vol. 1: Attachment* (2nd ed.). New York: Basic Books.

Bufalari, I., Aprile, T., Avenanti, A., Di Russo, F., & Aglioti, S. M. (2007). Empathy for pain and touch in the human somatosensory cortex. *Cerebral Cortex, 17*, 2553–2561.

Brennan, K. A., Clark, C. L., & Shaver, P. R. (1998). Self-report measurement of adult attachment: An integrative overview. In J.A. Simpson & W.S. Rholes (Eds.), *Attachment theory and close relationships* (pp. 46–76). New York: Guilford Press.

Cheng, Y., Lin, C. P., Liu, H. L., Hsu, Y. Y., Lim, K. E., Hung, D., & Decety, J. (2007). Expertise modulates the perception of pain in others. *Current Biology, 17*, 1708–1713.

Coke, J. S., Batson, C. D., & McDavis, K. (1978). Empathic mediation of helping: A two-stage model. *Journal of Personality and Social Psychology, 36*, 752–766.

Davis, M. H. (1980). A multidimensional approach to individual differences in empathy. *JSAS Catalogue of Selected Documents in Psychology, 10*, 85.

Decety, J., & Jackson, P. L. (2004). The functional architecture of human empathy. *Behavioral and Cognitive Neuroscience Reviews, 3*, 71–100.

Decety, J., & Lamm, C. (2006). Human empathy through the lens of social neuroscience. *The Scientific World Journal*, 6, 1146–1163.

Decety, J., & Lamm, C. (2007). The role of the right temporoparietal junction in social interaction: How low-level computational processes contribute to metacognition. *The Neuroscientist, 13*(6), 580–593. [doi:10.1177/1073858407304654]

de Vignemont, F., & Singer, T. (2006). The empathic brain: How, when, and why? *Trends in Cognitive Sciences, 10*, 435–441.

Dovidio, J. F., ten Vergert, M., Stewart, T. L., Gaertner, S. L., Johnson, J. D., Esses, V. M., et al. (2004). Perspective and prejudice: Antecedents and mediating mechanisms. *Personality and Social Psychology Bulletin, 30*, 1537–1549.

Eisenberg, N. (2000). Emotion, regulation, and moral development. *Annual Review of Psychology, 51*, 665–697.

Eisenberg, N., Guthrie, I. K., Cumberland, A., Murphy, B. C., Shepard, S. A., Zhou, Q., et al. (2002). Prosocial development in early adulthood: A longitudinal study. *Journal of Personality and Social Psychology, 82*, 993–1006.

Eisenberg, N., & Lennon, R. (1983). Sex differences in empathy and related capacities. *Psychological Bulletin, 94*, 100–131.

Eisenberg, N., & Miller, P. A. (1987). The relation of empathy to prosocial and related behaviors. *Psychological Bulletin, 101*, 91–119.

Feeney, B. C., & Collins, N. L. (2001). Predictors of caregiving in adult intimate relationships: An attachment theoretical perspective. *Journal of Personality and Social Psychology, 80*, 972–994.

Ferrari, P. F., Gallese, V., Rizzolatti, G., & Fogassi, L. (2003). Mirror neurons responding to the observation of ingestive and communicative mouth actions in the monkey ventral premotor cortex. *The European Journal of Neuroscience, 17*, 1703–1714.

Finlay, K. A., & Stephan, W. G. (2000). Improving intergroup relations: The effects of empathy on racial attitudes. *Journal of Applied Social Psychology, 30*, 1720–1737.

Fraley, R. C., & Shaver, P. R. (2000). Adult romantic attachment: Theoretical developments, emerging controversies, and unanswered questions. *Review of General Psychology, 4*, 132–154.

Frith, U., & Frith, C. D. (2003). Development and neurophysiology of mentalizing. *Philosophical Transactions of the Royal Society of London, 358*, 459–473.

Gallagher, H. L., & Frith, C. D. (2003). Functional imaging of "theory of mind." *Trends in Cognitive Sciences, 7*, 77–83.

Gallese, V. (2003). The manifold nature of interpersonal relations: The quest for a common mechanism. *Philosophical Transactions of the Royal Society of London, 358*, 517–528.

Gallese, V., Fadiga, L., Fogassi, L., & Rizzolatti, G. (1996). Action recognition in the premotor cortex. *Brain, 119*, 593–609.

Gillath, O., Bunge, S. A., Shaver, P. R., Wendelken, C., & Mikulincer, M. (2005). Attachment-style differences in the ability to suppress negative thoughts: Exploring the neural correlates. *Neuroimage, 28*, 835–847.

Gillath, O., Shaver, P. R., & Mikulincer, M. (2005). An attachment-theoretical approach to compassion and altruism. In P. Gilbert (Ed.), *Compassion: Its nature and use in psychotherapy* (pp. 121–147). London: Brunner-Routledge.

Grezes, J., & Decety, J. (2001). Functional anatomy of execution, mental simulation, observation, and verb generation of actions: A meta-analysis. *Human Brain Mapping, 12*, 1–19.

Gu, X., & Han, S. (2007). Attention and reality constraints on the neural processes of empathy for pain. *Neuroimage, 36*, 256–267.

Hart, A. J., Whalen, P. J., Shin, L. M., McInerney, S. C., Fischer, H., & Rauch, S. L. (2000). Differential response in the human amygdala to racial outgroup vs. ingroup face stimuli. *Neuroreport, 11*, 2351–2355.

Hewstone, M., Rubin, M., & Willis, H. (2002). Intergroup bias. *Annual Review of Psychology, 51*, 575–604.

Hoffman, M. L. (1981). The development of empathy. In J. P. Rushton & R. M. Sorrentino (Eds.), *Altruism and helping behavior: Social, personality, and developmental perspectives* (pp. 41–63). Hillsdale, NJ: Erlbaum.

Innocenti, G. M. (2007). Subcortical regulation of cortical development: Some effects of early, selective deprivations. *Progress in Brain Research, 164*, 23–37.

Jabbi, M., Swart, M., & Keysers, C. (2007). Empathy for positive and negative emotions in the gustatory cortex. *Neuroimage, 34*, 1744–1753.

Jackson, P. L., Brunet, E., Meltzoff, A. N., & Decety, J. (2006). Empathy examined through the neural mechanisms involved in imagining how I feel versus how you feel pain. *Neuropsychologia, 44*, 752–761.

Jackson, P. L., Meltzoff, A. N., & Decety, J. (2005). How do we perceive the pain of others? A window into the neural processes involved in empathy. *Neuroimage, 24*, 771–779.

Kerstenbaum, R., Farber, E. A., & Sroufe, L. A. (1989). Individual differences in empathy among preschoolers: relation to attachments history. In N. Eisenberg (Ed.), *Empathy and related emotional competence. New Directions for Child Development* (No. 44, pp. 51–64). San Francisco, CA: Jossey-Bass.

Keysers, C., & Gazzola, V. (2007). Integrating simulation and theory of mind: From self to social cognition. *Trends in Cognitive Sciences, 11*, 194–196.

Lamm, C., Batson, C. D., & Decety, J. (2007). The neural substrate of human empathy: Effects of perspective taking and cognitive appraisal. *Journal of Cognitive Neuroscience, 19*, 42–58.

Mehrabian, A., & Epstein, N. (1972). A measure of emotional empathy. *Journal of Personality, 40,* 525–543.

Mikulincer, M., Gillath, O., Halevy, V., Avihou, N., Avidan, S., & Eshkoli, N. (2001). Attachment theory and reactions to other' needs: Evidence that activation of the sense of attachment security promotes empathic responses. *Journal of Personality and Social Psychology, 81,* 1205–1224.

Mikulincer, M., & Shaver, P. R. (2007). Attachment in adulthood: Structure, dynamics, and change. New York: Guilford Press.

Mikulincer, M., Shaver, P. R., Gillath, O., & Nitzberg, R. A. (2005). Attachment, caregiving, and altruism: Boosting attachment security increases compassion and helping. *Journal of Personality and Social Psychology, 89,* 817–839.

Mitchell, J. P., Banaji, M. R., & Macrae, C. N. (2005a). General and specific contributions of the medial prefrontal cortex to knowledge about mental states. *Neuroimage, 28,* 757–762.

Mitchell, J. P., Banaji, M. R., & Macrae, C. N. (2005b). The link between social cognition and self-referential thought in the medial prefrontal cortex. *Journal of Cognitive Neuroscience, 17,* 1306–1315.

Mitchell, J. P., Heatherton, T. F., & Macrae C. N. (2002). Distinct neural systems subserve person and object knowledge. *Proceedings of the National Academy of Science, 99,* 15238–15243.

Mitchell, J. P., Macrae, C. N., & Banaji, M. R. (2006). Dissociable medical prefrontal contributions to judgments of similar and dissimilar others. *Neuron, 50,* 655–663.

Moriguchi, Y., Decety, J., Ohnishi, T., Maeda, M., Mori, T., Nemoto, K., et al. (2007). Empathy and judging other's pain: An fMRI study of alexithymia. *Cerebral Cortex, 17,* 2223–2234.

Morris, J. S., Frith, C. D., Perrett, D. I., Rowland, D., Young, A. W., Calder, A. J., & Dolan, R. J. (1996). A differential neural response in the human amygdala to fearful and happy facial expressions. *Nature, 383,* 812–815.

Morrison, I., Lloyd, D., di Pellegrino, G., & Roberts, N. (2004). Vicarious responses to pain in anterior cingulate cortex: Is empathy a multisensory issue? *Cognitive, Affective and Behavioral Neuroscience, 4,* 270–278.

Morrison, I., Peelen, M. V., & Downing, P. E. (2007). The sight of others' pain modulates motor processing in human cingulate cortex. *Cerebral Cortex, 17,* 2214–2222.

Mullen, B., Brown, R. J., & Smith, C. (1992). Ingroup bias as a function of salience, relevance, and status: An integration? *European Journal of Social Psychology, 22,* 103–122.

Ochsner, K. N., & Lieberman, M. D. (2001). The emergence of social cognitive neuroscience. *The American Psychologist, 56,* 717–734.

O'Doherty, J., Winston, J., Critchley, H., Perrett, D., Burt, D. M., & Dolan, R. J. (2003). Beauty in a smile: The role of medial orbitofrontal cortex in facial attractiveness. *Neuropsychologia, 41,* 147–155.

Penner, L. A. (2002). The causes of sustained volunteerism: An interactionist perspective. *Journal of Social Issues, 58*, 447–467.

Penner, L. A., Dovidio, J. F., Piliavin, J. A., & Schroeder, D. A. (2005). Prosocial behavior: Multilevel perspectives. *Annual Review of Psychology, 56*, 365–392.

Penner, L. A., Fritzsche, B. A., Craiger, J. P., & Freifeld, T. R. (1995). Measuring the prosocial personality. In J. Butcher & C. D. Spielberger (Eds.), *Advances in personality assessment* (Vol. 10, pp. 147–163). Hillsdale, NJ: Erlbaum.

Premack, D., & Woodruff, G. (1978). Does the chimpanzee have a theory of mind? *Behavioral and Brain Sciences, 1*, 515–526.

Preston, S. D., & de Waal, F. B. (2002). Empathy: Its ultimate and proximate bases. *Behavioral and Brain Sciences, 25*, 1–20.

Rizzolatti, G., Fadiga, L., Gallese, V., & Fogassi, L. (1996). Premotor cortex and the recognition of motor actions. *Cognitive Brain Research, 3*, 131–141.

Saarela, M. V., Hlushchuk, Y., Williams, A. C., Schürmann, M., Kalso, E., & Hari, R. (2007). The compassionate brain: Humans detect intensity of pain from another's face. *Cerebral Cortex, 17*, 230–237.

Sagi, A., & Hoffman, M. L. (1976). Empathic distress in newborns. *Developmental Psychology, 12*, 175–176.

Singer, T. (2006). The neuronal basis and ontogeny of empathy and mind reading: Review of literature and implications for future research. *Neuroscience and Biobehavioral Reviews, 30*, 855–863.

Singer, T., Seymour, B., O'Doherty, J., Kaube, H., Dolan, R. J., & Frith, C. D. (2004, February 20). Empathy for pain involves the affective but not sensory components of pain. *Science, 303*, 1157–1162.

Singer, T., Seymour, B., O'Doherty, J. P., Stephan, K. E., Dolan, R. J., & Frith, C. D. (2006, January 26). Empathic neural responses are modulated by the perceived fairness of others. *Nature, 439*, 466–469.

Sturmer, S., Snyder, M., & Omoto, A. M. (2005). Prosocial emotions and helping: The moderating role of group membership. *Journal of Personality and Social Psychology, 88*, 532–546.

Valiente, C., Eisenberg, N., Fabes, R. A., Shepard, S. A., Cumberland, A., & Losoya, S. H. (2004). Prediction of children's empathy-related responding from their effortful control and parents' expressivity. *Developmental Psychology, 40*, 911–926.

Van der Mark, I. L., van IJzendoorn, M. H., & Bakermans-Kranenburg, M. J. (2002). Development of empathy in girls during the second year of life: Associations with parenting, attachment, and temperament. *Social Development, 11*, 451–468.

Vescio, T. K., Sechrist, G. B., & Palolucci, M. P. (2003). Perspective taking and prejudice reduction: The mediational role of empathy arousal and situational attributions. *European Journal of Social Psychology, 33*, 455–472.

Wicker, B., Keysers, C., Plailly, J., Royet, J. P., Gallese, V., & Rizzolatti, G. (2003). Both of us disgusted in my insula: The common neural basis of seeing and feeling disgust. *Neuron, 40*, 655–664.

Winston, J. S., Strange, B. A., O'Doherty, J., & Dolan, R. J. (2002, February 19). Automatic and intentional brain responses during evaluation of trustworthiness of faces. *Nature Neuroscience*, 5, 277–283.

Zahn-Waxler, C., Radke-Yarrow, M., & King, R.A. (1979). Child rearing and children's prosocial initiations toward victims of distress. *Child Development*, 50, 319–330.

Zahn-Waxler, C., Radke-Yarrow, M., Wagner, E., & Chapman, M. (1992). Development of concern for others. *Developmental Psychology*, 28, 126–136.

II

PSYCHOLOGICAL PROCESSES

7

EMPATHY-RELATED RESPONDING: LINKS WITH SELF-REGULATION, MORAL JUDGMENT, AND MORAL BEHAVIOR

NANCY EISENBERG

In this chapter, I argue that it is important to distinguish between different empathy-related reactions, that individual differences in self-regulation play a role in sympathetic and altruistic behavior, and that self-regulation may account, in part, for the relations of sympathy with morality and various forms of social and psychological maladjustment. There is undoubtedly more to sympathy, moral judgment, and altruistic behavior than self-regulation, but self-regulation is an extremely important piece of the puzzle, and it is my main concern in this chapter.

I begin my analysis by defining empathy and distinguishing among various empathy-related emotional reactions (e.g., sympathy, personal distress). I then consider the developmental factors that contribute to individual differences in each of these emotional reactions, and I emphasize the role of self-regulation processes. Next, I zero in on one important self-regulation process or capacity—effortful control—and review evidence for its association with empathy. Finally, I review findings from my own and others' studies showing that self-regulatory capacities involved in empathy-related responding contribute broadly to prosocial and moral behavior.

DEFINITIONAL ISSUES: EMPATHY-RELATED RESPONDING

In any discussion of empathy-related responding, it is important to distinguish among various empathy-related emotional reactions. Batson (see chap. 1, this volume) first differentiated empathy from personal distress. He defined *empathy* as other-oriented concern, whereas *personal distress* is a self-oriented response to others' emotions or negative states. My colleagues and I have found it useful to draw an additional distinction. We define empathy as an affective response stemming from the apprehension or comprehension of another's emotional state or condition—a response that is identical, or very similar, to what the other person is feeling or might be expected to be feeling (see chap. 6, this volume). For example, if a girl views a sad boy and consequently feels sad herself, she is experiencing empathy. In contrast, *sympathy* is an affective response that may stem from empathy but can derive solely (or partly) from perspective taking or other cognitive processing, including retrieval of information from memory. Sympathy consists of feelings of sorrow or concern for the distressed or needy other rather than feeling the emotion the other person is experiencing or might be expected to experience. Our definition of sympathy is similar to what Batson (chap. 1, this volume) calls empathy. We view personal distress as also stemming from exposure to another's state, but it is conceptualized as a self-focused, aversive reaction to the vicarious experiencing of another's emotion (e.g., as discomfort or anxiety; see chap. 1, this volume; see also Eisenberg, Shea, Carlo, & Knight, 1991). This distress is associated with the egoistic motivation of making oneself, not necessarily the other person, feel better.

REGULATION AND EMPATHY-RELATED DEVELOPMENT

If sympathy and personal distress both frequently stem from empathy (vicarious emotional responding), what might account for the difference in their occurrence and in the motivations associated with them? Hoffman (1982) suggested that people sometimes experience empathic overarousal, and I (e.g., Eisenberg & Fabes, 1992) argued that empathic overarousal, if aversive, is experienced as personal distress. In other words, I believe that personal distress involves empathic arousal that is overly high and experienced as aversive, with the consequence that people who experience it tend to focus on relieving their own distress.

In support of the view that personal distress involves empathic overarousal, when empathy-inducing stimuli are highly evocative, personal distress is linked with higher levels of physiological arousal than is sympathy (for a review, see Eisenberg, Fabes, & Spinrad, 2006). Specifically, people exhibit higher skin conductance, and sometimes report more distress, in situations likely to elicit personal distress (in contrast to sympathy or baseline conditions; Eisenberg, Fabes, et al., 1988; Eisenberg, Fabes, Schaller, Carlo, & Miller, 1991; Eisenberg, Fabes, Schaller, Miller, et al., 1991; Eisenberg, Schaller, et al., 1988). Moreover, personal distress is sometimes associated with lower heart rate variability (the degree to which heart rate goes up and down), which can be viewed as a rough index of low or poor physiological regulation (see Fabes, Eisenberg, & Eisenbud, 1993). In addition, negative emotional arousal is associated with focusing on oneself (Wood, Saltzberg, & Goldsamt, 1990), which we have argued is the result of empathic overarousal. This self-focus is inherent to personal distress.

Although sympathy involves vicariously induced emotion, we assume that this vicarious affect is usually sufficiently modulated so that it is not experienced as aversive personal distress. If this assumption is correct, sympathy should be associated with individual differences in self-regulation (see chap. 9, this volume), especially the regulation of emotion, and with a moderate level of emotional arousal when experiencing vicarious emotion. The evidence just discussed is consistent with this view: (a) Skin conductance and heart rate are lower when people are viewing sympathy-inducing, in comparison with distressing, films (Eisenberg, Fabes, Schaller, Miller, et al., 1991; Eisenberg, Schaller, et al., 1988; also see Eisenberg, Fabes, Murphy, et al., 1996), and (b) higher situational sympathy (as indicated by a concerned facial expression) has been correlated with higher heart rate variability (which is related to a measure of physiological regulation, vagal tone; Fabes et al., 1993).

If our analysis of sympathy as distinct from personal distress is correct, then factors likely to contribute to individual differences in empathy-related responding include dispositional differences in susceptibility to vicarious negative emotions and differences in self-regulation. Self-regulation is especially likely to be involved in sympathy if the empathy-inducing stimulus is strong and vicarious arousal is high. However, it is important to note that individuals prone to more frequent and intense negative emotions are relatively likely to experience personal distress (e.g., Eisenberg et al., 1994; Mikulincer, Shaver, Gillath, & Nitzberg, 2005), although individuals prone to sympathy are also somewhat emotional and relatively prone to emotions such as sadness (Eisenberg et al., 1994). Conversely, people with psychopathic tendencies tend to be low in empathic responsivity (e.g., Frick, 1998) and are therefore unlikely to experience sympathy.

Although we believe that regulation is often required to modulate empathic arousal, regulation may not always be involved in sympathy. If a sympathy-inducing stimulus is not strong, regulation may be irrelevant to the modulation of vicariously induced emotion and the prevention of empathic overarousal. If cues regarding another's state or condition are subtle, a child who is attentionally well regulated may be relatively likely to experience empathy and sympathy, although not personal distress (due to the relatively nonevocative nature of subtle stimuli). In other words, when a person has to attend to and interpret mild cues to another person's state, the regulated individual may experience higher levels of empathic arousal than the less regulated individual (for data consistent with this argument, see Liew, Eisenberg, Losoya, Guthrie, & Murphy, 2003).

Self-regulatory processes may contribute in several ways to the likelihood of experiencing sympathy. First, as already noted, the ability to focus attention and process cues relevant to empathy and sympathy may sometimes be important for experiencing sympathy. In addition, the ability to modulate emotional arousal by shifting or refocusing one's attention may contribute to the ability to modulate empathic arousal and prevent empathic overarousal (see Derryberry & Reed, 2002; Eisenberg, Fabes, Murphy, et al., 1996). The executive attention involved in self-regulation (Posner & Rothbart, 2007) is also likely to be involved in integrating information, planning, and executing other mental activities that might help an individual interpret information about another and feel competent to deal with negatively valenced vicarious emotion. In addition, self-regulation may contribute to a person's ability to enact sympathy-based prosocial behavior, especially when there is a cost to the self and one is not naturally inclined to assist (see chap. 9, this volume).

CONCEPTIONS OF SELF-REGULATION

There are numerous, generally overlapping, definitions of *emotion-related regulation*. Eisenberg, Hofer, and Vaughan (2007) defined it as aspects of regulation relevant to the modulation of emotion and associated behavior. Eisenberg and Spinrad (2004) argued that emotion-related self-regulation involves the processes

> of initiating, avoiding, inhibiting, maintaining, or modulating the occurrence, form, intensity, or duration of internal feeling states, emotion-related physiological, attentional processes, motivational states, and/or the behavioral concomitants of emotion in the service of accomplishing affect-related biological or social adaptation or achieving individual goals. (p. 338)

Individual differences in temperamentally based effortful control are generally believed to contribute to the regulation of reactivity, including emotionality (e.g., Rothbart & Bates, 2006). Rothbart and Bates (2006) defined *effortful control*, a major dimension of temperament, as "the efficiency of executive attention—including the ability to inhibit a dominant response and/or to activate a subdominant response, to plan, and to detect errors" (p. 129). Effortful control involves the abilities to shift and focus attention as needed; to activate and inhibit behavior when required, especially when one does not feel like doing so; and to use other executive functioning skills needed to integrate information, plan, and modulate emotion and behavior. The capacity for effortful control is believed to be centered in the anterior cingulate gyrus but also involves regions of the prefrontal cortex (e.g., Posner & Rothbart, 2007). It is grounded in executive attention and is believed to involve other executive-functioning skills as well.

Eisenberg and colleagues (e.g., Eisenberg & Morris, 2002; see also Carver, 2005; Derryberry & Rothbart, 1988; Nigg, 2000) have sought to differentiate, conceptually and empirically, the regulatory processes involved in effortful control from other aspects of control/inhibition (or the lack thereof) that seem to be involuntary or so automatic that they often are not under voluntary control. They have labeled the latter *reactive control*, which includes processes that pertain to relatively involuntary motivational approach and avoidance systems of response reactivity, which at extreme levels result in impulsive undercontrol and rigid overcontrol. Measures typically tap (but are not confined to): (a) impulsivity or speed of response initiation (including surgent approach behaviors) and (b) overcontrol (rigid, constrained behavior) or behavioral inhibition (slow or inhibited approach, distress, or subdued affect in situations involving novelty or uncertainty; Derryberry & Rothbart, 1988; Kagan & Fox, 2006). These capacities are generally viewed as parts of reactivity (albeit more behavioral than emotional reactivity) by Rothbart and colleagues (see Rothbart, Ahadi, Hershey, & Fisher, 2001; Rothbart & Bates, 2006) rather than components of effortful control.

Pickering and Gray (1999) argued that approach and avoidance motivational systems related to impulsive and overly inhibited behaviors, respectively, are associated with subcortical systems, such as Gray's behavioral activation system (which involves sensitivity to cues of reward or cessation of punishment) and behavioral inhibition system (activated in situations involving novelty and stimuli signaling punishment or frustrative nonreward). Thus, reactive over- and undercontrol probably have somewhat different biological bases than effortful control, although subcortical and cortical systems are intimately connected.

INDIVIDUAL DIFFERENCES IN EFFORTFUL CONTROL ASSOCIATED WITH EMPATHY-RELATED RESPONDING

On the basis of this discussion of sympathy and the apparent role of effortful control (or self-regulation) in moral development more generally (e.g., Eisenberg et al., 2006), one would expect effortful control to be positively related to children's sympathy. Moreover, effortful control would seem to be of greater conceptual relevance to empathy-related responding than would reactive over- or undercontrol.

In a series of studies, we have found that individual differences in self-regulation are related to children's and adults' sympathy, personal distress, or both. In most cases, although not always, our indices of self-regulation were based on other-report measures (e.g., teachers' or parents' reports) or self-report measures of effortful control. However, in one study (Eisenberg et al., 1994), another questionnaire measure of emotion regulation was also used, and in another study (Eisenberg, Michalik, et al., 2007) we used behavioral indices of self-regulation.

On the basis of the notion that sympathy tends to involve optimal levels of regulation, we made the following predictions (Eisenberg & Fabes, 1992): (a) Self-regulation, and processes involved in the regulation of emotion (e.g., effortful control), relate in a positive, linear manner to sympathy; (b) conversely, low levels of regulatory capacities (especially those involved in modulating emotional arousal) are associated with personal distress; and (c) self-regulatory capacities are more predictive of sympathy for individuals prone to intense and frequent negative emotions than they are for less emotionally reactive people. In addition, we would expect reactive overcontrol and undercontrol (e.g., impulsivity) to be somewhat less consistently related to sympathy or personal distress than effortful control.

In general, we have obtained support for the hypothesis that individual differences in self-regulation predict individual differences in dispositional sympathy and personal distress. In an initial study with college students (Eisenberg et al., 1994), we found that self-reported dispositional personal distress was related to low levels of both self-reported regulation (behavioral and attentional) and friends' reports of undergraduate students' coping. Although self-reported sympathy was unrelated to regulation in zero-order correlations, it was significantly positively related to regulation when the effects of negative emotional intensity were controlled (for similar findings with a sample of older persons, see Okun, Shepard, & Eisenberg, 2000).

In another study (Eisenberg & Okun, 1996), the pattern of findings in a sample of older people was even more consistent with expectations. Self-reported regulation, especially attentional regulation, was positively related to the participants' sympathy and negatively related to their dispositional personal distress. Moreover, for women only (most of the older study participants were women), there was an interaction between negative emotional intensity and regulation (a composite of attentional and behavioral regulation) when predicting personal distress. Personal distress decreased with increasing level of regulation for women at all levels of negative emotional intensity, but particularly for women who were low or average in negative emotional intensity. Older women who were prone to intense negative emotionality appeared to be more likely than less emotional women to be overwhelmed by vicariously induced negative emotion, even if they were high in regulation. However, even these women showed a significant drop in personal distress as a function of increasing regulation; the drop was simply less dramatic than for women who were moderate or low in negative emotional intensity.

We have also found relations between self-regulation and dispositional empathy-related responding in children. In a study of 6- to 8-year-old school children, we obtained teachers' and children's reports of sympathy (on questionnaire measures) and parents' and teachers' reports of children's effortful control (as well as emotionality; Eisenberg, Fabes, Murphy, et al., 1996). Specifically, adults reported on children's abilities to shift and focus attention and to inhibit their overt behavior when needed. In general, adults' reports of children's regulation (combined with low impulsivity) were positively related to children's dispositional sympathy. Further, respiratory sinus arrhythmia, a marker of physiological regulation (Porges, Doussard-Roosevelt, & Maiti, 1994), was positively related to self-reported sympathy for boys. In 2- and 4-year follow-ups of these children, similar relations between adult-reported effortful control and children's dispositional sympathy were found, both within a given assessment time and across 2 or 4 years (Eisenberg et al., 1998; Murphy, Shepard, Eisenberg, Fabes, & Guthrie, 1999).

Similar findings have been obtained in other samples of children. For example, in a study of 4.5- to 7-year olds, children's reports of sympathy in response to an empathy-inducing film and self-reported dispositional sympathy were positively related to parent- and teacher-reported sympathy. Conversely, reported personal distress reactions to the film were negatively related to adults' reports of children's effortful control (Eisenberg, Michalik, et al., 2007). Moreover, over the next 8 years, positive relations between measures of dispositional sympathy and the adult-reported effortful control were often found within and across time (Eisenberg, Michalik, et al., 2007). In addition, in a study conducted in Java, Indonesia, there was also a positive relation between third graders' adult-reported sympathy and their effortful control (Eisenberg, Liew, & Pidada, 2001). This finding in Indonesia was replicated 3 years later, albeit primarily for boys (Eisenberg, Liew & Pidada, 2004).

In one of the United States longitudinal samples discussed previously, we examined whether there was an interaction between general emotional intensity (the general tendency to feel emotions strongly, without reference specifically to valence of the emotion) and effortful control when predicting teacher-reported child sympathy in early elementary school (Eisenberg, Fabes, Murphy, et al., 1996). Those children who were relatively unregulated were low in sympathy regardless of their level of general emotional intensity, probably because they were likely to be overwhelmed by their vicarious emotion. In contrast, among children moderate or relatively high in effortful control, sympathy increased with the level of general emotional intensity. Thus, children who were generally emotionally intense were sympathetic if they were at least moderately well-regulated. Such children would be expected to experience others' emotions vicariously yet not become overaroused and overwhelmed by the emotion. A similar interaction was noted 2 years later, but only for boys (Eisenberg et al., 1998; the sample was small, so statistical power was limited).

In a recent study (Eisenberg, Michalik, et al., 2007), we examined whether impulsivity (reactive undercontrol) demonstrated a similar, albeit reversed, relation with children's sympathy. The relations of children's dispositional sympathy to adult-reported and behavioral measures of effortful control and impulsivity were examined in a longitudinal study including five assessments spaced 2 years apart (mean age was 6 years at the first assessment). Especially for boys, relatively high levels of effortful control and growth in effortful control (using growth curve analyses) were related to high levels of adult-reported child sympathy in adolescence. There were also some positive correlations between behavioral measures of high effortful control and high sympathy.

In the same study, teacher-reported impulsivity was generally modestly negatively related to measures of teacher-reported sympathy for boys, and a decline in impulsivity was linked to boys' teacher-reported sympathy in adolescence. However, some findings suggested a positive association between impulsivity and children's self-reported sympathy; moreover, an increase versus decrease in impulsivity was related to higher levels of girls' parent-reported sympathy in adolescence. Thus, some impulsivity, or at least low levels of overcontrol, tended to be related to girls' sympathy. Overall, relations between impulsivity and youths' sympathy were less consistent and less frequent than were relations with effortful control. Moreover, effortful control, especially when reported by teachers, was more often a unique predictor of sympathy than was impulsivity (in regressions in which both effortful control and impulsivity were used to predict sympathy). Thus, effortful control and impulsivity appear to relate somewhat differently to sympathy.

In brief, across studies, we generally (albeit not always) have found that self-regulation is related to high dispositional (and sometime situational) sympathy and low personal distress. These results are consistent with data indicating that in childhood and adolescence, sympathy is related to the personality trait conscientiousness (which is partly a matter of regulation; Del Barrio, Aluja, & Garcia, 2004), as well as constructive modes of coping (McWhirter, Besett-Alesch, Horibata, & Gat, 2002) and self-reported efficacy in self-regulation (e.g., resisting peer pressure to engage in high-risk behaviors, not abusing alcohol and drugs, not engaging in theft and other transgressive activities) and in managing negative emotions (Bandura, Caprara, Barbaranelli, Gerbino, & Pastorelli, 2003). In addition, there is initial evidence that the joint contributions of general emotionality and regulation are sometimes useful for predicting individual differences in empathy-related reactions. Children who were prone to relatively intense emotions (both positive and negative) and who were well-regulated were especially high in sympathy. Although measures indicative of regulation tend to be positively related to sympathy, impulsivity is not consistently negatively related to sympathy.

RELATIONS OF EMPATHY-RELATED RESPONDING TO MORAL INDICES AND ADJUSTMENT

If sympathy involves optimal regulation, it is reasonable to expect sympathy to predict moral behaviors that involve self-denial or efforts to benefit another. In fact, in various studies, we have found that self-regulatory abilities are related to prosocial behaviors such as helping and sharing and prosocial moral reasoning, and to low aggression and externalizing problems.

Relation of Empathy-Related Responding to Prosocial Behavior

One reason the distinction between sympathy and personal distress is important is that the two kinds of emotional reactions are believed to relate differently to prosocial behavior, especially altruistic prosocial behavior (see chaps. 1 and 4, this volume). *Prosocial behavior* is frequently defined as voluntary, intentional behavior that benefits another. *Altruism* is a subtype of prosocial behavior; it is prosocial behavior motivated by factors other than egoistic or pragmatic concerns or the desire for approval (chap. 1, this volume). Generally, altruism is believed to be motivated by sympathy or moral values (see Eisenberg et al., 2006). Batson (chap. 1, this volume) argued that sympathy motivates altruistic behavior, whereas personal distress is associated with the self-focused motive of alleviating one's own distress. Personal distress predicts low levels of altruistic behavior if the actor can escape from the suffering person who is inducing the feelings of personal distress. If, however, helping is the easiest way to reduce the negative cues coming from the other person (because escape is difficult), personal distress could be positively related to prosocial action. In such situations, people may assist another to alleviate their own distress (chap. 1, this volume).

Because other-oriented prosocial behaviors are sometimes costly to the actor, one would expect prosocial behavior to be related to individual differences in self-regulation (see chap. 9, this volume). Although research on this topic is more limited than research on sympathy and personal distress, there is evidence that regulated children score higher on measures of prosocial behavior than do less regulated children (e.g., Eisenberg, Fabes, Guthrie, & Reiser, 2000; Eisenberg, Fabes, Karbon, Murphy, Carlo, et al., 1996; Eisenberg, Fabes, Karbon, Murphy, Wosinski, et al., 1996; for a review, see Eisenberg et al., 2006).

Relations of Sympathy and Personal Distress to Prosocial Behavior

In a series of empirical studies, often involving experimental manipulations, Batson (see chap. 1, this volume) demonstrated that adults induced to experience sympathy in situations in which escape from the needy, distressed other was easy were relatively likely to help the target of their sympathy, whereas personal distress generally was not associated with increased helping (and tended to predict less helping). However, the kinds of manipulations Batson used were not generally appropriate for, or did not work well with, children. Moreover, in many of his studies, Batson did not examine the relations between individual differences in sympathy (or personal distress) and individual differences in prosocial behavior. Thus, in a series of studies we used self-reports of empathy-related reactions, facial expressions, and physiological measures of sympathy and personal distress to examine the relations of these indices to children's helping or sharing behaviors in the same or a similar context.

In a first set of studies, we sought to validate our measure of sympathy and personal distress. Children and/or adults viewed videotape clips selected to elicit sympathy or distress, or, in one study, they talked about situations likely to induce sympathy or self-focused distress. The study participants generally exhibited more facial concerned attention in sympathy-inducing contexts and more distress in situations believed to elicit personal distress (or self-focused distress), and older children's and adults' self-reports were also somewhat consistent with the emotional context (Eisenberg, Fabes, et al., 1988; Eisenberg, Fabes, Schaller, Miller, et al., 1991; Eisenberg, Schaller, et al., 1988; for a review, see Eisenberg & Fabes, 1990). In two studies (Eisenberg, Fabes, et al., 1988; Eisenberg, Schaller, et al. 1988), younger children's self-reports of sympathy and personal distress were less differentiated and less contextually appropriate than those of older children and adults, although even young children's verbal reports of emotion in the evocative situations were more likely than chance to be consistent with the context (i.e., sympathy or distress inducing).

On the basis of the physiological literature (e.g., Cacioppo & Sandman, 1978), we had argued that heart rate acceleration was likely to reflect distress, whereas heart rate deceleration was likely to reflect interest in, and processing of, information coming from external stimuli—in this case, from the sympathy-inducing stimulus. Heart rate acceleration has also been linked to high arousal and to the processing of information that is internal rather than outside the self; consequently, it might tap self-focus. Skin conductance probably is a purer measure of emotional arousal than heart rate and therefore a good index of personal distress. On the basis of the emotion literature, we suggested that high skin conductance in fairly evocative contexts is more likely to accompany anxiety than sadness (which is involved in empathic feelings) and is expected to reflect an aversive state and the desire to avoid or reduce the impact of the situation rather than confront another's distress (Eisenberg & Fabes, 1990).

In several studies, we found evidence supporting our use of the physiological indices of empathy-related responding. In general, people tended to exhibit higher heart rate and/or skin conductance in the distress conditions than in the baseline conditions. Moreover, heart rate acceleration was typical at the evocative moments when study participants viewed distressing film clips, whereas heart rate deceleration occurred during the evocative sympathy-inducing clips (e.g., Eisenberg, Fabes, et al., 1988; Eisenberg, Schaller, et al., 1988; Eisenberg, Fabes, Schaller, Miller, et al., 1991; see also Eisenberg & Fabes, 1990; Eisenberg et al., 2006). However, it should be noted that skin conductance is likely to be associated with personal distress only if the empathy-inducing stimulus is relatively evocative. When it is subtle, a skin-conductance response is unlikely to indicate empathic overarousal (i.e., personal distress; Liew et al., 2003).

Once we had some evidence of the validity of our indices of sympathy and personal distress, we examined the association between children's and adults' responding to empathy-inducing films and their willingness to assist the needy or distressed individuals in the films or people with similar problems. Across the studies, we used a variety of measures of helping and sharing, although in all studies we sought to create situations in which it was easy to avoid contact with the needy or distressed person, and the experimenter would be unlikely to know what the person chose to do.

For example, children sometimes watched a film of a child who was injured, in the hospital, and talking about their experience. We measured heart rate and/or skin conductance while the children watched the film, taped and coded their facial reactions to the film, and when the film was over, we asked them to rate how they felt during the film. A little later, they had the opportunity to assist the child in the film or others like him or her by doing one of a variety of tasks (in different studies), including donating part of a payment or doing a boring task anonymously to help the children (e.g., packing toys for the children because they were bored at the hospital) rather than playing with attractive toys. As predicted, markers of sympathy were related to higher levels of prosocial behavior, whereas markers of personal distress were related to lower levels of prosocial behavior (although the findings for facial personal distress were generally obtained in studies of children and especially for boys; e.g., Eisenberg et al., 1989, 1990; Fabes, Eisenberg, Karbon, Troyer, & Switzer, 1994; Miller, Eisenberg, Fabes, & Shell, 1996). Facial and physiological markers were generally better predictors of prosocial responding than were children's self-reported reactions, especially in studies of younger children (e.g., Eisenberg et al., 1990; see Eisenberg & Fabes, 1990). Thus, sympathy and personal distress seemed to reflect quite different motivational states.

Dispositional sympathy has also been related to prosocial behavior in a variety of studies (see Eisenberg et al., 2006), including across time. Indeed, spontaneously emitted, costly prosocial behaviors in real-life preschool settings have predicted sympathy in adolescence and adulthood (Eisenberg et al., 1999, 2002), probably because these kinds of prosocial behavior are related to rudimentary other-oriented prosocial moral reasoning in preschool (which likely reflects empathy or sympathy; Eisenberg-Berg & Hand, 1979). Evidence from a variety of studies has suggested that the association between sympathy and prosocial behavior can be found not only with situational measures of the constructs but also with dispositional measures and across a variety of measures (observed, other-reported, self-reported) in multiple contexts (see Eisenberg et al., 2006, and related ideas in chap. 3, this volume).

Empathy-Related Responding and Moral Reasoning

If empathy-related responding, especially sympathy, is frequently the motive for other-oriented (altruistic) prosocial behavior, we would expect it to relate to children's judgments about moral issues (moral reasoning) as well as to prosocial behavior. This is because the beliefs and motives that contribute to moral decisions are believed to be reflected in the level of moral reasoning that a person expresses, at least within the range of levels that the child is capable of understanding (Eisenberg, 1986). Hoffman (1987) argued that sympathy or empathy contributes to the development of moral reasoning because it stimulates internalized moral judgments reflecting concern for others' welfare. Eisenberg (1986) further suggested that sympathy primes the use of preexisting other-oriented moral cognitions in given situations; thus, sympathy (and perhaps empathy) may affect the construction of moral judgments in specific situations, as well as its development. Even if children are not capable of understanding or expressing higher levels of moral judgment, it is logical to expect those prone to empathy and sympathy (especially the latter) to verbalize higher levels of rudimentary other-oriented concerns and fewer hedonistic, egoistic concerns than their less sympathetic peers.

An association between empathy-related vicarious responding and moral reasoning is likely to be especially evident in children's prosocial moral reasoning (in contrast to justice-oriented, Kohlbergian moral reasoning; Colby, Kohlberg, Gibbs, & Lieberman, 1983). Prosocial moral reasoning is reasoning about moral dilemmas in which one person's needs or desires conflict with those of others in a context in which the role of formal prohibitions, authorities' dictates, and formal obligations is minimal (Eisenberg, 1986; Eisenberg-Berg, 1979). Eisenberg, Zhou, and Koller (2001) hypothesized that empathy-related responding and prosocial moral reasoning are not only related but that prosocial moral reasoning also partly mediates the relation of sympathy to prosocial behavior.

In a number of studies, Eisenberg and colleagues have obtained findings consistent with the view that empathy-related responding is associated with prosocial or care-oriented moral reasoning. Skoe, Eisenberg, and Cumberland

(2002) found that adults' reports of experiencing sympathy when resolving moral conflicts were related to their care-related moral reasoning, especially when discussing a real-life moral dilemma. Moreover, in a longitudinal study from childhood through adolescence (and into adulthood), Eisenberg and colleagues (Eisenberg, Carlo, Murphy, & Van Court, 1995; Eisenberg et al., 1997; Eisenberg, Miller, Shell, McNalley, & Shea, 1991) repeatedly found within-time correlations between reported sympathy (or empathy at younger ages) and higher level prosocial moral reasoning, the greater use of empathy-related modes of prosocial moral reasoning, and the reduced use of hedonistic reasoning (Eisenberg, Miller, et al., 1991; Eisenberg et al., 1995). In addition, there were numerous relations between measures of prosocial moral judgment in early adulthood (ages 21–22, 23–24, or 25–26) and measures of sympathy or empathy at younger ages, including with empathy reported at ages 9 to 12. In contrast, personal distress was infrequently related to measures of prosocial moral judgment (Eisenberg et al., 2002).

Similar relations between sympathy and moral reasoning have been found in other samples of adolescents in the United States (e.g., Carlo, Eisenberg, & Knight, 1992) and Brazil (e.g., Eisenberg, Zhou, & Koller, 2001), as well as among preschoolers (e.g., Miller et al., 1996). In contrast to sympathy, Carlo, Koller, Eisenberg, DaSilva, and Frohlich (1996) found that personal distress was positively related to approval-oriented reasoning (a relatively immature type of reasoning) and negatively related to internalized and stereotypic moral reasoning (relatively advanced modes of moral judgment).

In a study in Brazil, Eisenberg, Zhou, and Koller (2001) examined the prediction that prosocial moral reasoning would mediate the relation between sympathy and prosocial behavior. In a structural equation model, sympathy (as well as cognitive perspective taking) predicted adolescents' level of prosocial moral reasoning, which in turn predicted their self-reported prosocial behavior (this prosocial measure correlated substantially with peer-reported prosocial behavior in another sample). In the model, perspective taking had a direct path to sympathy, and sympathy had a direct path, as well as a mediated path (through moral reasoning), to prosocial behavior. When a direct path was added to the model from perspective taking to prosocial behavior, it was not significant. Thus, although the model was based on concurrent, correlational data, the results are consistent with the view that sympathy contributes to prosocial behavior directly, as well as through its effects on prosocial moral reasoning.

Relations of Empathy-Related Responding to Antisocial Behavior

For multiple reasons, empathy-related responding, especially sympathy, should be related to low levels of externalizing problems, including aggression, delinquency, and antisocial behavior (see Miller & Eisenberg, 1988).

Feshbach (e.g., Feshbach & Feshbach, 1982) and others (e.g., Mehrabian & Epstein, 1972) have argued that people who tend to vicariously experience the negative emotions of others when they perceive cues of others' negative emotions are inclined to inhibit behaviors that have hurtful effects on others and to reduce their aggression in subsequent interactions. In addition, the same kinds of regulatory skills that have been linked to sympathy (e.g., effortful control) tend to negatively predict or correlate with externalizing problems/aggression (see Eisenberg, Spinrad, et al., 2004). It is likely that regulatory skills affect both sympathy and levels of externalizing behaviors and that sympathy also has direct effects on externalizing problems.

Psychologists have long recognized that deficits in empathy and remorse are common in individuals with antisocial personality disorders (*Diagnostic and Statistical Manual of Mental Disorders*, 4th ed., American Psychiatric Association, 1994; Frick, 1998; Lynam, 1997). Psychopaths or people with psychopathic traits appear to be less physiologically responsive to emotion-inducing stimuli (often mildly evocative slides) and to cues of others' distress than are nonpsychopaths (Blair, 1999; Levenston, Patrick, Bradley, & Lang, 2000; also see Hastings, Zahn-Waxler, Robinson, Usher, & Bridges, 2000).

Moreover, there is considerable empirical support for an inverse association between empathy or sympathy and externalizing problems (Miller & Eisenberg, 1988). For example, in a longitudinal study, we found that teachers' reports of 6- to 8-year-olds' dispositional sympathy were significantly correlated, within and across time, with teachers' reports of children's nonaggressive or socially appropriate behavior and with mothers' ratings of low levels of concurrent externalizing problems (including aggression and antisocial behavior; Murphy et al., 1999). We also have found similar links between children's dispositional sympathy and adults' reports of children's low levels of externalizing problems and fighting in Indonesia (Eisenberg, Liew, & Pidada, 2001). Similarly, Zhou et al. (2002) found that elementary school children's situational empathy in response to slides depicting negative facial expressions or people in negative situations was correlated with low levels of children's adult-reported externalizing problems. In a structural equation model, facial and self-reported empathy with the negative slides 2 years after the initial assessment had stronger unique relations with children's concurrent low levels of externalizing problems even when controlling for level of empathy 2 years before.

Children's aggressive behavior may also be related to their personal distress. In a study of kindergartners and third graders, Fabes et al. (1994) found that mothers' reports of children's aggressive coping were positively associated with markers of boys' (but not girls') personal distress (i.e., heart rate acceleration, facial distress) when reacting to a crying infant. Thus, children's empathy-related responding appears to be negatively associated with their aggressive, externalizing behavior, just as it is positively associated with their prosocial behavior.

CONCLUSIONS

On the basis of both conceptual analysis and empirical research, I conclude that individual differences in sympathy and personal distress are related to a wide range of prosocial and moral reactions, including having real concern for others' welfare and offering altruistic help when others need or request it. Moreover, individual differences in self-regulatory capabilities play an important part in sympathy and personal distress, and also contribute to prosocial behavior or antisocial behavior and externalizing symptoms of psychopathology. It seems very likely that some of the connections between sympathy and measures of moral behavior (and perhaps moral reasoning) are due to individual differences in self-regulation. Of course, there are likely to be other links among sympathy, moral reasoning, prosocial behavior, and low levels of externalizing symptoms, and these deserve continued study. In this chapter, I wanted only to suggest that self-regulatory processes are important components of moral emotions, judgments, and behaviors.

REFERENCES

American Psychiatric Association. (1994). *Diagnostic and statistical manual of mental disorders* (4th ed.). Washington, DC: Author.

Bandura, A., Caprara, G. V., Barbaranelli, C., Gerbino, M., & Pastorelli, C. (2003). Role of affective self-regulatory efficacy in diverse sphere of psychosocial functioning. *Child Development, 74*, 769–782.

Blair, R. J. R. (1999). Responsiveness to distress cues in the child with psychopathic tendencies. *Personality and Individual Differences, 27*, 135–145.

Cacioppo, J. T., & Sandman, C. A. (1978). Physiological differentiation of sensory and cognitive tasks as a function of warning processing demands and reported unpleasantness. *Biological Psychology*, 6, 181–192.

Carlo, G., Eisenberg, N., & Knight, G. P. (1992). An objective measure of adolescents' prosocial moral reasoning. *Journal of Research on Adolescence, 2*, 331–349.

Carlo, G., Koller, S. H., Eisenberg, N., DaSilva, M. S., & Frohlich, C. B. (1996). A cross-national study on the relations among prosocial moral reasoning, gender role orientations, and prosocial behaviors. *Developmental Psychology, 32*, 231–240.

Carver, C. S. (2005). Impulse and constraint: Perspectives from personality psychology, convergence with theory in other areas, and potential for integration. *Personality and Social Psychology Review*, 9, 312–333.

Colby, A., Kohlberg, L., Gibbs, J., & Lieberman, M. (1983). A longitudinal study of moral judgment. *Monographs of the Society for Research in Child Development, 48*(1-2, Serial No. 200).

Del Barrio, V., Aluja, A., & Garcia, L. (2004). Relationship between empathy and the Big Five personality traits in a sample of Spanish adolescents. *Social Behavior and Personality, 32*, 677–682.

Derryberry, D., & Reed, M. A. (2002). Anxiety-related attentional biases and their regulation by attentional control. *Journal of Abnormal Psychology, 111*, 225–236.

Derryberry, D., & Rothbart, M. K. (1988). Arousal, affect, and attention as components of temperament. *Journal of Personality and Social Psychology, 55*, 958–966.

Eisenberg, N. (1986). *Altruistic emotion, cognition, and behavior*. Hillsdale, NJ: Erlbaum.

Eisenberg, N., Carlo, G., Murphy, B., & Van Court, P. (1995). Prosocial development in late adolescence: A longitudinal study. *Child Development, 66*, 1179–1197.

Eisenberg, N., & Fabes, R. A. (1990). Empathy: Conceptualization, assessment, and relation to prosocial behavior. *Motivation and Emotion, 14*, 131–149.

Eisenberg, N., & Fabes, R. A. (1992). Emotion, regulation, and the development of social competence. In M. S. Clark (Ed.), *Review of personality and social psychology: Vol. 14._Emotion and social behavior* (pp. 119–150). Newbury Park, CA: Sage.

Eisenberg, N., Fabes, R. A., Bustamante, D., Mathy, R. M., Miller, P., & Lindholm, E. (1988). Differentiation of vicariously induced emotional reactions in children. *Developmental Psychology, 24*, 237–246.

Eisenberg, N., Fabes, R. A., Guthrie, I. K., & Reiser, M. (2000). Dispositional emotionality and regulation: Their role in predicting quality of social functioning. *Journal of Personality and Social Psychology, 78*, 136–157.

Eisenberg, N., Fabes, R. A., Karbon, M., Murphy, B. C., Carlo, G., & Wosinski, M. (1996). Relations of school children's comforting behavior to empathy-related reactions and shyness. *Social Development, 5*, 330–351.

Eisenberg, N., Fabes, R. A., Karbon, M., Murphy, B. C., Wosinski, M., Polazzi, L., et al. (1996). The relations of children's dispositional prosocial behavior to emotionality, regulation, and social functioning. *Child Development, 67*, 974–992.

Eisenberg, N., Fabes, R. A., Miller, P. A., Fultz, J., Mathy, R. M., Shell, R., & Reno, R. R. (1989). The relations of sympathy and personal distress to prosocial behavior: A multimethod study. *Journal of Personality and Social Psychology, 57*, 55–66.

Eisenberg, N., Fabes, R. A., Miller, P. A., Shell, C., Shea, R., & May-Plumlee, T. (1990). Preschoolers' vicarious emotional responding and their situational and dispositional prosocial behavior. *Merrill-Palmer Quarterly, 36*, 507–529.

Eisenberg, N., Fabes, R. A., Murphy, B., Karbon, M., Maszk, P., Smith, M., et al. (1994). The relations of emotionality and regulation to dispositional and situational empathy-related responding. *Journal of Personality and Social Psychology, 66*, 776–797.

Eisenberg, N., Fabes, R. A., Murphy, B., Karbon, M., Smith, M., & Maszk, P. (1996). The relations of children's dispositional empathy-related responding to their emotionality, regulation, and social functioning. *Developmental Psychology, 32,* 195–209.

Eisenberg, N., Fabes, R. A., Schaller, M., Carlo, G., & Miller, P. A. (1991). The relations of parental characteristics and practices to children's vicarious emotional responding. *Child Development, 62,* 1393–1408.

Eisenberg, N., Fabes, R. A., Schaller, M., Miller, P. A., Carlo, G., Poulin, R., et al. (1991). Personality and socialization correlates of vicarious emotional responding. *Journal of Personality and Social Psychology, 61,* 459–471.

Eisenberg, N., Fabes, R. A., Shepard, S. A., Murphy, B. C., Jones, S., & Guthrie, I. K. (1998). Contemporaneous and longitudinal prediction of children's sympathy from dispositional regulation and emotionality. *Developmental Psychology, 34,* 910–924.

Eisenberg, N., Fabes, R. A., & Spinrad, T. L. (2006). Prosocial behavior. In N. Eisenberg (Vol. Ed.) and W. Damon & R. M. Lerner (Series Eds.), *Handbook of child psychology: Vol. 3. Social, emotional, and personality development* (6th ed., pp. 646–718). New York: Wiley.

Eisenberg, N., Guthrie, I., Cumberland, A., Murphy, B. C., Shepard, S. A., Zhou, Q., & Carlo, G. (2002). Prosocial development in early adulthood: A longitudinal study. *Journal of Personality and Social Psychology, 82,* 993–1006.

Eisenberg, N., Guthrie, I. K., Fabes, R. A., Reiser, M., Murphy, B. C., Holgren, R., et al. (1997). The relations of regulation and emotionality to resiliency and competent social functioning in elementary school children. *Child Development, 68,* 295–311.

Eisenberg, N., Guthrie, I. K., Murphy, B. C., Shepard, S. A., Cumberland, A., & Carlo, G. (1999). Consistency and development of prosocial dispositions: A longitudinal study. *Child Development, 70,* 1360–1372.

Eisenberg, N., Hofer, C., & Vaughan, J. (2007). Effortful control and its socioemotional consequences. In J. J. Gross (Ed.), *Handbook of emotion regulation* (pp. 287–306). New York: Guilford Press.

Eisenberg, N., Liew, J., & Pidada, S. (2001). The relations of parental emotional expressivity with the quality of Indonesian children's social functioning. *Emotion, 1,* 107–115.

Eisenberg, N., Liew, J., & Pidada, S. (2004). The longitudinal relations of regulation and emotionality to quality of Indonesian children's socioemotional functioning. *Developmental Psychology, 40,* 790–804.

Eisenberg, N., Michalik, N., Spinrad, T. L., Hofer, C., Kupfer, A., Valiente, C., et al. (2007). Relations of effortful control and impulsivity to children's sympathy: A longitudinal study. *Cognitive Development, 22,* 544–567.

Eisenberg, N., Miller, P. A., Shell, R., McNalley, S., & Shea, C. (1991). Prosocial development in adolescence: A longitudinal study. *Developmental Psychology, 27,* 849–857.

Eisenberg, N., & Morris, A. S. (2002). Children's emotion-related regulation. In R. Kail (Ed.), *Advances in child development and behavior* (Vol. 30, pp. 190–229). Amsterdam: Academic Press.

Eisenberg, N., & Okun, M. (1996). The relations of dispositional regulation and emotionality to elders' empathy-related responding and affect while volunteering. *Journal of Personality, 64,* 157–183.

Eisenberg, N., Schaller, M., Fabes, R. A., Bustamante, D., Mathy, R., Shell, R., & Rhodes, K. (1988). The differentiation of personal distress and sympathy in children and adults. *Developmental Psychology, 24,* 766–775.

Eisenberg, N., Shea, C. L., Carlo, G., & Knight, G. (1991). Empathy-related responding and cognition: A "chicken and the egg" dilemma. In W. Kurtines & J. Gewirtz (Eds.), *Handbook of moral behavior and development: Vol. 2. Research* (pp. 63–88). Hillsdale, NJ: Erlbaum.

Eisenberg, N., & Spinrad, T. L. (2004). Emotion-related regulation: Sharpening the definition. *Child Development 75,* 334–339.

Eisenberg, N., Spinrad, T. L., Fabes, R. A., Reiser, M., Cumberland, A., Shepard, S. A., et al. (2004). The relations of effortful control and impulsivity to children's resiliency and adjustment. *Child Development, 75,* 25–46.

Eisenberg, N., Zhou, Q., & Koller, S. (2001). Brazilian adolescents' prosocial moral judgment and behavior: Relations to sympathy, perspective taking, gender-role orientation, and demographic characteristics. *Child Development, 72,* 518–534.

Eisenberg-Berg, N. (1979). The development of children's prosocial moral judgment. *Developmental Psychology, 15,* 128–137.

Eisenberg-Berg, N., & Hand, M. (1979). The relationship of preschoolers' reasoning about prosocial moral conflicts to prosocial behavior. *Child Development, 50,* 356–363.

Fabes, R. A., Eisenberg, N., & Eisenbud, L. (1993). Behavioral and physiological correlates of children's reactions to others' distress. *Developmental Psychology, 29,* 655–663.

Fabes, R. A., Eisenberg, N., Karbon, M., Troyer, D, & Switzer, G. (1994). The relations of children's emotion regulation to their vicarious emotional responses and comforting behavior. *Child Development, 65,* 1678–1693.

Feshbach, N. D., & Feshbach, S. (1982). Empathy training and the regulation of aggression: Potentialities and limitations. *Academic Psychology Bulletin, 4,* 399–413.

Frick, P. J. (1998). *Conduct disorders and severe antisocial behavior.* New York: Plenum.

Hastings, P. D., Zahn-Waxler, C., Robinson, J., Usher, B., & Bridges, D. (2000). The development of concern for others in children with behavior problems. *Developmental Psychology, 36,* 531–546.

Hoffman, M. L. (1982). Development of prosocial motivation: Empathy and guilt. In N. Eisenberg (Ed.), *The development of prosocial behavior* (pp. 281–313). New York: Academic Press.

Hoffman, M. L. (1987). The contribution of empathy to justice and moral judgment. In N. Eisenberg & J. Strayer (Eds.), *Empathy and its development* (pp. 47–80). Cambridge, England: University of Cambridge Press.

Kagan, J., & Fox, N. (2006). Biology, culture, and temperamental biases. In W. Damon & R. L. Lerner (Series Eds.) and N. Eisenberg (Vol. Ed.), *Handbook of child psychology: Vol. 3. Social, emotional, and personality development* (6th ed., pp. 167–225). New York: Wiley.

Levenston, G. K., Patrick, C. J., Bradley, M. M., & Lang, P. J. (2000). The psychopath as observer: Emotion and attention in picture processing. *Journal of Abnormal Psychology, 109*, 373–385.

Liew, J., Eisenberg, N., Losoya, S. H., Guthrie, I. K., & Murphy, B. C. (2003). Maternal expressivity as a moderator of the relations of children's vicarious emotional responses to their regulation, emotionality, and social functioning. *Journal of Family Psychology, 17*, 584–597.

Lynam, D. R. (1997). Pursuing the psychopath: Capturing the fledgling psychopath in a nomological net. *Journal of Abnormal Psychology, 106*, 425–438.

McWhirter, B. T., Besett-Alesch, T. M., Horibata, J., & Gat, I. (2002). Loneliness in high risk adolescents: The role of coping, self-esteem, and empathy. *Journal of Youth Studies, 5*, 69–84.

Mehrabian, A., & Epstein, N. A. (1972). A measure of emotional empathy. *Journal of Personality, 40*, 523–543.

Mikulincer, M., Shaver, P. R., Gillath, O., & Nitzberg, R. E. (2005). Attachment, caregiving, and altruism: Boosting attachment security increases compassion and helping. *Journal of Personality and Social Psychology, 89*, 817–839.

Miller, P. A., & Eisenberg, N. (1988). The relation of empathy to aggression and externalizing/antisocial behavior. *Psychological Bulletin, 103*, 324–344.

Miller, P. A., Eisenberg, N., Fabes, R. A., & Shell, R. (1996). Relations of moral reasoning and vicarious emotion to young children's prosocial behavior toward peers and adults. *Developmental Psychology, 32*, 210–219.

Murphy, B. C., Shepard, S. A., Eisenberg, N., Fabes, R. A., & Guthrie, I. K. (1999). Contemporaneous and longitudinal relations of young adolescents' dispositional sympathy to their emotionality, regulation, and social functioning. *Journal of Early Adolescence, 19*, 66–97.

Nigg, J. T. (2000). On inhibition/disinhibition in developmental psychopathology: Views from cognitive and personality psychology and a working inhibition taxonomy. *Psychological Bulletin, 126*, 230–246.

Okun, M. A., Shepard, S. A., & Eisenberg, N. (2000). The relations of emotionality and regulation to dispositional empathy-related responding among volunteers-in-training. *Personality and Individual Differences, 28*, 367–382.

Pickering, A. D., & Gray, J. A. (1999). The neuroscience of personality. In O. P. John & L. A. Pervin (Eds.), *Handbook of personality: Theory and research* (2nd ed., pp. 277–299). New York: Guilford Press.

Porges, S. W., Doussard-Roosevelt, J. A., & Maiti, A. K. (1994). Vagal tone and the physiological regulation of emotion. *Monographs of the Society for Research in Child Development, 59*(Serial No. 240), 167–186.

Posner, M. I., & Rothbart, M. K. (2007). Research on attention networks as a model for the integration of psychological science. *Annual Review of Psychology, 58*, 1–23.

Rothbart, M. K., Ahadi, S. A., Hershey, K. L., & Fisher, P. (2001). Investigations of temperament at three to seven years: The Children's Behavior Questionnaire. *Child Development, 72*, 1394–1408.

Rothbart, M. K., & Bates, J. E. (2006). Temperament. In N. Eisenberg (Vol. Ed.) and W. Damon & R. M. Lerner (Series Eds.), *Handbook of Child Psychology: Vol. 3. Social, emotional, personality development* (pp. 99–166). New York: Wiley.

Skoe, E., Eisenberg, N., & Cumberland, A. (2002). The role of reported emotion in real-life and hypothetical moral dilemmas. *Personality and Social Psychology Bulletin, 28*, 962–973.

Wood, J. V., Saltzberg, J. A., & Goldsamt, L. A. (1990). Does affect induce self-focused attention? *Journal of Personality and Social Psychology, 58*, 899–908.

Zhou, Q., Eisenberg, N., Losoya, S., Fabes, R. A., Reiser, M., Guthrie, I. K., et al. (2002). The relations of parental warmth and positive expressiveness to children's empathy-related responding and social functioning: A longitudinal study. *Child Development, 73*, 893–915.

8

GENETIC AND ENVIRONMENTAL INFLUENCES ON PROSOCIAL BEHAVIOR

ARIEL KNAFO AND SALOMON ISRAEL

Prosocial behavior, defined as voluntary behavior enacted with the intent of benefiting others (see chaps. 1 and 7, this volume), is central to human social functioning. At the species level, prosocial behavior has been explained in genetic terms (see chap. 2, this volume). At the individual level, however, only about a dozen studies have directly addressed the origins of individual differences in prosocial behavior using genetically informed research designs.

Typical prosocial behaviors include volunteering, sharing personal resources, providing instrumental help (especially costly help), and supporting others emotionally in times of distress. The obvious importance to human social functioning of empathy, helping, cooperation, and altruism has led to extensive research on the sources of individual differences in prosociality (e.g., Graziano, Habashik, Sheese, & Tobin, 2007; see also chaps. 3, 4, 7, 13,

Data collection was supported by Grant No. 31/06 from the Israel Science Foundation. The work of the second author was supported by a grant from the Israel National Institute for Psychobiology to the first author. We thank the families who participated in the study.

14, and 19, this volume). The considerable debates concerning the extent to which prosocial behaviors reflect altruism and the boundaries between prosocial behavior and empathy are beyond the scope of this chapter. For current purposes, we treat empathy, altruism, and prosocial behavior as related aspects of a single prosocial tendency.

Evidence exists for individual differences in the tendency to behave prosocially or empathically that are moderately consistent across situations and stable across time (Eisenberg et al., 1999; Knafo, Zahn-Waxler, Van Hulle, Robinson, & Rhee, 2008; see also chap. 3, this volume). In this chapter, we examine the interactions and correlations among genetic and environmental factors as they influence this tendency for prosocial behavior. We present evidence from twin studies demonstrating that individual differences in tendencies for prosocial behavior have a substantial heritable component. Next, we present evidence for a developmental pattern in which the heritability of prosocial behavior increases with age. We discuss potential explanations for this increase, such as changes in the role of theory-of-mind abilities needed for effective prosocial responding (for related ideas, see chap. 6, this volume). We then present recent evidence from molecular genetic studies to illustrate the role of genes in human altruism. Finally, we review different approaches to understanding changes in genetic influences during development and provide an example investigation of gene–environment interplay.

ENVIRONMENTAL INFLUENCES ON PROSOCIAL BEHAVIOR

Although the focus of this chapter is genetic influences on prosocial behavior, it is important to acknowledge the importance of the environment. Most of the genetic studies we describe here also refer to environmental influences without specifying their nature. That is, the amalgamation of psychobiological and social influences that affect prosocial behavior is described in terms of proportions of variance not accounted for by genetic factors. In this section, we briefly discuss these factors and refer readers to the vast literature on the topic.

Many environmental forces (e.g., siblings: Hastings, Utendale, & Sullivan, 2007; friends: Barry & Wentzel, 2006) may influence prosocial behavior. For example, training teachers to promote children's prosociality and self-discipline longitudinally increased children's prosocial behavior (Solomon, Watson, Delucchi, Scraps, & Battistich, 1988). There is also evidence for the positive influence of specially designed television programs (Calvert & Kotler, 2003).

Most of the environmental research on individual differences in prosociality has focused on parental influences (see Eisenberg, Fabes, & Spinrad, 2006; Hastings et al., 2007; Staub, 1979); here we summarize only the most consistent findings. Children's prosociality increases and persists when parents are warm, supportive, responsive, and sensitive to their children's needs. In contrast, lower prosociality is observed in children whose parents are authoritarian, strict, or punitive (Hastings et al., 2007).

Environmental variables can also have biological effects. In one study that distinguished between genetic and other prenatal biological factors, Hur (2007) grouped South Korean identical twin pairs according to whether they shared their chorion (the outer membrane of the amniotic sac). Chorion sharing may be used as a proxy variable for a variety of hormonal and other influences that tend to be shared more extensively by monochorionic twins. Hur found no influence of chorion sharing on parent-rated prosocial behavior. However, evidence for the influence of hormones on social behavior (Kosfeld, Heinrichs, Zak, Fischbacher, & Fehr, 2005) has suggested that the role of chemical environmental factors should be studied further.

GENETIC INFLUENCES AT THE INDIVIDUAL AND SPECIES LEVELS

From an evolutionary perspective, prosocial behavior is often viewed in terms of the costs and benefits of altruistic acts weighed against some criterion, such as genetic relatedness, likelihood of future interaction, or maintaining one's reputation (Nowak, 2006). Although there is still some disagreement concerning genetic versus cultural contributions to the large-scale emergence of cooperative social adaptations in human societies (Richerson & Boyd, 2005), many of the underlying cognitive and affective processes that contribute to these adaptations were likely to have been under selection pressure during evolution (see chap. 2, this volume). These evolutionary considerations suggest that altruism could have evolved as an innate human capacity.

Evolutionary pressures might also have increased diversity in the genetic tendencies for prosocial behavior. Nettle (2006) proposed that evolutionary forces maintain variability in partially heritable behavior. Variations in human personality can be viewed as the result of a tradeoff between fitness benefits and costs. Agreeableness, the trait most likely to relate to prosocial behavior (Eisenberg et al., 2006; Graziano et al., 2007; chap. 3, this volume), balances the social benefits of empathy and trust with the costs of increased susceptibility to cheating and failure to maximize selfish advantage (Nettle, 2006).

Consider the gene locus for the human dopamine receptor D4 (DRD4). Bachner-Melman, Gritsenko, Nemanov, Zohar, and Ebstein (2005) reported that the most common 4-repeat variant in the third exon (the part of the gene translated to RNA for coding protein) is associated with prosociality. But an alternative genotype may also have advantages. Ding et al. (2002) estimated that the 7-repeat variant in the third exon (associated with behavioral phenotypes such as extraversion, novelty seeking, and attention-deficit/hyperactivity disorder) is the result of a relatively recent (40,000 to 50,000 years ago) and rare mutation event that created a variant that increased in prevalence due to positive selection. The authors proposed that individuals with a DRD4 7-repeat allele might have had traits that endowed them with evolutionary advantages (e.g., multiple sexual partners, higher probability for mate selection), which under certain conditions would have expanded the frequency of the 7-repeat. Bachner-Melman et al. (2005) also suggested that the need for diverse behavioral phenotypes in human populations resulted in a balanced maintenance of both alleles.

INDIVIDUAL DIFFERENCES IN THE TENDENCY TO BEHAVE PROSOCIALLY ARE HERITABLE

There are two major methods of assessing genetic influences on individual differences in human behavior and personality. One approach, discussed later in this chapter, establishes relationships between a trait and variability in observed DNA sequences. The other approach uses genetically informative research designs to disentangle environmental and genetic effects on prosocial behavior. These designs (such as the adoption design) are intended to account for variance in the measured or observed (phenotypic) trait by looking at differences in the similarity between family members as predicted by differences in their genetic and/or environmental relatedness (Plomin, DeFries, McClearn, & McGuffin, 2001). The results are usually reported in terms of proportion of the variance accounted for by genetic and environmental factors.

Most studies of genetic and environmental contributions to individual differences in prosocial behavior have used the twin design, which compares monozygotic (MZ) twins, who share all of their genes, with dizygotic (DZ) twins, who share on average half of their genes. The twin method uses this genetic difference in conjunction with the equal environments assumption, that is, that MZ and DZ twins growing up in their biological families are equal in terms of how similar their environments are, in which case greater similarity of MZ twins indicates genetic influence (heritability). Similarity beyond this genetic effect is attributed to the environment the twins share (shared environment effect), and any further differences between the twins are ascribed to nonshared environment and measurement error (Plomin et al., 2001). One advantage of the twin design is that it simultaneously points to the importance of environmental and genetic influences.

From the few studies that have directly addressed the genetic and environmental contributions to individual differences in prosocial behavior, a meaningful developmental pattern emerges. There appears to be an increase in the heritability of prosocial behavior as children grow up, accompanied by a decrease in the importance of shared environment effects.[1] This increase in heritability goes hand in hand with the development of cognitive and affective abilities (e.g., perspective taking, language, and interpersonal skills) that are required to assess social situations, approach distressed others, and provide support. The increase in heritability may also indicate that although there is some longitudinal stability in prosocial tendencies (e.g., Knafo, Zahn-Waxler, et al., 2008), the prevalence and nature of these behaviors change with time, increasing the role of genetic factors in these behaviors.

Most studies conducted with children find both genetic and shared environment effects. Deater-Deckard, Dunn, O'Connor, Davies, and Golding (2001) reported modest heritability (.15) and modest shared environment effects (.18) on the basis of maternal reports using the prosocial behavior scale of the Strengths and Difficulties Questionnaire (SDQ; Goodman, 1997) and a stepfamily sibling design. A British twin study (Knafo & Plomin, 2006a) revealed genetic and shared environment effects on mother-reported prosocial behavior of children ages 2 to 7 years and similar findings using teacher reports at age 7 years. Evidence for genetic effects and some shared environment effects on prosocial behavior as measured with the SDQ was reported for 5- to 16-year-old British twins (Scourfield, John, Martin, & McGuffin, 2004), but for 2- to 9-year-old South Korean twins (Hur & Rushton, 2007), the genetic effects were not accompanied by shared environment effects.

Three studies have addressed genetic and environmental influences on children's reactions to adults in distress. Of particular interest are children's empathy displays, which include both a cognitive aspect, labeled *hypothesis testing*, whereby the child actively tries to understand the other person's problem, and an affective aspect, labeled *empathic concern*, which requires a child to have a vicarious emotional reaction to another person's expressed emotions (Zahn-Waxler, Schiro, Robinson, Emde, & Schmitz, 2001). Volbrecht et al. (2007) estimated the heritability of empathic concern for mother shown by children ages 19 to 25 months to be .30; for hypothesis testing it was .40. Shared environment effects were .19 and .24. A study of twins followed from 14 to 36 months of age also found moderate genetic effects on empathic concern and hypothesis testing (Zahn-Waxler et al., 2001), as well as evidence for both shared and nonshared environmental effects. Finally, an Israeli study of 44-month-old twins (Knafo et al., 2009) estimated moderate heritabilities (.19 to .44) for individual differences in empathy toward an examiner, and

[1]In reviewing the literature, we often encountered studies with a limited number of twin pairs (e.g., 292 in Volbrecht, Lemery-Chalfant, Aksan, Zahn-Waxler, & Goldsmith, 2007). In such studies it often seems that dropping shared environment effects does not affect model fit, so an alternative model is chosen. But model-fitting decisions often depend on statistical power. Because we are interested here in comparing studies, we describe results in terms of the raw, unfitted models. In addition, we chose not to review evidence concerning genetic and environmental contributions to prosocial behavior that occurs between twins or siblings (e.g., Lemery & Goldsmith, 2002), because in dyadic interactions between genetically-related individuals it is difficult to disentangle genetic and reciprocal environmental contributions to the relationship (see Knafo & Plomin, 2006a).

the nonshared environment and error accounted for the rest of the variance. No shared environment effects were reported in this last study.

In two of these three studies, children's prosocial acts (trying to help or comfort a distressed victim) were related to their empathy. Volbrecht et al. (2007) reported a heritability of .22 and a shared environment effect of .43. Zahn-Waxler et al. (2001) and a later report with a fuller sample found genetic effects for both hypothesis testing and empathic concern, and modest genetic effects for prosocial behavior (Knafo, Zahn-Waxler, et al., 2008). In this study, nonshared environmental effects largely accounted for the positive relationship between empathy and prosocial behavior. Because in the twin design, nonshared environmental effects represent the amalgamation of a wide set of variables (including measurement error) not captured by genetic or shared environment components, these underlying drivers may be the result of a vast array of different experiences that mold the developing child's prosocial orientation. Nevertheless, two prominent factors have been shown to influence nonshared environmental effects (Asbury, Dunn, Pike, & Plomin, 2003). The first is high-risk environment; for example, families with lower socioeconomic status or greater maternal depression tend to display greater nonshared environmental effect sizes. The second is differences in parental discipline, where a child consistently labeled as "the good kid" ends up fulfilling the parents' prophesy.

Studies of adults generally find genetic influences on prosocial behavior. Four self-report twin studies in Western countries all found genetic effects and nonshared environmental effects (Davis, Luce, & Kraus, 1994; Gillespie, Cloninger, Heath, & Martin, 2003; Matthews, Batson, Horn, & Rosenman, 1981; Rushton, Fulker, Neale, Nias, & Eysenck, 1986; for a review, see Knafo & Plomin, 2006a). A Japanese study (Ando et al., 2004) estimated heritability at .00 for empathy and found a meaningful (.27) shared environment effect. In contrast, genetic (heritability) effects of .41 and .34 were found for helpfulness and compassion, respectively, and the rest of the variance was accounted for by nonshared environment and error.

Thus, most twin studies using questionnaire measures converge on the finding that, at least in adolescence and adulthood, genes influence prosocial traits, as does the environment. The environmental influences, however, tend to be of the nonshared type, meaning that they cause twins growing up in the same family to be dissimilar rather than similar. One American study reached a different conclusion: Krueger, Hicks, and McGue (2001) found a moderate effect of shared environment on altruism (.35) and little genetic effect. Except for this one outlier study, the overwhelming majority of studies provide consistent evidence for the influence of both genes and environment on prosocial behavior, particularly by adolescence and beyond.

In a study by Cesarini et al. (2008), Swedish and American twins participated in an economic game called The Trust Game, with real monetary rewards. In this game, the first player (the investor) receives an initial allocation of monetary units and has the option of transferring all or some of them to the second player (the trustee). Any amount transferred is tripled by the experimenter, and the trustee can then either keep the tripled sum or choose to transfer all or part of it to the other player. Twins arrived together for the experimental session and were then seated separately and paired with unknown other players seated in a different room. In the Swedish sample, trustees' return of funds could be considered altruistic because the other player could not reciprocate the return of funds (although trustworthiness is also a function of the investor's decision). In this sample, the heritability of trustworthiness was estimated at .18 and the influence of the shared environment at .17 (Cesarini et al., 2008).

GENETIC EFFECTS ON PROSOCIAL BEHAVIOR INCREASE WITH AGE

Most of the literature reviewed in the previous section has suggested that shared environment effects on prosocial behavior steadily decrease from childhood to adolescence and into adulthood. In contrast, childhood studies generally indicate some degree of shared environment effects. A different pattern emerges for genetic effects. In their literature review, Knafo and Plomin (2006a) noted that the heritability of prosociality tended to be higher in adolescence and adulthood than in childhood, in line with the notion that the influence of shared environment usually decreases, and that heritability increases from infancy all the way into adulthood (Plomin et al., 2001).

Generalizing from these trends, Knafo and Plomin (2006a) expected a decline throughout childhood in the importance of the shared environment to prosocial behavior. Comparing genetic and environmental influences on children's parent-reported prosocial behavior with a longitudinal design, Knafo and Plomin (2006a) found that shared environment effects decreased from .47 on average at 2 years of age to .03 at age 7, and genetic effects increased from .32 on average to .61. In another longitudinal study (Knafo, Zahn-Waxler, et al., 2008), genetic influences on children's empathy (but not prosociality) were negligible at 14 and 20 months and increased by 24 to 36 months. In contrast, shared environment effects were large at the earlier ages but small by 36 months. Scourfield et al. (2004) reported a similar pattern with a wider age range.

For a cross-cultural comparison, we plotted the results from four studies in which parents rated twin children's prosocial behavior, using age-specific correlations whenever they were available. Figure 8.1 shows both cross-cultural similarities and differences in the contributions of genetics and shared environment to individual differences in children's parent-rated prosocial behavior. In both British samples, the younger ages appeared more to the right, indicating larger shared environment effects in the younger age periods (although the shared environment is estimated to be more influential by Knafo & Plomin, 2006a than by Scourfield et al., 2004). The same is true for the Korean samples (Hur & Rushton, 2007), on the basis of comparing children ages 2 and 3 years with older children. Both British samples show higher heritability in older children, but the Korean sample does not. Finally, interesting cross-cultural variability is demonstrated when results from age 3 years are compared. In all three countries, heritability at this age is estimated to fall between .43 and .58. However, the differential positions of the three subsamples on the *x*-axis represent the lack of shared environment effects in Israel, in contrast with modest shared environment effects in Korea, and substantial effects (.26) in the United Kingdom, calling for further cross-cultural consideration of the interaction of genetics and the environment with the cultural and ethnic context.

GENETICS AND THE ENVIRONMENT CAUSE BOTH CONTINUITY AND CHANGE IN PROSOCIAL BEHAVIOR

Having established that prosocial behavior is partly heritable, and that the genetic effects tend to increase with age (while shared environment effects decrease with age), we now address the dynamics of these changes. With a longitudinal adaptation of the Cholesky method (e.g., Gillespie & Martin, 2005), it is possible to use within-twin and between-twin multivariate variance-covariance matrices to decompose the variance within and between ages into a set of genetic, shared environment, and nonshared environment factors. The variance is decomposed so that at each age, genetic, shared environment, and nonshared environment components are estimated and their reappearance at later ages can be examined. To the extent that scores at later and younger ages load on the same factors, this indicates continuity. To the extent that scores at later ages do not load on the same factors as those at younger ages, this indicates change.

We are aware of only two studies in which the investigators estimated change and stability in the environmental and genetic contributions to prosociality. Both found that genetics contributed to both change and stability, shared environment contributed to stability but became less important with age, and the nonshared environment (which includes measurement error) contributed mainly to change (Knafo & Plomin, 2006a; Knafo, Zahn-Waxler, et al., 2008; the latter study followed up earlier analyses by Zahn-Waxler et al., 2001).

Regarding empathy, genetic effects were partially responsible for continuity, although new genetic effects emerged at the different ages, accounting for change as well (Zahn-Waxler et al., 2001). With a larger sample, it was possible to pinpoint the developmental period in which changes in the genetic influences occurred (Knafo, Zahn-Waxler, et al., 2008). At 14 months,

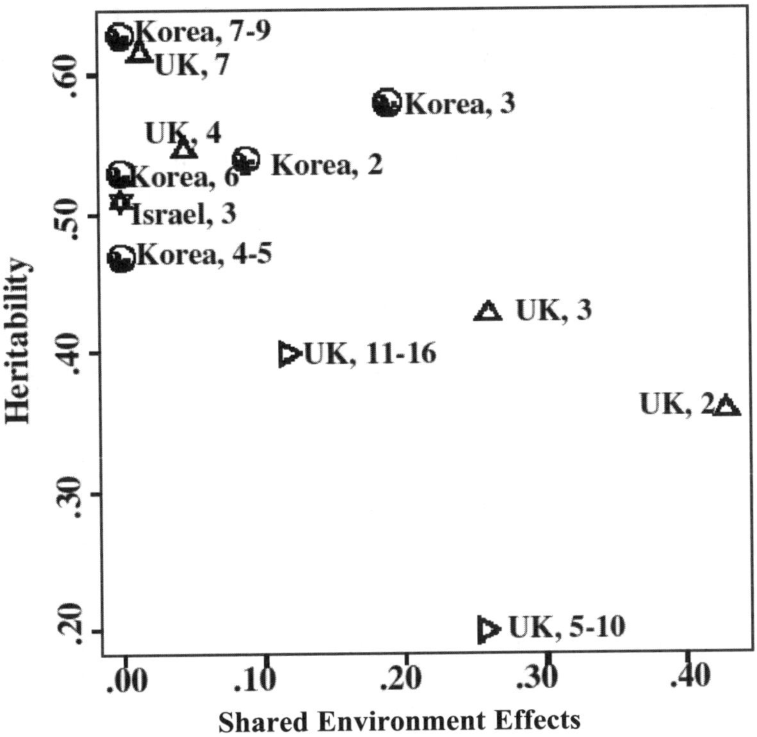

Figure 8.1. Cross-cultural similarities and differences in the contributions of genetics and shared environment to individual differences in children's parent-rated prosocial behavior.

no genetic effect was found on the overall empathy measure. The first genetic effects appeared at 20 months, accounting for 9% of the variance. These genetic effects were carried on, accounting for 16% of the variance at age 24 months. At that age a new genetic effect, distinct from the earlier genetic effect, emerged. This effect accounted for an additional 8% of the variance in empathy at 24 months (resulting in a heritability of .24 at this age). The genetic effect derived at 24 months accounted fully for the 25% heritability estimated at 36 months. This means that the main change in the genetic factors occurred between 20 and 24 months, which makes sense developmentally because this period includes major transitions in self–other differentiation, children's affective regulation, and cooperative play (e.g., Brownell & Carriger, 1990; Hay, 1979; Zahn-Waxler et al., 2001), all psychological variables relevant to empathy (Knafo, Zahn-Waxler, et al., 2008). This meshes well with previous research exploring the developmental scaling of theory-of-mind tasks (Wellman & Liu, 2004). Children first learn that others may have different desires than they do before they are able to recognize false beliefs. This scaling, which coincides with the development of executive function in the brain, may be influenced by genetic factors.

A study of mother-rated prosocial behavior also found that genetics accounted for both change and continuity (Knafo & Plomin, 2006a). Whereas Knafo, Zahn-Waxler, et al. (2008) found no new genetic effects on empathy from 24 to 36 months, with regard to prosocial behavior new genetic effects continued to emerge at 3, 4, and 7 years. This is not surprising because prosocial behavior has other predictors besides empathy (e.g., norm following). An interesting sex difference emerged in the transition from 4 to 7 years. The heritability of parent-rated prosocial behavior was similar for boys (.57) and girls (.55) at this age. However, most of the genetic variance in girls' prosocial behavior was stable and represented earlier genetic effects (.41), with the new genetic effects accounting for only 14% of the variance. In contrast, the new genetic effects for boys at this age accounted for 32% of the variance, more than half of the genetic influence at age 7 (Knafo & Plomin, 2006a). The dynamics of change in genetic effects are therefore quite different for girls and boys. Research on this phenomenon is still needed, focusing on potential moderators such as the transition to school that occurs in this period.

Environmental influences can also contribute to change as well as continuity. In the empathy study, a single strong (.43) shared environment effect was estimated at 14 months and was carried over, but it became increasingly weaker with age, until it contributed only 9% to the variance at 36 months (Knafo, Zahn-Waxler, et al., 2008). In the prosocial behavior study, a substantial effect of shared environment at age 2 years for boys (.44) and girls (.56) was also carried over but waned in importance in later years. There was also evidence for new effects at 3 and at 4 years, but they were progressively smaller in size, and at age 7 years no new significant effects were found (Knafo & Plomin, 2006a). Thus, both studies found early substantial and stable shared environment factors that became weaker with age. In both studies, the main contributions of the nonshared environment were unique at each age. This is not surprising because nonshared environment estimates include a component of error. Knafo and Plomin's (2006a) longitudinal analysis included 2,901 pairs, so they were able to detect minimal (1%–2%) contributions of the nonshared environment to continuity that are unlikely to reflect longitudinal measurement error.

WHERE ARE THE GENETIC EFFECTS TO BE FOUND?

Despite overwhelming evidence supporting the role of genetic factors in predicting prosocial behavior, very little is known about the specific genes involved. As with other complex traits, genes may influence prosocial behavior through small effects on different behavioral, cognitive, and affective components, in an additive or interactive manner. It would be unlikely for a single gene to have a strong influence on the normal variation in a complex trait (see Plomin et al., 2001). Nevertheless, there has been some progress in molecular genetic research into prosocial behavior and related traits. Initial hypotheses focused on the dopaminergic system (Tahir et al., 2000), associated with antisocial behavior and conduct disorder, as well as the serotonergic system, related to various affective processes likely to be involved in empathy (Hariri & Weinberger, 2003; Hastings, Zahn-Waxler, & McShane, 2006). Significant associations were also observed between self-reported altruism (based on the Selflessness Scale; Bachar et al., 2002) and genetic polymorphisms in the dopamine receptor D4 and D5 genes, as well as in the insulin-like growth factor 2 gene, which is involved in physical development and growth (Bachner-Melman et al., 2005).

Studies have highlighted the importance of oxytocin (OT) and arginine vasopressin (AVP), neuropeptides synthesized in the hypothalamus, released into the blood as hormones, and acting as neurotransmitters at synaptic targets in the brain. OT and AVP also serve important social functions, such as social bonding, parental care, social communication, and emotional reactivity (Fries, Ziegler, Kurian, Jacoris, & Pollak, 2005). Pharmacological administration of OT profoundly affects social behavior (e.g., Domes, Heinrichs, Michel, Berger, & Herpertz, 2007; Kosfeld et al., 2005). Genes involved in OT and AVP regulation, notably the OT receptor gene (OXTR) and vasopressin receptor gene (AVPR1a), are therefore likely candidates for genetic association with social behavior. Variability in these genes has been related to behavioral and social differences within and between other mammalian species (Hammock & Young, 2005). For example, male and female prairie voles (with longer variants of an AVPR1a polymorphism) form lifelong attachments, rear pups together, and show high levels of social interest, whereas males of the closely related montane vole species (with a shorter variant) do not show these behaviors (Lim et al., 2004; Young, Nilsen, Waymire, MacGregor, & Insel, 1999). Regarding humans, several studies (reviewed by Israel et al., 2008) found associations between the AVPR1a gene and a variety of social and nonsocial phenomena, from sibling relationships to creative dance and musical memory.

Recently, together with Gary Bornstein and Richard Ebstein, we investigated the relationship between altruism and the length of the AVPR1a RS3 region. We assigned individuals to the role of Player A in the Dictator Game, giving them the Shekel equivalent of $12. Player A was then asked if he or she wanted to share with Player B, a person Player A would never meet and who would never learn Player A's identity. More than 60% of the participants who had two copies of the "long" version of the RS3 region were "generous," donating at least half of their endowment. In comparison, less than 30% of individuals with two copies of the "short" version of the RS3 region donated generously (Knafo, Israel, et al., 2008). Variations in OXTR are also associated with altruism as measured in the dictator game and in a different paradigm, the Social Values Orientation task (Israel et al., 2009).

Other genes relevant to altruism, empathy, and other aspects of prosocial tendencies are likely to be discovered soon.

GENETIC AND ENVIRONMENTAL EFFECTS ARE OFTEN INTERTWINED

Genetic and environmental influences should not be viewed as opposing explanations for behavior (Plomin et al., 2001). Focusing on only one of them is comparable to watching a color film in black and white. The richness of development is derived in part from the multitude of possible correlations and interactions between genes and environment. Consider, for example, the steady age-related increase in the heritability of prosocial behavior. As Knafo and Plomin (2006a) noted, this increase may reflect in part environmental processes. For example, parents' behaviors are often influenced by their children's temperamental tendencies (Kochanska, Friesenborg, Lange, & Martel, 2004). Such evocative gene–environment correlations, in which children's genes operate through their behavior on the environment, are more likely as children grow up (Scarr & McCartney, 1983), and they end up contributing to the heritability estimate (Knafo & Plomin, 2006a).

The Knafo and Plomin study (2006b) also addressed the issue of gene–environment correlations. Children's relatively low prosocial behavior scores were related to parents' use of negative discipline and low affection. These associations were due mainly to children's genetic tendencies, implying that the genetically influenced low prosocial behavior evokes a negative reaction from parents. In contrast, parents' positive discipline and affection showed a moderate positive correlation with children's prosocial behavior. This correlation was due mainly to shared environment processes and to a lesser extent to genetic processes (Knafo & Plomin, 2006b).

Again, genetic and environmental effects are likely to interact (Bakermans-Kranenburg & van IJzendoorn, 2006). One approach to assessing gene–environment interactions (Caspi et al., 2002) compares the association between an environmental variable and a measured phenotype, across different genetic profiles. For example, one study looked at the interaction between insensitive parenting and children's DRD4 third exon. Bakermans-Kranenburg and van IJzendoorn (2006) reported a sixfold increase in externalizing behaviors in children who did not have the 7-repeat allele and were exposed to insensitive care, in comparison with children without this combination of risk factors. This is an important finding, especially as this polymorphism has been negatively associated with self-reported altruism (Bachner-Melman et al., 2005).

Another approach to gene–environment interactions involves investigating the relative genetic contributions to individual differences in prosocial behavior across different levels of a measured environmental variable, such as parental discipline or socioeconomic status (e.g., Turkheimer, Haley, Waldron, D'Onofrio, & Gottesman, 2003). Changes in heritability across levels of the environmental variable suggest that the magnitude of genetic effects is influenced by the environment. With regard to prosociality, the presence of other siblings is an especially interesting environmental variable. First, older or younger siblings are among the first people children have to share with, from a very early age (Hay, 1994). Second, some older siblings are often expected to take care of their younger siblings, thereby providing the latter with a model of prosocial behavior (Eisenberg et al., 2006). Third, there is no simple relationship between number of siblings or birth order and prosociality (i.e., no main effect for number of siblings on prosocial behavior). For example, sharing may be more common, and spontaneous help less common, in large families (for a review, see Eisenberg et al., 2006).

To illustrate gene–environment interactions, we focused on the presence of additional siblings.[2] In the Longitudinal Israeli Study of Twins (LIST; Knafo, 2006), parents of all Hebrew-speaking twins born in Israel in 2004 and 2005 were sent questionnaires around the twins' third birthday for details concerning study design and zygosity assessment, see Knafo, 2006; here we present data from the first 491 families). For current purposes the number of siblings was reduced to three levels (no additional siblings, one additional sibling, and two or more additional siblings). Mothers rated their twins' prosocial behavior using the SDQ scale. No association was found between the number and sex of additional siblings and children's prosocial behavior.

Table 8.1 presents the twin correlations with mother-reported prosocial behavior, separately for MZ and DZ twins. MZ correlations tended to be substantially higher than DZ correlations, indicating a genetic influence on prosocial behavior. Next we ran a series of model-fitting procedures, using MZ and DZ data to estimate genetic and environment effects, with twins' sex and age as covariates. Although there is evidence for genetic influence on prosocial behavior in this sample, a gene-by-environment interaction also emerged from the findings. Clear differences were found between families in which twins were the only children and families in which there were additional siblings. In the former, an additive genetic effect of .23 and a nonshared environment effect of .77 accounted for individual differences. In families with additional children, a larger genetic effect of .64 to .72 was found (estimated as a dominant, nonadditive genetic effect, due to the strong MZ correlation and the negligible DZ correlation). Further analyses showed that split-

[2]It may seem counterintuitive to consider the presence of additional siblings in families of twins, in which no child is a single child. However, the fact that the additional siblings are older or younger than the twins is important: Older siblings are often expected to behave prosocially toward their younger siblings, and they can be viewed as role models (Garner, Jones, & Palmer, 1994). In addition, it has been suggested that taking the perspective of the younger sibling contributes to the development of prosocial behavior (Eisenberg et al., 2006). Research suggests that the presence of an additional sibling of the same age (i.e., a twin) does not improve children's theory of mind, but having an older or younger sibling does (Cassidy, Fineberg, Brown, & Perkins, 2005).

TABLE 8.1
Twin Correlations in Mother-Rated Prosocial Behavior According to Presence of Additional Siblings

Siblings	Twin correlation: MZ twins	Twin correlation: DZ twins	Genetic influence	Nonshared environmental influences and error
No additional siblings	.25	.10	.23 (.01–.44)	.77 (.56–.99)
One additional sibling	.78**	.02	.64 (.31–.81)	.36 (.19–.69)
Two or more additional siblings	.71**	.21*	.72 (.56–.82)	.28 (.18–.44)
One, two, or more additional siblings	.73**	.09	.70 (.56–.79)	.30 (.21–.44)
Total	.54**	.10	.54 (.40–.65)	.46 (.35–.60)

Note. Numbers in parentheses represent 95% confidence intervals. Best-fitting models are presented (details of each analysis and model fitting procedure are available from the authors). No significant shared environment effects were found. All genetic effects (except for the group with no additional siblings) are nonadditive (dominant genetic influences). MZ = monozygotic; DZ = dizygotic.
*$p < .05$ (1-tailed). **$p < .01$.

ting these families into two groups, those with younger or older siblings and those with different numbers of additional siblings, had little effect, indicating that the mere presence of additional siblings was associated with increased heritability.

This finding illustrates how the environment can moderate the effects of genes on children's behavior. One possibility is that in families with additional children, parents' attention is divided among more children, and the parents are constrained in their ability to influence children consistently. This may result in increased differences between children due to their genetic propensities. Another possibility is that when families include more children, the number of opportunities children have to demonstrate prosocial behavior increases due to more frequent social interactions with different people (e.g., siblings and their friends), in which case their decisions to help or share represent their genetically influenced tendencies more purely. Alternative explanations may be proffered, but we should not lose sight of the central point that gene × environment interactions may be important and should be investigated in greater detail.

CONCLUSIONS

We have reviewed seven studies of children and seven of adults, and all but one of them provides evidence for the heritability of prosocial behavior. Initial evidence from molecular genetic studies supports this conclusion, although more research elucidating the psychobiological processes responsible for the genetic effects is still needed. The heritability of prosocial behavior tends to increase with age, although the reasons for this increase are unclear. The environmental influences are also important, and our cross-cultural comparison suggests a need for further twin research in additional countries. Such studies will increase our understanding of environmental effects across cultures. Finally, genetic and environmental influences should not be seen as competing, but as complementary explanations of individual differences in prosocial behavior.

REFERENCES

Ando, J., Suzuki, A., Yamagata, S., Kijima, N., Maekawa, H., Ono, Y., et al. (2004). Genetic and environmental structure of Cloninger's temperament and character dimensions. *Journal of Personality Disorders, 18*, 379–393.

Asbury, K., Dunn, J., Pike, A., & Plomin, R. (2003). Nonshared environmental influences on individual differences in early behavioral development: A monozygotic twin differences study. *Child Development, 74*, 933–943.

Bachar, E., Latzer, Y., Canetti, L., Gur, E., Berry, E. M., & Bonne, O. (2002). Rejection of life in anorexic and bulimic patients. *International Journal of Eating Disorders, 31*, 42–48.

Bachner-Melman, R., Gritsenko, I., Nemanov, L., Zohar, A. H., & Ebstein, R. P. (2005). Dopaminergic polymorphisms associated with self-report measures of human altruism: A fresh phenotype for the dopamine D4 receptor. *Molecular Psychiatry, 10*, 333–335.

Bakermans-Kranenburg, M. J., & van IJzendoorn, M. H. (2006). Gene–environment interaction of the Dopamine D4 receptor (DRD4) and observed maternal insensitivity predicting externalizing behavior in preschoolers. *Developmental Psychobiology, 48*, 406–409.

Barry, C. M., & Wentzel, K. R. (2006). Friend influence on prosocial behavior: The role of motivational factors and friendship characteristics. *Developmental Psychology, 42*, 153–163.

Brownell, C. A., & Carriger, M. S. (1990). Changes in cooperation and self-other differentiation during the second year. *Child Development, 61*, 1164–1174.

Calvert, S. L., & Kotler, J. A. (2003). The Children's Television Act: Can media policy make a difference? *Journal of Applied Developmental Psychology, 24*, 375–380.

Caspi, A., McClay, J., Moffitt, T. E., Mill, J., Martin, J., Craig, W. I., et al. (2002, August 2). Role of genotype in the cycle of violence in maltreated children. *Science, 297*, 851–854.

Cassidy, K. W., Fineberg, D., Brown, K., & Perkins, A. (2005) Theory of mind may be contagious, but you don't catch it from your twin. *Child Development, 76*, 97–106.

Cesarini, D., Dawes, C. T., Fowler, J. H., Johannesson, M., Lichtenstein, P., & Wallace, B. (2008). Heritability of cooperative behavior in the trust game. *Proceedings of the National Academy of Sciences, USA, 105*, 3721–3726.

Davis, M. H., Luce, C., & Kraus, S. J. (1994). The heritability of characteristics associated with dispositional empathy. *Journal of Personality, 62,* 369–391.

Deater-Deckard, K., Dunn, J., O'Connor, T. G., Davies, L., & Golding, J. (2001). Using the stepfamily genetic design to examine gene-environment processes in child and family functioning. *Marriage and Family Review, 33,* 131–156.

Ding, Y. C., Chi, H. C., Grady, D. L., Morishima, A., Kidd, J. R., Kidd, K. K., et al. (2002). Evidence of positive selection acting at the human dopamine receptor D4 gene locus. *Proceedings of the National Academy of Sciences, USA, 99,* 309–314.

Domes, G., Heinrichs, M., Michel, A., Berger, C., & Herpertz, S. C. (2007). Oxytocin improves "mind-reading" in humans. *Biological Psychiatry, 61,* 731–733.

Eisenberg, N., Fabes, R. A., & Spinrad, T. (2006). Prosocial development. In N. Eisenberg (Vol. Ed.) and W. Damon & R. M. Lerner (Series Eds.), *Handbook of child psychology: Vol. 3. Social, emotional, and personality development* (6th ed., pp. 646–718). New York: Wiley.

Eisenberg, N., Guthrie, I. K., Murphy, B. C., Shepard, S. A., Cumberland, A., & Carlo, G. (1999). Consistency and development of prosocial dispositions: A longitudinal study. *Child Development, 70,* 1360–1372.

Fries, A. B., Ziegler, T. E., Kurian, J. R., Jacoris, S., & Pollak, S. D. (2005). Early experience in humans is associated with changes in neuropeptides critical for regulating social behavior. *Proceedings of the National Academy of Sciences, USA, 102,* 17237–17240.

Garner, P. W., Jones, D. C., & Palmer, D. J. (1994). Social cognitive correlates of preschool children's sibling caregiving behavior. *Developmental Psychology, 30,* 905–911.

Gillespie, N. A., Cloninger, C. R., Heath, A. C., & Martin, N. G. (2003). The genetic and environmental relationship between Cloninger's dimensions of temperament and character. *Personality and Individual Differences, 35,* 1931–1946.

Gillespie, N. A., & Martin, N. G. (2005). Multivariate genetic analysis. In B. S. Everitt & D. C. Howell (Eds.), *Encyclopedia of statistics in behavioral science* (pp. 1363–1370). Chichester, England: Wiley.

Goodman, R. (1997). The Strengths and Difficulties Questionnaire: A research note. *Journal of Child Psychology and Psychiatry, 38,* 581–586.

Graziano, W. G., Habashi, M. M., Sheese, B. E., & Tobin, R. M. (2007). Agreeableness, empathy, and helping: A person × situation perspective. *Journal of Personality and Social Psychology, 93,* 583–599.

Hammock, E. A. D., & Young, L. J. (2005, June 10). Microsatellite instability generates diversity in brain and sociobehavioral traits. *Science, 308,* 1630–1634.

Hariri, A. R., & Weinberger, D. R. (2003). Functional neuroimaging of genetic variation in serotonergic neurotransmission. *Genes, Brain, and Behavior, 2,* 341–349.

Hastings, P. D., Utendale, W. T., & Sullivan, C. (2007). The socialization of prosocial development. In J. E. Grusec & P. D. Hastings (Eds.), *Handbook of socialization* (pp. 638–664). New York: Guilford Press.

Hastings, P. D., Zahn-Waxler, C., & McShane, K. E. (2006). We are, by nature, moral creatures: Biological bases of concern for others. In M. Killen & J. Smetana (Eds.), *Handbook of moral development* (pp. 483–516). Mahwah, NJ: Erlbaum.

Hay, D. F. (1979). Cooperative interactions and sharing between very young children and their parents. *Developmental Psychology, 15*, 647–653.

Hay, D. F. (1994). Prosocial development. *Journal of Child Psychology and Psychiatry and Allied Disciplines, 35*, 29–71.

Hur, Y.-M. (2007). Effects of the chorion type on prosocial behavior in young twins. *Twin Research and Human Genetics, 10*, 773–777.

Hur, Y.-M., & Rushton, J. P. (2007). Genetic and environmental contributions to prosocial behaviour in 2- to 9-year-old South Korean twins. *Biology Letters, 3*, 664–666.

Israel, S., Lerer, E., Shalev, I., Uzefovsky, F., Reibold, M., Bachner-Melman, R., et al. (2008). Molecular genetic studies of the arginine vasopressin 1a receptor (AVPR1a) and the oxytocin receptor (OXTR) in human behavior: From autism to altruism with some notes in between. *Progress in Brain Research, 170*, 435–449.

Israel, S., Lerer, E., Shalev, I. Uzefovsky, F., Riebold, M., Laiba, E., et al. (2009, May 20). The oxytocin receptor (*OXTR*) contributes to prosocial fund allocations in the Dictator Game and the Social Values Orientation Task. *PLoS ONE*.

Knafo, A. (2006). The Longitudinal Israeli Study of Twins (LIST): Children's social development as influenced by genetics, abilities, and socialization. *Twin Research and Human Genetics*, 9, 791–798.

Knafo, A., Israel, S., Darvasi, A., Bachner-Melman, R., Uzefovsky, F., Cohen, L., et al. (2008). Individual differences in allocation of funds in the Dictator Game and postmortem hippocampal mRNA levels are correlated with length of the arginine vasopressin 1a receptor (AVPR1a) RS3 promoter-region repeat. *Genes, Brain, and Behavior, 7*, 266–275.

Knafo, A., & Plomin, R. (2006a). Prosocial behavior from early to middle childhood: Genetic and environmental influences on stability and change. *Developmental Psychology, 42*, 771–786.

Knafo, A., & Plomin, R. (2006b). Parental discipline and affection, and children's prosocial behavior: Genetic and environmental links. *Journal of Personality and Social Psychology*, 90, 147–164.

Knafo, A., Zahn-Waxler, C., Davidov, M., Van Hulle, C., Robinson, J., & Rhee, S. H. (2009). Empathy in early childhood: Genetic, environmental and affective contributions. *Annals of the New York Academy of Sciences*.

Knafo, A., Zahn-Waxler, C., Van Hulle, C., Robinson, J., & Rhee, S. H. (2008). The developmental origins of a disposition toward empathy: Genetic and environmental contributions. *Emotion, 8*, 737–752.

Kochanska, G., Friesenborg, A. E., Lange, L. A., & Martel, M. M. (2004). The parent's personality and the infant's temperament as contributors to their emerging relationship. *Journal of Personality and Social Psychology*, 86, 744–759.

Kosfeld, M., Heinrichs, M., Zak, P. J., Fischbacher, U., & Fehr, E. (2005, June 2). Oxytocin increases trust in humans. *Nature, 435*, 673–676.

Krueger, R. F., Hicks, B. M., & McGue, M. (2001). Altruism and antisocial behavior: Independent tendencies, unique personality correlates, distinct etiologies. *Psychological Science, 12*, 397–402.

Lemery, K. S., & Goldsmith, H. H. (2002). Genetic and environmental influences on preschool sibling cooperation and conflict: Associations with difficult temperament and parenting style. *Marriage and Family Review, 33*, 77–99.

Lim, M. M., Wang, Z., Olazabal, D. E., Ren, X., Terwilliger, E. F., & Young, L. J. (2004, June 17). Enhanced partner preference in a promiscuous species by manipulating the expression of a single gene. *Nature, 429*, 754–757.

Matthews, K. A., Batson, C. D., Horn, J., & Rosenman, R. H. (1981). "Principles in his nature which interest him in the fortune of others . . .": The heritability of empathic concern for others. *Journal of Personality, 49*, 237–247.

Nettle, D. (2006). The evolution of personality variation in humans and other animals. *American Psychologist, 61*, 622–631.

Nowak, M. A. (2006, December 8). Five rules for the evolution of cooperation. *Science, 314*, 1560–1563.

Plomin, R., DeFries, J. C., McClearn, G. E., & McGuffin, P. (2001). *Behavioral genetics* (4th ed.). New York: Worth.

Richerson, P. J., & Boyd, R. (2005). *Not by genes alone: How culture transformed human evolution*. Chicago: University of Chicago Press.

Rushton, J. P., Fulker, D. W., Neale, M. C., Nias, D. K. B., & Eysenck, H. J. (1986). Altruism and aggression: The heritability of individual differences. *Journal of Personality and Social Psychology, 50*, 1192–1198.

Scarr, S., & McCartney, K. (1983). How people make their own environments: A theory of genotype → environmental effects. *Child Development, 54*, 424–435.

Scourfield, J., John, B., Martin, N., & McGuffin, P. (2004). The development of prosocial behaviour in children and adolescents: A twin study. *Journal of Child Psychology and Psychiatry, 45*, 927–935.

Solomon, D., Watson, M. S., Delucchi, K. L., Scraps, E., & Battistich, V. (1988). Enhancing children's prosocial behavior in the classroom. *American Educational Research Journal, 25*, 527–554.

Staub, E. (1979). *Positive social behavior and morality: Socialization and development* (Vol. 2). New York: Academic Press.

Tahir, E., Yazgan, Y., Cirakoglu, B., Ozbay, F., Waldman, I., & Asherson, P. J. (2000). Association and linkage of DRD4 and DRD5 with attention deficit hyperactivity disorder (ADHD) in a sample of Turkish children. *Molecular Psychiatry, 5*, 396–404.

Turkheimer, E., Haley, A., Waldron, M., D'Onofrio, B., & Gottesman, I. I. (2003). Socioeconomic status modifies heritability of IQ in young children. *Psychological Science, 14*, 623–628.

Volbrecht, M. M., Lemery-Chalfant, K., Aksan, N., Zahn-Waxler, C., & Goldsmith, H. H. (2007). Examining the familial link between positive affect and empathy development in the second year. *Journal of Genetic Psychology, 168*, 105–129.

Wellman, H., & Liu, D., (2004). Scaling of theory-of-mind tasks. *Child Development*, 75, 523–541.

Young, L. J., Nilsen, R., Waymire, K. G., MacGregor, G. R., & Insel, T. R. (1999, August 19). Increased affiliative response to vasopressin in mice expressing the V1a receptor from a monogamous vole. *Nature*, 400, 766–768.

Zahn-Waxler, C., Schiro, K., Robinson, J. L., Emde, R. N., & Schmitz, S. (2001). Empathy and prosocial patterns in young MZ and DZ twins: Development and genetic and environmental influences. In R. N. Emde & J. K. Hewitt (Eds.), *Infancy to early childhood: Genetic and environmental influences on developmental change* (pp. 141–162). New York: Oxford University Press.

9

THE EFFORTFUL AND ENERGY-DEMANDING NATURE OF PROSOCIAL BEHAVIOR

MATTHEW T. GAILLIOT

Living in a complex society requires that people work together, cooperate, and help one another. Hence, prosocial behavior is a necessity in modern life. Helping others is not always easy, however, and it can demand effort and energy (see chaps. 7 and 19, this volume). In addition, although theorists agree that human beings have an innate capacity for prosocial behavior (see chaps. 1, 2, and 4, this volume), other innate tendencies and cultural factors may predispose people toward selfishness and reduced altruism. In this chapter, I focus on *self-regulation* (or *self-control*)—the capacity that allows a person to exert effort when necessary to resolve conflicts arising from competing thoughts and behavioral tendencies (e.g., by overriding one thought or behavior with another)—and propose that self-regulation is necessary for increased prosociality, to the extent that factors such as selfishness that decrease prosociality must be overridden (see chap. 7, this volume).

I begin by reviewing evidence indicating that prosocial behavior requires energy-expending self-regulation efforts. I then analyze the relation between self-regulation and energy expenditure, the involvement of glucose metabolism in self-regulation, and the effects of self-regulation and glucose depletion on subsequent effortful behavior. Next, I present conceptual arguments and review initial findings showing that self-regulation and glucose depletion impair prosocial behavior and that increases in glucose can facilitate such behavior. Finally, I speculate beyond the range of studies conducted to date in an effort to spur additional research on energy, metabolism, and prosocial behavior.

HELPING AS EFFORTFUL AND ENERGY-DEMANDING

Several lines of thinking and evidence suggest that prosocial behavior is effortful. Helping others requires additional thought and action that a person would not otherwise have to engage in, and it therefore requires additional effort. As shown by Simpson and Beckes (see chap. 2, this volume), evolutionary theories have suggested that helping is an innate tendency that has evolved through selection. However, evolutionary theory has also suggested that people are inherently selfish and think of others' needs as less important than their own and those of their relatives (Dawkins, 1976). Therefore, helping others should sometimes, and perhaps often, require that a person exert effort to overcome or suspend other, more selfish innate tendencies. For example, a student might have to stop studying to help someone fix a flat tire. Of course, people view the world from their own perspective, and helping others requires taking others' perspectives (see chap. 6, this volume), which might also require effort. For many reasons, then, helping requires energy and effort.

SELF-REGULATION: EFFORTFUL AND ENERGY DEMANDING

Self-regulation allows people to achieve their goals, maintain good physical and mental health, and get along well with others (Shoda, Mischel, & Peake, 1990; Tangney, Baumeister, & Boone, 2004). Although maintaining good self-control is generally desirable, people do not possess an unlimited, unwavering capacity for self-control. Instead, self-control is limited. Several experimental studies, as well as other evidence, have demonstrated that exerting self-control at one point in time impairs later self-control (Baumeister, Heatherton, & Tice, 1994; Baumeister, Vohs, & Tice, 2007; Muraven & Baumeister, 2000). In the laboratory, participants were divided into two groups. In the first group, members were given a task that required self-control to complete (e.g., resisting sweet food). In the second group, members were given a task that did not require self-control (e.g., watching a video). After this, participants were given a second task, this time requiring self-control from participants in both groups. The typical finding was that participants who completed the initial self-control task exhibited less self-control on the second task, compared with participants who completed an initial task that did not require self-control. Findings that fit this pattern are listed in Table 9.1.

GLUCOSE AND SELF-REGULATION

Why are people worse at self-control after they have exerted self-control? One reason is that exerting self-control can metabolize glucose, the brain's primary source of energy, removing it from the bloodstream faster than it is replenished. This claim is supported by studies in which blood-glucose levels decrease as participants exert self-control (e.g., perform a Stroop task, engage in effortful conversations, or try to look away from attractive stimuli) but not when participants do not exert self-control (e.g., sit and watch a video, engage in less effortful conversations; Fairclough & Houston, 2004; Gailliot, Baumeister, et al., 2007). Self-control requires more glucose than processes that involve less self-control (Gailliot & Baumeister, 2007a). The decrease in glucose levels in the bloodstream thus undermines self-control: There simply is too little glucose, which leads to suboptimal self-control. Likewise, after having exerted self-control, ingesting a drink containing glucose improves self-control and eliminates the typical impairments found after exerting self-control (Gailliot, Baumeister, et al., 2007).

Prosocial Behavior, Self-Regulation, and Glucose

In recent studies, participants who exerted self-control (e.g., by changing a habitual routine or effortfully looking away from attractive stimuli), compared with participants who had not exerted self-control but instead completed a different task that did not require self-control, indicated in questionnaire reports that they would be less likely to donate food or money to people in need, and they volunteered for fewer hours to help stuff envelopes and complete other helpful office tasks (Gailliot, Baumeister, Maner, & DeWall, 2006; see also Gailliot, Baumeister, et al., 2007). However, when participants had consumed a glucose drink, before or after the initial self-control task, exerting self-control on the initial task did not reduce helping (Gailliot, Baumeister, et al., 2006; see also Gailliot, Plant, et al., 2007). This pattern of findings suggests that people are less helpful after they have exerted self-control and that increasing glucose levels can increase helping behavior.

Other evidence is consistent with the idea that mental effort, akin to self-control, reduces helping behavior later on. Relative to participants who completed an easy listening task, participants who completed a difficult listening task were less helpful with another experiment (Sherrod & Downs, 1974). Being in a larger crowd of people (which can be more stressful and

TABLE 9.1
Tasks, Domains, and Self-Controlled Behaviors That Impaired by Prior Self-Control, That Impair Subsequent Self-Control, or Both

Task or Domain	Reference
Simulated automobile driving for 8 hours	Ryan & Warner, 1936
Controlling visual or auditory attention	DeWall, Baumeister, Stillman, & Gailliot, 2006; Gailliot & Baumeister, 2006; Gailliot, Baumeister, et al., 2007a; Gailliot, Schmeichel, & Baumeister, 2006; Govorun & Payne, 2006; see Hockey, 1983; Inzlicht, McKay, & Aronson, 2006; Oaten & Cheng, 2005; Richeson, Baird, et al., 2003; Richeson & Shelton, 2003; Richeson & Trawalter, 2005; Rotton, Olszewski, Charleton, & Soler, 1978; Schmeichel, Vohs, & Baumeister, 2003; Sherrod & Downs, 1974; Stucke & Baumeister, 2006; Trawalter & Richeson, 2006; Vohs, Baumeister, & Ciarocco, 2005; Wallace & Baumeister, 2002; Webb & Sheeran, 2003
Cursing	Hockey, 1983
Being exposed to uncontrollable noise	Glass & Singer, 1972
Mental persistence (on math problems or word fragments)	Frankenhaeuser & Lundberg, 1977; Gailliot, Baumeister, et al., 2007a; Gailliot & Baumeister, 2006; Vohs, Baumeister, & Ciarocco, 2005
Physical persistence (breath holding, handgrip)	Ciarocco, Sommer, & Baumeister, 2001; Finkel et al., 2006; Inzlicht, McKay, & Aronson, 2006; Muraven & Slessareva, 2003; Muraven, Tice, & Baumeister, 1998; Seeley & Gardner, 2003; Vohs, Baumeister, & Ciarocco, 2005
Persistence on impossible tasks (figure tracing, puzzles)	Baumeister, Bratslavsky, Muraven, & Tice, 1998; Ciarocco, Sommer, & Baumeister, 2001; Cohen & Spacacan, 1978; Moller, Deci, & Ryan, 2006; Muraven & Slessareva, 2003; Muraven, Tice, & Baumeister, 1998; Rotton, Olszeqski, Charleton, & Soler, 1978; Wallace & Baumeister, 2002; Webb & Sheeran, 2003; Vohs & Schmeichel, 2003
Emotion regulation (suppressing or amplifying emotions, including sadness, happiness, disgust)	Baumeister, Bratslavsky, Muraven, & Tice, 1998; Finkel & Campbell, 2001; Shamosh & Gray, 2007; Muraven & Slessareva, 2003; Muraven, Tice, & Baumeister, 1998; Vohs, Baumeister, & Ciarocco, 2005; Schmeichel, Vohs, & Baumeister, 2003; Gailliot, Schmeichel, & Maner, 2007; Schmeichel, Demaree, Robinson, & Pu, 2005
Motor control (staying still while watching a film)	Finkel et al., 2006; Stucke & Baumeister, 2006
Thought suppression (of thoughts of white bears, death, or sex)	Gailliot & Baumeister, 2007b; Gailliot, Baumeister, et al., 2007; Gailliot, Schmeichel, & Baumeister, 2006; Gailliot, Schmeichel, & Maner, 2007; Muraven, Baumeister, & Tice, 1999; Muraven, Collins, & Nienhaus, 2002; Muraven & Slessareva, 2003; Muraven, Tice, & Baumeister, 1998; Oaten & Cheng, 2005; Seeley & Gardner, 2003; Vohs, Baumeister, & Ciarocco, 2005; Vohs & Schmeichel, 2003

Dietary restraint and healthy eating	Baumeister, Bratslavsky, Muraven, & Tice, 1998; DeWall, Baumeister, Stillman, & Gailliot, 2006; Kahan, Polivy, & Herman, 2003; Muraven & Slessareva, 2003; Stirling & Yeomans, 2004; Stucke & Baumeister, 2006; Vohs & Heatherton, 2000
Drinking (alcohol) restraint	Muraven, Collins, & Nienhaus, 2002; Muraven, Collins, Shiffman, & Paty, 2005
Sexual restraint (sexual infidelity)	Gailliot & Baumeister, 2007b
Aggressive restraint	DeWall, Baumeister, Stillman, & Gailliot, 2006; Stucke & Baumeister, 2006
Monetary restraint (shopping, buying lottery tickets)	Bruyneel, Dewitte, Franses, & Dekimpe, 2005; Vohs & Faber, 2007
Overriding habits (of crossing out letters for a laboratory task)	Baumeister, Bratslavsky, Muraven, & Tice, 1998; DeWall, Baumeister, Stillman, & Gailliot, 2006; Gailliot & Baumeister, 2007a
Suppressing stereotypes and related responses	Gailliot, Plant, Butz, & Baumeister, 2007; Gordijn, Hindriks, Koomen, Dijksterhuis, Van Knippenberg, 2004; Govorun & Payne, 2006
Effortful interracial interactions	Richeson, Baird, et al., 2003; Richeson & Shelton, 2003; Richeson & Trawalter, 2005; Richeson, Trawalter, & Shelton, 2005; Trawalter & Richeson, 2006
Impression management (e.g., leaving a phone message)	Miyamoto & Schwarz, 2006; Vohs, Baumeister, & Ciarocco, 2005
Relationship accommodation	Finkel & Campbell, 2001
Social coordination	Finkel et al., 2006
Ostracizing others and being rejected	Baumeister, DeWall, Ciarocco, & Twenge, 2005; Ciarocco, Sommer, & Baumeister, 2001
Stereotype threat	Inzlicht, McKay, & Aronson, 2006
Regulating speech	Muraven & Slessareva, 2003

hence more mentally demanding than being in a smaller crowd of people) reduced instances of helping a person find a lost contact lens (Cohen & Spacacan, 1978). It is possible that other factors, aside from self-control (e.g., difficult tasks, crowding, stress), that influence glucose levels also influence prosocial behavior. Factors associated with suboptimally low glucose levels are likely to be associated with reduced helping, whereas factors associated with optimal glucose levels are likely to be associated with increased helping.

Glycogen and Prosocial Behavior: Increasing Prosocial Behavior

It is plausible that helping behavior is decreased when glycogen—glucose stored in the brain—is low. Glycogen use is similar to glucose use in that exerting self-control may decrease brain glycogen, rendering the brain less efficient and effective when glycogen levels are low (Gailliot, 2008). However, ironically, glycogen also exhibits a "rebound" effect; that is, stored glycogen reserves in the brain rise to higher levels if they are repeatedly and chronically depleted (Gailliot, 2008). This may explain why practicing self-control causes self-control to be less easily fatigued (Baumeister, Gailliot, DeWall, & Oaten, 2006; Gailliot, Plant, Butz, & Baumeister, 2007; Oaten & Cheng, 2005, 2006a, 2006b). Exerting self-control repeatedly might deplete brain glycogen, thereby causing brain glycogen reserves to increase later on. This process may be one means by which prosocial behavior increases with practice. Exerting self-control, including while helping others, might decrease glycogen, causing glycogen levels to increase over time, thereby increasing helping behavior when glycogen stores otherwise would have been low.

The idea that repeated glycogen depletion can increase helping behavior parallels the idea that helping requires people to learn how to help with repeated exposures to opportunities to help. Following exertion of self-control and initial glucose depletion, a person may lack the energy to help the first time he or she encounters someone in need of help. However, the person may be more able to help a needy other after repeatedly being exposed to similar helping situations because of the expansion of glycogen stores in the brain, which allow more energy to be expended.

Upon subsequent exposures, the person develops a schema or learns how to help and respond, so he or she is more likely to respond by helping. Decreases in glucose and perhaps glycogen might follow initial helping situations, as the person learns how to help in that situation. The amount of metabolites used up during the learning process might be related to the amount of metabolites needed to form the new neuronal connections created during the process of learning to help. This idea fits with data indicating that decreases in glucose, or ego-depletion (Baumeister, Bratslavsky, Muraven, & Tice, 1998; Muraven, Tice, & Baumeister, 1998), are associated with greater learning. Specifically, among participants performing a Stroop color-naming task, larger decreases in glucose were associated with larger increases in improvement, assessed when participants completed the same Stroop task 2 weeks later (Gailliot, 2007).

The depletion of glucose might occur at least partly because people learn as they exert self-control. Learning self-control might require relatively large amounts of metabolites (e.g., glucose, glycogen), because additional metabolites would be required for the neural growth underlying the learning of self-control.

ENERGY AND PROSOCIAL BEHAVIOR

In this section, I speculate about additional possible links among energy, metabolism, and prosocial behavior. One idea is that other kinds of energy might help to explain prosocial behavior. People are biological organisms, and life is sustained though the acquisition and use of metabolic energy. Much of the human psyche might therefore be related to metabolism. Therefore, helping behavior, which is effortful and metabolically demanding, might be reduced when metabolic stores throughout the brain and body are low or less easily distributable (e.g., when liver glycogen stores are adequate but ineffectively distributed to brain processes involved in self-control). Eating healthily, for example, might increase helping because it improves metabolism. Vitamins and minerals help to catalyze metabolic processes, thereby allowing the extraction of additional metabolic energy from a given amount of resources.

Metabolic demands other than those that support helping behavior could plausibly divert metabolism from helping-related brain processes. Examples of these demands are reproduction (which requires the building of certain hormones) and experiencing or resisting physical illness (e.g., growing cancer cells, fighting pathogens). This idea is supported by studies indicating that metabolic needs of one biological process can be met by decreasing metabolic supplies to other processes (Gailliot, 2009). For instance, evidence has suggested that increases in brain size and metabolism are met by decreases in the size and metabolism of the gut, muscles, and other tissues.

Air is obviously important to metabolism (e.g., the brain uses oxygen as a primary resource), so the contents of the air may influence prosocial behavior. Levels of oxygen, carbon dioxide, and pollutants, for example, might influence helping behavior by influencing metabolism. Higher levels of carbon dioxide might undermine metabolic processes, given that carbon dioxide is a waste product of brain activity, and thereby decrease helping behavior.

Helping behavior might be increased when internal metabolic processes are displaced from the individual into the external environment. For instance, friends help a person cope with stress (e.g., by providing solutions to problems), and this can be viewed as reducing the metabolic demand the individual would experience to cope without social support (e.g., having to think about the problem at greater length). Increased social support may therefore increase helping behavior (see chap. 3, this volume). Tools, and perhaps culture more broadly, might also increase helping by displacing metabolic demands. Metabolic demands of thermoregulation (i.e., keeping the body at a constant temperature) and transportation (e.g., walking) are met by tools such as air conditioners, heaters, bicycles, and automobiles. These may increase helping by freeing up metabolic resources for processes underlying prosocial behavior. This suggests an optimistic possibility: Modern environments, which are often denigrated because they increase demands and stress, might compensate to some extent by making prosocial behavior easier to perform.

Improved metabolic efficiency might also increase helping behavior. For instance, as people learn and develop skills (e.g., playing the computer game Tetris), the amount of metabolic energy required to use those skills decreases (Haier, Siegel, Tang, Abel, & Buchsbaum, 1992). Such improved efficiency may free up metabolism for processes that would increase prosocial behavior. Other factors that increase efficiency (e.g., observing efficient, rather than less efficient, models so as to behave later in more efficient ways) might also increase helping.

Other ideas are more speculative, yet could prove useful. One is that the self can be viewed as an entity possessing a strength that is relative to the nonself (the world, external factors). When the self is weakened (e.g., because of stress or illness), the nonself has a stronger influence. For example, weakening the self by wearing a heavy, versus a light, backpack makes traversing a certain distance more tiring (Proffitt, Stefanucci, Banton, & Epstein, 2003). Strengthening the self physically, by taking medications that reduce physical pain, has been found to reduce the impact of negative social events (DeWall & Baumeister, 2007), as if the self becomes stronger and the external environment has a weaker influence.

Finally, to speculate even further, an energy perspective on money might be relevant to prosocial behavior. Money can be viewed as a symbol of prior energy expended (e.g., pay for previous work) and of future energy acquisition (e.g., the potential to acquire food, the potential to save energy by taking a taxi rather than walking). In this sense, money is intrinsically intertwined with metabolism. Money represents factors that will cause one to acquire, save, and use different amounts of metabolites. The muscles will use fewer metabolites while taking a taxi than walking, and the additional monetary cost of taking a taxi thus intertwines with metabolism.

CONCLUSION

To summarize, prosocial behavior can be effortful and may be reduced or made less feasible by low levels of metabolic energy (glucose). When glucose levels are above suboptimal, helping should be easier and more common. Metabolism and energy more broadly might be important to consider when studying prosocial motivation and behavior. Factors that influence helping behavior might include levels of stored metabolites, the displacement or relinquishment of internal metabolic demands, air content, and efficiency of other metabolic processes.

REFERENCES

Baumeister, R. F., Bratslavsky, E., Muraven, M., & Tice, D. M. (1998). Ego depletion: Is the active self a limited resource? *Journal of Personality and Social Psychology, 74*, 1252–1265.

Baumeister, R. F., DeWall, C. N., Ciarocco, N. J., & Twenge, J. M. (2005). Social exclusion impairs self-regulation. *Journal of Personality and Social Psychology, 88*, 589–604.

Baumeister, R. F., Gailliot, M. T., DeWall, C. N., & Oaten, M. (2006). Self-regulation and personality: Strength-boosting interventions and trait moderators of ego depletion. *Journal of Personality, 74*, 1773–1802.

Baumeister, R. F., Heatherton, T. F., & Tice, D. M. (1994). *Losing control: How and why people fail at self-regulation*. San Diego, CA: Academic Press.

Baumeister, R. F., Vohs, K., & Tice, D. M. (2007). The strength model of self-control. *Current Directions in Psychological Science, 16*, 351–355.

Bruyneel, S., Dewitte, S., Franses, P. H. B. F., & DeKimpe, M. G. (2005). *Why consumers buy lottery tickets when the sun goes down on them: The depleting nature of weather-induced bad moods*. Unpublished manuscript, Catholic University of Leuven, Leuven, Belgium.

Ciarocco, N. J., Sommer, K. L., & Baumeister, R. F. (2001). Ostracism and ego depletion: The strains of silence. *Personality and Social Psychology Bulletin, 27*, 1156–1163.

Cohen, S., & Spacapan, S. (1978). The aftereffects of stress: An attentional interpretation. *Environmental Psychology and Nonverbal Behavior, 3*, 43–57.

Dawkins, R. (1976). *The selfish gene*. London: Oxford University Press.

DeWall, C. N., & Baumeister, R. F. (2007). *Acetaminophen reduces psychologically hurt feelings and pain*. Unpublished manuscript.

DeWall, C. N., Baumeister, R. F., Stillman, T. F., & Gailliot, M. T. (2006). Violence restrained: Effects of self-regulation and its depletion on aggression. *Journal of Experimental Social Psychology, 43*, 62–76.

Fairclough, S. H., & Houston, K. (2004). A metabolic measure of mental effort. *Biological Psychology, 66*, 177–190.

Finkel, E. J., & Campbell, W. K. (2001). Self-control and accommodation in close relationships: An interdependence analysis. *Journal of Personality and Social Psychology, 81*, 263–277.

Finkel, E. J., Campbell, W. K., Brunell, A. B., Dalton, A. N., Scarbeck, S. J., & Chartrand, T. L. (2006). High-maintenance interaction: Inefficient social coordination impairs self-regulation. *Journal of Personality and Social Psychology, 91*, 456–475.

Frankenhaeuser, M., & Lundberg, U. (1977). The influence of cognitive set on performance and arousal under different noise loads. *Motivation and Emotion, 1*, 139–149.

Gailliot, M. T. (2007). *Ego depletion and glucose depletion might be caused by learning*. Unpublished manuscript.

Gailliot, M. T. (2008). Unlocking the energy dynamics of executive functioning: Linking executive functioning to brain glycogen. *Perspectives on Psychological Science, 3*, 139–149.

Gailliot, M. T. (2009). *A limited energy theory of human functioning: Thought and behavior as constrained by metabolic tradeoffs.* Manuscript submitted for publication.

Gailliot, M. T., & Baumeister, R. F. (2007a). The physiology of willpower: Linking blood glucose to self-control. *Personality and Social Psychology Review, 11*, 303–327.

Gailliot, M. T., & Baumeister, R. F. (2007b). Self-regulation and sexual restraint: Dispositionally and temporarily poor self-regulatory abilities contribute to failures at restraining sexual behavior. *Personality and Social Psychology Bulletin, 33*, 173–186.

Gailliot, M. T., Baumeister, R. F., DeWall, C. N., Maner, J. K., Plant, E. A., Tice, D. M., et al. (2007). Self-control relies on glucose as a limited energy source: Willpower is more than a metaphor. *Journal of Personality and Social Psychology, 92*, 325–336.

Gailliot, M. T., Baumeister, R. F., Maner, J. K., & DeWall, C. N. (2006). *Helping behavior is reduced by prior self-regulation and increased by glucose-containing drinks.* Unpublished manuscript.

Gailliot, M. T., Plant, E. A., Butz, D. A., & Baumeister, R. F. (2007). Increasing self-regulatory strength can reduce the depleting effect of suppressing stereotypes. *Personality and Social Psychology Bulletin, 33*, 281–294.

Gailliot, M. T., Schmeichel, B. J., & Maner, J. K. (2007). Differentiating the effects of self-control and self-esteem on reactions to mortality salience. *Journal of Experimental Social Psychology, 43*, 894–901.

Glass, D. C., & Singer, J. E. (1972). *Urban stress: Experiments on noise and social stressors.* New York: Academic Press.

Gordijn, E. H., Hindriks, I., Koomen, W., Dijksterhuis, A., & Van Knippenberg, A. (2004). Consequences of stereotype suppression and internal suppression motivation: A self-regulation approach. *Personality and Social Psychology Bulletin, 30*, 212–224.

Govorun, O., & Payne, B. K. (2006). Ego-depletion and prejudice: Separating automatic and controlled components. *Social Cognition, 24*, 111–136.

Haier, R. J., Siegel, B., Tang, C., Abel, L., & Buchsbaum, M. S. (1992). Intelligence and changes in regional cerebral metabolic rate following learning. *Intelligence, 16*, 415–426.

Hockey, R. H. (1983). *Stress and fatigue in human performance.* New York: Wiley.

Inzlicht, M., McKay, L., & Aronson, J. (2006). Stigma as ego depletion: How being the target of prejudice affects self-control. *Psychological Science, 17*, 262–269.

Kahan, D., Polivy, J., & Herman, C. P. (2003). Conformity and dietary disinhibition: A test of the ego-strength model of self-regulation. *International Journal of Eating Disorders, 32*, 165–171.

Miyamoto, Y., & Schwarz, N. (2006). When conveying a message may hurt the relationship: Cultural differences in the difficulty of using an answering machine. *Journal of Experimental Social Psychology, 42*, 540–547.

Moller, A. C., Deci, E. L., & Ryan, R. M. (2006). Choice and ego-depletion: The moderating role of autonomy. *Personality and Social Psychology Bulletin, 32*, 1024–1036.

Muraven, M., & Baumeister, R. F. (2000). Self-regulation and depletion of limited resources: Does self-control resemble a muscle? *Psychological Bulletin, 126*, 247–259.

Muraven, M., Collins, R. L., & Neinhaus, K. (2002). Self-control and alcohol restraint: An initial application of the self-control strength model. *Psychology of Addictive Behaviors, 16*, 113–120.

Muraven, M., Collins, R. L., Shiffman, S., & Paty, J. A. (2005). Daily fluctuations in self-control demands and alcohol intake. *Psychology of Addictive Behaviors, 19*, 140–147.

Muraven, M., & Slessareva, E. (2003). Mechanisms of self-control failure: Motivation and limited resources. *Personality and Social Psychology Bulletin, 29*, 894–906.

Muraven, M., Tice, D. M., & Baumeister, R. F. (1998). Self-control as a limited resource: Regulatory depletion patterns. *Journal of Personality and Social Psychology, 74*, 774–789.

Oaten, M., & Cheng, K. (2005). *Improvements in self-control from financial monitoring.* Unpublished manuscript.

Oaten, M., & Cheng, K. (2006a). Longitudinal gains in self-regulation from regular physical exercise. *British Journal of Health Psychology, 11*, 717–733.

Oaten, M., & Cheng, K. (2006b). Improved self-control: The benefits of a regular program of academic study. *Basic and Applied Social Psychology, 28*, 1–16.

Proffitt, D. R., Stefanucci, J., Banton, T., & Epstein, W. (2003). The role of effort in perceiving distance. *Psychological Science, 14*, 106–112.

Richeson, J. A., Baird, A. A., Gordon, H. I., Heatherton, T. F., Wyland, C. L., Trawalter, S., & Shelton, J. N. (2003). An fMRI investigation of the impact of interracial contact on executive function. *Nature Neuroscience*, 6, 1323–1328.

Richeson, J. A., & Shelton, J. N. (2003). When prejudice does not pay: Effects of interracial contact on executive function. *Psychological Science, 14*, 287–290.

Richeson, J. A., & Trawalter, S. (2005). Why do interracial interactions impair executive function? A resource depletion account. *Journal of Personality and Social Psychology*, 88, 934–947.

Richeson, J. A., Trawalter, S., & Shelton, J. N. (2005). African Americans' implicit racial attitudes and the depletion of executive function after interracial interactions. *Social Cognition, 23*, 336–352.

Rotton, J., Olszewski, D., Charleton, M., & Soler, E. (1978). Loud speech, conglomerate noise, and behavioral aftereffects. *Journal of Applied Psychology*, 63, 360–365.

Ryan, A. H., & Warner, M. (1936). The effect of automobile driving on the reactions of the driver. *The American Journal of Psychology*, 48, 403–421.

Schmeichel, B. J., Demaree, H. A., Robinson, J. L., & Pu, J. (2006). Ego depletion by response exaggeration. *Journal of Experimental Social Psychology*, 42, 95–102.

Schmeichel, B. J., Vohs, K. D., & Baumeister, R. F. (2003). Intellectual performance and ego depletion: Role of the self in logical reasoning and other information processing. *Journal of Personality and Social Psychology*, 85, 33–46.

Seely, E. A., & Gardner, W. L. (2003). The "selfless" and self-regulation: The role of chronic other-orientation in averting self-regulatory depletion. *Self and Identity, 2*, 103–117.

Shamosh, N. A., & Gray, J. R. (2007). The relation between fluid intelligence and self-regulatory depletion. *Cognition and Emotion, 21*, 1833–1843.

Sherrod, D. R., & Downs, R. (1974). Environmental determinants of altruism: The effects of stimulus overload and perceived control on helping. *Journal of Experimental Social Psychology, 10*, 468–479.

Shoda, Y., Mischel, W., & Peake, P. K. (1990). Predicting adolescent cognitive and self-regulatory competencies from preschool delay of gratification: Identifying diagnostic conditions. *Developmental Psychology, 26*, 978–986.

Stirling, L. J., & Yeomans, M. R. (2004). Effects of exposure to a forbidden food on eating in restrained and unrestrained women. *International Journal of Eating Disorders, 35*, 59–68.

Stucke, T. S., & Baumeister, R. F. (2006). Ego depletion and aggressive behavior: Is the inhibition of aggression a limited resource? *European Journal of Social Psychology, 36*, 1–13.

Tangney, J. P., Baumeister, R. F., & Boone, A. L. (2004). High self-control predicts good adjustment, less pathology, better grades, and interpersonal success. *Journal of Personality, 72*, 271–322.

Trawalter, S., & Richeson, J. A. (2006). Regulatory focus and executive function after interracial interactions. *Journal of Experimental Social Psychology, 42*, 406–412.

Vohs, K. D., Baumeister, R. F., & Ciarocco, N. J. (2005). Self-regulation and self-presentation: Regulatory resource depletion impairs impression management and effortful self-presentation depletes regulatory resources. *Journal of Personality and Social Psychology, 88*, 632–657.

Vohs, K. D., & Faber, R. J. (2007). Spent resources: Self-regulatory resource availability affects impulse buying. *Journal of Consumer Research, 33*, 537–547.

Vohs, K. D., & Heatherton, T. F. (2000). Self-regulatory failure: A resource-depletion approach. *Psychological Science, 11*, 249–254.

Vohs, K. D., & Schmeichel, B. J. (2003). Self-regulation and the extended now: Controlling the self alters the subjective experience of time. *Journal of Personality and Social Psychology, 85*, 217–230.

Wallace, H. M., & Baumeister, R. F. (2002). The effects of success versus failure feedback on further self-control. *Self and Identity, 11*, 35–41.

Webb, T. L., & Sheeran, P. (2003). Can implementation intentions help to overcome ego-depletion? *Journal of Experimental Social Psychology, 39*, 279–286.

10

HELPING RELATIONS AS STATUS RELATIONS

ARIE NADLER, SAMER HALABI, GAL HARAPZ-GORODEISKY, AND YAEL BEN-DAVID

Most, if not all, human societies tell us that we should be sensitive to the plight of our fellow human beings, and if we fail to respond to others in need, we are likely to incur social costs and be labeled *immoral.* This emphasis on the importance of helping others has also been reflected in social psychological research. As the chapters in this volume indicate, for almost 50 years social psychological research has been concerned with specifying the conditions under which helping is more or less likely, the psychological forces that propel this behavior, and the demographic and personality characteristics that foster it. Social psychologists have paid less attention to the fact that helping relations also imply different power relations between an agent who has more knowledge or resources and a recipient who is dependent on help. This view of helping relations has important implications for the conceptualization of prosocial behavior. These conceptual and applied implications are discussed toward the end of this chapter.

Preparation of this chapter was supported by the Argentina Chair for Research in the Social Psychology of Conflict and Cooperation, Tel Aviv University.

Our research team has pursued work on this topic within the *threat to self-esteem* model of seeking and receiving help (Nadler & Fisher, 1986) and the more recent *helping relations as status relations* model (Nadler, 2002). The two models differ in that the first focuses on interpersonal helping relations and the second on intergroup helping relations, but they are related in two major respects: (a) both view helping relations as power relations, and (b) both consider the consequences of social inequality for the willingness to seek and receive help and not only to helping others.

We begin this chapter by addressing the general link between helping and unequal power between helper and recipient, continue with a brief discussion of the threat to self-esteem model of reactions to help, and then devote most of the chapter to our more recent research based on viewing intergroup helping as status relations (i.e., Intergroup Helping as Status Relations [IHSR] model). This model explains how groups use helping relations as implicit mechanisms to create, maintain, or challenge status relations among them.

HELPING AND POWER: SOCIAL INEQUALITY IN HELPING AND THE THREAT TO SELF-ESTEEM MODEL OF REACTIONS TO HELP

The process of human development is one of gradual movement from complete reliance on powerful others to self-reliance. This process is often stormy and conflictual (e.g., in adolescence), and it reaches its conclusion when we have become independent and learned to be proud of our achievements as our own. Later in life, as we grow frail in body and mind, we lament our need to become dependent on more powerful others. In general, self-reliance implies strength, and dependence on others implies weakness. This fact finds expression in the positive value assigned to independence in various cultures around the globe. The Koran states: "A charitable deed must be done as a duty man owes to man, so that it conveys no idea of the superiority of the giver or the inferiority of the receiver." The Jewish prayer book instructs us to pray to God to "not make us need others' gifts or loans" (cited in Nadler & Fisher, 1986, p. 82). Societies seem to have a conflicted attitude toward helping relations: They tell us to give a helping hand to all who are in need, but they warn us about seeking or accepting help when we ourselves are in need (for related ideas, see chap. 11, this volume).

The link between helping and power is echoed in the behavioral and social sciences in general and in social psychology in particular. In the field of animal behavior, research on helping in groups of babblers (i.e., small birds that live in intricate social systems) indicates that helping within a group is unidirectional and downward: The more dominant member in the group displays its advantage by sharing with lower status members (Zahavi, 1997). This downward helping has been viewed as an example of the "handicap principle" (Zahavi, 1997), which states that individual animals advertise their genetic fitness by expending energy in the short run to gain long-term genetic advantages (for a review of evolutionary perspectives on prosocial behavior, see chap. 2, this volume). In applying this principle to human altruism, Boone (1998) noted that "expenditure of time or energy in altruistic behavior signals the sender's ability to bear the short-term costs of cooperation . . ." and therefore results in increased status (p. 12). On the intergroup level, Alexis de Tocqueville (1835/1956), in his book *Democracy in America*, written 200 years ago, observed that members of advantaged groups exercise their dominance over low-status groups by providing them with assistance, and Marcel Mauss (1907/1954), in a classic essay entitled "The Gift," described the custom of Potlach, whereby tribal leaders confer lavish gifts on other tribal leaders to signify their clan's superiority.

Research in social psychology has also noted the association between helping and status. Van Vugt and his colleagues reported that helping within the group is motivated by the helper's desire to obtain status in the group (Hardy & Van Vugt, 2006; Van Vugt & De Cremer, 1999), and Brown and Smart (1991) reported that people remedy injuries to their self-esteem by helping others. Research on reactions to help and willingness to seek it indicates that when receiving help implies inferiority on ego-central dimensions, people in need prefer to continue to suffer hardships rather than seek assistance (Nadler, 1991). Under such conditions of implied weakness or inferiority, people who receive help respond negatively to its receipt (Fisher, Nadler, & Whitcher-Alagna, 1982).

The view that being dependent on others implies relative weakness and being able to provide help implies strength and higher status is the underlying conceptual building block of the threat to self-esteem model of reactions to help (Nadler & Fisher, 1986). The model begins with the observation that receiving help is a mixed blessing as far as a recipient's self-esteem is concerned. On the one hand, in addition to the instrumental benefits of allowing the recipient to overcome his or her predicament, it can be a message of caring from the helper. When this is the case, recipients are said to respond favorably to receiving aid (i.e., to feel good about themselves and have positive perceptions of and feelings toward the helper), and help is said to be a self-supportive experience for the recipient. On the other hand, receiving help can be experienced as self-threatening, because it may convey a message about the recipient's lower standing relative to the helper. When this occurs, recipients feel bad about themselves, view the helper unfavorably, and work to terminate the self-threatening dependency.

Self-help efforts to regain independence are made when recipients believe they can regain self-reliance by investing in such efforts. Research within this model indicates that characteristics of (a) the help (e.g., its ego-centrality; Nadler & Fisher, 1986), (b) the recipient (e.g., dispositional self-esteem; Nadler, 1997), and (c) the helper (e.g., his or her similarity to the recipient;

Nadler & Fisher, 1986) determine the amount of self-threat experienced, the recipient's willingness to seek or receive aid, and the consequences of receiving it.

This body of research reflects a shift from the more common emphasis on trying to understand who gives help to whom and why to research designed to illuminate the other side of the helping relationship: the recipients and their willingness to seek and receive help. Moreover, this research portrays helping relations as complex and multifaceted rather than uniformly positive, which casts doubt on the universal advocacy of providing help (for a discussion of egoistic motives for prosocial behavior, see chap. 1, this volume).

Recently, the model of IHSR (Nadler, 2002; Nadler & Halabi, 2006) has extended this view on helping relations to the analysis of intergroup relations. The model builds on an integration of key concepts from research on helping relations and research on social identities (Turner & Reynolds, 2001). It is based on the idea that when social identity is salient, people's behavior is partially explicable by their group membership and needs to be analyzed in terms of theories concerning intergroup relations.

INTERGROUP HELPING AS STATUS RELATIONS: THE MODEL AND SUPPORTIVE RESEARCH

The model suggests (a) that by giving to an outgroup, ingroup members maintain their group's positive distinctiveness; (b) that willingness to receive help from the outgroup signifies acceptance of the receiving group's lower status; and (c) that by refusing to seek or receive help from the outgroup, the low-status group members challenge the existing social inequality. Such reluctance to be dependent on the high-status group is an expression of the low-status group's motivation for equality with the outgroup.

Before proceeding to explain the model and provide evidence for it, we should note that we do not claim that people give to outgroup members only because they want to assert their superiority or that people are willing to be dependent on an outgroup only because they accept their group's relatively low social standing. Although group members in need of help often misperceive assistance from rival outgroups as driven by ulterior motives (Fisher, Nadler, Little, & Saguy, 2008), help across group boundaries is often driven by empathy and genuine caring (see, e.g., chap. 20, this volume). We often help people from other ethnic groups or cultures because of our common humanity and not to assert the ingroup's positive distinctiveness. Yet, as was the case with interpersonal helping, intergroup helping is a multifaceted phenomenon. It can be driven by empathy and caring or by a desire to maintain dominance and social advantage. A full understanding of intergroup helping necessitates attention to both aspects.

The model suggests that the dynamics of intergroup helping viewed in terms of status relations depend on characteristics of the social structure (i.e., security of status relations), the help (i.e., autonomy or dependency orientation of the help), and the individual group member (i.e., ingroup identification; Nadler, 2002; Nadler & Halabi, 2006). In the following section, we outline the model's three layers and then describe briefly some of the data that support its assertions.

Structural Characteristics: Security of Intergroup Status Relations

Social identity theory tells us that secure status relations are viewed as stable and legitimate, and insecure relations are perceived as illegitimate and unstable. To make this important distinction clearer, we consider status relations between men and women in past centuries and at present. In the past, men's social advantage over women was a secure social phenomenon. When a status hierarchy is secure, neither the high- nor the low-status group is motivated to accomplish change in the status quo. When a status hierarchy is perceived as insecure, members of high-status groups remain motivated to defend their social advantage, but members of low-status groups view their disadvantaged position as changeable and are therefore motivated to change the status quo (Tajfel & Turner, 1986). The reasons for changes in perceived status security may include large-scale cultural changes (e.g., a shift from a stratified to an egalitarian social ideology) or perception by either or both of the low- and high-status groups that the existing hierarchy is changeable.

How is the phenomenon of perceived security of status hierarchy reflected in intergroup helping relations? When status relations are secure, members of advantaged groups are expected to care for members of the lower status group and help them whenever help is needed. Members of low-status groups, in contrast, are expected to be receptive to the high-status group's help. Under such conditions, repeated instances of a unidirectional downward flow of assistance are consistent with, and behaviorally solidify, the status hierarchy.

To continue the previous example, in past centuries when status relations between men and women were perceived as secure, women were routinely helped by men to confront daily economic challenges. This help contributed to the institutionalization and maintenance of gender inequality.

When status relations are perceived as insecure, members of the high-status group are expected to defend their social advantage by reinforcing the low-status group's dependence by assisting them even when assistance is not requested. Turning to the low-status group, when status relations are insecure, dependency on the high-status group's help is inconsistent with the motivation for equality, and members of the low-status group are therefore unlikely to seek or receive help from the high-status group. An example of this is the criticism sometimes leveled at affirmative action programs: Because assistance is given on the basis of membership in a social category (e.g., people of color), such programs may amplify the view of the receiving group as being dependent on and relatively inferior to the giving group (Pratkanis & Turner, 1996, 1999). Yet these dynamics depend on the second building block of the model, which is the autonomy- or dependency-oriented nature of help.

Characteristics of the Help: Dependency- Versus Autonomy-Oriented Help

Dependency-oriented help consists of providing recipients with full solutions to their problem. Recipients of such help are viewed as relatively weak and unable to help themselves. They are viewed by the helper and themselves as chronically dependent on outside sources to overcome their difficulties. *Autonomy-oriented help* consists of giving recipients assistance in the form of tools they can use to solve the problem on their own. When helpers provide such help, they view the needy others as able to help themselves (Nadler, 1997, 1998).

Autonomy-oriented help is unique in circumventing the self-threat inherent in dependency. The recipient is helped but retains self-control and a large measure of independence. To use a well-known metaphor, dependency-oriented help consists of giving cooked fish to the hungry, whereas autonomy-oriented help consists of giving them fishing rods and teaching them how to fish. The merits of autonomy-oriented help were noted by Maimonides, a Jewish physician and philosopher who in the 13th century described the highest form of generosity as giving those in need a loan or teaching them a skill so that they will not need to ask for assistance again in the future (Maimonides, 1998).

In our research, we obtained evidence for the lesser effectiveness of dependency-oriented help. In one study, we measured three different styles of dealing with difficulties among high school students: (a) seeking dependency-oriented help (asking for solutions to the problem), (b) seeking autonomy-oriented help (asking for instructions on how to solve the problem on one's own), and (c) avoiding seeking help. We subsequently correlated these expressed behavioral preferences with students' grade point average (GPA) at the end of the school year and found that stronger preference for dependency-oriented help predicted a lower GPA at the end of the school year (Harpaz-Gorodeisky & Nadler, 2008).

Within this perspective to intergroup helping relations, we argue that the way in which group members use helping relations to maintain or challenge intergroup status relations in secure and insecure status hierarchies depends on the dependency or autonomy orientation of the help. Regarding members of the high-status group, when status relations are secure, dependency-oriented assistance will be the normative behavior of "taking care" of those who are lesser than one. An example of this is when, in previous centuries, men took care of all the financial needs of women. Such a normatively based downward provision of dependency-oriented assistance has reinforced and solidified gender inequality. In contrast, in insecure status hierarchies, the low-status group is viewed by the high-status group as threatening to bring it down from its lofty perch of social privilege. Under these conditions the high-status group is motivated to defend against this threat by giving dependency-oriented help to the low-status group. The paternalistic behavior of men toward women during the past century, when gender inequality was increasingly challenged, constitutes an example of efforts by the high-status group to maintain its relatively advantaged position by taking care of the threatening low-status group (Jackman, 1994). On the other hand, low-status groups are expected to welcome dependency-oriented help when status relations are viewed as secure. Under these conditions, they expect the high-status group to take care of them. When status relations are insecure, members of low-status groups are expected to resist dependency-oriented help from the high-status outgroup. The objections of women to what they viewed as men's paternalism are illustrative of this (Jackman, 1994). Under these conditions, members of low-status groups are expected to be receptive to help only when it is viewed as a tool to expedite future independence and equal status (i.e., autonomy-oriented help).

Characteristics of Individual Group Members

The third layer of the model suggests that these relationships will be affected by group members' individual characteristics. Consistent with much research within the social identity perspective, these patterns are likely to be affected by the level of ingroup identification (Ellemers, Spears, & Doosje, 1999). In addition, people with a dispositional need for relatively stratified social environments, assessed with measures of social dominance orientation (SDO; Sidanius & Pratto, 1999) or authoritarianism (Altemeyer, 1982), are more likely than people with more egalitarian tendencies to use helping as a tool to establish social dominance.

Table 10.1 summarizes this analysis: When intergroup status relations are secure, the high-status group is expected to provide dependency-oriented help to the low-status group whenever it needs it, and members of low-status groups are expected to be receptive to such help. When status relations are insecure, members of the high-status group will give the low-status group dependency-oriented help even when this help is neither requested nor needed. Under these conditions of status insecurity, members of low-status groups are expected to avoid seeking dependency-oriented help from the high-status outgroup and react negatively to its receipt. They will be receptive only to autonomy-oriented help. Finally, these patterns are expected to be

TABLE 10.1
Intergroup Helping Relations as Affected by Perceived Legitimacy and Stability of Power Relations Between Groups

Variable	High-status group	Low-status group
	Low perceived legitimacy and stability of differential power	
Motivation	• High motivation to reassert power and diffuse threat to social dominance	• High motivation to challenge existing hierarchy
Behavior	• Increased effort to provide dependency-oriented help to low-status outgroup	• No help seeking from high-status outgroup • Unwillingness to receive assumptive help from high-status outgroup • Greater willingness to seek and receive autonomy-oriented help
	High perceived legitimacy and stability of differential power	
Motivation	• Medium to low motivation of the high-status group to assert power	• Low motivation to challenge existing hierarchy. Dependency on the high-status group is relatively nonthreatening to social identity.
Behavior	• High level of giving dependency-oriented help to low-status outgroup	• High level of seeking dependency-oriented help from high-status out-group • Willingness to receive dependency-oriented help from high-status outgroup

affected by relevant personal characteristics of group members. In the next section, we review empirical findings that bear on the validity of the model.

HELPING AND STATUS: EMPIRICAL FINDINGS

We begin this section with findings demonstrating that group members respond to a threat to their group identity by helping the outgroup that initiated the threat. Because such help is thought to be motivated by group members' tendency to defend against threat to their social identity, we call it *defensive helping* (Nadler, Harpaz-Gorodeisky, & Ben-David, in press). Support for the assertion that helping can be a means of maintaining a group's positive identity creates an empirical background for examining hypotheses based on the IHSR, the model that deals with helping relations between high- and low-status groups. The studies to be described here tested the model's hypothesis that when status relations are insecure, members of low-status groups are unwilling to seek or receive dependency-oriented help from the high-status group. We close this empirical section by describing a recent experiment indicating, in line with the IHSR model, that under conditions of status insecurity, the high-status group maintains its social advantage by giving dependency-oriented help to the low-status group. This experiment also demonstrates that by inducing a common identity within the low-status outgroup, defensive helping (i.e., giving dependency-oriented help to the source of threat) disappears and is replaced by the giving of autonomy-oriented help.

Defensive Helping: Giving Help to Defend Against Threat to Social Identity

In the first phase of our research, we sought to substantiate the assertion that group members can remedy threat to ingroup identity by giving help to the source of the threat. In the language of social identity theory, group members achieve positive ingroup distinctiveness by positive means such as helping the outgroup. Consistent with research conducted within the social identity perspective, the motivation for defensive helping should be highest when group members experience threat to social identity and have a high level of ingroup identification. Our aim was to substantiate this phenomenon and, by doing so, to lend empirical support to our assertion that group members can defend against threats to social identity by making the source of threat dependent on their help. For example, members of a reputable team suffer a threat to their group's relative advantage when learning that another team had solved an important problem which their group had failed to solve. The concept of defensive helping suggests that they will try to remedy this threat by giving the source of the threat (i.e., the outgroup) assistance in solving a subsequent problems even when they had not been asked to do so. By using such a tactic, the more reputable team makes an implicit statement about the outgroup's relative disadvantage, which finds expression in its need to be dependent on their group's assistance. Further, because high ingroup identifiers experience a higher level of threat when their group's advantage is questioned than do low ingroup identifiers, their motivation to remedy these threats through defensive helping is also expected to be higher.

Recent research examined this proposition in two experimental studies (Nadler et al., in press, Studies 1 & 2). The first was a 2 (high vs. low threat to social identity) × 2 (high vs. low ingroup identification) minimal group experiment in which participants who had or had not been induced to identify with the ingroup experienced a high or a low level of threat to their group identity from an outgroup. The main dependent measure was the amount of help participants gave to the outgroup member. A significant

Threat to Social Identity × Ingroup Identification interaction indicated that in line with our prediction, high identifiers who had experienced a high level of threat to the ingroup's identity gave the most help to this source of threat. We interpret this result as indicating that the high identifiers in the high-threat condition who had experienced the greatest threat to their social identity defended against this threat and upheld their positive ingroup distinctiveness by helping the source of threat.

Although this finding is consistent with expectations, it is open to alternative interpretations. One such alternative is that high identifiers whose social identity was threatened experienced more negative affect than did their counterparts in the other experimental conditions, and they gave more help to remedy their negative mood (e.g., Cialdini, Darby, & Vincent, 1973). This interpretation would suggest that the increased helping in the high-identification, high-threat condition reflects an individual-level process of remedying a negative mood rather than an intergroup behavior aimed to increase the ingroup's positive distinctiveness.

To examine this alternative, and to replicate the initial finding and extend its external validity, we ran a second experiment using real groups. In this experiment, high school students could provide help to a student from another school that had been previously presented as posing a threat to participants' social identity (i.e., the other school had been described as outperforming their school on important dimensions) or to a student from another school that had been presented as not posing a similar threat (i.e., the other school had been described as similar to their school on these dimensions). Because defensive helping is help given to the source of threat to social identity, we reasoned that if our interpretation of defensive helping was valid, more help would be given to a member of an outgroup that was the source of threat to social identity than to a member of an outgroup that did not pose such a threat. If, however, increased helping is driven by individual-level processes such as remedying a negative mood, more help should be given by high identifiers who experienced threat to their ingroup identity, regardless of whether the outgroup that was the target of help was or was not the source of the threat, than by high identifiers who had not experienced a threat to identity.

Participants could give the students from the other school help on eight problems that they had been said to have difficulties with. We found that participants gave significantly more help to an outgroup that had posed a threat to social identity than to an outgroup that had not, or to an outgroup in a no-threat control condition ($M = 6.36$, $SD = 1.03$; $M = 3.63$, $SD = 1.3$; and $M = 3.50$, $SD = 0.89$, respectively). This finding corroborates the concept of defensive helping. Further, consistent with the findings of the first experiment, defensive helping characterized the behavior of high ingroup identifiers. Finally, the findings indicate that defensive help is given without much regard for the recipient's actual state of need. High identifiers in the outgroup source of threat condition provided help on difficult problems and on easy problems. Participants in the other conditions gave help according to need. They helped more on difficult than easy problems.

Beyond ingroup members' level of ingroup identification, research has indicated that group members' level of social dominance orientation (SDO; Sidanius & Pratto, 1999) also moderates the phenomenon of defensive helping. Because members of high-status groups who are high on SDO are more likely to be threatened by challenges to their group's status than are those low on SDO, they are more likely to engage in defensive helping. This hypothesis was supported in a study by Halabi, Dovidio, and Nadler (2008) that focused on defensive helping of the high-status group within the context of Israeli society. We found that high SDO Israeli Jews gave Israeli Arabs (i.e., high- and low-status groups in Israeli society, respectively) more dependency-oriented help than did low SDO participants. Conversely, participants who scored low on the SDO scale tended to give more autonomy-oriented help. These findings indicate that individuals who are motivated to uphold their group's high status in a stratified social setting do so by giving dependency-oriented help to the low-status group.

Taken together, these experiments demonstrate the validity of the concept of defensive helping and corroborate the link between helping and status. This link is important because social identity research has tended to consider only negative and injurious means (e.g., discrimination) used by group members to cope with threats to social identity. Our findings set the stage for an examination of predictions derived from the IHSR, which says that this and related phenomena depend on the perceived security of status relations and the autonomy- or dependency-oriented nature of the help. Here, we consider two major predictions. The first is that members of disadvantaged groups will be reluctant to seek or receive help from a high-status group when status relations are perceived as insecure and help is dependency oriented. The second is that when status relations are insecure and the advantaged position of the high-status group is threatened, its members will defend their group's high status by giving dependency-oriented help to the low-status group.

Receptivity of Low-Status Group Members to Help: Effects of Perceived Stability of Status Relations and Autonomy- or Dependency-Oriented Nature of the Help

To examine the receptivity of the low-status group members to help from the high-status group under conditions of secure and insecure status relations, we first conducted a minimal group experiment that was followed by studies using real groups. Our main prediction was that because depending on the high-status group when status relations are unstable is inconsistent with the low-status group members' motivation for greater equality with the high-status group, receipt of help under these conditions will threaten group members' social identity. This will lead to characteristic reactions such as devaluation of and discrimination against the high-status helper. We obtained support for this prediction in a 2 (help vs. no help) × 2 (stable vs. unstable status) minimal group experiment: Members of low-status groups who had been induced to view status relations with the high-status group as unstable and later received help from that out-group experienced the highest level of threat to their social identity and exhibited the greatest level of discrimination against it (Nadler & Halabi, 2006, Experiment 1).

A second experiment examined the same hypothesis with real groups. In this experiment, Israeli Arabs, who are a low-status group in Israeli society, received help from an Israeli Arab or an Israeli Jew to complete a scholastic task. Prior to that, half of the participants received information that the status differences between Israelis and Arabs in Israel have been narrowing in the past decade. The other half were informed that the status differences between the two groups have remained unchanged. These communications created the unstable and stable status relations conditions, respectively.

The results supported our prediction. Arab participants who were told that their group was making headway in closing the gap with the higher status Israeli Jews responded most negatively to help from an Israeli Jew. They had the lowest affect scores (M = 4.3, *SD* = 0.67, with the other Ms ranging from 5.3 to 5.5), the highest ingroup favoritism score (M = 554, *SD* = 334, with the other Ms ranging from 200 to 295), and the lowest evaluation of the outgroup (M = 2.7, *SD* = 0.98, with the other Ms ranging between 4.3 and 4.5). Other experiments in this research program indicated, in line with the model's prediction, that this phenomenon of negative reactions to receiving help from a high-status out-group under conditions of status instability is especially true for members of low-status groups who identify strongly with their group.

In another experiment, we examined the model's predictions that when status relations are perceived as unstable, members of low-status groups will be most reluctant to seek needed help from a member of the outgroup, and that this reluctance will be more characteristic of *high ingroup* identifiers and occur only when help is dependency oriented. This experiment is particularly important because it examines the interaction between variables that represent the three conceptual layers in the IHSR model: the structural level of security of status relations (i.e., stability of status relations), the type of help (i.e., autonomy- or dependency-oriented help), and individual group members' characteristics (i.e., ingroup identification).

We ran an experiment in which high school students, who had or had not been induced to identify with their school (i.e., by writing a paragraph about the unique attributes of their school or a paragraph on a neutral topic, respectively), could seek autonomy- or dependency-oriented help (i.e., seek a hint or the solution to difficult math problems, respectively) from a member of another school that was higher in academic status than their own school (i.e., a school reputed to be the most prestigious high school in northern Israel). Further, half of the participants were under the impression that the scholastic differences between the two schools had been stable over the years, and the other half thought these differences were consistently narrowing. The results fully supported our predictions. The least help seeking occurred when high identifiers perceived the status relations to be unstable. This reluctance to seek help was indexed by willingness to seek dependency-oriented help. Specifically, although no participant in the unstable status/high identification cell was willing to seek dependency-oriented help from the high-status group, participants in the other three cells showed a similar medium-level degree of willingness to seek dependency-oriented help from members of the high-status group. There were no differences in help seeking when help was autonomy oriented.

Dependency- and Autonomy-Oriented Help Given by the High-Status Group: Effects of Status Stability and Self-Categorization

We now describe a recent experiment that supports the model's hypothesis that high-status group members give dependency-oriented help to the low-status group when the status relation between the groups is unstable. This increase in defensive helping is not expected to occur with autonomy-oriented help. Another purpose of the experiment was to study the role of self-categorization processes as mechanisms that can be used to reduce defensive helping. Consistent with theoretical and empirical work on the common ingroup identity model proposed by Gaertner and Dovidio (2000), inclusion of a low-status group that threatens the high-status group's advantaged position in a larger common group should reduce the motivation of the high-status group to maintain its advantaged position by defensively helping the low-status group.

We conducted a field experiment with real groups to explore these hypotheses (Nadler et al., in press, Study 3). We set up a computer interaction between Israeli high school students in a prestigious high school in the Negev region of Israel (the high-status group) and a member of a high school from the same region with substantially lower academic status (the low-status group). The status difference between the two schools was ascertained by an independent check with a group of teachers from the region. Participants belonged to the high-status school. Half of them received information that the status differences between them and the lower status outgroup was narrowing, and the other half received information that the difference had remained unchanged over the past 5 years. This constituted the manipulation of perceived status instability and stability, respectively.

Further, one third of the participants were exposed to a manipulation that highlighted the uniqueness of their school compared with other schools in the Negev region (the salient ingroup identity condition), and another third was exposed to information that stressed the uniqueness of schools in the Negev region compared with other schools in the country (the common ingroup identity condition). Since both the ingroup and the outgroup were situated in the Negev, this manipulation induced a common ingroup identity with the outgroup. The last third of the participants, in the control condition, were exposed to neutral information.

Participants later interacted with a student from the low-status outgroup who was said to experience difficulties in solving mathematical problems, and they were able to provide them with dependency- or autonomy-oriented help (i.e., a hint that might allow the recipient to solve the problem on his or her own vs. an obvious clue that would lead everyone to the correct answer, respectively). The amount of autonomy- and dependency-oriented help that was given to the outgroup member served as the main dependent measure.

A significant 2 (stable vs. unstable status) × 3 (in-group identity, common identity, control) interaction indicated, in line with our predictions, that the most dependency-oriented help was given to the outgroup when status relations had been described as unstable *and* ingroup identity had been made salient. It is important that the least dependency-oriented help was given to the outgroup when status relations had been described as unstable and a common group identity had been induced. There were no differences between the three identity conditions in the stable-status condition.

A mirror-image empirical picture emerged for the measure of autonomy-oriented help. A significant 2 × 3 interaction indicated that in the unstable status condition most autonomy-oriented help was given to the outgroup when it was perceived as sharing a common identity with the ingroup. The least autonomy-oriented help was given to the outgroup in the condition in which the identity of the ingroup had been made salient. No differences were observed among the three identity groups in the stable status condition.

SUMMARY AND CONCLUSIONS

The findings support the view that intergroup helping relations are, in part, social mechanisms through which group members maintain or challenge existing status hierarchies. Regarding the giving of help, the phenomenon of defensive helping indicates that group members remedy threats to the ingroup by giving help to the outgroup that poses the threat. Moreover, the finding that such help is given on problems that are perceived as either easy or difficult suggests that such helping constitutes the helper's wish to assert his or her superior social position rather than being a response to the recipient's difficulties.

This research also supports the major assertions of the IHSR model of intergroup helping. In the face of information that status relations are unstable, a high-status group works to maintain its advantage by giving more dependency-oriented help to the low-status group, and low-status groups avoid seeking such help and respond negatively to its receipt.

Finally, self-categorization processes play an important role. When status relations are unstable and the high- and low-status groups share a common ingroup identity, the pattern of helping changes dramatically. Under these conditions, members of the high-status group adopt a helping strategy that promotes the recipient's future self-reliance by providing autonomy-oriented help. The velvet glove that humiliates the recipient through dependency-oriented help changes to a helping hand that makes it more likely that the recipient will climb the ladder toward future self-reliance.

Security of Status Relations: The Conceptual Link Between the Threat to Self-Esteem Model and the IHSR Model

The evidence gathered thus far indicates that helping relations are multicausal and multifaceted. It reminds us that although helping is often driven by genuine caring for the recipient and is an expression of the nobler side of human nature (see chap. 1, this volume), it can also be an expression of social inequality. Both our early work on the threat to self-esteem aroused by being helped and the more recent work guided by the IHSR model tell the same story. In interpersonal and intergroup interactions, helping can humiliate recipients or support and empower them. The concept of *security of status relations* is central at both levels of analysis, and it is a conceptual link between the two models of helping relations. Although this concept was developed within the context of research on intergroup relations, it is also applicable to the analysis of interpersonal helping relations. On both levels of analysis, when recipients' lower social position (e.g., low status within the group, disadvantaged position within society) is perceived as both legitimate and stable, dependency is viewed as consistent with recipients' social standing and their expectations and self-definition. Under these conditions, being helped is not self-threatening. Dependency on more powerful others conforms to the recipients' and benefactors' expectations. Helping interactions between parents and their children, an experienced manager and a new employee, or a teacher and a student are typical of dependency relationships. Social inequality and the ensuing dependency of the weaker party on the stronger one are often consensual.

The situation is different when status differences between two individuals or two groups are perceived by the less powerful participants as illegitimate, unstable, or both. Under these conditions, recipients desire and expect equality, and being helped is inconsistent with these expectations and therefore self-threatening. Our early research, which indicates that people find reliance on similar others who serve as a frame of reference for self-judgments to be self-threatening, corroborates this line of reasoning (Nadler, Fisher, & Ben-Itzhak, 1983). Further, the finding that people with high self-esteem are more threatened by dependency than those with low self-esteem is also consistent with this conception (Nadler, 1997). In fact, people with higher self-esteem are more likely to view dependency on others as unstable and illegitimate.

This emphasis on the security of status relations connects the threat to self-esteem and IHSR models of helping relations. Both models contend that when status relations are secure, dependency of the weak on the strong is consistent with expectations and is therefore a source of support for the recipient. When these hierarchical relations are insecure, dependency is inconsistent with self-expectations and is threatening to self-esteem. By the same token, dependency on another group when status relations are perceived as insecure is threatening to social identity. In both cases individuals and group members are likely to shy away from seeking help and respond negatively to its receipt.

Both models tell us that the degree of threat to self-esteem or social identity inherent in receiving help shapes recipients' behavioral responses. If the level of threat is high, whether viewing themselves as individuals or group members, people shy away from seeking help. In cases in which threatening help is offered, the threat to self-esteem model of reactions to help predicts that if recipients believe they can change the situation of uneasy dependency and attain independence, they will do so by attempting to help themselves. Thus, because self-threatening help induces negative affect (Nadler & Fisher, 1986), receiving it will be a greater source of discomfort in the short term than receiving nonthreatening help. But because the receipt of self-threatening help motivates recipients to invest more in self-help efforts than the receipt of nonthreatening help, it is also more likely to lead to long-term independence. The same is expected to hold for intergroup helping relations. Under conditions of status insecurity, members of low-status groups who are offered help may try to end their dependency on the higher status group. Thus, help that is given to a group with insecure low status (i.e., perceptions that inferiority is illegitimate and/or unstable) is a precursor of change toward independent coping on both the interpersonal and intergroup levels.

The Meaning of Help: Transient or Chronic Dependency

The receipt of help can denote either transient or chronic recipient dependency. Some of the characteristics of help addressed by our research illuminate this distinction. Dependency-oriented help signals chronic dependency. Such help is predicated on the belief that the recipient is not strong enough to contribute to solving the problem (Brickman et al., 1982). Autonomy-oriented help signals that the recipient's dependency is transient, and it encourages the recipient to help solve the problem.

Another characteristic of help that is linked with chronic dependency is its assumptive nature (Schneider, Major, Luthanen, & Crocker, 1996).

Assumptive help is given without waiting for the recipient to ask for it and implies the helper's assumption that the recipient cannot solve the problem autonomously and needs help. Such help is more likely to imply chronic dependency than is help given in response to the recipient's request. In our research, the helping was assumptive. This raises the possibility that under conditions similar to the ones we have studied, receiving help would not have been a source of threat to self-esteem or social identity if it had been given in response to the recipient's request.

A final characteristic of help that is related to its implications for chronic or transient dependency is the ease or difficulty of the task on which help is given. When help is given assumptively on easy problems, it implies more chronic dependency than when it is given only on difficult problems on which almost anyone would need help.

Final Comments

We conclude by addressing two general issues raised by viewing helping relations as power relations. The first concerns the definition of a helpful act, which depends on whether we adopt the recipient's or the helper's perspective. The second concerns the implications of this approach for social change on the interpersonal and intergroup levels. Regarding the first issue, the definition of help, it is important to consider the conditions under which receiving help implies chronic dependency. Is assistance really helpful if it is driven by the helper's caring and empathy but encourages long-term dependency? From the helper's perspective it is, but from the recipient's perspective it may not be.

The view of helping relations as power relations has important conceptual and applied implications. On the conceptual level, it deepens the understanding of the motivational dynamics that underlie phenomena such as giving, seeking, or receiving help. The amount and kind of help that is given or is sought after can reflect the helper's and the recipient's desire to maintain their position in the social hierarchy. Thus for example, individuals and groups may give dependency-oriented help in order to maintain perceptions of individual or group's relative worthiness, and people in need who desire greater equality may be receptive to help only when it is autonomy-oriented. This emphasis on the links between helping and power relations has implications for the long-term consequences of helping relations. It focuses on specifying the conditions under which helping relations constitute equality-based social relations in which help is viewed as a response to a transient state of need, which will result in an ultimate mutual independence. Alternatively, the need for help is viewed as an indication of chronic dependence and relative inferiority and helping as reinforcing inequality. These alternative views of helping have important implications for social contexts such as affirmative action programs (Nadler, 2009), international aid (Fisher et al., 2008), or peace-building projects (Nadler & Saguy, 2004). On a societal level, the shift from an inequality-based helping interaction to an equality-based interaction is characteristic of periods of large-scale social change (e.g., when relations between the genders or ethnic groups become less rigidly stratified, or when two rival groups move from a competitive to a cooperative mode of interaction). The same thing happens between individuals (e.g., during times of organizational change, when an employee begins to expect greater equality with a supervisor). In these and similar instances, tensions related to helping may anticipate social change or be associated with it once status relations begin to change.

REFERENCES

Altemeyer, B. (1982). *Right-wing authoritarianism*. Winnipeg, Canada: University of Manitoba Press.

Boone, J. L. (1998). The evolution of magnanimity: When it is better to give than to receive. *Human Nature*, 9, 1–21.

Brickman, P., Rabinowitz, V. C., Karuza, J., Coates, D., Cohn, E., & Kidder, L. (1982). Models of helping and coping. *American Psychologist, 37*, 368–384.

Brown, J. D., & Smart, S. A. (1991). The self and social conduct: Linking self-representations to prosocial behavior. *Journal of Personality and Social Psychology*, 60, 368–375.

Cialdini, R. B., Darby, B. L., & Vincent, J. E. (1973). Transgression and altruism: A case for hedonism. *Journal of Experimental Social Psychology*, 9, 502–516.

de Tocqueville, A. (1956). *Democracy in America: Mentor book edition*. New York: New American Library. (Original work published in 1835)

Ellemers, N., Spears, R., & Doosje, B. (Eds.). (1999). *Social identity: Context, commitment, content*. Oxford, England: Blackwell.

Fisher, J. D., Nadler, A., Little, J. S., & Saguy, T. (2008). Help as a vehicle to reconciliation with particular reference to help for extreme health needs. In A. Nadler, T. Malloy, & J. D. Fisher (Eds.), *The social psychology of intergroup reconciliation* (pp. 447–471). New York: Oxford University Press.

Fisher, J. D., Nadler, A., & Whitcher-Alagna, S. (1982). Recipient reactions to aid: A conceptual review. *Psychological Bulletin, 91*, 27–54.

Gaertner, S. L., & Dovidio, J. F. (2000). *Reducing intergroup bias: The common ingroup identity model*. Philadelphia: Psychology Press.

Halabi, S., Dovidio, J. F., & Nadler, A. (2008). When and how high status groups offer help: Effects of social dominance orientation and status threat. *Political Psychology, 29*, 841–858.

Hardy, C., & Van Vugt, M. (2006). Nice guys finish first: The competitive altruism hypothesis. *Personality and Social Psychology Bulletin, 32*, 1402–1413.

Harpaz-Gorodeisky, G., & Nadler, A. (2008). *Help seeking styles and their links to school performance*. Unpublished manuscript.

Jackman, M. R. (1994). *The velvet glove: Paternalism and conflict in gender, class and race relations*. Berkeley: University of California Press.

Maimonides, M. (1998). *The Mishneh Torah*. New York: Rambam/Maimonides and Moznaim Publishers.

Mauss, M. (1954). *The gift: Forms and functions of exchange in archaic societies*. Glencoe, IL: Free Press. (Original work published 1907)

Nadler, A. (1991). Help-seeking behavior, psychological costs, and instrumental benefits. In M. S. Clark (Ed.), *Review of personality and social psychology* (Vol. 12, pp. 290–312). New York: Sage.

Nadler, A. (1997). Autonomous and dependent help seeking: Personality characteristics and the seeking of help. In B. R. Sarason, I. G. Sarason, & G. Pierce (Eds.), *Handbook of personality and social support* (pp. 258–302). New York: Plenum.

Nadler, A. (1998). Relationship, esteem, and achievement perspectives on autonomous and dependent help seeking. In S. A. Karabenick (Ed.), *Strategic help seeking: Implications for learning and teaching* (pp. 61–95). Mahwah, NJ: Erlbaum.

Nadler, A. (2002). Inter-group helping relations as power relations: Helping relations as affirming or challenging inter-group hierarchy. *Journal of Social Issues*, 58, 487–503.

Nadler, A. (in press). Interpersonal and intergroup helping: Implications for real world contexts. In S. Strumer & M. Snyder (Eds.), *The psychology of prosocial behavior: Group processes, intergroup relations and helping*. Oxford, England: Blackwell.

Nadler, A., & Fisher, J. D. (1986). The role of threat to self-esteem and perceived control in recipient reaction to help: Theory development and empirical validation. In L. Berkowitz (Ed.), *Advances in experimental social psychology* (pp. 81–121). New York: Academic Press.

Nadler, A., Fisher, J. D., & Ben-Itzhak, S. (1983).With a little help from my friend: Effects of single or multiple act aid as a function of donor and task characteristics. *Journal of Personality and Social Psychology*, *44*, 310–321.

Nadler, A., & Halabi, S. (2006). Intergroup helping as status relations: Effects of status stability, identification, and type of help on receptivity to high-status group's help. *Journal of Personality and Social Psychology*, *91*, 97–110.

Nadler, A., Harpaz-Gorodeisky, G., & Ben-David, Y. (2009). Defensive helping: Threat to group identity, ingroup identification, status stability, and common group identity as determinants of intergroup help-giving. *Journal of Personality and Social Psychology*.

Nadler, A., & Saguy, T. (2004). Trust building and reconciliation between adversarial groups: A social psychological perspective. In H. Langholtz and Chris E. Stout (Eds.), *The psychology of diplomacy* (pp. 29–47). Westport, CT: Praeger.

Pratkanis, A. R., & Turner, M. E. (1996). The proactive removal of discriminatory barriers: Affirmative action as effective help. *Journal of Social Issues, 52,* 111–132.

Pratkanis, A. R., & Turner, M. E. (1999). The significance of affirmative action for the souls of white folk: Further implications of a helping model. *Journal of Social Issues, 55,* 787–815.

Schneider, M. E., Major, B., Luhtanen, R., & Crocker, J. (1996). Social stigma and the potential costs of assumptive help. *Personality and Social Psychology Bulletin, 22,* 201–209.

Sidanius, J., & Pratto, F. (1999). *Social dominance: An intergroup theory of social hierarchy and oppression.* New York: Cambridge University Press.

Tajfel, H., & Turner, J. C. (1986). The social identity theory of intergroup behavior. In W. G. Austin & S. Worchel (Eds.), *The social psychology of intergroup relations* (pp. 7–24). Chicago: Nelson-Hall.

Turner, J. C., & Reynolds, K. J. (2001). The social identity perspective in intergroup relations: Theories, themes, and controversies. In R. Brown & S. L. Gaertner (Eds.), *Intergroup processes* (pp. 133–153). Oxford, England: Blackwell.

Van Vugt, M., & De Cremer, D. (1999). Helping the group or helping yourself? Social motives and group identity in resource dilemmas. *Journal of Personality and Social Psychology, 76,* 587–599.

Zahavi, A. (1997). *The handicap principle: A missing piece of Darwin's Puzzle.* New York: Oxford University Press.

11

COMPASSIONATE CALLOUSNESS: A TERROR MANAGEMENT PERSPECTIVE ON PROSOCIAL BEHAVIOR

GILAD HIRSCHBERGER

In the spring of 1942, Joseph Zeligman, a young German Jew, fled Nazi Germany to the neighboring Netherlands to seek refuge from Nazi persecution. He arrived with a group of other refugees at a small Dutch village and asked the local priest for a place to hide. The priest led the group to one of the farmers in his parish and asked the farmer to hide them in his barn. "Father," the farmer pleaded, "I sympathize with these people and appreciate and admire your efforts to help them, but if the Nazis discover that I am hiding Jews, they will kill us all. I cannot risk the lives of my wife and children for strangers I do not know." "The concerns you raise are grave," responded the priest, "and there is no question that your fear is justified. You would be endangering your family, and I certainly understand and respect your decision." As he turned to walk away the priest exclaimed, "It all comes down to a question of faith." Several minutes later the farmer came running after the priest. "Father, please come back, I will help these people and provide them with shelter." For the following 3 years until the war ended, Joseph Zeligman and eight other Jewish refugees hid in the barn, where they were cared for by the farmer.

The decision to help this group of Jewish refugees and save their lives involved feelings of compassion tainted with self-protective fears. The story of Joseph Zeligman illustrates the dilemma many rescuers face when helping persecuted victims, especially when the decision to help becomes a life or death question not only for the people needing rescue but also for the rescuers. This chapter provides a social psychological perspective on some of the processes evident in the rescue of Zeligman and his group. It is an attempt to shed light on the ambivalence aroused by requests for help and the determinants of the decision to help or not to help. In considering these issues, I adopt the perspective of terror management theory (TMT; Greenberg, Pyszczynski, & Solomon, 1997) to explain the existential underpinnings of the action tendencies people experience and exhibit toward others in need, because recent terror management research has provided insight into the processes that promote or impede prosocial behavior. Here, I focus mainly on the contrast between organ donation and charitable contributions, and on helping people with physical disabilities compared with helping nondisabled people. These examples help to illuminate the reasons underlying the ambivalence people often experience following requests for prosocial behavior when personal death is salient.

AMBIVALENT REACTIONS TO REQUESTS FOR HELP

Behaviors intended to serve others' needs are exalted by most if not all human cultures. People who display kindness and compassion toward others and are willing to sacrifice their personal resources for the benefit of others are held in the highest esteem and often serve as exemplars of cultural and religious values (see chap. 1, this volume). However, despite the high value placed on prosocial behavior, there is often considerable reluctance to engage in such behavior. This reluctance is not uniform, however; there are specific causes and circumstances that inhibit compassionate and caring responses.

Classic studies of bystander interventions in emergencies (e.g., Darley & Latané, 1968) and Darley and Batson's (1973) research on Good Samaritans indicate that seemingly trivial factors may impede prosocial behavior. If acting prosocially reinforces important norms and values and increases the helper's positive emotions and self-esteem, then it may seem odd that variables such as the presence of other people or the pressure of time constraints should stand in the way of achieving such valued benefits.

Over the past few years, research has revealed some of the reasons people disengage from prosocial behavior and has suggested that egoistic concerns may sometimes override prosocial inclinations (see chaps. 1, 4, 5, and 7, this volume). In one study, when participants could not justify their behavior as being consistent with their self-interest, they were reluctant to behave prosocially (Holmes, Miller, & Lerner, 2002). In other cases, the disengagement from prosocial behavior seems to be a defensive maneuver designed to protect the self from threat (see chap. 10, this volume). A series of studies found that the threat of social exclusion significantly reduced prosocial behavior, implying that when the focus shifts from the plight of others to self-focused threats, the capacity for empathic understanding is impaired (Twenge, Baumeister, DeWall, Ciarocco, & Bartels, 2007; see also chap. 1, this volume).

However, egotistical and self-protective concerns do not always entail a reluctance or refusal to behave prosocially. In fact, such seemingly self-focused concerns may, in some cases, have the opposite effect and increase prosocial behavior. Such is the case when prosocial behavior restores self-esteem after a failure (e.g., Brown & Smart, 1991), regulates negative affect (Cialdini et al., 1997), or enables one group to maintain superiority over another while appearing to be benevolent (see chap. 10, this volume). Thus, prosocial behavior can serve numerous human needs, some of which are selfish and others of which reflect genuine empathy (e.g., chap. 1, this volume).

Because prosocial behavior is highly regarded by society, people cannot simply refrain from prosocial behavior without rationalizing their decision. According to Crandall (2000), people must be able to justify their rejecting, avoidant, and disparaging behavior toward others as somehow fair, appropriate, and judicious. Similarly, Bandura (1998) contended that inhumane treatment of others requires moral disengagement, which facilitates emotional distancing and self-justification. Primo Levi (1981), a well-known author and Holocaust survivor, observed that the operators of gas chambers reduced their victims to subhuman objects, not only because of inherent cruelty but also because it was necessary to dehumanize their victims in order to kill them without being overwhelmed by guilt. These processes of justification, dehumanization, and moral disengagement are elaborate rationalizations that enable the observer to reject and gain distance from the other without experiencing severe pangs of conscience.

Because so many different behaviors fall into the prosocial category, it is not surprising that variables that predict prosocial behavior in one setting are unable to do so with other types of prosocial behavior in other settings (see chap. 1, this volume). Although ambivalence seems to characterize many people's reactions to calls for prosocial behavior, some activities more than others seem to elicit mixed emotions, and some prosocial opportunities arouse greater reluctance than others. This ambivalence is clearly evident in the dissonance between attitudes and behaviors concerning posthumous organ donations.

The Organ Donation Dilemma

The general reluctance to donate organs, despite positive attitudes toward organ donation (e.g., Nolan & Spanos, 1989), is an example of ambivalence about prosocial actions. This particular discrepancy between attitudes and behavior is perplexing because posthumous organ donation imposes no tangible cost, unlike other charitable behaviors that carry a tangible cost in money, effort, or time. Even if consent to donate organs is obtained when one is alive, the actual donation takes place after death—when one no longer needs physical organs. Thus, the willingness to donate organs posthumously should exceed willingness to engage in other forms of prosocial behavior that exert real, tangible costs. Organ donation presents an opportunity to benefit others, endorse important personal and cultural values, and be regarded highly by society at no personal cost. We obviously need an alternative to a rational account of the discrepancy between positive attitudes toward organ donation and the relatively low rate of actually allowing one's organs to be used after one dies.

Ambivalence Toward Disability

People with physical disabilities are a stigmatized group that elicits considerable ambivalence and discomfort among nondisabled peers. Research has revealed that emotional reactions to people with physical disabilities include both negative and positive emotions (e.g., Livneh, 1985). People may experience a sense of aversion and disgust, and at the same time display a desire to be egalitarian and fair (e.g., Jones et al., 1984; Scheier, Carver, Schulz, Glass, & Katz, 1978). In addition, they may experience denigrating emotional reactions, such as pity, that convey concern for the other together with condescension and emotional distancing (Florian, Mikulincer, & Hirschberger, 2000; Lazarus, 1991). As Livneh (1985) eloquently stated, "People with disabilities are construed as objects of ambivalence, triggering momentary, fluctuating favorable and unfavorable feelings of compassion and sympathy but also of aversion and distaste" (p. 37).

The apparent similarity in the ambivalence about organ donation and the ambivalence about people with physical disabilities raises a question: Is there a common process that may explain the similar reactions to two phenomena that at first sight seem to have little in common? One common denominator might be fear of death. Research has indicated that fear of death is related to both negative attitudes toward disabilities (e.g., Livneh, 1985) and reluctance to donate organs (e.g., Cleveland & Johnson, 1970). I examine this link between fear of death and inhibition of prosocial behavior from the perspective of TMT.

TERROR MANAGEMENT THEORY

TMT (Greenberg et al., 1997) contends that the need to manage the anxiety evoked by awareness of mortality lies at the heart of human motivation. The unique human predicament of having a life-sustaining drive, like all other creatures, but also possessing awareness of death creates an intolerable paradox: People cherish life but are aware that life is transient and temporary. Inability to escape this fate could render humans helpless and consumed with terror. But they have devised elaborate symbolic defense mechanisms that remove thoughts of death from consciousness. This "denial of death," as Becker (1973) called it, is an ongoing dynamic process that enables psychological equanimity much of the time.

According to TMT, two primary defense mechanisms ward off awareness of mortality: cultural worldview validation and self-esteem enhancement. Cultural worldviews are belief systems that imbue the world with meaning and structure. They offer answers to basic existential questions, such as wondering about the meaning and purpose of life and puzzling over what happens after death. The second defense mechanism, self-esteem, depends on successfully living up to cultural prescriptions and ideals. Together, these defenses offer the solace, in many cases, of literal immortality (in an afterlife), as well as the possibility of symbolic immortality (contributing to the group or one's culture in ways that survive one's physical death).

These terror management defenses have been conceptualized in a dual process model of *proximal* and *distal* defenses (Pyszczynski, Greenberg, & Solomon, 1999). The initial defenses, proximal defenses, focus on conscious death concerns and attempts to remove them from awareness. This may be achieved by actively suppressing death concerns, distracting oneself, shifting to an external focus of attention, avoiding self-reflective thought, or biasing inferential processes to deny one's vulnerability (Pyszczynski et al., 1999). The second line of defense, the distal defenses, comes into play only after people are distracted from death-related thoughts, and these thoughts begin to resurface but remain outside of focal attention (Pyszczynski et al., 1999). Distal defenses are symbolic in nature and consist of attempts to embed oneself in a symbolic meaning structure that offers death transcendence (Pyszczynski et al., 1999). The cultural worldview defense and self-esteem have been identified as primary distal terror management mechanisms.

Terror management researchers have primed thoughts of death (termed *mortality salience*) and examined cultural worldview defenses. They have obtained support for their hypotheses that mortality salience would increase motivation to (a) support punishment of social transgressors (e.g., Florian & Mikulincer, 1997), (b) exhibit positive reactions to one's ingroup and negative reactions to an outgroup (e.g., Greenberg et al., 1990), and (c) react aggressively against anyone who threatens their worldview (e.g., Hirschberger & Ein-Dor, 2006).

A body of TMT research that is particularly relevant to this chapter shows that human physicality poses a threat to terror management defenses. That is, reminders of the human body (e.g., the physical aspects of sex; breastfeeding) become aversive when mortality is salient (e.g., Cox,

Goldenberg, Arndt, & Pyszczynski, 2007; Goldenberg, McCoy, Pyszczynski, Greenberg, & Solomon, 2000; Goldenberg, Pyszczynski, McCoy, Greenberg, & Solomon, 1999). In addition, reminders of death amplify feelings of disgust toward body products or animals and strengthen the belief that humans are distinct from animals (Goldenberg et al., 2001).

People with physical disabilities are a stark reminder of human frailty and of one's susceptibility to devastating injury and to death. Thus, attitudes toward disability should be negative to the extent that one is concerned about death. Similarly, posthumous organ donation requests are an unsettling reminder of one's susceptibility to an untimely, tragic death. Early research has indicated an inverse relationship between fear of death and attitudes toward disability (e.g., Livneh, 1985), and between fear of death and the willingness to donate organs (Cleveland & Johnson, 1970). These findings provide the substrate for my contention that people with physical disabilities, or a request to donate one's organs after death, draw attention to the physical and vulnerable nature of human life, and as such are likely to become aversive when mortality is made salient.

Several terror management studies have examined whether the disruption of a terror management defense will result in an upsurge of death-related cognitions. These studies have found that inducing people to think about the physical aspects of sex (e.g., Goldenberg et al., 1999), problems in close relationships (e.g., Florian, Mikulincer, & Hirschberger, 2002), or threats to one's worldview (e.g., Schimel, Hayes, Williams, & Jahrig, 2007) increase the accessibility of death-related cognitions. These studies, recently conceptualized in terms of the death-thought accessibility (DTA) hypothesis (Schimel et al., 2007), have provided a method for identifying stimuli that elicit death awareness or salience and thereby pose a threat to terror management processes. In the next section, I demonstrate the applicability of TMT to prosocial behavior and argue that existential concerns may in some cases promote compassionate and caring responses, and in other cases induce callousness and reluctance to behave prosocially.

TERROR MANAGEMENT AND PROSOCIAL BEHAVIOR

> When your fear touches someone's pain it becomes pity; when your love touches someone's pain it becomes compassion. —Stephan Levine

Prosocial behavior is an important culturally influenced phenomenon that maintains solidarity and contributes to a sense of social cohesion. From a TMT perspective, prosocial behavior is a way to validate one's worldview and attain self-esteem; as such, it bolsters terror management defenses. As stated in one of the early summaries of TMT: "Providing help to those in need, especially those who are deemed praiseworthy of help within the culture, is one example of how meeting cultural standards of value provides individuals with a sense of personal value" (Solomon, Greenberg, & Pyszczynski, 1991, p. 120).

This notion of prosocial behavior as a means of defending against death is also rooted in many cultural and religious beliefs. For example, at the entrance to every Jewish graveyard a charity box stands inscribed with King Solomon's ancient proclamation, "Charity saves from death" (Proverbs 11:4). Similarly, in Charles Dickens' *A Christmas Carol*, Ebenezer Scrooge, a bitter old miser, undergoes a process of redemption after a frightening encounter with the Ghost of Christmas during which he visualizes his own lonely death. In line with this idea— that death reminders might increase prosocial behavior—Jonas, Schimel, Greenberg, and Pyszczynski (2002) conducted two studies to determine whether subtle reminders of death would strengthen prosocial attitudes and behavior. In Study 1, pedestrians were stopped in front of a funeral parlor (the mortality salience condition) or three blocks away (the control condition) and were asked questions pertaining to attitudes toward charitable organizations. Participants expressed more positive attitudes toward charitable causes in the mortality salience condition than in the control condition. Study 2 replicated the findings of Study 1 but focused on actual charitable behaviors. Participants primed with death reminders donated more money to a charitable cause than those in a control condition, but only to an ingroup (American) cause, not an international one. These studies provide initial evidence that death primes amplify prosocial attitudes and behavior.

Research following up these studies indicates that mortality salience does not have a uniform effect on prosocial tendencies, and that some people are more likely than others to respond to death primes with increased prosocial attitudes and values. A series of studies conducted by Joireman and Duell (2005) showed that people with a proself value orientation (those who were more inclined to promote themselves rather than help others) responded to mortality salience with stronger endorsement of self-transcendent values (for a review of theory and research on values and prosocial behavior, see chap. 12, this volume). However, individuals with a prosocial value orientation, who are habitually inclined to behave prosocially, did not change their value orientations following mortality salience.

Similarly, Joireman and Duell (2007) had participants complete Schwartz's (1992) value scale and found that participants with low self-transcendent values (characterized by values of self-enhancement and less concern for others) responded to mortality salience with more positive evaluations of charitable organizations. However, participants scoring high on self-transcendent values (characterized by more benevolent and universal values) did not change their evaluations following mortality salience. Both series of studies (Joireman & Duell, 2005, 2007) indicated that mortality salience affects prosocial values and attitudes mostly among people who are habitually inclined not to help others. The authors explained that such people, who are usually driven to serve their own interests, experience uncomfortable dissonance between their attitudes and the predominant values of their cultural worldview that become more accessible when death is made salient. Because prosocial behavior is endorsed by the worldview, self-focused individuals are motivated to shift their concern to others and close the gap between the culture's prescriptions and their own inclinations.

Do these findings suggest that mortality salience is a cure for egotism, and that once primed with death the Ebenezer Scrooges of the world will transform into Mother Teresas? Although the evidence seems to provide an affirmative answer, other evidence has suggested that the truth is more complicated. For example, Joireman and Duell (2005, Studies 2a and 2b) gave participants either a positive description of a proself individual ("works hard to reach her goals") or a negative description of a prosocial individual ("gets really involved with other people's problems") and examined whether these descriptions moderated the effect of mortality salience on self-transcendent values. They found that whereas a negative prosocial description did not reduce the endorsement of self-transcendent values among prosocials following mortality salience, a positive proself description reduced self-transcendent values among proselfs when death was salient. These findings suggest that people with a pro-self orientation will reduce, not increase, their endorsement of prosocial values when death is salient if they are provided with ample justification to do so. It seems that these people experience ambivalence about prosocial behavior when death is salient, and this ambivalence is resolved depending on the context.

THE DEATH–DISABILITY REJECTION HYPOTHESIS

The findings reviewed in this chapter thus far hint at the possibility that the link between death reminders and prosocial tendencies is not as simple as it seems. In fact, another line of terror management research has suggested that there are instances in which awareness of death is an impediment to prosocial behavior. In the past few years, research has consistently shown that mortality salience induces negative emotions, cognitions, and behavior toward people with physical disabilities. The first study along these lines found that when primed with death, male participants responded with less compassion toward people with physical disabilities (Hirschberger, Florian, & Mikulincer, 2005, Studies 1 & 2). Moreover, a description of a person with a physical disability elicited greater accessibility of death-related thoughts and greater fear of personal death (Hirschberger et al., 2005, Studies 3 & 4) than a description of a nondisabled person. It is interesting that these findings were obtained only when the person with a physical disability was described as an ingroup member (Israeli Jew) but not when the target was described as an outgroup member (Arab). Thus, the rejection of people with physical disabilities when death is salient cannot be attributed to the rejection and derogation of outgroup members found in previous terror management studies. It is actually the ingroup status of the victim and his or her similarity to the participant that amplifies the sense of personal threat when death is salient.

Because prosocial behavior and the fair treatment of people with illnesses and disabilities are important in most cultural worldviews, people cannot simply distance themselves emotionally from stigmatized others, especially when mortality is salient and worldview values are highly accessible. To do so, people must find ways to justify the rejection and mistreatment of others. To better understand the role of moral justification in the process of disengagement from people with physical disabilities, I (Hirschberger, 2006) examined whether the awareness of personal death induces greater blaming of people who suffered a severe physical injury. Blaming the victim may be experienced as a valid and morally defensible reason for turning away from people with physical disabilities without feeling callous or ruthless.

However, there are disagreements in the research literature on blame attributions regarding the conditions that elicit greater attributions of blame. Rational decision models such as Weiner's (1980) contend that people who are perceived to be responsible for their condition elicit more blame, whereas people who are perceived to be innocent victims elicit more sympathy. Recent developments in attribution theory have raised questions about the applicability of normative attribution models to all situations. According to the culpable control model (Alicke, 2000), when observers are motivationally biased they process information in a blame-validation mode—they may be motivated to blame the other to the extent that this bias favors their own immediate psychological needs. This conceptualization is consistent with motivational theories of attribution, such as the defensive attribution hypothesis (Shaver, 1970), which posits that outcome severity (i.e., degree of injury) is associated with greater attributions of blame, and with the just world hypothesis (Lerner, 1980), which suggests that innocent victims elicit greater blame. Predictions based on these two theories are directly opposite from predictions based on Weiner's (1980) model.

I (Hirschberger, 2006) hypothesized that mortality salience would induce a blame validation mode (Alicke, 2000), which would in turn bias the normative attribution process described by Weiner (1980). Specifically, mortality salience was hypothesized to induce a self-protective motivational state that would lead to blaming severely injured innocent victims. This defensive maneuver would enable individuals primed with thoughts of personal death to deny that tragic outcomes may be the result of random forces over which one has little or no control. Moreover, it would justify emotional distancing from innocent victims.

Three studies (Hirschberger, 2006, Studies 1–3) examined the effects of mortality salience on attributions of blame. In the first study, following a death prime, participants were randomly assigned to read a description of a day in the life of a person with a disability or parallel descriptions of a nondisabled person and a negatively portrayed other. In the second and third studies, an accident was described and participants were randomly assigned to read that the outcome of the accident was either mild (i.e., a broken limb) or severe (i.e., irreversible spinal cord injury). The third study also manipulated victim responsibility and portrayed a driver as either responsible (he drove through a red traffic light) or innocent (he drove through a green traffic light). In all three studies, attribution of blame was the dependent variable.

The results supported both normative and defensive models of attribution. When death was not salient, (a) less blame was attributed to a victim suffering from severe consequences than to a victim suffering mild consequences, and (b) less blame was attributed to innocent victims compared with victims responsible for their condition. These findings are consistent with Weiner's (1980) normative model. However, as expected, mortality salience biased the normative attribution process and induced more defensive processing. Specifically, the defensive model was supported by the following results: Death primes led to greater attributions of blame toward a victim suffering from a severe injury, but not toward a victim suffering from a mild injury or a negatively portrayed other, and to more attributions of blame toward an explicitly innocent victim suffering from a severe injury, but not toward a victim who could be held accountable for a severe injury, or toward any victim (innocent or accountable) incurring a mild injury. These findings indicate that under mortality salience conditions, innocent victims who are severely injured pose a threat to terror management mechanisms. A fourth study examining the impact of injury severity and victim responsibility on the accessibility of death-related cognition further validated this conclusion and indicated that severely injured innocent victims illicit the highest level of death-related cognitions (Hirschberger, 2006, Study 4). The findings from these four studies delineate two important components of victim blaming when death is salient: an irreversibly severe injury and an innocent victim. Only when the injury becomes a permanent physical disability and when the victim is clearly innocent are terror management mechanisms compromised, and observers feel compelled to resort to defensive blaming.

The results of these studies are also consistent with previous research indicating that mortality salience increases motivation to search for disparaging information about victims among participants high in personal need for structure (Landau et al., 2004). The findings also raise the possibility that the emotional distancing from people with physical disabilities found by Hirschberger et al. (2005) involves a process of moral justification in the form of victim blaming, which enables nondisabled observers to distance themselves from victims with little or no remorse. Future research should investigate this possibility in a single study to examine whether attributions of blame mediate the link between death salience and disability rejection.

Following the two studies on the emotional and cognitive processes involved in disability rejection when mortality is salient, we set out to examine whether the impact of mortality salience on the rejection of people with physical disabilities would also be seen in behavior. Our first such study (Hirschberger, Ein-Dor, & Almakias, 2008) was conducted at the central library of a large university. A female research assistant randomly handed out fliers to female students several meters from the entrance to the library. The fliers displayed the logo of the Kalima Institute, a fictional organization created for the purpose of the study that served as a mortality salience manipulation. In the mortality salience condition, the flier read: "Are you concerned about death? We can help! Call us and we can ease your suffering both physically and spiritually." In the control condition, the flier read: "Are you dealing with back or muscle pain? We can help! Call us and we can ease your suffering both physically and spiritually" (see Greenberg, Solomon, & Arndt, 2008, for further information on control conditions in terror management studies). The words *death* and *back or muscle pain* were printed in bold letters. As the participant entered the library, another research assistant approached her. In half of the cases the research assistant was seated in a wheelchair, and in the other half she approached the participant walking. When she reached the participant, she introduced herself as a psychology student working on a class research project and asked whether the participant would be willing to complete a questionnaire for her. The dependent measure was whether the participant consented or declined. The results indicated that when the research assistant was walking, death primes increased the percentage of people willing to help, a finding consistent with previous TMT studies on prosocial behavior (Jonas et al., 2002). When the research assistant was seated in a wheelchair, however, death primes had the opposite effect and led to a lower percentage of people agreeing to help.

Encouraged by these initial behavioral results, we were interested in examining whether more subtle behaviors would also reveal the death–disability rejection effect on helping behavior. For this purpose we focused on eye-movement behavior, which is reliably related to the early stages of visual attention (Findlay & Gilchrist, 2003). Recent research on eye-movements indicates that motivational and emotional processes may be revealed by eye-movement decisions (Balcetis & Dunning, 2006). In our study (Hirschberger, Ein-Dor, Caspi, Arzouan, & Zivotofsky, 2008, Study 2), participants were seated in front of a computer screen and, following a subliminal mortality salience procedure in which the word *death* or *pain* was briefly displayed (on the basis of Arndt, Greenberg, Pyszczynski, & Solomon, 1997), were presented with a series of picture matrices. Each matrix contained either four neutral pictures or three neutral pictures and one picture of a severely injured person. While participants were looking at the pictures, a camera followed their eye movements to determine where they were focusing their gaze. We found that death primes led to shorter gazes at the physical injury pictures but did not affect gaze duration for the neutral pictures. These results provide further evidence for our contention that death primes lead to emotional, cognitive, and behavioral disengagement from people with physical disabilities. The results also indicate that the death–disability rejection link occurs at the attentional level and that once a target person is identified as physically injured, the process of disengagement begins.

If attitudes toward disability are inextricably linked to deep-seated existential concerns, is there any hope for fundamentally changing the social status of people with physical disabilities? To answer this question, Ben-Naim, Weissman, and Hirschberger, (2008) conducted a study based on the contact hypothesis (e.g., Pettigrew, 1988) to determine whether interpersonal contact would lead nondisabled people to evaluate peers with disabilities more favorably when death was salient. Participants were primed with death or dental pain and were seated in a room with a research confederate who sat either in a wheelchair or in a regular chair. They were then assigned to one of two tasks: an individual task that would be completed in parallel, such that participant and confederate were each working on their own task, or a cooperative task that required the participant and the confederate to collaborate. Following completion of the task, the participant was asked to evaluate the confederate on a list of traits. In the individual task condition, mortality salience induced a more negative evaluation of the confederate in a wheelchair compared with the control condition. However, when participant and confederate engaged in a cooperative task, there were no significant differences in confederate evaluation between the mortality salience and the control conditions. This finding demonstrates the power of interpersonal contact in attenuating the death–disability rejection link.

THE COMPASSION EFFECT

If reactions to physical disability are negative, especially when death is salient, where is the supposed ambivalence between prosocial inclinations and self-protective concerns? The reliable replication of the death–disability rejection effect across a number of experimental paradigms using self-report, cognitive, and behavioral measures may suggest that there is no ambivalence at all. Rather, people with physical disabilities may be consistently treated in a negative manner. However, a closer look at our findings indicates that when death is not salient, observers' reactions to people with physical disabilities are often more positive than they are even toward nondisabled persons. For example, severely injured innocent victims elicited lower attributions of blame than did mildly injured victims in the death nonsalient condition (Hirschberger, 2006, Studies 2 & 3). Similarly, in the behavioral study of helping, participants responded more favorably to the request for help from the confederate in a wheelchair than from the walking confederate when death was not salient (Hirschberger, Ein-Dor, & Almakias 2008, Study 3), and in the study examining the moderating role of contact on the death–disability rejection process, the most favorable confederate evaluations were received by the confederate in a wheelchair in the death nonsalient condition (Ben-Naim et al., 2008). However, under mortality salience conditions, reactions to people with physical disabilities turned negative, resulting in emotional distancing, greater attributions of blame, greater reluctance to help, and more negative evaluations. The dramatic difference in attitudes and emotional reactions to disability between death salient and death nonsalient conditions suggests that normative compassionate responses to disability are overturned when death is salient because defensive needs override other-oriented concerns.

POSTHUMOUS ORGAN DONATIONS? OVER MY DEAD BODY!

Is the effect of mortality salience on the disinclination to behave prosocially limited to interactions with people with physical disabilities? Posthumous organ donation is a unique category of prosocial behavior that on the one hand entails no immediate tangible costs but on the other hand requires a donor to contemplate the eventuality of death. Research has indicated that stimuli related to death, such as human physicality, become aversive primarily under mortality salience conditions (e.g., Goldenberg et al., 2001). Similarly, research on the death–disability rejection link has indicated that emotional, cognitive, and behavioral disengagement from a person with a disability is accompanied by a greater accessibility of death thoughts (e.g., Hirschberger, 2006; Hirschberger et al., 2005). Thus, we (Hirschberger, Ein-Dor, & Almakias, 2008) hypothesized that because requests for organ donation probably arouse death awareness, donating one's organs will seem especially aversive under mortality salience conditions. To verify that this effect is specific to organ donation and not to other kinds of prosocial behavior, we compared contributions to an organ donation organization with donations of money to the poor.

Our first study (Hirschberger, Ein-Dor, & Almakias, 2008, Study 1), based on self-reports, was designed to determine whether mortality salience increases willingness to contribute to a charitable organization but reduces willingness to contribute to an organ donation organization. Following two open-ended questions about death or physical pain, participants read a description of either an organ donation organization or a charitable organization for the poor. Then, they were asked a series of questions about whether they would be willing to donate to the organization or volunteer to work for it. Mortality salience increased prosocial inclinations toward the charitable organization, validating earlier findings concerning terror management and prosocial behavior (Jonas et al., 2002). However, mortality salience had an opposite effect on willingness to contribute to the organ donation organization. In this case, as expected, death primes led to decreased willingness to contribute to the organization.

To explore the possibility that the results may reflect differences in negative affect elicited by the two organizations, we asked another sample of participants to read the organization descriptions and then to complete a measure of positive and negative affect (positive and negative affect schedule; Watson, Clark, & Tellegen, 1988) and a word-stem completion task assessing the accessibility of death-related thoughts. There were no significant differences in positive or negative affect between the organ donation and charitable donation organizations, but the organ donation organization elicited significantly greater death-thought accessibility compared with the charitable donation organization. This finding is consistent with the research on reactions to disability described earlier, which also revealed a relation between the disinclination to behave prosocially and elevated death-related cognitions.

In the next step of our investigation, we (Hirschberger, Ein-Dor, & Almakias, 2008, Study 2) examined whether the influence of mortality salience on attitudes toward prosocial causes would also be reflected in actual behavior. To do so, we used donation booths borrowed from Adi, an organ donation organization, and A Caring Heart, a charitable organization for the poor. The study was conducted in a central location on campus where many student activities take place. A research assistant handed out the mortality salience and pain salience fliers (described earlier) in random order. Fifteen meters away from the first research assistant, a second research assistant sat at a booth and solicited those who received fliers to come and make a donation. Research assistants were blind to experimental conditions and recorded only a sticker color that indicated to which condition the participant was assigned. In half of the cases, the booth belonged to A Caring Heart and participants were asked to make a monetary donation of 10 Israeli shekels (approximately U.S. $2.50). In the other half, the booth belonged to the Adi organization and participants were asked to sign an organ donation card. The dependent measure was whether participants consented or declined to donate to the organization. As expected, the results indicated that mortality salience increased the percentage of participants donating to a charitable organization but decreased the percentage of participants signing an organ donation card.

COMPASSIONATE CALLOUSNESS: THE OPERATING MECHANISMS

The findings reviewed so far provide convergent evidence across a range of methodologies, research paradigms, and populations that existential concerns play a role in prosocial behavior. However, these findings also indicate that the effect of death awareness on prosocial behavior may have diametrically opposite effects depending on the target population and the nature of the prosocial cause involved. Specifically, mortality salience increases prosocial attitudes and behavior toward charitable causes. But mortality salience also leads to (a) withdrawal of compassion from people with physical disabilities, (b) greater attributions of blame toward severely injured innocent victims, (c) stronger motivation to disparage innocent victims, (d) a lower rate of positive responses to a request for help from a person seated in a wheelchair, (e) a lower rate of agreeing to sign an organ donation card, and (f) greater gaze aversion from pictures of physically injured people.

The research described here illustrates two terror management scenarios: (a) successful execution of the terror management process, resulting in distal, symbolic defenses driving death-thoughts out of awareness; and (b) disruption of the terror management processes caused by reactivation of death-thoughts, which induces greater reliance on proximal defenses such as distancing and denial to remove thoughts of death. In both cases, death primes at first temporarily increase the level of death awareness, activating proximal defenses (Pyszczynski et al., 1999). In the case of charitable donations and helping a person without a disability, the normal terror management sequence takes place and distal defenses (i.e., compassion, social justice) are successfully used if death awareness reemerges. These defenses effectively remove thoughts of death from awareness. However, in the cases of posthumous organ donation and helping a person with a physical disability, the target needing help rekindles death awareness, rather than buffering against it, and the typical terror management process is thwarted. Consequently, the individual is stripped of the ability to rely on distal, symbolic defenses and instead must rely on proximal defense mechanisms for removing the threat of death awareness. Distancing from people with physical disabilities and walking away from an organ donation booth are two examples of concrete, proximal attempts to reduce one's exposure to death.

CONCLUSION

The growing body of research on terror management and prosocial attitudes and behavior has identified and clarified two reactions to others' needs (see also chaps. 1, 4, 5, and 7, this volume). One reaction is other focused and reflects a genuine desire to address the others' needs and provide help. The other reaction is self-focused and reflects the need to protect oneself and disengage from threat. This conclusion is in keeping with Stefan Zweig's (1938/1982) thinking on human responses to suffering in his novel, *Beware of Pity*:

> There are two kinds of pity: one, the weak and sentimental kind, which is really no more than the heart's impatience to be rid as quickly as possible of the painful emotion aroused by the sight of another's unhappiness, that pity which is not compassion, but only an instinctive desire to fortify one's own soul against the sufferings of another; and the other, the only one that counts, the unsentimental but creative kind, which knows what it is about and is determined to hold out, in patience and forbearance, to the very limit of its strength and even beyond. (p. vi)

The research reviewed here suggests that the inclination to behave prosocially when personal death is salient may be thwarted when the prosocial cause rekindles thoughts of death. In such cases, observers shift their gaze, feel less compassionate, attribute more blame, and ultimately refuse to help. The findings shed light on the dilemma facing the Dutch farmer described at the beginning of this chapter who eventually decided to help the Jewish refugees. He was motivated to help but also very aware of the possibility that he would die as a result. Research has not yet identified protective factors that might overturn this initial reaction. Future research should focus on the Dutch farmer's eventual decision to help because it is important to clarify the conditions that promote prosocial behavior when existential concerns and self-protective motives interfere with compassion and care for others in need.

REFERENCES

Alicke, M. D. (2000). Culpable control and the psychology of blame. *Psychological Bulletin, 126*, 556–574.

Arndt, J., Greenberg, J., Pyszczynski, T., & Solomon, S. (1997). Subliminal exposure to death-related stimuli increases defense of the cultural worldview. *Psychological Science, 8*, 379–385.

Balcetis, E., & Dunning, D. (2006). See what you want to see: Motivational influences on visual perception. *Journal of Personality and Social Psychology, 91*, 612–625.

Bandura, A. (1998). Mechanisms of moral disengagement. In W. Reich (Ed.), *Origins of terrorism: Psychologies, ideologies, theologies, states of mind* (pp. 161–191). New York: Cambridge University Press.

Becker, E. (1973). *The denial of death*. New York: Free Press.

Ben-Naim, S., Weissman, G., & Hirschberger, G. (2008). Strained interaction: Evidence that interpersonal contact moderates the death–disability rejection link. *Rehabilitation Psychology, 53*, 464–470.

Brown, J. D., & Smart, S. A. (1991). The self and social conduct: Linking self-representations to prosocial behavior. *Journal of Personality and Social Psychology, 60*, 368–384.

Cialdini, R. B., Brown, S. L., Lewis, B. P., Luce, C., & Neuberg, S. L. (1997). Reinterpreting the empathy–altruism relationship: When one into one equals oneness. *Journal of Personality and Social Psychology, 73*, 481–494.

Cleveland, S. E., & Johnson, D. L. (1970). Motivation and readiness of potential human tissue donors and non-donors. *Psychosomatic Medicine, 32*, 225–231.

Cox, C. R., Goldenberg, J. L., Arndt, J., & Pyszczynski, T. (2007). Mother's milk: An existential perspective on negative reactions to breastfeeding. *Personality and Social Psychology Bulletin, 33*, 110–122.

Crandall, C. S. (2000). Ideology and lay theories of stigma: The justification of stigmatization. In T. F. Heatherton, R. E. Kleck, M. R. Hebl, & J. G. Hull (Eds.), *The social psychology of stigma* (pp. 126–152). New York: Guilford Press.

Darley, J. M., & Batson, C. D. (1973). From Jerusalem to Jericho: A study of situational and dispositional variables in helping behavior. *Journal of Personality and Social Psychology, 27*, 100–108.

Darley, J. M., & Latané, B. (1968). Bystander intervention in emergencies: Diffusion of responsibility. *Journal of Personality and Social Psychology, 10*, 202–214.

Findlay, J. M., & Gilchrist, I. D. (2003). *Active vision: The psychology of looking and seeing*. New York: Oxford University Press.

Florian, V., & Mikulincer, M. (1997). Fear of death and the judgment of social transgressions: A multidimensional test of terror management theory. *Journal of Personality and Social Psychology, 73*, 369–380.

Florian, V., Mikulincer, M., & Hirschberger, G. (2000). The anatomy of a problematic emotion: Conceptualizing and measuring of the experience of pity. *Imagination, Cognition, and Personality, 19*, 3–12.

Florian, V., Mikulincer, M., & Hirschberger, G. (2002). The anxiety buffering function of close relationships: Evidence the relationship commitment acts as a terror management mechanism. *Journal of Personality and Social Psychology, 82*, 527–542.

Goldenberg, J. L., McCoy, S. K., Pyszczynksi, T., Greenberg, J., & Solomon, S. (2000). The body as a source of self-esteem: The effects of mortality salience on identification with one's body, interest in sex, and appearance monitoring. *Journal of Personality and Social Psychology, 79*, 118–130.

Goldenberg, J. L., Pyszczynski, T., Greenberg, J., Solomon, S., Kluck, B., & Cornwell, R. (2001). I am not an animal: Mortality salience, disgust, and the denial of human creatureliness. *Journal of Experimental Psychology: General, 130*, 427–435.

Goldenberg, J. L., Pyszczynski, T., McCoy, S. K., Greenberg, J., & Solomon, S. (1999). Death, sex, love, and neuroticism: Why is sex such a problem? *Journal of Personality and Social Psychology, 77*, 1173–1187.

Greenberg, J., Pyszczynski, T., & Solomon, S. (1997). Terror management theory of self-esteem and cultural worldviews: Empirical assessments and conceptual refinements. In P. M. Zanna (Ed.), *Advances in experimental social psychology* (Vol. 29, pp. 61–141). San Diego, CA: Academic Press.

Greenberg, J., Pyszczynski, T., Solomon, S., Rosenblatt, A., Veeder, M., Kirkland, S., et al. (1990). Evidence for terror management theory II: The effects of mortality salience on reactions to those who threaten or bolster the cultural worldview. *Journal of Personality and Social Psychology*, *58*, 308–318.

Greenberg, J., Solomon, S., & Arndt, J. (2008). A basic but uniquely human motivation: Terror management. In J. Shah (Ed.), *Handbook of motivation science* (pp. 114–134). New York: Guilford Press.

Hirschberger, G. (2006). Terror management and attributions of blame to innocent victims: Reconciling compassionate and defensive responses. *Journal of Personality and Social Psychology*, *91*, 832–844.

Hirschberger, G., & Ein-Dor, T. (2006). Defenders of a lost cause: Terror management and violent resistance to the disengagement plan. *Personality and Social Psychology Bulletin*, *32*, 761–769.

Hirschberger, G., Ein-Dor, T., & Almakias, S. (2008). The self-protective altruist: Terror management and the ambivalent nature of prosocial behavior. *Personality and Social Psychology Bulletin*, *34*, 666–678.

Hirschberger, G., Ein-Dor, T., Caspi, A., Arzouan, Y., & Zivotofsky, A. Z. (2008). *Looking away from death: Eye tracking evidence for unconscious terror management.* Unpublished manuscript.

Hirschberger, G., Florian, V., & Mikulincer, M. (2005). Fear and compassion: A terror management analysis of emotional reactions to physical disability. *Rehabilitation Psychology*, *50*, 246–257.

Holmes, J. G., Miller, D. T., & Lerner, M. J. (2002). Committing altruism under the cloak of self-interest: The exchange fiction. *Journal of Experimental Social Psychology*, *38*, 144–151.

Joireman, J., & Duell, B. (2005). Mother Teresa versus Ebenezer Scrooge: Mortality salience leads proselfs to endorse self-transcendent values (unless proselfs are reassured). *Personality and Social Psychology Bulletin*, *31*, 307–320.

Joireman, J., & Duell, B. (2007). Self-transcendent values moderate the impact of mortality salience on support for charities. *Personality and Individual Differences*, *43*, 779–789.

Jonas, E., Schimel, J., Greenberg, J., & Pyszczynski, T. (2002). The Scrooge effect: Evidence that mortality salience increases prosocial attitudes and behavior. *Personality and Social Psychology Bulletin*, *28*, 1342–1353.

Jones, E. E., Farina, A., Hastorf, A. H., Markus, H., Miller, D. T., & Scott, R. A. (1984). *Social stigma: The psychology of marked relationships*. New York: Freeman.

Landau, M. J., Johns, M., Greenberg, J., Pyszczynski, T., Martens, A., Goldenberg, J. L., & Solomon, S. (2004). A function of form: Terror management and structuring the social world. *Journal of Personality and Social Psychology*, *87*, 190–210.

Lazarus, R. S. (1991). *Emotion and adaptation*. New York: Oxford University Press.

Lerner, M. J. (1980). *The belief in a just world: A fundamental delusion*. New York: Plenum Press.

Levi, P. (1981). *Se questo é un uomo* [If this is a man]. Torino, Italy: Einaudi.

Livneh, H. (1985). Death attitudes and their relationship to perceptions of physically disabled persons. *Journal of Rehabilitation*, *51*, 38–41.

Nolan, B. E., & Spanos, N. S., (1989). Psychosocial variables associated with willingness to donate organs. *Canadian Medical Association Journal*, *14*, 27–32.

Pettigrew, T. F. (1998). Intergroup contact theory. *Annual Review of Psychology*, *49*, 65–85.

Pyszczynski, T., Greenberg, J., & Solomon, S. (1999). A dual process model of defense against conscious and unconscious death-related thoughts: An extension of terror management theory. *Psychological Review*, *106*, 835–845.

Scheier, M. F., Carver, C. S., Schultz, R., Glass, D. C., & Katz, I. (1978). Sympathy, self-consciousness, and reactions to the stigmatized. *Journal of Applied Social Psychology*, *8*, 270–282.

Schimel, J., Hayes, J., Williams, T., & Jahrig, J. (2007). Is death really the worm at the core? Converging evidence that worldview threat increases death-thought accessibility. *Journal of Personality and Social Psychology*, *92*, 789–803.

Shaver, K. G. (1970). Defensive attribution: Effects of and relevance on the responsibility assigned for an accident. *Journal of Personality and Social Psychology*, *14*, 101–113.

Schwartz, S. H. (1992). Universals in the content and structure of values: Theoretical advances and empirical tests in 20 countries. In M. Zanna (Ed.), *Advances in experimental social psychology* (pp. 1–65). San Diego: Academic Press.

Solomon, S., Greenberg, J., & Pyszczynski, T. (1991). A terror management theory of social behavior: The psychological functions of self-esteem and cultural worldviews. In L. Berkowitz (Ed.), *Advances in experimental social psychology* (Vol. 24, pp. 93–159). New York: Academic Press.

Twenge, J. M., Baumeister, R. F., DeWall, C. N., Ciarocco, N. J., & Bartels, J. M. (2007). Social exclusion decreases prosocial behavior. *Journal of Personality and Social Psychology*, *92*, 56–66.

Watson, D., Clark, L. A., & Tellegen, A. (1988). Development and validation of brief measures of positive and negative affect: The PANAS Scales. *Journal of Personality and Social Psychology*, *54*, 1063–1070.

Weiner, B. (1980). A cognitive (attribution)-emotion-action model of motivational behavior: An analysis of help giving. *Journal of Personality and Social Psychology*, *39*, 186–200.

Zweig, S. (1982). *Beware of pity*. New York: Plume Books. (Original work published 1938)

12

BASIC VALUES: HOW THEY MOTIVATE AND INHIBIT PROSOCIAL BEHAVIOR

SHALOM H. SCHWARTZ

In 1970, clerical workers in Wisconsin received a mailed survey from New York about attitudes toward organ transplantation, ostensibly part of a national study. Included among many questions was a measure of the disposition to deny responsibility for the consequences of one's behavior and the following question: "If a stranger to you needed a bone marrow transplant and you were a suitable donor, would you feel a moral obligation to donate bone marrow?" Three months later, those who had replied received an appeal letter from a Wisconsin transplant specialist. He asked them to join a pool of potential bone marrow donors by providing local doctors with blood samples for typing and inclusion in a national donor bank. Four levels of response ranged from "not interested, don't contact me again" to "have your doctor call me for an appointment." Among respondents who were inclined to deny personal responsibility, as measured earlier, the personal norm did not correlate with volunteering ($r = .01$); among those inclined to accept responsibility, the personal norm correlated substantially ($r = .44$, $p < .01$) with volunteering (Schwartz, 1973).

Studies like this one (summarized in Schwartz, 1977, and Schwartz & Howard, 1984) investigated aspects of my theory of moral–decision making and altruistic behavior. The key concept in this theory was the *personal norm*—the sense of obligation people presumably feel when encountering another in need (i.e., their sense of what they ought to do regardless of what others expect). The theory postulated that people typically generate personal norms when faced with decisions about how to act. They do this by weighing the possible consequences of taking different actions for their relatively stable values. The sense of obligation to act that people feel depends on whether they perceive an act as likely to promote attainment of their high priority values or to undermine these values. But when the theory was proposed, I wrote (Schwartz, 1977), "to identify in advance [a person's priority system of values] . . . that might link abstract values to specific feelings of obligation in particular situations is probably an impossible task" (p. 234).

In this chapter, I describe some of my efforts during the past 30 years to accomplish this "impossible" task. I outline my general theory of basic values and the implications of this theory for the full range of prosocial behaviors. I first discuss the nature and content of the basic values that both motivate and inhibit prosocial behavior. I then explain the structure of congruent and conflicting relations among these values, analyzing how trade-offs between competing values in this structure affect prosocial behavior. I next examine the dynamic roots of this near-universal structure to clarify why particular values affect prosocial behavior as they do and follow with an exploration of the mechanisms that link values to prosocial behavior. I end the chapter with a set of studies that use values to predict a variety of prosocial behaviors and attitudes.

My values theory concerns the basic values that people in all cultures are likely to recognize. It identifies 10 motivationally distinct values and specifies the conflicts (e.g., benevolence vs. power) and compatibilities (e.g., conformity, security) among them. The *structure of values* refers to these relations of conflict (opposition) and compatibility (congruence). Similar value structures exist across culturally diverse groups, suggesting that there is a universal organization of human motives. But even if the types of human motivation that values express and the structure of their relations are universal, individuals and groups differ substantially in the relative importance they attribute to particular values. That is, their value priorities or hierarchies differ.

THE NATURE OF VALUES

My conception of values (Schwartz, 1992, 2006) includes the following six main features:

1. Values are beliefs linked inextricably to affect. When values are activated, they become infused with feeling. People who value independence highly are aroused if their independence

is threatened, feel despair when they are helpless to protect it, and are happy when they can exercise or use it.

2. Values refer to desirable goals that motivate action. People for whom social order, justice, and helpfulness are important values are motivated to pursue these goals.
3. Values transcend specific actions and situations. Obedience, for example, is a value relevant at work and school, as well as with family, friends, or strangers. This feature distinguishes values from narrower concepts such as norms and attitudes, which usually refer to specific actions, objects, or situations.
4. Values serve as standards. They guide the selection or evaluation of actions, policies, events, and people, including oneself. As bases of self-evaluation, values are central to the self-concept. People decide what is good or bad, justified or illegitimate, and worth doing or avoiding on the basis of possible consequences for their cherished values.
5. Values are ordered by importance relative to one another to form a relatively stable ordered system of priorities. This hierarchical feature also distinguishes values from norms and attitudes.
6. The relative importance of multiple values guides any action or attitude. For example, the relative importance of four values, tradition and conformity versus hedonism and stimulation, typically guides church attendance and religiosity. More generally, underlying any action or attitude is a trade-off between the competing values that are relevant to it.

These features characterize all values. What distinguishes one value from another is the goal or motivation it expresses. The values theory defines 10 broad values according to the motivation that each expresses. These values are likely to be universal because they are grounded in universal requirements of human existence—of individuals as biological organisms, of coordinated social interaction, and of group survival and welfare. To cope successfully with these requirements, individuals must articulate appropriate goals, communicate with others about them, and gain cooperation in their pursuit. Values are socially desirable concepts that represent these goals cognitively. They are the vocabulary used to express the goals in social interaction. Following are definitions of the 10 values in terms of the broad goals they express:

- *Conformity*—restraint of actions, inclinations, and impulses likely to upset or harm others and to violate social expectations or norms;
- *Tradition*—respect, commitment, and acceptance of the customs and ideas provided by one's culture or religion;

- *Benevolence*—preserving and enhancing the welfare of people with whom one is in frequent personal contact;
- *Universalism*—understanding, appreciation, tolerance, and protection regarding the welfare of all people and of nature;
- *Self-Direction*—independent thought and action: choosing, creating, exploring;
- *Stimulation*—excitement, novelty, and challenge in life;
- *Hedonism*—pleasure or sensuous gratification for oneself;
- *Achievement*—personal success through demonstrating competence according to social standards;
- *Power*—social status and prestige, control or dominance over people and resources; and
- *Security*—safety, harmony, and stability of society, of relationships, and of self.

Each of the 10 values might be relevant to prosocial behavior under some conditions. The values that affect prosocial behavior most frequently across contexts, however, are universalism, benevolence, conformity, security, and power. Benevolence values concern the welfare of the ingroup, whereas universalism values concern the welfare of all. Benevolence values are socialized in the family and other primary groups. Universalism values probably arise and can be socialized effectively only after people encounter others outside the extended primary group with whom they must get along. Development of the aspect of universalism values concerned with nature may require awareness of the scarcity of natural resources.

Benevolence and conformity values both promote cooperative and supportive social relations. However, benevolence values motivate actions to promote the welfare of others out of concern for them. In contrast, conformity values motivate prosocial behavior in order to avoid negative outcomes for self. Both values may motivate the same helpful act.

Finally, security and power values typically oppose prosocial behavior. With their motivation to maintain a stable, protective environment, security values focus on one's own rather than others' needs, and they deter prosocial actions that might entail risk. The pursuit of dominance over people and accumulation of resources inherent in power values justifies self-serving behavior even at the expense of others. Power values emphasize self-interest and competitive advantage more strongly than does achievement, the other self-enhancement value. Achievement is particularly associated with the pursuit of social approval. This may temper self-interest and even elicit prosocial behavior in situations where acting prosocially will bring public acclaim.

In the field of prosocial behavior, both Staub (e.g., 1984) and Eisenberg (e.g., chap. 7, this volume) have used the term *personal goals* much as I use the term *values*. They discuss hierarchies of goal importance, activation of goals, links of goals to emotion and the self-concept, and competition between "goals of a moral nature" that motivate prosocial behavior and other goals (Eisenberg, 1986, p. 204). Goals of a moral nature primarily express benevolence and universalism and sometimes tradition or conformity values. Personal goals are less abstract than basic values, and the structure of relations among values plays a central role in my theorizing but not in work on personal goals.

THE STRUCTURE OF VALUE RELATIONS

The structure of relations among the 10 values derives from the fact that actions in pursuit of any value have consequences that conflict with some values but are congruent with others. For example, pursuing power values typically conflicts with pursuing universalism values. Seeking dominance for self tends to obstruct actions aimed at granting equality to others. But pursuing both achievement and power values is usually possible, so the two are congruent or compatible. Demonstrating one's personal success can strengthen one's status and authority over others.

Actions in pursuit of values have practical, psychological, and social consequences. Practically, choosing an action alternative that promotes one value (e.g., vigorously pursuing ambitions—achievement) may contravene or violate a competing value (sacrificing a career so one's spouse can get ahead—benevolence). The person who faces the choice may sense that such alternative actions are psychologically dissonant. Others may impose social sanctions by pointing to practical and logical inconsistencies between an action and other values the person professes. Of course, people can and do pursue competing values but not in a single act. They do so through different acts, at different times, and in different settings.

Although the theory distinguishes 10 values, it postulates, at a more basic level, that values form a continuum of related motivations. This continuum gives rise to a circular structure (see Figure 12.1). The order in which the values are listed previously in this chapter is their order around the motivational circle; conformity and security close the circle. The closer any two values are around the circle, the more similar are their underlying motivations; the more distant they are, the more antagonistic are their motivations. Analyses in 81 countries, using three different instruments to measure values, provided near-universal support for the circular structure of the 10 values (Schwartz, 2006, 2007b).

Two bipolar dimensions summarize the oppositions between competing values. One dimension contrasts *openness to change* and *conservation* values. It captures the conflict between values that emphasize independence of thought, action, and feelings and readiness for change (self-direction, stimulation), and values that emphasize order, self-restriction, preservation of the

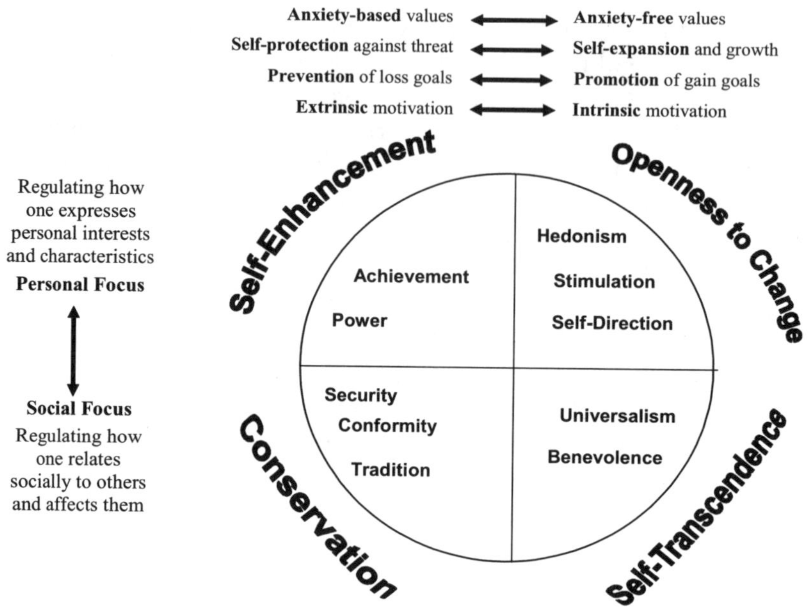

Figure 12.1. Dynamic contrasts that underlie the circular structure of relations among 10 values.

past, and resistance to change (security, conformity, tradition). The second dimension contrasts *self-enhancement* and *self-transcendence* values. This dimension captures the conflict between values that emphasize concern for the welfare and interests of others (universalism, benevolence) and values that emphasize pursuit of self-interests and relative success and dominance over others (power, achievement). Hedonism shares elements of both openness to change and self-enhancement.

As goals, values influence all motivated behavior. Their structure provides a framework for relating all 10 values to behavior. It makes clear that behavior entails a trade-off between competing values. All intentional behavior has positive implications for expressing, upholding, or attaining some values but negative implications for values across the structural circle in opposing positions. Trying to understand the value bases of prosocial behavior by considering only values that might foster it overlooks the equally important contribution of the values that oppose such behavior. Relations of value priorities to prosocial behavior illustrate this.

ROOTS OF THE STRUCTURE OF VALUES

First, to shed more light on the nature of the motivations that values represent, consider possible roots of the near-universal structure of values.

This further clarifies the relevance of values to prosocial behavior. Previously, I discussed the first dynamic principle that organizes values. Actions that express or pursue a value usually have practical, psychological, or social consequences that conflict with values on the opposite side of the motivational circle and are congruent with values adjacent in the circle. When people choose to behave, they experience these conflicting and congruent consequences. Their repeated choices reinforce the circular structure of value relations.

Figure 12.1 points to other dynamic principles. Values in the top section (power, achievement, hedonism, stimulation, self-direction) primarily regulate how people express personal interests and characteristics. Values in the bottom section (benevolence, universalism, tradition, conformity, security) primarily regulate how people relate socially to others and affect their interests. Correlations of value priorities with worry about societal problems (macro-worries) support this interpretation (Schwartz, Sagiv, & Boehnke, 2000). Respondents in seven samples from Israel, Germany, and Russia reported their values and indicated the extent to which they worry about poverty, hunger, intergroup conflict, destruction of the environment, and international wars in the world at large and in the wider society. Such macro-worries represent a social focus, a prosocial concern with preserving the interests of others. In all seven samples, universalism values correlated most strongly with macro-worries ($M\ r = .49$); the mean correlations of the other social-focused values were all positive and significant as well. In contrast, power values correlated most negatively with macro-worries ($M\ r = -.37$), and the mean correlations of all the other personal-focused values were also negative.

Links between values and anxiety help to explain other aspects of the value structure. Pursuit of values on the left in Figure 12.1 aims to cope with anxiety due to uncertainty in the social and physical world. People seek to avoid conflict (conformity) and to maintain order (tradition, security) or actively to control threat (power). Values on the right (hedonism, stimulation, self-direction, universalism, benevolence) express more anxiety-free motivations. Achievement values do both: Meeting social standards successfully may control anxiety and may affirm one's sense of competence.

If people are preoccupied with pursuing values that control anxiety, they have fewer psychic resources available to help others (see similar ideas in chaps. 1, 4, 5, and 7, this volume). Relative freedom from anxiety frees up such resources, though it is not sufficient to direct resources toward the welfare of others. Data from the European Social Survey (ESS) are relevant to this issue.[1]

[1]The ESS is a semiannual, face-to-face survey of large, representative national samples in European and neighboring countries. It includes a scale to measure the 10 basic human values discussed here. This chapter draws on data from the first round of the ESS in 2002–2003.

Analyses of these data support the assumption that conservation and self-enhancement values reflect greater personal anxiety than self-transcendence and openness values, whereas the latter reflect greater comfort with life. Responses of representative national samples from 24 to 26 countries to three items reflect a degree of comfort in life rather than anxiety: "How happy are you?" "How satisfied are you with life as a whole?" and "How often have you felt cheerful and in good spirits in the last two weeks?" Responses to all three items correlated positively with all of the self-transcendence and openness values and negatively with all of the self-enhancement and conservation values. Negative correlations were strongest for security and power values, and positive correlations were strongest for hedonism and either benevolence or self-direction values.

Agreement with items that measure micro-worries—worries about one's personal health, safety, social acceptance, success, and finances and those of close others—points to anxiety. In the cross-national study of worries (Schwartz et al., 2000), self-enhancement and hedonism values correlated positively with micro-worries, whereas self-transcendence and self-direction values correlated negatively. This suggests that people who emphasize self-transcendence and self-direction values are relatively free of the personal anxiety that might sap resources needed for prosocial behavior. It further suggests negative relations of self-enhancement and hedonism values to prosocial behavior.

Mikulincer et al. (2003) identified bases of self-transcendence values that are consistent with this reasoning. In three studies building on attachment theory (see chaps. 4, 14, and 19, this volume), the researchers examined the effects of contextual and chronic activation of a sense of having a secure base on the endorsement of self-transcendence values. Priming a sense of secure attachment increased the importance that participants attributed to universalism and benevolence values as measured both by self-reports and by spontaneously generated "most important values." In addition, in all three studies, a measure of dispositional avoidant attachment correlated negatively with endorsement of these self-transcendence values.

Mikulincer et al. (2003) noted that avoidant attachment entails chronic mistrust of others and avoidance of interdependence and closeness. Persons who are low on avoidant attachment have more positive representations of others than do persons high on avoidance. Seeing others as benign and supportive may promote a more sensitive caregiving orientation and a greater desire to protect and promote others' welfare. Thus, universalism and benevolence values should be higher among individuals who share a positive outlook on human nature. Mikulincer et al. (2003) did not study attachment bases of self-enhancement values. The logic of the value circle suggests, however, that they are grounded in high avoidance. Hence, self-enhancement values should be higher among individuals who share a generally negative outlook on human nature (some studies already suggest that they are; see, e.g., Mikulincer & Shaver, 2001; chaps. 4, 13, and 18, this volume).

Responses to three items in the ESS support these ideas. Participants were asked whether "most people can be trusted" versus "you can't be too careful," "most people try to take advantage of you" versus "most people try to be fair," and "people are mostly helpful" versus "people mostly look out for themselves." Universalism and benevolence values correlated most positively with believing that most people are trustworthy, fair, and helpful; power and security values correlated most negatively. Moreover, the openness values correlated positively and the remaining self-enhancement and conservation values correlated negatively with viewing human nature as positive. These different views of human nature inherent in value priorities are likely to influence prosocial behavior.

Mikulincer et al. (2003) found no relation of chronic attachment anxiety to endorsement of self-transcendence values. Attachment anxiety implicates people's working model of self—how worthy, competent, and socially desirable they believe they are. The authors suggested that the positive model of self that accompanies low attachment anxiety may reduce worries about self and lead people to engage in autonomous exploration and risk-taking activities. It may not, however, enable them to transcend the self and contribute to the welfare of people and society. Hence, attachment anxiety is unrelated to self-transcendence values. The negative association of attachment anxiety with the sense of self-worth suggests that it may relate to conservation values positively and to openness values negatively. Future research should test these speculations.

Finally, values on the left of Figure 12.1 may also be seen as largely expressing extrinsic motivation: Attainment of these values is contingent on obtaining social approval and material rewards (self-enhancement), on meeting the expectations of others and avoiding the sanctions they may impose (conformity, tradition), or on receiving protection and care (security). Values on the right largely express intrinsic motivation: Behavior based on these values is rewarding in itself, providing satisfaction or pleasure through expressing autonomy and competence (openness) or nurturance and relatedness (self-transcendence).

MECHANISMS THAT LINK VALUES TO PROSOCIAL BEHAVIOR

The discussion thus far has described the motivational goals of the ten basic values and some of their dynamic roots. But what mechanisms link value priorities to prosocial behavior? I turn next to an examination of processes through which values can influence behavior.

Value Activation

Values affect behavior only if they are activated and if, at some level of awareness, they are experienced as relevant in the context (Verplanken & Holland, 2002). Activation may or may not entail self-conscious thought about the value. The more accessible a value (i.e., the more easily it comes to mind), the more likely it is to be activated. Because more important values are more accessible (Bardi, 2000), they relate more to behavior. Schwartz (1977) posited four steps in the activation of personal norms that apply equally to basic values.

The first step in the activation of values is a conscious awareness of need. Self-transcendence values direct attention to others' needs. The finding that self-transcendence values correlate positively and self-enhancement values negatively with worrying about societal poverty and environmental destruction reflects this directing of attention. Chronic individual differences in valuing others' welfare may have effects similar to those Batson, Eklund, Chermok, Hoyt, and Ortiz (2007) demonstrated by manipulating the extent of valuing another's welfare. Greater manipulated valuing increased the perceived need of others, empathic concern for them, increased perspective taking, imagining their feelings, and helping (see chap. 1, this volume). Benevolence values may increase perception of need, empathic concern, and perspective taking in relation to members of one's ingroup; universalism may do the same in relation to outgroup members and strangers. Moreover, self-enhancement values may reduce perception of need, perspective taking, empathy, and thereby helping. Universalism and benevolence values correlate positively and power and achievement values negatively with indexes of empathic concern and of perspective taking (Silfver, Helkama, Lönnqvist, & Verkasalo, 2008).

Verplanken and Holland (2002, Study 3) tested relations of environmental values (two universalism value items) to information seeking. This study demonstrated how values can direct attention. When the values were first primed in an unrelated task, students who strongly endorsed the values sought twice as much information about the environmental impact of television sets than did students who did not endorse such values. Values also affect interpretation of the situation of need. For example, self-transcendence values incline bystanders to see an assault as a situation requiring help, whereas security values incline them to see it as a situation in which to avoid harm.

The second step in the activation of values is awareness of viable actions that can relieve need. Values may not affect this step, but they do matter for the third critical step—perceiving oneself as able to help. Caprara and Steca (2007) hypothesized that self-transcendence values positively influence self-efficacy beliefs relevant to prosocial behavior. They reasoned that the more people value others' welfare, (a) the more they strive to develop abilities to help others and (b) the more important it is to them to believe that they possess these abilities that are congruent with the self-ideal embodied in their self-transcendence values. Analyses of data from a large convenience sample of the Italian population aged 20 through 90 supported this reasoning with regard to four types of self-efficacy: beliefs in one's ability to manage one's own negative affect and positive affect, to manage social relationships, and to sense other's feelings. The best predictive model included direct, positive effects of self-transcendence values on prosocial behavior (sharing, helping, taking care of, and feeling empathic with others) and on all four types of self-efficacy, and indirect effects of values on behavior through self-efficacy beliefs.

The final step in the activation of values is sensing some responsibility to become involved. Research has identified accountability, role requirements, distinctive suitability, and direct appeals as elicitors of responsibility (as summarized in Schwartz, 1977). The impact of value priorities on feeling responsibility has yet to be studied empirically. Values that focus the person on relations to others may also be conducive to feeling responsibility to be involved. Self-transcendence values link the self to others in order to promote their welfare; conformity and tradition values link the self to others in order to meet their expectations. Values that focus the person on expressing personal interests and characteristics may have the opposite effect. Self-enhancement values legitimize attending to own needs and avoiding involvement with others' who are needy; involvement with others' need is usually irrelevant to pursuit of openness values.

Values as a Source of Motivation

Once people recognize feasible actions to help another and feel at least a minimum of responsibility, their values provide motivation to act. Values induce valences on possible actions (Feather, 1995). Actions become more attractive, and more valued subjectively, to the extent that they promote attainment of valued goals. High-priority values are central to the self-concept. Sensing that an action will attain them sets off an automatic, positive, affective response; sensing that an action threatens them sets off a negative affective response.

As noted, actions have implications for multiple values. The balance of positive and negative affective responses resulting from the trade-off between opposing values determines the attractiveness of an action. Universalism, self-direction, and stimulation values may induce positive valences on protesting police brutality against immigrants, for example; security, conformity, and tradition values may induce negative valences. The attractiveness of this activity depends on the importance of each of these values to a person and on their perceived relevance.

At this point in the processes leading to prosocial behavior, all 10 values may come into play. People implicitly consider the implications of actions for each of the values they perceive to be relevant (i.e., the values that are activated). Prosocial actions express self-transcendence values and elicit anticipated positive self-evaluation as good and moral. Implications of such actions for self-enhancement and security values elicit concern about material or physical costs. And implications for conformity and tradition values elicit attention to social costs or benefits. A prosocial action may also have implications for openness values, if it is perceived as limiting or enhancing freedom (self-direction), excitement (stimulation), or pleasure (hedonism). The resultant motivation is a product of (a) the importance of each of the values that is implicated, (b) the magnitude of the anticipated impacts of the action on the attainment or expression of these values, and (c) the perceived probability that these impacts will in fact be forthcoming.

Anticipating the possibility of acting prosocially typically activates self-transcendence values. It is also likely to activate the motivationally opposed values that the action may harm. Prediction of behavior on the basis of values should take account of the importance of the values opposed to the behavior as well as those that promote it. Failure to consider opposing values has led to underestimating the influence of values on behavior in past research. A study of cooperative behavior illustrated the importance of trade-offs between competing values in guiding prosocial behavior (Schwartz, 1996). Students chose one of three alternatives for allocating money between self and a member of their group. They learned they would receive the amount of money they allocated to self plus the amount their partner allocated to them. The cooperative choice was to take just a little more for themselves than they gave to their partner. The other two choices were both uncooperative, either maximizing the size of the difference between what they took and what they gave to their partner or maximizing what they took for themselves.

In this experiment with students, cooperation was more a matter of conventional thoughtfulness and decency than social justice. Hence, benevolence rather than universalism values related most strongly to cooperation. Power values related most strongly to noncooperation because they emphasize competitive advantage and legitimize maximizing own gain even at the expense of others. Splitting the sample at the median on benevolence and on power values and crossing these subsamples yielded four groups. In the group that valued benevolence highly and gave low importance to power values, 87% cooperated. This was twice the rate in any other group. Thus, to elicit a high level of cooperation required both high priority for values that promote cooperation (benevolence) and low priority for values that oppose it (power).

Lönnqvist, Leikas, Paunonen, Nissinen, and Verkasalo (2006) illustrated interactions between conformity values and both self-transcendence and self-enhancement values in predicting prosocial behavior. People who attribute high importance to conformity values are especially sensitive and vulnerable to social norms and constraints. They are therefore less likely to behave in ways consistent with their other values. Those low in conformity values, in contrast, are more likely to ignore social pressures and to act in a manner consistent with their other values. Finnish military cadets rated members of their platoon on the disposition to prosocial behavior. Among those for whom conformity values were highly important, prosocial behavior did not relate to value priorities. Among those for whom conformity values were unimportant, both universalism and benevolence values predicted more prosocial behavior and power values predicted less.

A second study in Lönnqvist et al. (2006) examined relations of value priorities to anticipated feelings that motivate value-consistent or -inconsistent behavior. It built on my assumption (Schwartz, 1977) that people anticipate self-blame for failing to behave consistently with activated self-transcendence values that motivate them. When motivated mainly by social expectations, people anticipate less self-blame. The authors applied this reasoning to a situation in which people's behavior led to negative consequences. They suggested that people feel less regret if they have acted consistently with their self-transcendence values and more regret if they have acted inconsistently with these values. This applies, however, only to those low on conformity values, because they are motivated by their own values and not by social expectations. For these people, self-satisfaction from value-consistent behavior should weaken regret over negative outcomes, whereas self-blame from value-discrepant behavior should increase regret.

In a test of these hypotheses, Finnish students read about a person who decided to attend an antiwar demonstration (an action congruent with universalism values) and a second person who harshly reprimanded a subordinate (an action in conflict with universalism and benevolence values). Both people were assaulted and suffered a mild concussion because of their action. Students rated how much regret they themselves would anticipate if they performed these two actions and suffered the same consequences. The higher the students' universalism values, the less regret they anticipated for attending the antiwar demonstration despite the negative consequences—but, as hypothesized, only if they were also low in conformity values. Similarly, the higher their universalism or benevolence values, the more regret they anticipated for reprimanding their subordinate, but again only if they were low in conformity values. These studies illustrate how values that motivate conformity combine with values that motivate promoting others' welfare to affect motivation for prosocial behavior.

By evaluating the implications of specific prosocial acts for all their relevant, activated values, people identify the material, social, moral, and other psychological costs and benefits of these potential behaviors. This evaluation often occurs quickly and outside conscious awareness. If the balance of anticipated costs and benefits clearly favors either action or inaction, a decision is made. A cost–benefit assessment that does not clearly favor action or inaction generates internal conflict and arousal. The decision is delayed, and people try to reduce the conflict.

The easiest way to reduce decisional conflict is to weaken the motivation for the specific prosocial action that is based on self-transcendence values—the personal norm or feeling of moral obligation. Reinterpreting the situation to deactivate self-transcendence values can do this. A person can reinterpret the need as less serious, the possible helping actions as less effective, his or her own abilities as less efficacious, and him- or herself as less responsible due to extenuating circumstances. A person can also reinterpret the various costs of action as greater. Schwartz (1977) and Schwartz and Howard (1984) summarized studies that illustrate how situational and dispositional variables that promote these defensive processes reduce the association between individual differences in value-based personal norms and subsequent prosocial behavior.

Much prosocial behavior requires planning and persistence (see chaps. 7 and 9, this volume). Theory and research on the ways goals lead to action (e.g., Gollwitzer, 1996) identify another set of mechanisms through which value priorities affect behavior. Goals that are more important induce a stronger motivation to plan. The more important a value, the more likely it is that people will form action plans that can lead to its expression in behavior. Planning focuses people on the pros of desired actions rather than the cons. It enhances their belief in their ability to reach the valued goal and increases their persistence in the face of obstacles and distractions. By promoting planning, value importance increases value-consistent behavior.

PREDICTING PROSOCIAL BEHAVIOR AND ATTITUDES FROM VALUE PRIORITIES: EXEMPLARY STUDIES

Having outlined processes through which values may influence behavior, I next examine several studies that used values to predict behavior or attitudes. I begin with a study that examined everyday behaviors that are relevant to each of the 10 basic values. I then present three studies of socially significant prosocial behavior in which the trade-off between competing values was an important predictor. The section ends with a study of the role of values as determinants of voting for political parties that differ in their commitment to the social welfare of the population.

Everyday Behavior

Bardi and Schwartz (2003) generated sets of behaviors that primarily express one of the 10 values. Intimate partners or close peers rated how frequently a participant had performed each behavior in the past year, relative to their opportunities to perform it. The average frequency of the set of items that expressed each value indexed behavior. Each behavior set correlated most highly with the value it was intended to express and most negatively with an opposing value, except the most positive correlation of conformity with tradition values.

Some behaviors correlated more strongly with the value they express than did others, reflecting how normative pressure undermines value-behavior relations. The most frequently performed (most normative) behaviors in the group studied—security, conformity, benevolence, and achievement—exhibited relatively weak correlations with values (M r = .29, across three studies). Correlations of behavior with the two values that were least important to the group, tradition (.59) and stimulation (.57), were the strongest. This illustrates how the absence of social pressure enables individuals to express their unique values more freely.

Participation in Prosocial Organizations

Respondents in the 21 national samples of the ESS indicated the degree of their involvement, if any, in organizations that work to protect the environment, foster peace, or fight for animal rights. I indexed participation by combining membership, donating, active involvement, and volunteer work. The motivational circle of values implies that correlations between values and participating in such organizations—devoted to well-being in the world at large—should be most positive for universalism values and decline in both directions around the circle to most negative for power values (see Figure 12.1). As shown in Figure 12.2, the correlations fit this pattern. Correlations with basic values are not strong because many factors influence such long-term prosocial behavior. Nonetheless, both hierarchical regression and multilevel modeling revealed that only education predicted participation more strongly than did universalism, security, and tradition values, which, in turn, predicted more strongly than age, gender, and income (Schwartz, 2007b).

Attitudes Toward Immigration

With the ESS data, I examined relations between basic values and attitudes toward immigration among people in 15 European countries. Three items measured attitudes toward accepting outgroup immigrants: those of a different race or ethnic group, from poorer European, and from non-European countries. Opposition to outgroup immigrants likely reflects concern with protecting personal and social security, preserving European Christian traditions, and maintaining Western norms. Thus, security, tradition, and conformity values should motivate opposition to immigration. In contrast, self-direction and stimulation values may motivate acceptance of immigration because people who attribute importance to them are open to change and should feel less threatened; they might even welcome enrichment of their society. Moreover, those who cherish universalism values, with their goals of acceptance, appreciation, and concern for the welfare even of those who are different, should most accept immigration.

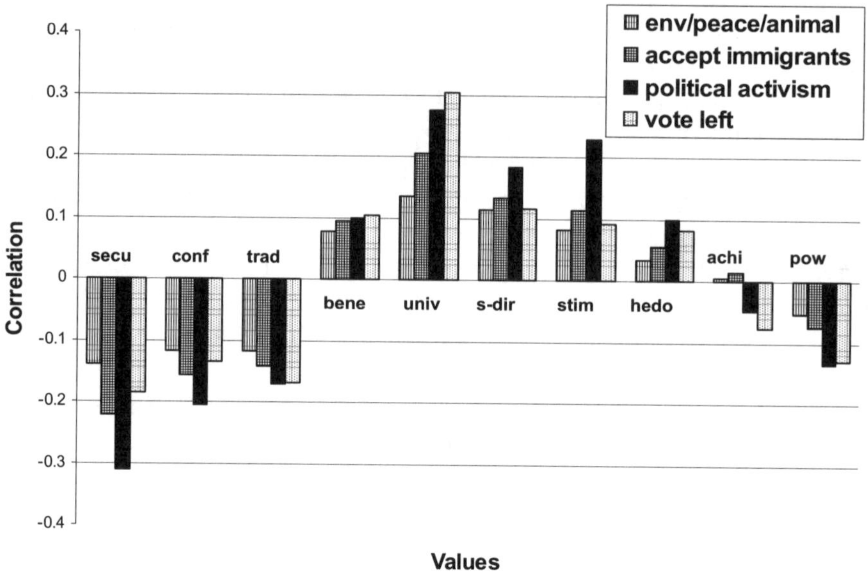

Figure 12.2. Correlations of the 10 basic values with socially significant behavior and attitudes. env = environment; secu = security; conf = conformity; trad = tradition; bene = benevolence; univ = universalism; s-dir = self-direction; stim = stimulation; hedo = hedonism; achi = achievement; pow = power.

The pattern of correlations in Figure 12.2 fully supports the hypotheses. Universalism values correlate most positively with acceptance values and most negatively with security values. The order of correlations follows the order of the motivational circle of values, with the openness values correlating positively and the conservation values negatively. A hierarchical regression revealed that security values accounted for most variance in acceptance of immigration, followed in order by education, universalism, conformity, and being foreign born. Age, gender, household income, religiosity, urban/rural, and unemployment of 3 or more months did not contribute.

Political Activism

Using the ESS data from France, I constructed an index of political activism—the number of legal acts (e.g., boycotting a product, displaying a sticker, contacting a politician, participating in a public demonstration) performed in the past 12 months. These acts largely support causes aimed at improving the general welfare, so I viewed them as prosocial. Universalism values should correlate most strongly with activism because they promote social justice and environmental preservation—goals of much activism. Security and conformity should correlate most negatively because activism is risky and change oriented. I also included an index of subjective political efficacy to test its interaction with value-based motivation.

Figure 12.2 portrays the pattern of correlations. Universalism correlated most positively and security most negatively. Stimulation values correlated more positively than expected from their position in the motivational order of values. This deviation indicates that pursuing excitement also motivates political activism. A hierarchical regression revealed that universalism values were the strongest predictor of activism, followed in order by education, stimulation, self-direction, income, benevolence, and security. Age, gender, and marital status did not contribute. Universalism, self-direction, and stimulation values interacted with self-efficacy, indicating that the more capable people felt, the more their value-based motivations led to action.

Participation in prosocial organizations, acceptance of immigrants, and political activism in support of social justice and the environment are prosocial behaviors whose targets are outside the circle of ingroup members. The findings affirm the distinction between the two values that most frequently promote prosocial behavior, universalism and benevolence: Universalism values express concern for the welfare of all others and of nature; benevolence values express concern for those to whom one is close. In comparative tests of the predictive power of these two values, universalism contributed significantly to predicting each of the variables both across countries and within almost every country studied; benevolence rarely added significantly (Schwartz, 2007a).

Voting

Finally, consider the voting process for the two main coalitions in the 2006 Italian elections. The right promoted entrepreneurship, a market economy, security, and traditional values. These policies have consequences compatible with self-enhancement and conservation values, power and security in particular. But these consequences may conflict with self-transcendence values. The left advocated social welfare, justice, equality, and tolerance even of groups that might disturb the conventional social order. These policies have consequences compatible with self-transcendence values but conflicting with self-enhancement and conservation values. The motivational circle of values implies correlations with voting for the left that are most positive for universalism and decline in both directions around the circle to most negative for power and security values (see Figure 12.1).

Italian adults' values, measured 1 month before the election, correlated with actual voting for the left in a pattern reflecting the motivational circle of values (see Figure 12.1). Universalism correlated most positively and security most negatively with voting for the left. A stronger than expected negative correlation for tradition values reflects the religious orientations of the main rightist parties. Neither age, nor gender, nor marital status, nor income explained additional variance in voting beyond that explained by values (Schwartz, Caprara, & Vecchione, 2009).

CONCLUSIONS

The values theory identifies 10 basic, motivationally distinct values that people in virtually all cultures implicitly recognize. Especially striking is the emergence of the same circular structure of relations among values across cultures and measurement instruments. I discussed several dynamic processes that may account for this structure.

The values theory makes clear that behavior entails a trade-off between competing values. Almost any behavior has positive implications for expressing, upholding, or attaining some values, but negative implications for the values across the structural circle in opposing positions. People tend to behave in ways that balance their opposing values. They choose alternatives that promote higher as opposed to lower priority values. Consequently, the order of positive and negative associations between any specific behavior and the 10 values tends to follow the order of the value circle. Figure 12.2 illustrates this for four prosocial behaviors. Sinusoid curves with different peaks and low points emerge for other types of behavior (e.g., bullying, delinquency).

Once activated, values affect prosocial behavior most critically through influencing the direction of motivation. But differences in value importance may also affect which values, if any, are activated in the first place. Valuing others' welfare may increase attention to need, empathy and perspective-taking, self-efficacy for helping, and even acceptance of personal responsibility to act. Moreover, if a decision to act prosocially is made, stronger self-transcendence values may enhance planning and persistence in the face of obstacles.

The priority people assign to each of the 10 values provides insight into the weight they are likely to give to the full range of costs and benefits inherent in decisions. The power of the values theory for understanding prosocial (and other) behavior derives in large measure from this fact. The priority of self-transcendence values suggests the importance that moral considerations will have in decisions—anticipated self-pride or blame. The priority of conservation and self-enhancement values suggests how an individual will weigh different kinds of social and material considerations—anticipated social approval or disapproval, physical and material gains or losses. The priority of openness values identifies how an individual will weigh the opportunities or threats that a behavior implies for his or her freedom, creativity, curiosity, arousal, or pleasure.

By encompassing the various competing forces that motivate behavior, the values approach can integrate different motivational theories. Indeed, the 10 types of values and their interrelations may point the way toward a unifying theory of human motivation (Bilsky & Schwartz, 2008; Schwartz, 2006). The analysis of the roots of the value structure, the dynamic processes that give rise to the near-universal pattern of motivational conflicts and congruencies, is a first step in this direction.

This chapter has demonstrated the key role that values play in prosocial behavior. Yet, significant gaps in the research are waiting to be filled. In particular, studies are needed on the involvement of values in the four steps related to value activation. Given the role of values, scholars and practitioners will want to reexamine the question of how to change values. The value self-confrontation method that Rokeach (1973) developed for this purpose has received little attention in recent decades. An interesting idea that has been investigated only minimally is that power and security values become more important to the extent that people feel they cannot attain them, whereas self-transcendence and openness values become more important the more opportunities there are to attain them (Schwartz, 2006; Schwartz, Bardi, & Bianchi, 2000). This has implications both for socialization and education and for political and economic policy. It suggests that increasing the importance of the values that promote prosocial behavior and decreasing the importance of the values that oppose it depend on giving people opportunities to control their environment and to benefit others.

REFERENCES

Bardi, A. (2000). *Relations of values to behavior in everyday situations*. Unpublished doctoral dissertation, The Hebrew University, Jerusalem.

Bardi, A., & Schwartz, S. H. (2003). Values and behavior: Strength and structure of relations. *Personality and Social Psychology Bulletin, 29*, 1207–1220.

Batson, C. D., Eklund, J. H., Chermok, V. L., Hoyt, J. L., & Ortiz, B. G. (2007). An additional antecedent of empathic concern: Valuing the welfare of the person in need. *Journal of Personality and Social Psychology, 93*, 65–74.

Bilsky, W. & Schwartz, S. H. (2008). Measuring motivations: Integrating content and method. *Personality and Individual Differences, 44*, 1738–1751.

Caprara, G. V., & Steca, P. (2007). Prosocial agency: The contribution of values and self–efficacy beliefs to prosocial behavior across ages. *Journal of Social and Clinical Psychology, 26*, 218–239.

Eisenberg, N. (1986). *Altruistic emotion, cognition, and behavior*. Hillsdale, NJ: Erlbaum.

Feather, N. T. (1995). Values, valences, and choice: The influence of values on the perceived attractiveness and choice of alternatives. *Journal of Personality and Social Psychology, 68*, 1135–1151.

Gollwitzer, P. M. (1996). The volitional benefits of planning. In P. M. Gollwitzer & J. A. Bargh (Eds.), *The psychology of action* (pp. 287–312). New York: Guilford Press.

Lönnqvist, J.-E., Leikas, S., Paunonen, S., Nissinen, V., & Verkasalo, M. (2006). Conformism moderates the relations between values, anticipated regret, and behavior. *Personality and Social Psychology Bulletin, 32*, 1469–1481.

Mikulincer, M., Gillath, O., Sapir-Lavid, Y., Yaakobi, E., Arias, K., Tal-Aloni, L., & Bor, G. (2003). Attachment theory and concern for others' welfare: Evidence that activation of the sense of secure base promotes endorsement of self-transcendence values. *Basic and Applied Social Psychology, 25*, 299–312.

Mikulincer, M., & Shaver, P. R. (2001). Attachment theory and intergroup bias: Evidence that priming the secure base schema attenuates negative reactions to out-groups. *Journal of Personality and Social Psychology, 81*, 97–115.

Rokeach, M. (1973). *The nature of human values*. New York: Free Press.

Schwartz, S. H. (1973). Normative explanations of helping behavior: A critique proposal and empirical test. *Journal of Experimental Social Psychology, 9*, 349–364.

Schwartz, S. H. (1977). Normative influences on altruism. In L. Berkowitz (Ed.), *Advances in experimental social psychology* (Vol. 10, pp. 221–279). New York: Academic Press.

Schwartz, S. H. (1992). Universals in the content and structure of values: Theory and empirical tests in 20 countries. In M. P. Zanna (Ed.), *Advances in experimental social psychology* (Vol. 25, pp. 1–65). New York: Academic Press.

Schwartz, S. H. (1996). Value priorities and behavior: Applying a theory of integrated value systems. In C. Seligman, J. M. Olson, & M. P. Zanna (Eds.), *The psychology of values: The Ontario Symposium* (Vol. 8, pp. 1–24). Hillsdale, NJ: Erlbaum.

Schwartz, S. H. (2006). Les valeurs de base de la personne: Théorie, mesures et applications [Basic human values: Theory, measurement, and applications]. *Revue Française de Sociologie, 47*, 249–288.

Schwartz, S. H. (2007a). Universalism values and the inclusiveness of our moral universe. *Journal of Cross Cultural Psychology, 38*, 711–728.

Schwartz, S. H. (2007b). Value orientations: Measurement, antecedents, and consequences across nations. In R. Jowell, C. Roberts, R. Fitzgerald, & G. Eva (Eds.), *Measuring attitudes cross-nationally: Lessons from the European Social Survey* (pp. 161–193). London: Sage.

Schwartz, S. H., Bardi, A., & Bianchi, G. (2000). Value adaptation to the imposition and collapse of Communist regimes in Eastern Europe. In S. A. Renshon & J. Duckitt (Eds.), *Political psychology: Cultural and cross cultural perspectives* (pp. 217–237). London: Macmillan.

Schwartz, S. H., Caprara, G. V., & Vecchione, M. (2009). Basic values, core political values and political preference. Manuscript submitted for publication.

Schwartz, S. H., & Howard, J. (1984). Internalized values as motivators of altruism. In E. Staub, D. Bar-Tal, J. Karylowski, & J. Reykowski (Eds.), *Development and maintenance of prosocial behavior* (pp. 229–255). New York: Plenum.

Schwartz, S. H., Sagiv, L., & Boehnke, K. (2000). Worries and values. *Journal of Personality, 68*, 309–346.

Silfver, M., Helkama, K., Lönnqvist, J.-E., & Verkasalo, M. (2008). The relation between value priorities and proneness to guilt, shame, and empathy. *Motivation and Emotion, 32*, 69–80.

Staub, E. (1984). Steps toward a comprehensive theory of moral conduct: Goal orientation, social behavior, kindness and cruelty. In J. Gewirtz & W. Kurtines (Eds.), *Morality, moral development, and moral behavior: Basic issues in theory and research* (pp. 241–260). New York: Wiley.

Verplanken, B., & Holland, R. W. (2002). Motivated decision making: Effects of activation and self-centrality of values on choices and behavior. *Journal of Personality and Social Psychology*, *82*, 434–447.

III

PROSOCIAL EMOTIONS

13

COMPASSIONATE LOVE AS A PROSOCIAL EMOTION

BEVERLEY FEHR

A newspaper headline reads: "Why I gave a stranger a kidney" (Gulli, 2005). The article features an interview with Trent Fenwick, a resident of Kelowna, British Columbia, who decided to donate one of his kidneys after learning that a man in Chicago—a father with a 2-year-old son and a 3-month-old daughter—needed a donor. When asked why he would make such an enormous sacrifice, Mr. Fenwick explained that "if you've ever had a sick family member, you would do anything." Indeed, cases of people donating organs to save loved ones are plentiful. But why go to such great lengths for a stranger? Trent Fenwick's response: "Your heart's desire is to give, so you give in whatever way you are at peace about."

The focus of this chapter is compassionate love (Post, Underwood, Schloss, & Hurlbut, 2002; Underwood, 2002). This kind of love is exemplified by humanitarian icons such as Mother Teresa and ordinary citizens such as Trent Fenwick. It is also a kind of love that is experienced in people's

I am grateful to the Fetzer Institute for supporting the research reported in this chapter. Preparation of the chapter also was supported by a grant from the Social Sciences and Humanities Research Council of Canada. I would like to thank Susan Sprecher, Lynn Underwood, and the editors for their constructive, helpful comments.

closest, most intimate relationships (see Fehr & Sprecher, in press; Sprecher & Fehr, 2005). Nevertheless, compassionate love has been largely overlooked by social scientists, despite having been nominated as one of four fundamental kinds of love (Berscheid, 1985, 2006). However, in the last 5 or 6 years, the tide has turned. A pivotal event was a meeting of a World Health Organization working group in 1998. Lynn Underwood, then vice president of the Fetzer Institute, and other members of the group chose the term *compassionate love* to capture a prosocial emotion that moves one to give freely of oneself with the intention of benefiting another (Underwood, 2002, 2009). Underwood went on to formulate a model of compassionate love (including antecedents, dynamics, and outcomes) to guide scholarly work on this topic. There now exists a handbook of compassionate love in which Underwood's model is used as an overarching framework within which to situate current research on this topic (Fehr, Sprecher, & Underwood, 2009).

This chapter offers an overview of this nascent area of investigation. The central assumptions are that compassionate love is a prosocial emotion and that prosocial actions are a behavioral manifestation of this kind of love. In the words of Underwood (2009), "Observing altruistic actions such as organ donation, volunteering, helping behaviors, and supporting or caring for others . . . are important ways to assess compassionate love" (p. 16). Certainly, compassionate love can be expressed in other ways as well. For example, Underwood (2002, 2009) pointed out that simply communicating a caring attitude can have the effect of soothing another, even before any prosocial actions have been taken. It is also the case that prosocial behavior can be motivated by any number of factors (e.g., self-gratification), not just compassionate love. In this chapter, I take the view that compassionate love is an important determinant of prosocial behavior and, as such, is deserving of research attention.

I begin by addressing the fundamental question: What is compassionate love? Both experts' and laypeople's answers to this question are discussed. Next, I present research on compassionate love, using a simplified version of Underwood's (2009) model as a heuristic for organizing and integrating existing research. The model starts with the individual person, nested in his or her social and cultural environment. Characteristics of the person are linked to motivation and discernment processes, which entail the accurate perception of another's needs and appropriate motives for responding to them. Motivation and discernment, in turn, lead to compassionate love fully expressed.

In the first part of the chapter, I present basic research on this prosocial kind of love (Berscheid, 2006). The specific aims are to understand the meaning of compassionate love, paint a profile of the kind of person most likely to experience or express this kind of love, identify sociocultural factors that influence its expression, and identify the motivations that give rise to this kind of love. The focus then shifts from basic research to applied research designed to increase compassionate love toward close others as well as strangers or even all of humanity. Finally, I end with a discussion of issues to be resolved in this area of research and with suggestions for future work in this promising line of inquiry.

COMPASSIONATE LOVE: WHAT IS IT?

Scholars in this fledgling area have made considerable efforts to define the construct of compassionate love. As shall be seen, research also has been conducted examining laypeople's conceptions of this kind of love.

Experts' Definitions

According to Underwood (2009), the term *compassionate love* refers to a kind of love that involves giving of oneself for the good of another. This kind of love comprises five elements: free choice for the other; valuing the other at a fundamental level; openness and receptivity; an accurate understanding of oneself, the other, and the situation; and a response of the "heart"—an accurate emotional understanding of the situation.

Scholars from a variety of disciplines have generated other definitions and conceptualizations of compassionate love. These were compiled by Shacham-Dupont (2003), who examined the extent of commonality across definitions. Compassionate love was variously defined as an attitude; specific behaviors; cognitive predispositions; an expression of the neural-based bonding system; a dyadic phenomenon; and a "complex functional whole including appraisals, appreciations, patterned physiological responses, action tendencies, and instrumental behaviors" (p.14). Features or elements of compassionate love included altruism (e.g., "a type of sharing that is selfless"), helpfulness (e.g., "helping, or willingness to help, someone in distress"), care and concern (e.g., "observable, meaningful behaviors that demonstrate concern and care for the welfare of the others"), empathy, sympathy, tenderness, and so on (p. 13). Selflessness and sacrifice were also prominent themes in these definitions (e.g., put the needs of others over individual needs). Although there were some similarities in these definitions, equally striking was the diversity—both in terms of what compassionate love is (e.g., an attitude, behavior, cognition) and in terms of its elements or features.

Laypeople's Conceptions of Compassionate Love

The failure of experts to agree on a definition suggests that compassionate love, like other kinds of love, may not be amenable to a classical definition, whereby concepts are defined in terms of individually necessary and jointly sufficient attributes. Instead, compassionate love may be better understood as a *prototype concept*. This term comes from prototype theory as put forth by Eleanor Rosch (1973; for a review, see Mervis & Rosch, 1981), who argued that many natural language concepts cannot be classically defined but instead are organized around their clearest cases or best examples. Members of a category can be ordered in terms of their degree of resemblance to these prototypical cases. Boundaries between categories are blurry, with members of one category shading into members of neighboring categories. Rosch (1973) showed, for example, that apples and oranges are considered prototypical members of the category *fruit*, whereas figs and pomegranates are nonprototypical. Some members of the category *fruit* (e.g., tomato) overlap with the adjacent category *vegetable*.

Although Rosch's (1973) work focused primarily on natural object categories, her theory inspired prototype analyses of a variety of concepts, including emotion in general and specific emotions, such as anger and love (e.g., Aron & Westbay, 1996; Fehr, 1988; Fehr & Russell, 1984; Shaver, Schwartz, Kirson, & O'Connor, 1987; for a review, see Fehr, 2005). In fact, love is the concept that has been most extensively analyzed from a prototype perspective (Fehr, 2006). For example, in one program of research (Fehr & Russell, 1991), participants were asked to list the varieties of love (compassionate love was listed as a type of love, albeit with relatively low frequency). Consistent with a prototype perspective, some types (e.g., maternal love, friendship) were considered highly representative of the concept of love, whereas other types (e.g., patriotic love, infatuation) were considered less so. Moreover, this prototype structure affected information processing in predictable ways. For example, in a reaction-time study, participants were quick to verify that prototypical instances were, in fact, types of love, but required more deliberation to confirm the category membership of nonprototypical instances.

In other research, Fehr (1988) hypothesized that the features of love might show a similar prototype organization such that some attributes would be considered more representative of the concept than others. Consistent with a prototype conceptualization, features such as trust, caring, friendship, respect, and compassion were regarded as central to the concept of love in general; features such as excitement, uncertainty, and gazing at the other were regarded as peripheral (i.e., nonprototypical). Once again, this prototype structure was reflected in various information-processing tasks and in the kinds of judgments people made about close relationships. This prototype of love proved replicable by other researchers, using diverse samples (for reviews, see Fehr, 1993, 2006).

Subsequently, researchers conducted prototype analyses of specific kinds of love, including romantic love (e.g., Regan, Kocan, & Whitlock, 1998) and the concept of *being in love* (Lamm & Wiesmann, 1997; Luby & Aron, 1990). Once again, there was evidence that these kinds of love were organized as prototype concepts, such that some features were regarded as more central to the concept than others.

Fehr and Sprecher (in press) conducted a series of studies to determine whether compassionate love is also a prototype concept. In their first study, participants were asked to generate features of compassionate love. Identical and highly synonymous responses were combined, creating 59 features listed by more than one participant. The prototype of compassionate love included cognitions (e.g., worrying, thinking about the other all the time), feelings and emotions (e.g., feeling happiest when with the person, feeling sad when apart), behaviors (e.g., doing anything for the other, hugging), and motives (e.g., wanting to make the other happy, wanting to spend time with the other). The feature caring was listed most frequently, followed by trust, helping, understanding, and wanting to spend time with the other.

In a second study, we gathered prototypicality ratings to determine whether compassionate love is structured as a prototype concept, such that some features are considered more central to the concept than others. The features that received the highest ratings were trust, honesty, caring, understanding, and support. It is interesting that these features are central to the concept of love itself (Fehr, 1988). The features that received the lowest prototypicality ratings were the following: do anything for the other, put other ahead of self, and make sacrifices for the other. In other words, these characteristics were regarded as part of the concept but residing on its periphery. The findings suggest that in the minds of laypeople, compassionate love is, first and foremost, a kind of love. The peripheral features serve a diagnostic function in specifying that this kind of love involves giving of oneself for the good of another.

In our remaining studies, we sought to verify the prototype structure of compassionate love, using a variety of methods. For example, in one study, we used reaction times to test the hypothesis that participants would be quick to confirm that prototypical features are part of the concept but would require more deliberation when deciding whether nonprototypical features belonged. The results supported predictions. In another study, we focused on memory for prototypical versus nonprototypical features of compassionate love. Consistent with our hypothesis, participants were more likely to recall prototypical features, even when they had not been presented. False memory effects were less likely to occur for nonprototypical features.

In another study, we examined logical inferences. We hypothesized that when the concept of compassionate love was activated, people would be more likely to infer that prototypical, rather than nonprototypical, features characterize a relationship. For example, when told that "Pat experiences compassionate love for Chris," participants inferred that Pat was likely to trust Chris, care about Chris, be concerned about Chris's well-being, and so on. They were less likely to assume that nonprototypical features, such as Pat putting Chris first or making sacrifices for Chris, would apply to the relationship.

These studies suggest that laypeople have rich and complex knowledge of the concept of compassionate love. The findings are consistent with the view that compassionate love is organized as a prototype concept, such that some features are seen as more representative of the concept than others. Put another way, it would appear that the concept of compassionate love is not definable in terms of a necessary and sufficient set of criterial features. The implication is that experts are not likely to uncover a classical definition of compassionate love because such a definition may not exist.

In addition to speaking to definitional issues, prototype analyses reveal the meaning that laypeople attribute to various concepts. This kind of information is important because people rely on these conceptions when deciding how to behave and how to interpret others' behavior (e.g., Kelley, 1983). Our studies revealed that laypeople regard compassionate love as a supremely prosocial kind of love, exemplified by caring, understanding, and supportiveness. One implication is that if these features are present, people will be more likely to interpret their experience as compassionate love, and, consequently, be more likely to engage in compassionate behaviors. It is interesting that the cost of compassionate love (e.g., sacrifice), which is a critical feature in many experts' definitions, was peripheral in lay conceptions of the construct. Thus, for ordinary people, compassionate love revolves primarily around benevolence to others; the costs of extending that benevolence are secondary.

COMPASSIONATE LOVE: A WORKING MODEL

In addition to explicating what compassionate love is, scholars have explored how compassionate love "works." The focus has been on individual-level factors that promote compassionate love, the role of the social and cultural context in which the individual is embedded and, finally, the motivations underlying the expression of compassionate love. Research on each of these topics is discussed in this section.

The Individual

Researchers have examined two kinds of individual-level factors: demographic correlates of compassionate love and the role of attachment in the expression of compassionate love. Six demographic variables have received the most attention: gender, age, race/ethnicity, education level, income, and religiosity/spirituality (see Fehr et al., 2009). The most extensive analyses of the demographic markers of compassionate love have been conducted with national survey data gathered in the United States. For example, Smith (2009) analyzed U.S. General Social Survey data collected in 2002 and 2004. Several demographic variables were correlated with two indices of compassionate love: altruistic love (measured by a short version of the Agape love-style scale; Hendrick & Hendrick, 1986) and altruistic behaviors (e.g., helping others with housework, donating money to charity, giving blood). (Altruistic values and empathy were also included, but were conceptualized as motivational variables, and therefore are discussed in the section on Motivation and Discernment.) Marks and Song (2009) also examined demographic correlates of compassionate love using data from the National Survey of Midlife in the United States (1995) and the National Survey of Families and Households (1987–1993). These researchers examined a number of acts of compassionate love, such as volunteerism; contributing to the well-being of others; and providing various kinds of support (emotional, instrumental, caregiving) to primary kin, secondary kin, and friends. (Marks and Song also examined variables that they considered motivational: altruistic normative obligation, normative obligation to kin and normative obligation to friends; see section on Motivation and Discernment.)

Gender

Women appear to be the more compassionate sex. For example, in Smith's (2009) analysis, women generally scored higher than men on measures of altruistic behaviors, although the opposite was true for altruistic love (assessed with a modified Agape love-style scale; Hendrick & Hendrick, 1986). In Marks and Song's (2009) analysis, women scored higher than men on the item "overall personal contribution to the well-being of others" and on measures of emotional support provided to primary kin and to secondary kin and friends. For example, women reported having spent an average of 95.7 hr providing emotional support to primary kin in the last month, compared with an average of 54.2 hr reported by men. Women also scored higher than men on a measure of instrumental support to primary kin. The exception was the provision of instrumental support to secondary kin and friends, where men outscored women. The number of hours spent in volunteer activities did not differ by gender.

In research that has assessed compassionate love directly (using the Compassionate Love Scale; Sprecher & Fehr, 2005), women consistently score higher than men (Sprecher & Fehr, 2005; Sprecher, Fehr, & Zimmerman, 2007). This gender difference holds across targets (family and friends, strangers/humanity), with one exception—gender differences are not found when the target is one's romantic partner (Fehr, 2008). These findings are generally consistent with the larger social psychological literature showing that women express more empathy toward others and provide more emotional support than do men (e.g., Eagly & Crowley, 1986; Taylor, 2002; see also chap. 3, this volume).

Age

Smith (2009) found that altruistic love increased with age, whereas altruistic behavior declined. In Marks and Song's analysis, respondents who were 55 to 64 years of age had the highest score on the "contribution to the well-being of others" variable. Young adults (ages 25–34) reported the highest levels of emotional support to primary kin and secondary kin, whereas the eldest group in the study (young–old adults, ages 65–74) reported the lowest levels. The findings were similar for instrumental support provision. Sprecher and Fehr (2005) did not find age differences in compassionate love scores, although the age range was limited, given their college student sample. Although it is premature to draw firm conclusions, it would seem that the experience of compassionate love increases with age (e.g., increased altruistic love, promoting the well-being of others), but the ability to perform compassionate acts may be hampered by limitations of mobility and health in later life.

Education

In Smith's (2009) analysis, effects of education were generally nonsignificant. Marks and Song (2009) found that those with the most education (16 or more years of schooling) scored higher on the "contribution to the well-being of others" question than did those with less education. Emotional support to primary kin, secondary kin, and friends increased with education level, but, inexplicably, those with the highest education reported the lowest levels of support provision. A similar pattern was found for instrumental support. In contrast, those who were highly educated reported more volunteerism than those with less education. In short, in research conducted so far, there is not a clear link between education level and compassionate love.

Income

Income was not significantly related to altruistic love, nor to altruistic behaviors, in Smith's (2009) analyses. Similarly, Marks and Song (2009) did not find significant relations between income and volunteerism, overall contribution to others' well-being, or provision of emotional and instrumental support to different targets.

Race/Ethnicity

The findings for race/ethnicity have been inconsistent. Smith (2009) found that White Americans scored highest on altruistic love but Black Americans scored highest on altruistic behaviors. Marks and Song (2009) obtained some significant omnibus effects for race/ethnicity in their analyses, but specific comparisons between groups were generally not significant. African Americans had the highest mean rating on the "contribution to the well-being of others" item and also tended to report the highest levels of provision of emotional support to primary kin, secondary kin, and friends, as well as instrumental support to secondary kin and friends. The researchers caution that these effects may have been due to a few extreme scores. Latinos scored highest on the measure of instrumental support to primary kin; non-Hispanic Whites scored lowest. Finally, Latinos reported significantly lower levels of volunteerism than did the other racial and ethnic groups examined.

Religiosity/Spirituality

In Smith's (2009) analysis, altruistic love and altruistic behaviors did not vary as a function of religious identification. However, these variables were positively associated with religious involvement. The strongest relations were found for an item assessing time spent in prayer. Altruistic love and behaviors also were significantly correlated with daily spiritual experiences (e.g., finding strength or comfort in one's faith, as assessed by the Daily Spiritual Experiences Scale; Underwood & Teresi, 2002).

Sprecher and Fehr (2005; Study 2) found links between religiosity/spirituality and compassionate love, using multiple measures, including frequency of church attendance, self-ratings of religiosity and spirituality, and the Daily Spiritual Experiences Scale. The correlations were small to moderate, and generally were higher for compassionate love for strangers/ humanity than for close others. In fact, measures of religiosity/spirituality were uncorrelated with compassionate love for a specific close other (generally a romantic partner; Sprecher & Fehr, 2005, Study 3).

Other research has indicated that spirituality, rather than religion per se, is associated with compassionate love. Graber and Mitcham (2009) interviewed 24 hospital-based physicians and nurses who had been nominated by peers as being particularly compassionate. All but one reported holding strong spiritual, but not necessarily religious, beliefs.

In summary, the compassionate person is likely to be female, spiritually oriented, and older rather than younger (although perhaps lacking the health or strength to act on this capacity for love). The compassionate person could be a member of any racial or ethnic group, may or may not be well educated, and may or may not be wealthy. Thus, it does not appear that the capacity for compassionate love is strongly constrained by demographic variables. One implication is that it should be possible to foster compassionate love in all people, although those who are female, spiritual, and older may be less in need of intervention to promote this kind of love.

Attachment

The individual-level variable that has received the most extensive research attention is attachment (see chaps. 4 and 14, this volume). Mikulincer, Shaver, and their colleagues have examined the effects of being loved, protected, and comforted by others (beginning with parents during infancy) on the capacity to love and respond compassionately to others' needs. Moreover, the role of attachment in the expression of compassionate behavior has been explored in a variety of relational contexts. For example, in the literature on parent–child relationships, there is consistent evidence that secure parents are sensitive and attuned to their infant's needs. They also exhibit greater responsiveness and less distress when interacting with their child compared with insecure parents (for a review, see, e.g., Mikulincer, Shaver, & Gillath, 2009). Attachment-related differences also have been found in studies of caregiving for elderly parents. Adult children who are secure are more caring and provide more emotional support than do those who are insecure. They also report less caregiver burden (e.g., Mikulincer & Shaver, 2007; Mikulincer et al., 2009; for similar findings regarding caregivers of people with disabilities, see Giesbrecht, 2009).

Attachment-related differences have also been examined in dating and romantic relationships (see chap. 19, this volume). Self-report and laboratory interaction studies have shown that secure partners are more sensitive, responsive, comforting, and supportive than their less secure counterparts. Although compassionate love per se has not been the target construct in these studies, the effects are replicated when compassionate love is measured directly. For example, Sprecher and Fehr (2007) found that secure attachment was positively correlated with compassionate love toward one's romantic partner, whereas avoidant attachment was negatively associated with compassionate love. (Anxious attachment was also negatively correlated with compassionate lover, but the association was weak.)

Attachment-related differences in the expression of compassionate love (or variables that serve as proxies for compassionate love) have been found in many contexts beyond the realm of close relationships, including altruistic helping, reactions to a stranger's distress, prosocial motives and behaviors, and volunteerism. For example, Gillath et al. (2005) examined behaviors and motives related to volunteering among young adults in Israel, the Netherlands, and the United States. Across countries, avoidant attachment was correlated with engaging in fewer volunteer activities and spending less time on such activities. Anxious attachment was not associated with participating in volunteer activities but was associated with self-serving motives for volunteering.

In a series of laboratory experiments, Mikulincer, Shaver, Gillath, and Nitzberg (2005) examined the decision to help a stranger in distress. In this research, a female confederate performed tasks that became progressively more aversive. She was informed that for the next task, she would have to hold a live tarantula—a prospect that appeared to cause her considerable upset. Participants were given an opportunity to relieve the woman's suffering by taking her place for the remaining tasks. Those who were more avoidant expressed less compassion for the woman and were less willing to help by taking her place. Anxious attachment was uncorrelated with compassion and willingness to help but was positively associated with personal distress in response to the woman's suffering.

In conclusion, there is mounting evidence that those who are low in attachment anxiety and avoidance (i.e., are secure) are more likely to engage in prosocial actions, including performing acts of compassion, than those who are high on these dimensions.

The Social Context

Although contextual factors have not received much research attention, the few studies that have been conducted support Underwood's (2002, 2009) claim that the expression of compassionate love is affected by the sociocultural context in which individuals are embedded. Volling, Kolak, and Kennedy (2009) examined an important milieu for promoting compassionate love, namely, the family. Participants were members of two-parent families with at least two young children. The parents were asked to report on their relationship with one another, their parenting and socialization practices, their children's sibling relationship, and each child's empathic concern. In addition, Volling et al. observed sibling interaction in the laboratory, as well as the children's response to an adult's need. Four compassionate behaviors (on the part of the children) were assessed during laboratory sessions: comfort, sharing, cooperation, and helping (e.g., a research assistant "accidentally" dropped a box of paper clips).

The results indicated that the family environment played a role in fostering compassionate love. Specifically, love between the parents was correlated with older siblings' empathic concern (as rated by the parents). Parental socialization practices also played a role in the development of empathic concern. For example, the father's encouragement of the expression of negative emotions was associated with younger siblings' empathic concern. This research also highlighted the role of siblings in socializing compassionate love. Positive involvement of older siblings with their younger sibling (as indicated by parents' reports) was correlated with the younger child's empathic concern. Further, the greater the empathic concern of the older child, the more likely it was that both children helped the research assistant who dropped her paper clips.

Compassionate love also takes different forms, depending on the target—for example, a close other, a stranger, or all of humanity. Sprecher and Fehr (2005) found that compassionate love for close others was more strongly associated with the provision of social support (e.g., emotional support, practical support) than was compassionate love for strangers/humanity. In contrast, spirituality and engaging in volunteer activities were more strongly associated with compassionate love for strangers/humanity than with compassionate love for close others.

Even within the same relationship, compassionate love is manifested differently depending on contextual factors. In the context of early marriage, compassionate love takes the form of globally adoring the partner while accepting the partner's specific strengths and weaknesses (Neff & Karney, 2009). In an end-of-life context, compassionate love toward one's partner takes a very different form. Roberts, Wise, and Du Benske (2009) conducted interviews with terminal cancer patients and their family caregivers (most often a spouse). Confrontation with death generally fostered compassionate love, which in this context took the form of caring for the other physically and emotionally, healing and forgiving (working through past transgressions and finding a way to move on), and letting go. (See chap. 11, this volume, for other findings related to mortality and altruism.) The authors concluded that "for caregivers of someone with a life-limiting illness, the *ultimate act of compassionate love* may be letting go, allowing and accepting death" (Roberts et al., p. 328, italics added).

The relevance of an independent versus interdependent sociocultural context to compassionate love was explored by Giesbrecht (2009) in a large-scale study of support staff who work with people who have cognitive and/or physical disabilities. Two caregiving environments were examined: l'Arche communities, in which disabled people live and receive treatment based on an interdependent ethic of care; and community living organizations, which are based on an independent ethic of care. In l'Arche communities, the goal is to develop mutual relationships between caregivers and the clients, on the basis of their common humanity. To facilitate this development, caregivers live with the disabled individuals in their care. In independent community living organizations, the goal for caregivers is to foster self-sufficiency and independence in their clients. Giesbrecht predicted and found that l'Arche support staff exhibited more compassionate care than community living staff. Thus, the endorsement of an interdependent versus an independent ethic of care influenced the expression of compassionate love (for other findings regarding situational contexts and helping behavior, see chap. 3, this volume).

Finally, Vaughan et al. (2009) explored whether compassionate love is facilitated in a collectivist culture (in this case, the Javanese in Indonesia) that values displays of interpersonal harmony and the avoidance of conflict (for other studies of cultural values related to prosocial motives and behavior, see chap. 12, this volume). Vaughan et al. hypothesized that empathy-related responding (a composite of sympathy and perspective taking) would predict prosocial behavior and cross-religion friendship. The participants were adolescents who completed measures of empathy-related responding, prosocial behavior, and their friendship networks. Parents and teachers also rated the adolescents on these variables. There was evidence that empathy-related responding was associated with prosocial behavior, but the prediction that adolescents who scored high on this variable would be more likely to have cross-religion friends was not supported. Overall, findings from this culture did not differ greatly from those obtained in research conducted in Western samples.

In conclusion, the limited evidence so far suggests that social and relational contexts that are loving, caring, and supportive are likely to facilitate the expression of compassionate love. Further research is needed to more fully explicate the role of relationship type as well as the role of culture in shaping this important emotion.

MOTIVATION AND DISCERNMENT

In Underwood's (2009) model, individual and social factors set the stage for the next step on the path toward compassionate love: motivation and discernment. She argued that to reach the ultimate goal of compassionate love fully expressed, a person must accurately perceive the potential recipient's need for compassionate love. Moreover, actions based on that perception must be motivated by other-centered, benevolent motives. Research on motivation has focused on two questions: Who is most likely to exhibit the kinds of prosocial motives that promote compassionate love? and What motives are most closely linked to the expression of compassionate love?

Who Is Most Likely to Report Compassionate Motivation?

In Marks and Song's (2009) analysis of U.S. survey data, three variables were considered motivational: altruistic normative obligation (e.g., paying for health care so that there is universal access), normative obligation to family (e.g., dropping one's own plans in response to one's child's need), and normative obligation to friends (e.g., raising a friend's child if the friend dies). On each of these measures, women scored higher than men. Young and early midlife adults scored lower than later midlife and young–old (45–75 years) adults. Race/ethnicity, education, and income generally did not show significant effects (with some exceptions).

In another analysis of national survey data, Smith (2009) conceptualized empathy (assessed with Davis's, 1996, empathy scale) and altruistic values (e.g., "People should be willing to help the less fortunate") as motives for compassionate acts. Consistent with Marks and Song's (2009) findings, women scored higher than men on these variables. Both empathy and altruistic values tended to increase with age. There were no significant differences in empathy as a function of education, income, or race. However, altruistic values tended to increase as education and income increased. Both empathy and altruistic values were associated with religious involvement and spirituality (for additional findings concerning empathic concern and altruistic helping, see chap. 1, this volume).

Finally, Mikulincer, Shaver, and their colleagues found that avoidant attachment is negatively associated with prosocial motives for engaging in compassionate acts (e.g., Mikulincer, Shaver, & Gillath, 2009). For example, in their analysis of volunteerism, Gillath et al. (2005) found that avoidance was negatively associated with altruistic and exploration-oriented motives for volunteerism. Anxious attachment was linked with egoistic or self-enhancement motives (e.g., wanting to be accepted, seeking distraction from personal problems).

In conclusion, research on who is most likely to report compassionate motivations mirrors the findings for who is most likely to experience compassionate love, namely, those who are female, spiritual, older and relatively low in attachment avoidance and anxiety (i.e. those who are securely attached).

What Motives Are Most Closely Tied to the Expression of Compassionate Love?

The construct of motivation is frequently partitioned into self- versus other-focused reasons for engaging in compassionate acts. For example, Omoto, Malsch, and Barraza (2009) assessed self-focused motives for volunteering (e.g., "to feel better about myself") and other-focused motives (e.g., "to help members of a particular community"). Other-focused motivation was more strongly correlated with conceptualizing volunteerism as an expression of compassionate love than was self-focused motivation ($r = .74$ vs. $r = .47$). Other-oriented motivation also was more strongly correlated with empathic concern than was self-oriented motivation ($r = .35$ vs. $r = .23$).

In their qualitative analysis of compassionate hospital clinicians, Graber and Mitcham (2009) identified four levels of patient–client interaction, characterized by differing degrees of focus on self versus other. They concluded that "compassion occurs primarily and most often when clinicians' focus is not on themselves, but on the well-being and interests of their patients" (p. 361). Along similar lines, Roberts and colleagues (2009) identified two motivational processes that facilitated compassionate love in the face of the impending death of a loved one: a shift to genuine other-centered goals, as opposed to defensive, self-serving goals, and a shift in priorities, allowing relationships to have precedence.

In conclusion, there is a common thread in the studies just reviewed: People whose actions are motivated by a desire to enhance the well-being of another, not of the self, are on the path to compassionate love fully expressed.

CAN COMPASSIONATE LOVE BE INCREASED?

Given the array of prosocial outcomes associated with compassionate love, it would seem important to develop interventions to increase this kind of love. Fortunately, there are already a number of promising avenues.

One successful method is to prime attachment security (for reviews, see Mikulincer & Shaver, 2007; chap. 14, this volume). For example, in a series of studies in which attachment security was primed in various ways (e.g., recalling personal memories, seeing a picture of a supportive interaction), participants read about a student who had lost her parents and sister in a car accident. Those who received a security prime (rather than a positive affect or a neutral prime) reported less self-oriented personal distress and greater empathy (e.g., compassion, sympathy, warmth) for the bereaved student. In another series of studies, security priming was found to reduce negative reactions to out-group members (Mikulincer & Shaver, 2001). Mikulincer and Shaver (2007) maintained that attachment security diminishes the need for defensive self-protection, thereby allowing a person's caregiving system to become fully active (see chap. 4, this volume).

Other approaches to increasing compassionate love include education and raising awareness. For example, Graber and Mitcham (2009) suggested that compassion can be fostered among hospital clinicians through the training of communication skills and empathic listening skills, and through exposure to compassionate role models. They emphasized that experiential methods (e.g., role playing, learning to put oneself in another's shoes) are likely to be more effective than passive learning (e.g., attending lectures on the importance of compassion).

Finally, Wright, Aron, and their colleagues (for a review, see Brody, Wright, Aron, & McLaughlin-Volpe, 2009) have examined the role of cross-group friendships in the creation of compassionate love—defined in this work as positive attitudes toward outgroup members (for other ways of fostering positive intergroup attitudes, see chap. 20, this volume). For example, in a study by Wright and Van Der Zande (1999), White women engaged in several interactions with either a White woman or a woman who was Asian or Latina. During the interactions, the participants engaged in closeness and friendship-building exercises. Later, White participants in the cross-group friendship condition reported more positive attitudes toward their partner's ethnic group as a whole, and even more positive attitudes toward minorities in general, than did White participants who were paired with a White partner.

Overall, there is good reason to believe that compassionate love can be enhanced in the real world. This is an important area for further research and experimental interventions.

COMPASSIONATE LOVE: CONCEPTUAL ISSUES AND FUTURE DIRECTIONS

Research on compassionate love has made remarkable progress in a brief period of time. There are, however, a number of issues that need to be addressed if scholarly work in this area is to flourish and grow. A crucial step is to situate compassionate love in the nomological net of related constructs, such as altruism, empathy, sympathy, social support, tenderness, and caregiving, not to mention compassion and love. Compassionate love must be conceptually and empirically distinguished from these other concepts if it is to stand on its own scientifically. Put another way, a case needs to be made that social science "needs" the concept of compassionate love, over and above existing prosocial concepts. Underwood (2002, 2009) has argued that the current lexicon of prosocial concepts does not adequately capture compassionate love as she conceptualizes it—namely, as a kind of love that is centered on the good of the other and that is intended to relieve distress as well as help the other flourish and grow. She has meticulously articulated points of similarity and difference between compassionate love and other prosocial concepts. For example, she specified that the term *compassion* refers more narrowly to responding to another's suffering, whereas *compassionate love* also includes efforts to enhance the growth and well-being of another. She also suggested that compassionate love is distinguishable from altruism on the basis of motivation—altruistic acts can be performed for self-centered or other-centered reasons, whereas compassionate love is motivated predominantly by the latter. However, additional conceptual analysis and precise scientific research is required to demonstrate that compassionate love is not simply redundant with other prosocial concepts and to elucidate the contribution that this made by the inclusion of this construct in the literature. It is possible, for example, that compassionate love could take on the status of a "central organizing construct," as has been ascribed to the concept of perceived partner responsiveness in the close relationships literature (e.g., Reis, Clark, & Holmes, 2004). Obviously, much empirical and conceptual work needs to be done before any such claims could be made.

As a starting point, it would be valuable to correlate compassionate love scales with measures of other prosocial concepts to examine convergent and discriminant validity. Preliminary steps in this direction were taken by Sprecher and Fehr (2005), although they examined only a small number of prosocial concepts. Another option would be to conduct prototype analyses in which participants list features of compassionate love as well as related constructs (e.g., empathy, sympathy, social support, compassion, love in general) to identify features unique to compassionate love and reveal areas of overlap with other prosocial concepts. Such analyses have been conducted to clarify the relation between love and commitment; love, liking, and being in love; and intimacy and sexual intimacy. Prototype analyses have also proven useful for revealing the hierarchical structure of concepts (e.g., identifying which concepts are superordinate; which concepts are basic; and which are lower level, subordinate categories). Analyses along the lines of those conducted on the hierarchical organization of emotions concepts (see, e.g., Shaver et al., 1987) could prove useful in revealing whether compassionate love should be construed as an overarching, higher order prosocial concept. Although these kinds of analysis are confined to laypeople's definitions and concepts, lay conceptions frequently do inform experts' conceptualizations and provide useful information in their own right.

A related, but even thornier, task is specifying where other prosocial concepts fit in models of compassionate love. This point can be illustrated with the concept of empathy. Some scholars conceptualize empathy as an individual-level variable. For example, Vaughan et al. (2009) proposed a model in which empathy-related responding leads to motivation and discernment, which, in turn, leads to compassionate love fully expressed. However, in other research, empathy is classified as a motivation and discernment variable (e.g., Graber & Mitcham, 2009; Smith, 2009; Volling et al., 2009). Obviously, it is difficult to integrate findings if the same construct does double duty (i.e., as an antecedent and as a motivational variable) in models of compassionate love. It will be important in future work to gather the kind of data that will allow researchers to test whether empathy is an individual-level variable, a motivation and discernment variable, an outcome variable, or a part of the construct of compassionate love. A first step would be to compare the predictive power of various models, depending on where empathy is placed in the causal chain. Similar analyses would be required for other prosocial concepts (e.g., sympathy, compassion, altruism) to determine where these fit in models of compassionate love.

Thus, a pressing issue for future research will be to clarify the status of compassionate love vis á vis other prosocial concepts. Fortunately, social scientists possess the methodological tools to take on this challenge.

CONCLUSION

In conclusion, the purpose of this chapter was to paint—or at least sketch—a picture of research on a fledgling but flourishing topic, compassionate love. Scholars have made important strides in identifying the individual and social-contextual factors that facilitate the experience and expression of this prosocial emotion. Further, some of the underlying motives have been explicated. Although intervention efforts have not directly targeted compassionate love, the literature on security priming and cross-group friendship formation offers hope that compassionate love can be enhanced. Further research on compassionate love is encouraged because it has the potential to broaden our understanding of prosocial emotions, and ultimately to make the world a more humane, caring place.

REFERENCES

Aron, A., & Westbay, L. (1996). Dimensions of the prototype of love. *Journal of Personality and Social Psychology*, *70*, 535–551.

Berscheid, E. (1985). Interpersonal attraction. In G. Lindzey & E. Aronson (Eds.), *The handbook of social psychology* (3rd ed., vol. 2; pp.413–484). New York: Random House.

Berscheid, E. (2006). Searching for the meaning of "love." In R. J. Sternberg & K. Weis (Eds.), *The new psychology of love* (pp. 171–183). New Haven, CT: Yale University Press.

Brody, S., Wright, S. C., Aron, A., & McLaughin-Volpe, T. (2009). Compassionate love for individuals in other social groups. In B. Fehr, S. Sprecher, & L. G. Underwood (Eds.), *The science of compassionate love: Theory, research, and applications* (pp. 283–308). West Sussex, England: Wiley-Blackwell.

Davis, M. H. (1996). *Empathy: A social psychological approach.* Boulder, CO: Westview Press.

Eagly, A. H., & Crowley, M. (1986). Gender and helping behavior: A meta-analytic review of the social psychological literature. *Psychological Bulletin, 100,* 283–308.

Fehr, B. (1988). Prototype analysis of the concepts of love and commitment. *Journal of Personality and Social Psychology, 55,* 557–579.

Fehr, B. (1993). How do I love thee . . . ? Let me consult my prototype. In S. Duck (Ed.), *Understanding personal relationships: Vol. 1. Individuals in relationships* (pp. 87–120). Newbury Park, CA: Sage.

Fehr, B. (2005). The role of prototypes in interpersonal cognition. In M. W. Baldwin (Ed.), *Interpersonal cognition* (pp. 180–206). New York: Guilford Press.

Fehr, B. (2006). A prototype approach to studying love. In R. J. Sternberg & K. Weis (Eds.), *The new psychology of love* (pp. 225–246). New Haven, CT: Yale University Press.

Fehr, B. (2008, February). *Compassionate love: Conceptual, measurement, and relational issues.* Paper presented at the Close Relationships Preconference, Society for Personality and Social Psychology, Albuquerque, NM.

Fehr, B., & Russell, J. A. (1984). Concept of emotion viewed from a prototype perspective. *Journal of Experimental Psychology: General, 113,* 464–486.

Fehr, B., & Russell, J. A. (1991). The concept of love viewed from a prototype perspective. *Journal of Personality and Social Psychology, 60,* 425–438.

Fehr, B., & Sprecher, S. (in press). Prototype analysis of compassionate love. *Personal Relationships.*

Fehr, B., Sprecher, S., & Underwood, L. (Eds.). (2009). *The science of compassionate love: Theory, research, and applications.* Malden, MA: Blackwell/Wiley.

Giesbrecht, N. D. (2009). Caregiving in sociocultural context. In B. Fehr, S. Sprecher, & L. G. Underwood (Eds.), *The science of compassionate love: Theory, research, and applications* (pp. 373–402). West Sussex, England: Wiley-Blackwell.

Gillath, O., Shaver, P. R., Mikulincer, M., Nitzberg, R. E., Erez, A., & van IJzendoorn, M. H. (2005). Attachment, caregiving, and volunteering: Placing volunteerism in an attachment-theoretical framework. *Personal Relationships, 12,* 425–446.

Graber, D. R., & Mitcham, M. D. (2009). Compassionate clinicians: Exemplary care in hospital settings. In B. Fehr, S. Sprecher, & L. G. Underwood (Eds.), *The science of compassionate love: Theory, research, and applications* (pp. 345–372). West Sussex, England: Wiley-Blackwell.

Gulli, C. (2005, September, 17). Why I gave a stranger a kidney. *National Post*, p. A1.

Hendrick, C., & Hendrick, S. (1986). A theory and method of love. *Journal of Personality and Social Psychology, 50*, 392–402.

Lamm, H., & Wiesmann, U. (1997). Subjective attributes of attraction: How people characterize their liking, their love, and their being in love. *Personal Relationships, 4*, 271–284.

Luby, V., & Aron, A. (1990, July). *A prototype structuring of love, liking, and being in-love.* Paper presented at the International Conference on Personal Relationships, Oxford, England.

Marks, N. F., & Song, J. (2009). Compassionate motivation and compassionate acts across the adult life course: Evidence from US national studies. In B. Fehr, S. Sprecher, & L.G. Underwood (Eds.), *The science of compassionate love: Theory, research, and applications* (pp. 121–158). West Sussex, England: Wiley-Blackwell.

Mervis, C. B., & Rosch, E. (1981). Categorization of natural objects. *Annual Review of Psychology, 32*, 89–115.

Mikulincer, M., & Shaver, P. R. (2001). Attachment theory and intergroup bias: Evidence that priming the secure base schema attenuates negative reactions to outgroups. *Journal of Personality and Social Psychology, 81*, 97–115.

Mikulincer, M., & Shaver, P. R. (2007). *Attachment in adulthood: Structure, dynamics, and change.* New York: Guilford Press.

Mikulincer, M., Shaver, P. R., & Gillath, O. (2009). A behavioral systems perspective on compassionate love. In B. Fehr, S. Sprecher, & L. G. Underwood (Eds.), *The science of compassionate love: Theory, research, and applications* (pp. 201–222). West Sussex, England: Wiley-Blackwell.

Mikulincer, M., Shaver, P. R., Gillath, O., & Nitzberg, R. A. (2005). Attachment, caregiving, and altruism: Boosting attachment security increases compassion and helping. *Journal of Personality and Social Psychology*, 89, 817–839.

Neff, L. A., & Karney, B. R. (2009). Compassionate love in early marriage. In B. Fehr, S. Sprecher, & L. G. Underwood (Eds.), *The science of compassionate love: Theory, research, and applications* (pp. 201–222). West Sussex, England: Wiley-Blackwell.

Omoto, A. M., Malsch, A. M., & Barraza, J. A. (2009). Compassionate acts: Motivations for and correlates of volunteerism among older adults. In B. Fehr, S. Sprecher, & L.G. Underwood (Eds.), *The science of compassionate love: Theory, research, and applications* (pp. 257–282). West Sussex, England: Wiley-Blackwell.

Post, S. G., Underwood, L. G., Schloss, J. P., & Hurlbut, W. B. (Eds.). (2002). *Altruism and altruistic love: Science, philosophy, and religion in dialog.* New York: Oxford University Press.

Reis, H. T., Clark, M. S., & Holmes, J. G. (2004). Perceived partner responsiveness as an organizing construct in the study of intimacy and closeness. In D. J. Mashek

& A. Aron (Eds.), *Handbook of closeness and intimacy* (pp. 201–225). New York: Oxford University Press.

Regan, P. C., Kocan, E. R., & Whitlock, T. (1998). Ain't love grand! A prototype analysis of the concept of romantic love. *Journal of Social and Personal Relationships, 15*, 411–420.

Roberts, L. J., Wise, M., & DuBenske, L. L. (2009). Compassionate family caregiving in the light and shadow of death. In B. Fehr, S. Sprecher, & L. G. Underwood (Eds.), *The science of compassionate love: Theory, research, and applications* (pp. 311–344). West Sussex, England: Wiley-Blackwell.

Rosch, E. (1973). On the internal structure of perceptual and semantic categories. In T. E. Moore (Ed.), *Cognitive development and the acquisition of language* (pp. 111–144). New York: Academic Press.

Shacham-Dupont, S. (2003). Compassion and love in relationships: Can they coexist? *Relationship Research News, 2*, 13–15.

Shaver, P., Schwartz, J., Kirson, D., & O'Connor, C. (1987). Emotion knowledge: Further explorations of a prototype approach. *Journal of Personality and Social Psychology, 52*, 1061–1086.

Smith, T. W. (2009). Loving and caring in the United States: Trends and correlates of empathy, altruism, and related constructs. In B. Fehr, S. Sprecher, & L. G. Underwood (Eds.), *The science of compassionate love: Theory, research, and applications* (pp. 81–120). West Sussex, England: Wiley-Blackwell.

Sprecher, S., & Fehr, B. (2005). Compassionate love for close others and humanity. *Journal of Social and Personal Relationships, 22*, 629–651.

Sprecher, S., & Fehr, B. (2007). *General and relationship-specific attachment as predictors of compassionate love for a romantic partner.* Unpublished manuscript, Illinois State University, Normal, IL.

Sprecher, S., Fehr, B., & Zimmerman, C. (2007). Expectation for mood enhancement as a result of helping: The effects of gender and compassionate love. *Sex Roles, 56*, 543–549.

Taylor, S. E. (2002). *The tending instinct: Women, men, and the biology of our relationships*. New York: Henry Holt.

Underwood, L. G. (2002). The human experience of compassionate love: Conceptual mapping and data from selected studies. In S. G. Post, L. G. Underwood, J. P. Schloss, & W. B. Hurlbut (Eds.), *Altruism and altruistic love: Science, philosophy, and religion in dialogue* (pp. 72–88). Oxford, England: Oxford University Press.

Underwood, L. G. (2009). Compassionate love: A framework for research. In B. Fehr, S. Sprecher, & L.G. Underwood (Eds.), *The science of compassionate love: Theory, research, and applications* (pp. 3–26). West Sussex, England: Wiley-Blackwell.

Underwood, L. G., & Teresi, J. (2002). The Daily Spiritual Experience Scale: Development, theoretical description, reliability, exploratory factor analysis, and preliminary construct validity using health-related data. *Annals of Behavioral Medicine, 24*, 22–33.

Vaughan, J., Eisenberg, N., French, D.C., Purwono, U., Suryanti, T. A., & Pidada, S. (2009). Testing aspects of compassionate love in a sample of Indonesian adolescents. In B. Fehr, S. Sprecher, & L.G. Underwood (Eds.), *The science of compassionate love: Theory, research, and applications* (pp. 405–430). West Sussex, England: Wiley-Blackwell.

Volling, B. L., Kolak, A. M., & Kennedy, D. E. (2009). Empathy and compassionate love in early childhood: Developmental and family influence. In B. Fehr, S. Sprecher, & L.G. Underwood (Eds.), *The science of compassionate love: Theory, research, and applications* (pp. 161–200). West Sussex, England: Wiley-Blackwell.

Wright, S. C., & van Der Zande, C. C. (1999, October). *Bicultural friends: When cross-group friendships cause improved intergroup attitudes*. Paper presented at the Society for Experimental Social Psychology conference, St. Louis, MO.

14

DOES GRATITUDE PROMOTE PROSOCIAL BEHAVIOR? THE MODERATING ROLE OF ATTACHMENT SECURITY

MARIO MIKULINCER AND PHILLIP R. SHAVER

As part of a general turn toward positive psychology (e.g., Seligman, 2002), psychological researchers have begun to examine the nature and effects of classical virtues, one of which is gratitude. Emmons and McCullough (2004), for example, portrayed gratitude as a remedy for many of life's hardships and a way to achieve peace of mind, happiness, physical health, and improved social relationships. The sacred writings of the three major monotheistic faiths, Judaism, Christianity, and Islam, as well as Buddhist and Hindu writings, emphasize the desirability and benefits of gratitude (Emmons & Crumple, 2000). Even before the advent of positive psychology, Graham (1988) and Peterson and Stewart (1996) reported that people who feel more grateful after receiving a benefit are later more likely to help the benefactor and other people as well. Even earlier, Baron (1984) found that grateful people are less likely to engage in hostile, destructive behavior. In short, gratitude seems to foster prosocial behavior, which makes it relevant to the present volume.

For centuries, gratitude was a prominent topic in philosophy, and philosophers could be divided into two groups—those who glorified gratitude and those who viewed it as tinged with egoistic motives and feelings of obligation (McCullough, Emmons, & Tsang, 2002). In other words, gratitude, like empathy (see chap. 1, this volume), has a mixed reputation. It may lead naturally to prosocial behavior, but it may also be contaminated or distorted by selfish, self-protective motives. If so, the link between gratitude and prosocial behavior may not be either simple or straightforward.

From ancient Greek philosophers to contemporary thinkers, gratitude has often been viewed as an important contributor to harmonious relationships (McCullough et al., 2002). The prominent child psychoanalyst Melanie Klein (1957) suggested that the development of gratitude in childhood goes hand in hand with the development of generosity because a grateful person wishes to benefit others by sharing the gifts he or she has received. In a more recent analysis, Tsang (2006) suggested that "the receipt of a benefit from another may trigger the norm of reciprocity, which states that individuals should help, as well as refrain from harming, people who have helped them" (p. 139). And Bartlett and DeSteno (2006) claimed that gratitude contributes to trust, which is especially likely to develop when a benefactor engages in costly acts of generosity (see chap. 17, this volume).

We are interested here in the possibility that the beneficial effects of gratitude on prosocial behavior are moderated by attachment insecurity. In our previous work (e.g., Mikulincer, Shaver, Gillath, & Nitzberg, 2005), we found that attachment insecurity interferes in various ways with prosocial attitudes and behavior. Thus, it seems likely that insecurity will also disrupt the otherwise normative link between gratitude and prosocial behavior. We begin by considering evidence for that normative link in general. We then explain parts of attachment theory (Bowlby, 1982; see also chaps 4 and 19, this volume) in sufficient detail to allow their use in our examination of gratitude. Next, we review some of our previous work on attachment insecurity and prosocial caregiving, which provides a model for research on gratitude and prosocial behavior. We then present new research, including two previously unpublished studies, on the moderation of the gratitude–altruism link by two forms of attachment insecurity, attachment anxiety and avoidance. We explain how these attachment insecurities affect both the texture of gratitude experiences and the effects of such experiences on prosocial behavior.

GRATITUDE AND PROSOCIAL BEHAVIOR

In psychology, gratitude has been portrayed in diverse ways, as a positive emotion, a personality trait, a positive attitude toward others, a moral virtue, and a constructive approach to interpersonal relations (e.g., Emmons

& McCullough, 2004; Weiner, 1985). Emmons and McCullough (2004) concluded, despite these different perspectives, that gratitude can be conceptualized in terms of three propositions. First, the object of gratitude is always an "other," whether a human being, a nonhuman natural being (e.g., an animal, the weather), or a supernatural being (e.g., God). Second, gratitude is a response to a perceived personal benefit (e.g., a material, emotional, or spiritual gain) resulting from another's actions, a benefit that has not necessarily been earned or deserved. Third, gratitude stems from appraising the benefactor's actions as intentionally designed to benefit the recipient, even if the intention is metaphorical, as in the case of good weather ("Thank you for not raining on my parade"). Agreeing with this conception, Tsang (2006) defined *gratitude* as "a positive emotional reaction to the receipt of a benefit that is perceived to have resulted from the good intentions of another" (p. 139).

Given her psychoanalytic perspective, Klein (1957) focused on the mother–infant relationship and equated the ability to feel gratitude with the ability to love. She proposed that warm, comforting interactions with a sensitive, responsive, and supportive caregiver foster positive mental representations of others (an idea taken up later by Bowlby, 1973, who had studied under Klein). These positive representations soften or dilute destructive emotions, such as greed and envy, and cause infants to feel they have received a unique gift from their mother that they wish to keep. This feeling makes it easier, later on, to feel grateful for other people's kindness and generosity. Klein (1957) also viewed gratitude as part of a child's assimilation of a "good object" (mental representation of another person), which enriches the self and provides inner resources for coping with frustrations and hardships without bitterness.

Viewing gratitude as an inner resource is also part of positive psychology (e.g., Seligman, 2002). Happiness and life satisfaction are viewed not only as consequences of luck or genetics but also as results of personal strengths shaped by social experiences and of deliberate personal effort. The capacity for gratitude is one of these strengths, which can improve physical and mental health (Emmons & McCullough, 2004). In support of this view, Emmons and McCullough (2003) found that priming thoughts of gratitude each day over a period of weeks measurably improved people's sense of health and well-being.

McCullough et al. (2002) constructed a self-report scale to measure individual differences in dispositional gratitude (the Gratitude Questionnaire-6; GQ-6). They viewed the "grateful disposition" as a tendency to recognize others' generous contributions to one's own well-being and to feel thankful. People who score high on dispositional gratitude are expected to feel more grateful than low scorers following positive events, and to feel grateful for more aspects of, or more people in, their lives. In support of this view, Watkins, Woodward, Stone, and Kolts (2003) found that grateful people tended to experience greater "abundance" in their lives, feel grateful for others' contributions to their personal well-being, and appreciate even small pleasures in life.

McCullough et al. (2002) found, in support of a hypothesized link between dispositional gratitude and prosocial behavior, that people who scored higher on the GQ-6 were more empathic toward others who were distressed. Moreover, such people engaged more frequently in prosocial behavior and were rated as more generous and helpful by their friends and relatives (McCullough et al., 2002). As mentioned earlier, Graham (1988) and Peterson and Stewart (1996), studying state rather than dispositional gratitude, found that people who felt more grateful after being benefited by another person were more likely to be helpful later on. Because these findings were based on self-reports of helping behavior and on cross-sectional research designs, however, they do not provide strong evidence for the causal hypothesis that gratitude increases the occurrence of helping behavior rather than merely being correlated with it.

Bartlett and DeSteno (2006) and Tsang (2006) recently overcame these methodological limitations by experimentally manipulating gratitude and then assessing actual helping behavior. In Bartlett and DeSteno's (2006) study, participants in a gratitude condition performed a tedious, repetitive, aversive eye-hand coordination task and were informed after completing it that, because of a computer problem, they would need to perform it again. Just then, a confederate (the "benefactor"), who had completed the task without any difficulty, solved the computer problem and made it unnecessary for the study participant to repeat the task. This gratitude condition was compared with a neutral condition (in which there was no computer problem and the confederate merely conversed briefly with participants) and a positive mood condition (in which participants watched a humorous video clip after the tedious task). At the end of the experiment, participants were approached by either the confederate or a stranger and asked if they would be willing to help with a cognitively taxing problem-solving survey. Time spent on the survey was the index of helping behavior. Bartlett and DeSteno (2006) found that participants in the gratitude condition spent more time helping the benefactor or the stranger than participants in the neutral and positive mood conditions. Moreover, this effect was mediated by feelings of gratitude and could not be explained by other measured positive emotions.

In Tsang's (2006) study, participants performed three rounds of a resource-distribution task with a confederate and received, by "chance," less money than the confederate in the first round. In the second round, the confederate in the gratitude condition gave most of the money he or she had gained (9 out of 10 dollars) and wrote to the participant, "I saw that you didn't get a lot in the last round—that must've been a bummer" (p. 142). In the control condition, participants received $9 by chance. All participants received $10 in the third round and were asked to distribute the money between themselves and the confederate and to write the reasons for their distribution decision. Participants in the gratitude condition gave more money to the confederate than did participants in the chance condition and were more likely to write that they were expressing appreciation or gratitude.

Although these two studies demonstrated that experimental manipulations of gratitude can facilitate prosocial behavior, they did not take into account the possibility that people differ in their reactions to receiving a valued benefit from others. For example, one person may react to the benefit with appreciation, whereas another may mistrust the benefactor's intentions. Hence, one person may express gratitude as a means of strengthening his or her relationship with the benefactor, whereas another may believe that such an expression is a threat to his or her sense of personal freedom and dignity ("I was so weak that I needed help"). In addition, the designers of these studies did not consider that research participants may differ in relationship history, their mental representations of other people, or their disposition to feel empathic concern for other's needs (see chaps. 1, 4, and 7, this volume). Such individual differences may moderate people's reactions to generous behavior and the extent to which gratitude leads to prosocial behavior.

We believe that attachment theory (Bowlby, 1973, 1982), the framework motivating our research (for a review, see Mikulincer & Shaver, 2007), offers an integrative explanation of individual differences that affect the link between gratitude and prosocial behavior. The theory deals specifically with the long-term effects of relationship history, beginning in infancy, on mental representations of others, empathic concern, and prosocial behavior. In the next section, we explain key components of the theory.

ATTACHMENT THEORY AND THE MENTAL REPRESENTATION OF OTHERS

According to attachment theory (Bowlby, 1982), human infants are born with a repertoire of behaviors (*attachment behaviors*) designed by evolution to assure proximity to supportive others (*attachment figures*) because such proximity protects an infant from physical and psychological dangers and threats and fosters emotional stability (good affect regulation) and healthy exploration. Bowlby (1973) also proposed that experiences with particular attachment figures produce fairly stable individual differences in mental representations of the self and others and a broadly applied *attachment style*—a systematic pattern of relational expectations, emotions, and behaviors that results from a particular attachment history (Fraley & Shaver, 2000). Research, beginning with Ainsworth, Blehar, Waters, and Wall (1978) and continuing through recent studies by social and personality psychologists (reviewed by Mikulincer & Shaver, 2007) has indicated that individual differences in attachment style can be measured along two orthogonal dimensions, attachment-related *anxiety* and *avoidance* (Brennan, Clark, & Shaver, 1998). A person's position on the anxiety (or anxious attachment) dimension indicates the degree to which he or she worries that a partner will not be available and responsive in times of need. A person's position on the avoidance dimension indicates the extent to which he or she distrusts relationship partners' goodwill and strives to maintain behavioral independence and emotional distance from partners. People who score high on these dimensions are said to be insecure, or to have an insecure attachment style.

Mikulincer and Shaver (2007) proposed that variations along the dimensions of attachment anxiety and avoidance reflect both a person's sense of attachment security and the ways in which he or she deals with distress. People who score low on both dimensions hold internalized representations of comforting attachment figures, which create a continuing sense of attachment security, positive self-regard, and reliance on constructive strategies of affect regulation. Those who score high on either attachment anxiety or avoidance possess internalized representations of frustrating or unavailable attachment figures and hence suffer from a continuing sense of attachment insecurity. These insecure individuals rely on what Cassidy and Kobak (1988) called *secondary attachment strategies* (contrasted with the primary strategy of seeking proximity to an attachment figure in times of need). These strategies involve either hyperactivating or deactivating the attachment system in an attempt to regulate distress. High scores on the attachment anxiety dimension are associated with hyperactivating strategies: energetic attempts to attain greater proximity, support, and love combined with a lack of confidence that it will be provided. High scores on avoidant attachment are associated with deactivating strategies—inhibition of proximity-seeking tendencies, denial of attachment needs, maintenance of emotional and cognitive distance from others, and compulsive reliance on oneself as the only reliable source of protection.

According to attachment theory, differences in attachment histories are evident in a person's mental representations of others (Bowlby, 1973; Shaver & Hazan, 1993), which Bowlby called *internal working models of others*. Whereas security-enhancing interactions with available and responsive attachment figures promote a positive working model of others, emotionally painful, frustrating interactions with cold, unavailable, or rejecting attachment figures weaken a person's sense of security and contribute to negative working models of other people. These models are gradually generalized across interactions with a particular attachment figure and then combined with models of other partners to create general models that can have a top-down or schematic effect on perceptions of and expectations about others.

Bowlby's (1973) conceptualization of working models of others implies that insecure individuals, who score high on one or both attachment-insecurity dimensions, are likely to harbor negative beliefs about other people's intentions and traits. We (Mikulincer & Shaver, 2007) have shown how avoidant strategies exacerbate negative views of others by diverting attention away from attachment-relevant information, including information about others' positive traits, intentions, and actions. In this way, genuine signals of a partner's love and support or the receipt of a valued benefit from the partner can be missed. And even when noticed, these positive actions can easily be forgotten and remain inaccessible when later appraisals of the partner are made.

Anxious, hyperactivating strategies are associated with complex, ambivalent mental representations of others. Although anxiously attached people have a history of frustrating interactions with attachment figures, they still believe that if they intensify their proximity-seeking efforts, they may force relationship partners to pay attention and provide adequate support (Mikulincer & Shaver, 2007). This hopeful attitude stems from previous relationships in which parents or other relationship partners were sometimes responsive and sometimes not, thereby placing the anxiously attached person on a partial reinforcement schedule that inadvertently rewards persistence in proximity seeking (Shaver & Hazan, 1993). As a result, anxiously attached people, unlike avoidant ones, do not form a simple negative view of others and decide that proximity seeking is hopeless. They tend instead to take some of the blame for relationship partners' unreliable attention, which lowers their self-confidence, but they also tend to become angry or jealous when a partner seems not to care enough (Mikulincer & Shaver, 2007). In other words, they hold out hope for true love and security while doubting their ability to attain and hold onto them.

Numerous studies have shown that people who score relatively high on measures of attachment anxiety and avoidance tend to describe relationship partners in less positive trait terms (e.g., Levy, Blatt, & Shaver, 1998), to perceive partners as less supportive (e.g., Ognibene & Collins, 1998), and to feel less trusting than their less anxious peers (e.g., Hazan & Shaver, 1987). In addition, people high on attachment anxiety or avoidance have more negative expectations about their partner's behavior (e.g., Baldwin, Fehr, Keedian, Seidel, & Thomson, 1993) and tend to explain their partner's negative behavior in less positive, less tolerant terms (e.g., Collins, 1996).

ATTACHMENT INSECURITIES, CAREGIVING, AND PROSOCIAL BEHAVIOR

Beyond conceptualizing the attachment system, Bowlby (1982) proposed that human beings are innately equipped with another system aimed at providing nurturance (the *caregiving behavioral system*). Theoretically, the caregiving system evolved because providing care for dependent or injured individuals (e.g., infants, frightened or injured family members) increased inclusive fitness (see chap. 4, this volume). Its operation is most evident in parents' emotional and behavioral reactions to their offspring's signals of need or distress. But we believe this system is also the innate foundation of empathy, compassion, and prosocial behavior.

According to Bowlby (1982), there is a dynamic interplay between the attachment system and the caregiving system, by which the natural tendency to provide care to dependent or needy others can be suppressed or overridden by attachment insecurity. Under conditions of threat, adults often think of turning to others for support and comfort rather than thinking first of providing care to others. At such times they are likely to be so focused on their own vulnerability that they lack the mental resources necessary to attend compassionately to other people's need for help. Only when relief is attained and a sense of attachment security is restored can a person fully direct attention and energy to other behavioral systems. Only a relatively secure person can easily perceive others not only as sources of security and support but also as human beings who themselves need and deserve support. An insecure person may have difficulty finding the mental resources necessary to provide sensitive and effective care to others. On this basis, Kunce and Shaver (1994), Mikulincer and Shaver (2007), and others (e.g., Simpson, Rholes, & Nelligan, 1992; chap. 19, this volume) have argued that attachment-related insecurities impede altruistic helping, whereas attachment security makes empathy, compassion, and prosocial behavior more likely.

Recently, we have begun to examine associations between attachment security, on the one hand, and prosocial feelings and behaviors, on the other. For example, Mikulincer et al. (2001) found that contextual heightening of the sense of attachment security increased compassionate responses to others' suffering. They also found that higher scores on avoidant attachment were negatively associated with empathic reactions to others' suffering. Higher scores on the anxiety dimension were associated with personal distress in response to another's suffering, but not with empathic responses. (The distinction between empathic concern and personal distress is discussed by Batson in chap. 1, this volume.) In other studies (Mikulincer et al., 2003), experimentally engendered security increased the endorsement of two "self-transcendence values" (see chap. 12, this volume), benevolence and universalism, which encourage prosocial behavior. In these studies, higher scores on the avoidance dimension were negatively associated with endorsement of these values.

Attachment insecurities are also negatively related to offering care to a mate. Individuals who score high on anxiety or avoidance are less sensitive to their romantic or marital partner's needs, report less cooperative caregiving, and spontaneously offer less comfort and reassurance to their distressed partner (e.g., Feeney & Collins, 2001; Simpson et al., 1992). For example, Simpson et al. (1992) unobtrusively videotaped dating couples while the female partner waited to undergo a stressful procedure, finding that secure men recognized their partner's worries and provided more emotional support and more supportive comments if their partner showed higher levels of distress. In contrast, men who scored high on avoidance actually provided less support as their partner's distress increased.

In an attempt to examine attachment-and-caregiving dynamics in the wider social world, Gillath et al. (2005) examined associations between attachment insecurities, involvement in altruistic volunteer activities, and motives for volunteering. The findings were similar across the three countries that were sampled—the United States, Israel, and the Netherlands. Avoidant attachment was associated with engaging in fewer volunteer activities, devoting less time to such activities, and being less motivated by desires to express altruistic values and to learn about oneself and the world. Attachment anxiety was not generally related to engaging or not engaging in volunteer activities or to devoting more or less time to such activities, but it was associated with more egoistic reasons for volunteering.

In a recent series of studies, Mikulincer et al. (2005) examined the actual decision to help or not to help a person in distress. In the first two experiments, participants watched a confederate while she performed a series of aversive tasks. As the study progressed, the confederate became increasingly distressed, and the actual participant was given an opportunity to take her place, in effect sacrificing self for the welfare of another. Shortly before this scenario unfolded, participants were primed with either representations of attachment security (the name of a participant's security provider) or attachment-unrelated representations (the name of a mere acquaintance or the name of a familiar person who was not an attachment figure). This priming was conducted at either a subliminal or a supraliminal level. Both kinds of security induction increased participants' compassion and willingness to take the distressed person's place. This made us wonder whether gratitude, another prosocial emotion, might work similarly to empathy and compassion.

ATTACHMENT INSECURITIES AND GRATITUDE

From an attachment perspective, the experience of gratitude should be similar to feelings of being protected, accepted, and valued, in which case it should contribute to working models of others as available, responsive, supportive, and loving (Bowlby, 1973; Shaver & Hazan, 1993). In other words, attachment security should be associated with dispositional gratitude. In contrast, avoidant individuals would be expected to react with less gratitude to others' generous behavior. They tend not to believe in others' goodwill even when it is demonstrated, and they do not wish to depend on or be supported by other people (Mikulincer & Shaver, 2007). Moreover, expressions of gratitude toward a relationship partner can be interpreted as a sign of closeness or dependence, which is incongruent with avoidant people's preference for emotional distance and self-reliance. People who score high on attachment anxiety are expected to react ambivalently to others' generous behavior. They tend not to believe they deserve others' kindness and tend to worry that they will not be able to reciprocate fully or meet a partner's needs and expectations. This, in turn, may contaminate gratitude with fear and anxiety (Mikulincer & Shaver, 2007).

Mikulincer, Shaver, and Slav (2006) tested these ideas in two recent studies. In the first study, 142 Israeli undergraduates completed the Experiences in Close Relationships inventory (ECR; Brennan et al., 1998), a measure of attachment-related anxiety and avoidance; they also completed the GQ-6 scale (McCullough et al., 2002) and the Gratitude Experience Scale (GES)—a 29-item measure we created to tap the subjective experience of gratitude. In the GES, participants were asked to recall a specific situation in which they felt grateful to someone and then rate the extent to which they experienced each of several feelings, thoughts, and wishes (security feelings, happiness and love, narcissistic threats, generosity and positive outlook on life, a sense of distrust in the other's goodwill, a sense of inferiority and vulnerability, feelings of obligation).

In line with predictions based on attachment theory, both attachment anxiety and avoidance contributed uniquely to explaining variance in dispositional gratitude and in the experience of gratitude. In particular, avoidant attachment was inversely associated with dispositional gratitude and with feelings of security, happiness/love, and generosity. Moreover, avoidant attachment was positively associated with the experience of narcissistic threats and distrust while feeling grateful. Although attachment anxiety was not significantly associated with dispositional gratitude, it was positively related to security feelings, happiness/love, and generosity, and to narcissistic threats and feelings of inferiority and obligation. In other words, anxious attachment was associated with ambivalent experiences of gratitude.

In the second study, we examined whether the observed attachment-gratitude links also occurred in marital relationships and could be observed in daily reactions to specific partner behaviors. For this purpose, 55 newlywed couples (both husbands and wives) completed the ECR inventory, the GQ-6, and the GES. In addition, they completed a questionnaire each evening for 21 days, listed positive and negative behaviors exhibited by the partner that day, and rated the extent to which they felt grateful to their spouse during that day.

The results for the GQ-6 and the GES replicated the findings of the first study, again illustrating avoidant people's generally negative characterization of gratitude experiences and anxious people's ambivalent experiences. For both husbands and wives, avoidant but not anxious attachment predicted lower levels of daily gratitude toward one's partner across the 21-day study period. It is interesting that husbands' avoidant attachment interacted with daily perceptions of wife's behavior in determining daily gratitude. Whereas less avoidant husbands reported more gratitude on days when they perceived more positive spousal behavior, more avoidant husbands reported relatively low levels of gratitude even on days when they noticed their wife's positive behavior. In other words, a husband's avoidant orientation not only inhibited gratitude overall, it also interfered with feeling grateful for a wife's specific beneficial behavior on a particular day.

Overall, Mikulincer et al.'s (2006) findings indicate that attachment insecurities are related to reductions in or distortions of gratitude. Avoidant attachment is related to lower levels of gratitude, even in relational contexts that might make gratitude seem natural. Anxious attachment has a more complex signature: It does not necessarily eliminate gratitude, but it sullies gratitude with conflicting feelings that may erode its beneficial effects.

DO ATTACHMENT INSECURITIES MODERATE THE LINK BETWEEN GRATITUDE AND PROSOCIAL BEHAVIOR?

On the basis of the findings reviewed so far, we hypothesized that the receipt of a valued benefit from another person, and even the expression of gratitude per se, is not sufficient to increase the likelihood of prosocial behavior. Rather, the link between gratitude and prosocial behavior is likely to depend on a person's attachment orientation: Attachment security should allow gratitude to strengthen prosocial behavior, and attachment insecurities should erode the natural compassion and altruism one would otherwise expect to see following receipt of a valued benefit from another person.

As explained earlier, people who have enjoyed a gratifying history of interactions with attachment figures and who generally feel secure and valued as a result tend to hold positive beliefs about other people's goodwill and character traits, and to be predisposed to feel empathic concern for others' needs and to engage in prosocial behavior aimed at alleviating others' suffering. Moreover, they are likely to express gratitude following the receipt of a valued benefit from another person and to experience gratitude as positive. Hence, for securely attached people, the receipt of a valued benefit from another person and the resulting experience of gratitude should increase the likelihood of prosocial behavior. The secure person's positive mental representations of others should make it easy to perceive the valued benefit as a manifestation of other's goodwill. Moreover, the secure person's familiarity with true empathic concern and endorsement of the norms of reciprocity and fairness should encourage them to help others even when prosocial behavior is somewhat costly in the short term.

In contrast, avoidant attachment should reduce gratitude and break the natural link between being benefited and wishing to benefit others. Avoidant people's negative models of others should raise doubts about the benefactor's intentions and interfere with the experience and expression of gratitude. Moreover, their wish to maintain interpersonal distance and to avoid interdependence should further inhibit any empathic concern for others and tendency to act generously after being benefited themselves.

Although attachment anxiety has not been found to inhibit gratitude, it may still interfere with the prosocial effects of this virtue. As explained earlier, attachment-anxious people possess ambivalent models of others and are not confident of others' goodwill, even after receiving a valued benefit. They are so focused on their worries and doubts—their personal distress (see chaps. 1 and 7, this volume)—that they may have insufficient resources for attending to other people's needs. Moreover, because they experience gratitude as involving mixed, ambivalent feelings (of being loved and supported but also inadequate and indebted), they may not be able to attend confidently to another person's needs even after being the recipient of an act of kindness.

In two previously unpublished studies, we examined the hypothesized role of attachment insecurities in moderating the link between gratitude and prosocial behavior. In the first study, 80 Israeli undergraduate students (59 women and 21 men) completed the ECR measure of attachment anxiety and avoidance during regular class time. Some weeks later, they came to the laboratory individually and were randomly assigned to one of two conditions. In the gratitude condition ($n = 40$), participants received the gratitude exercise developed by Emmons and McCullough (2003). They were asked to think and write about the many things in their life, large or small, for which they might feel grateful (e.g., supportive relationships, sacrifices another person has made for them). In the control condition ($n = 40$), participants were asked to think and write about their typical day and the kinds of things that usually happen, in as much detail as possible in the time allowed. Following this exercise, the experiment seemed to end. But after leaving the room, each participant was approached by a confederate who asked if he or she would be willing to help with a cognitively taxing problem-solving survey (identical to the one used by Bartlett & DeSteno, 2006). The major dependent variable was the time spent working on the survey, which we interpret as a measure of helpful behavior.

A hierarchical regression analysis examining the unique and interactive effects of the gratitude exercise (a dummy variable contrasting the gratitude condition with the control condition), avoidant attachment, and attachment anxiety revealed significant main effects for the all three predictors. Replicating previous findings, participants in the gratitude condition spent more time helping with the survey than did participants in the control condition ($\beta = .38$, $p < .01$), and more anxious and/or avoidant participants spent less time helping (βs of $-.37$ and $-.32$, ps $< .01$). However, the main effects were qualified by significant interactions between gratitude and avoidant attachment ($\beta = -.17$, $p < .01$) and between gratitude and attachment anxiety ($\beta = -.19$, $p < .01$). Simple slope tests examining the nature of the significant interactions revealed that the gratitude exercise led to more helping behavior than the control condition mainly when participants scored relatively low on anxiety and/or avoidance (βs of .57 and .55, *ps* < .01). This prosocial effect of the gratitude exercise was lower when attachment anxiety or avoidance was relatively high (βs of .19 and .21, *ps* < .05). As expected, attachment insecurities of either the anxious or avoidant variety disrupted the link between gratitude and prosocial behavior.

In the second study, we primed representations of attachment security or attachment insecurities and examined whether and how these manipulations moderated the gratitude-behavior link. For this purpose, 120 Israeli undergraduates (93 women and 27 men) participated in a two-phase laboratory experiment. They were divided into eight experimental conditions, with 15 participants in each. In the first phase, we primed representations of a particular interpersonal relationship: a security-enhancing relationship, an avoidance-enhancing relationship, an anxiety-enhancing relationship, or a neutral relationship. In the security, anxiety, and avoidance conditions, participants received the prototypic description of either secure, anxious, or avoidant relational attitudes and feelings (taken from Hazan & Shaver's, 1987, descriptions) and were asked to think and write about their experiences in an actual close relationship that best fit this description. For example, in the security priming condition, participants were asked to think and write about a close relationship in which "you found it relatively easy to get close to your partner and were comfortable depending on him/her and having him/her depend on you. You did not worry about being abandoned or about the partner getting too close to you." Participants in the neutral priming condition were asked to think and write about a student they knew but with whom they did not have a close relationship.

In the second phase of the second study, participants performed Tsang's (2006) resource distribution task with a confederate. Each priming group was then randomly subdivided into two conditions—gratitude and chance—according to whether or not the confederate intentionally gave them a large amount of money and wrote them a generous note. The amount of money participants gave to the confederate in the third round was used as a measure of prosocial behavior. The entire procedure, including instructions, the gratitude vs. chance manipulation, and the dependent variable, was identical to that developed by Tsang (2006).

A two-way analysis of variance with priming condition (security, avoidance, anxiety, neutral) and gratitude manipulation (gratitude, chance) as the independent factors and amount of money given to the confederate as the dependent variable revealed a significant interaction between priming and gratitude, $F(3, 112) = 3.03$, $p < .05$. Simple main effect tests indicated that participants in the gratitude condition gave more money to the confederate than did participants in the chance condition only when they were primed with neutral (M = 4.93 vs. M = 3.66) or secure attachment representations (M = 6.53 vs. M = 4.20), but not when they were primed with anxious or avoidant representations (Ms of 2.33 and 3.20 vs. 2.53 and 2.80). Additional simple main effect tests revealed that security priming caused participants in the gratitude condition to give more money to the confederate than given in the neutral condition (M = 6.53 vs. M = 4.93).

In line with our predictions, priming insecure attachment representations, either anxious or avoidant, interfered with the prosocial effect of the gratitude induction. Moreover, priming a sense of attachment security strengthened the prosocial effects of the induction, suggesting that even short-term attachment security (induced in this case by memories of a good relationship) strengthens the connection between the receipt of benefits and generous behavior. The two new studies support our belief that gratitude and its links with prosocial behavior are complex and dependent on other factors, especially attachment security. It is relatively easy for a secure person to be generous, especially after being rewarded by someone else. It is difficult for an insecure person not to feel ambivalent about receiving a benefit from another person, and difficult for the insecure person to turn his or her benefit, through gratitude, into a benefit for someone else. To an important extent, moral virtue depends on feeling loved, valued, and cared for, both in the moment and over the years.

CONCLUDING COMMENTS

As explained in the initial sections of this chapter, research on gratitude indicates that it is a scientifically supported route to the enhancement of prosocial behavior (e.g., Emmons, 2007). Our own studies confirm this conclusion, but they also show that the character of gratitude differs as a function of attachment security or insecurity, as do gratitude's links with prosocial behavior. People differ in attachment style, which includes mental representations of self and others based on a person's history of social experiences. Our previous research showed that attachment style and experimentally augmented attachment security or insecurity affects prosocial attitudes, emotions, and behaviors. Here we add that it affects the quality of gratitude experiences and the link between gratitude and prosocial behavior.

Avoidant attachment is inversely related to dispositional gratitude and seems to dampen or eliminate positive aspects of gratitude such as feelings of security, happiness, love, and generosity while sullying it with distrust and threatened self-esteem. Avoidance also reduces or eliminates the beneficial effects of a mate's positive behavior on a given day, and interferes with the prosocial effects of receiving benefits from another person. Attachment anxiety is associated with ambivalent experiences of gratitude: It is positively related to feelings of security, happiness, love, and generosity, but also to feelings of inferiority and obligation. Like avoidance, attachment anxiety reduces the beneficial effects on prosocial behavior of receiving help or rewards from another person. The resulting reduction in prosocial behavior follows automatically from dispositional forms of attachment insecurity, but it can also be induced situationally by priming people with representations or reminders of insecure attachment experiences. Conversely, the beneficial effects of attachment security on the link between gratitude and prosocial behavior can be brought about through experimental security inductions. Future studies should examine whether experimental security primes can overcome dispositional barriers to gratitude and therefore increase prosocial behavior even in people who are not generally inclined to feel grateful.

We can confidently recommend gratitude as a route to prosocial behavior, along with empathy, which is discussed in several chapters of this volume. But we should also recommend other methods of authentically bolstering people's sense of security, because this sense provides a foundation for every kind of prosocial emotion and behavior studied to date.

REFERENCES

Ainsworth, M. D. S., Blehar, M. C., Waters, E., & Wall, S. (1978). *Patterns of attachment: Assessed in the Strange Situation and at home*. Hillsdale, NJ: Erlbaum.

Baldwin, M. W., Fehr, B., Keedian, E., Seidel, M., & Thomson, D. W. (1993). An exploration of the relational schemata underlying attachment styles: Self-report and lexical decision approaches. *Personality and Social Psychology Bulletin, 19*, 746–754.

Baron, R. A. (1984). Reducing organizational conflict: An incompatible response approach. *Journal of Applied Psychology, 69*, 272–279.

Bartlett, M. Y., & DeSteno, D. (2006). Gratitude and prosocial behavior: Helping when it costs you. *Psychological Science, 17*, 319–325.

Bowlby, J. (1973). *Attachment and loss: Vol. 2. Separation: Anxiety and anger*. New York: Basic Books.

Bowlby, J. (1982). *Attachment and loss: Vol. 1. Attachment* (2nd ed.). New York: Basic Books. (Original work published 1969)

Brennan, K. A., Clark, C. L., & Shaver, P. R. (1998). Self-report measurement of adult attachment: An integrative overview. In J. A. Simpson & W. S. Rholes (Eds.), *Attachment theory and close relationships* (pp. 46–76). New York: Guilford Press.

Cassidy, J., & Kobak, R. R. (1988). Avoidance and its relationship with other defensive processes. In J. Belsky & T. Nezworski (Eds.), *Clinical implications of attachment* (pp. 300–323). Hillsdale, NJ: Erlbaum.

Collins, N. L. (1996). Working models of attachment: Implications for explanation, emotion, and behavior. *Journal of Personality and Social Psychology, 71*, 810–832.

Emmons, R. A. (2007). *Thanks!: How the new science of gratitude can make you happier*. New York: Houghton Mifflin.

Emmons, R. A., & Crumple, C. H. (2000). Gratitude as a human strength: Appraising the evidence. *Journal of Social and Clinical Psychology, 19*, 56–69.

Emmons, R. A., & McCullough, M. E. (2003). Counting blessings versus burdens: An experimental investigation of gratitude and subjective well-being in daily life. *Journal of Personality and Social Psychology, 84*, 377–389.

Emmons, R. A., & McCullough, M. E. (Eds.). (2004). *The psychology of gratitude*. New York: Oxford University Press.

Feeney, B. C., & Collins, N. L. (2001). Predictors of caregiving in adult intimate relationships: An attachment theoretical perspective. *Journal of Personality and Social Psychology, 80*, 972–994.

Fraley, R. C., & Shaver, P. R. (2000). Adult romantic attachment: Theoretical developments, emerging controversies, and unanswered questions. *Review of General Psychology, 4*, 132–154.

Gillath, O., Shaver, P. R., Mikulincer, M., Nitzberg, R. A., Erez, A., & van IJzendoorn, M. H. (2005). Attachment, caregiving, and volunteering: Placing volunteerism in an attachment-theoretical framework. *Personal Relationships, 12*, 425–446.

Graham, S. (1988). Children's developing understanding of the motivational role of affect: An attributional analysis. *Cognitive Development, 3*, 71–88.

Hazan, C., & Shaver, P. R. (1987). Romantic love conceptualized as an attachment process. *Journal of Personality and Social Psychology, 52*, 511–524.

Klein, M. (1957). *Envy and gratitude*. London: Free Press.

Kunce, L. J., & Shaver, P. R. (1994). An attachment-theoretical approach to caregiving in romantic relationships. In K. Bartholomew & D. Perlman (Eds.), *Advances in personal relationships: Attachment processes in adulthood* (Vol. 5, pp. 205–237). London: Jessica Kingsley.

Levy, K. N., Blatt, S. J., & Shaver, P. R. (1998). Attachment styles and parental representations. *Journal of Personality and Social Psychology, 74*, 407–419.

McCullough, M. E., Emmons, R. A., & Tsang, J. (2002). The grateful disposition: A conceptual and empirical topography. *Journal of Personality and Social Psychology, 82*, 112–127.

Mikulincer, M., Gillath, O., Halevy, V., Avihou, N., Avidan, S., & Eshkoli, N. (2001). Attachment theory and reactions to others' needs: Evidence that activation of the sense of attachment security promotes empathic responses. *Journal of Personality and Social Psychology, 81*, 1205–1224.

Mikulincer, M., Gillath, O., Sapir-Lavid, Y., Yaakobi, E., Arias, K., Tal-Aloni, L., & Bor, G. (2003). Attachment theory and concern for others' welfare: Evidence that activation of the sense of secure base promotes endorsement of self-transcendence values. *Basic and Applied Social Psychology, 25*, 299–312.

Mikulincer, M., & Shaver, P. R. (2007). *Attachment in adulthood: Structure, dynamics, and change*. New York: Guilford Press.

Mikulincer, M., Shaver, P. R., Gillath, O., & Nitzberg, R. A. (2005). Attachment, caregiving, and altruism: Boosting attachment security increases compassion and helping. *Journal of Personality and Social Psychology, 89*, 817–839.

Mikulincer, M., Shaver, P. R., & Slav, K. (2006). Attachment, mental representations of others, and gratitude and forgiveness in romantic relationships. In M. Mikulincer & G. S. Goodman (Eds.), *Dynamics of romantic love: Attachment, caregiving, and sex* (pp. 190–215). New York: Guilford Press.

Ognibene, T. C., & Collins, N. L. (1998). Adult attachment styles, perceived social support, and coping strategies. *Journal of Social and Personal Relationships, 15,* 323–345.

Peterson, B. E., & Stewart, A. J. (1996). Antecedents and contexts of generativity motivation and midlife. *Psychology and Aging,* 11, 21–33.

Seligman, M. E. P. (2002). *Authentic happiness: Using the new positive psychology to realize your potential for lasting fulfillment.* New York: Simon & Schuster.

Shaver, P. R., & Hazan, C. (1993). Adult romantic attachment: Theory and evidence. In D. Perlman & W. Jones (Eds.), *Advances in personal relationships* (Vol. 4, pp. 29–70). London: Jessica Kingsley.

Simpson, J. A., Rholes, W. S., & Nelligan, J. S. (1992). Support seeking and support giving within couples in an anxiety-provoking situation: The role of attachment styles. *Journal of Personality and Social Psychology, 62,* 434–446.

Tsang, J. (2006). Gratitude and prosocial behavior: An experimental test of gratitude. *Cognition and Emotion, 20,* 138–148.

Watkins, P. C, Woodward, K., Stone, T., & Kolts, R. L. (2003). Gratitude and happiness: Development of a measure of gratitude, and relationships with subjective well-being. *Social Behavior and Personality, 31,* 431–452.

Weiner, B. (1985). An attributional theory of achievement motivation and emotion. *Psychological Review,* 92, 548–573.

15

THE MALLEABILITY OF FORGIVENESS

JOHAN C. KARREMANS AND PAUL A. M. VAN LANGE

Forgiveness is not an emotion, it's a decision.
—Randall Worley

The basic idea that forgiveness is a "decision," often reached after a process of thought, evaluation, and judgment, is one that seems widely accepted in the scientific literature on forgiveness (see chap. 18, this volume). Pastor Worley is not alone in his view of forgiveness; the scientific literature also portrays *forgiveness* as a deliberative process in which people consciously and actively seek to overcome their negative thoughts, feelings, and behavioral tendencies toward a transgressor in order to regain a more positive stance, despite the transgressor's hurtful actions (e.g., Baumeister, Stillwell, & Wotman, 1990; McCullough, Pargament, & Thoresen, 2000; chap. 18, this volume). Surely, in some cases people do actively decide to forgive their offenders and may actually succeed in transforming their negative feelings into more positive ones toward the offender. At other times, however, people may have difficulty forgiving their offenders and find themselves unable to get rid of their hurt feelings, despite their intention to forgive someone. Moreover, a person may have consciously forgiven an offender at a certain time, yet still experience negative feelings afterwards—for instance, when something reminds him or her of the offense.

Indeed, findings from longitudinal research in which people report their level of forgiveness regarding a past offense on several occasions suggest that forgiveness fluctuates considerably (McCullough, Fincham, & Tsang, 2003).

Although people generally display roughly linear increases in forgiveness over extended periods of time, on different measurement occasions the level of forgiveness often deviates from what would be expected on the basis of the linear trend: On some days the level of forgiveness may be higher, and on other days lower. Thus, as noted by McCullough and colleagues, forgiveness is not likely to be a simple, continuous phenomenon. Once a person decides to forgive an offender, his or her negative feelings toward the offender are likely to fluctuate, even if they generally decrease over time.

One of the reasons why forgiveness may be rather labile is that although some offenses are unambiguously terrible and unacceptable (e.g., rape) many and perhaps most offenses can be interpreted in different ways. For example, failure to keep a secret may be attributable to a "weak moment," or it may be viewed as a deliberate attempt to damage someone's reputation. Even offenses that are generally unacceptable, or that clearly violate rules or norms (e.g., cheating on one's partner), can be softened by circumstances (e.g., "He drank too much") or downward social comparison (e.g., "Compared with other men, he's not that bad"). Such interpretive latitude provides the offended person with a means to adopt various perspectives on the offense, although this may occur in an implicit, automatic fashion, as we argue later.

The causes of fluctuations in forgiveness, called *temporary* forgiveness (McCullough et al., 2003), have received remarkably little attention in the research literature. This is unfortunate because temporary fluctuations may have important consequences for a relationship (and for the individual, as we discuss later), even in the long run. For example, imagine Bob, who has been cheated on by his girlfriend Jessica. Bob decided to forgive Jessica, and his negative feelings toward her have diminished somewhat since that decision. However, when something reminds him of the incident, Bob realizes that his negative feelings toward Jessica have become much stronger again. One might say that Bob experiences a drop in his level of forgiveness. And despite things going fairly well in the relationship since Bob decided to forgive Jessica, this temporary drop in forgiveness is likely to decrease Bob's prorelational motivation and behavior (e.g., willingness to sacrifice for the partner, cooperation; Karremans & Van Lange, 2004). This in turn may frustrate Jessica (who thought Bob had forgiven her), causing a drop in her prorelational motivation and behavior as well (cf. Wieselquist, Rusbult, Foster, & Agnew, 1999; see also chap. 17, this volume). In this manner, a temporary drop in forgiveness can initiate a downward cycle of reciprocity that ultimately threatens the well-being and stability of the relationship.

In an alternative—and more optimistic—scenario, Bob generally cannot and will not forgive Jessica for what she did, suffering the hurt whenever recalling her infidelity. Then one day Bob realizes that his negative feelings toward her have become less intense and that his thoughts and feelings toward her are much more positive again. He experiences a temporary rise in his level of forgiveness. This temporary increase in forgiveness may set the stage for reconciliatory behavior on Bob's part. Jessica in turn may express gratitude for Bob's forgiving attitude, and mutual trust and confidence in the relationship may be reestablished.

These examples of Bob's rising and falling forgiveness illustrate that forgiveness is not always and entirely driven by conscious and deliberative decisions. In the first scenario, despite Bob's willingness to forgive his partner, he later finds that he has not really succeeded in doing so. In the latter scenario, despite Bob's reluctance to forgive Jessica, at some point he realizes that he has actually forgiven her after all. Furthermore, it shows that there can be a clear distinction between one's decision to forgive and one's actual level of forgiveness viewed in emotional terms (Worthington and colleagues make a similar distinction between what they term *decisional* and *emotional* forgiveness; Worthington, Witvliet, Pietrini, & Miller, 2007).

In this chapter, we argue that a person's inclination to forgive an offender as well as the level of actual forgiveness (i.e., an actual reduction of negative thoughts, feelings, and behavior; see chap. 18, this volume) are at least partially influenced by situational circumstances and may also be affected by unconscious processes. Although we do not wish to discard the possibility that deliberative processes influence forgiveness, we argue that deliberative decisions tell only part of the story and do not provide a complete understanding of the forgiveness process. Instead, there may be hidden forces at play that significantly influence one's level of forgiveness toward an offender, and a decision or inclination to forgive may not be as self-determined as one thinks (see also Karremans & Van Lange, 2009).

To provide evidence for this general idea, we first review recent research findings demonstrating that subtle situational cues can have a substantial influence on both a person's inclination to forgive and the person's temporary level of forgiveness regarding a past offense. We then discuss how such apparently minor, temporary changes in forgiveness can have important consequences. We close by outlining some theoretical and practical implications of our analysis and research. We adopt a *malleability* approach to forgiveness, arguing that forgiveness, rather than being a linear process initiated by conscious intentions, is best considered to be a malleable state driven—at least partly—by unconscious affective processes.

We should also note that we developed our view of the forgiveness process with an eye to offenses that are relatively common—that is, that tend to occur with some regularity in the context of close and nonclose relationships, such as incidents in which one person makes the other feel uncomfortable, ashamed, or irritated or hurt by, for example, insulting, sharing secrets with others, saying something inappropriate, failing to take into account the other's preferences in a joint decision, or failing to meet the terms of an agreement or even promise. Although we think that some of our lines of reasoning may, over time, also be relevant to understanding severe or very severe offences (e.g., rape or physical abuse), in this chapter we focus mainly on the relatively common offenses that also tend to have important effects on people and their relationships, at least when they would not enter the forgiveness process.

INFLUENCING TEMPORARY FORGIVENESS THROUGH SUBTLE SITUATIONAL CUES

In recent years, a number of studies have used priming techniques to influence temporary levels of forgiveness regarding either a past offense or hypothetical offenses. In one of the first demonstrations of subtle situational influences on forgiveness, Karremans and Van Lange (2005) examined the association between people's justice values and their inclination to forgive others. This issue is interesting because reading different literatures may result in making different predictions regarding this association. On the one hand, several authors in the forgiveness literature have argued that justice values may be essential in obstructing a person's inclinations to forgive (e.g., Enright, Gassin, & Wu, 1992; Exline & Baumeister, 2000; Exline, Worthington, Hill, & McCullough, 2003). According to these scholars, justice conceptions entail an eye-for-an-eye approach to the offender, which clearly hinders reconciliatory motives. On the other hand, the available theoretical and empirical literature on social justice suggests that justice conceptions are much broader than retribution alone. For example, justice values are usually associated with the belief that conflicts should be settled fairly (i.e., that there should be procedural justice; Tyler, 1987) or the belief that resources should be distributed fairly (i.e., distributive justice; Adams, 1965). In other words, conceptions of justice influence concerns for others' welfare.

On the basis of our assumption that justice values are often much more prosocial than is generally assumed in the forgiveness literature (an idea that is empirically supported by findings concerning human values; see chap. 12, this volume), Karremans and Van Lange (2005) set out to test the idea that the activation or salience of justice values would increase, rather than decrease, people's inclinations to forgive. In the first study, to cognitively activate different values, some participants were asked to write down their thoughts when thinking about the concept of justice, other participants wrote their thoughts about the concept of helpfulness (a prosocial value), still others wrote their thoughts about the concept of ambition (a self-oriented rather than a prosocial value), and the remaining participants did not write down thoughts regarding a value. Subsequently, all participants completed the Transgression Narrative Test of Forgiveness (TNTF), a scenario-based measure of people's inclinations to forgive, developed and validated by Berry, Worthington, Parrot, O'Connor, and Wade (2001).

Results were in line with expectations. Participants for whom the values of justice and helpfulness were activated by means of the thought-listing task displayed significantly greater inclinations to forgive compared with participants for whom the value of ambition was activated or for whom no value was activated (Karremans & Van Lange, 2005, Study 1). Moreover, content coding of participants' justice descriptions confirmed that most participants came up with very prosocial ideas about the concept, most of which referred to principles of both procedural and distributive justice. These findings are in line with the general idea that a person's inclination to forgive depends on specific features of the context.

The next two studies were designed to replicate these findings using more subtle situational cues to activate the concept of justice. Specifically, participants in both studies were primed with a universal symbol of justice, Lady Justitia, the Roman goddess of justice. In one study, half of the participants were first exposed to a picture of Lady Justitia, while the other half were exposed to a control picture (of a trumpet). Participants primed with justice, compared with the control group, subsequently had higher scores on the TNTF (Karremans & Van Lange, 2005, Study 2). In the next study, justice was primed even more subtly. All participants completed the TNTF, but in the experimental condition this forgiveness measure was printed on paper bearing a watermark picture of Lady Justitia. In two control conditions, the paper contained a watermark logo of the university (all participants were university students) or did not contain a watermark at all. Again, participants for whom justice was made salient, even in this subtle manner, displayed stronger inclinations to forgive compared with participants for whom the concept was not made salient (Karremans & Van Lange, 2005, Study 3). Together, these findings support the idea that situational cues can alter one's decision or inclination to forgive, and the latter two studies suggest that people are not aware of such influences. In none of the studies did participants report any suspicion regarding the hypotheses; in particular, they did not guess that the studies examined whether justice primes influenced their inclinations to forgive.

In another line of research suggesting the role of subtle and nonconscious processes in forgiveness, Karremans and Aarts (2007) examined the link between closeness and forgiveness. Although previous research has established an almost intrinsic link between level of closeness toward an offender and forgiveness, deliberative processes are often regarded as the mechanism responsible for this association (e.g., Finkel, Rusbult, Hannon, Kumashiro, & Childs, 2002; McCullough et al., 1998). The argument goes as follows: An offended person who is close and committed to the offender (e.g., a romantic partner, a good friend) will attempt to see the other's harmful act and underlying motives in a less negative light (e.g., the partner may not have acted intentionally). Such deliberative attribution processes will result in greater forgiveness (i.e., a reduction of negative thoughts, feelings, and behavior toward the offender).

However, as argued by Karremans and Aarts (2007), over the course of a close and committed relationship, people are likely to learn that forgiving responses (compared with retributive responses) to the partner's harmful acts generally result in more positive outcomes (including individual as well as relationship well-being; Karremans, Van Lange, Ouwerkerk, & Kluwer, 2003). If conflicts arise repeatedly in a close relationship (as they generally seem to do; Brehm, Miller, Perlman, & Campbell, 2002), forgiveness may eventually occur in a relatively habitual and nondeliberative fashion. That is, the positive outcomes that accompany forgiveness may reinforce a person for automatically exhibiting forgiving rather than retributive responses to a partner's negative acts. In other words, forgiveness as a response to a close other's negative behavior may become part of the mental representation of the relationship with that person (Baldwin, 1992; Fitzsimons & Bargh, 2003).

Karremans and Aarts (2007) tested this prediction in a series of experiments, the first two of which are most relevant to the present chapter. If forgiveness is indeed part of the mental representation of the relationship with the close other, cognitively activating the relationship representation should automatically increase people's inclination and willingness to forgive (cf. Fitzsimons & Bargh, 2003). In these studies, participants were asked to indicate their inclination to forgive, in general, a number of negative behaviors (e.g., lies, insults) that were presented sequentially on a computer screen. Unbeknownst to the participants, right before each negative behavior either the name of a close other or the name of a nonclose other was flashed on the screen for 23 ms, which was outside participants' awareness (i.e., subliminal). Participants had provided these names before their inclination to forgive the negative behaviors was measured. Thus, while responding to the negative behaviors, for half of the participants the mental representation of a close relationship was activated, whereas for the other half the mental representation of a nonclose relationship was activated.

The results of both studies provided good support for the central prediction. Those who were subliminally primed with the name of a close other displayed a greater inclination to forgive the behaviors than did those who were primed with the name of a nonclose other (and, in one of the studies, compared with participants who were primed with a random letter string). In addition, the second study revealed that the close versus nonclose primes did not differentially affect participants' evaluation of the severity of the behaviors. That is, the close other prime did not lead to significantly lower, or higher, ratings of severity of the offenses, suggesting that the close prime did not simply result in a general positivity effect. Together, the findings demonstrate that people's inclination to forgive a particular behavior does not depend solely on the content of the behavior itself. Although a person may consciously weigh certain features of the behavior (e.g., its severity, its likelihood of being intentional) when deciding whether it should be forgiven, the findings indicate that this is only part of the story. Participants in these studies were not aware of the closeness primes, yet the primes influenced their inclination to forgive beyond the effects of any conscious deliberative processes.

A recent series of experiments by Wohl and McGrath (2007) on the influence of subjective temporal distance from an offense on forgiveness provided further evidence for the claim that subtle situational cues may influence forgiveness. Time may be considered the "mother" of all determinants of forgiveness, and as noted, longitudinal research generally reveals that forgiveness increases as time passes (McCullough et al., 2003). Wohl and McGrath (2007), however, did not examine the objective temporal distance from the offense but rather the effects of participants' subjective perception of the elapsed time since the offense on willingness to forgive it (controlling for the actual temporal distance from the event).

Participants in one study were asked to imagine a hypothetical offense that occurred 1 month before or, in another study, to recall a real offense that they experienced about 1 month before (Wohl & McGrath, 2007, Studies 2 and 3). Suppose (for the sake of simplicity) that both studies were conducted in April, so the hypothetical and real offenses took place in March. The subjective perception of how long ago the offense took place was manipulated using the following procedure. Participants in the subjectively temporally close condition were asked to mark when the offense took place on a time line ranging from November to April. Participants in the subjectively temporally distant condition marked when the offense took place on a time line ranging from February to April. That is, participants in the latter condition placed the mark further away from the right side of the scale—that is, further away from the present (April). As expected, participants reported higher levels of forgiveness (i.e., were less likely to desire revenge or to avoid the transgressor) regarding both the hypothetical offense and the actually experienced offense, when the time since the offense was manipulated to seem further in the past.

A last example of the malleability of forgiveness comes from recent research by Karremans and Smith (2007), who explored the role of power in forgiveness. Although power is an intrinsic aspect of interpersonal relations, the effects of power on forgiveness have received little attention (but see Aquino, Tripp, & Bies, 2006). It was hypothesized that the experience of power (i.e., experiencing that one is able to control outcomes and resources for oneself and others; Keltner, Gruenfield, & Anderson, 2003) should facilitate forgiveness, but only toward an offending partner to whom one is strongly committed. This prediction was based on recent research suggesting that the experience of high power causes people to become more goal-directed (e.g., Galinsky, Gruenfeld, & Magee, 2003; Guinote, 2007). Because strong commitment by definition implies that one has the goal to maintain the relationship, the increased goal-directedness engendered by a person's experience of high power (compared with low power) would lead him or her to focus on the goal of maintaining the relationship with the offending partner, resulting in a greater willingness to forgive.

Most relevant to the present chapter, in one study a relatively high sense of power was induced by means of priming. That is, in one condition participants were asked to recall an instance in which they had power over others, whereas in another condition participants recalled an instance in which others had power over them. As previous research has shown, such primes temporarily induce differential levels of experienced power (e.g., Galinsky et al., 2003; Smith & Trope, 2006). Subsequently, participants reported their inclinations to forgive a number of hypothetical offenses, in some cases in which the protagonist was a close other (a good friend), and in other cases where the protagonist was not close (an acquaintance). In line with predictions, participants who were primed with high power (compared with low power) displayed greater inclinations to forgive, especially in cases in which a close other had behaved badly.

Together, the reviewed studies provide compelling evidence that level of forgiveness (in some of the studies operationalized as a reduction in revenge toward and avoidance of the offender) is at least partly influenced by subtle environmental inputs. Situational reminders of power, closeness, social justice, and the subjective passing of time all affect people's inclinations to forgive, including cases in which there was an actual past offense. Moreover, results of some of the studies suggest that people are often unaware of these influences and that their level of forgiveness may go up or down without awareness of the causes of the fluctuations. These findings are especially interesting in light of previous theorizing and research on the factors determining forgiveness, which has typically focused on the features of the offense itself (e.g., severity, intentionality) or on the relationship between the offended person and the transgressor (e.g., commitment, closeness, apologies; for an overview, see McCullough et al., 1998). However, and most strikingly, in each of the aforementioned studies level of forgiveness was influenced by temporary variations in factors essentially unrelated to the offense, while the offense itself, and the relationship with the offender, remained constant. In other words, the very same offense can be more or less forgiven depending on the offended person's situation. In sum, these findings suggest that, at least in addition to the role of deliberative processes, unconscious and implicit processes may often influence a person's level of forgiveness regarding a past offense.

THE EFFECTS OF TEMPORARY FLUCTUATIONS: HOW A SMALL CHANGE CAN HAVE PROFOUND CONSEQUENCES

Considering its apparent malleability, is there any behavioral predictive value left to forgiveness? Do fluctuations in forgiveness occur unnoticed, residing only in the offended person's mind? Or can changes in forgiveness resulting from subtle situational inputs still have major consequences? A number of recent studies have suggested the latter. That is, although forgiveness can be relatively easily influenced by subtle changes in the environment, the resulting changes in level of forgiveness seem to affect, just as easily, a number of both individual and relationship outcomes (e.g., Karremans & Van Lange, 2008; Karremans, Van Lange, & Holland, 2005; Karremans et al., 2003; Witvliet, Ludwig, & Vander Laan, 2001).

One of the first and most intriguing demonstrations of the impact of temporary changes in forgiveness comes from a study by Witvliet et al. (2001). Participants in this study were asked to recall an incident in which they felt hurt by someone, and subsequently they were asked to imagine a forgiving response toward the offender or to imagine an unforgiving response toward the offender. During these imagery tasks, participants' physiological reactions were monitored, providing an online assessment of the immediate effects of participants' forgiving or unforgiving thoughts. Participants reported higher levels of forgiveness during the forgiving imagery task than during the unforgiving imagery task, and these fluctuating levels of forgiveness were associated with physiological changes. Higher levels of forgiveness were associated with less facial tension in the corrugator (brow) muscle region, lower heart rate and blood pressure, and lower skin conductance—each being a physiological indicator associated in other studies with physical health. Thus, merely imagining forgiving or unforgiving responses influenced temporary levels of forgiveness and concomitant physiological responses.

In a study by Karremans et al. (2003), in which the association between forgiveness and psychological well-being was examined, participants were led to believe that they had forgiven an offender. Participants were told that because people find it generally difficult to introspect on and thus to determine clearly their level of forgiveness toward an offender, scientists from the United States had devised an instrument by which one's true level of forgiveness could be measured. In fact, participants completed an implicit association task (Greenwald & Banaji, 1995) with the name of the offender as a target, after which they received false feedback regarding their response times. In the forgiveness condition, participants were told that they had displayed faster responses when the name of the offender was coupled with positively valenced words than when the name was coupled with negatively valenced words, indicating that "at least at an implicit level, you seem to have forgiven the other." In the unforgiveness condition, their responses were allegedly faster when the name of the offender was coupled with negative words than when it was coupled with positive words, indicating that "you have not entirely forgiven the other." This manipulation significantly affected participants' temporary level of forgiveness, with greater forgiveness in the forgiveness condition. More important, these temporary increases in forgiveness were associated with several indicators of psychological well-being, including state self-esteem, satisfaction with life, and positive and negative affect.

Not only can temporary fluctuations influence individual well-being, recent research has suggested that such fluctuations may have important consequences for a person's relationship with an offender. Karremans and Van Lange (2008) demonstrated that thinking of forgiven versus unforgiven offenses subtly influences the way people speak about their relationship with the offender. When thinking of forgiven offenses (compared with thinking of unforgiven offenses), people tend to speak, literally, more in terms of "we" and "us" when describing their relationship with the offender. Although on the surface such an effect may appear rather minor, such subtle differences in language use reflect differences in self–other overlap (Agnew, Van Lange, Rusbult, & Langston, 1998) and are related to several indicators of relationship quality (Acitelli & Young, 1996; Aron, Aron, & Smollan, 1992; Simmons, Gordon, & Chambless, 2005).

Finally, it appears that different levels of forgiveness regarding a particular past offense can have consequences beyond the relationship with the offender, as research by Karremans, Van Lange, and Holland (2005) has suggested. They demonstrated that for people who are thinking about past offenses, their current level of forgiveness regarding the offense affects cognitions, feelings, and behavior toward others who have nothing to do with the offense. For example, in one study participants who were reminded of a forgiven offense reported stronger feelings of relatedness toward other people in general than participants who were reminded of unforgiven offenses. Another study demonstrated that recalling forgiven offenses (compared with unforgiven offenses) affected the amount of money participants donated to a charity organization. Although these studies did not examine the effects of fluctuating levels of forgiveness regarding a single past offense, they raise the possibility that temporary ups and downs in forgiveness (as described earlier) can create different levels of a more generalized prosocial mind-set. In other words, a person who currently experiences relatively high levels of forgiveness toward an offender may not only respond more positively to the offender but may also be at least temporarily more inclined to behave in a prosocial manner toward others as well.

Together, the findings suggest that although forgiveness can be influenced by the environment quite easily, the resulting changes have important consequences ranging from effects on health to behavioral responses that spill over to other relationships (for a more extensive overview, see Karremans & Van Lange, in press). Put differently, a person who has forgiven an offense, compared with a person who has not forgiven an offense, may be a rather different person, behaving, feeling, and thinking differently in relation to his or her social environment (see chap. 18, this volume). As such, forgiveness is not only central to individual healing processes, as is often claimed in the psychological literature, it also may be key to explaining a host of interpersonal motives and behaviors that have been overlooked by social scientists.

THEORETICAL IMPLICATIONS OF THE MALLEABILITY OF FORGIVENESS

Although there is good evidence, as demonstrated here, that forgiveness is influenced by unconscious and implicit processes, it is important to recognize that several other research findings have suggested an association between deliberative processes and forgiveness. Finkel et al. (2002), for example, examined the link between commitment and forgiveness and found that this association was, at least partially, mediated by cognitive interpretations of the offense. Their research suggests that people in close relationships are more likely to discount dispositional causes for an offense, to find external explanations for the offense, and therefore to forgive. Fincham, Paleari, and Regalia (2002) showed that the relation between marital satisfaction and forgiveness is mediated by causal and responsibility attributions regarding the offense. McCullough, Root, and Cohen (2006) demonstrated that participants who wrote about personal benefits resulting from a transgression subsequently reported higher levels of forgiveness (compared with control conditions in which participants wrote about a topic unrelated to the offense or wrote about negative features of the offense). Writing about the benefits led to increased cognitive processing of the event (e.g., greater insight, clearer cause-and-effect relations, and so on), which in turn facilitated forgiveness. Such findings suggest that deliberative processes occurring after an offense can facilitate forgiveness and that forgiveness may sometimes involve thoughtful and effortful processes.

But do people spontaneously engage in conscious and effortful processing with the aim of forgiving a relationship partner? Surely it is possible that, following an offense, people may sometimes spontaneously contemplate the reasons for the offender's behavior. If so, motivated reasoning—induced, for example, by strong commitment to the offender—may elicit more benign attributions regarding the offender's behavior. People may sometimes spontaneously consider the personal benefits of a transgression, as participants did in the study by McCullough et al. (2006) described in the previous paragraph. Both forms of active and deliberative processing may result in forgiveness. At the same time, it is questionable whether people always (or even often) engage in such active and deliberative thinking about an offense. Actually, it may be quite rare for people to actively make attributions or indulge other considerations regarding the offense (cf. Haidt, 2001). Is such higher order cognitive processing really necessary if we are to forgive our offenders, especially those to whom we feel close?

Granted, deliberative (e.g., attribution) processes may determine a person's level of forgiveness when he or she actively reflects on the offense and the motives and intentions of the offender (again, we do not want to disregard this possibility). At the same time, it is possible (even plausible, we think) that deliberative processes sometimes follow rather than precede forgiveness (Karremans & Aarts, 2007). For example, a person may make benign attributions of responsibility (i.e., "It was not really his fault") only after more intuitive and implicit processes have diminished negative feelings toward the offender. One may see the benefits of a transgression only after one has intuitively forgiven the other. Such a forgiveness-attribution sequence is congruent with the general idea that reasoning processes are often guided by intuitive affective processes rather than vice versa (e.g., Damasio, 1994; Haidt, 2001; Wilson, 2002). For example, in his social intuitionist model, Haidt (2001) proposed that moral judgment depends largely on automatic and intuitive affective responses rather than reasoning. According to the model, a particular immoral act automatically elicits an affective evaluative response followed by a moral reasoning process, which helps a person justify his or her moral judgment. Although this may give a person the illusion that his or her judgment is based on the moral reasoning he or she engaged in, ultimately it is the intuitive affective response that determines the judgment.

In fact, the emerging view in the social-psychological literature is that most of our attitudes, judgments, goals, and even behaviors are elicited automatically or intuitively and are driven largely by automatic evaluation (affective) processes (Bargh, 1994; Greenwald & Banaji, 1995; Zajonc, 1980). Is the process of forgiveness an exception? We believe not. Similar to the process that leads to moral judgment as just described, deliberative attribution processes may often serve as post hoc explanations for one's level of forgiveness. The research findings reviewed in this chapter suggest that situational circumstances may affect one's level of forgiveness even outside of awareness. If a person has no conscious access to the reasons for his or her forgiving attitude toward an offender, it is difficult to retain the idea that for most offenses, forgiveness is the exclusive (or even primary) result of a careful and deliberate process. We should note, however, that to date there is no direct evidence in support of such an intuitive forgiveness-attribution sequence. An important challenge for future research is to disentangle these two processes and to explore the different ways in which automatic and deliberative processes interact in determining forgiveness.

IMPLICATIONS AND FUTURE DIRECTIONS

In recent years, there has been a rising interest in the therapeutic application of forgiveness interventions. In an overview of the effectiveness of such interventions, Baskin and Enright (2004) found that individuals who took part in forgiveness interventions were more likely to forgive than were members of waiting list control groups, and they enjoyed better emotional health. However, the underlying mechanisms are not yet clear, and although reappraisal, perspective taking, or other cognitive strategies may be responsible for the increases in forgiveness and health (e.g., Fincham et al., 2002), other factors such as the qualities of the counselor, or the attention or social support clients received during the intervention, may also have contributed to its effectiveness. In fact, although there has been little research on the effects of third parties in the forgiveness process, perceived social support may be an important and powerful facilitator of forgiveness. Social support may help a person overcome the stress resulting from an offense (Pasch & Bradbury, 1998), and this reduction in negative feelings may in turn—possibly through misattribution processes (Van den Bos, 2003)—facilitate forgiveness toward the offender.

It is interesting that Baskin and Enright (2004) found that decision-based interventions were not particularly effective (e.g., Al-Mabuk, Enright, & Cardis, 1995; McCullough & Worthington, 1995), suggesting that, in line with our analysis, a decision to forgive does not in itself evoke actual forgiveness; that is, it does not necessarily decrease negative feelings toward the offender. Still, it is important to acknowledge that most of the research reviewed here, which deemphasized the role of deliberative processes in forgiveness, is not concerned with the kind of traumatic experiences often recounted in counseling settings. However, we would argue that an exclusive focus on the cognitive aspects of an offense, or on the decision to forgive an offender, may not maximize the chances of forgiveness interventions being effective. And even if interventions do show improvements in forgiveness, given the malleability of forgiveness it is questionable whether the improvement is likely to be stable and long lasting. As McCullough et al. (2006) wondered regarding their forgiveness writing intervention: "Did [it] create long-term changes . . . or did the reductions in revenge and avoidance motivations . . . dissipate a few moments after participants left?" (p. 895).

Recently, researchers have begun to explore a phenomenon possibly even more complex than interpersonal forgiveness: intergroup forgiveness (see chap. 21, this volume). So far, this research has examined the role of intergroup contact or common group identification in facilitating intergroup forgiveness and reconciliation (e.g., Hewstone, Cairns, Voci, Hamberger, & Niens, 2006; Hewstone et al., 2004; Wohl & Branscombe, 2005). Although there may be several other factors that help members of one group to forgive another, forgiveness at the intergroup level may fluctuate at least as much as it does at the interpersonal level. Although at some point negative feelings associated with a group of people (e.g., Whites in South Africa as perceived by Blacks) may subside, as indicated, for example, by negotiations and an end to hostilities, such periods of apparent forgiveness can be followed by a sudden outbreak of further conflict, often without clear or demonstrable reasons (e.g., the conflicts between Catholics and Protestants in Northern Ireland, Palestinians and Israelis, or, on a smaller scale, gang rivalry in Los Angeles). Similar to the ways in which subtle situational changes may affect interpersonal forgiveness, subtle societal changes may subtly affect intergroup forgiveness and reconciliation, making it difficult to understand and at the same time extremely important to study.

CONCLUSIONS

To portray forgiveness exclusively as a conscious decision is unrealistic when one understands that subtle influences can affect forgiveness in powerful ways. Evidence is growing that such influences can be largely unconscious. In light of the scores of studies reviewed in this chapter, we suggest that forgiveness is most accurately conceptualized as a state that is subject to fluctuations rooted in subtle or unconscious reminders of the offense, the partner and his or her qualities, the relationship, and other factors. This notion of malleability is increasingly used to understand phenomena such as moral judgment, and it may be the case that cognitions often serve to rationalize or interpret and label intuitive feelings that are actually responsible for variations in forgiveness. Clearly, the malleability approach can be viewed in terms of cost-effectiveness. If relatively small, inexpensive means can be used to yield powerful benefits of forgiveness, then the benefits for the forgiver (as well as the offender and the relationship between the two people) may easily outweigh the costs. One might speculate that a relatively high and stable level of forgiveness regarding a specific past offense is likely to occur only if one has repeatedly experienced the state of forgiveness. This possibility, which needs to be researched further, has important implications for forgiveness interventions.

REFERENCES

Acitelli, L. K., & Young, A. M. (1996). Gender and thought in relationships. In J. Fitness & G. J. O. Fletcher (Eds.), *Knowledge structures in close relationships: A social psychological approach* (pp. 147–168). Hillsdale, NJ: Erlbaum.

Adams, J. S. (1965). Inequity in social exchange. In L. Berkowitz (Ed.), *Advances in experimental social psychology* (Vol. 2, pp. 267–299). New York: Academic Press.

Agnew, C. R., Van Lange, P. A. M., Rusbult, C. E., & Langston, C. A. (1998). Cognitive interdependence: Commitment and the mental representation of close relationships. *Journal of Social and Psychological Psychology, 74*, 939–954.

Al-Mabuk, R. H., Enright, R. D., & Cardis, P. A. (1995). Forgiving education with parentally love-deprived late adolescents. *Journal of Moral Education, 24*, 427–444.

Aquino, K., Tripp, T. M., & Bies, R. J. (2006). Getting even or moving on? Power, procedural justice, and types of offense as predictors of revenge, forgiveness, reconciliation, and avoidance in organizations. *Journal of Applied Social Psychology, 91*, 653–668.

Aron, A., Aron, E., & Smollan, D. (1992). Inclusion of Other in the Self Scale and the structure of interpersonal closeness. *Journal of Science and Pathological Psychology, 63*, 596–612.

Baldwin, M. W. (1992). Relational schemas and cognition in close relationships. *Journal of Social and Personal Relationships, 12*, 547–552.

Bargh, J. A. (1994). The Four Horsemen of automaticity: Awareness, efficiency, intention, and control in social cognition. In R. S. Wyer, Jr., & T. K. Srull (Eds.), *Handbook of social cognition* (2nd ed., pp. 1–40). Hillsdale, NJ: Erlbaum.

Baskin, T. W., & Enright, R. D. (2004). Intervention studies on forgiveness: A meta-analysis. *Journal of Counselling and Development, 82*, 79–91.

Baumeister, R. F., Stillwell, R., & Wotman, S. R. (1990). Victim and perpetrator accounts of interpersonal conflict: Autobiographical narratives about anger. *Journal of Personality and Social Psychology, 59*, 994–1005.

Berry, J. W., Worthington, E. L., Jr., Parrot, L., III, O'Connor, L. E., & Wade, N. G. (2001). Dispositional forgivingness: Development and construct validity of the Transgression Narrative Test of Forgivingness (TNTF). *Personality and Social Psychology Bulletin, 27*, 1277–1290.

Brehm, S. S., Miller, R. S., Perlman, D., & Campbell, S. M. (2002). *Intimate relationships* (3rd ed.). New York: McGraw-Hill.

Damasio, A. (1994). *Descartes' error: Emotion, reason, and the human brain.* New York: Grosset/Putman.

Exline, J. J., & Baumeister, R. F. (2000). Expressing forgiving and repentance: Benefits and barriers. In M. McCullough, K. Pargament, & C. Thoresen (Eds.), *Forgiving: Theory, research, and practice* (pp. 133–155). New York: Guilford Press.

Exline, J. J., Worthington, E. L., Jr., Hill, P., & McCullough, M. E. (2003). Forgiveness and justice: A research agenda for social and personality psychology. *Personality and Social Psychology Review, 7*, 337–348.

Enright, R. D., Gassin, E. A., & Wu, C. (1992). Forgiveness: A developmental view. *Journal of Moral Education, 21*, 99–114.

Fincham, F. D., Paleari, G., & Regalia, C. (2002). Forgiveness in marriage: The role of relationship quality, attributions, and empathy. *Personal Relationships, 9*, 27–37.

Finkel, E. J., Rusbult, C. E., Hannon, P. A., Kumashiro, M., & Childs, N. M. (2002). Dealing with betrayal in close relationships: Does commitment promote forgiveness? *Journal of Personality and Social Psychology, 82*, 956–974.

Fitzsimons, G. M., & Bargh, J. A. (2003). Thinking of you: Nonconscious pursuit of interpersonal goals associated with relationship partners. *Journal of Personality and Social Psychology, 84*, 148–164.

Galinsky, A. D., Gruenfeld, D. H., & Magee, J. C. (2003). Power and action. *Journal of Personality and Social Psychology, 85*, 453–466.

Greenwald, A. G., & Banaji, M. R. (1995). Implicit social cognition: Attitudes, self-esteem, and stereotypes. *Psychological Review, 102*, 4–27.

Guinote, A. (2007). Power and goal pursuit. *Personality and Social Psychology Bulletin*, *33*, 1076–1087.

Haidt, J. (2001). The emotional dog and its rational tail: A social intuitionist approach to moral judgment. *Psychological Review*, *108*, 814–834.

Hewstone, M., Cairns, E., Voci, A., Hamberger, J., & Niens, U. (2006). Intergroup contact, forgiveness, and experience of "The Troubles" in Northern Ireland. *Journal of Social Issues*, *62*, 99–120.

Hewstone, M., Cairns, E., Voci, A., McLernon, F., Niens, U., & Noor, M. (2004). Intergroup forgiveness and guilt in Northern Ireland: Social psychological dimensions of "The Troubles." In N. R. Branscombe & B. Doosje (Eds.), *Collective guilt: International perspectives* (pp. 193–215). New York: Cambridge University Press.

Karremans, J. C., & Aarts, H. (2007). The role of automaticity in forgiving close others. *Journal of Experimental Social Psychology*, *43*, 902–917.

Karremans, J. C., & Smith, P. (2007). *The association between power and forgiveness: The moderating role of commitment*. Unpublished manuscript.

Karremans, J. C., & Van Lange, P. A. M. (2004). Back to caring after being hurt: The role of forgiveness. *European Journal of Social Psychology*, *34*, 207–227.

Karremans, J. C., & Van Lange, P. A. M. (2005). Does activating justice help or hurt in promoting forgiveness? *Journal of Experimental Social Psychology*, *41*, 290–297.

Karremans, J. C., & Van Lange, P. A. M. (2008). The role of forgiveness in shifting from Me to We. *Self and Identity*, *7*, 75–88.

Karremans, J. C., & Van Lange, P. A. M. (2009). Forgiveness in personal relationships: Its malleability and powerful consequences. *European Review of Social Psychology*, *19*, 202–241.

Karremans, J. C., Van Lange, P. A. M., & Holland, R. W. (2005). Forgiveness and its associations with prosocial thinking, feeling, and doing beyond the relationship with the offender. *Personality and Social Psychology Bulletin*, *31*, 1315–1326.

Karremans, J. C., Van Lange, P. A. M., Ouwerkerk, J. W., & Kluwer, E. S. (2003). When forgiveness enhances psychological well-being: The influence of interpersonal commitment. *Journal of Personality and Social Psychology*, *84*, 1011–1026.

Keltner, D., Gruenfeld, D. H., & Anderson, C. (2003). Power, approach, and inhibition. *Psychological Review*, *110*, 265–284.

McCullough, M. E., Fincham, F. D., & Tsang, J. A. (2003). Forgiveness, forbearance, and time: The temporal unfolding of transgression-related interpersonal motivations. *Journal of Personality and Social Psychology*, *84*, 540–555.

McCullough, M. E., Pargament, K. I., & Thoresen, C. E. (2000). The psychology of forgiveness: History, conceptual issues, and overview. In M. McCullough, K. Pargament, & C. Thoresen (Eds.), *Forgiveness: Theory, research and practice* (pp. 1–14). New York: Guilford Press.

McCullough, M. E., Rachal, K. C., Sandage, S. J., Worthington, E. L., Jr., Wade Brown, S., & Hight, T. L. (1998). Interpersonal forgiving in close relationships:

II. Theoretical elaboration and measurement. *Journal of Personality and Social Psychology, 75*, 1586–1603.

McCullough, M. E., Root, L. M., & Cohen, A. D. (2006). Writing about the benefits of forgiveness facilitates forgiveness. *Journal of Counseling and Clinical Psychology, 74*, 887–897.

McCullough, M. E., & Worthington, E. L. (1995). Promoting forgiveness: A comparison of two brief psychoeducational interventions with a waiting-list control. *Counseling and Values, 40*, 55–68.

Pasch, L. A., & Bradbury, T. N. (1998). Social support, conflict, and the development of marital dysfunction. *Journal of Consulting and Clinical Psychology, 66*, 219–230.

Simmons, R. A., Gordon, P. C., & Chambless, D. L. (2005). Pronouns in marital interaction: What do "you" and "I" say about marital health? *Psychological Science, 16*, 932–936.

Smith, P. K., & Trope, Y. (2006). You focus on the forest when you are in charge of the trees: Power priming and abstract information processing. *Journal of Personality and Social Psychology, 90*, 578–596.

Tyler, T. R. (1987). Conditions leading to value expressive effects in judgments of procedural justice: A test of four models. *Journal of Personality and Social Psychology, 52*, 333–344.

Van den Bos, K. (2003). On the subjective quality of social justice: The role of affect as information in the psychology of justice judgments. *Journal of Personality and Social Psychology, 85*, 482–498.

Wieselquist, J., Rusbult, C. E., Foster, G. A., & Agnew, C. R. (1999). Commitment, pro-relationship behavior, and trust in close relationships. *Journal of Personality and Social Psychology, 77*, 942–966.

Wilson, T. D. (2002). *Strangers to ourselves: Discovering the adaptive unconscious.* Cambridge, MA: Harvard University Press.

Witvliet, C. V. O., Ludwig, T. E., & Vander Laan, K. L. (2001). Granting forgiveness or harboring grudges: Implications for emotion, physiology, and health. *Psychological Science, 121*, 117–123.

Wohl, M. J. A., & Branscombe, N. R. (2005). Forgiveness and collective guilt assignment to historical perpetrator groups depends on level of social category inclusiveness. *Journal of Personality and Social Psychology, 88*, 288–303.

Wohl, M. J. A., & McGrath, A. L. (2007). The perception of time heals all wounds: Temporal distance affects willingness to forgive following an interpersonal transgression. *Personality and Social Psychology Bulletin, 33*, 1023–1035.

Worthington, Jr., E. L., Witvliet, C. V. O., Pietrini, P., & Miller, A. J. (2007). Forgiveness, health, and well-being: A review of evidence for emotional versus decisional forgiveness, dispositional forgivingness, and reduced unforgiveness. *Journal of Behavioral Medicine, 30*, 291–302.

Zajonc, R. B. (1980). Feeling and thinking: Preferences need no inferences. *American Psychologist, 35*, 151–175.

16

THE SUBJECTIVE EXPERIENCE OF GENEROSITY

ELIANE SOMMERFELD

When I first became interested in generosity, I was familiar with the Freudian notion that there is a close connection between generosity and its opposite, parsimony or stinginess, because of a process of reaction formation and sublimation (Freud, 1908). Nevertheless, I was not satisfied with the idea that generosity is purely a defense against an underlying tendency toward miserliness (for a similar view, see chap. 5, this volume). Although generosity may sometimes function as a defense, I had the clinical impression that people often transcend selfishness and give to others without knowing what, if anything, they might receive in return. That belief made a positive psychological perspective (e.g., Peterson & Seligman, 2004) attractive because positive psychology has broadened the scientific view of human nature, making it acceptable to study a phenomenon such as generosity.

Generous deeds are among the building blocks of good social relations. However, although extensive theoretical and empirical work has been devoted to the topics of helping behavior and prosocial attitudes, there is no systematic research on the subjective experiences of people when they act generously. I therefore decided to begin my exploration of generosity with a phenomenological approach, which requires no a priori assumptions about what generosity is or how it is experienced by different people. This is the approach taken by Mikulincer, Shaver, and Slav (2006) in their examinations of the experience of other prosocial tendencies, such as gratitude and forgiveness.

Following some basic conceptual considerations, in this chapter I review findings for my program of research on what people are thinking and feeling when they engage in behavior that they perceive as generous. I describe the construction of a new self-report measure based on my phenomenological explorations of generosity, and I show how the new measure relates to other individual-difference measures. I conclude with a brief discussion of the theoretical implications of my research.

CONCEPTUAL CONSIDERATIONS

How should *generosity* be defined? Is it a trait, a behavior, a feeling, or an attitude? In the antique Latin poem *Psychomachia* [Fight for Mansoul], written by Prudentius (trans. 1949), which describes the battle between vices and virtues, generosity is defined as willingness to give and nobility of thought or action. In Aristotle's *Nicomachean Ethics* (trans. 1934), generosity is defined, according to the golden mean principle, as the balance between miserliness and prodigality. Assisting others who are in need is encouraged in all religions (see chap. 1, this volume). For example, the Talmud claims that "deeds of kindness are equal in weight to all the commandments" (*Talmud Yerushalmi*, Pe'ah, 1:1).

Considering these ancient statements about the importance of generosity and kindness, it is surprising that the term *generosity* is rare, if not completely absent, in modern psychology. During the 1960s and 1970s, psychological studies were conducted on "helping behavior" and "altruism," but as far as I know there were no published studies of generosity. More recently, Van Lange, Ouwerkerk, and Tazelaar (2002) used the term *generosity* when discussing social interactions characterized by a conflict between self-interest and the interests of others. They defined generosity as behaving more cooperatively than one's partner, rather than behaving in an eye-for-an-eye, reciprocally punishing fashion.

In studies by sociologists and economists, one sometimes finds the term *generosity* used to describe the extent to which individuals share their money and other assets, and at other times to describe certain kinds of cooperative decisions in economic games (e.g., Bendor, Kramer, & Swistak, 1996; Kollock, 1993). In these studies, costs and benefits of generous behavior are manipulated and a participant's cooperative decisions are used as an index of his or her overall generosity. Generous decisions have been found to be affected by many contextual factors, such as the social distance between the decision maker and other parties (e.g., the other player, the experimenter), the monetary cost of a generous action, and certain rules or norms of reciprocity (for a recent example, see Cox & Deck, 2006). These studies have contributed to our understanding of generous behavior, but they are based on inferring generosity from people's decisions to behave in certain ways under certain conditions. It is unclear how well these studies represent experiences and behaviors that occur in daily life in more natural settings.

Even within positive psychology, use of the term *generosity* has been limited. Peterson and Seligman (2004) used it in their classification of character strengths and virtues related to kindness. The other terms they mentioned in that context are *nurturance*, *care*, and *altruistic love*, all being cases of a person acting without "assurance of reciprocity, reputational gains, or any other benefits to the self" (Peterson & Seligman, 2004, p. 326). It is important to note, however, that the concept of *character strength* encourages dichotomous thinking: A person either does or does not have this strength or quality (although presumably it could be nurtured and developed over time). Why not consider instead that generosity is a kind of behavior or experience not restricted to people with a generous character?

If one assumes that generous behavior is a part of most people's social repertoire, individual differences might exist not only in the overall level of generous behavior but also in how a particular person feels when acting generously. For example, individuals who are prosocially motivated might be more oriented toward others' needs and more likely to experience joy and satisfaction in helping others (see chap. 3, this volume). But individuals who are more self-centered and concerned with their own needs and deprivations might be more ambivalent about helping and might construe acts of generosity as sacrifices or instances of exploitation (see chaps. 1 and 6, this volume).

Following this line of thought, I decided to explore the experiential aspects of generous behavior, initially adopting a phenomenological approach. Several studies have used this approach to explore other kinds of experiences. For example, Mikulincer et al. (2006) conducted a phenomenological study of the experience of gratitude and revealed that when people feel grateful toward someone, they experience a multifaceted blend of happiness, love, and security, together with self-focused fears, feelings of vulnerability and obligation, and distrust of the benefactor's intentions (see chap. 14, this volume). My aim was to explore the elements of the experience of generosity, relying on people's own understanding of the concept.

STUDYING THE EXPERIENCE OF GENEROSITY

My research project consisted of three phases. In the first phase, I used open-ended questionnaires to elicit thoughts and feelings that participants spontaneously mention when recalling examples of their own experiences of generosity. These thoughts and feelings were content analyzed to create a series of experience categories. In the second phase, I constructed a self-report scale to measure individual differences in the experiences revealed in the first phase of the project. I then conducted a preliminary factor analysis of responses to this self-report scale. In the third phase, I administered a refined version of the scale to a large pool of participants, conducted a new factor analysis, and examined associations between scores on the extracted factors and a number of potentially related psychological constructs.

Extraction of Units of Meaning From Responses to the Open-Ended Questionnaire

An open-ended questionnaire was designed to help participants reflect on an event in which they were generous toward another person. Sixty-one subjects (ages 22–44) from a regional college in the central region of Israel were asked to recall an event in which they were generous toward another person and to write a detailed description of their experiences during the event. Specifically, they were asked to describe what happened, what they and the other person did, and what they were thinking and feeling during and after the recalled event. Generous deeds included giving material aid, such as money or alms (31%); giving emotional aid, such as guidance or support (23%); giving physically effortful help (23%); creating a more pleasant or enjoyable situation (16%); and offering a solution to a problematic situation (15%).

Participants' descriptions were content analyzed. First, each description was broken into small units of meaning while retaining as much of the participant's original wording as possible. This resulted in a list of 257 units of meaning. Next, these units were grouped according to semantic similarity, which resulted in a list of 33 categories. Table 16.1 shows the 33 categories, the number participants who reported thoughts or feelings in each category, and examples of units extracted from participants' descriptions.

Initial Exploration of the Factor Structure of the Experience of Generosity

A pool of 58 items was constructed on the basis of the content analysis of participants' descriptions of their thoughts and feelings during generous acts. These items included 1 to 2 representative sentences (units) from each of the 33 categories listed in Table 16.1. The 58 items were then administered to a new sample of 289 Israeli undergraduates (ages 19–45). They were first instructed to describe in their own words an event in which they were generous toward another person. Then they were asked to read each of the 58 items and rate the extent to which it was representative of their thoughts and feelings during the recalled event. These ratings were made on a 7-point scale, ranging from 1 (*not at all*) to 7 (*very much*). An exploratory factor analysis with varimax rotation revealed that 34 of the 58 items could be

TABLE 16.1
First Formulation of the Components of the Experience of Generosity

Examples (with gendered pronouns retained)	*N* (%) mentioning component	Component
I felt good about my successful help; I felt useful to him.	34 (56)	1. Satisfaction due to feelings of self-efficacy
I thought that if I were in her situation I would need help; I felt his suffering as if it were mine; I imagined the terrible emotions he must have been feeling.	16 (26)	2. Empathy and identification with the other
I felt sorry for him; I felt love and compassion for him.	12 (20)	3. Feelings of pity, compassion, and love for the other
I could not ignore someone in his situation and pass by without helping; I felt that it was urgent and that I could not pass by and do nothing to help.	12 (20)	4. Feelings of emergency and inability to avoid acting
I felt happy; I was delighted; I sang all the way home.	12 (20)	5. Joy and elevated mood as a result of helping
The lady thanked me many times after that; he didn't know what to do in order to thank me for what I did for him.	12 (20)	6. Interpreting the other's behavior as signifying that he/she felt a debt was being created
I felt happy to see the old man smiling; I was happy to see that the child was feeling good.	10 (16)	7. Feeling happy about the happiness of the other
I wanted to help her; I had good intentions to help him.	10 (16)	8. Wishing to help
I was disappointed because I had to give up something that was important to me; I was happy to help, but I had to double my pace afterwards; I felt that I was giving her my time.	10 (16)	9. Conflict due to the costs and loss involved in giving to the other
I felt that it was hard and that I wanted it to be over; I felt that my hand was hurting me and I was a bit sorry.	10 (16)	10. Feeling the nuisance and burden of the situation
Although I didn't have to do it, I went out of my way to help him; I gave him all that I could and more, although it was not convenient for me.	9 (15)	11. Measuring the amount of giving, and considering it to require extraordinary effort
I felt that I couldn't really solve his problem; I felt bad that I could not help him more; I felt that I didn't help her enough so she will still be alone and depressed.	8 (13)	12. Feelings of inadequacy, helplessness, or shorthandedness
I felt guilty that we are all so healthy and he is so miserable; I felt uncomfortable about being spoiled when there is so much suffering in the world.	8 (13)	13. Conscientiousness and self-criticism

continues

TABLE 16.1
Continued

I thought how sad it is that something like that can happen to anyone in our country; I thought that there is so much poverty and suffering in the world; I thought that in our lives we are always running, and that it is these moments that give meaning to our lives.	8 (13)	14. Existential thoughts about the world, the society, and the meaning of life
I felt proud about the person that I am; I felt good about me, because I did a good deed; I felt very satisfied about myself, because I did the right thing.	8 (13)	15. Narcissistic feelings and heightened self-esteem as a result of doing the morally correct thing
I felt that one day I'll also need help; I'll be paid for my help by God.	7 (11)	16. The profitability of giving to others
I felt that she was laughing and having a good time; I saw him being happy about what I did.	7 (11)	17. Tracking the other's joy after the helpful deed
I felt happy because I got him out of trouble; I was glad that nothing bad happened to him.	7 (11)	18. Satisfaction of being able to prevent suffering and distress
I felt that he was completely helpless and depressed; He looked like he was really desperate.	7 (11)	19. Perception of the other as feeling depressed and in despair
It is an obligation to help others; You ought to help other people.	5 (8)	20. The moral obligation of helping other people
I was frightened but I went to help him right away; It took me some seconds to respond.	5 (8)	21. The encounter with the other's distress was shocking/required quick adaptation
I thought that I shouldn't leave him to the dangers he might be faced with; I didn't give him money because I was sure that he would use it on drugs.	5 (8)	22. Parenting or patronizing attitude toward the other, seeing the other as not being capable of looking after him- or herself
I wanted to make him feel better; I hoped that he would feel happier.	4 (7)	23. Willing to elevate someone's mood
He wasn't willing to receive my help, but I insisted; I didn't give up and I stayed with her, although she told me to go away.	4 (7)	24. The need to overcome the other's rejection of what you are trying to offer
I felt relief after helping him; I felt better because I couldn't stand the fact that she was suffering so much.	4 (7)	25. Relief of tension as a result of helping someone in need
It passed and I didn't think about it afterwards; I didn't think it was very important.	4 (7)	26. Evaluation of the event as transient and meaningless
I felt bad all day afterwards; After that I felt moody and sad all day long.	3 (5)	27. Negative impact of the whole incident on the helper's mood
I felt that she took advantage of my good intentions; He was happy that he received help without paying for it.	3 (5)	28. Feelings of being exploited by the other

After that event I felt that I wanted to help her again; I felt that I would be glad to help him again in the future.	3 (5)	29. Giving as a reinforcer of motivation to give again and again
I thought that other people would not care as much as I did; I felt good about myself because it was revealed that I am a nice guy and not apathetic.	3 (5)	30. Narcissistic feelings and heightened self-esteem as a result of being special in comparison to others
I saw her as weaker than me; I felt good about the fact that I knew how to help someone in trouble.	3 (5)	31. Narcissistic feelings and heightened self-esteem as a result of the perceived gap between the self and the person in need
I wanted him to feel pleased; I wanted him to know that I gave him the best that I could.	2 (3)	32. Wanting the other to be pleased
I felt that they wanted my help; I felt that he needed me.	2 (3)	33. Being needed by the other

grouped into five factors that explained 49.5% of the total variance. Twenty-four items were excluded at this point because of their relatively low loadings (< .40) on all of the factors or their relatively high loadings (> .40) on more than one factor. The five factors were labeled *prosocial orientation* (11 items, Cronbach's α = .89), *personal cost/burden* (10 items, α = .82), *self-criticism/guilt* (6 items, α = .72), *expectations of other's positive response* (3 items, α = .79), and *narcissistic concerns* (4 items, α = .64). By *narcissistic*, used in the psychoanalytic sense, I mean self-congratulatory or pride inducing; I do not intend for the term to be judgmental or pathologizing.

Refining the Factor Structure

To determine whether the five factors would replicate, I administered the 34-item self-report questionnaire to a different and larger sample using a Hebrew-language Internet site (http://www.midgam.com; Ayalon, 2009) designed to collect data for psychology studies. Participants register on the site, provide sociodemographic information, and receive an individual code that allows investigators to avoid repetitive participation. The site calls for participants to respond to various self-report scales to receive feedback about themselves and gain greater self-awareness. Participants are assumed to respond frankly in order to receive reliable feedback. For my study, participants were asked to focus on an event in which they were generous to another person; they were then asked to rate the extent to which each of the 34 items was representative of their thoughts and feelings during the recalled event. Ratings were made on the previously described 7-point scale. Five hundred eighty-one participants (27% men and 73% women, ages 14–62, *Mdn* age = 25 years) responded to the questionnaire, and a second factor analysis with varimax rotation was performed on the 34 items. This analysis revealed a

TABLE 16.2
Factor Analysis of the Experience of Generosity Questionnaire (N = 581)

Item	Factor 1	Factor 2	Factor 3	Factor 4
Factor 1. Emotional cost and burden				
1. I had thoughts about the personal cost that I incurred by helping the other.	.75			
2. I felt that the event weighed down heavily on me.	.75			
3. I felt that the other did not appreciate what I did for him/her.	.75			
4. I felt that the other exploited me.	.69			
5. I wanted the other to appreciate what I did for him.	.67			
6. I thought I would be rewarded for my help.	.66			
7. I felt that I was doing something that demanded a special effort on my part.	.66			
8. I felt that I wanted the event to end rapidly.	.65			
9. After the event I was left with a bad feeling.	.64			
10. I felt that I hesitated about helping or not.	.60			
11. I thought that there are people who ask for help even when they can manage by themselves.	.54			
12. I felt that I gave up something that was important to me.	.50			
13. I hoped the other would be pleased with me.	.41			
Factor 2. Prosocial orientation				
14. I felt I wanted to help.		.80		
15. I felt good about assisting someone in trouble.		.74		
16. I hoped that what I was doing would make the other feel better.		.74		
17. I felt that I had good intentions for the other.		.73		
18. I wanted to give the other a good feeling.		.71		
19. I was satisfied that my help assisted the other.		.69		
20. I felt good about being able to give to the other.		.66		
21. I cared about the other person.		.66		
22. I was happy that I succeeded in helping.		.65		
23. I was happy to rescue the other from a distressing situation.		.55		
Factor 3. Narcissistic gratification				
24. I felt that the other was grateful to me.			.79	
25. I felt that I was a special person by virtue of helping others.			.66	
26. I felt that the other was pleased with my help.			.66	
27. I felt that the other was happy about my behavior.			.59	
Factor 4. Guilt and self-accusation				
28. I felt uncomfortable about not being able to assist more.				.63

29. I wanted to feel that I and the other were equals				.53
30. I had thoughts about Israeli society.				.52
31. I criticized myself for not being more generous.				.51
32. I thought that there is an obligation to help others.				.44
33. I felt guilty for being in a better situation than the other.				.44
34. After helping I felt a relief.				.41
Explained variance (%)	21.5	18.6	5.3	4.3
Cronbach's alpha	.88	.89	.72	.68

similar, although not quite identical, factor structure of the experience of generosity. The 34 items were grouped into four factors (with eigenvalues > 1) this time, and they accounted for 49.7% of the item variance. The results of the factor analysis are shown in Table 16.2.

The meaning of the factors was similar in the two samples, even though there were some differences in item locations and loadings. Both analyses suggested that when people act generously toward others, they experience a complex set of both positive and negative thoughts and feelings concerning the other and the self (see also chaps. 1 and 4, this volume). In other words, people are often motivated by genuine empathy and caring for others in distress, and when they provide assistance they feel good about themselves and experience a boost in self-esteem and personal satisfaction. Nevertheless, some may also be preoccupied with negative thoughts and feelings about what for them is a difficult situation, feel guilty for not helping as much as they should, feel they are being exploited by the other person, or just feel that they are losing something valuable while acting generously.

Pearson correlations between scales based on the four factors were computed to determine whether there were indeed four distinct factors or just two: a combination of the emotional cost and the guilt factors and a combination of the prosocial orientation and narcissistic gratification factors. Correlations ranged between .03 and .48, implying that it is worthwhile to retain the four-factor structure. The emotional cost and guilt factors were moderately associated, $r(579) = .42$, $p < .01$, suggesting that they are two related but still distinct sources of distress that arise during prosocial behavior. The prosocial orientation and narcissistic gratification factors were also moderately related, $r(579) = .48$, $p < .01$, implying that an individual may feel positively about others but not necessarily obtain narcissistic gratification from acting generously.

Exploring Associations Between the Experience of Generosity and Other Variables

The complex structure of the experience of generosity raised questions about possible correlates of the four factors. Because I believe that the experience of generosity, like that of other subjective experiences, is shaped by a combination of personality, cultural socialization, and personal history, I examined associations between the generosity-experience factors and major personality traits (Costa & McCrae's, 1992, Big Five traits), moral attitudes and ideologies, and participants' recollections of their relationships with parents during childhood. In addition, because acts of generosity occur within interpersonal settings, I wanted to see whether the generosity-experience factors are associated with interpersonal styles and concerns, such as attachment styles, social anxieties, and experiences of loneliness. Finally, because Peterson and Seligman (2004) viewed generosity as a core virtue that sustains well-being and happiness, I wanted to examine associations between the generosity-experience factors and measures of mood, mental health, and life satisfaction.

Four scores were computed for each of the 581 participants by averaging items on each factor, and correlations between these scores and other theoretically relevant psychological variables were examined. As described previously, the Experience of Generosity Questionnaire (EGQ) was posted on an Internet site, allowing participants to respond not only to it but also to many other self-report scales. Examining the correlations between these variables allowed me to better understand the meaning of individual differences in generosity experiences while assessing the convergent and discriminant validity of the new EGQ.

The Experience of Generosity and Demographic Variables

Significant differences between men (n = 152) and women (n = 409) were found on the emotional cost/burden factor, $t(559) = 2.16$, $p < .05$, and on the prosocial orientation factor, $t(559) = -2.39$, $p < .05$. Men reported more emotional costs (M = 3.18, *SD* = 1.21) and a weaker prosocial orientation (M = 6.13, *SD* = .08) than women (M = 2.94, *SD* = 1.19; M = 6.30, *SD* = .74, respectively). No significant differences were found between married, single, divorced, or widowed participants on any of the four factors. In addition, religiosity was not significantly associated with any of them.

The Experience of Generosity and the Big Five Personality Traits

I used the 300-item Hebrew version of the IPIP-NEO inventory (Goldberg, 1999; International Personality Item Pool, 2001) to assess the Big Five personality traits—openness to experience, conscientiousness, agreeableness, extraversion, and neuroticism (Costa & McCrae, 1992)—and to examine their associations with the four generosity experience factors. As can be seen in Table 16.3, the emotional cost/burden factor of the generosity measure was associated with scores on all six facets of neuroticism and with lower scores on two facets of agreeableness (morality and altruism) and one facet of conscientiousness (self-efficacy). The prosocial orientation factor of the EGQ was associated with the artistic interests facet of openness to expe-

TABLE 16.3
Experience of Generosity, the Big Five Personality Factors, and Their Facets

Personality trait	Emotional cost/burden	Prosocial orientation	Narcissistic gratification	Guilt/self-accusation
Neuroticism	.30**	−.02	−.01	.18*
Anxiety	.30**	.07	,03	.22*
Anger	.21*	−.12	−.04	.03
Depression	.20*	−.02	−.08	.14
Self-consciousness	.18*	.03	.07	.09
Immoderation	.29**	−.05	−.04	.16
Vulnerability	.27**	−.01	.03	.22*
Extraversion	−.05	.03	.02	−.03
Friendliness	−.15	.13	.12	−.08
Gregariousness	.01	−.01	.02	.01
Assertiveness	.07	.06	.08	−.01
Activity level	.02	−.04	−.08	−.03
Excitement-seeking	−.08	−.03	−.07	.03
Cheerfulness	−.06	.02	−.01	−.05
Openness to experience	−.02	.27**	.07	.10
Imagination	.10	−.05	−.10	.01
Artistic interests	.01	.41**	.21*	.25**
Emotionality	−.11	.16	.12	.07
Adventurousness	−.12	.09	−.05	.04
Intellect	−.08	.14	−.11	−.02
Liberalism	−.17	.20*	.14	−.05
Agreeableness	−.28**	.46**	.26**	.20*
Trust	−.19*	.19*	.18*	−.03
Morality	−.25**	.39**	.19*	.19*
Altruism	−.18*	.34**	.19*	.10
Cooperation	−.14	.42**	.21*	.20*
Modesty	−.17	.11	.05	.14
Sympathy	−.12	.34**	.17	.18*
Conscientiousness	−.13	.40**	.13	.10
Self-efficacy	−.20*	.19*	.10	−.08
Orderliness	−.01	.28**	.05	.13
Dutifulness	−.17	.43**	.28**	.15
Achievement-striving	−.07	.28**	.11	.08
Self-discipline	−.10	.25**	.01	.07
Cautiousness	−.05	.27**	.05	.10

Note. $N = 127$. $^{*}p < .05$. $^{**}p < .01$.

rience, higher scores on most of the facets of agreeableness (trust, morality, altruism, cooperation, and sympathy), and higher scores on all of the conscientiousness facets. Participants who reported having received more "narcissistic supplies" during their generosity experiences scored higher on most of the agreeableness facets (trust, morality, altruism, cooperation, and sympathy), artistic interests, and dutifulness. The guilt/self-accusation factor of the EGQ was associated with anxiety, vulnerability, artistic interests, and three facets of agreeableness (morality, cooperation, and sympathy).

The associations between agreeableness facets and the narcissistic component of the EGQ may seem somewhat surprising, but they are compatible with positive psychologists' view of human nature (e.g., Peterson & Seligman, 2004) because helping others can provide a sense of self-satisfaction, expansion, and growth (see chap. 4, this volume). It is possible that this self-benefit is experienced mainly by agreeable people. In contrast, relatively neurotic individuals may have difficulty experiencing the self-benefits that are potentially available from acts of generosity. Rather, such people may experience these acts as additional sources of guilt and remorse because not enough was done for the other or it was not done well enough.

Moral Attitudes and Ideologies

In the first phase of my research, some participants spontaneously reported feeling a moral obligation to help others; experiencing self-criticism; and having existential concerns about the world, society, and the meaning of life during or after their generous act (see Table 16.1). These meaning units seem to reflect a moral or ethical approach to life, which encouraged me to examine possible associations between the four generosity factors and participants' endorsement of moral attitudes and ideologies assessed with Forsyth's (1980) measure of ethical ideologies (the 20-item Ethics Position Questionnaire) and the 20-item MACH-IV measure of Machiavellianism (Christie & Geis, 1970).

Ethical ideologies are defined as sets of beliefs, attitudes, and values that provide a framework for considering ethical dilemmas (Barnett, Bass, & Brown, 1994). Forsyth (1980) suggested that these ethical ideologies are organized around two orthogonal dimensions: relativism and idealism. *Relativism* refers to the extent to which a person rejects the possibility of formulating or relying on universal moral rules when making moral judgments. *Idealism* refers to the extent to which a person assumes that desirable consequences can always be obtained by morally "right" action. As can be seen in Table 16.4, significant associations were found only between idealism and the prosocial orientation and narcissistic gratification factors of the EGQ. Idealistic participants reported having a more prosocial orientation and higher levels of narcissistic gratification during generosity experiences. It therefore seems that believing morally "right" actions lead to desirable consequences is associated with prosocial attitudes and higher levels of narcissistic gratification from helping others.

Machiavellianism is a tendency to deceive and manipulate others for personal gain. It refers to a person's willingness to achieve goals with little regard for morality (Henning & Six, 1977). Machiavellianism is also negatively associated with social cooperation (Paal & Bereczkei, 2007). Therefore, I wanted to see how it was associated with the four EGQ factors. Significant correlations were found between Machiavellianism and the emotional cost/burden and guilt/self-accusation factors of the generosity measure, $r(134) = .26$, $p < .01$ and $r(134) = .19$, $p < .05$, respectively. The more a participant had a Machiavellian view of interpersonal relations, the more he or she felt

TABLE 16.4
Experience of Generosity in Relation to Other Psychological Variables

Variable	Emotional cost/burden	Prosocial orientation	Narcissistic gratification	Guilt/self-accusation
Ethical ideologies ($N = 134$)				
Idealism	.13	.47**	.35**	.15
Relativism	.14	−.07	.07	.10
Machiavellianism ($N = 127$)	.26**	−.10	−.07	.19*
Attachment orientations ($N = 283$)				
Anxiety	.47**	−.01	−.01	.17**
Avoidance	.21**	−.18**	−.07	.10
Social anxiety ($N = 118$)	.18*	−.09	−.03	.15
Loneliness ($N = 173$)				
Isolation	.20*	−.20*	−.20*	−.03
Relational connectedness	−.12	.20**	.17*	−.03
Collective connectedness	−.12	.13	.16*	.05
Perception of parents ($N = 173$)				
Father's warmth	−.09	.12	.20**	.05
Father's control	.13*	−.15*	−.12	−.07
Mother's warmth	−.08	.10	.13	−.02
Mother's control	.12	−.15*	−.15*	−.08
Self-construal ($N = 125$)				
Independent	.18	.09	.12	.05
Interdependent	.12	.16	.12	.20*
PANAS ($N = 168$)				
Positive	−.25**	.14	.12	−.06
Negative	.30**	−.11	−.12	.13
DASS ($N = 96$)				
Depression	.21*	.01	−.02	.24*
Anxiety	.28**	.15	.05	.41**
Stress	.30**	.10	.01	.25*
Life satisfaction ($N = 168$)	−.25**	.19*	.18*	−.05

Note. PANAS = Positive and Negative Affect Schedule; DASS = Depression, Anxiety, and Stress Scales.
$^*p < .05$. $^{**}p < .01$.

that generosity entails emotional costs and burdens, and the more he or she was bothered by guilt and self-accusation while acting generously. These findings emphasize the aversive nature of generosity in the case of Machiavellian individuals.

Generosity Experience and Attachment

I administered the 36-item Experiences in Close Relationships—Revised inventory (Fraley, Waller, & Brennan, 2000), which measures attachment anxiety and avoidance. Attachment anxiety was significantly associated with the emotional cost/burden and guilt/self-accusation factors of the EGQ (see Table 16.4). In addition, avoidant attachment was significantly associated with the emotional cost/burden factor of the generosity measure and with lower scores on the prosocial orientation factor. Thus, it seems that people who score high on one or both dimensions of insecure attachment are more likely to emphasize the emotional costs and burdens of generosity. Attachment-anxious people also tended to be troubled by self-accusation and self-criticism, whereas avoidant people tended to be less guided by prosocial motives. These findings are compatible with the negative appraisals of self associated with attachment anxiety and the negative appraisals of others associated with avoidant attachment (chap. 14, this volume).

Generosity Experience and Social Anxiety

Social anxiety is defined as fear and avoidance of social situations in which a person might be exposed to negative evaluations (Kashdan, 2007). Although it might seem reasonable to assume that the generous acts reported by study participants were not threatening in this way, because the participants presumably decided to help others, it is still possible that social anxiety is associated with specific facets of the experience of generosity. Participants completed the 30-item Social Interaction Self-Statement Test (Glass, Merlluzi, Bireve, & Larsen, 1982), which taps the extent to which people perceive the social environment to be threatening and a source of tension. I found that participants' level of social anxiety was associated with the perceived emotional cost/burden of generosity (see Table 16.4). That is, individuals who are more sensitive to social threats may have emotional difficulties even in benign interpersonal interactions.

Generosity Experience and Loneliness

How do lonely people feel when they act generously? *Loneliness* is defined as the subjective experience of deficits in the quality or quantity of social relationships and the accompanying feelings of tension and distress (Peplau & Perlman, 1982). To measure loneliness, I used the revised UCLA Loneliness Scale (Hawkley, Browne, & Cacioppo, 2005), which taps three different aspects of loneliness: (a) isolation (feelings of being rejected and withdrawn from society), (b) relational connectedness (feelings of interpersonal proximity, closeness, and support), and (c) collective connectedness (feelings of belonging and affiliation). Higher scores on the first factor and lower scores on the second and third factors indicate greater loneliness. As can be seen in Table 16.4, the perceived emotional cost/burden of generous acts was significantly associated with feelings of isolation. Additionally, the EGQ prosocial orientation factor was inversely related to the feeling of isolation and positively related to feelings of relational connectedness. The narcissistic gratification factor of the generosity experience measure was also inversely associated with feelings of isolation and positively associated with feelings of relational and collective connectedness. The experience of guilt/self-accusation was not significantly related to any of the loneliness scores (see Table 16.4). These findings imply that people who feel more connected to the interpersonal and social environment tend to be prosocially motivated to engage in generous acts, to feel empathy for others, and to receive narcissistic gratification from helping others. The opposite seems to be true for isolated individuals; helping others in the context of feelings of loneliness and isolation seems to be tied up with negative feelings and emotional burden.

Generosity Experience and Perception of Parents

Authoritative, permissive, and authoritarian parenting styles are predictive of different trajectories in personality development (Baumrind, 1967). Children who are exposed to a more sensitive, responsive, nonpunitive, and nonauthoritarian parenting style tend to develop higher levels of affective and cognitive empathy toward needy others and to engage more often in prosocial behavior (e.g., see chap. 7, this volume; Eisenberg, Lennon, & Roth, 1983; Kestenbaum, Farber, & Sroufe, 1989). This optimal parenting style includes two elements: (a) parental responsiveness, warmth, and supportiveness and (b) moderate demandingness and control (Maccoby & Martin, 1983). Participants completed the 25-item Parental Bonding Instrument (Parker, Tupling, & Brown, 1979), which assesses perceptions of mothers and fathers along the dimensions of parental warmth and parental control. As can be seen in Table 16.4, perception of paternal warmth was significantly associated with the narcissistic gratification factor of generous experiences. Perception of parental control was inversely correlated with the prosocial orientation factor of the EGQ and positively correlated with experiencing generous acts as costly and burdensome. Perception of maternal control was significantly associated with a less prosocial orientation and with the narcissistic gratification factor of the EGQ (see Table 16.4).

These initial findings imply that parental control interferes with prosocial motivation and empathy and makes it more likely that generous behavior will be experienced as emotionally burdensome. In addition, people who were reared by a warm and sensitive father tend to obtain narcissistic gratification from acting generously.

Generosity Experience and Self-Construal

Self-construal refers to the ways in which people perceive themselves in relation to others. Markus and Kitamaya (1991) identified two kinds of self-construal: independent and interdependent. People who construe themselves as independent view themselves as unique and separate from their interpersonal context. People who construe themselves as interdependent perceive themselves as woven into their social context and tend to conform to social norms and group expectations. I administered the 24-item Self-Construal Scale (Singelis, 1994), tapping independent and interdependent forms of self-construal, and found a significant positive association between interdependent self-construal and the guilt/self-accusation factor of the generosity experience measure (see Table 16.4). It seems that for people who construe themselves as connected to others, their sense of duty and responsibility for others' welfare is so strong that guilt feelings accompany acts of generosity.

Generosity Experience and Mood

I also examined associations between the EGQ and participants' mood states. Participants completed the 20-item Positive and Negative Affect Schedule (PANAS; Watson, Clark, & Tellegen, 1988), which assesses positive and negative affect with two separate scales (PA and NA). PA reflects the extent to which a person feels enthusiastic, active, and alert. NA is a measure of subjective distress or negative mood (Watson et al., 1988). I asked participants to think about their feelings during the past month. Only the emotional cost/burden factor of the EGQ was significantly associated with higher NA and lower PA (see Table 16.4), implying that this factor captures the affective component of the generosity experience.

I also included the Depression, Anxiety, and Stress scales (Lovibond & Lovibond, 1995). The Depression scale assesses dysphoria, hopelessness, devaluation of life; the Anxiety scale assesses autonomic arousal, situational anxiety, and subjective experience of anxious affect; and the Stress scale is sensitive to levels of chronic nonspecific arousal. The three scores were associated with the emotional cost/burden and guilt/self-accusation factors of the generosity experience measure (see Table 16.4). These findings can be interpreted in terms of individuals' generally negative mood or emotional disregulation during generosity experiences.

Generosity Experience and Life Satisfaction

In the previous section, I reported findings concerning positive and negative affect. Now I turn to *life satisfaction*—the process by which individuals assess the quality of their lives using their own criteria (e.g., Diener, Emmons, Larsen, & Griffin, 1985). I asked participants to complete the 5-item Satisfaction with Life Scale (Diener et al., 1985). There was a significant negative correlation between life satisfaction and the emotional cost/burden factor of the EGQ; there were significant positive associations between life satisfaction and the prosocial orientation and narcissistic gratification factors of the EGQ (see Table 16.4). These results reinforce the conclusion that holding a prosocial orientation and obtaining narcissistic gratification while acting generously toward others are closely related to a person's overall subjective well-being.

Some Additional Findings: Generosity Experience, Obsessions, and Money

In the opening paragraph of this chapter, I mentioned the classical psychoanalytic notion that a generous character may result from reaction formation and sublimation of unconscious stinginess, harking back to the anal phase of psychosexual development (Freud, 1908). In his account of anal eroticism, Freud mentioned three character traits: orderliness, parsimony (frugality), and obstinacy. In my study, participants completed the following measures of some of these traits: (a) the Obsessive-Compulsive Inventory

TABLE 16.5
Experience of Generosity, Obsessions, and Money-related Beliefs and Behaviors

Variable	Emotional cost/burden	Prosocial orientation	Narcissistic gratification	Guilt/self-accusation
Obsessive thoughts and compulsive behaviors (*N* = 195)				
Fear of contamination	.18*	.12	.07	.25**
Urge to check	.12	−.07	−.04	.04
Obsessional thoughts	.17*	.01	−.04	.16*
Hoarding	.21**	−.01	−.13	.11
Ordering	.15*	.05	.08	.05
Neutralizing activities	.09	.03	.01	.12
Obsessive beliefs (*N* = 172)				
Responsibility	.20**	.09	.01	.33**
Perfectionsim	.16*	.12	.05	.21**
Controlling	.25**	.02	.01	.27**
Money beliefs and behaviors (*N* = 170)				
Obsession	.24**	−.04	.05	.17*
Power	.21**	−.08	−.04	.21**
Retention	.28**	.06	.14	.27**

Note. *p < a.05. **p < .01.

(Foa et al., 2002), which assesses the frequency of different kinds of obsessive thoughts and compulsive behaviors (fear of contamination, urge of checking, obsessional thoughts, hoarding, ordering, and neutralizing activities); (b) the Obsessive Beliefs Questionnaire (Obsessive-Compulsive Cognitions Working Group, 2005), which measures three cognitive aspects of obsession–compulsion: overestimation of responsibility for thoughts, perfectionism (i.e., intolerance of ambiguity), and the importance of controlling thoughts; and (c) the Money Beliefs and Behaviors Scale (Furnham, 1984), which measures obsession (i.e., excessive preoccupation with money), power (i.e., the belief that money can purchase power, prestige, and control over others), and retention (i.e., parsimony and hoarding).

With regard to obsessive thoughts and compulsive behaviors (Obsessive-Compulsive Inventory), I found that the emotional cost/burden and guilt/self-accusations factors of the generosity experience measure were significantly associated with fear of contamination and obsessional thoughts (see Table 16.5). The emotional cost/burden factor was also significantly associated with hoarding and ordering (see Table 16.5). The emotional cost/burden and guilt/self-accusation factors of the EGQ were significantly associated with all three obsessional beliefs: overestimation of responsibility for thoughts, intolerance of ambiguity, and the importance of controlling thoughts (see Table 16.5). All three attitudes toward money were also significantly associated with scores on the emotional cost/burden and guilt/self-accusations factors of the generosity experience (see Table 16.5).

Taken together, these findings reveal an association between obsessive thoughts and compulsive behaviors, obsessional beliefs, and obsessions concerning money, on the one hand, and, on the other hand, the more negative qualities of generosity experiences—perceived emotional cost/burden and the experience of guilt/self-accusation when acting generously. In his paper "Character and Anal Erotism," Freud (1908) mentioned that he had clinically encountered patients with a constellation of prominent characteristics; they were tidy, clean, trustworthy, parsimonious, and obstinate. Freud assured his readers that "no theoretical expectation played any part in that impression" (p. 169), but he tried to understand it on the basis of his psychosexual theory. My findings are compatible with Freud's observations and with conclusions reached by contemporary investigators of the psychology of money (Furnham & Argyle, 1998): "Money is clearly symbolic and imbued with moral and emotional meaning" (p. 60). The associations I observed between obsessions concerning money and negative qualities of experienced generosity reflect basic psychological insecurities, some probably having to do with maintenance of control in general, but others concerned with other people's perceived unreliability and unavailability in times of need. These perceptions suggest to some individuals that they need to earn and hoard money so as to cope with life's slings and arrows without having to rely on other people.

CONCLUSIONS

I have found generosity experiences to be complex, containing both positive and negative aspects. While engaging in self-classified generous acts, people not only encounter needy others, they also encounter aspects of themselves—their moral attitudes, interpersonal schemas, coping strategies, and emotional states (for related ideas, see chap. 3). People may experience positive feelings associated with helping others, including the pride associated with being good, kind, and moral. But they may also feel emotionally burdened, annoyed, or self-critical. The four-factor structure of experiences of generosity seems likely to be reliable because it appeared in two different participant samples, one of university students and one of respondents to a Web site. Nevertheless, the findings need to be replicated in other cultures and checked for generalizability.

The associations between the factors of generosity experiences and other psychological constructs explored here indicate that individual differences in the experience of generosity are related to other extensively studied psychological processes. It is unclear at present how the variables are causally interrelated and how best to interpret their associations. I hope this chapter stimulates further research that deepens our understanding of generosity, an important human virtue.

REFERENCES

Ayalon, A. (2009). *Midgam Project*. Retrieved March 12, 2009, from http://www.midgam.com/info.asp

Barnett, T., Bass, K., & Brown, G. (1994). Ethical ideology and ethical judgment regarding ethical issues in business. *Journal of Business Ethics, 13*, 469–480.

Baumrind, D. (1967). Child care practices anteceding three patterns of preschool behavior. *Genetic Psychology Monographs, 75*, 43–88.

Bendor, J., Kramer, R. M., & Swistak, P. (1996). Cooperation under uncertainty: What is new, what is true, and what is important. *American Sociological Review, 61*, 333–338.

Costa, P. T., Jr., & McCrae, R. R. (1992). *NEO PI-R professional manual*. Odessa, FL: Psychological Assessment Resources.

Cox, J. C., & Deck, C. A. (2006). When are women more generous than men? *Economic Inquiry, 44*, 587–598.

Cristie, R., & Geis, F. L. (1970). *Studies in Machiavellianism*. New York: Academic Press.

Diener, E., Emmons, R. A., Larsen, R. J., & Griffin, S. (1985). The Satisfaction with Life Scale. *Journal of Personality Assessment, 49*, 71–75.

Eisenberg, N., Lennon, R., & Roth, K. (1983). Prosocial development in childhood: A longitudinal study. *Developmental Psychology, 19*, 846–855.

Foa, E. B., Huppert, J. D., Leiberg, S., Langner, R., Kichic, R., Hajcak, G., et al. (2002). The Obsessive Compulsive Inventory: Development and validation of a short version. *Psychological Assessment, 14*, 485–496.

Forsyth, D. R. (1980). A taxonomy of ethical ideologies. *Journal of Personality and Social Psychology, 39*, 175–184.

Fraley, R. C., Waller, N. G., & Brennan, K. A. (2000). An item response theory analysis of self-report measures of adult attachment. *Journal of Personality and Social Psychology, 78*, 350–365.

Freud, S. (1908). Character and anal erotism. In J. Strachey (Ed.), *The standard edition of the complete psychological works of Sigmund Freud* (Vol. 9, pp. 167–175). London: Hogarth Press.

Furnham, A. (1984). Many sides of the coin: The psychology of money usage. *Personality and Individual Differences, 5*, 501–509.

Furnham, A., & Argyle, M. (1998). *The psychology of money*. London: Routledge.

Glass, C. R., Merluzzi,T. V., Biever, J. L., & Larsen, K. H. (1982). Cognitive assessment of social anxiety: Development and validation of a self-statement questionnaire. *Cognitive Therapy and Research , 6*, 37–55.

Goldberg, L. R. (1999). A broad-bandwidth, public domain, personality inventory measuring the lower-level facets of several five-factor models. In I. Mervielde, I. Deary, F. De Fruyt, & F. Ostendorf (Eds.), *Personality psychology in Europe, Vol. 7* (pp. 7–28). Tilburg, The Netherlands: Tilburg University Press.

Hawkley, L. C., Browne, M. W., & Cacioppo, J. T. (2005). How can I connect with thee? Let me count the ways. *Psychological Science, 16*, 798–804.

Henning, H. J., & Six, B. (1977). Konstruktion einer Machiavellismus-skala [Construction of a new Machiavellianism Scale]. *Zeitschrift fur Sozial Psychologie, 8*, 185–198.

International Personality Item Pool. (2008). *A scientific collaboration for the development of advanced measures of personality traits and other individual differences*. Retrieved May 2, 2009, from http://ipip.ori.org

Kashdan, T. B. (2007). Social anxiety spectrum and diminished positive experiences: Theoretical synthesis and meta-analysis. *Clinical Psychology Review, 27*, 348–365.

Kestenbaum, R., Farber, E. A., & Sroufe, L. A. (1989). Individual differences in empathy among preschoolers: Relation to attachment history. In N. Eisenberg (Ed.), *New directions for child development: Vol. 44. Empathy and related emotional responses* (pp. 51–64). San Francisco, CA: Jossey-Bass.

Kollock, P. (1993). "An eye for an eye leaves everyone blind": Cooperation and accounting systems. *American Sociological Review, 58*, 768–786.

Lovibond, P. F., & Lovibond, S. H. (1995). *Manual for the Depression Anxiety Stress Scales* (2nd. ed.). Sydney, Australia: Psychology Foundation.

Maccoby, E. E., & Martin, J. A. (1983). Socialization in the context of the family: Parent–child interaction. In P. H. Mussen (Ed.) & E. M. Hetherington (Vol. Ed.), *Handbook of child psychology: Vol. 4. Socialization, personality, and social development* (4th ed., pp. 1–101). New York: Wiley.

Markus, H. R., & Kitayama, S. (1991). Culture and the self: Implications for cognition, emotion, and motivation. *Psychological Review, 98*, 224–253.

Mikulincer, M., Shaver, P. R., & Slav, K. (2006). Attachment, mental representations of others, and gratitude and forgiveness in romantic relationships. In M. Mikulincer & G. S. Goodman (Eds.), *Dynamics of romantic love: Attachment, caregiving, and sex* (pp. 190–215). New York: Guilford Press.

Obsessive Compulsive Cognitions Working Group. (2005). Psychometric validation of the Obsessive Beliefs Questionnaire and Interpretation of Intrusions Inventory: Part 2. Factor analyses and testing of a brief version. *Behavior Research and Therapy, 43*, 1527–1542.

Paal, T., & Bereczkei, T. (2007). Adult theory of mind, Machiavellianism, and cooperation: The effect of mindreading on social relation. *Personality and Individual Differences, 43*, 541–551.

Parker, G., Tupling, H., & Brown, L. B. (1979). A parental bonding instrument. *British Journal of Medical Psychology, 52*, 1–10.

Peplau, L. A. & Perlman, D. (1982). *Loneliness: A source book of current theory, research, and therapy*. New York: Wiley.

Peterson, C., & Seligman, M. E. P. (2004). *Character strengths and virtues: A classification and handbook*. New York: Oxford University Press/Washington, DC: American Psychological Association.

Singelis, T. M. (1994). The measurement of independent and interdependent self-construals. *Personality and Social Psychology Bulletin, 20*, 580–591.

Van Lange, P. A. M., Ouwerkerk, J. W., & Tazelaar, M. J. A. (2002). How to overcome the detrimental effects of noise in social interaction: The benefits of generosity. *Journal of Personality and Social Psychology, 82*, 768–780.

Watson, D., Clark, L. A., & Tellegen, A. (1988). Development and validation of brief measures of positive and negative affect: The PANAS scales. *Journal of Personality and Social Psychology, 54*, 1063–1070.

IV

PROSOCIAL BEHAVIOR AT THE RELATIONAL LEVEL

17

PROSOCIAL MOTIVATION AND BEHAVIOR IN CLOSE RELATIONSHIPS

CARYL E. RUSBULT AND CHRISTOPHER R. AGNEW

Why are people in close relationships motivated to go beyond their own self-interest and act in a manner that benefits their partner? Some theorists would point to person factors in answering this question, specifying various personality dimensions as particularly relevant (see chaps. 3, 4, 7, and 19, this volume). Others would take a social cognitive approach, emphasizing the manner in which relationship cognitions guide prosocial activity (see chaps. 1, 10, and 18, this volume). In this chapter, we advance a different approach. We review findings from a long-standing program of research on prosocial behavior in close relationships from an interdependence perspective. We make three main points.

First, we suggest that the structure of interdependence between persons should be an important concern for social and behavioral scientists interested in understanding prosocial motivation and behavior. That is, it is important for us to understand the manner in which each person's actions influence the other's well-being. We suggest that *diagnostic situations* are particularly meaningful and important in understanding prosocial actions, in that in such situations the individual's direct self-interest is pitted against the interests of the partner.

Second, we suggest that behaving to the benefit of one's partner in such situations rests on key structural features of relationships. Specifically, behaving prosocially rests on the degree to which the individual is dependent on a relationship and, accordingly, experiences strong commitment to it. We emphasize the concepts of dependence and commitment because we believe psychologists typically place too much weight on positive affect in relationships, on concepts such as liking versus disliking, positive versus negative attitudes, and the like. Note that for the purposes of this chapter, we are focusing on prosocial behavior that occurs within the bounds of a given relationship.

Third, we propose that in interdependent relationships, each person's actions have implications for the partner. Thus, we should understand prosocial behavior not so much by examining individual-level cognition, personality, or motivation but by examining the relationship between individuals—by understanding the implications of each person's thoughts, traits, and motives for those of the partner. In short, we are going to suggest that psychology, particularly social psychology, should be more truly social in character when attempting to understand prosocial motives and behavior in interpersonal contexts.

INTERDEPENDENCE STRUCTURE: RELEVANCE OF DIAGNOSTIC SITUATIONS

How is interdependence structure relevant to understanding prosocial motivation? In the following paragraphs we introduce the concept of outcome correspondence, suggesting that situations with noncorrespondent outcomes are particularly diagnostic. Diagnostic situations afford the expression of an individual's motives, in that such situations pit individual interests against the interests of the partner and relationship. Partners frequently exhibit transformation of motivation in such situations, departing from their direct self-interest by exhibiting prorelationship motives and acts.

Diagnostic Situations and Transformation of Motivation

Sometimes involvement with a relationship partner is simple. When partners' goals correspond and their preferences are compatible, partners can readily achieve desirable outcomes, such as intimacy, companionship, sexual gratification, and security. Such a situation is described by interdependence theorists as one involving high *correspondence of outcomes* (e.g., Kelley et al., 2003; Rusbult, Arriaga, & Agnew, 2001; Rusbult & Van Lange, 2003). The true test of a relationship arises when outcomes are not correspondent—when partners encounter dilemmas involving conflicted interaction, incompatible preferences, or extrarelationship temptation. Holmes and Rempel

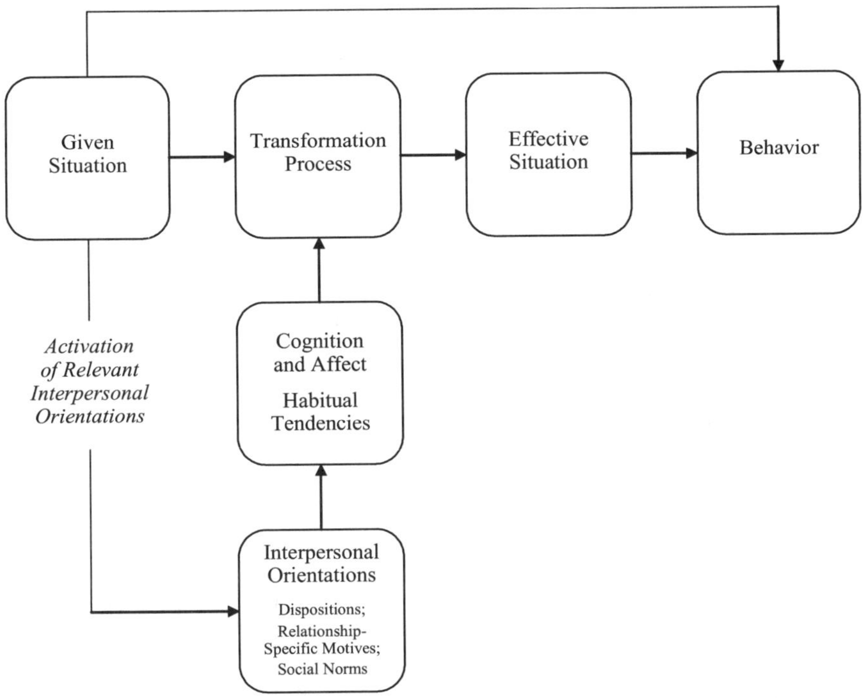

Figure 17.1. Transformation of motivation process.

(1989) termed such dilemmas *diagnostic situations*. A diagnostic situation is an interdependence dilemma—a situation in which the individual's direct self-interest is incompatible with the interests of the relationship. Diagnostic situations are termed *diagnostic* because behavior in such situations communicates the individual's broader motives. They are diagnostic in that when a partner behaves well in a dilemma of this sort, such behavior communicates the partner's prorelationship motives, revealing that the partner is willing to depart from his or her immediate self-interest to promote one's own well-being and the well-being of the relationship.

According to interdependence theory, behaving well in diagnostic situations rests on *transformation of motivation*, or the psychological process whereby an individual comes to react to a given situation not on the basis of direct self-interest but on the basis of broader considerations, such as long-term goals, social or personal values, norms, or the well-being of a partner or relationship (Arriaga & Holmes, 2009; Kelley et al., 2003). How does transformation of motivation come about? To begin with, an individual encounters a specific *given situation*, which describes outcome interdependence based on direct self-interest (see Figure 17.1). In the given situation, individuals sometimes react on the basis of that which is dictated by direct self-interest. Alternatively, the given pattern may then activate any of several possible interpersonal orientations, which embody stable transformational tendencies. For example, a given pattern may activate specific dispositions (attachment style; see chap. 14, this volume), relationship-specific motives (commitment), or social norms (e.g., "Do unto others. . ."). Relevant orientations may yield habitual transformation tendencies, or the transformation process may be mediated by orientation-colored cognitive interpretations and affective reactions. That is, the process may be automatic or may involve systematic cognitive activity. The transformation process yields what is referred to using interdependence terminology as the *effective situation*, which represents preferences based on such broader considerations. Effective preferences directly guide behavior in interpersonal contexts.

For example, in a situation between Hillary and Bill involving an act of betrayal by Bill, Hillary must decide whether to (a) pursue her "gut level," given preferences (i.e., preferences based on direct self-interest) and seek revenge, or (b) inhibit this impulse, exhibit pro-relationship transformation, and react in a constructive manner (i.e., preferences based on broader considerations). If Hillary sets aside her direct self interest and forgives Bill, Bill will likely recognize that she is motivated by prorelationship concerns, and their relationship will be maintained or improved.

Empirical Evidence of the Transformation Process

Do important phenomena involve conflict between self-interest and the interests of a relationship? Does behaving well in such situations involving a partner rest on prorelationship transformation of motivation? Research relevant to understanding accommodative behavior has suggested an affirmative answer to these questions. Rusbult, Verette, Whitney, Slovik, and Lipkus (1991) defined *accommodation* as the tendency, when a partner enacts a potentially destructive behavior, to (a) inhibit impulses to react destructively in turn and (b) instead, react in a constructive manner. We suggest that from a perfectly self-interested point of view, people are not inclined to accommodate. Rather, accommodation rests on transformation of motivation, which involves taking account of broader considerations, considerations such as concern for the well-being of a partner, goals for the future of the relationship, and broader social norms.

To the extent that this is true, and to the extent that "taking account of broader considerations" rests on active cognitive activity, variations in reaction time should reveal the discrepancy between given versus effective preferences. In situations requiring transformation of motivation, compared with participants given plentiful reaction time, those given limited reaction time should exhibit substantially more destructive, self-interested behavior. In one study we conducted in our laboratory (Yovetich & Rusbult, 1994), participants heard hypothetical situations in which partners enacted constructive or destructive behaviors. Participants were given either limited or plentiful time in which to react. We then measured the proportion of times the participant chose a constructive response. Consistent with expectations, when confronted with destructive partner acts, participants exhibited more constructive behavioral responses given plentiful reaction time (i.e., time for transformation) than given limited reaction time (i.e., no time for transformation). When confronted with constructive partner acts whereby no transformation is necessary, the probability of constructive behavior did not differ for limited versus plentiful reaction time. Thus, accommodation does involve conflict between self-interest and the interests of the relationship, and behaving well in accommodative dilemmas does rest on prorelationship transformation.

Past research has explored the transformation process using both experimental and nonexperimental methods, a variety of measurement techniques, a variety of participation populations, and a variety of paradigms. For example, paradigms have varied the presence versus absence of transformation-relevant concern (e.g., explicit directions to consider oneself only vs. consider oneself in a relationship), the degree of interdependence-relevant concern (e.g., acquaintance vs. close-other interaction), and the resources available for the transformation process (e.g., manipulating state of mental depletion vs. nondepletion). Research has examined the responses individuals consider enacting ("gut level," given preferences) versus the behavior they actually enact (transformed, effective preferences) as well as preferences under conditions of limited time (given preferences) versus plentiful time (effective preferences; e.g., Rusbult et al., 1991). But what motivates individuals to make the necessary transformation in response to an interdependence dilemma, a situation in which one's own well-being is pitted against the well-being of one's relationship? We consider this question in the next section.

PRORELATIONSHIP MOTIVATION: COMMITMENT AS A CENTRAL MOTIVE

In the following paragraphs we introduce the concept of commitment, outlining the character of this motive and describing its origins in interdependence structure. Commitment has its origins in the nature of an individual's dependence on a given partner, and plays a key role in promoting prorelationship motivation.

Commitment, Dependence, and the Investment Model

We have argued that commitment is a key variable in understanding relationships. Commitment embodies one's history of interdependence, guides present behavior, and shapes goals for future behavior. *Commitment* is defined as the sense of allegiance that individuals develop toward the objects of their dependence. Commitment comprises three components: (a) intent to persist, (b) psychological attachment, and (c) long-term orientation (cf. Rusbult & Buunk, 1993; Arriaga & Agnew, 2001).

According to the investment model of commitment (Rusbult, 1983; Rusbult, Martz, & Agnew, 1998), people become committed because they are dependent on their relationships—because (a) they are satisfied with the relationship, as the relationship gratifies the individual's most important needs (companionship, intimacy, sexuality; Drigotas & Rusbult, 1992); (b) they believe their alternatives are poor, as their most important needs could not be gratified independent of the relationship (in an alternative relationship, by friends or kin); and (c) they have invested many important resources in the relationship, such as time and effort, shared friendship network, and material possessions.

Being dependent means that you "need" a relationship; the relationship gratifies important needs, those needs cannot be gratified elsewhere, and you have invested a good deal in the relationship. Accordingly, we suggest that commitment should powerfully predict tendencies to persist at a given line of behavior, to remain involved in a relationship, to continue at a specific job or career, to continue using a given product, and so on.

Empirical Evidence of Commitment and Persistence in Relationships

Does commitment emerge as a consequence of dependence, and does it promote persistence? With respect to close relationships, numerous studies have provided evidence for the bases of dependence described here: satisfaction, alternatives, and investments (Le & Agnew, 2003; Rusbult et al., 1998). We briefly describe one such study. Individuals provided self-report measures of the investment model variables on 13 separate occasions over the course of an academic year. About a third of the relationships ended during this time. The data provided on multiple research occasions are not independent, so they were analyzed using hierarchical linear modeling. We used growth curve analysis to transform data for each variable into trend scores, that is, scores representing linear change over time in each model variable. Increases over time in feelings of satisfaction, decreases over time in perceived quality of alternatives, and increases over time in the magnitude of investments each significantly predicted increases over time in commitment. Figure 17.2 displays mean trend scores for each variable as a function of later relationship fate—for voluntary stayers; for voluntary leavers; and for "the abandoned," whose partners ended the relationship. As can be seen, commitment increased over time among stayers and declined among voluntary leavers; commitment increased marginally among the abandoned. Parallel supportive evidence was obtained for all investment model variables. For example, among the abandoned, investment size increased over time to the

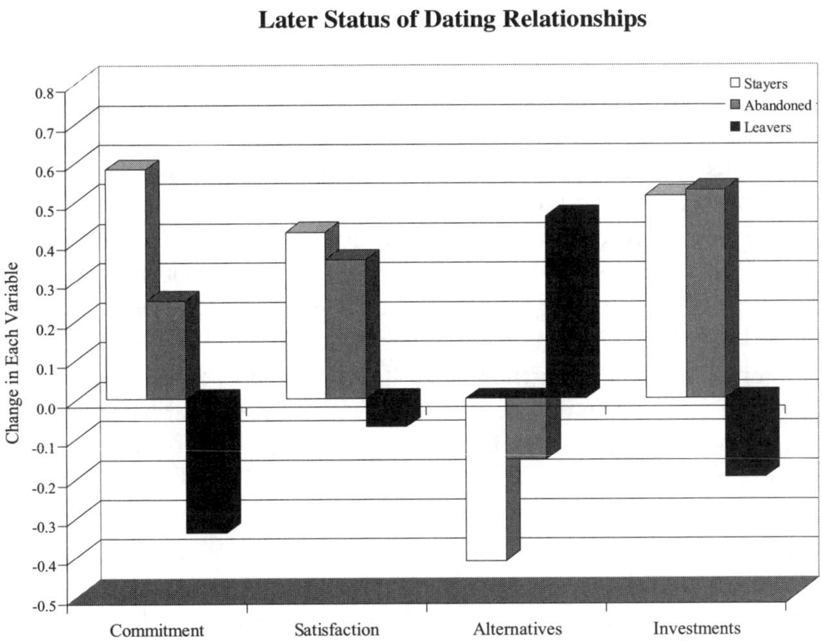

Figure 17.2. Investment model prediction of relationship fate.

same extent as it did for voluntary stayers, thereby entrapping the abandoned in not-completely-satisfying relationships that their partners ultimately ended. Importantly, of the four variables that we examined, commitment was by far the strongest predictor of later relationship fate.

The investment model has been tested using both experimental and nonexperimental methods (e.g., Agnew, Hoffman, Lehmiller, & Duncan, 2007); using a variety of measurement techniques and a variety of populations (e.g., Bui, Peplau, & Hill, 1996); in a variety of cultures; and across multiple domains, for example, not only in the context of close relationships but also in organizational settings and in the domain of consumer behavior (cf. Le & Agnew, 2003).

COMMITMENT AND RELATIONSHIP MAINTENANCE MECHANISMS

Beyond being a potent predictor of persistence in a relationship, commitment also promotes other behaviors that reflect prorelationship orientation. Committed individuals are willing to exert effort and endure cost for the good of their relationships, departing from immediate self-interest for the good of the relationship. Commitment predicts both behavioral and cognitive maintenance processes. For example, in addition to examining the association of commitment with accommodation, past research has examined behavioral tendencies for committed individuals to (a) sacrifice immediate self-interest for the good of the relationship (e.g., Van Lange et al., 1997) and (b) forgive a partner's acts of betrayal (e.g., Finkel, Rusbult, Kumashiro, & Hannon, 2002). Research has also focused on cognitive tendencies to derogate attractive and tempting relationship alternatives (Johnson & Rusbult, 1989); to exhibit positive illusions regarding one's relationship (i.e., to perceive one's relationship as better than, and not as bad as, other relationships; e.g., Van Lange, Rusbult, Semin-Goossens, Goerts, & Stalpers, 1999); and to become more cognitively interdependent with respect to mental representations of the partner and self (e.g., Agnew, Van Lange, Rusbult, & Langston, 1998). We describe illustrative findings regarding two behavioral and two cognitive mechanisms that are particularly relevant to prosocial action and motivation.

Behavioral Maintenance Mechanisms

Committed individuals engage in diverse behavioral maintenance mechanisms, exhibiting prorelationship acts that are costly and effortful for the individual yet promote the interests of the partner and relationship. In the following paragraphs we discuss two such behavioral mechanisms, reviewing theory and research regarding willingness to sacrifice and forgiveness of betrayal.

Willingness to Sacrifice

One tendency often exhibited by members of a couple is a general willingness to sacrifice for their partner. We define *willingness to sacrifice* as the tendency, when partners' outcome preferences are noncorrespondent, to (a) forego otherwise desirable behaviors, (b) engage in otherwise undesirable behaviors, or (c) both (e.g., see Van Lange et al., 1997). Across a series of studies using a variety of methods (both experimental and nonexperimental) and a variety of participant populations (undergraduates, married partners), past research manipulated or measured (a) the three bases of dependence (i.e., satisfaction, alternatives, and investments), (b) commitment level, (c) willingness to sacrifice, and (d) couple well-being (Van Lange et al., 1997). Consistent with expectations, it was found that (a) all three bases of dependence accounted for unique variance in predicting commitment, (b) commitment predicted willingness to sacrifice, and (c) willingness to sacrifice predicted couple well-being. Moreover, causal modeling analyses revealed that commitment fully mediates any associations of the three bases of dependence with willingness to sacrifice (e.g., satisfaction does not exert any direct effect on sacrifice), and willingness to sacrifice partially mediates the association of commitment with couple well-being. Sacrifice does not fully mediate the effects of commitment because it promotes couple well-being via a variety of mechanisms, including accommodation, forgiveness, and other mechanisms previously described.

Forgiveness of Betrayal

We define *forgiveness* as the inclination, when a partner departs from the norms of decency and fairness that are assumed to govern the relationship, to (a) forego desire for retribution and demands for atonement and (b) instead react in a more constructive, less judgmental manner. Forgiveness involves the resumption of prebetrayal patterns of interaction (see chap. 18, this volume). Does strong commitment promote forgiveness? We assume that level of commitment exhibits some day-to-day variation and that people are capable of experiencing feelings of greater or lesser commitment to a given relationship. Accordingly, past research used a simple priming technique to temporarily activate low versus high feelings of commitment (Finkel et al., 2002). The experiment was described as two separate studies. In Study 1, low versus high commitment was primed by asking participants to answer open-ended questions that brought to mind thoughts regarding either independence or dependence (low vs. high commitment). After priming, in Study 2, forgiveness was measured; specifically, participants indicated how they would react to a series of hypothetical partner betrayals. Both destructive and constructive reactions to betrayal were assessed. Consistent with expectations, compared with participants in the low commitment priming condition, those in the high commitment priming condition were (a) significantly less likely to react to betrayal in a destructive manner (i.e., with exit or neglect responses) and (b) nonsignificantly more likely to react in a constructive manner (i.e., with voice or loyalty responses; see Figure 17.3). Commitment inhibits destructive impulses more powerfully than it promotes constructive acts. It is interesting that destructive actions are more harmful to relationships; commitment is particularly powerful in inhibiting destructive impulses.

Cognitive Maintenance Mechanisms

In addition to the behavioral mechanisms described above, committed individuals also engage in diverse cognitive maintenance mechanisms, exhibiting mental maneuvers that serve to sustain or strengthen relationships. In the following sections, we discuss two such cognitive mechanisms, reviewing theory and research regarding perceived superiority and cognitive interdependence.

Perceived Superiority

Commitment to a partner also fuels cognitive maintenance mechanisms. In the literature regarding self processes, there is abundant evidence that individuals' perceptions of themselves are somewhat more positive than a strictly veridical view of the world can support. For example, individuals evalu-

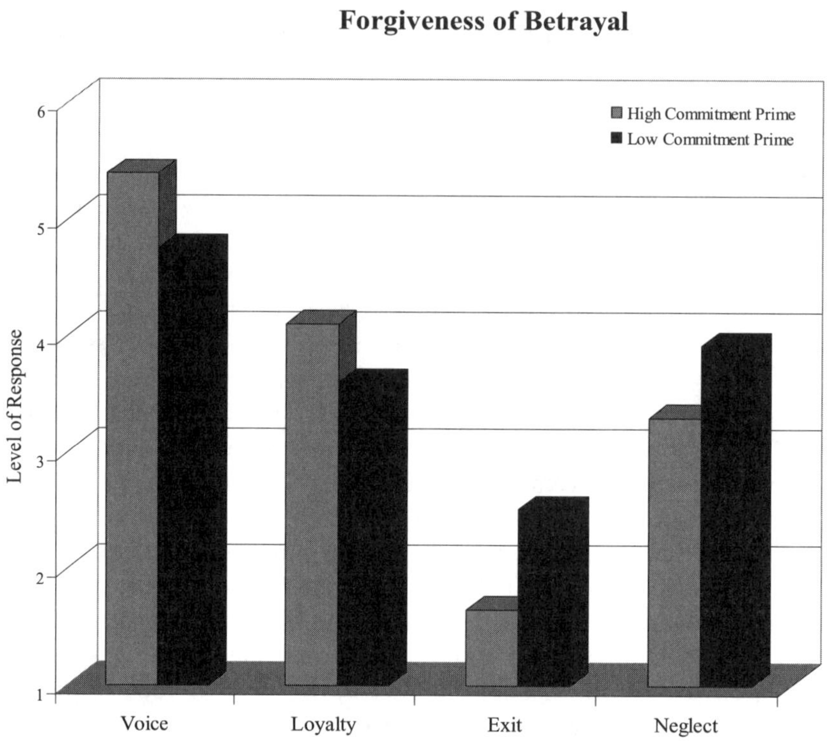

Figure 17.3. Priming commitment to influence forgiveness of betrayal.

ate themselves in exceedingly positive ways, perceive that they possess greater control over events than they truly do, and hold exceptionally optimistic beliefs regarding the future. Do people engage in parallel forms of illusion regarding intimate partners and relationships? As evidenced by recent research on this question, the answer is a resounding yes.

For example, past research has examined perceived superiority. *Perceived superiority* describes the tendency to perceive one's relationship as better than others' relationships. Using a simple thought-listing task, individuals were asked to record all of the thoughts that spontaneously come to mind regarding relationships, their own or others (Rusbult, Van Lange, Wildschut, Yovetich, & Verette, 2000). Four key tendencies are evident in individuals' thought lists. First, they have more positive thoughts about their own than about other relationships. Second, they possess fewer negative thoughts about their own than about other relationships. Third, they have more positive than negative thoughts about their own relationship. And fourth, they possess more negative than positive thoughts about others' relationships. Moreover, these tendencies are greater to the extent that individuals are more committed.

Is perceived superiority a motivated process? A variety of techniques have been used to test this claim. First, perceived superiority is evident beyond concrete indices of relationship quality. Also, this tendency is not attributable to self-esteem; it rests on commitment. And to separate "reality from illusion," instructional sets have been varied (accuracy instructions vs. no instructions vs. threat instructions). Consistent with expectations, the association of commitment level with positive illusion (total perceived superiority) is stronger to the extent that psychological threat is stronger (e.g., Rusbult et al., 2000).

Cognitive Interdependence

As individuals become increasingly committed to a relationship and develop relationship-specific cognition, affect, and behavioral responses, they come to think of their partners as part of themselves and to regard themselves as part of a collective unit that includes the partner. We use the label *cognitive interdependence* to describe this relational self—a sense of self that includes relationship-specific cognitive, affective, and behavioral structures, along with an explicit consideration of the self as part of the relationship (e.g., Agnew & Etcheverry, 2006; Agnew et al., 1998). Cognitive interdependence may be thought of as a habit of thinking that supports prorelationship motivation and behavior. The existing literature both indirectly and directly supports the assertion that cognitive interdependence characterizes committed relationships. For example, actor–observer differences in attribution are more attenuated for close partners than for strangers, in that compared to close partners, strangers take more credit than their interaction partners for successes and blame the partner more for failures (e.g., Sedikides, Campbell, Reeder, & Elliot, 1998). Similarly, individuals tend to reflect others' successes when the other is close, in that compared to strangers, close partners rejoice in their partners' successes and are unlikely to feel threatened by such successes (Beach et al., 1998). The existence of reflected experiences of success and parallel patterns of self-partner attribution is compatible with the notion that commitment results in cognitive restructuring, including incorporation of a close partner into one's sense of self.

Past research has directly tested whether strong commitment to a relationship is associated with a relatively pluralistic, other-inclusive cognitive representation of the self-in-relationship. For example, in a two-wave longitudinal investigation of romantic relationships, Agnew et al. (1998) found cognitive interdependence to increase hand in hand with commitment level. The more romantically committed individuals became, the greater was the tendency to think about the relationship in a pluralistic, other-inclusive manner, as reflected, for example, in the spontaneous use of plural pronoun cognitions (e.g., "we," "us," "our," "ours") to describe oneself and one's relationship. In addition, the more romantically committed individuals became, the more they came to regard themselves as "blended" with the partner, as revealed in perceived overlap in mental representations of self and partner (as measured with the Inclusion-Of-Other-In-The-Self Scale; Aron, Aron, & Smollan, 1992). Furthermore, romantically committed individuals tended to regard their relationships as relatively central to who they are and what their lives are about.

The effects of commitment and cognitive interdependence were also found to be reciprocal: Earlier commitment was significantly associated with increases over time in levels of cognitive interdependence, and earlier cognitive interdependence was significantly associated with increases over time in commitment level. Such reciprocal causal associations were anticipated, in that key processes in ongoing relationships unfold over extended periods of time. Such cyclical patterns have considerable adaptive value in the context of an ongoing involvement. Although the field of social psychology has tended to emphasize models of unidirectional cause-and-effect, we believe that models of mutual cyclical influence may be a more suitable means of understanding causal processes in ongoing relationships (Wieselquist, Rusbult, Foster, & Agnew, 1999). We discuss this point further in the following section.

INTERDEPENDENCE AND INTERACTION: COMMITMENT, TRUST, AND MUTUAL CYCLICAL GROWTH

Interdependence theory suggests that partners are interdependent not only at the level of specific interactions but also at the level of broader motives (i.e., the transformations that partners apply in deciding how to behave in specific interactions). Given the centrality of commitment in promoting prorelationship behavior, it would be adaptive for partners to attend to one another's commitment. Why? First, dependence and commitment place the individual in a vulnerable position: The more you need something, the more you stand to lose. People attend carefully to risky, dangerous situations. Second, commitment promotes the sorts of prorelationship behavior on which the very existence of a relationship rests. People attend carefully to how much others are willing to "contribute" to social entities (groups or dyads). Third, given that prorelationship acts tend to be guided by reciprocity, it is adaptive to have a good sense of a partner's motivation toward prorelationship behavior. Fourth, given that mutuality of commitment represents balance of power, and given that balance of power is a stable pattern, it is adaptive to have a good understanding of the extent of a partner's commitment.

Commitment, Trust, and Mutual Cyclical Growth

We suggest that trust is an implicit gauge of the strength of a partner's commitment. Following Holmes and Rempel (1989), *trust* is defined not as a personal disposition but as a relationship-specific motive, as the abstract, positive expectation that the partner can be relied on to care for one and be responsive to one's needs, now and in the future. Trust has three components: (a) *predictability*—belief that the partner's behavior is consistent, not volatile; (b) *dependability*—belief that the partner can be counted on to be cooperative and essentially benevolent; and (c) *faith*—conviction that the partner is intrinsically motivated to be caring and belief that the partner's motives go beyond instrumental reasons for benevolence.

According to Holmes and Rempel (1989), John develops trust as a consequence of observing Mary behave well in the sorts of diagnostic situations described earlier. Developing trust is essentially a matter of uncertainty reduction, or in our language, trust represents confidence in the strength of a partner's commitment. What are the consequences of enhanced trust? We suggest that as individuals become increasingly trusting, they become increasingly willing to take risks and make themselves vulnerable by becoming dependent on their relationships. They not only become more satisfied but are also likely to drive away or derogate tempting alternatives and invest in their relationships in material and nonmaterial ways.

For an illustration of the process by which trust and commitment inspire mutual growth, see Figure 17.4. First, dependence yields strong commitment. Second, strong commitment induces prorelationship behaviors, such as accommodation. Third, the partner's observation of such behavior yields perceived prorelationship behavior. Fourth, perceived prorelationship behavior (in diagnostic situations) induces strong partner trust. Fifth, strong trust makes the partner increasingly willing to become dependent on the relationship. Then the cycle begins again. We are describing a process of mutual cyclical growth, a process whereby each person's dependence, commitment, and prorelationship acts operate on one another and feed back on one another in such a manner as to promote the continued health and vitality of the relationship (or, alternatively, to send a relationship into a spiral of deterioration).

Empirical Evidence of Commitment, Trust, and Mutual Cyclical Growth

We used data from two longitudinal studies to test our model (Wieselquist, Rusbult, Foster, & Agnew, 1999). Study 1 was a three-wave longitudinal study of dating relationships, and Study 2 used data from a six-wave longitudinal study of marital relationships. Both studies obtained measures of each construct outlined in Figure 17.4. All analyses examined main effects of participant sex, main effects of time, and all two- and three-factor interactions of each model variable with sex and time. In testing model links, we examined concurrent simple associations, residualized lagged simple associations, and concurrent mediation analyses.

Does trust reflect the strength of partner commitment? First, we examined the association of each person's commitment with the partner's trust. This is not a direct link in the model, but it embodies our claim that trust is

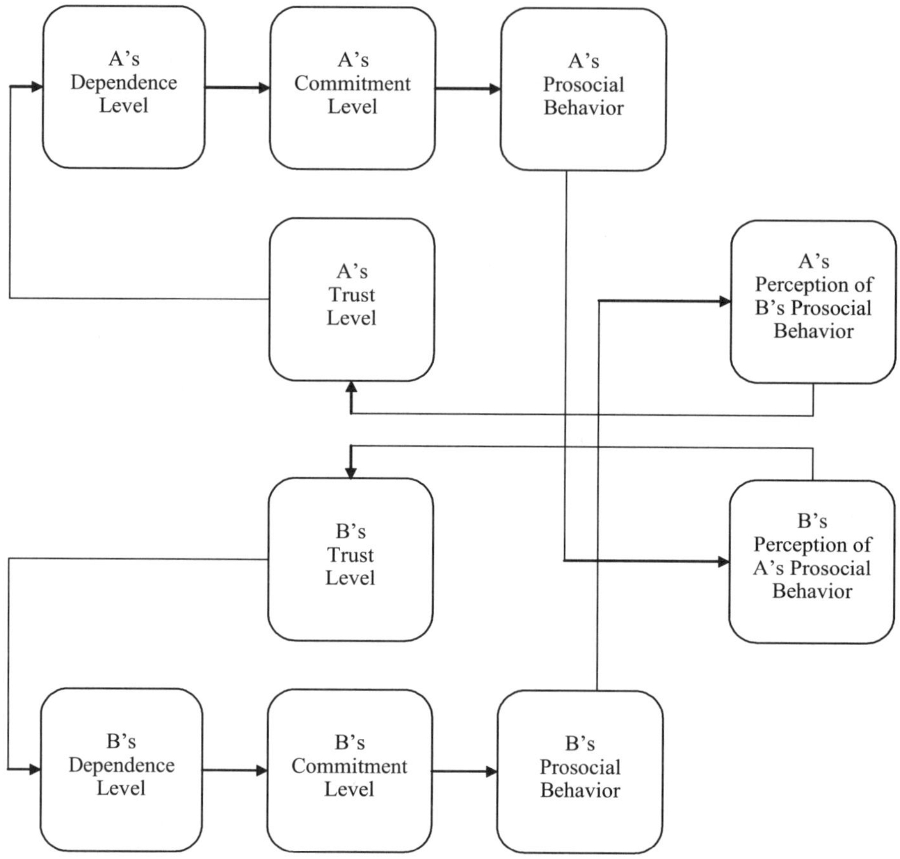

Figure 17.4. Model of commitment, trust, and mutual cyclical growth.

an implicit gauge of partner commitment. Each person's commitment was found to be associated with the partner's trust level concurrently. Also, each person's earlier commitment predicted change over time in partner trust level.

Next, we examined the simple associations between contiguous model variables (see Figure 17.4). All five concurrent associations were significant in both studies, and most residualized lagged associations were significant. Earlier measures of presumed predictors tended to account for change over time in their presumed consequences (8 of 10 associations).

In subsequent mediation analyses, we obtained good support for our model of direct and indirect associations. All presumed proximal predictors exhibited significant associations with criteria. All presumed distal predictors exhibited significant associations with criteria. However, in mediation analyses, when we examined the simultaneous associations of each criterion with its presumed proximal and distal predictors, presumed proximal predictors accounted for unique variance, whereas coefficients for presumed distal predictors declined substantially.

For further evidence that the findings were specific to the relational constructs we proposed and not to any relational constructs, we also examined attachment variables. Commitment, dependence, and trust are clearly relevant to the issues of caregiving, care seeking, and felt security, which are at the heart of attachment theory (e.g., see chap. 14, this volume). When we examine attachment variables along with the proximal interdependence predictor, interdependence predictors continue to account for unique variance. Attachment appears to operate "at the margins"; most associations with attachment style are in the predicted direction, but these variables accounted for little of the variance in key criteria.

Theoretical Implications of the Model

This model has a number of important theoretical implications. First, regarding the link between A's accommodation and B's perception of A's accommodation, disparities between the given situation and effective situation serve as the basis for attributional activity, revealing transformation-relevant motives. Departures from direct self-interest are meaningful. This link does not simply reflect projection ("I accommodate, my partner accommodates"), as the perception of a partner's accommodation was found to be more powerfully related to the partner's report of his or her accommodation than to one's own report of one's own accommodation. Although a social constructionist would suggest that perception is an internal, individual process that occurs inside one's mind, interdependence theory states that these processes are very real and are perceivable by both partners.

Second, when we place the interests of a relationship above personal interests in diagnostic situations, our partners trust us. Thus, trust is a function of the individual, partner, and situation. Situations provide opportunities to display prorelationship motives—one cannot know that a partner is trustworthy unless his or her motives are tested. Individuals must "pass the test" in diagnostic situations, and partners must perceive such acts, recognizing disparities from given preferences. Third, with respect to the trust–dependence link, strong trust frees individuals from anxiety, allowing them to risk increased dependence. Trusting individuals not only become increasingly satisfied, they also become more willing to drive away or derogate alternatives and more willing to invest in the relationship in material and nonmaterial ways.

Fourth, it is important to note that trust is a product of the relationship, not a personal disposition. When we find that our partners do not trust us or will not commit to us, we often turn to personality as an explanation ("He has been hurt badly in the past"). What is more important than our history of dependence is what transpires in a specific relationship.

One final implication concerning the model as a whole: It is useful to conceptualize commitment and trust as aspects of what might be termed *rela-*

tionship regulation. Dependence yields commitment, which promotes prorelationship acts; when partners perceive such acts, they develop increased trust and become increasingly willing to become dependent. Thus, changes in each person's actions and motives trigger complementary changes in the partner. Adaptations such as these reside at the heart of an interdependence analysis of prosocial behavior.

Over time, the process exhibited in Figure 17.4 yields mutuality. Equity theory, too, suggests that mutuality is beneficial. The problem with an equity analysis is that according to equity theory, equally low dependence should be as healthy as equally high dependence. However, our results cannot be explained by this sort of analysis because growth requires more than 50/50 reciprocity. Partners must sometimes be willing to give more than the other, with each taking it on faith that the partner enacts as many prorelationship acts as he or she does. Moreover, equity theory suggests that mutuality results from conscious attention to fairness. We suggest that it results from lawful interdependence processes and that partners' behavior may have little to do with fairness per se. Indeed, from our perspective there is a higher form of "goodness" than justice: benevolence.

SUMMARY AND CONCLUSIONS

Interdependence structure is important. This chapter has highlighted two properties of situation structure: correspondence level (as in diagnostic situations) and dependence level (as a function of satisfaction, alternatives, and investments). Why is it important to attend to situation structure? First, situations afford the display of motives. For example, John knows that Mary is committed, and he trusts her precisely because she accommodates and sacrifices, because she departs from her direct self-interest for the good of the relationship. Second, social cognition is "all about" understanding (a) situation structure per se, along with (b) the implications of one's own and others' behavior in specific situations. Too much social cognition research studies "free floating" cognition that is unhinged from the interpersonal setting to which it is relevant. Third, psychologists talk a lot about person–situation interactions but do not often study the situation per se. For example, the most popular marital therapy is cognitive behavioral, in which clinicians work on partners' social skills and cognitions during conflict. Often, the problem faced by couple members is not so much that partners are thinking about the situation wrong. Rather, the problem is the problematic situations that they confront. To help couples, clinicians need to spend as much time on their circumstances of interdependence as on their social skills and cognition.

Commitment is a central motive in interdependence theory. Commitment embodies partners' interdependence histories and motivates departures from direct self-interest in interdependence dilemmas. Focusing on commitment represents a departure from a large body of relationship research that emphasizes the role of positive affect in shaping an individual's interpersonal behavior. However, considering solely the extent to which an individual is "feeling good" provides an incomplete understanding of interpersonal behavior. Structural dependence and motives such as commitment play equally important roles in guiding behavior. In fact, commitment predicts continuation of behavior better than any other variable we have examined.

Departures from direct self-interest are not only visible but also provide meaningful information. To begin with, partners are reasonably in touch with their interdependence; for example, they perceive one another's acts of accommodation with some degree of accuracy. The field of psychology places a good deal of emphasis on cognitive bias and the extent to which human perception and cognition are "constructive processes." Of course, perception and cognition are colored by motivation and error. But departures from direct self-interest are surely meaningful. Social and behavioral scientists must find a better way of describing and predicting behavior, including that which is not driven purely by the situation or by self-interest.

Many theories of relationships emphasize the disappearance or transcendence of self-interest, arguing that with increasing closeness (a) people no longer distinguish between self-interest and partner interests, or (b) people behave well simply because the partner needs it. Although people often behave well in interdependence dilemmas, such behavior is antithetical to self-interest. The continued existence and compelling nature of self-interest is precisely what makes prosocial behavior interesting.

To misquote the Gestalt psychologists, prosocial behavior in close relationships is more than the sum of its part(ner)s. Much of contemporary psychology, even social psychology, is focused on the individual. Psychologists expend an enormous amount of energy studying individual-level cognitions, and we still tend to explain behavior in terms of individual-level processes. For example, we study "self" processes (e.g. self-esteem, self-regulation) or individual personality. Interdependence theory principles provide a solid basis for understanding truly social psychological phenomena, providing a particularly compelling account of prosocial motivations and behaviors. In so doing, it helps keep the "social" in social psychology.

REFERENCES

Agnew, C. R., & Etcheverry, P. E. (2006). Cognitive interdependence: Considering self-in-relationship. In K. D. Vohs & E. J. Finkel (Eds.), *Self and relationships: Connecting intrapersonal and interpersonal processes* (pp. 274–293). New York: Guilford Press.

Agnew, C. R., Hoffman, A. M., Lehmiller, J. J., & Duncan, N. T. (2007). From the interpersonal to the international: Understanding commitment to the "War on Terror." *Personality and Social Psychology Bulletin*, *33*, 1559–1571.

Agnew, C. R., Van Lange, P. A. M., Rusbult, C. E., & Langston, C. A. (1998). Cognitive interdependence: Commitment and the mental representation of close relationships. *Journal of Personality and Social Psychology, 74,* 939–954.

Aron, A., Aron, E. N., & Smollan, D. (1992). Inclusion of Other in the Self Scale and the structure of interpersonal closeness. *Journal of Personality and Social Psychology, 63,* 596–612.

Arriaga, X. B., & Agnew, C. R. (2001). Being committed: Affective, cognitive, and conative components of relationship commitment. *Personality and Social Psychology Bulletin, 27,* 1190–1203.

Arriaga, X. B., & Holmes, J. G. (2009). Transformation of motivation. To appear in H. T. Reis & S. Sprecher (Eds.), *Encyclopedia of human relationships* (pp. 1641–1644). Thousand Oaks, CA: Sage.

Beach, S. R. H., Tesser, A., Fincham, F., Jones, D. J., Johnson, D., & Whitaker, D. J. (1998). Pleasure and pain in doing well, together: An investigation of performance-related affect in close relationships. *Journal of Personality and Social Psychology, 74,* 923–938.

Bui, K. T., Peplau, L. A., & Hill, C. T. (1996). Testing the Rusbult model of relationship commitment and stability in a 15-year study of heterosexual couples. *Personality and Social Psychology Bulletin, 22,* 1244–1257.

Drigotas, S. M., & Rusbult, C. E. (1992). Should I stay or should I go? A dependence model of breakups. *Journal of Personality and Social Psychology, 62,* 62–87.

Finkel, E. J., Rusbult, C. E., Kumashiro, M., & Hannon, P. A. (2002). Dealing with betrayal in close relationships: Does commitment promote forgiveness? *Journal of Personality and Social Psychology, 82,* 956–974.

Holmes, J. G., & Rempel, J. K. (1989). Trust in close relationships. In C. Hendrik (Ed.), *Review of personality and social psychology* (Vol. 10, pp. 187–219). Newbury Park, CA: Sage.

Johnson, D. J., & Rusbult, C. E. (1989). Resisting temptation: Devaluation of alternative partners as a means of maintaining commitment in close relationships. *Journal of Personality and Social Psychology, 57,* 967–980.

Kelley, H. H., Holmes, J. G., Kerr, N., Reis, H. T., Rusbult, C. E., & Van Lange, P. A. M. (2003). *An atlas of interpersonal situations.* New York: Cambridge University Press.

Le, B., & Agnew, C. R. (2003). Commitment and its theorized determinants: A meta-analysis of the Investment Model. *Personal Relationships, 10,* 37–57.

Rusbult, C. E. (1983). A longitudinal test of the investment model: The development (and deterioration) of satisfaction and commitment in heterosexual involvements. *Journal of Personality and Social Psychology, 45,* 101–117.

Rusbult, C. E., Arriaga, X. B., & Agnew, C. R. (2001). Interdependence in close relationships. In G. J. O. Fletcher & M. S. Clark (Eds.), *Blackwell handbook of social psychology, Vol.2: Interpersonal processes* (pp. 359–387). Oxford, England: Blackwell.

Rusbult, C. E., & Buunk, B. P. (1993). Commitment processes in close relationships: An interdependence analysis. *Journal of Social and Personal Relationships, 10,* 175–204.

Rusbult, C. E., Martz, J. M., & Agnew, C. R. (1998). The Investment Model Scale: Measuring commitment level, satisfaction level, quality of alternatives, and investment size. *Personal Relationships, 5*, 357–391.

Rusbult, C. E., & Van Lange, P. A. M. (2003). Interdependence, interaction, and relationships. *Annual Review of Psychology, 54*, 351–375.

Rusbult, C. E., Van Lange, P. A. M., Wildschut, T., Yovetich, N. A., & Verette, J. (2000). Perceived superiority in close relationships: Why it exists and persists. *Journal of Personality and Social Psychology, 79*, 521–545.

Rusbult, C. E., Verette, J., Whitney, G. A., Slovik, L. F., & Lipkus, I. (1991). Accommodation processes in close relationships: Theory and preliminary empirical evidence. *Journal of Personality and Social Psychology, 60*, 53–78.

Sedikikes, C., Campbell, W. K., Reeder, G. D., & Elliot, A. J. (1998). The self-serving bias in relational context. *Journal of Personality and Social Psychology, 74*, 378–386.

Van Lange, P. A. M., Rusbult, C. E., Drigotas, S. M., Arriaga, X. B., Witcher, B. S., & Cox, C. L. (1997). Willingness to sacrifice in close relationships. *Journal of Personality and Social Psychology, 72*, 1373–1395.

Wieselquist, J., Rusbult, C. E., Foster, C. A., & Agnew, C. R. (1999). Commitment, pro-relationship behavior, and trust in close relationships. *Journal of Personality and Social Psychology, 77*, 942–966.

Yovetich, N. A., & Rusbult, C. E. (1994). Accommodative behavior in close relationships: Exploring transformation of motivation. *Journal of Experimental Social Psychology, 30*, 136–164.

18

FORGIVENESS: INTEGRAL TO A SCIENCE OF CLOSE RELATIONSHIPS?

FRANK D. FINCHAM

If we really want to love, we must learn how to forgive.

—Mother Teresa

It is easier to forgive an enemy than to forgive a friend.

—William Blake

Paradoxically, fulfillment of our deepest needs occurs in intimate relationships, in which we are also likely to experience emotional injuries. For if there is one certainty in life, it is that romantic partners are not perfect, despite our tendency to idealize them (e.g., Murray, Holmes, & Griffin, 1996); it is a rare person who has never felt "wronged," "let down," "betrayed," or "hurt" by a relationship partner. In close relationships, we voluntarily make ourselves most vulnerable to another human being by linking the realization of our needs, aspirations, and hopes to the goodwill of our relationship partner (for related ideas, see chap. 17, this volume). Rendering ourselves vulnerable makes possible the profound sense of well-being that can be experienced in close relationships. But at the same time, the imperfection of any partner means that hurt or injury is virtually inevitable, and when it occurs, the hurt is particularly poignant precisely because we have made ourselves vulnerable.

In the face of such injury, negative feelings (e.g., anger, resentment, disappointment) are common. Motivation to avoid the source of the harm,

The author is grateful to Steven Beach and Steven Graham for their helpful comments on an earlier draft of this chapter.

or even a desire to retaliate or seek revenge, is also typical. Indeed, some have argued that retaliation in such circumstances "is deeply ingrained in the biological, psychological, and cultural levels of human nature" (McCullough & vanOyen Witvliet, 2002, p. 446), a position consistent with Aristotle's (trans. 1939) view of anger as "a longing, accompanied by pain, for a real or apparent revenge for a real or apparent slight" (p. 173). This creates a particular challenge because hurts inflicted by an intimate partner have the potential to corrode, disrupt, and even end the relationship.

Understanding how partners respond to such hurt is critical to understanding intimate relationships. One means of dealing with such hurt is through forgiveness, which is likely the basis for Mother Teresa's statement cited at the beginning of this chapter. At the same time, the fact that the hurt occurs in a context in which we have intentionally made ourselves vulnerable is probably why William Blake asserted that forgiving an intimate other may be more difficult than forgiving an enemy.

EMERGENCE OF RESEARCH ON FORGIVENESS IN CLOSE RELATIONSHIPS

In light of the observations just offered, it is perhaps surprising that the study of forgiveness is a relative latecomer to the literature on close relationships. The first published data that specifically focused on forgiveness in intimate relationships appear to have emerged only in 2000. In this regard, research on close relationships has followed the lead of the broader scientific literature. Before 1985 only five studies on forgiveness had been published (Worthington, 1998). By 1998, McCullough, Exline, and Baumeister were able to provide an annotated bibliography on forgiveness that contained 46 studies. It is perhaps not surprising that these authors noted that "scientific understanding of the concept of forgiveness is quite limited" (p. 194). The relative lack of research on forgiveness likely reflects this construct's association with religion. This association did not engender hostility or disdain toward forgiveness in the social sciences, but it may have caused it to seem insufficiently relevant, important, or amenable to scientific study (McCullough et al., 1998).

The astute reader may note, however, that relationship researchers have long recognized that the less than ideal behavior of intimates toward each other poses a challenge for relationships, suggesting that we may have been researching forgiveness all along but just calling it something else. This observation demands attention and is therefore briefly addressed.

The closest construct to forgiveness in intimate relationship research is *accommodation* or the willingness to respond to potentially destructive partner behavior by inhibiting "tendencies to react destructively" and instead to "engage in constructive reactions" (Rusbult, Verette, Whitney, Slovik, &

Lipkus, 1991, p. 53; see also chap. 17, this volume). However, potentially destructive partner behavior may take many forms, and only when this behavior represents a perceived "wrong" is forgiveness relevant. In addition, accommodation might occur because potentially destructive partner behavior is construed in such a way that its destructive nature is ignored, overlooked, or downplayed, or when fully recognized, is condoned or excused. Under these circumstances, forgiveness is not a relevant concern. Thus, although accommodation and forgiveness overlap under certain conditions, accommodation is a much broader construct than forgiveness. Accommodation therefore cannot be equated with forgiveness.

Given this historical context, why has psychological research on forgiveness flourished recently, with 52 peer reviewed articles containing "forgive" or "forgiveness" in their title appearing in 2007 alone (PsycINFO). In the late 1980s the zeitgeist in psychology began to change to accommodate the study of human strengths and virtues. This shift ultimately culminated in the formal naming of a field of positive psychology in 1998 by the then APA president, Martin Seligman. The emergence of positive psychology contributed to a propitious environment for the growth of forgiveness research. Just as important, in 1998 the Templeton Foundation made available $10 million for research on forgiveness. Given these developments, the explosion of forgiveness research in the past decade was inevitable.

Finally, it is noteworthy that the emergence of positive psychology occurred almost simultaneously with the coming of age or what Berscheid (1999) called the *greening of relationship science*. Although a consensus definition is yet to emerge, the study of forgiveness in close relationships has proceeded in isolation from the broader positive psychology literature, but in this regard it appears to be no different from its parent literature on close relationships.

WHAT IS FORGIVENESS AND HOW IS IT STUDIED?

How researchers conceptualize a construct shapes how it is measured and used in subsequent research. It therefore behooves us to clarify exactly what is meant by forgiveness.

Conceptualizing Forgiveness

Because it is a complex construct, considerable effort has been expended on conceptualizing forgiveness and discerning how it might best be studied. Although a consensus has yet to emerge, central to various approaches to forgiveness is the idea of a freely chosen motivational transformation in which the desire to seek revenge and to avoid contact with the transgressor is overcome. This position is consistent with many philosophical writings that define *forgiveness* as the forswearing of resentment toward the wrongdoer. Notice the idea of effort by the forgiver embodied in this view (for an alternative view of forgiveness as a nonconscious process, see chap. 15, this volume). To forgive entails a struggle to overcome the negative feelings that result from being wrongfully harmed, and the magnitude of this struggle differs across individuals. This view immediately distinguishes forgiveness from related constructs such as forgetting (i.e., passive removal of the offense from consciousness; to forgive is more than not thinking about the offense), condoning (i.e., no longer viewing the act as a wrong and removing the need for forgiveness), and pardon (granted only by a representative of society such as a judge). Thus, the common phrase "forgive and forget" is misleading because forgiveness is possible only in the face of a remembered wrong.

It is this latter observation that helps undermine Nietzsche's (1887) argument that forgiveness is a sign of weakness. As noted, forgiveness requires the victim to acknowledge adverse treatment that entitles him or her to justifiably feel negatively toward the transgressor; it thus requires the strength to assert a right, the right to better treatment than that shown by the transgressor. Absent such assertion, conciliatory actions can reflect factors such as condoning of the transgressor's behavior, a strategic ploy, a desire to appease the transgressor, and so on. Accordingly, it is incorrect to label such behaviors *forgiveness*. In addition to asserting one's claim to a position of moral authority vis-à-vis the transgressor, forgiveness requires the strength to relinquish this position of moral authority and release the transgressor from the debt incurred by the transgression. As anyone who has attempted to forgive knows, forgiving is not easy; in fact, it may prove extraordinarily difficult because it involves working through, not avoiding, emotional pain. It is little surprise then that Mahatma Ghandi (2000) asserted that "the weak can never forgive. Forgiveness is the attribute of the strong" (p. 301).

It may be argued that forgiving subverts the course of justice and that when forgiveness occurs justice is not served. In the aftermath of a transgression, it is common for victims to experience a "moral injury" in the sense that their beliefs about what is right and wrong have been assailed. This experience may lead to a strong desire to set the scale of justice back in balance. Forgiveness does not preclude doing so, and the pursuit of justice (e.g., appropriate punishment, compensation) can be justified on numerous grounds, such as a necessary corrective to shape future behavior, to protect others from danger, and so on. There is thus no contradiction between forgiving a transgressor and pursuing justice (for further discussion, see Exline, Worthington, Hill, & McCullough, 2003).

Finally, in the relationship context, forgiveness needs to be distinguished from reconciliation. Although an inherently interpersonal construct, forgiveness occurs primarily within the individual. It is known to be influenced by interpersonal events, such as expressions of remorse by the wrongdoer, but the motivational change involved occurs largely at the intraindividual level.

Reconciliation, in contrast, restores a relationship between persons and is a dyadic process that requires appropriate participation by both parties: It involves the restoration of violated trust and requires the goodwill of both partners. Forgiveness increases the likelihood of reconciliation but is not synonymous with it. There is no contradiction involved in forgiving a wrongdoer and also ending one's relationship with the person. Likewise, reconciliation can occur without forgiveness, further emphasizing the need to distinguish between the two actions.

Operationalizing Forgiveness

Most research on forgiveness has focused on forgiveness either as a response to a specific transgression or as a personality trait (forgivingness). In both cases it has been operationalized as the reduction of negative motivational tendencies toward the transgressor. Perhaps the most widely used offense-specific measure is McCullough, Rachal, et al.'s (1998) and McCullough, Worthington, and Rachel's (1997) Transgression-Related Interpersonal Motivation (TRIM) Inventory. The TRIM comprises 12 items that assess the motivation to seek revenge and to avoid the offender. Although McCullough and colleagues assumed that revenge motives and avoidant motives are distinct dimensions, others assumed that they are indistinguishable in the close relationship context (e.g., Worthington & Wade, 1999). In such relationships, the desire to even the score and the desire to maintain a significant physical and psychological distance from the offending partner can often coexist.

In a similar vein, the most widely used measure to assess the disposition to forgive others is the Dissipation-Rumination Scale, which Caprara (1986) developed to study aggression. The 15 Likert-type items are positively related to retaliation after a transgression. A more recent measure specifically developed to assess dispositional forgiveness, the Transgression Narrative Test of Forgivingness (Berry, Worthington, Parrott, O'Connor, & Wade, 2001), reflects sophisticated use of item-response scaling and is one of the very few measures to use spouse reports to validate responses (self and partner ratings correlated .60). It asks a single question about forgiveness after each of five scenarios. The scale thus relies on a respondent's understanding of the construct of forgiveness.

It is interesting that laypersons tend to view positive features as more representative of forgiveness than a decrease in negativity (Kearns & Fincham, 2005). In this regard, they appear to be closer to the view of philosophers who have noted that forgiveness is "an attitude of real goodwill towards the offender as a person" (Holmgren, 1993, p. 34) or "the attitude of respect which should always characterize interpersonal behavior" (Downie, 1971, p. 149). There is a lack of agreement among researchers on whether forgiveness requires a benevolent or positive response (e.g., compassion, empathy) to the offender or whether the absence of negative responses (e.g., resentment, anger, avoidance) is sufficient (Exline et al., 2003; Fincham, 2000). Indeed, forgiveness may be unidimensional in noncontinuing relationships but have both positive and negative elements in continuing close relationships (Worthington, 2005).

Because the positivity view of forgiveness cannot be inferred from the absence of unforgiveness, it is worth noting that both dimensions have been built into two measures specifically designed to assess forgiveness in close relationships. The nine-item Relationship Forgiveness Scale—Event (Fincham, Beach, & Davila, 2004) assesses retaliation (e.g., "I did something to even the score"), withdrawal (e.g., "I didn't want to have anything to do with her/him"), and benevolence (e.g., "It was easy to feel warmly again toward my partner"). The Relationship Forgiveness Scale—Disposition (Fincham & Beach, 2002) assesses the general tendency to forgive the partner while tapping both retaliation and benevolence. As will soon be evident, positive and negative dimensions of forgiveness have different correlates. Before turning to findings on forgiveness in relationships, we note that the TRIM has been expanded to include a positive dimension. An initial longitudinal study showed that in the first few weeks following a transgression, avoidance and revenge motivation decreased, whereas benevolence motivation did not change (McCullough, Fincham, & Tsang, 2003).

WHAT HAVE WE LEARNED ABOUT FORGIVENESS IN CLOSE RELATIONSHIPS?

A thorough review of what has been learned about forgiveness in close relationships is beyond the scope of this chapter, so what follows is only a brief overview of major findings (see Fincham, Hall, & Beach, 2005). Studies have shown that forgiveness is robustly and positively related to core relationship constructs. But in the absence of an integrative theory of forgiveness in close relationships, available research tends to be somewhat fragmented. Given the centrality of relationship satisfaction in relationship research, it is not surprising that substantial attention has been given to the association between relationship satisfaction and forgiveness.

Relationship Satisfaction

Several studies have documented a positive association between relationship satisfaction and forgiveness (e.g., Fincham, 2000; Paleari, Regalia, & Fincham, 2005). It appears that the association between forgiveness and relationship quality is bidirectional. There is emerging evidence that marital quality predicts later forgiveness (Fincham & Beach, 2007; Paleari et al., 2005), as well as data showing that forgiveness predicts later marital satisfaction (e.g., Fincham & Beach, 2007). Among newlyweds, McNulty (2008) found a more complex longitudinal relationship in that more forgiveness led to a smaller decline in satisfaction over time and less forgiveness led to a greater reduction in satisfaction, but only for spouses married to partners who infrequently engaged in negative behavior. Among spouses married to partners who frequently engaged in negative behavior, increased forgiveness appeared to be harmful over time for marital satisfaction, whereas decreased forgiveness appeared to be beneficial.

Relationship satisfaction also appears to influence documented differences between victim and perpetrator perspectives on transgressions, which may explain why forgiveness and satisfaction are related. Specifically, victims tend to overlook details that facilitate forgiving and embellish their memories with details that make forgiving more difficult, whereas transgressors tend to embellish details, such as extenuating circumstances, that facilitate forgiving (Stillwell & Baumeister, 1997). However, individuals in highly satisfying relationships are less likely to exhibit these self-serving biases than individuals in less satisfying relationships (Kearns & Fincham, 2005). Existing data are consistent with a causal sequence in which relationship quality leads to more benign interpretations of a transgression, which in turn promote forgiveness. Relationship satisfaction may therefore help to meet the challenge forgiveness poses whereby the victimized partner has to cancel a debt that is often perceived as bigger than the debt acknowledged by the transgressing partner.

Although the association between satisfaction and forgiveness is robust, the mechanism underlying this link remains unclear. McCullough, Rachal, et al. (1998) proposed several possible mechanisms, including a greater likelihood of confession and apology in satisfied intimate relationships, leading to more forgiveness. Another possibility is that commitment facilitates forgiveness.

Commitment

Because both commitment and forgiveness are believed to promote prorelationship motives, it is perhaps not surprising that the two constructs are positively related (e.g., McCullough, Rachal, et al., 1998; see also chap. 17, this volume). As suggested, the forgiveness–commitment association could be driven by commitment, as highly committed individuals may be more motivated to forgive simply because they intend to remain in their current relationship. In fact, some experimental data show that greater commitment facilitates forgiveness (chap. 17, this volume). On the other hand, it is also plausible that following a relational transgression, forgiveness has to occur for damaged closeness and commitment to be restored: It is difficult for the hurt individual to feel close to his or her offending partner if he or she still harbors a grudge about the transgression. Consistent with this viewpoint,

Tsang, McCullough, and Fincham (2006) offered longitudinal evidence that forgiveness promotes increases in commitment, although they also found limited evidence that effects also ran in the opposite direction. Finally, there is evidence that attributions may mediate the association between commitment and forgiveness, as committed individuals tend to interpret their partners' betrayals in a more benevolent manner, which may thereby promote forgiveness.

Attributions

As in the broader forgiveness literature, attributions or explanations for the offending behavior predict forgiveness among intimates (e.g., Friesen, Fletcher, & Overall, 2005). Fincham, Paleari, and Regalia (2002) found that benign attributions predicted forgiveness both directly and indirectly through lessening negative emotional reactions to the transgression and increasing empathy toward the transgressing spouse. Similarly, adolescents' attributions for negative parent behavior were directly related to forgiving and indirectly related through affective reactions to the behavior (Paleari et al., 2003). It is interesting that attributions moderate the well-established impact of transgression severity on forgiveness. Among dating partners, perceived transgression severity was strongly related to forgiveness only when conflict-promoting attributions (e.g., inferring greater intent, selfish motivation, blameworthiness) were made for partner behavior. When benign attributions were made, severity was not significantly related to forgiveness (Fincham, Jackson, & Beach, 2005). Finally, forgiveness mediates the association between attributions and behavior toward one's spouse (Fincham, 2000) or romantic partner (Eaton & Struthers, 2006), whereas adolescent forgiving is associated with a decreased likelihood of subsequent parent–adolescent conflict (Paleari et al., 2003).

Conflict

In addition to the link between forgiveness and conflict noted previously, unresolved conflict provides a potential mechanism that links forgiveness and relationship satisfaction. Specifically, it can be argued that transgressions that are not forgiven may spill over into future conflicts and, in turn, impede their resolution, thereby putting the couple at risk of developing the negative cycle of interaction that characterizes distressed relationships. Supporting this line of reasoning, retaliation and avoidance among husbands and a lack of benevolence among wives were linked to ineffective conflict resolution (Fincham et al., 2004). Moreover, for wives the positive dimension of forgiveness or benevolence predicted husbands' reports of better conflict resolution 12 months later, controlling for initial levels of conflict resolution and degree of hurt (Fincham, Beach, & Davila, 2007).

Empathy

Empathy is a relationship construct that appears to play an important role in the forgiveness process (e.g., McCullough, Rachal et al., 1998), and its connection to forgiveness was mentioned earlier. There is some evidence that empathy is a better predictor of forgiveness for husbands than wives, potentially because empathic behavior tends to be less common for men in relationships and therefore more influential (Fincham et al., 2002). The importance of empathy is further emphasized by the substantial body of research on promoting forgiveness in relationships in which attempts to increase empathy play a central role.

Applied Research on Inducing Forgiveness

Several interventions, typically delivered in the context of psychoeducational groups or relationship-enrichment programs, have been shown to increase forgiveness in romantic relationships. Although an initial analysis of 14 studies documented a linear relationship between intervention length and its efficacy (Worthington, Sandage, & Berry, 2000), a more recent meta-analysis of 27 studies showed that although amount of time spent in the intervention predicted efficacy, intervention status (full vs. partial vs. no intervention) predicted outcome over and beyond intervention duration (Wade, Worthington, & Meyer, 2005). Most of the interventions included helping couples understand what forgiveness is and is not (87%), encouraging them to recall the hurt (95%), and helping victims empathize with the offending partner (89%). Of these components, amount of time spent on empathy was reliably related to intervention effect size.

In a field in which it is difficult to do experimental research, intervention studies have the potential to provide much needed information on mechanisms involved in forgiveness. To date, however, this potential remains largely untapped because the dismantling of these multicomponent interventions to determine the active ingredients for changing forgiveness is notably absent. Also absent are data on the impact of induced forgiveness on relationship outcomes. Thus, the potential of applied research to advance understanding of forgiveness remains unrealized.

TOWARD A MORE COMPLETE UNDERSTANDING OF FORGIVENESS AMONG INTIMATES

Although the need for an integrative theory of forgiveness in close relationships should by now be quite obvious, space limitations preclude its realization in the present context. The remainder of the chapter is therefore devoted to identifying some critical issues overlooked in relationship forgiveness research that are critical to advancing such a theory.

Relationships Have a History: Specific Hurts and Hurtful Relationships

The imperfection of relationship partners necessarily gives rise to a history of hurts in any relationship. This means that forgiveness may not pertain to a particular transgression even when it appears to do so. Rather, the specific transgression in question may (knowingly or unknowingly) represent the accumulated hurts of numerous, functionally equivalent prior acts. The task of forgiveness is potentially rendered more difficult because it may now pertain to forgiving multiple harm-doing events, a possibility that has been ignored in research. The importance of this oversight is easily illustrated.

Consider a couple in which one partner has been unfaithful. The aggrieved partner is unlikely to respond similarly to the transgression without regard to whether this is the first instance or the tenth time the partner has been unfaithful. In the latter case, the aggrieved partner may be experiencing ongoing hurt from the prior transgressions, making this transgression fundamentally different than it would be for a partner experiencing it for the first time. In short, the history of infidelity may transform the "wrong" that needs to be forgiven into one that involves not a hurtful event, or even a series of events, but a "hurtful relationship." A hurtful relationship carries with it a variety of broader concerns than does a single event, and it may arise in a variety of ways.

For instance, an aggrieved spouse may frequently be reminded of the harm resulting from a specific act (e.g., an adulterous one-night stand) by the partner's behavior (e.g., his or her comment on the appearance of an opposite-sex friend or stranger) because it can be viewed symbolically. In this event, the pain is likely to be experienced afresh and may be viewed as a new hurt, ultimately leading the spouse to conclude that he or she is in a hurtful relationship. The transition from a perceived hurtful event to a hurtful relationship is likely to be influenced by the extent to which a broad range of behaviors can be interpreted as symbolic of a prior transgression, by the spouse's proclivity to interpret the partner's behavior as symbolic of the transgression, and by the partner's attempts to avoid behaving in ways that lend themselves to such interpretation.

At a minimum, it will be important in future research to determine whether the identified transgression has occurred previously in the relationship and if so, to ascertain how it was dealt with. For example, if it included an apology by the transgressor and a statement that it would not happen again, the event would be viewed differently than if these accommodations had not occurred. Similarly, given a prior attempt(s) to ensure that the transgressing partner is aware of the previously inflicted injury, or the extent of the injury, forgiving the harm can be hypothesized to be less likely than in the absence of such attempts. In both the case of a prior apology and the victim's attempt to raise the transgressor's awareness, the occurrence of a subsequent similar transgression is likely to increase the probability that the injured spouse will view the relationship as hurtful. Finally, a broader perspective on the history of hurt reminds us that a hurtful partner's behavior may be experienced quite differently when it is functionally or symbolically similar to hurts experienced in other close relationships (e.g., at the hands of parents or a past partner). In such cases, it may be easier for the aggrieved partner to draw broader conclusions about the hurtful nature of the relationship.

Relationships Include Implicit Processes: Explicit and Implicit Forgiveness

The idea that forgiveness requires effort by the forgiver has important implications that need to be made explicit if they are to receive systematic research attention. First, it makes sense to talk about degrees of forgiveness when the referent is the accomplishment of forgiveness. Second, the accomplishment of forgiveness may or may not be achieved regardless of effort. Third, aggrieved partners likely use cues about their effort to make inferences about forgiveness, and those inferences may or may not be correct.

For example, it can be hypothesized that after exerting effort that leads to some positive interactions with the partner, a person may infer that he or she has forgiven the partner even though hurt feelings are not fully resolved. For this person, it is easy to imagine circumstances (e.g., a reminder of the transgression) that prompt negative thoughts related to forgiveness, making them relatively more accessible than positive thoughts. In contrast, for partners who have worked through the hurt and completely forgiven the partner, positive thoughts about forgiveness should be relatively more accessible regardless of situational cues. This accessibility effect should moderate the associations between forgiveness and related constructs.

To investigate such implicit forgiveness processes, Terzino, Fincham, and Cross (2008) had partners complete a priming task designed to bring to mind thoughts about a recent transgression. The partners then completed an 80-item lexical decision task in which target stimuli comprised five positive (e.g., *reconcile*, *understanding*, *compassion*, *acceptance*, *empathy*) and five negative (e.g., *retaliation*, *grudge*, *avoid*, *withdraw*, *revenge*) forgiveness-related terms. The difference in mean reaction time between positive and negative forgiveness words was computed to identify completed forgivers (positive words < negative words) and uncompleted forgivers (positive words > negative words). There was no mean difference between the two groups on self-reported forgiveness, commitment, closeness after the offense, or general closeness.

As hypothesized, implicit forgiveness moderated the relationship between forgiveness and commitment and closeness: The measures were highly correlated among completed forgivers (*r*s from .45 to .61) and unrelated among uncompleted forgivers (*r*s from .01 to .14). It therefore appears that a useful distinction can be made between explicit forgiveness and implicit forgiveness. Unlike explicit forgiveness, which can be accomplished relatively quickly, implicit forgiveness, like any automatic process, requires extensive practice to develop.

Types of Forgiveness

The finding just described concerning uncompleted forgiveness helps to illuminate why it is not uncommon to find a spouse who says and believes that he or she has forgiven the partner but who discovers that resentment or a desire for revenge is instigated during an interaction with the partner. When this happens with sufficient force or frequency, it is likely to result in a subjective experience of ambivalence and prompt reflection on the effort to forgive, which leads to the inference that forgiveness has not yet been fully accomplished. It is possible to characterize such ambivalent forgiveness in terms of the two forgiveness dimensions described earlier, because it appears to reflect high levels of both positives and negatives.

Accordingly, there may be heuristic value in identifying "types" of forgiveness defined by positive and negative forgiveness dimensions (see Figure 18.1). As just described, *ambivalent forgiveness* is characterized by an increase in positive behavior and affect toward the partner even though some negative motivation (e.g., a desire to teach him or her a lesson) continues. *Completed forgiveness* involves change on both forgiveness dimensions and is most likely to result in relationship repair. Probably important to complete forgiveness is the transition from the backward-looking victim role to a future orientation, one of the defining criteria of whether people adjust well following victimization (Holman & Silver, 2005). *Detached forgiveness* occurs when a partner finds that he or she is less motivated to punish and avoid but not more motivated to engage with the partner. Because the lack of positive motivation may not have the same perceptual salience as the presence of negative motivations and negative interactions, detached forgiveness is a potential stopping point in the forgiveness process. However, the relative absence of positives might set the stage for deteriorating relationship satisfaction and result in a devitalized relationship characterized by indifference (Fincham & Linfield, 1997).

Nonforgiveness occurs when, following a transgression, the victim is no less motivated to avoid or punish the partner and is not motivated to approach the partner. Such an individual is unlikely to characterize him- or herself as having "forgiven." However, in cases in which an individual had previously taken some initial behavioral steps toward forgiveness, any claim he or she makes about having forgiven may be either self-deceptive or promissory. In the former case, one might characterize the forgiveness as "hollow."

		Positive Dimension	
		High	Low
Negative Dimension	High	Ambivalent forgiveness	Nonforgiveness
	Low	Completed forgiveness	Detached forgiveness

Figure 18.1. Forgiveness Typology Resulting From a Bidimensional Conception of Forgiveness. From *Handbook of Forgiveness* (p. 215), by E. L. Worthington, 2005, New York: Routledge. Copyright 2005 by Taylor & Francis. Reprinted with permission.

Hollow forgiveness may be particularly difficult to resolve because the individual may assert that he or she has satisfied the requirements of forgiveness and may see little need to continue any process of forgiveness. Promissory forgiveness, on the other hand, might reflect an individual at a very early, but potentially productive, stage of the forgiveness process. It suggests an openness to continued change in motivation toward the partner, but this has the potential to create misunderstanding between partners, a topic considered in the next section.

It remains to be made explicit that the typology just outlined raises the question of whether there are natural points of discontinuity in the forgiveness process. Finding evidence of discontinuity sets the stage for identification of the "point of discontinuity" and for an intensive investigation of the transition between states. Taxometrics (Waller & Meehl, 1998) provides a method to determine whether persons displaying forgiveness beyond a certain point behave in a qualitatively different manner from those displaying less forgiveness along a particular dimension. Although ignored thus far, the issue of types versus continua has the potential to change the future of forgiveness research.

Relationships Involve Communication: Expressed Forgiveness and Private Forgiveness

Initiating forgiveness and only later fully achieving it has the potential to set up interesting dynamics in an ongoing relationship, especially when the person verbally expresses forgiveness to the partner. There is the temptation to equate such statements with forgiveness even though they can be no more than a promissory note. Even when worded as such (though in the normal course of events one expects "I forgive you" to occur more commonly than "I want to try to forgive you"), the harm-doer is likely to experience the statement as performative and be puzzled, annoyed, or angry when incompletely resolved feelings of resentment about the harm-doing intrude upon subsequent discourse or behavior in the relationship. Thus, the words "I forgive you" can signal the beginning of a process yet be viewed as the end of the matter by the transgressor, who is likely to be only too willing to put the transgression in the past. The timing of such a verbalization, and where the speaker stands in regard to our typology of forgiveness, is likely to be particularly important. For example, the verbalization may have a different effect depending on whether the speaker is seen as ambivalent or detached.

Communication between partners about transgressions has been largely overlooked in forgiveness research (but see Kelley, 1998). Yet it is through such communication that the view of the victim communicated by the wrongdoing can be directly repudiated by the transgressor. Recognition of the bidirectional nature of communication also focuses attention on the victim's behavior. The extent of vacillation between positions in the space defined by the earlier described typology, and the duration of occupying a particular space, is likely to influence the victim's behavior. In short, how the victim responds to recurrent feelings of hurt—the subsequent inevitable hurts that result from a relationship with an imperfect partner, and so on—is likely to be important for understanding forgiveness.

Forgiveness-related communication is also important because genuinely motivated attempts to tell the partner that he or she is forgiven can easily be seen as, for instance, a putdown or a form of retaliation, and it might in itself end up being a source of hurt. And because the victim loses more than the transgressing partner gains from the transgression, such communication requires some skill to avoid it being seen as an overreaction and a possible source of conflict.

In short, there is a need to study both the process and the outcome of communication about transgressions, especially statements of forgiveness, and to distinguish these situations from one in which forgiveness occurs in the absence of any verbalized statements of forgiveness. The importance of such research is emphasized by the recent finding that positive attributions and relationship quality independently predicted higher private forgiveness, whereas only relationship quality predicted expressed forgiveness (Friesen et al., 2005).

Relationships: An Antidote to the Same-Source Variance Problem

As with the broader literature on forgiveness, most research on forgiveness in relationships is limited by the problem of same-source variance. This is because indices of forgiveness and its correlates are obtained from a single source, typically the victim. This obscures whether forgiveness reflects something about the forgiver or the partner's forgivability, or something about their relationship. When these effects were disaggregated, reactions to spouse transgressions were determined largely by relationship-specific factors rather than by individual tendencies toward forgivingness or the offending partner's forgivability (Hoyt, Fincham, McCullough, Maio, & Davila, 2005). Moreover, greater attention to the specific relationship in which forgiveness takes place suggests that it is intrinsically different across relationships (Maio, Thomas, Fincham, & Carnelley, 2008).

The availability of analytic techniques such as the actor-partner interdependence model (Kenny, Kashy, & Cook, 2006) has the potential to advance understanding of forgiveness in relationships. But even without the use of such techniques progress can be made by obtaining data from both partners. For example, showing that spouse-reported forgiveness predicts partner-reported outcomes is an improvement over most current data on forgiveness in relationships.

The Dark Side of Forgiveness

Forgiveness has been viewed in the relationship literature almost exclusively in a positive light. However, the finding that women in shelters (Burton, Gordon, & Porter, 2004) and those who experience dating violence (Katz, Street, & Arias, 1997) are more likely to return to their partner to the extent that they forgive him or her highlights the possible downside of forgiveness. That forgiveness has a dark side becomes patently obvious when the philosophers Murphy and Hampton (1988) remind us that "forgiveness is the sort of thing that one does for a reason, and where there are reasons there is a distinction between good ones and bad ones" (p. 15).

Forgiveness lends itself to abuse, as one realizes when recalling that a transgression places the aggrieved partner in a position of moral superiority vis-à-vis the transgressor. Undoubtedly some in relationships succumb to the temptation to abuse this position, though in the absence of data this must remain speculative. Although one might expect such behavior to occur more frequently in relationships that are dysfunctional, it is probably not exclusive to such relationships. It would therefore be useful to identify the conditions under which forgiveness is used to manipulate the partner or even as a weapon to exact revenge. Failure to do so will result in an incomplete picture of forgiveness in relationships.

CONCLUSION

This chapter has covered considerable ground, demonstrating that a good deal has been learned about forgiveness in relationships in a relatively short time. This fact alone suggests an answer to the question posed in the chapter title. The philosopher Boleyn-Fitzgerald's (2002) conclusion that forgiveness is "arguably the most important virtue for controlling anger" (p. 483), which, together with Mother Teresa's observation, and most important, the data cited in this chapter, indicates that forgiveness needs to be integral to a complete science of close relationships. At the same time, it is apparent that William Blake's observation about the difficulty of forgiving those with whom we are in a close relationship is equally true. The challenge this poses for research on forgiveness in relationships is immense. Several issues that need to be addressed in the service of meeting this challenge were therefore identified, including the history of hurts in the relationship, the implicit versus explicit nature of forgiveness, types of forgiveness, the communication of forgiveness, and the potential downside of forgiveness.

REFERENCES

Aristotle. (1939). *Rhetoric*. Cambridge, MA: Harvard University Press.

Berscheid, E. (1999). The greening of relationship science. *American Psychologist, 54*, 260–266.

Berry, J. W., Worthington, E. L., Parrott, L., O'Connor, L. E., & Wade, N. G. (2001). Dispositional forgivingness: Development and construct validity of the Transgression Narrative Test of Forgivingness (TNTF). *Personality and Social Psychology Bulletin, 27*, 1277–1290.

Boleyn-Fitzgerald, P. (2002). What should "forgiveness" mean? *The Journal of Values Inquiry, 36*, 483–498.

Burton, S., Gordon, K., & Porter, L. (2004). Predicting the intentions of women in domestic violence shelters to return to partners: Does forgiveness play a role? *Journal of Family Psychology, 18*, 331–338.

Caprara, G. V. (1986). Indicators of aggression: The dissipation-rumination scale. *Personality and Individual Differences, 7*, 763–769.

Downie, R. S. (1971). *Roles and values*. London: Methuen.

Eaton, J., & Struthers, C. W. (2006). The reduction of psychological aggression across varied interpersonal contexts through repentance and forgiveness. *Aggressive Behavior, 32*, 195–206.

Exline, J. J., Worthington, E. L., Jr., Hill, P., & McCullough, M. E. (2003). Forgiveness and justice: A research agenda for social and personality psychology. *Personality and Social Psychology Review, 7*, 337–348.

Fincham, F. D. (2000). The kiss of the porcupines: From attributing responsibility to forgiving. *Personal Relationships, 7*, 1–23.

Fincham, F. D., & Beach, S. R. H. (2002). Forgiveness in marriage: Implications for psychological aggression and constructive communication. *Personal Relationships, 9*, 239–251.

Fincham, F. D., & Beach, S. R. H. (2007). Forgiveness and marital quality: Precursor or consequence in well-established relationships. *Journal of Positive Psychology, 2*, 260–268.

Fincham, F. D., Beach, S. R., & Davila, J. (2004). Forgiveness and conflict resolution in marriage. *Journal of Family Psychology, 18*, 72–81.

Fincham, F. D., Beach, S. R. H., & Davila, J. (2007). Longitudinal relations between forgiveness and conflict resolution in marriage. *Journal of Family Psychology, 21*, 542–545.

Fincham, F. D., Hall, J. H., & Beach, S. R. H. (2005). 'Til lack of forgiveness doth us part: Forgiveness in marriage. In E. L. Worthington (Ed.), *Handbook of forgiveness* (pp. 207–226). New York: Routledge.

Fincham, F. D., Jackson, H., & Beach, S. R. H. (2005). Transgression severity and forgiveness: Different moderators for objective and subjective severity. *Journal of Social and Clinical Psychology, 24*, 860–875.

Fincham, F. D., & Linfield, K. J. (1997). A new look at marital quality: Can spouses feel positive and negative about their marriage? *Journal of Family Psychology, 11*, 489–502.

Fincham, F. D., Paleari, G., & Regalia, C. (2002). Forgiveness in marriage: The role of relationship quality, attributions and empathy. *Personal Relationships, 9*, 27–37.

Friesen, M. D., Fletcher, G. J. O., & Overall, N. C. (2005). A dyadic assessment of forgiveness in intimate relationships. *Personal Relationships, 12*, 61–77.

Ghandi, M. (2000). *The collected works of Mahatma Gandhi* (2nd rev. ed., Vol. 51, pp. 301– 302). Retrieved April 2, 2008, from http://www.gandhiserve.org/cwmg/cwmg.html

Holman, H. E., & Silver, R. C. (2005). Future-oriented thinking and adjustment in a nationwide longitudinal study following the September 11th terrorist attacks. *Motivation and Emotion, 29*, 389–410.

Holmgren, M. R. (1993). Forgiveness and the intrinsic value of persons. *American Philosophical Quarterly, 30*, 342–352.

Hoyt, W. T., Fincham, F., McCullough, M. E., Maio, G., & Davila, J. (2005). Responses to interpersonal transgressions in families: Forgivingness, forgivability, and relationship-specific effects. *Journal of Personality and Social Psychology, 89*, 375–394.

Katz, J., Street, A., & Arias, I. (1997). Individual differences in self-appraisals and responses to dating violence scenarios. *Violence and Victims, 12*, 265–276.

Kearns, J. N., & Fincham, F. D. (2005). Victim and perpetrator accounts of interpersonal transgressions: Self-serving or relationship-serving biases? *Personality and Social Psychology Bulletin, 31*, 321–333.

Kelley, D. (1998). The communication of forgiveness. *Communication Studies, 49*, 1–17.

Kenny, D. A., Kashy, D. A., & Cook, W. L. (2006). *Dyadic data analysis*. New York: Guilford Press.

Maio, G. R., Thomas, G., Fincham, F. D., & Carnelley, K. (2008). Unraveling the role of forgiveness in family relationships. *Journal of Personality and Social Psychology, 94*, 307–319.

McCullough, M. E., Exline, J. J., & Baumeister, R. F. (1998). An annotated bibliography of research on forgiveness and related concepts. In E. L. Worthington

(Ed.), *Dimensions of forgiveness: Psychological research and theological perspectives* (pp. 193–317). Philadelphia: Templeton Press.

McCullough, M. E., Fincham, F. D., & Tsang, J. (2003). Forgiveness, forbearance, and time: The temporal unfolding of transgression-related interpersonal motivations. *Journal of Personality and Social Psychology, 84*, 540–557.

McCullough, M. E., Rachal, K. C., Sandage, S. J., Worthington, E. L., Jr., Brown, S. W., & Hight, T. L. (1998). Interpersonal forgiving in close relationships: II. Theoretical elaboration and measurement. *Journal of Personality and Social Psychology, 75*, 1586–1603.

McCullough, M. E., & vanOyen Witvliet, C. (2002). The psychology of forgiveness. In C. R. Snyder & S. J. Lopez (Eds.), *Handbook of positive psychology* (pp. 446–458). Oxford, England: Oxford Psychology Press.

McCullough, M. E., Worthington, E. L., Jr., & Rachal, K. C. (1997). Interpersonal forgiving in close relationships. *Journal of Personality and Social Psychology, 73*, 321–336.

McNulty, J. K. (2008). Forgiveness in marriage: Putting the benefits into context. *Journal of Family Psychology, 22*, 171–175.

Murphy, J., & Hampton, J. (1988). *Forgiveness and mercy*. New York: Cambridge University Press.

Murray, S. L., Holmes, J. G., & Griffin, D. W. (1996). The benefits of positive illusions: Idealization and the construction of satisfaction in close relationships. *Journal of Personality and Social Psychology, 70*, 79–98.

Nietzsche, F. W. (1887). *The genealogy of morals*. London: Society for Promoting Christian Knowledge.

Paleari, G., Regalia, C., & Fincham, F. D. (2003). Adolescents' willingness to forgive parents: An empirical model. *Parenting: Science and Practice, 3*, 155–174.

Paleari, G., Regalia, C., & Fincham, F. D. (2005). Marital quality, forgiveness, empathy, and rumination: A longitudinal analysis. *Personality and Social Psychology Bulletin, 31*, 368–378.

Rusbult, C. E., Verette, J., Whitney, G. A., Slovik, L. F., & Lipkus, I. (1991). Accommodation processes in close relationships: Theory and preliminary empirical evidence. *Journal of Personality and Social Psychology, 60*, 53–78.

Stillwell, A. M., & Baumeister, R. F. (1997). The construction of victim and perpetrator memories: Accuracy and distortion in role-based accounts. *Personality and Social Psychology Bulletin, 23*, 1157–1172.

Terzino, K., Fincham, F. D., & Cross, S. (2008). *But do you* really *forgive me? An implicit test of forgiveness*. Unpublished manuscript.

Tsang, J., McCullough, M.E., Fincham, F. D. (2006). Forgiveness and the psychological dimension of reconciliation: A longitudinal analysis. *Journal of Social and Clinical Psychology, 25*, 404–428.

Wade, N. G., Worthington, E. L., Jr., & Meyer, J. E. (2005). But do they work?: A meta-analysis of group interventions to promote forgiveness. In E. L. Worthington, Jr. (Ed.), *Handbook of forgiveness* (pp. 423–440). New York: Routledge.

Waller, N. G., & Meehl, P. E. (1998). *Multivariate taxometric procedures*. Thousand Oaks, CA: Sage.

Worthington, E. L. (1998). Introduction. In E. L. Worthington (Ed.), *Dimensions of forgiveness: Psychological research and theological perspectives* (pp. 1–5). Philadelphia: Templeton Press.

Worthington, E. L. (2005). More questions about forgiveness: Research agenda for 2005-2015. In E. L. Worthington (Ed.), *Handbook of forgiveness* (pp. 557–575). New York: Routledge.

Worthington, E. L., Sandage, S. J., & Berry, J. W. (2000). Group interventions to promote forgiveness. In M. E. McCullough, K. Pargament, & C. Thoreson (Eds.), *Forgiveness: Theory, research, and practice* (pp. 228–253). New York: Guilford Press.

Worthington, E. L., & Wade, N. (1999). The psychology of unforgiveness and forgiveness and implications for clinical practice. *Journal of Social and Clinical Psychology, 18*, 385–418.

19

RESPONDING TO NEED IN INTIMATE RELATIONSHIPS: SOCIAL SUPPORT AND CAREGIVING PROCESSES IN COUPLES

NANCY L. COLLINS, MÁIRE B. FORD, ANAMARIE C. GUICHARD, HEIDI S. KANE, AND BROOKE C. FEENEY

Human beings are hardwired to nurture, protect, and promote the welfare of others, as argued in several other chapters in this volume. This propensity to care for others is most visible in our closest relationships, in which individuals routinely sacrifice their own needs—even their own health—to respond to the needs of their spouses, children, and other loved ones. Indeed, one defining feature of intimate relationships is the expectation that romantic partners will take care of each other in times of adversity and be mutually responsive to one another's needs. These expectations are made explicit in traditional weddings, when partners vow to love one another in good times and bad, in sickness and in health.

In attachment theory, Bowlby (1982, 1988) recognized the profound importance of caregiving in adult close relationships, and he suggested that healthy and secure intimate relationships are possible only when relationship partners acknowledge, and respect, the crucial role they play as caregivers to one another. Nevertheless, romantic partners differ considerably in their ability and willingness to provide sensitive care to one another, and many intimate relationships fail to provide partners with the deep sense of emotional security that is necessary for optimal functioning. After all, responding to the needs of others is often difficult, involving a good deal of responsibility and consuming considerable cognitive, emotional, and sometimes tangible resources. Not everyone is equally skilled at providing responsive care or equally motivated to do so. Thus, although mutual caring and responsiveness is widely understood as the ideal in intimate relationships, many relationships fall short of this ideal.

Why are some individuals more willing, and better able, to be effective caregivers in their romantic relationships? Are there systematic individual differences in patterns of caregiving, and if so, what are the personal and interpersonal dynamics that explain these differences? To address these questions, we use attachment theory as a framework for studying social support and caregiving processes in couples. We conceptualize social support as an interpersonal process that occurs at the interface of two distinct behavioral systems: the attachment system and the caregiving system. Our approach explores both the normative patterns of support and care that occur in intimate relationships and the ways in which these patterns are shaped by important individual differences in attachment style. Most of our research examines how romantic partners help one another cope with stressful life events (a process called *safe haven support*), but we also explore how partners help one another pursue their personal goals and engage in autonomous exploration (a process called *secure base support*; Feeney & Collins, 2004). Throughout our work, we study social support as a dyadic process involving the mutual influence of careseekers and caregivers. In this chapter, we highlight the role of the caregiver, that is, the person who provides emotional and instrumental aid to a loved one in need.

In some ways, the study of prosocial behavior in close relationships is no different from the study of prosocial behavior in relationships between strangers; and our research on social support in intimate relationships can be viewed as a microcosm of many of the more general social and psychological processes discussed in other chapters in this volume. But despite the similarities, there are also important differences between research on helping strangers and our research on helping close relationship partners. Here we highlight three differences that are important for the present discussion.

First, research on helping strangers has typically focused on providing instrumental aid to others in need, such as volunteering time, donating money, or providing tangible assistance in an emergency. Although instrumental support is also vital in close relationships, our work places greater emphasis on emotional forms of support such as comfort, reassurance, encouragement, and validation, especially when one partner in a relationship is undergoing psychological or social stress. In addition, because emotional support is somewhat difficult to define objectively, we often assess it from multiple perspectives by obtaining reports from support providers, support recipients, and objective coders.

Second, the outcome of interest in most studies of prosocial behavior is whether people help (e.g., donate money) or how much they help (e.g., the amount of money they donate). In contrast, our research with couples is more concerned with the quality rather than the quantity of support offered (e.g., Do caregivers listen sympathetically, do they offer advice in ways that enhance rather than diminish their partner's self-esteem?). Thus, one goal of our research has been to specify the features of effective (and ineffective) caregiving and to identify the skills, resources, and motives that are necessary for individuals to be sensitive and responsive to the emotional and instrumental needs of others.

Finally, unlike helping among strangers, social support processes in couples are embedded in relationships that have both a past and a future. Hence, it is difficult to understand social support and caregiving dynamics without reference to other relationship features such as the caregiver's level of trust, commitment, and interdependence. At the same time, we are also interested in understanding the impact of social support on relationship quality and individual health and well-being. Attachment theory emphasizes the importance of responsive caregiving for the development and maintenance of secure and well-functioning relationships, and this topic has been an important focus of our research.

Thus, compared with the broader helping literature, our research on social support in couples places greater emphasis on the interpersonal antecedents and consequences of this special form of prosocial behavior.

This chapter provides an overview of our research on social support and caregiving processes in couples. We begin by describing two behavioral systems— attachment and caregiving—that are relevant to understanding caregiving dynamics in couples. We then discuss theory and research on the caregiving behavioral system. In so doing, we discuss the normative activation of the caregiving system, individual differences in the capacity for responsive care, and mechanisms that may explain these differences. Finally, we review our research on caregiving in adult intimate relationships and discuss implications of these findings for individual and relationship well-being.

ATTACHMENT AND CAREGIVING

Attachment theory provided an ideal framework for studying social support and caregiving processes in intimate relationships because it stipulates that the need for security is one of the most fundamental of all basic needs (for individuals of all ages), and it provides a basis for understanding the complex interpersonal dynamics involved in two interrelated components of human nature: attachment (support seeking) and caregiving (support giving). We briefly discuss these two behavioral systems as a backdrop for our discussion of caregiving processes.

Attachment Behavioral System

Attachment theory regards the propensity to form strong emotional bonds with particular individuals as a basic feature of human nature—present in infants and continuing through adulthood. According to the theory, infants enter the world equipped with an innate attachment behavioral system that promotes safety and survival through contact with nurturing caregivers. The attachment system becomes activated most strongly in adversity, so that when frightened, anxious, tired, or ill, a child will tend to seek protection and care from an attachment figure, typically a parent (Bowlby, 1973, 1982; Bretherton, 1985). Moreover, the quality of the relationship that develops between parent and child is expected to be largely determined by the parent's emotional availability and responsiveness to the child's attachment needs (Ainsworth, Blehar, Waters, & Wall, 1978). The child's ability to rely on an attachment figure as a safe haven of comfort and support when distressed, and as a secure base for exploration when not distressed, is considered a key component of secure attachment bonds and a predictor of healthy emotional development.

Although attachment theory was originally developed to explain parent–child bonds, Bowlby (1982) emphasized that the attachment system continues to operate across the life span and that attachment behavior is not limited to children. Attachment behavior in adulthood can be seen most clearly when adults face stressful or threatening events. For example, adults often seek proximity to significant others in response to illness, pain, fatigue, fear of new situations, feelings of attack or rejection by others, achievement problems or failures, and threats of loss. Attachment behavior, and an associated increase in desire for support and care, is the norm in these situations and is considered neither childish nor immature.

Although the need for security is believed to be universal, individuals develop characteristic strategies for coping with distress and regulating feelings of security; these strategies are thought to be contingent, at least in part, on an individual's history of regulating distress with attachment figures (Kobak & Sceery, 1988; Mikulincer & Shaver, 2007; see also chap. 14, this volume). This has led researchers to identify different attachment styles in infants and adults, which are defined by two roughly orthogonal dimensions: attachment anxiety and avoidance (Ainsworth et al., 1978; Bartholomew & Horowitz, 1991; Mikulincer & Shaver, 2007). *Attachment anxiety* reflects the degree to which individuals worry about being rejected, abandoned, or unloved. *Avoidant attachment* reflects the degree to which individuals wish to limit intimacy and interdependence with others. These two dimensions can be used to define a secure attachment style, characterized by low anxiety and avoidance, and various insecure attachment styles (i.e., preoccupied, fearful avoidant, dismissing avoidant), characterized by high anxiety, high avoidance, or both.

These attachment styles can be understood in terms of rules that regulate the attachment system and guide responses to emotionally distressing situations (Mikulincer & Shaver, 2007). Secure attachment is organized by rules that allow acknowledgment of distress and turning to others for comfort when needed. Avoidant attachment is organized by rules that restrict acknowledgment of distress and inhibit dependence on others (i.e., a *deactivating* strategy), whereas anxious attachment is organized by rules that direct attention toward distress and attachment figures in a hypervigilant manner that inhibits autonomy and self-reliance (i.e., a *hyperactivating* strategy). As we discuss in the following section, these different strategies for coping with one's own distress have important implications for how individuals respond to the emotional distress of others.

Caregiving Behavioral System

The propensity to care for the needs of others is regarded by attachment theory as another major component of human nature (see chap. 4, this volume). Whereas the attachment system is a normative safety-regulating system that reduces the risk of the self coming to harm, the caregiving system is a safety regulating system that reduces the risk of a close other coming to harm. From a normative perspective, the caregiving system alerts individuals to the needs of others and motivates them to provide protection, comfort, and assistance to those who are dependent on them; hence, the caregiving behavioral system will be activated most strongly when a close other is facing adversity. However, the caregiving and attachment behavioral systems within an individual will be antithetical, such that sensitive and responsive caregiving is most likely to occur when the caregiver's own attachment needs have been satisfied and the attachment system has been deactivated (Bowlby, 1982, 1988).

Although the caregiving behavioral system is most often discussed in the context of parent–child relationships (see George & Solomon, 2008), Bowlby (1988) recognized the importance of caregiving in adult pair bonds and suggested that secure and well-functioning intimate relationships are possible only when relationship partners accept (and value) their roles as caregivers to one another. In the sections that follow, we examine the caregiving behavioral system in depth by considering the normative processes that activate and motivate caregiving behavior in close relationships, and the ways in which these processes are shaped by individual differences in the caregiver's working models of attachment and caregiving.

CAREGIVING: NORMATIVE PROCESSES

If attachment bonds are to function effectively, the attachment behavior of one partner must be coordinated with the caregiving behavior of his or her attachment figure. For example, just as infants are motivated to remain in close proximity to their parents, parents feel a strong urge to remain close to their infants and young children; they routinely monitor their whereabouts and remain ready to respond on short notice should any threat arise.

Effective caregiving involves more than simply monitoring a partner's whereabouts and remaining alert to signs of distress. According to attachment theory, caregiving serves two major functions: (a) meeting the dependent partner's need for security by responding to signals of distress or potential threat (providing a safe haven); and (b) supporting the attached person's autonomy and exploration when not distressed (providing a secure base). We find it useful to distinguish between safe haven and secure base support because they have different antecedents, interpersonal forms, and consequences. In the rest of this chapter, we focus on safe haven caregiving dynamics, the subject of most of our empirical work (for our comprehensive theoretical model that incorporates both safe haven and secure base caregiving, see Feeney & Collins, 2004).

Safe Haven Caregiving Processes

Safe haven support occurs when a caregiver supports a partner's need to "come in" to the relationship for comfort and assistance in times of adversity (Feeney & Collins, 2004). Caregivers provide a safe haven for their relationship partners when they respond sensitively and appropriately to their partners' needs for proximity, reassurance, and/or assistance. The specific kind of care provided in any situation will, of course, depend on the nature of the stressful event but may include (a) encouraging communication of thoughts and feelings, (b) showing interest in the partner's problems and validating his or her concerns, (c) conveying a sense of confidence in a partner's ability to handle the stressful situation, (d) affirming the partner's worth and reassuring the partner that he or she is loved and valued, (e) providing physical closeness and affection, (f) providing instrumental assistance (task assistance, tangible resources), and (g) conveying continued availability. Thus, safe-haven caregiving behaviors are those that restore an attached partner's felt security by reducing emotional distress and supporting the partner's own coping efforts, as well as behaviors that convey (and provide) availability and assistance if needed.

Key Features of Effective Caregiving

Regardless of the specific form of support being offered, we (Collins, Guichard, Ford, & Feeney, 2006) have suggested that effective caregiving is

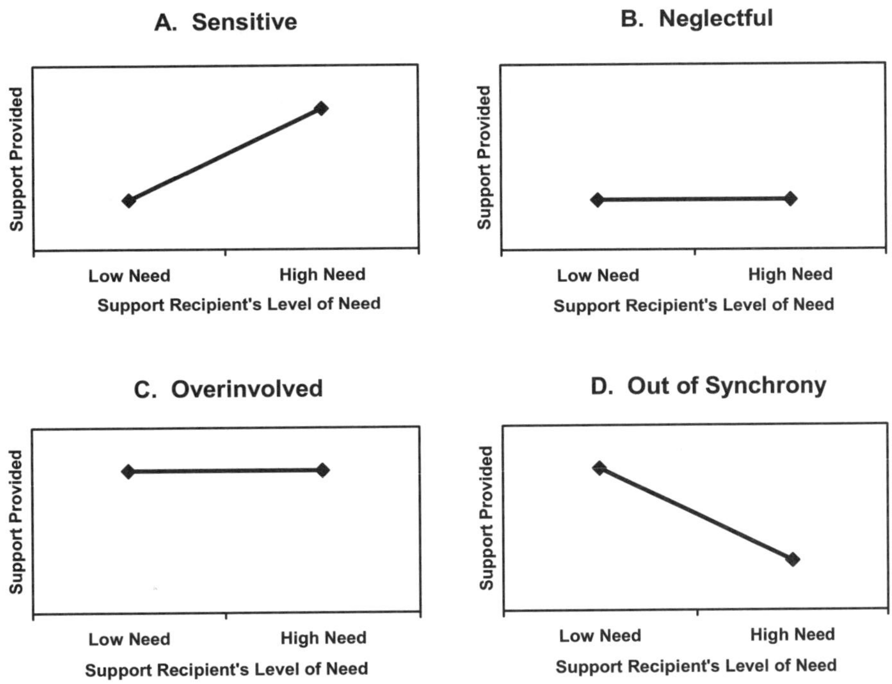

Figure 19.1. Patterns of sensitive care (A) and various forms of insensitive care (B, C, D) provided in response to a partner's need.

characterized by two features: (a) sensitivity to the partner's signals and (b) interpersonal responsiveness. The first feature, *sensitivity*, refers to the degree to which the caregiver's behavior is in synchrony with, and appropriately contingent on, the partner's needs. A sensitive caregiver takes cues from the careseeker, allows the careseeker to pace interventions, is attuned to the careseeker's signals, interprets them correctly, and responds promptly and appropriately. In contrast, insensitive caregivers may not notice the careseeker's signals or may misinterpret them, interfere with activities in an arbitrary way, or respond late, inappropriately, or not at all to a need for support. Thus, insensitive caregivers may be neglectful, overinvolved, intrusive, or otherwise out of sync with their partner's needs. Figure 19.1 illustrates these various patterns of sensitive and insensitive care.

The second feature of effective caregiving is *interpersonal responsiveness*, which refers to the manner in which support is provided. Specifically, responsive care is provided in a way that leads the recipient to feel understood, validated, and cared for (Reis & Patrick, 1996). To accomplish this goal, caregivers must offer support in a way that expresses generous intentions, protects their partner's esteem, validates their partner's feelings and needs, respects their partner's point of view, and conveys acceptance and understanding. Being responsive is not always easy, and even well-intended support efforts can have unintended negative consequences (Gleason, Iida, Shrout, & Bolger, 2008; Nadler, 1991; Rini, Dunkel-Schetter, Hobel, Glynn, & Sandman, 2006). For example, caregivers may offer support in a way that makes their partner feel weak or inadequate, that induces guilt or indebtedness, or that makes their partner feel like a burden. Caregivers may also minimize or discount their partner's problem or blame the partner for his or her misfortune.

Effective caregiving requires skills and resources and so is likely to be easier for some people than for others, and in some relationships compared with others. To understand systematic differences in patterns of caregiving, we began by identifying three broad categories of factors that seem likely to enhance the provision of sensitive and responsive care: (a) skills and abilities, (b) resources, and (c) motivation.

Skills and Abilities

If caregivers are to provide sensitive and responsive care, they must possess a variety of skills and abilities that enable them to accurately discern the needs of others and to respond flexibly to a wide range of situations. For example, they must have the ability to take the perspective of others (Batson, Early, & Salvarani, 1997) and to accurately decode verbal and nonverbal signals (Noller, 2006). Caregivers must also know how to provide the appropriate type and amount of support, and they must hold adaptive attitudes, beliefs, and expectations about providing support to others. Effective self-regulation and emotion regulation skills are also necessary for responsive caregiving (Eisenberg, Hofer, & Vaughan, 2007). For a variety of reasons, individuals who have difficulty regulating their own emotions—especially distress-related emotions—are likely to have difficulty responding to the needs of others. For instance, those who have difficulty modulating negative affect may become overaroused, which may interfere with their ability to plan and enact effective helping behaviors (see chap. 7, this volume), whereas those who are uncomfortable with emotional distress may direct their attention away from distressing stimuli, which may lead them to distance themselves from the person in need (Cassidy, 1994).

Resources

Effective caregiving requires adequate cognitive, emotional, and material resources. If individuals are stressed, overwhelmed with personal responsibilities, and experiencing time constraints, their caregiving behavior is likely to suffer because they may be self-focused and short of cognitive and emotional resources necessary to discern and attend to the needs of others (Vinokur, Price, & Caplan, 1996; Wood, Saltzberg, & Goldsampt, 1990). In addition, if self-regulatory resources are depleted (see chap. 9, this volume), caregivers may be less able to inhibit unhelpful support behaviors (e.g., criticism) and may lack the patience needed to be cooperative and nonintrusive in their caregiving efforts.

Motivation

Finally, even if caregivers have appropriate skills and sufficient resources for providing care, they may or may not be motivated to deploy those resources in the service of others. We distinguish between two different aspects of motivation: (a) an individual's overall degree of motivation to provide care (conceptualized as the degree of felt responsibility for responding to another's needs) and (b) the specific form of that motivation (conceptualized in terms of altruistic versus egoistic motivation).

Because caregiving often involves a good deal of responsibility, as well as substantial cognitive, emotional, and material resources (and sometimes personal sacrifice), individuals must be motivated to accept this responsibility and to share their resources with others in need (Mills, Clark, Ford, & Johnson, 2004). If caregivers are not sufficiently motivated, they may provide either low levels of care or ineffective forms of care that are out of sync with their partner's needs.

Individuals differ in the degree to which their caregiving efforts are motivated by *altruistic* concerns (i.e., the desire to promote another's welfare), or *egoistic* concerns (i.e., the desire to promote one's own welfare; Feeney & Collins, 2003; see also chap. 1, this volume). Caregivers who are motivated by altruistic concerns are likely to be more effective because their caregiving efforts will be guided by their partner's needs rather than their own needs. They will be more attuned to their partner's signals, more willing to expend effort to respond appropriately to these signals, and more likely to provide support in a manner that expresses their benevolent motives. In contrast, caregivers who are motivated by egoistic concerns are likely to be less effective because they are focused on their own needs rather than on the needs of their partner. For example, caregivers who are motivated to provide care to reduce their own distress, or out of a sense of obligation (to avoid sanctions for not helping), are likely to be controlling rather than cooperative in their caregiving efforts and may provide support in a manner that expresses a sense of burden. Likewise, caregivers who are motivated to provide care in order to be loved or needed may become overinvolved or intrusive in their caregiving efforts and may express dissatisfaction if others fail to show adequate gratitude or appreciation.

CAREGIVING: INDIVIDUAL DIFFERENCES

Although caring for close others is presumed to be a universal human tendency, people differ in the degree to which their caregiving systems are sensitive to (easily triggered by) the needs of others and in the way they enact their caregiving tendencies. Although caregiving behavior, like attachment behavior, is to some degree preprogrammed (meaning that it is ready to develop along certain lines when conditions support it), Bowlby (1982, 1988) emphasized that the details and system parameters are affected by experience, especially by experiences with major care providers (Kunce & Shaver, 1994). Thus, while the caregiving system is theoretically distinct from the attachment system, the two systems are thought be linked both developmentally and behaviorally (George & Solomon, 2008; see also chap. 4, this volume).

Interface of the Attachment and Caregiving Behavioral Systems

Figure 19.2 summarizes our assumptions about the intrapersonal links between the attachment and caregiving systems, and it provides a framework for understanding individual differences in the capacity for effective caregiving. We assume that the attachment behavioral system has both a direct influence (Path a) on the caregiving system (skills, resources, motivation) and an indirect influence (Paths b–c) mediated by relationship characteristics (e.g., interdependence, commitment, and trust). Furthermore, we assume that features of the caregiving system will shape caregiving responses (cognitive, affective, physiological, and behavioral) in specific episodes of care (Path d). Space does not permit a full discussion of our theoretical framework, but it is useful to elaborate on some of its important features.

Direct Links Between Attachment and Caregiving

Consider Path a. The caregiving and attachment systems are linked in at least two ways: Working models of attachment shape working models of caregiving, and the dynamics of the attachment system influence the dynamics of the caregiving system. As discussed in the next section, we conceptualize the first link as *distal*, and the second link as *proximal*.

Working Models of Attachment Shape Working Models of Caregiving

If caregiving is regulated by its own behavioral system, then individuals should develop internal working models of caregiving that guide the caregiving system. Furthermore, because people first learn about seeking and giving care in the context of their own experiences of being cared for by attachment figures, working models of attachment (which guide support-seeking behavior and the regulation of personal distress) are likely to shape working models of caregiving (which should consist of rules that guide caregiving behaviors and the regulation of a significant other's distress).

Thus, in terms of distal influence, we assume that the quality of care a person receives during childhood and adolescence shapes many of the skills, resources, and motives necessary for effective caregiving. Support for this assumption is provided in multiple literatures. First, children who come from

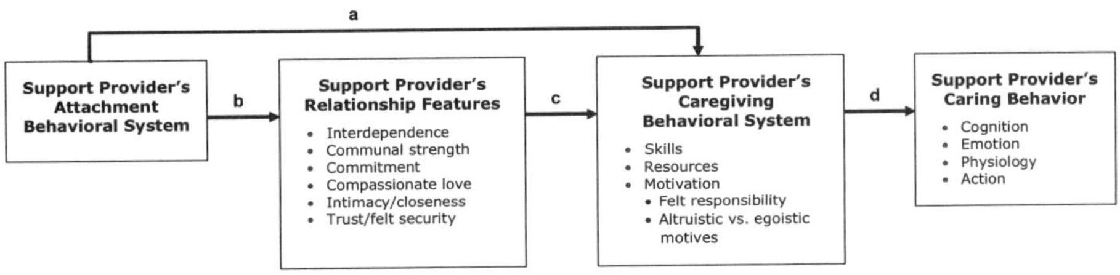

Figure 19.2. Summary of the intrapersonal links between the attachment and caregiving behavioral systems within the support provider.

secure and loving homes show more empathic concern for others, behave in more sympathetic ways toward peers in distress, and are more prosocially oriented (see chap. 7, this volume). Second, research on caregiving in intimate relationships shows that adults who recall their parents as having been warm and responsive are warmer and more responsive toward their romantic partners (Feeney & Collins, 2003; Kunce & Shaver, 1994). Finally, research on parenting behavior shows that parents' memories of their attachment experiences with their own parents predict the quality of their caregiving behavior toward their children (Hesse, 2008). Together, previous experiences are likely to guide cognition (e.g., attention, memory, social inferences), emotion (e.g., empathy, personal distress, anger), physiology, and behavior in specific situations that call for caregiving (see Figure 19.2, Path d).

Dynamics of the Attachment System Influence the Dynamics of the Caregiving System

In terms of proximal influence, the attachment and caregiving systems are likely to be interrelated in at least two ways. First, as noted earlier, Bowlby (1982, 1988) suggested that it is only when attachment needs have been met, and the attachment system is deactivated, that individuals can turn their attention fully to other behavioral systems. Thus, caregiving may be impaired if the caregiver's own feelings of security are threatened (which may deplete cognitive and emotional resources and may activate egoistic or self-protective emotions and motives). Felt security (dispositional or situational) should therefore facilitate one's ability to be responsive to the needs of others (Mikulincer, Shaver, Gillath, & Nitzberg, 2005; Murray, Holmes, & Collins, 2006). Second, because an intimate partner is both a target of one's care and a source of one's own care and security, activation of the caregiving system is likely to activate the attachment behavioral system.

Thus, the caregiving system may sometimes operate in the service of current attachment needs, and these needs are often incompatible with optimal caregiving. For example, individuals who are anxious about being rejected may become overinvolved in caregiving behavior in order to create dependence (to become indispensable to their partner) or to satisfy their own need to be close to their partner. In contrast, avoidant caregivers may fail to notice or respond to other's distress in the service of their own need to deactivate attachment concerns.

Indirect Links Between Attachment and Caregiving

Working models of attachement should have directed effect on the caregiving system by shaping relationship features (see Figure 19.2, Path b), which, in turn, directly affect the caregiving system (Path c). For example a caregiver who is comfortable with emotional expressiveness and interdependence (i.e., one who is low in avoidance) is more likely to develop a relationship that is high in intimacy, commitment, and compassionate love, which fosters felt responsibility for the partner's welfare and altruistic motives for providing support (see chaps. 13 and 17, this volume). A caregiver who is worried about being rejected (i.e., one who is high in attachment anxiety) may find it difficult to trust his or her partner and may have doubts about the partner's love and commitment. As a result, such a person is likely to pursue self-protective goals in the relationship (proceeding with caution, attempting to prevent hurt or betrayal), which may undermine communal norms, deplete cognitive resources, and increase egoistic motives for helping (e.g., helping in order to ensure the partner's love and commitment) that can interfere with other-oriented emotions and actions (see chap. 1, this volume; Clark, Graham, Williams, & Lemay, 2008; Murray et al., 2006).

Individual Differences in Patterns of Caregiving

As the previous discussion makes clear, there are many reasons to expect a close connection between attachment and caregiving dynamics in adulthood, and to expect that individual differences in attachment style will be important for understanding effective and ineffective caregiving processes in couples. Secure caregivers—who are confident that they are loved, comfortable with intimacy and interdependence, and effectively regulate their emotions—will be better equipped to provide responsive care because they have more of the necessary skills and resources for attending to the signals of others and responding flexibly to needs as they arise and because their own attachment needs are less likely to interfere with their caregiving activities. In addition, secure individuals are likely to have more adaptive beliefs and attitudes about careseeking and caregiving, which increases their sense of responsibility for the welfare of others and motivates them to provide help and support for altruistic reasons.

In contrast, the caregiving behavior of insecure adults is likely to be impaired; different forms of insecurity should be linked to different patterns of care and different underlying dynamics. Anxious individuals, who are worried about being rejected and have a hyperactivating style of emotion regulation, may have some of the motives and skills necessary for effective caregiving (e.g., compassion for others, comfort with emotional expression) but may lack some of the resources and adaptive motivation needed to be truly sensitive to the needs of others. For example, they may be preoccupied with their own attachment needs and highly self-focused, which leaves them with fewer cognitive and emotional resources for responding to their partners' needs. In addition, anxious individuals may be highly motivated to provide care to their partner but may do so for largely egoistic reasons (to satisfy their own attachment needs). Avoidant individuals, who value self-reliance and have a deactivating style of emotion regulation, are likely to lack many of the skills needed for effective caregiving and are less likely to develop the deep sense of compassionate love, commitment, and interdependence that is necessary for understanding their partner's needs and feeling responsible for their partner's welfare. Moreover, their need to minimize attachment concerns will tend to direct their attention away from a partner who is in distress and to provide support for relatively egoistic reasons.

In the following sections, we review empirical evidence, mostly from our own research program, relevant to safe haven caregiving behavior in couples. We begin by describing studies on normative processes and then review studies on attachment-style differences in caregiving.

EMPIRICAL EVIDENCE FOR SAFE HAVEN PROCESSES

In the following sections, we review empirical evidence, mostly from our own research program, relevant to safe haven caregiving behavior in couples. We begin by describing studies on normative processes and then review studies on attachment-style differences in caregiving.

Normative Processes

We began our research on safe haven caregiving by conducting an observational study in which we videotaped couples while one member (the "support seeker") disclosed a recent personal concern to his or her partner (the "caregiver"; Collins & Feeney, 2000). Caregivers in this study showed evidence of sensitivity by matching their overall support effort, and specific support behaviors, to the needs expressed by their partners. For example, when support seekers' needs were greater and more clearly expressed (as evidenced by higher levels of emotional and instrumental disclosure), caregivers responded with greater support effort and more helpful forms of support (more behavioral responsiveness, more emotional and instrumental support). In addition, careseeking and caregiving behaviors were coordinated such that the type of help offered (emotional or instrumental) was matched to the type of help sought.

We obtained further evidence for normative safe haven processes by investigating within-person variability in support-seeking and caregiving behavior in a daily diary study of couples (Collins & Feeney, 2005). In this study, both members of romantic couples completed a nightly diary for 21 days in which they recorded stressful events, support-seeking and caregiving behavior, and relationship quality each day. Results indicated that individuals sought more support from their partners on days when they experienced more stressful events (normative activation of the attachment system), and partners responded by providing more support on days when support seekers expressed greater need (normative activation of the caregiving system).

To provide more definitive evidence of caregiving dynamics, we created a laboratory paradigm to examine sensitivity and responsiveness to needs by experimentally manipulating a caregiver's perceptions of their partner's support needs (Feeney & Collins, 2001). We created a stressful event (a speech task) for one member of the couple and then manipulated the caregiver's perception that his or her partner was either extremely distressed about the upcoming speech task (the high-need condition) or not at all distressed (the low-need condition) by showing the caregiver a false stress questionnaire that had ostensibly been completed by his or her partner. From a normative perspective, the caregiving behavioral system should be activated with greater intensity when the partner is perceived to be in greater distress. Consistent with this assumption, when caregivers were separated from their partner and allowed to write the partner a private message, they wrote more supportive messages (as judged by their partners and by independent raters) in the high-need condition than in the low-need condition.

We extended and replicated these findings in a recent study using the same laboratory paradigm but with a broader range of outcome variables (Collins, Ford, Guichard, Kane, & Feeney, 2008, Study 1). Results showed that caregivers in the high-need condition, relative to those in the low-need condition, wrote messages that were more emotionally supportive, experienced greater empathic concern for their partner, and were more mentally focused on their partner while completing their own individual activity (a puzzle task). These results show that caregivers modulated their support efforts in line with their partner's needs by deploying greater cognitive, emotional, and behavioral resources when their partners needed them most.

Individual Differences: Attachment Style and Patterns of Caregiving

We turn now to studies showing that these normative reactions are often moderated by individual differences in attachment style, and that adults with different attachment styles show substantially different patterns of caregiving behavior. In the first study to explore this issue, Kunce and Shaver (1994) developed an adult Caregiving Questionnaire that assesses four caregiving dimensions: (a) proximity (e.g., "When my partner seems to want or need a hug, I'm glad to provide it"), (b) sensitivity (e.g., "I'm very good at recognizing my partner's needs and feelings, even when they're different from my own"), (c) cooperation vs. control (e.g., "I tend to be too domineering when trying to help my partner"), and (d) compulsive caregiving (e.g., "I tend to get overinvolved in my partner's problems and difficulties"). Using this measure, each attachment style was associated with a unique pattern of caregiving. Secure adults reported low levels of compulsive (overinvolved) and controlling caregiving, and high levels of proximity and sensitivity. In contrast, preoccupied individuals reported high levels of proximity and compulsive caregiving, but low levels of sensitivity and cooperation, suggesting that although they are capable of providing affectionate care, their caregiving efforts may be intrusive and out of sync with their partner's needs. Finally, dismissing-avoidant individuals reported low levels of proximity, sensitivity, and compulsive care, whereas fearful-avoidant individuals reported low levels of proximity and sensitivity but high levels of compulsive caregiving.

This basic pattern of findings has been replicated in other self-report studies. For example, in a large sample of couples we found that avoidant individuals described themselves as less responsive and more controlling in their caregiving style, whereas anxious individuals were more compulsive and controlling (Feeney & Collins, 2001). These patterns were also corroborated by partner reports. For example, when we asked couple members to describe their partner's caregiving style, both men and women rated avoidant partners as less responsive, and men rated anxious female partners as less responsive (Kane et al., 2007).

Observational studies have provided converging evidence for these patterns. In a series of studies, Simpson, Rholes, and colleagues (Rholes, Simpson, & Orina, 1999; Simpson, Rholes, & Nelligan, 1992) showed that attachment avoidance was associated with less effective caregiving behavior. In these studies, they unobtrusively videotaped couples after telling the female member of each couple that she would be participating in an anxiety-provoking laboratory procedure (the exact nature of the procedure was not revealed to the women, although they were shown a darkened laboratory chamber with physiological recording equipment in it). Men who were low in avoidance were more sensitive and responsive to their partner's needs during the waiting/stress period—they provided more reassurance, more emotional support, and more supportive comments when their partners showed higher levels of distress (Simpson et al., 1992). In contrast, those who were high in avoidance provided less support as their partner's level of distress increased. They also expressed more anger toward their partners during the stress period and interacted less positively with them during the recovery period, especially when their partners sought more social support (Rholes et al., 1999). These findings suggest that avoidant men found their partner's expressions of need to be aversive and that they responded to their own discomfort by distancing themselves from their partner.

We also examined individual differences in caregiving behavior in the observational study described previously, in which one member of each couple described a personal stressor to his or her partner (Collins & Feeney, 2000). We found that individuals who were high in attachment anxiety were less effective caregivers; they provided less instrumental support, were less responsive listeners, and exhibited more negative caregiving behavior, especially when their partner's needs were less clearly expressed. These findings provided the first behavioral evidence that attachment anxiety limits one's ability to be a good caregiver.

From an attachment theoretical perspective, sensitive caregiving should be appropriately contingent on a partner's needs; thus, caregivers should show increased support effort in response to greater need (see Figure 19.1, Panel A). As already mentioned, caregivers did, on average, write more supportive message to their partners when they believed their partners were more distressed about an upcoming speech task (Feeney & Collins, 2001). However, this normative increase in support did not occur for everyone in this study. Avoidant caregivers provided low levels of emotional support in both the high- and low-need conditions (see Figure 19.1, Panel B) and provided more instrumental support in the low-need condition than in the high-need condition (see Figure 19.1, Panel D). In contrast, anxious caregivers showed some responsiveness, but they were not always in synch with their partner's needs; they provided more instrumental support in the high-need condition than in the low-need condition (see Figure 19.1, Panel A), but they provided the same relatively high level of emotional support regardless of their partner's need (a pattern of over-involvement; see Figure 19.1, Panel C).

We extended these findings in two recent studies using a similar paradigm and a more diverse set of outcomes (Collins, Ford, Guichard, Kane, & Feeney, 2008). In the first study, secure individuals (low anxiety and avoidance) showed clear evidence of responsiveness. They experienced more emotional empathy and were more cognitively focused on their partner (thinking about their partner's feelings, being distracted by thoughts of their partner while working on their own puzzle task) in the high-need condition (when they were led to believe that their partner was highly distressed about an upcoming speech task) than in the low-need condition (when they were led to believe that their partner was not at all distressed about the task). They also provided more behavioral support in the high-need condition, as evidenced by an increase in the number of times they checked a computer monitor for messages from their partner and by an increased willingness to switch tasks with their partner (volunteering to give the speech in place of their partner). In contrast, anxious caregivers showed clear evidence of being out of sync with their partner's needs; they failed to increase their support behavior in response to their partner's distress, and showed high levels of empathy, mental distraction, and partner focus regardless of their partner's level of need (a pattern of overinvolvement). Anxious caregivers also reported more negative affect and more negative dispositional attributions about their partner (perceiving their partner as weak and emotionally unstable) in the high-need condition than in the low-need condition, perhaps because they depend heavily on their partners as a source of their own care and therefore felt threatened when their partner was emotionally needy and required more care. Finally, avoidant caregivers showed a clear pattern of relative neglect; regardless of their partner's level of need, they were less behaviorally supportive and reported less emotional empathy, less partner focus, and less mental distraction. We replicated this basic pattern of findings in a second study using a sample of married couples and a slightly modified procedure in which we measured (rather than manipulated) the partner's level of speech anxiety.

Taken together, these studies provide clear evidence that secure individuals are more sensitive to the needs of others and better able to modulate their cognitive, emotional, and behavioral resources in ways that are contingent on their partner's expression of distress. In contrast, avoidant caregivers are relatively neglectful and unmotivated to provide support, whereas anxious caregivers are motivated to provide care but have difficulty modulating their cognitive, emotional, and behavioral responses in accordance with their partner's needs.

Mechanisms Explaining Individual Differences in Caregiving

In addition to identifying individual differences in patterns of caregiving, we have been interested in identifying the specific mechanisms that explain these differences (see Figure 19.2, Paths a–c). We began by investigating a variety of skills (empathic abilities, support knowledge), resources (chronic self-focus), motivational factors (communal orientation, specific motivations for caring), and relationship features (commitment, closeness, trust) that may mediate attachment differences in self-reported caregiving patterns in couples (Feeney & Collins, 2001). Results of mediation analyses indicated that avoidant caregivers were unresponsive and controlling because they lacked knowledge about how to support others, had a weak prosocial orientation toward others, lacked emotional closeness and interdependence with their partner, and had low trust in their partner. Other analyses revealed that anxious caregivers were overinvolved and controlling because they had a high sense of relationship interdependence but lacked trust in their partner's love and commitment and had relatively selfish motives for caring for their partner.

Motivations for Caregiving

We have argued that individuals with different attachment styles will develop different motives for taking care of their partners (see Figure 19.2, Path a) and that these motives will influence their caregiving efforts (see Figure 19.2, Path d). To test these assumptions, we developed a Motivations for Caregiving Questionnaire that measures altruistic and egoistic reasons for providing (or not providing) help and support to a romantic partner

(Feeney & Collins, 2003; see also Feeney & Collins, 2001). Using this measure, we found that secure individuals (those low in avoidance and anxiety) were more likely to help their partners for altruistic reasons and less likely to help for egoistic reasons. In contrast, avoidant individuals helped their partners for relatively egoistic reasons (e.g., because they felt obligated to help and wanted to avoid sanctions for not helping, because they expected to get something explicit in return), whereas anxious individuals helped for both egoistic and altruistic reasons (e.g., because they felt concern for their partner's welfare, but also because they wanted to gain their partner's love or make their partner dependent on them). This pattern may explain why anxious individuals tend to express a mixture of effective and ineffective caregiving behaviors in their close relationships. Although they have been shown to be warm, approachable, and empathic toward others (perhaps driven by their altruistic concerns for the welfare of others), they have also been shown to be overinvolved and sometimes controlling in their caregiving efforts (perhaps driven by their desire to be appreciated by others and to increase their partner's dependence).

Consistent with these ideas, this study also demonstrated that egoistic and altruistic motives predicted the quality of support that was provided in the relationship (see Figure 19.2, Path d). For example, individuals who endorsed altruistic motives for helping their partner were more likely to have a responsive caregiving style, whereas those who endorsed egoistic motives were more likely to have an unresponsive or overinvolved caregiving style. Taken together, these results suggest that the underlying motives that people have for helping play a vital role in determining the quality of care that is provided.

IMPLICATIONS OF CAREGIVING FOR HEALTH, WELL-BEING, AND RELATIONSHIP FUNCTIONING

Thus far, this chapter has focused on the factors that facilitate or impede effective caregiving in couples, but attachment theory also highlights the benefits of responsive care for individual health and well-being, and for relationship functioning. Just as a secure parent–child relationship provides an optimal environment for children to thrive, a secure and caring intimate relationship in adulthood should provide the optimal environment for men and women to thrive. When partners provide responsive support to one another in times of adversity, not only do they foster an environment of kindness and goodwill in their relationship, they also provide one another with diagnostic evidence of their love and commitment. It is precisely because individuals typically need support when they are weakest and most vulnerable (when their social capital is at its lowest) that social support interactions provide such a critical testing ground for judging their partner's intrinsic motivation to care for them (Collins & Feeney, 2004). Thus, a sense of felt security in adult relationships should depend in large part on the degree to which individuals feel confident that their partner will be available and responsive when needed.

On the basis of these assumptions, another goal of our research has been to understand the importance of responsive caregiving for the development and maintenance of secure and satisfying relationships in adulthood, as well as in the health and emotional well-being of couple members. In several studies, we have found that small acts of caring (or neglect) can have immediate effects on well-being and relationship functioning. For example, in our daily diary study (Collins & Feeney, 2005), both men and women felt happier and more secure in their relationship (more loved and valued) on days when their partner provided more caring support, and these positive effects lingered the following day. Likewise, in our observational study of couples in which one partner disclosed a personal worry to the other, we found that support recipients experienced immediate improvements in emotional well-being (increases in positive mood) when their partner provided more responsive support (Collins & Feeney, 2000). In a more recent study (Collins et al., 2008), we found that spouses felt more secure in their marriage (more confident of their partner's love and commitment) when they perceived their partner as a responsive caregiver and support provider. In addition, when spouses actually received more responsive support from their partner after a stressful speech task (as assessed through self-report and observational coding), they felt more secure immediately after the interaction (i.e., calmer, more secure, and more valued and accepted by the partner).

In addition to these correlational studies, two experimental studies showed that caring support can have immediate effects on emotional well-being and relationship functioning. In one study, we created a frightening cliff-walking task for one member of each couple in an immersive virtual environment and then experimentally manipulated the partner's attentiveness and emotional support in the virtual world (Kane, McCall, Collins, & Blascovich, 2008). Relative to those with an inattentive/neglectful partner, those with an attentive partner reported feeling more loved and valued by their partner and less anxious during their cliff-walking task. In addition, those who had been exposed to an inattentive/neglectful partner kept greater physical distance between themselves and their partner during a subsequent, unrelated task in the virtual world. These findings suggest that responsive support can reduce stress and foster relationship security, and that unresponsiveness can erode physical and emotional closeness between partners. In another study, we manipulated the quality of support given by romantic partners by having them send prewritten messages before and after their partner participated in a stressful speech task (Guichard & Collins, 2008). Support recipients who received high support were in a better mood after their speech had higher state self-esteem and felt more satisfied with their relationship compared with those who received low support (or no support). When support recipients were then given a chance to help their partners on a subsequent task, those who had received high support were more willing to help in return. These findings indicate that caring support can lead to immediate improvements in well-being and relationship satisfaction and that small acts of kindness can foster an environment of reciprocal compassion and helping.

CONCLUSION

The purpose of this chapter was to review theory and research on social support and caregiving in close relationships from an attachment theoretical perspective. Although we focused exclusively on caregiving behavior in couples, these findings suggest broader implications of attachment theory for understanding other forms of prosocial behavior within other kinds of relationships. For example, as discussed by Shaver et al. (chap. 4, this volume), attachment theory is useful for understanding prosocial behavior toward strangers and for identifying factors that may reduce discrimination and intergroup hostility. As our review attachment and caregiving processes are deeply intertwined, and understanding how people care for others (in the broadest sense) requires that researchers also understand how caregivers regulate their own attachment needs. We hope that this chapter helps to build bridges with other work on prosocial behavior, as discussed in other chapters in this volume, and moves the field toward more refined and integrative theoretical models.

REFERENCES

Ainsworth, M., Blehar, M., Waters, E., & Wall, S. (1978). *Patterns of attachment: A psychological study of the Strange Situation.* Hillsdale, NJ: Erlbaum.

Bartholomew, K., & Horowitz, L. M. (1991). Attachment styles among young adults: A test of a four-category model. *Journal of Personality and Social Psychology, 61,* 226–244.

Batson, C. D., Early, S., & Salvarani, G. (1997). Perspective taking: Imagining how another feels versus imagining how you would feel. *Personality and Social Psychology Bulletin, 23,* 751–758.

Bowlby, J. (1973). *Attachment and loss: Vol. 2. Separation.* New York: Basic Books.

Bowlby, J. (1982). *Attachment and loss: Vol. 1. Attachment* (2nd ed.). New York: Basic Books.

Bowlby, J. (1988). *A secure base.* New York: Basic Books.

Bretherton, I. (1985). Attachment theory: Retrospect and prospect. *Monographs of the Society for Research in Child Development, 50*(1-2, Serial No. 209), 3–35.

Cassidy, J. (1994). Emotion regulation: Influences of attachment relationships. *Monographs of the Society for Research in Child Development*, 59(2–3), 228–283.

Clark, M. S., Graham, S. M., Williams, E., & Lemay, E. P. (2008). Understanding relational focus of attention may help us understand relational phenomena. In J. P. Forgas & J. Fitness (Eds.), *Social relationships: Cognitive, affective, and motivational processes* (pp. 131–146). New York: Psychology Press.

Collins, N. L., & Feeney, B. C. (2000). A safe haven: An attachment theory perspective on support-seeking and caregiving in intimate relationships. *Journal of Personality and Social Psychology*, *78*, 1053–1073.

Collins, N. L., & Feeney, B. C. (2004). An attachment theory perspective on closeness and intimacy: Normative processes and individual differences. In D. Mashek & A. Aron (Eds.), *Handbook of Closeness and Intimacy* (pp. 163–187). Mahwah, NJ: Erlbaum.

Collins, N. L., & Feeney, B. C. (2005, May). *Attachment processes in intimate relationships: Support-seeking and caregiving behavior in daily interaction*. Paper presented at the meeting of the American Psychological Society, Los Angeles, CA.

Collins, N. L., Ford, M. B., Guichard, A. C., Kane, H. S., & Feeney, B. C. (2008). *Responding to need in intimate relationships: Cognitive, emotional, and behavioral responses to partner distress*. Unpublished manuscript, University of California, Santa Barbara.

Collins, N. L., Guichard, A., Ford, M., & Feeney, B. (2006). Responding to need in intimate relationships: Normative processes and individual differences. In M. Mikulincer & G. Goodman (Eds.), *Dynamics of romantic love: Attachment, caregiving, and sex* (pp. 149–189). New York: Guilford Press.

Eisenberg, N., Hofer, C., & Vaughan, J. (2007). Effortful control and its socioemotional consequences. In J. Gross (Ed.), *Handbook of emotion regulation* (pp. 287–306). New York: Guilford Press.

Feeney, B. C., & Collins, N. L. (2001). Predictors of caregiving in adult intimate relationships: An attachment theoretical perspective. *Journal of Personality and Social Psychology*, *80*, 972–994.

Feeney, B. C., & Collins, N. L. (2003). Motivations for caregiving in adult intimate relationships: Influences on caregiving behavior and relationship functioning. *Personality and Social Psychology Bulletin*, *29*, 950–968.

Feeney, B. C., & Collins, N. L. (2004). Interpersonal safe haven and secure base caregiving processes in adulthood. In W. S. Rholes & J. A. Simpson (Eds.), *Adult attachment: Theory, research, and clinical implications* (pp. 300–338). New York: Guilford Press.

George, C., & Solomon, J. (2008). The caregiving system: A behavioral systems approach to parenting. In J. Cassidy & P. R. Shaver (Eds.), *Handbook of attachment: Theory, research, and clinical applications* (2nd ed., pp. 833–836). New York: Guilford Press.

Gleason, M. E. J., Iida, M., Shrout, P. E., & Bolger, N. (2008). Receiving support as a mixed blessing: Evidence for dual effects of support on psychological outcomes. *Journal of Personality and Social Psychology*, *94*, 824–838.

Guichard, A., & Collins, N. (2008, February). *The influence of social support and attachment style on performance, self-evaluations, and interpersonal behaviors.* Poster presented at the meeting of the Society for Personality and Social Psychology, Albuquerque, NM.

Hesse, E. (2008). The Adult Attachment Interview: Protocol, method of analysis, and empirical studies. In J. Cassidy & P. R. Shaver (Eds.), *Handbook of attachment: Theory, research, and clinical applications* (2nd ed., pp. 552–598). New York: Guilford Press.

Kane, H. S., Jaremka, L. M., Guichard, A. C., Ford, M. B., Collins, N. L., & Feeney, B. C. (2007). Feeling supported and feeling satisfied: How one partner's attachment style predicts the other partner's relationship experiences. *Journal of Social and Personal Relationships, 24,* 535–555.

Kane, H., McCall, C., Collins, N., & Blascovich, J. (2008, February). *The effects of social support from a significant other in an immersive virtual environment.* Poster presented at the meeting of the Society for Personality and Social Psychology, Albuquerque, NM.

Kobak, R. R., & Sceery, A. (1988). Attachment in late adolescence: Working models, affect regulation, and perception of self and others. *Child Development, 59,* 135–146.

Kunce, L. J., & Shaver, P. R. (1994). An attachment-theoretical approach to caregiving in romantic relationships. In K. Bartholomew & D. Perlman (Eds.), *Advances in personal relationships: Vol. 5. Attachment processes in adulthood* (pp. 205–237). London: Jessica Kingsley.

Mikulincer, M., & Shaver, P. R. (2007). *Attachment in adulthood: Structure, dynamics, and change.* New York: Guilford Press.

Mikulincer, M., Shaver, P. R., Gillath, O., & Nitzberg, R. E. (2005). Attachment, caregiving, and altruism: Boosting attachment security increases compassion and helping. *Journal of Personality and Social Psychology,* 89, 817–839.

Mills, J., Clark, M. S., Ford, T. E., & Johnson, M. (2004). Measurement of communal strength. *Personal Relationships, 11,* 213–230.

Murray, S. L., Holmes, J. G., & Collins, N. L. (2006). Optimizing assurance: The risk regulation system in relationships. *Psychological Bulletin, 132,* 641–666.

Nadler, A. (1991). Help-seeking behavior: Psychological costs and instrumental benefits. In M. S. Clark (Ed.), *Review of personality and social psychology: Vol. 12. Prosocial behavior* (pp. 290–311). Newbury Park, CA: Sage.

Noller, P. (2006). Nonverbal communication in close relationships. In V. Manusov & M. L. Patterson (Eds.), *The Sage handbook of nonverbal communication* (pp. 403–420). Thousand Oaks, CA: Sage Publications.

Reis, H. T., & Patrick, B. C. (1996). Attachment and intimacy: Component processes. In E. T. Higgins, & A. W. Kruglanski (Eds.), *Social psychology: Handbook of basic principles* (pp. 523–563). New York: Guilford Press.

Rholes, W. S., Simpson, J. A., & Orina, M. M. (1999). Attachment and anger in an anxiety-provoking situation. *Journal of Personality and Social Psychology, 76,* 940–957.

Rini, C., Dunkel-Schetter, C., Hoblel, C. J., Glynn, L. M., & Sandman, C. A. (2006). Effective social support: Antecedents and consequences of partner support during pregnancy. *Personal Relationships, 13*, 207–229.

Simpson, J. A., Rholes, W. S., & Nelligan, J. S. (1992). Support seeking and support giving within couples in an anxiety-provoking situation: The role of attachment styles. *Journal of Personality and Social Psychology, 62*, 434–446.

Vinokur, A. D., Price, R. H., & Caplan, R. D. (1996). Hard times and hurtful partners: How financial strain affects depression and relationship satisfaction of employed persons and their spouses. *Journal of Personality and Social Psychology, 71*, 166–179.

Wood, J. V., Saltzberg, J. A., & Goldsamt, L. A. (1990). Does affect induce self-focused attention? *Journal of Personality and Social Psychology, 58*, 899–908.

V

PROSOCIAL BEHAVIOR AT THE GROUP AND SOCIETAL LEVELS

20

EMPATHY AND INTERGROUP RELATIONS

JOHN F. DOVIDIO, JAMES D. JOHNSON, SAMUEL L. GAERTNER,
ADAM R. PEARSON, TAMAR SAGUY, AND LESLIE ASHBURN-NARDO

Empathy has received increasing empirical attention in the study of intergroup relations. Much of this research has focused on the potential of interventions that generate empathy for improving intergroup attitudes and reducing intergroup bias. Specifically, this work typically explores how empathy mediates the effects of various manipulations, such as direct instructions to imagine how an outgroup member feels on participants' attitudes toward the outgroup as a whole. In this chapter, we offer complementary perspectives on the role of empathy in intergroup relations. In addition, we examine other potential roles of empathy in intergroup relations, considering the direct impact of intergroup empathy on behavior and how intergroup attitudes can moderate the arousal of empathy and its subsequent intergroup impact.

We consider three perspectives on the relations among empathy, intergroup attitudes, and group membership. Our goal is not to test these as com-

Preparation of this chapter was supported by NSF Grant #BCS-0613218 awarded to the first and third authors.

peting models, but rather to explore the range of ways empathy can play an important role in intergroup relations. In addition, we acknowledge that many alternative models are not only possible but also likely. All three of our models, however, share a common feature. In each, we hypothesize that empathy, specifically in the form of an other-oriented emotion (empathic concern; see chap. 1, this volume) that is associated with altruistic motivation, is a proximal predictor of intergroup orientations. That is, empathy is a significant mediator by which different social factors, such as intergroup contact and perceptions of common identity, shape intergroup attitudes and behavior.

There are several reasons why we propose that empathy is likely to play a role in intergroup behavior, potentially beyond any mediating effect on intergroup attitudes. First, intergroup attitudes are only a moderate predictor of intergroup discrimination (Dovidio, Brigham, Johnson, & Gaertner, 1996). Also, interventions, such as intergroup contact, which robustly improve intergroup attitudes, frequently do not translate into actual support for policies that when implemented would promote equality between groups (Dixon, Durrheim, & Tredoux, 2005). Second, intergroup behavior is motivated substantially by affective reactions. As Weiner (1980) observed, "Attributions guide our feelings, but emotional reactions provide the motor and direction for behavior" (p. 186). And third, empathy has unique interpersonal and thus, potentially, intergroup qualities. At the interpersonal level, empathizing with a member of the group may produce a "self-other merging" (Cialdini, Brown, Lewis, Luce, & Neuberg, 1997; see also chap. 6, this volume), in which the member becomes included more fully as part of his or her self-representation. To the extent that one's representations of ingroup members and one's self-representation are also closely related (Smith & Henry, 1996), these more positive orientations may generalize to the group as a whole.

Here, we explore three models that explicate the role of empathy as a mediator of intergroup behavior and its relation to intergroup attitudes. Model 1 depicts the arousal of empathic concern (e.g., the experience of sympathy, compassion, concern) as a mediator of the effect of various bias interventions, such as perspective-taking manipulations (Batson et al., 1997), on reductions of intergroup bias. In the second model, we explore how empathic concern can influence intergroup behavior over and above the influence of attitudes. In this section, we emphasize the fundamental role of social categorization in this process and examine both prosocial and punitive behavior within and across group boundaries. Finally, we explore a third model in which intergroup attitudes moderate the effects of positive and negative intergroup exposure on empathy and subsequent intergroup prosocial behavior.

We emphasize that we do not present these as competing models. We acknowledge that intergroup relations are very complex and are shaped by a number of different forces over time. Therefore, we suggest and present evidence that each of these models may be correct, reflecting different facets of intergroup relations. Each of these approaches, however, converges on a central conclusion: Empathy can substantially shape intergroup responses; thus, it is an important factor to consider in interventions and programs designed to improve intergroup relations and promote lasting harmony.

BIAS INTERVENTIONS, EMPATHY, AND INTERGROUP ATTITUDES

We begin by considering Model 1 in Figure 20.1, which represents one of the more established frameworks for studying empathy and intergroup relations, a framework that emphasizes the causal role of empathy in prejudice reduction (Batson et al., 1997). Several studies provide converging evidence that interventions designed to influence the perspective that people adopt and their tendency to empathize with a member of another group can substantially affect intergroup attitudes. Finlay and Stephan (2000), for instance, varied whether participants adopted an empathic or an objective perspective while they read a series of short essays ostensibly written by Black college students describing their personal experiences with discrimination (e.g., being falsely accused of wrongdoing, being denied check-writing privileges). This study revealed that Whites who were instructed to empathize with the Black person (by imagining either how the writer of the essay would feel or how they themselves would feel in such a situation) showed lower levels of bias in their evaluations of Whites versus Blacks compared with those in a control condition who were instructed to attend objectively to the details of the essay.

Other research has more directly illuminated the mediating role of empathy in this process. In a study by Batson and colleagues (1997), participants who were instructed to focus on how a target person felt (rather than on facts about the person's problem) while listening to an interview with a member of a stigmatized group subsequently exhibited more positive attitudes toward the target person's group (people suffering from AIDS, homeless people, or convicted murderers). In other work, Batson, Chang, Orr, and Rowland (2002) showed that focusing on a particular group member's feelings, in this case a drug addict's feelings as he described his misfortunes (how he became addicted, got arrested, and spent time in prison), elicited higher levels of empathic concern (e.g., feeling sympathetic) than did focusing on the facts of the person's situation. Stronger feelings of empathic concern, in turn, increased caring about the person's welfare, which then mediated improved attitudes toward the group as a whole.

Vescio, Sechrist, and Paolucci (2003) also used the Batson et al. (1997) perspective-taking manipulation in a study in which White participants listened to an interview of a Black man who displayed stereotype-confirming or

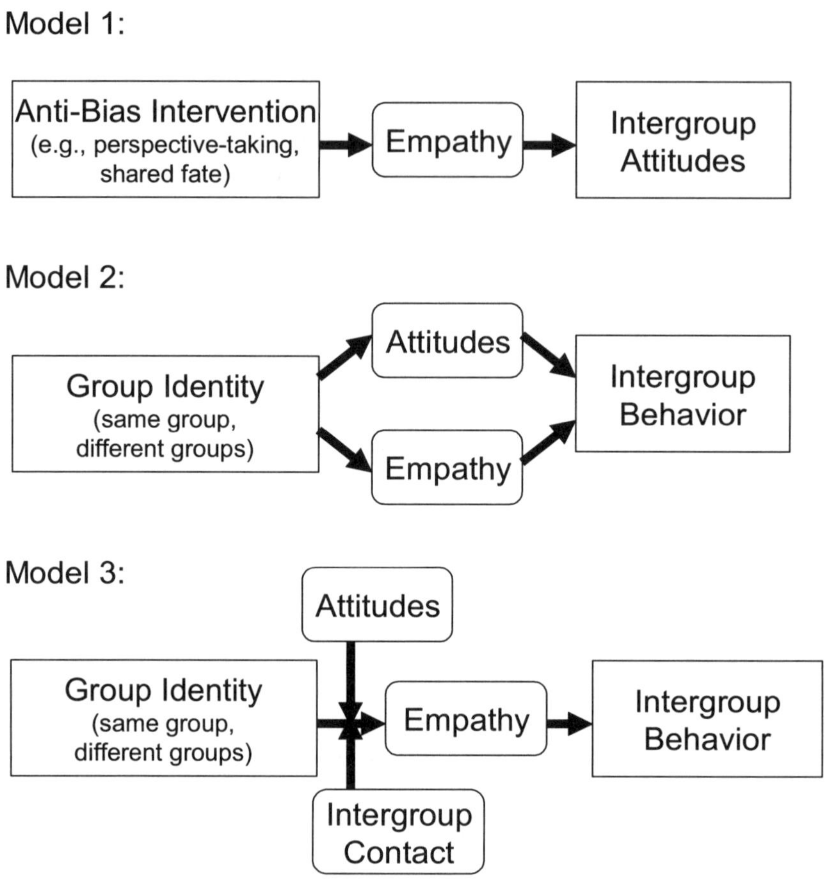

Figure 20.1. Three models of the relations among identity, empathy, attitudes, and intergroup behavior.

-disconfirming attributes while discussing challenges associated with being Black. These researchers similarly found that participants who focused on how the interviewee felt subsequently reported more positive attitudes toward Blacks as a group than did those who adopted an objective perspective and focused on the factual information while listening to the interview, regardless of whether the person exhibited stereotypic or nonstereotypic traits. It is important that the difference in racial attitudes among empathy-focused versus objectively focused participants was mediated by feelings of empathic concern for the interviewee. Dovidio et al. (2004, Study 1) further found that instructing Whites to take the perspective of victims (versus being objective) promoted feelings of injustice in response to viewing acts of racial discrimination, which subsequently mediated reductions in racial bias.

In a subsequent study (Dovidio et al., 2004, Study 2), we found that an indirect intervention designed to amplify the salience of a common racial identity produced parallel results. Whites who were led to believe that both Blacks and Whites were the common enemy of terrorists were more sensitive to injustice while viewing racially discriminatory acts than were those who were led to believe that Whites were the primary targets of terrorism, and these greater feelings of injustice again mediated a decrease in prejudice toward Blacks.

Taken together, these studies offer convergent evidence that taking the perspective of a member of another group can improve even well-crystallized intergroup attitudes, such as Whites' attitudes toward Blacks in the United States. Moreover, a range of empathically motivated reactions, such as feelings of compassion (Batson et al., 1997) or outrage at injustice (Dovidio et al., 2004), have been shown to critically mediate this process of prejudice reduction.

Whereas the approach represented in Model 1 emphasizes the importance of interpersonal processes (feeling empathy for another individual) on intergroup attitudes, the second perspective, which we discuss in the following section, considers group-level processes more explicitly. Specifically, Model 2 in Figure 20.1 proposes that group membership can influence both intergroup attitudes and empathy, and that these two factors can independently influence intergroup responses.

FROM GROUP IDENTITY TO INTERGROUP BEHAVIOR: EMPATHY AND ATTITUDES

The primary approach we have used, the common ingroup identity model (Gaertner & Dovidio, 2000), draws on the theoretical foundations of social identity theory (Tajfel & Turner, 1979). This strategy emphasizes the process of recategorization, in which the goal is to reduce bias by systematically altering the perception of intergroup boundaries, redefining who is conceived of as an ingroup member. If members of different groups are induced to conceive of themselves as a single superordinate group rather than as two separate groups, attitudes toward former outgroup members are expected to become more positive through processes involving pro—ingroup bias, thereby reducing intergroup bias (see Gaertner & Dovidio, 2000; chap. 10, this volume). A common ingroup identity can be achieved by increasing the salience of existing superordinate memberships (e.g., a school, a company, a nation) or by introducing factors perceived to be shared by different groups (e.g., common goals or fate).

Considerable empirical support has been obtained for the common ingroup identity model in laboratory and field experiments involving temporary and enduring groups (see Gaertner & Dovidio, 2000). For example, with respect to prosocial behavior, in one study (Dovidio et al., 1997) we brought two laboratory-formed minimal groups into contact under conditions that were designed to foster recategorization as one group (e.g., integrated seating, same-colored T-shirts) or to maintain their identities as different groups (e.g., segregated seating, different-colored T-shirts). Later in the study, in our examination of helping, participants were escorted to separate rooms and informed that they would be listening to an audiotape of one of the previous participants in the study. The person on the tape was presented as either a member of participants' original artificial subgroup category (e.g., a trait "overestimator" vs. "underestimator") or a member of the other group. In the audiotape, the person mentioned that she was unable to complete an important project because of an illness. At the conclusion of the session, participants were given an opportunity to help the person in need by posting advertisements to recruit participants for the other person's project.

The results provided support for the facilitating role of recategorization in intergroup helping. As expected, in the two-group condition, which reinforced the original group memberships, participants were more helpful (i.e., agreed to distribute more ads for the other person) toward an ingroup than an outgroup member. In the one-group condition, in contrast, no bias against initial outgroup members emerged.

Evidence of the effectiveness of establishing a common group identity for promoting intergroup helping has also been obtained outside of the laboratory. In a field experiment (Nier, Gaertner, Dovidio, Banker, & Ward, 2001, Study 2) conducted at the University of Delaware football stadium prior to a game between the University of Delaware and Westchester State University, Black and White interviewers wearing either a University of Delaware or a Westchester State hat approached White fans from both universities just before they entered the stadium. These fans were asked whether they would be willing to be interviewed about their food preferences. We found that whereas White fans were significantly more likely to help a Black interviewer who shared their university affiliation than a Black interviewer ostensibly from the other university (59% vs. 36%), they showed no significant difference in their likelihood of helping a White interviewer ostensibly from their own (44%) or a rival university (37%). These findings, together with those of the preceding study, offer converging support for the idea that outgroup members will be treated more favorably when they are perceived as members of a common ingroup.

However, these studies do not directly illuminate the processes—specifically, the potential effect of intergroup attitudes and empathic concern—that mediate the effect of recategorization on intergroup prosocial behavior. Thus, we conducted another experiment in which we manipulated the salience of same- or different-group membership and tested both attitudes and empathic concern as possible mediators of the link between recategorization and intergroup prosocial behavior.

In this experiment, White college students from Colgate University viewed a videotape that portrayed an interview with a Black male student (actually a confederate), with whom they anticipated interacting in a subsequent session. After a series of responses to questions designed to create a positive impression of the confederate, the interviewer inquired about how the confederate viewed himself in general. The confederate's response was systematically constructed to reflect either a common group membership ("I see myself primarily as a Colgate student") or different group membership ("I see myself primarily as a Black person"). The confederate then discussed a serious illness (pneumonia) that made him fall behind schedule in his senior project, which he needed to complete for graduation. The confederate explained that he needed students to complete questionnaires to help him finish the project. After the experimental session was allegedly concluded, a measure of helping behavior was obtained. The experimenter casually mentioned that the professor in charge of this study had asked her to give a sealed envelope to participants. Inside the envelope was a note from the professor informing participants that a letter was attached containing a request for their help but stressing that participants were not obligated to comply with this request. The letter was a request from the Black confederate who had been interviewed in the video to help distribute posters across campus for his project. The number of posters that participants agreed to distribute was our primary measure of helping. Additional dependent measures in the study included attitudes toward the confederate and empathic concern aroused by the person's problem. We expected that White participants would have more positive attitudes, respond with greater empathic concern, and be more helpful when the confederate expressed a common group identity (Colgate) than a different group identity (Black; see Dovidio et al., 1997).

The results of this study were generally consistent with our hypotheses. Responses were much more positive in the one-group condition than in the two-group condition for all three measures: attitudes, empathic concern, and helping. However, the results of mediation analyses revealed that whereas empathic concern significantly mediated the effect of a common group representation (compared with a different group representation) on helping, attitudes toward the confederate showed no significant mediating effect on helping behavior. These results not only replicate and extend our earlier work on recategorization and prosocial behavior but also directly illuminate underlying mechanisms. That is, consistent with the research of Stürmer, Snyder, and Omoto (2005), prosocial behavior toward others categorized as members of one's ingroup is motivated more strongly by feelings of empathy than by favorable attitudes.

Although we have focused on the roles of shared identity and empathy in promoting more direct forms of helping, to the extent that empathy sensitizes people to the needs of others and to concerns about injustice (Dovidio et al., 2004), it may also promote punitiveness toward individuals who are seen as unjustly causing the suffering of others. To examine this possibility, Pearson and Dovidio (2008) investigated how individual differences in empathy can influence the treatment of outgroup members who exhibit morally reprehensible behavior. In particular, we hypothesized that when people learned of the unjust harming of another (e.g., a violent assault) by an outgroup member, those who are characteristically higher in empathic concern (the Empathic Concern subscale of the Davis, 1983, Interpersonal Reactivity Index) would show more punitive reactions and report less empathic concern for the perpetrator than did those lower in trait empathy.

In this study, participants were college students who indicated affiliation with one of two rival major league baseball teams, the Boston Red Sox or the New York Yankees, in an ostensibly unrelated prior study. Data were collected at a large East Coast university uniquely situated midway between New York and Boston at the start of the 2005 American League play-off series. Participants read a newspaper article modeled after real police reports that described an assault on a male victim by a fan near Fenway Park in Boston or near Yankee Stadium in New York. The article depicted the perpetrator of the assault as a fan of the participants' rival team (outgroup perpetrator), describing the assailant as having just come from a game wearing either Red Sox or Yankees apparel, depending on whether participants had previously self-identified as Yankees or Red Sox fans, respectively. In all versions of the article, the victim was described as unidentified with either sports team (wearing generic clothing with no visible sports team affiliation). To manipulate the ostensible justification for the attack, in one version of the article the incident was described as having been provoked and potentially justified (provocation condition). Witnesses were reported to have seen the victim laugh at the assailant and shout an obscenity before being assaulted. In the other version of the article (no-provocation condition), the attack was portrayed as morally unjustified; no such instigating context was mentioned. The primary dependent measures were empathic concern (e.g., compassion, sympathy) for the victim and perpetrator of the crime, as well as recommendations for the length of prison sentence the perpetrator should serve.

The results largely confirmed our predictions. Although no main effect of provocation condition on length of sentence was found, the predicted Trait Empathy × Provocation interaction was obtained. Whereas participants lower (i.e., −1 *SD*) in empathic concern showed no significant difference in sentencing recommendations between the unprovoked and provoked conditions, those higher (+1 *SD*) in empathic concern recommended significantly longer sentences when the attack was described as unprovoked than when it could be justified by provocation. Furthermore, lack of empathy for the perpetrator, but not empathy for the victim, was found to mediate this effect. Whereas participants low in trait empathy reported no difference in empathy for the perpetrator as a function of condition, those higher in trait empathy reported significantly less empathy for the perpetrator when the attack was described as unprovoked versus provoked, and this differential empathic response mediated sentencing recommendations.

Together, these findings suggest a provocative new direction for intergroup empathy research. Whereas much of the research on empathy and intergroup responses has focused on positive behaviors, such as reductions in prejudice and the promotion of prosocial actions, this latter study indicates that empathic concern may also be important for "empathic punitiveness." Furthermore, in subsequent work, we have found that this punitiveness occurs uniquely for assailants who are members of an outgroup, but not for ingroup assailants (Pearson & Dovidio, 2008), suggesting that shared group membership may confer an empathic advantage by buffering sensitivity to injustice committed by a member of one's ingroup. Thus, identifying who is "out" of one's group may be as critical a condition for empathic punitiveness as being an ingroup member is for empathically motivated prosocial behavior (Stürmer et al., 2005).

In the next section, we consider an alternative perspective on the relationship between empathy and intergroup attitudes. Namely, we examine how preexisting intergroup attitudes can moderate the consequences of exposure to members of another group, affecting empathy and subsequent behavior toward the outgroup (see Figure 20.1, Model 3). This model differs notably from Model 2 by treating prior intergroup attitudes and the nature of intergroup encounters as moderators of empathic responses toward outgroup members.

MODERATORS OF EMPATHIC RESPONSES: ATTITUDES AND CONTEXT

In two studies, we investigated the impact of positive, negative, or neutral interracial contact on subsequent empathic concern and responsiveness to the needs of an outgroup member. Although intergroup contact is generally effective for improving intergroup attitudes (Pettigrew & Tropp, 2006), the nature of that contact can substantially moderate its effect. In particular, whereas positive intergroup contact has been shown to reduce intergroup bias, contact resulting in negative outcomes can exacerbate bias. Our focus in the present studies was on the responses of Blacks, a group that reports frequent experiences with prejudice, to Whites. In this research, in contrast to the perspectives offered by the two models of intergroup empathy reviewed in previous sections, we considered the potential moderating role of intergroup attitudes in this process. In particular, we examined the interactive effects of the nature of outgroup exposure—positive, negative, or neutral—and individual differences in Blacks' discriminatory expectations of Whites (Johnson & Lecci, 2003) on prosocial responding.

Blacks often anticipate discrimination from Whites (Johnson & Lecci, 2003; Mendoza-Denton, Downey, Purdie, Davis, & Pietrzak, 2002) and typically try to avoid situations in which they may experience stigma. Johnson and Lecci (2003), however, demonstrated individual differences in these expectations among Blacks, reflected in responses on the Ingroup-Directed Stigmatization and Discriminatory Expectations Scale (e.g., "I believe that most Whites would discriminate against Blacks if they could get away with it"; Johnson & Lecci, 2003). We hypothesized that individual differences in Blacks' discriminatory expectations of Whites would influence the impact of exposure to behavior by a White individual that was racially positive (a strong statement opposing bias), negative (a statement opposing affirmative action and supporting symbols that Blacks find offensive), or neutral (and unrelated to race) on supportive and prosocial responses to other Whites.

In the first of the pair of studies conducted to test this hypothesis (Johnson, Ashburn-Nardo, Spicer, & Dovidio, 2008), Black participants who had been pretested on the Ingroup-Directed Stigmatization and Discriminatory Expectations Scale read an essay ostensibly written by a White male college student for a study described as investigating perceptions of student writing quality. Participants were randomly assigned to one of three conditions (negative, neutral, positive). In the negative exposure condition, participants read an essay in which the writer indicated support for the Confederate flag, Southern culture, and antiaffirmative action beliefs. In the positive exposure condition, the essay indicated opposition to the display of the Confederate flag, Southern culture, or any negative beliefs regarding Blacks. In the neutral (control) condition, the essay discussed the role of student government at 4-year universities. Thus, our research involved exposure to, but not direct personal contact with, an outgroup member.

As part of an ostensibly unrelated study described as assessing responses to "real life" stories, participants later read about the plight of a pregnant White female college student ("Susan") who was seeking a late semester withdrawal from all of her courses because of pregnancy. Participants were presented with excerpts of a letter from Susan to the dean explaining her situation and describing the pain, suffering, and confusion she had endured as a result of the pregnancy. Finally, participants reported their feelings of empathic concern (e.g., sympathy, compassion) for Susan and their support for granting her a withdrawal.

We predicted that the effects of outgroup exposure on empathic concern and prosocial attitudes would depend on participants' discriminatory expectations. For participants who were low in discriminatory expectations, we anticipated that negative exposure would decrease and positive exposure would increase empathic concern and prosocial attitudes, relative to the neutral (control) condition. We predicted a similar pattern for participants who were high in discriminatory expectations—except in the positive exposure condition. For these participants, the benefits of positive exposure were expected to be attenuated. Because such behavior is inconsistent with these participants' strong discriminatory expectations, we predicted that this information would be discounted and, thus, would only minimally influence

Blacks' intergroup orientations. As in prior research (see chap. 1, this volume), we further anticipated that prosocial attitudes toward the White person in need would be mediated by empathic concern.

The results were supportive of our predictions. Compared with the control condition, participants who were low in discriminatory expectations responded with greater support for Susan following positive exposure and with less support following negative exposure. For Black participants who had strong discriminatory expectations of Whites, negative exposure yielded less support for granting the White student's request for withdrawal, and positive exposure had no effect on such support, relative to the control condition. These findings underscore the fact that even well-intentioned actions of an outgroup member toward a stigmatized target may have little impact on intergroup behavior if perceivers hold chronic negative expectations concerning the outgroup.

Furthermore, as hypothesized, empathic concern played a critical mediating role. Blacks' empathic concern for Susan, the White student in distress, paralleled the pattern of results for support, showing the same significant effects. In addition, when tests for mediated moderation were performed, controlling for empathic concern significantly reduced the Exposure × Discriminatory Expectations interaction effect on prosocial attitudes. The results of this study provide direct evidence of how differing intergroup expectations, specifically Blacks' expectations of discrimination by Whites, can critically influence empathic and prosocial responses toward outgroup members.

Although these findings are consistent with our hypotheses, other explanations are plausible. It could be the case, for example, that negative outgroup exposure, perhaps because it creates general feelings of negative affect or powerlessness, would cause Blacks to be unwilling to help any person in need, regardless of race. In a second study (Johnson et al., 2008, Study 2), we therefore investigated how discriminatory expectations and negative, positive, or neutral exposure to a White person might influence subsequent prosocial responding to a White versus a Black person in need.

As in the previous study, Black participants who varied in discriminatory expectations of Whites were exposed, using the same essays as those used in the previous experiment, to a White writer's comments showing evidence of racial bias (negative exposure), statements that opposed bias (positive exposure), or discussion of student government (racially neutral exposure). Participants then read a passage regarding the "true story" of a local college student who was the victim of a family tragedy. In this case, the essay described "Ron," a 26-year-old local college student whose parents were killed in a car accident, leaving him to raise his younger brother and sister alone. To vary Ron's perceived group membership, a photograph of the writer showing a White or Black student was included with the essay. Empathic concern was again assessed, and rather than measuring prosocial attitudes, participants' willingness to provide assistance to Ron was assessed. Specifically, participants read excerpts from a letter describing Ron's plight and were informed that the letter was to be distributed among any individuals who the participants thought might provide assistance to Ron. Participants were told that Ron needed help stuffing envelopes to distribute the letter and were asked to indicate their willingness to help by checking on a 7-point scale the number of hours they were willing to commit (ranging from 1 = *0 hours* to 7 = *6 hours*).

We hypothesized that for White targets, the results would replicate those of the previous study. However, for Black targets, the literature suggests at least two possible outcomes. On the one hand, given that outgroup exposure and discriminatory expectations are race-specific to Whites, one might predict null results when the person in need is Black. Indeed, many studies demonstrate the tendency to help others because of perceived similarity and/or shared group membership (e.g., Levine, Prosser, Evans, & Reicher, 2005) and underscore the importance of empathy for ingroup members (Stürmer et al., 2005). On the other hand, outgroup exposure—particularly when negative and presented to Blacks with higher expectations for discrimination—might increase prosocial orientations toward Black targets. For example, perceived discrimination may enhance feelings of commonality among Blacks, which, in turn, may increase prosocial behavior (Dovidio et al., 1997).

The results for prosocial commitment and empathy replicate and extend those of the previous study in which the patterns of findings for these two measures paralleled one another. For prosocial commitment, as illustrated in Figure 20.2, a significant three-way Exposure × Discriminatory Expectations × Race of the Person in Need interaction was revealed. As illustrated in the upper panel of Figure 20.2, when the person in need was White, among Black participants who reported lower discriminatory expectations, those who received negative interracial exposure volunteered significantly less time, and those who received positive exposure volunteered significantly more time than did those in the neutral exposure condition. For participants who anticipated greater discrimination from Whites, the negative exposure condition elicited less prosocial commitment than the neutral exposure condition, whereas positive exposure had no effect relative to the neutral condition. It is important to note that as in the previous study, empathic concern mediated the effects of the independent variables on prosocial commitment.

When the person in need was Black (Figure 20.2, bottom panel), prosocial commitment among Black participants who reported relatively low expectations of discrimination were unaffected by the type of interracial exposure. However, for participants who were high in discriminatory expectations, those who received negative exposure were subsequently more helpful to a Black person in need compared with those in the neutral exposure condition. For these participants, the positive exposure did not relate to prosocial commitment for an ingroup member in need. Thus, for stigmatized persons

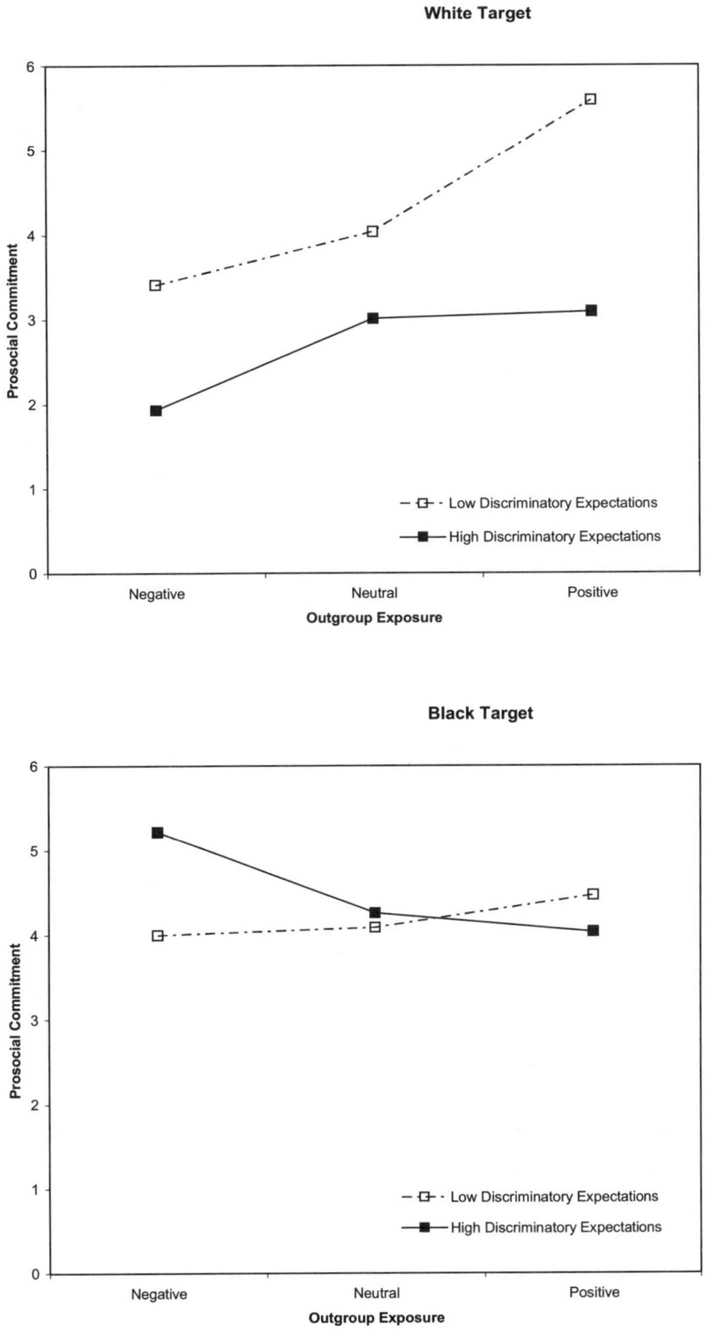

Figure 20.2. Effects of Blacks' positive, neutral, or negative exposure to one White person on prosocial support for another White person. From "The role of Blacks' discriminatory expectations in their prosocial orientations toward Whites" by J. D. Johnson, L. Ashburn-Nardo, V. Spicer, and J. F. Dovidio, 2008, *Journal of Experimental Social Psychology, 44*, 1503. Copyright 2008 by Elsevier. Reprinted with permission.

with chronic expectations of discrimination, negative contact not only decreased prosocial responses toward the outgroup but also increased prosocial responses toward the ingroup. Overall, then, this study provides further evidence of the consequential effects of Blacks' discriminatory expectations of bias and interracial exposure on their prosocial responses, but in this case not only toward Whites but toward Blacks as well.

CONCLUSION

In this chapter, we have explored ways that empathy can be aroused in intergroup contexts and the role it can play in reducing prejudice and shaping both punitive and prosocial intergroup behavior. Our goal was straightforward: to illustrate the potential range of ways empathy can be important in intergroup relations. We recognize that our models are simplified, distilling complex intergroup relations by focusing on only a few elements, and we readily acknowledge that many other models are plausible. Indeed, other chapters in this volume implicate other viable models. For instance, empathy can improve intergroup attitudes, which then produce more positive intergroup interaction (see chap. 1, this volume; see also Batson et al., 2002). In addition, future research might integrate several additional elements, suggested by other chapters in this volume, into our models. These additional facets could include (a) the relationship between empathy and intergroup forgiveness (chap. 15, this volume), (b) the potentially different impact of empathy on intergroup relations for majority and minority groups (chap. 21, this volume), and (c) the relationship of empathy to intergroup helping that produces empowerment or promotes dependency (chap. 10, this volume). We have found, for example, that among Whites who identify relatively strongly with their racial group, feelings of empathic concern relate to more support for policies of social change that will benefit Blacks, even if the change comes at some cost to Whites (Saguy & Dovidio, 2008). The significance of empathy, which is well-established in interpersonal relationships, thus holds enormous additional potential for improving intergroup relationships in stable, fundamental, and enduring ways.

REFERENCES

Batson, C. D., Chang, J., Orr, R., & Rowland, J. (2002). Empathy, attitudes, and action: Can feeling for a member of a stigmatized group motivate one to help the group? *Personality and Social Psychology Bulletin, 28*, 1656–1666.

Batson, C. D., Polycarpou, M. P., Harmon-Jones, E., Imhoff, H. J., Mitchener, E. C., Bednar, L. L., et al. (1997). Empathy and attitudes: Can feeling for a member of a stigmatized group improve feelings toward the group? *Journal of Personality and Social Psychology*, *72*, 105–118.

Cialdini, R. B., Brown, S. L., Lewis, B. P., Luce, C., & Neuberg, S. L. (1997). Reinterpreting the empathy-altruism relationship: When one into one equals oneness. *Journal of Personality and Social Psychology*, *73*, 481–494.

Davis, M. H. (1983). The effects of dispositional empathy on emotional reactions and helping: A multidimensional approach. *Journal of Personality*, *51*, 167–184.

Dixon, J. A., Durrheim, K., & Tredoux, C. (2005). Beyond the optimal strategy: A "reality check" for the contact hypothesis. *American Psychologist*, *60*, 697–711.

Dovidio, J. F., Brigham, J. C., Johnson, B. T., & Gaertner, S. L. (1996). Stereotyping, prejudice, and discrimination: Another look. In C. N. Macrae, C. Stangor, & M. Hewstone (Eds.), *Stereotypes and stereotyping* (pp. 276–319). New York: Guilford Press.

Dovidio, J. F., Gaertner, S. L., Validzic, A., Matoka, K., Johnson, B., & Frazier, S. (1997). Extending the benefits of re-categorization: Evaluations, self-disclosure and helping. *Journal of Experimental Social Psychology*, *33*, 401–420.

Dovidio, J. F., ten Vergert, M., Stewart, T. L., Gaertner, S. L., Johnson, J. D., Esses, V. M., et al. (2004). Perspective and prejudice: Antecedents and mediating mechanisms. *Personality and Social Psychology Bulletin*, *30*, 1537–1549.

Finlay, K. A., & Stephan, W. G. (2000). Improving intergroup relations: The effects of empathy on racial attitudes. *Journal of Applied Social Psychology*, *30*, 1720–1737.

Gaertner, S. L., & Dovidio, J. F. (2000). *Reducing intergroup bias: The Common Ingroup Identity Model*. Philadelphia: The Psychology Press.

Johnson, J. D., Ashburn-Nardo, L., Spicer, V., & Dovidio, J. F. (2008). The role of Blacks' discriminatory expectations in their prosocial orientations toward Whites. *Journal of Experimental Social Psychology*, *44*, 1498–1505.

Johnson, J. D., & Lecci, L. (2003). Assessing anti-White attitudes and predicting perceived racism: The Johnson-Lecci scale. *Personality and Social Psychology Bulletin*, *29*, 299–312.

Levine, M., Prosser, A., Evans, D., & Reicher, S. (2005). Identity and emergency intervention: How group membership and inclusiveness of group boundaries shape helping behavior. *Personality and Social Psychology Bulletin*, *31*, 443–453.

Mendoza-Denton, R., Downey, G., Purdie, V. J., Davis, A., & Pietrzak, J. (2002). Sensitivity to status-based rejection: Implications for African American students' college experience. *Journal of Personality and Social Psychology*, *83*, 896–918.

Nier, J. A., Gaertner, S. L., Dovidio, J. F., Banker, B. S., & Ward, C. M. (2001). Changing interracial evaluations and behavior: The effects of a common group identity. *Group Processes and Intergroup Relations*, *4*, 299–316.

Pearson, A. R., & Dovidio, J. F. (2008). [Effects of empathy for the victim and perpetrator on punishment].Unpublished raw data, Department of Psychology, Yale University, New Haven, CT.

Pettigrew, T. F., & Tropp, L. (2006). A meta-analytic test of intergroup contact theory. *Journal of Personality and Social Psychology*, *90*, 751–783.

Saguy, T., & Dovidio, J. F. (2008). [Intergroup empathy and support for social policies that benefit the outgroup]. Unpublished raw data, Department of Psychology, University of Connecticut, Storrs.

Smith, E. R., & Henry, S. (1996). An ingroup becomes part of the self: Response time evidence. *Personality and Social Psychology Bulletin*, *22*, 635–642.

Stürmer, S., Snyder, M., & Omoto, A. M. (2005). Prosocial emotions and helping: The moderating role of group membership. *Journal of Personality and Social Psychology*, *88*, 532–546.

Tajfel, H., & Turner, J. C. (1979). An integrative theory of intergroup conflict. In W. G. Austin & S. Worchel (Eds.), *The social psychology of intergroup relations* (pp. 33–48). Monterey, CA: Brooks/Cole.

Vescio, T. K., Sechrist, G. B., & Paolucci, M. P. (2003). Perspective taking and prejudice reduction: The mediational role of empathy arousal and situational attributions. *European Journal of Social Psychology*, *33*, 455–472.

Weiner, B. (1980). A cognitive (attribution)–emotion–action model of motivated behavior: An analysis of judgments of help-giving. *Journal of Personality and Social Psychology*, *39*, 186–200.

21

A NEEDS-BASED MODEL OF RECONCILIATION: PERPETRATORS NEED ACCEPTANCE AND VICTIMS NEED EMPOWERMENT TO RECONCILE

NURIT SHNABEL AND ARIE NADLER

In the year 2000, Israeli Jews grappled with the meaning and consequences of the apology offered by Pope John Paul II to victims of two millennia of persecution by the Catholic Church. They also received an apology from Argentinean President Fernando de la Rua for Argentina's tolerance of Nazi immigrants after World War II and its disinterest in helping bring them to justice. Three years earlier, in 1997, Ehud Barak, then the head of Israel's labor party (and later Israel's prime minister) apologized to Mizrahi Jews—those of non-European origin—for their maltreatment by labor-led governments throughout the years. The discussion of this somewhat controversial act was salient in Israeli public discourse. But the extensive use of apologies in the public sphere was not limited to Israeli or Jewish issues: In 1998, both United Nations Secretary-General Kofi Annan and former president Bill

Preparation of this chapter and the research reported in it were supported by a Fellowship from the Fulbright Foundation awarded to the first author and by the second author's Argentina Chair for Research on Social Psychology of Conflict and Cooperation at Tel Aviv University.

Clinton apologized for the United Nations' and America's failure to prevent the Rwandan genocide, and Japanese representatives apologized on several occasions for Japanese aggression during World War II.

Apologies and public acknowledgments of wrongdoing may be viewed as prosocial acts designed to soften painful memories and repair damaged relations. Past research on prosocial behavior has focused on benevolent actions of one individual, which are intended to promote the well-being of another individual (i.e., helping behavior). This emphasis is evident in the majority of contributions to the present volume. Our chapter addresses a different kind of prosocial action. It is concerned with the ways in which ameliorative behaviors such as apology or forgiveness promote the well-being of ailing relationships (e.g., between two adversaries who are locked in conflict). Our analysis thus extends the limits of the term *prosocial behavior* from the well-being of individuals to the well-being of relationships.

The increasing use of such ameliorative prosocial behavior in the public sphere made us wonder what it is about the *apology–forgiveness cycle* (a term suggested by Tavuchis, 1991) that makes it such an important social mechanism. Examining the language of apology, Tavuchis noted that

> we commonly say that one owes, gives, offers, receives, accepts, etc., an apology, implying thereby that something almost tangible is being bartered. . . . The apology itself—without any other objective consideration—constitutes both the medium of exchange and the symbolic *quid pro quo* for, as it were, compensation. (p. 33)

As social psychologists, we believe that this observation points to the exchange of certain symbolic emotional resources between victims and perpetrators engaged in an apology–forgiveness cycle. Trying to understand the nature of these resources and the way in which their exchange, through social interaction, may promote reconciliation led us to formulate the needs-based model of reconciliation, which is the focus of the present chapter.

We use the needs-based model as a framework for understanding both interpersonal and intergroup reconciliation processes. Obviously, these levels of analysis are different in some ways (Insko, Kirchner, Pinter, Efaw, & Wildschut, 2005). Nevertheless, there are sufficient similarities between the two levels of analysis to support our belief that the needs-based model applies to general processes of reconciliation (i.e., processes common to both the interpersonal and the intergroup levels).

We begin the chapter by distinguishing between reconciliation and conflict resolution. We then present the needs-based model of reconciliation, a theoretical framework that considers the unique emotional needs of victims and perpetrators and the ways in which satisfaction of these needs promotes reconciliation. We continue by describing a series of experiments that provide empirical evidence for the model's validity in both the interpersonal and the intergroup realms. Finally, we conclude by discussing the theoretical and practical implications of the needs-based model and suggesting directions for future research.

DISTINGUISHING RECONCILIATION FROM CONFLICT RESOLUTION

Social psychologists draw distinctions between the concepts of *conflict resolution* and *reconciliation*. The concept of conflict resolution is based on the realist approach to conflict and its resolution. According to the realist viewpoint, "disputes between persons and between groups are grounded in conflicts of material interests" (Scheff, 1994, p. 3). In international conflicts, these interests may relate to scarce natural resources (such as land); in intrasocietal conflicts, they may stem from tight budgets; and in conflicts between groups of children, they deal with pocket knives (Sherif, Harvey, White, Hood, & Sherif, 1961). The realist viewpoint has generated many theoretical and empirical insights regarding the antecedents of conflicts and ways to end them (Jones, 1998; Pruitt, 1998).

Reconciliation, in contrast, is a relatively new term in the social psychological literature (Nadler, Malloy, & Fisher, 2008; Rouhana, 2004). It differs from the concept of conflict resolution in two main respects: First, it emphasizes symbolic and emotional motives and processes rather than tangible and objective interests. Second, it focuses on the healing of relations rather than merely terminating the conflict. In other words, reconciliation "must include a changed psychological orientation towards the other" (Staub, Pearlman, Gubin, & Hagengimana, 2005, p. 301); involve "a willingness to come together to work, play, or live in an atmosphere of trust" (Exline & Baumeister, 2000, p. 136); and "may occur only once the parties have resolved the emotional issues that may have left them estranged" (Shnabel & Nadler, 2008, p. 116). We summarize these aspects by defining *reconciliation* as the process of removing conflict-related emotional barriers that block the way to healing a discordant relationship (Nadler & Shnabel, 2008).

Reconciliation theorists are often critical of the conflict resolution perspective because of its one-sided emphasis on conflicts over tangible interests. They emphasize that an end to a conflict cannot be achieved merely by satisfying the instrumental goals of opponents (e.g., wishing to maximize one's outcomes; see chap. 17, this volume). Instead, satisfying the conflicting parties' emotional needs (e.g., the need to regain feelings of self-worth and self-control; Kelman, 2004) is also necessary. Similarly, theoreticians of negotiation processes stress that negotiations may become deadlocked if they focus on the material issues that separate parties and ignore the less tangible issues related to the parties' conflict-related emotional needs (Zubek, Pruitt, Peirce, McGillicuddy, & Syna, 1992).

The process of addressing the emotional barriers that impede reconciliation (i.e., the unsatisfied psychological needs) was termed by Nadler and his colleagues (Nadler, 2002; Nadler & Liviatan, 2004; Nadler & Saguy, 2004; Nadler & Shnabel, 2008) the *socio-emotional route to reconciliation*, which is contrasted with the *instrumental route to reconciliation*.[1] One way in which these emotional barriers can be removed is the apology–forgiveness cycle. We believe that the kinds of apologies mentioned at the beginning of this chapter indicate a growing use of this cycle, suggesting an increasing awareness of the necessity of dealing with the emotional aspects of conflicts in order to heal damaged relations between victims and perpetrators. If these issues are not attended to, agreements to end a conflict may collapse, and the conflict may reignite (Kelman, 2008; Nadler, 2002).

NEEDS-BASED MODEL OF RECONCILIATION

During conflicts, especially protracted ones, parties inflict pain and humiliation on each other (see chap. 22, this volume). These emotions thwart the basic psychological needs of victims and perpetrators (e.g., the need to view oneself as worthwhile and just). Until these threats are removed, they act as emotional barriers to ending the conflict. We conceptualize the process of socioemotional reconciliation in general, and of the apology–forgiveness cycle in particular, as a process of social exchange between parties that ameliorates these threats to victims' and perpetrators' satisfaction of basic psychological needs. Reconciliation is expected to remove socioemotional barriers that impede the end of conflict and to allow adversaries to rehabilitate their relationship.

Before continuing to describe the model, we need to clarify our usage of the terms *perpetrators* and *victims*. First, in many conflicts, the distinction between the victim and the perpetrator is not clear-cut, and both parties claim to be victims of their adversary's wrongdoings. Yet because one party is often more likely to be viewed as the perpetrator and the other as the victim (i.e., the more and less powerful parties, respectively), our theoretical analysis rests on the distinction between victims and perpetrators. (We revisit this issue and its implications for our model toward the end of this chapter.) Second, our analysis applies to actors who are direct perpetrators or victims of aggressive acts as well as to those who perceive themselves as being victims or perpetrators by virtue of their affiliation with an aggressive or victimized group. Research shows that group members can feel victimized because oth-

[1]It should be noted that these two processes are not mutually exclusive. Rather, it is often the case that instrumental reconciliation, in the sense of building trust and forming a pragmatic partnership between former adversaries, is a necessary step that allows socioemotional reconciliation to occur (e.g., dealing with the painful past; Nadler & Liviatan, 2006). Yet, we distinguish between these two processes for the sake of conceptual clarity.

ers in their group have been victimized, or they can feel guilty because of past violence perpetrated by their group (e.g., Doosje, Branscombe, Spears, & Manstead, 1998).

Building on the distinction between victims and perpetrators, the needs-based model of reconciliation asserts that in a victimization episode, damage to the psychological resources of victims (i.e., individuals or group members who perceive themselves or their group as having been victimized by the outgroup) and perpetrators (i.e., individuals or group members who perceive themselves or their group as having perpetrated harm and suffering) is asymmetrical. Victims feel inferior with respect to their level of power (Foster & Rusbult, 1999), honor (Scheff, 1994), self-esteem (Scobie & Scobie, 1998), and perceived control (Baumeister, Stillwell, & Heatherton, 1994), and they may therefore experience feelings of victimization or anger (McCullough et al., 1998). In contrast, perpetrators suffer from a sense of moral inferiority (Exline & Baumeister, 2000; Zechmeister & Romero, 2002) and may experience guilt (Baumeister et al., 1994), shame (Exline & Baumeister, 2000), or remorse (North, 1998). This array of emotional states has been said to reflect perpetrators' "anxiety over social exclusion" (Baumeister et al., 1994, p. 246) because if perpetrators are viewed as guilty by others, they face the threat of being rejected from the moral community to which they belong (Tavuchis, 1991).

From a broader perspective, these impaired emotional resources can be subsumed under the human need for power and the human need for love and belonging, two needs that constitute the core of interpersonal experience (Bennis & Shepard, 1956). Using the terminology of resource theory, which classifies the resources that are exchanged in social interactions into six categories (love, status, services, goods, information, and money; Foa & Foa, 1980), we suggest that the resource most threatened in the case of victims falls into the category of *status* (i.e., the need for relative power), whereas the resource most threatened for perpetrators is in the category of *love* (i.e., the need for relatedness).

Deprivation of psychological resources corresponds with a motivational state in which the individual experiences his or her deficit as a need that must be fulfilled. For victims, there is an enhanced need to restore a sense of power, which increases power-seeking behavior (Foster & Rusbult, 1999). To achieve this goal, victims are likely to want perpetrators to acknowledge responsibility for the injustice they have caused. This acknowledgement creates a kind of debt that only the victim can cancel, and it returns a sense of control to the victim, who may then determine whether the perpetrator will be forgiven and reaccepted into the moral community (Akhtar, 2002; Minow, 1998; Schönbach, 1990). For this reason, victims often try to induce perpetrators to feel guilty, with perpetrators' guilt serving as an admission of the debt owed to victims, thus allowing even a relatively powerless group or person "to get his or her way" (Baumeister et al., 1994, p. 247).

The perpetrator, compared with the victim, exercises more power and control during the victimization episode. Nevertheless, when perpetrators are accused of violating conventional moral standards or deviating from group norms, they may fear exclusion from the moral community to which they belong. The concept of *moral community* was coined by Tavuchis (1991) in his analysis of the power of apologies to amend broken relationships. The community includes psychologically relevant others (i.e., both individuals and groups) who share with the individual or group in question a particular set of norms and values. Membership in this moral community is "predicated upon our knowledge, acceptance and conformity to specific and general norms" (Tavuchis, 1991, p. 8). Most, if not all, moral communities hold that one should not harm another person or group of people unjustifiably, unnecessarily, or disproportionately. Consequently, the perception that the perpetrators have inflicted such harm or humiliation may threaten their membership in the relevant moral community and arouse fears of exclusion (Tavuchis, 1991).[2] Anxiety over social exclusion increases perpetrators' motivation to perceive themselves as acceptable people (Baumeister, Stillwell, & Wotman, 1990), as well as their need to have others express empathy for their emotional distress (McCullough, Worthington, & Rachal, 1997) and understanding of the circumstances that compelled them to act in a socially unacceptable way (Nadler & Liviatan, 2004, 2006). This understanding, in turn, restores perpetrators' public moral image (i.e., their sense of being perceived as moral individuals) and helps them feel "rehumanized" (Staub et al., 2005). Empathy and understanding of the perpetrator's perspective are therefore a kind of gift that victims can offer to those who have offended them, which culminates in the victims explicitly granting forgiveness (Enright, Freedman, & Rique, 1998). In line with this reasoning, Carlsmith and Gross (1969) reported that participants who delivered an electric shock to a confederate tended to offer more help to the confederate following the experiment than did those who did not deliver the shock. This behavior may be interpreted as an effort by perpetrators to replenish their resources of approval and love or acceptance (Foa & Foa, 1980).

The needs for empowerment and acceptance can be fulfilled in ways other than the apology–forgiveness cycle. For example, perpetrators may empower their victims by acknowledging the victims' achievements and capabilities (competence is often treated as form of empowerment; Brookings & Bolton, 2000; Menon & Hartmann, 2002; Vardi, 2000; Yiannakis & Melnick, 2001) or, in the case of intergroup conflicts, by expressing feelings of respect for the victimized group's culture and values. Similarly, social acceptance of perpetrators may be expressed by willingness to form friendships

[2]It should be noted that the designated moral community may or may not include the victims themselves. For example, it is possible that during the Apartheid regime in South Africa, the international community constituted the group of significant others (e.g., due to the international embargo) more than did South African Blacks. In contrast, in the case of Barak's apology to Mizrahi Jews, the victims themselves constituted the relevant group of significant others.

with them, work with them, or in the case of intergroup conflict, to cooperate with them on joint projects of an economic or cultural nature. This greater willingness to engage in positive encounters with the perpetrators is facilitated by public acts of remorse by the perpetrators (e.g., the public remorse expressed by the German Chancellor Willy Brandt toward victims of the Holocaust) and by the general attenuation of the traumatic event that occurs over the years (partly because many of the direct victims and perpetrators have died). For example, although during the 1950s and 1960s many Israelis were unwilling to visit Germany or buy German products, their current willingness to do so may reflect their enhanced acceptance of Germany and Germans as part of the moral community of nations.

The understanding that empowerment and acceptance meet basic needs that can be manifested in different ways (mainly, but not only, through the apology–forgiveness cycle) makes the needs-based model parsimonious and applicable to a variety of contexts. Regardless of the specific ways in which empowerment or acceptance is manifested, when a successful social exchange between victims and perpetrators takes place, both sides satisfy their emotional needs and cease to feel weaker than, or morally inferior to, their counterpart. This generates a process of symbolic erasure of the roles of victim and perpetrator, which places the involved parties on a more equal footing (North, 1998) and thus leads to increased willingness to reconcile with one's opponent (Nadler & Shnabel, 2008). This progression along the socioemotional route to reconciliation is summarized in Figure 21.1.

EMPIRICAL EVIDENCE SUPPORTING THE NEEDS-BASED MODEL OF RECONCILIATION

We begin our review of evidence supporting the model by describing five experiments (Shnabel & Nadler, 2008) that tested the model at the interpersonal level. We then describe two experiments (Nadler & Liviatan, 2006; Shnabel, Nadler, Ullrich & Dovidio, 2009) that tested the model at the intergroup level.

To test the hypotheses that a victimization episode impairs different psychological resources for victims and perpetrators, and that this impairment evokes different emotional needs, we devised the "creativity test" experimental paradigm in which participants were randomly assigned to one of two roles: "writers," who composed marketing slogans for a list of products, or "judges," who evaluated these slogans. To control for information about success or failure, in both experimental and control dyads, writers were informed that they had failed their "test," whereas judges were informed that they had passed it. What varied between the experimental and control dyads were the instructions provided to participants. In the experimental dyads, judges were advised to be strict in their evaluations and were informed that being too

	Role: Victim	Role: Perpetrator
Impaired emotional resource:	Sense of power (Power)	Moral image (Belongingness)
	↓	↓
Resource sought from partner:	Empowerment (e.g., victim wants partner to apologize for causing injustice)	Acceptance (e.g., perpetrator wants partner to express forgiveness)
	↓	↓
Restore balance by:	Restored sense of power	Restored moral image
	↓	↓
Resulting in:	Increased willingness to reconcile	

Figure 21.1. The needs-based model of reconciliation.

lenient could harm their own chances of passing the test. By the end of the session, participants (i.e., judges and writers) were told that the judges passed the test, whereas writers failed it due to the harsh evaluations they received from their judges. In the control dyads, judges were advised to be relatively lenient. Participants were later informed that the judges passed the test whereas writers failed it due to the decision of an external committee. Thus, in both dyads (i.e., experimental and control conditions) judges passed the test and writers failed it. However, in the experimental dyad, but not in the control dyad, judges' success was gained at the expense of the writers, as they deliberately failed their partners to improve their own chances of passing the test.

Following the assignment of participants to the different experimental conditions, we measured their sense of power and moral image (i.e., whether they thought their partners viewed them as moral) and compared the reactions of participants in the experimental dyads with those of participants in the control dyads. The findings supported the hypothesis that after a victimization episode, victims would suffer a decrease in their sense of power and perpetrators would suffer a decrease in their self-perceived moral image. Consistent with the model's predictions, the decrease in perpetrators' moral image was associated with a parallel increase in need for social acceptance, which found expression in a greater desire for victims to understand the perpetrators' perspective and to express empathy toward them. Victims, on the other hand, expressed a greater need for power and justice (i.e., wanting perpetrators to acknowledge that the victims had been wronged).

It should be noted that this support for the model's predictions was obtained in an experiment in which the roles of victim and perpetrator were induced simultaneously, in a single experimental situation, using identical, mirror-image scenarios. This is the first experiment known to us that has accomplished this. Past experiments have induced victimization that was then studied from the perspective of either the victim or the perpetrator, but not both. Therefore, such studies have not been able to provide experimental tests of hypotheses regarding the dynamics of victim–perpetrator interactions.

To provide external validity for these findings, we sought to replicate them in real-life settings. We had participants recall a personal episode in which they had either hurt or been hurt by a significant other. Thus, participants were induced to enter the perpetrator or victim role in a real-life interpersonal context. Subsequently, we asked participants to rate their sense of power and moral image in the conflict episode, as well as their needs for power, justice, empathy, and social acceptance by the antagonist. The findings replicated the results of the experiment described earlier. Participants who had thought about themselves as victims had lower ratings of power and expressed greater needs for justice and power than did those who had thought about themselves as perpetrators. In contrast, those who had thought about themselves as perpetrators had lower ratings of moral image and expressed a greater need for acceptance.

Next we tested the model's prediction that victims' readiness to reconcile with an adversary would be enhanced by satisfying their need for power, and that perpetrators' readiness to reconcile would be enhanced by satisfying their need for acceptance. In the first experimental test of this hypothesis, we again used the creativity-test paradigm to randomly assign participants to the role of victim or perpetrator. Participants then received a message from their counterpart that increased the sense of either empowerment or social acceptance. Following this, their sense of power, moral image, and willingness to reconcile were measured. Our model predicts that because an empowering message satisfies the victims' need for power, it will increase their willingness to reconcile, whereas a message of acceptance will increase the willingness of perpetrators to reconcile. The findings supported these predictions. An empowering message restored victims' sense of power and increased their willingness to reconcile more than a message of acceptance, whereas a message of acceptance restored perpetrators' moral image and increased their willingness to reconcile more than an empowering message. The message of acceptance did not affect victims' sense of power, and the message of empowerment did not affect perpetrators' moral image.

In a subsequent study, we had participants react to two versions of the same vignette. The vignette depicted an incident that pilot testing had shown to be highly typical and relevant to the participants' lives (a supervisor's refusal of a seemingly legitimate request by an employee). In one version, the protagonist was the perpetrator, and in the other, he or she was the victim. Participants were asked to imagine themselves in the place of the protagonists. In the story, the antagonist approaches the protagonist some time after the offense has been committed and conveys a message of empowerment, acceptance, empowerment and acceptance, or neither. Participants were randomly assigned to one of the eight experimental conditions, and then the dependent variables (sense of power, moral image, and willingness to reconcile) were measured. The findings of the previous study were replicated.

In a final study in this research program, we sought to examine the full range of the model's predictions by measuring individuals' sense of power, moral image, and willingness to reconcile both before and after they received a message of empowerment or acceptance from an adversary. Participants were asked to read a vignette describing an event in which the protagonist discovered that his or her attractive job in an organization had been taken over by a fellow worker. Half of the participants were asked to assume the role of the perpetrator (i.e., the person who took the job) and the other half were asked to assume the role of the victim (i.e., the person who lost the job). They were then asked to fill out the first set of dependent measures. Consistent with earlier findings, perpetrators felt a greater threat to their moral image and had a stronger need for social acceptance than did victims, who experienced a greater threat to their sense of power and expressed a stronger need for power and justice. Several days later, participants received the second part of the vignette, in which they learned that the antagonist in the story made a verbal statement to the protagonist that expressed either empowerment or acceptance. The second set of dependent measures was then readministered. In line with the model's predictions, the increase in victims' sense of power between the first and second administration was greater in the empowerment condition than in the acceptance condition, and their willingness to reconcile was also greater in the empowerment than in the acceptance condition. For perpetrators, the increase in their moral image and willingness to reconcile was greater in the acceptance than in the empowerment condition.

In light of the consistent support for the needs-based model at the interpersonal level, we turned to assessing its predictions in the context of intergroup conflicts. Arguably, interpersonal conflicts and intergroup conflicts can be fundamentally different with regard to the degree of suffering and the complexity of the processes involved in bringing about an end to the conflict (see chaps. 20 and 22, this volume). Yet we maintain that the needs-based model is quite general and is equally applicable to analyses of interpersonal and intergroup contexts. In fact, the idea that victims and perpetrators have different needs that must be met before the two can reconcile was suggested as an explanation for the findings of a recent study that examined willingness to reconcile in one of the most protracted conflicts in recent history—the Israeli–Palestinian conflict (Nadler & Liviatan, 2006). Further, the social identity perspective (Tajfel & Turner, 1979) and self-categorization theory (Turner, Hogg, Oakes, Reicher, Wetherell, 1987) suggest that the psychology of individuals is influenced by salient group memberships. According to these theories, when a given ingroup–outgroup distinction is salient, people define themselves less in terms of their unique characteristics as individuals and more in terms of prototypical attributes of their ingroup. In support of this idea, research has indicated that individuals can feel guilty (e.g., Branscombe et al., 1998) or victimized because of something that has happened to other members of their group. These conceptual analyses and empirical findings further narrow the gap between the interpersonal and intergroup analyses of conflict and conflict resolution and reconciliation. Hence, in the second phase of our research, we sought to examine the needs-based model in intergroup contexts.

The first experiment (Shnabel et al., 2009) focused on relations between Germans and Jews. Because of historical events during the 20th century, primarily the Holocaust, we reasoned that in the context of this intergroup relationship both Jewish and German (non-Jewish) participants would perceive Jews as victims and Germans as perpetrators. In line with the needs-based model, we hypothesized that Jewish participants, even though they were not personally victims of the Holocaust (having not been alive at that time), would feel an enhanced need for power in the context of German–Jewish relations and would therefore have a greater willingness to reconcile following an empowering message conveyed by a German representative than following an accepting message. The opposite pattern was predicted for German participants, who were hypothesized to have a greater willingness to reconcile following a message of acceptance from a Jewish representative than following a message of empowerment.

To test these hypotheses, we exposed Jewish and German participants to two speeches, allegedly made by the outgroup's representatives. The central message conveyed in the speech was either the acceptance or empowerment of the participants' ingroup. The order in which the speeches were presented was counterbalanced. We then measured the extent to which each message was perceived as empowering and accepting, as well as participants' willingness to reconcile following its presentation.

To assess these hypotheses, we used messages that were identically phrased for Jewish and German participants in a within-participants experimental design, so that each participant was exposed to both kinds of messages. This allowed for an assessment of our hypothesis but required the blunting of the messages so that they would sound credible to both groups. For example, a message from the German representative to the Jewish sample, such as "The lesson from the Holocaust is that nowadays Jews should be strong," would not have been appropriate or believable when reverse-phrased for the German group. For this reason, we used subtler messages that would suit both samples, such as: "Nowadays, it is the [Germans'/Jews'] right to be strong and proud of their country and to have the power to determine their own fate" (in the empowerment message) or "We, the [Germans/Jews], should accept the [Jews/Germans] and remember that we are all human beings" (in the acceptance message).

Participants rated the extent to which each speech conveyed a message of acceptance and empowerment of their ingroup as well as their own consequent willingness to reconcile. Preliminary results provide general support for our hypotheses. Participants from both samples perceived the acceptance and empowerment messages as intended and, as expected, whereas Jews were more willing to reconcile following the message of empowerment than following a message of acceptance, Germans were more willing to reconcile following the message of acceptance than the message of empowerment.

Although the pattern of results provides empirical support for the needs-based model, the fact that participants were not randomly assigned to the role of victims or perpetrators gives rise to an alternative explanation—that the difference in the effects of the different types of messages is attributable to cultural differences between the two groups. To rule out this possibility, we replicated this experiment in the context of relations between Israeli Jews and Israeli Arabs. Because both Jews and Arabs often perceive themselves as the real victims of the Jewish–Arab conflict (Nadler, 2002), we focused on a historical event for which there is a consensus among Jewish and Arab Israelis as to the victimization of Arabs by the Jewish side: the Kefar Kasem massacre. In this event, which took place in October of 1956, 43 unarmed Arab civilians were killed by the Jewish–Israeli border patrol for violating a curfew that had recently been imposed. Using the same experimental design as the one used in the German–Jewish study, we exposed Israeli Arabs and Jews to speeches conveying messages of empowerment or acceptance ostensibly made by representatives of their outgroup on the 50th anniversary of the massacre. Again, following each speech participants rated the extent to which it conveyed acceptance and empowerment of their ingroup as well as their consequent willingness to reconcile. Preliminary results provide further support for the needs-based model: While Arabs were more willing to reconcile following a message of empowerment, Jews were more willing to reconcile following a message of acceptance.

Taken together, the findings of the two studies suggest that it is the social role in a specific context, rather than general cultural values, which influenced the extent to which Israeli Jews perceived different types of messages as more or less conciliatory. In the context of German–Jewish relations, in which Jews identify with the social role of the victim, an empowering message was found to be more conciliatory, whereas in the context of the Kefar Kasem massacre, in which Israeli Jews were placed in the social role of the perpetrator, it was the message of acceptance that had a more conciliatory effect. It should be emphasized that in both of the historical events we used in our research (i.e., the Holocaust and the Kfar Kasem massacre), there was general consensus concerning the identity of the victims and the perpetrators. This was necessary to test the predictions of the needs-based model, but it limits the conclusions to cases in which such a clear distinction exists. We discuss this issue at greater length later in this chapter.

To summarize, the three main tenets of the model—that (a) victimization episodes impair victims' sense of power and perpetrators' moral image; (b) consequently, victims experience an enhanced need for empowerment and perpetrators experience an enhanced need for acceptance; and (c) restoring these impaired emotional resources via an appropriate message from the adversary (e.g., apology or forgiveness) promotes victims' and perpetrators' willingness to reconcile—were validated at the interpersonal and intergroup levels.

IMPLICATIONS OF THE NEEDS-BASED MODEL

Our focus on the emotional motives underlying the reconciliation process comes on the heels of a relatively long period during which these motives were neglected in favor of more instrumental concerns. Yet both within and outside the field of social psychology, there is a growing understanding that the emotional factors that help to repair relationships between victims and perpetrators have practical meaning for achieving reconciliation and therefore should not be ignored. Informed by both theory and data, we outline in the following paragraphs three practical principles that follow from the model.

First, it should be acknowledged that victims and perpetrators are likely to have different emotional needs and consequently different perspectives, preferences, and goals. One issue on which victims and perpetrators are particularly likely to disagree is the severity of the damage or impairment caused to victims. Research indicates that victims and perpetrators have different perspectives on the same victimization episode (see chap. 18, this volume). Although perpetrators are concerned about whether others view them as moral actors, they often avoid feelings of guilt by minimizing the immoral implications of their actions or denying responsibility for them (Mikula, 2002). In fact, even actions that seem senselessly cruel may be perceived by perpetrators as having at least some redeeming purpose or merit (Baumeister, 1996).

This contrasts with victims' tendency to emphasize the injustice that they have suffered and the perpetrator's responsibility for it. This phenomenon was labeled the *magnitude gap* by Exline and Baumeister (2000). The experience of these gaps between individuals or group members having differential social roles (victims or perpetrators) is often overwhelming. The mere understanding that these divergent perspectives are common may reduce uncertainty, limit miscommunication and misperception, and decrease some of the anxiety aroused in the course of promoting genuine attempts to understand the other's perspective (see chap. 20, this volume).

Second, victims' need for power should be acknowledged. Because of their social role, victims experience an enhanced need for power, which can be gratified in several ways, such as receiving respect, bolstering pride or status, and having the perpetrators admit the injustice done to the victims. Yet perpetrators too often patronizingly dismiss this need, perceiving victims as too sensitive to issues of status, respect, or historical injustice. The remark of Uri Or, a member of the labor party referring to Ehud Barak's apology to Mizrahi Jews, that it is impossible to have a "normal conversation" with Mizrahi parliament members because they are so easily offended (Ben-Simon, 1998) illustrates this kind of dismissal. In other instances, implemented policies fail to pay sufficient attention to the needs of victims in a way that truly empowers the victims. For example, research on "defensive helping" has shown that under certain conditions members of the more powerful group may help a disadvantaged group in a way that increases its dependency on the advantaged group (Halabi, Dovidio, & Nadler, 2008; Nadler, 2002; see also chap. 10, this volume). In contrast, the Truth and Reconciliation Commissions (TRCs) in South Africa provide an example of a policy that genuinely empowers victims, through the use of restorative justice procedures. In contrast, restorative justice practices (i.e., practices that focus on rectifying relationships and personal connections damaged by victimization; Wachtel & McCold, 2001) may effectively empower victims. These procedures may include, for example, an organized encounter between the victim and the perpetrator and the involvement of the victim in determining, or at least influencing, the appropriate punishment. The empowering potential of the use of restorative justice procedures was illustrated by Gobodo-Madikizela (2003), who argued in her analysis of the psychological consequences of the TRCs: "The decision to forgive can paradoxically elevate a victim to a position of strength as the one who has the key to the perpetrator's wish . . . the victim becomes the gatekeeper to what the outcast desires" (p. 117).

Restorative justice procedures are also related to our third principle: The need of perpetrators for acceptance should be acknowledged. Because of their social position, perpetrators are often stronger and more influential than their victims (or at least were stronger historically, when the offense took place). For this reason, victims are often reluctant to express empathy toward their perpetrators, even when perpetrators experience emotional distress (Cottrell & Neuberg, 2005; Cuddy, Fiske, & Glick, 2007). Nevertheless, perpetrators' needs should not be ignored. In particular, acknowledging the dark side of one's identity (i.e., admitting immoral behavior committed by oneself or one's ingroup) is likely to evoke high levels of threat (Wohl, Branscombe, & Klar, 2006). It is therefore important that even when issues of injustice are raised, perpetrators should not be made to feel totally rejected but rather should be morally validated and socially accepted, at least to some extent. This idea is reflected in Staub et al.'s (2005) claim, based on their work with Hutus and Tutsis following the genocide in Rwanda, that "coming to see and understand the influences that led to the perpetrators' actions, however horrible those actions, and to the bystanders' passivity, can also lead survivors of violence to be more open to reconciliation with the perpetrator group" (p. 304). The To Reflect and Trust intervention (Maoz & Bar-On, 2002), aimed at promoting reconciliation between groups of former victims and perpetrators (e.g., Jews and Germans) by developing mutual empathy, is another illustration of this principle.

FUTURE RESEARCH DIRECTIONS

The needs-based model of reconciliation offers a general theoretical framework for understanding the emotional aspects of socioemotional reconciliation and suggests a number of issues for future research. The first of these is the goal of incorporating variables into the model that may moderate the effects hypothesized by it. For example, Nadler and Liviatan (2006) found that the effects of different types of messages (acceptance vs. empowerment) from a Palestinian representative on Jews' willingness to reconcile were moderated by Jews' level of trust in Palestinians' intentions. Specifically, Jews showed a differential response to different kinds of messages only in the presence of high level of trust; in the absence of trust, message type had no effect. Similarly, relevant personality traits such as the need for self-enhancement (see chap. 12, this volume) or social dominance orientation (Sidanius & Pratto, 1999) may have a moderating effect. For example, individuals who score high on social dominance orientation may be affected more strongly by an empowerment message, even when they hold the social role of the perpetrator. Other variables that have been shown to influence group members' willingness to reconcile, such as collective guilt (Doosje et al., 1998) and level of social categorization (Wohl & Branscombe, 2005), may also act as moderators.

A second direction for further research would involve investigating the capacity of third-party intermediaries to fulfill the needs of victims and perpetrators in place of the adversaries themselves. Research on the role of third parties has traditionally suggested that their involvement can facilitate quicker and more effective conflict resolution (Rubin, 1980). Yet third parties' contributions to socioemotional reconciliation still await empirical investigation. According to resource theory (Foa & Foa, 1980), some of the resources that are exchanged in social interactions are more fungible than others; that is, they can more easily be supplied in another form or by another party. For example, money and people connected with money are highly fungible, whereas love is not: A person can easily substitute a new bank teller for an old one, but it is not so easy to replace a loved romantic partner. Because love (acceptance) and status (power)—the resources at the heart of the needs-based model—are not generally fungible, it is possible that third parties may be unable to restore the impaired elements of the adversaries' identities. In other words, only the adversaries themselves can relay the messages necessary to satisfy each other's emotional needs in a manner that successfully promotes reconciliation. Even if third parties successfully replenish victims' or perpetrators' impaired emotional resources, this replenishment, by itself, will not restore harmony to the troubled relationship. We have obtained some initial empirical support for this hypothesis by showing that messages of empowerment or acceptance from a third party not only fail to increase but may even decrease victims' and perpetrators' willingness to reconcile.

A third, and perhaps the most essential, new research direction would be to illuminate how the processes described in the needs-based model can be set in motion. The model addresses the effects on reconciliation of restoring impaired emotional resources related to individuals' and groups' self-identity. Our experiments showed that when victims felt empowered by their perpetrators and perpetrators felt accepted by their victims, their willingness to reconcile increased. However, in all of these experiments we—the researchers—were the ones who manipulated these messages. In reality, however, for these messages to be exchanged, the involved parties must first change their perceptions of their adversaries.

In particular, rather than viewing their victims as incompetent and unequal social actors who make illegitimate claims, perpetrators need to view their victims as autonomous, capable, and equal, and to admit having injured them unjustly. Victims, on the other hand, need to understand the perpetrators' perspective and realize that their transgressions are not evidence of a fundamentally evil nature. Rather, perpetrators are often people who found themselves in circumstances in which most others, including the victims, might have behaved similarly (Staub et al., 2005). In addition, most members of a perpetrating group are not themselves direct aggressors but bystanders or constituents of a system with whose offenses they are only indirectly associated. This realization will allow victims to view their perpetrators as acceptable social actors and to feel at least some empathy toward them, rather than reject them or view them as cold and immoral. This idea is consistent with Kelman's (2008) view of reconciliation as a process of identity change, consisting of the removal of the negation of the other as an element in one's own identity. In other words, the needs-based model provides useful insights regarding which messages victims and perpetrators should transmit to their adversaries to effectively promote their adversaries' willingness to reconcile, but it is still necessary to learn how to get victims and perpetrators to endorse and transmit these messages.

In summary, conflict and reconciliation are complex, multicausal phenomena involving multiple material interests and psychological motives. Our model highlights the importance of attending to the different emotional needs of both sides of a conflict. Appreciation of these differences is likely to increase our sensitivity to each adversary's needs and desires, and it may promote a better understanding of the processes of both interpersonal and intergroup reconciliation.

Before we close, we should note that our discussion of socioemotional reconciliation and the needs-based model rests on the assumption of a clear distinction between perpetrators and victims. As noted earlier, such a clear-cut distinction was necessary to increase conceptual clarity in this relatively brief chapter. In the real world, however, some conflicts generate consensus as to who is the victim and who is the perpetrator, but many do not. Under such circumstances, both parties should recognize what decades of social psychological research have shown: Viewing oneself as a victim or perpetrator is a psychological construal that may change over time and across contexts. Sometimes it helps to allow both parties to view themselves as victims *and* perpetrators, and to encourage the initiation of simultaneous and reciprocal apology–forgiveness cycles in which each party admits its own wrongdoing and grants forgiveness to its former adversary.

REFERENCES

Akhtar, S. (2002). Forgiveness: Origins, dynamics, psychopathology, and technical relevance. *Psychoanalytic Quarterly, 71*, 175–212.

Baumeister, R. F. (1996). *Evil: Inside human violence and cruelty*. New York: Henry Holt.

Baumeister, R. F., Stillwell, A. M., & Heatherton, T. F. (1994). Guilt: An interpersonal approach. *Psychological Bulletin, 115*, 243–267.

Baumeister, R. F., Stillwell, A. M., & Wotman, S. R. (1990). Victim and perpetrator accounts of interpersonal conflict: Autobiographical narratives about anger. *Journal of Personality and Social Psychology, 59*, 994–1005.

Ben-Simon, D. (1998, July 29). Why apology, what apology. *Haaretz*, p. 1.

Bennis, W. G., & Shepard, H. A. (1956). A theory of group development. *Human Relations, 9*, 415–437.

Brookings, J. B., & Bolton, B. (2000). Confirmatory factor analysis of a measure of intrapersonal empowerment. *Rehabilitation Psychology, 45*, 292–298.

Carlsmith, J. M., & Gross, A. E. (1969). Some effects of guilt on compliance. *Journal of Personality and Social Psychology, 11*, 232–239.

Cottrell, C. A., & Neuberg, S. L. (2005). Different emotional reactions to different groups: A sociofunctional threat-based approach to "prejudice." *Journal of Personality and Social Psychology, 88*, 770–789.

Cuddy, A. J. C., Fiske, S. T., & Glick, P. (2007). The BIAS map: Behaviors from intergroup affect and stereotypes. *Journal of Personality and Social Psychology, 92*, 631–648.

Doosje, B., Branscombe, N. R., Spears, R., & Manstead, A. S. R. (1998). Guilty by association: When one's group has a negative history. *Journal of Personality and Social Psychology, 75*, 872–886.

Enright, R. D., Freedman, S., & Rique, J. (1998).The psychology of interpersonal forgiveness. In R. D. Enright & J. North (Eds.), *Exploring forgiveness* (pp. 46–62). Madison: University of Wisconsin Press.

Exline, J. J., & Baumeister, R. F. (2000). Expressing forgiveness and repentance: Benefits and barriers. In M. E. McCullough, K. I. Pargament, & C. E. Thoresen (Eds.), *Forgiveness: Theory, research, and practice* (pp. 133–155). New York: Guilford Press.

Foa, E. B., & Foa, U. G. (1980). Resource theory: Interpersonal behavior as exchange. In K. J. Gergen, M. S. Greenberg, & R. H. Willis (Eds.), *Social exchange: Advances in theory and research* (pp. 77–94). New York: Plenum.

Foster, C. A., & Rusbult, C. E. (1999). Injustice and powerseeking. *Personality and Social Psychology Bulletin, 25*, 834–849.

Gobodo-Madikizela, P. (2003). *A human being died that night: A South African story of forgiveness*. New York: Houghton Mifflin.

Halabi, S., Dovidio, J. F., & Nadler, A. (2008). When and how high status groups offer help: Effects of social dominance orientation and status threat. *Political Psychology, 29*, 841–858.

Insko, C. A., Kirchner, J. L., Pinter, B., Efaw, J., & Wildschut, T. (2005). Interindividual–intergroup discontinuity as a function of trust and categorization: The paradox of expected cooperation. *Journal of Personality and Social Psychology, 88*, 365–385.

Jones, E. (1998). Major developments in five decades of social psychology. In D. T. Gilbert, S. T. Fiske, & G. Lindzey (Eds.), *The handbook of social psychology* (4th ed., Vol. 1, pp. 3–57). New York: McGraw-Hill.

Kelman, H. C. (2004). The nature of international conflict: A sociological–psychological perspective. In H. J. Langholtz & C. E. Stout (Eds.), *The psychology of diplomacy* (pp. 59–77). Westport, CT: Praeger.

Kelman, H. C. (2008). Reconciliation from a social-psychological perspective. In A. Nadler, T. Malloy, & J. D. Fisher (Eds.), *The social psychology of intergroup reconciliation* (pp. 15–37). New York: Oxford University Press.

Maoz, I., & Bar-On, D. (2002). From working through the Holocaust to current ethnic conflicts: Evaluating the TRT group workshop in Hamburg. *Group, 26*, 29–48.

McCullough, M. E., Rachal, K. C., Sandage, S. J., Worthington, E. L., Brown, S. W., & Hight, T. L. (1998). Interpersonal forgiving in close relationships: II. Theoretical elaboration and measurement. *Journal of Personality and Social Psychology, 75*, 1586–1603.

McCullough, M. E., Worthington, E. L., & Rachal, K. C. (1997). Interpersonal forgiving in close relationships. *Journal of Personality and Social Psychology, 73*, 321–336.

Menon, S. T., & Hartmann, L. C. (2002). Generalizability of Menson's empowerment scale: Replication and extension with Australian data. *International Journal of Cross Cultural Management, 2*, 137–153.

Mikula, G. (2002). Perspective-related differences in interpretations of injustice in close relationships. In C. F. Graumann & W. Kallmeyer (Eds.), *Perspective and perspectivation in discourse* (pp. 251–262). Amsterdam: John Benjamins.

Minow, M. (1998). *Between vengeance and forgiveness: Facing history after genocide and mass violence*. Boston: Beacon.

Nadler, A. (2002). Post resolution processes: Instrumental and socio-emotional routes to reconciliation. In G. Salomon & B. Nevo (Eds.), *Peace education: The concept, principles, and practices around the world* (pp. 127–141). Mahwah, NJ: Erlbaum.

Nadler, A., & Liviatan, I. (2004). Intergroup reconciliation processes in Israel: Theoretical analysis and empirical findings. In N. R. Branscombe & B. Doosje (Eds.), *Collective guilt: International perspectives* (pp. 216–235). New York: Cambridge University Press.

Nadler, A., & Liviatan, I. (2006). Intergroup reconciliation: Effects of adversary's expressions of empathy, responsibility, and recipients' trust. *Personality and Social Psychology Bulletin, 32*, 459–470.

Nadler, A., Malloy, T., & Fisher, J. D. (Eds.). (2008). *The social psychology of intergroup reconciliation*. New York: Oxford University Press.

Nadler, A., & Saguy, T. (2004). Reconciliation between nations: Overcoming emotional deterrents to ending conflicts between groups. In H. Langholtz & C. E. Stout (Eds.), *The psychology of diplomacy* (pp. 29–46). New York: Praeger.

Nadler, A., & Shnabel, N. (2008). Intergroup reconciliation: The instrumental and socio-emotional paths and the needs-based model of socio-emotional reconciliation. In A. Nadler, T. Malloy, & J. D. Fisher (Eds.), *Social psychology of intergroup reconciliation* (pp.37–56). New York: Oxford University Press.

North, J. (1998). The "ideal" of forgiveness: A philosopher's exploration. In R. D. Enright & J. North (Eds.), *Exploring forgiveness* (pp. 15–34). Madison: University of Wisconsin Press.

Pruitt, D. G. (1998). Social conflict. In D. T. Gilbert, S. T. Fiske, & G. Lindzey (Eds.), *The handbook of social psychology* (4th ed., Vol. 2, pp. 470–503). New York: McGraw-Hill.

Rouhana, N. N. (2004). Group identity and power asymmetry in reconciliation processes: The Israeli-Palestinian case. *Peace and Conflict: Journal of Peace Psychology, 10*, 33–52.

Rubin, J. Z. (1980). Experimental research on third-party intervention in conflict: Toward some generalizations. *Psychological Bulletin, 87*, 379–391.

Scheff, T. J. (1994). *Bloody revenge: Emotions, nationalism, and war*. Boulder, CO: Westview.

Schönbach, P. (1990). *Account episodes: The management or escalation of conflict*. New York: Cambridge University Press.

Scobie, E. D., & Scobie, G. E. W. (1998). Damaging events: The perceived need for forgiveness. *Journal for the Theory of Social Behaviour, 28*, 373–401.

Sherif, M., Harvey, O. J., White, B. J., Hood, W. R., & Sherif, C. W. (1961). *Intergroup cooperation and competition: The Robbers Cave experiment*. Norman, OK: University Book Exchange.

Shnabel, N., & Nadler, A. (2008). A needs-based model of reconciliation: Satisfying the differential emotional needs of victim and perpetrator as a key to promoting reconciliation. *Journal of Personality and Social Psychology, 94*, 116–132.

Shnabel, N., Nadler, A., Ullrich, J., & Dovidio, J. F. (2009). Promoting reconciliation through satisfaction of the emotional needs of victimized and perpetrating group members: The Needs-Based Model of Reconciliation. *Personality and Social Psychology Bulletin*. doi: 10.1177/0146167209336610

Sidanius, J., & Pratto, F. (1999). *Social dominance: An intergroup theory of social hierarchy and oppression*. New York: Cambridge University Press.

Staub, E., Pearlman, L. A., Gubin, A., & Hagengimana, A. (2005). Healing, reconciliation, forgiving and the prevention of violence after genocide or mass killing: An intervention and its experimental evaluation in Rwanda. *Journal of Social and Clinical Psychology, 24*, 297–334.

Tajfel, H., & Turner, J. C. (1979). An integrative theory of intergroup conflict. In W. G. Austin & S. Worchel (Eds.), *The social psychology of intergroup relations* (pp. 33–48). Monterey, CA: Brooks/Cole.

Tavuchis, N. (1991). *Mea culpa: A sociology of apology and reconciliation*. Stanford, CA: Stanford University Press.

Turner, J. C., Hogg, M. A., Oakes, P. J., Reicher, S. D., & Wetherell, M. S. (1987). *Rediscovering the social group: A self-categorization theory*. Oxford, England: Basil Blackwell.

Vardi, Y. (2000). Psychological empowerment as a criterion for adjustment to a new job. *Psychological Reports, 87*, 1083–1093.

Wachtel, T., & McCold, P. (2001). Restorative justice in everyday life. In J. Braithwaite & H. Strang (Eds.), *Restorative justice and civil society* (pp. 114–129). Melbourne, Australia: Cambridge University Press.

Wohl, M. J. A., & Branscombe, N. R. (2005). Forgiveness and collective guilt assignment to historical perpetrator groups depend on level of social category inclusiveness. *Journal of Personality and Social Psychology*, 88, 288–303.

Wohl, M. J. A., Branscombe, N. R., & Klar, Y. (2006). Collective guilt: Emotional reactions when one's group has done wrong or been wronged. *European Review of Social Psychology, 17*, 1–37.

Yiannakis, A., & Melnick, M. J. (2001). *Contemporary issues in sociology of sport*. Champaign, IL: Human Kinetics.

Zechmeister, J. S., & Romero, C. (2002). Victim and offender accounts of interpersonal conflict: Autobiographical narratives of forgiveness and unforgiveness. *Journal of Personality and Social Psychology, 82,* 675–686.

Zubek, J. M., Pruitt, D. G., Peirce, R. C., McGillicuddy, N. B., & Syna, H. (1992). Disputant and mediator behaviors affecting short-term success in mediation. *Journal of Conflict Resolution, 36,* 546–572.

22

OVERCOMING PSYCHOLOGICAL BARRIERS TO PEACEMAKING: THE INFLUENCE OF BELIEFS ABOUT LOSSES

DANIEL BAR-TAL AND ERAN HALPERIN

One of the fundamental questions that preoccupies students of conflict resolution, as well as negotiators who attempt to resolve international conflicts, is how to overcome the psychological barriers to peacemaking in cases of serious and violent conflicts. Such conflicts concern real goods, such as territories, natural resources, and the right to self-government, and disagreements about basic values. In attempting to resolve such conflicts, it is necessary to address the incompatibility of some of the adversaries' positions, but it is also necessary to consider and deal with the important social-psychological foundations of the conflict that feed and maintain the evolved culture of conflict. These foundations are quite rigid and resistant to change, and they fuel continued conflict and create almost insurmountable barriers to conflict resolution.

This chapter examines ways of overcoming the psychological barriers to peaceful resolution of conflicts and outlines preliminary ideas that may be

We thank Rinat Arviv-Abramovich, Corinna Gayer, Tamir Magal, Nimrod Rosler, Keren Sharvit, Ofer Shinar, Eitan Spigel, Shiri Tal, and Doron Tzur for comments on an earlier draft of this chapter.

useful in stimulating further theory development and empirical research. We begin by briefly examining the nature of intractable conflicts and the associated cultures of conflict. The bulk of the chapter then addresses ways of overcoming the psychological barriers to conflict resolution, focusing on the extent to which thoughts about losses involved in a conflict can destabilize ("unfreeze") rigid beliefs and attitudes toward the conflict and lead to its reevaluation and resolution. Finally, we discuss other kinds of beliefs and attitudes that can move conflicted parties toward development of an ethos of peace, which is necessary for lasting conflict resolution and reconciliation.

CULTURE OF CONFLICT AND PSYCHOLOGICAL BARRIERS TO CONFLICT RESOLUTION

Conflicts are a natural part of intergroup relations, but we are interested here in conflicts that are prolonged, harsh, and violent—ones that are often called *intractable*.[1] In these conflicts, each of the opposing groups has typically evolved a culture of conflict based on shared societal beliefs,[2] an ethos of conflict, collective memories, and shared collective emotions (Bar-Tal, 2007a). Collective memories of a conflict involve a history shared by group members that summarizes how the conflict arose and evolved to its present state (e.g., Cairns & Roe, 2003; Wertsch, 2002). An ethos of conflict provides a unique, general, dominant orientation to a society in times of conflict (Bar-Tal, 2000a; Bar-Tal & Salomon, 2006).[3] The societal beliefs based on collective memory and an ethos of conflict are selective, biased, and distorted because their major function is to justify one side's position in the conflict rather than to provide an objective account of reality. The beliefs fuel intractable conflict by portraying one's own group very positively and as an unjustly injured or mistreated victim, while delegitimizing the opponent. Beyond societal beliefs, intractable conflicts are also fueled by collective emotional tendencies. The most notable such reaction is fear and apprehension with respect to the rival (Bar-Tal, 2001), but also important are anger toward and hatred of the opponent (e.g., de Rivera & Paez, 2007; Halperin, 2008; Petersen, 2002).

[1]Intractable conflicts can be characterized as violent, lasting at least 25 years, centering on goals perceived as necessary for existence, being viewed as unresolvable because of their zero-sum nature, greatly preoccupying society members, and involving parties who are heavily invested in continuing the conflict (Bar-Tal, 1998).

[2]Societal beliefs are defined as shared cognitions about topics and issues of special concern to a society and about its unique characteristics (Bar-Tal, 2000a).

[3]Bar-Tal (2000a, 2007a) proposed that the challenges of an intractable conflict lead to the development of an ethos of conflict that consists of the following eight themes of societal beliefs: the justness of the society's goals, security, positive collective self-image, the group's victimization, the illegitimacy of the adversary's goals, patriotism, societal unity, and conceptions of peace.

These beliefs and emotions are disseminated to all members of a society, maintained by societal institutions, transmitted to new generations by socialization processes, and suffused throughout all kinds of cultural productions (Ross, 1998). As a result, they amount to a rigid, change-resistant culture of conflict (e.g., Bar-Tal, 2007b). This cognitive–emotional–cultural system enables members of a society to cope with the challenges and strains of the conflict, but it also perpetuates the conflict, thereby constituting a major obstacle to peacemaking.

Attempts to resolve an intractable conflict require major changes in societal beliefs and collective emotional reactions, which of course cannot be changed overnight. They are familiar, deeply rooted, and held with great confidence, and they have fulfilled many functions for a society during the conflict and have been continuously supported by mass media and other societal institutions (for an analysis of the Jewish society in Israel, see, e.g., Bar-Tal, 2007b). Even when leaders of rival groups seem to resolve a conflict peacefully and have signed a peace agreement, the cultures of conflict may live on in group members' minds and interfere with peaceful relations and reconciliation efforts. Hence, changing collective cognitions and emotions from ones that support conflict to ones that support reconciliation presents one of the most important challenges to anyone who aspires to live in a peaceful world.

The rigidity of cultures of conflict is an example of what Kruglanski (2004) called *cognitive freezing* (see also Kruglanski & Webster, 1996; Kunda, 1990). When freezing has occurred, information is subjected to top-down processing. That is, information that fits the reigning cognitive-emotional structure is encoded and accepted as valid; incongruent information is unattended, rejected, and forgotten, or even when absorbed, is processed in a biased and distorted manner (Bar-Tal, 2007a). According to Kruglanski (2004), cognitive freezing is maintained by "specific needs for closure," which cause group members "to freeze on their prior knowledge if such knowledge was congruent with their needs" (pp. 17–18). Cognitive freezing encourages tunnel vision with respect to a conflict, precluding consideration of ways to resolve it (see Bar-Tal & Halperin, in press, for a more complete analysis of the barriers to peaceful conflict resolution).

To achieve conflict resolution and lasting peace, an alternative repertoire of collective cognitions and emotions must be constructed and disseminated among members of a society. This repertoire should include proposals for conflict resolution that can be accepted by both sides, beliefs that a peaceful agreement can be reached and implemented, a sense of trust in the rival, goals of forming peaceful relations with the rival, and eventually, recognition of the importance of reconciliation and readiness to carry it out (J. Bar-Siman-Tov, 2004; de Rivera, 2008). We realize, of course, that this is bound to be a long, complex, and nonlinear process. Moreover, in most intractable conflicts, the process begins with only a small minority of society's members who have the courage to present new alternatives to the majority—a majority that is likely to react initially with mistrust, hostility, devaluation, and rejection.

According to Lewin's (1947/1976) classic ideas, every process of cognitive change, in individuals and groups, requires *cognitive unfreezing* and destabilizing of the dominant cognitive-emotional structure (see also Kruglanski, 2004). In Figure 22.1, we depict the process of reevaluation and change of the beliefs and emotions that fuel a conflict. In this figure, changes in sociocultural contexts ("stimulating contexts") make salient the potential losses involved in the conflict, increase the accessibility of cognitions and emotions related to these losses, and then cause members of the society, or at least some of them, to entertain fundamental questions and worries about continuing the conflict. These questions can become the most effective force for reevaluating and changing the culture of conflict.

We focus here on the first part of the process—the emergence of beliefs about losses entailed by conflict, beliefs that can bring about the unfreezing and reevaluation of strongly held beliefs. We will sidestep a discussion of changes in sociocultural contexts that increase the accessibility of these beliefs because it would take us beyond the scope of the present chapter. Changing the beliefs and emotions that fuel a conflict depends on processes occurring both within each rival group and between the groups. Here, however, we focus mainly on the realization within a group that perpetuating a conflict entails losses for the group. This realization paves the way for changes in beliefs and emotions related to the conflict, which in turn makes communication and cooperation with the rival more likely.

THE UNFREEZING PROCESS

The most important factor in the unfreezing process is the arousal of motivation to reevaluate long-held beliefs and attitudes, to search for new ideas and information, and to consider the new alternatives. The second stage involves accepting and adopting new beliefs that facilitate peacemaking that eventually become the foundation for a culture of peace.

The unfreezing process usually begins with an appearance of a new idea (or ideas) inconsistent with previously held beliefs, an idea that creates some kind of tension, dissonance, dilemma, or internal conflict, thereby stimulating people to move away from their previous stance and search for new information (e.g., Bartunek, 1993; Kruglanski, 1989). In the cases we are considering here, the new idea, which we call the *instigating belief*, has to contradict the accepted belief that it is necessary to continue the conflict because it, or its imagined outcome, is beneficial, even crucial, for one's group. We propose that the instigating beliefs that motivate people to unfreeze previous beliefs and attitudes require recognition of the incompatibility between a desired

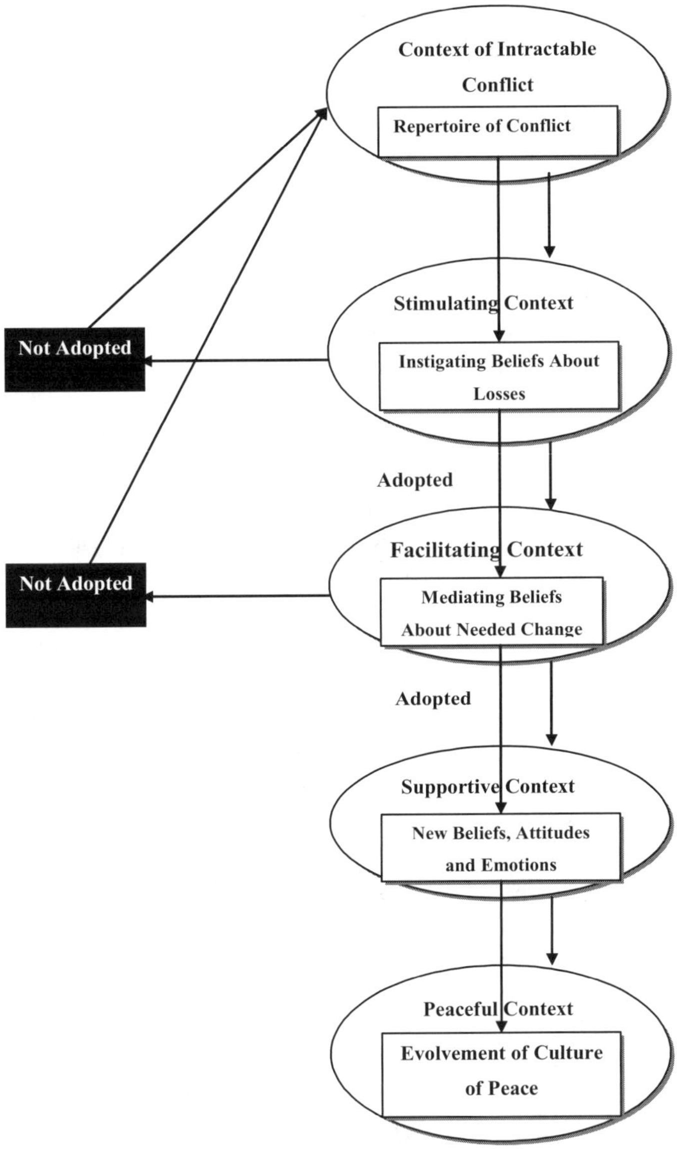

Figure 22.1. Process of overcoming the psychological barriers and constructing the culture of peace.

future, on the one hand, and the emerging future or current state of the society, on the other. In other words, motivation to reevaluate firmly held beliefs and consider alternatives is based on realizing that continuation of the conflict will not lead to a better or desired future but may drastically reduce the chances of the desired future coming about (Bartunek, 1993). Instigating beliefs may appear spontaneously in some group members' minds without any special surrounding circumstances, but usually they arise because of changes in the sociocultural context.

If unfreezing is to occur, forces that push for change (which we call *driving forces*) must be stronger than restraining forces (see Marcus, 2006, for elaboration). One of the most important challenges for anyone attempting to remove or attenuate psychological barriers to peace is to identify both kinds of forces and strengthen the driving forces while weakening the restraining forces. According to Marcus (2006), unfreezing a culture of conflict requires that members of a society have confidence in the inner strength of their society and its ability to cope with expected challenges that the peace process may present. (This is similar to Bandura's, 1997, well-known individual-level concept of self-efficacy.)

Kruglanski and his colleagues (Freund, Kruglanski, & Shpitzajzen, 1985; Kruglanski & Freund, 1983) proposed that two key mechanisms underlie the process of unfreezing. The first is fear of invalidity, defined by Kunda (1990) as *accuracy motivation*. When people are afraid of holding inaccurate beliefs or attitudes and of making a faulty decision (i.e., when they believe they will be held responsible for their decision), they may open their minds, unfreeze previously firm beliefs, process information more thoroughly, and search for more valid information. The second mechanism is recognizing that the current beliefs interfere with the attainment of important goals (Tetlock, Peterson, & Lerner, 1996). Both mechanisms contribute to cognitive unfreezing by emphasizing the costs of holding invalid cognitions or the benefits of cognitive openness (Kruglanski, 2004). Hence, increasing the salience of validity concerns or highlighting the costs of misperceptions or of biased, distorted information processing may foster openness and influence people to consider alternative beliefs about a conflict and new ways to end it (Kruglanski & Webster, 1996).

Another way to encourage unfreezing is related to emotions. In an early protection motivation theory, Rogers (1983) suggested that fear appeals are effective in changing attitudes if they are not overwhelming and they convince people that the negative consequences of holding onto a belief or an associated mode of conduct will be severe. An early meta-analysis of fear studies found that the use of fear appeals was associated with increased persuasion (Boster & Mongeau, 1984). Similarly, according to affective intelligence theory (Marcus & MacKuen, 1993), moderate levels of "surveillance system" emotions, such as fear and anxiety, can move people to reassess their attitudes and search for additional information and new alternatives (Marcus, 2006). Valencia (2008), who examined the effects of various emotions on peace negotiations in the Basque Country (a semiautonomous region of Spain), found that in some cases fear can increase people's support for negotiations with terrorists. Overall, it seems that moderate use of fear of negative consequences might be useful in unfreezing cognitions and emotions that fuel conflicts.

INSTIGATING BELIEFS ABOUT LOSSES

As already mentioned, we suspect that the most effective instigator of an unfreezing process is contemplation of severe losses made likely by continuation of a conflict.[4] This idea is based partly on Kahneman and Tversky's (1979) prospect theory, which has been adapted to apply to conflict situations (e.g., Boettcher, 2004; Geva & Mintz, 1997; Levy, 1997). According to prospect theory, people are more reluctant to lose what they already have than they are motivated to gain what they do not have (Tversky & Kahneman, 1986). In the language of prospect theory, the value function is steeper on the loss side than on the gain side. The theory's claim about the larger impact of imagined losses than of imagined gains has also been part of other theories. One example is conservation of resources theory (Hobfoll, 1989), which states that losing resources through a traumatic event evokes greater distress than an equivalent failure to gain new resources. A similar negativity bias has been noted within the literature on persuasion: Negative events and information tend to be more closely attended, better remembered, and more able to produce attitude change than positive events and information (for a review, see Cacioppo & Berntson, 1994).

One way to emphasize the potential losses associated with continuing a conflict and to reduce the emphasis on losses associated with a peaceful settlement is to reframe the reference point. Prospect theory proposes that people react more strongly to changes in assets than to net asset levels; that is, they react to gains and losses from a reference point rather than to the absolute values of gains or losses (e.g., Kahneman & Tversky, 1979; Tversky & Kahneman, 1986). In most cases, the reference point is the status quo, but in some situations it can be a person's "aspiration level" (Payne, Laughhunn, & Crum, 1981) or a desired goal (Heath, Larrick, & Wu, 1999). Very often, members of societies involved in a conflict are socialized to believe in the feasibility of future gains from the conflict or even the victory of their group over the rival (Bar-Tal, 2007a). The alternative possibility of paying a high price for continuing the conflict or being defeated is often ignored. As a result, when the compromises required by a peaceful settlement of the conflict are compared with the society's aspirations, or even with the status-quo (mostly for the stronger group), they are perceived as requiring an enormous loss.

To unfreeze the conflicting parties' cultures of conflict, negotiators or mediators should encourage new reference points. The potential losses of continuing the conflict should be presented very concretely, as relevant to

[4]The motivation to reevaluate attitudes and behavior within the context of a conflict does not always stem from gain–loss considerations. There are members in every society who judge the situation from a moral perspective. Yet, according to Kohlberg's (1984) theory of moral development, most people do not reach the highest stages of moral development, so the subgroup that makes judgments based on a high level of moral development is a small minority.

individual members of a society and to their collective well-being, as blocking the satisfaction of basic needs and as having a high probability of occurring. When compared with the new reference point, the losses entailed by peaceful compromise may seem acceptable. Because both societies have to give up some of their aspirations and dreams to achieve an end to conflict, the principles involved in selecting instigating beliefs (i.e., beliefs that can unfreeze the culture of conflict) are similar for both sides, although the content of the beliefs may differ, especially if the two societies are unequal in certain respects (see chap. 10, this volume).

POTENTIAL FUTURE LOSSES

According to prospect theory, thinking about losses entailed or threatened if the conflict is continued is likely to be more effective in unfreezing beliefs than thinking about the benefits of peace. People find it difficult to imagine peace after living through years of brutal conflict; the vision of peace is clouded by ambiguity, uncertainty, and perceived risk (Mitzen, 2006). Hence, instead of highlighting the advantages of peace, it may be necessary to arouse fear by pointing out that the losses incurred if the conflict continues would be greater than the losses incurred by accepting a peaceful solution. This is especially important for the stronger participant in the conflict because that side may have gained a great deal from years of struggle and may not want to give any of it up to attain peace.[5]

In many cases, the conflict has continued because at least one side believes that "time is on our side" and eventually "we will win or at least improve our gains from a settlement." Therefore, it is important for negotiators to stress that "time is not on your side" and the future may bring greater costs rather than benefits. For the stronger party in the conflict, beliefs such as "We don't have the resources to continue the conflict" or "We may pay a heavy price if the conflict continues" can change the reference point for comparing expected losses from peace with expected losses from continued conflict or defeat.

This movement of the reference point and the subsequent cognitive unfreezing process were illustrated in the peacemaking processes of Northern Ireland, South Africa, and the Middle East. With reference to Northern Ireland, Mac Ginty and Darby (2002) argued that in the early 1990s, people on the unionist side of the conflict began to expect increased losses if they refused to negotiate, and the unionist leaders decided to enter negotiations to

[5]The lion's share of our discussion focuses on the beliefs of members of the more powerful side of a conflict, because in most cases the radical reevaluations of alternatives, as well as most compromises, are required from the side that holds most of the tangible and intangible resources. The side that has military, economic, and political advantages has more to lose by ending the conflict.

gain greater influence over a possible agreement. Mac Ginty and Darby quoted a statement by a senior Orangeman that, according to them, reflected a view shared by many unionists: "Every time something comes along it is worse than what came before" (p. 23). Concerning the South African conflict, Mufson (1991) pointed out that when President F. W. de Klerk and his associates realized that "White South Africans' bargaining position would only grow weaker with time" (p. 124), they opened negotiations and made every effort to move as quickly as possible toward an agreement.

In an attempt to mobilize public support for the Israeli–Palestinian peacemaking process, Ehud Olmert, Israel's Prime Minister, said, "If the day comes when the two-state solution collapses and we face a South African–style struggle for equal voting rights . . . then, as soon as that happens, the state of Israel is finished" (Ben, Landau, Ravid, & Rosner, 2007, para. 1). On another occasion he said,

> Israel needs to internalize that even its supportive friends on the international stage conceive of the country's future on the basis of the 1967 borders and with Jerusalem divided. . . . If Israel will have to deal with a reality of one state for two peoples . . . [it] could bring about the end of the existence of Israel as a Jewish state. That is a danger one cannot deny; it exists, and is even realistic. (Keinon & Horovitz, 2008, paras. 1 & 4)

Recently this line of thinking was tested experimentally with the Israeli Jewish population. The results clearly showed that exposure to information about losses inherent to the conflict induces a higher willingness to acquire new information about possible solutions to the conflict, a higher willingness to reevaluate current positions about it, and more support for compromises than exposure to neutral information or to information about possible gains derived from a peace agreement (Gayer, Tal, Halperin, & Bar-Tal, 2008).

Similar, although not identical, beliefs about future losses may motivate reevaluation of existing beliefs on the weaker side of a conflict, which is militarily, economically, and politically at a disadvantage. For members of the less advantaged society, cognitive unfreezing can be motivated by a wish to end the losses and suffering. Alternatively, unfreezing can result from believing that in the current stage of the conflict, the gains of a near-term peace agreement are larger than the gains possibly available in the future, after the conflict has continued to deplete resources.

This kind of reasoning was evident in a speech by Mahmoud Abbas, president of the Palestinian National Authority, during the Annapolis Conference attended by Palestinian and Israeli leaders in November 2007. Abbas stressed that what Palestinians could get at that time was better than what they could expect to get if the peace process were delayed: "The possibilities offered by today's conference must not be wasted. This window of opportunity might never open again . . . we must not lose this opportunity that might never be repeated" (para. 8). He pointed to the necessity of achieving peace so as to end the Palestinians' suffering:

> This is how we will end occupation and long years of suffering for our refugees . . . to Palestinian mothers who are awaiting the return of their jailed sons; to the children who are dreaming of a new life and a prosperous and more peaceful future; to our brave prisoners and to all of my sons and daughters wherever you are: Have faith in tomorrow and the future because an independent Palestine is coming. (Abbas, 2007, paras. 17 & 27)

COLLATERAL THREATS AND UNACHIEVED GOALS

Another way to unfreeze a culture of conflict is to emphasize imminent threats to society that although unrelated to the conflict itself, may result from continuing the conflict. This places the conflict into a broader perspective and highlights possible collateral damage from the conflict, such as depletion of limited resources that could be used to meet other important goals. An example of such a collateral threat occurred in South Africa. According to Sisk (1989), the rise in the late 1980s of a reactionary right-wing party, the Conservative Party, accelerated the peace process because it forced Whites in general and members of the governing National Party to reassess their views of the conflict and develop an alternative perspective on the apartheid regime. The rise of the new party caused National Party leaders to realize that if they did not act immediately they might lose their long-standing control of the government. This new threat instigated a notable unfreezing of the apartheid policy toward Black South Africans.

In the case of the Israeli–Palestinian conflict, then Israeli Prime Minister Ehud Barak used consideration of emerging global threats to convince Israelis of the urgency of achieving a peace agreement, even if they had to make huge compromises. Barak frequently argued that international terrorism, the growth of Islamic fundamentalism, and the possible acquisition of nuclear weapons by Islamic countries outweighed any potential Israeli achievements in future negotiations with the Palestinians (Sher, 2001).

PAST AND PRESENT LOSSES

Another method of unfreezing a culture of conflict is to focus on past losses, emphasizing the enormous price that a society involved in the conflict has paid over the years. Often the cost includes an enormous number of deaths—the loss of untold community and family members who can never be brought back to life, a loss for which there is no adequate compensation.

The cost may also be tallied in terms of huge financial investments that have deprived the society of many important contributions to the general welfare (e.g., Swirski, 2005). This may lead to public discussion of how resources invested in the conflict (human, financial, societal, and psychological) could have been invested differently. Such a discussion can cause people to view the continuing conflict as a vain and tragic waste. By themselves, these discussions and debates may not convince people that peace is desirable, but they may motivate them to unfreeze existing beliefs and begin to reevaluate their investments in the conflict.

Discussions of past losses seem to have been among the most important factors in changing the American public's opinions about the war in Vietnam (Burstein & Freudenburg, 1978). The main theme of antiwar messages by both demonstrators and antiwar politicians was the huge cost of the war, whether calculated in terms of lost lives or lost financial resources (Small, 1987). Similar, though not identical, issues are being raised in the United States by critics of the war in Iraq. At the time of this writing, it is impossible to be certain of the outcome of these discussions, but certainly there has been a notable shift in American public opinion. Although the wars in Vietnam and Iraq may not meet the criteria for "intractable conflicts," we use them as examples because they illustrate how emphasizing past and continuing costs can destabilize war-related public opinion.

AWARENESS OF LOSSES ATTRIBUTABLE TO CLOSEDMINDEDNESS

For both sides of a conflict, becoming aware of the rigidity of one's own beliefs about a conflict may initiate an unfreezing process. That is, once the members of a society (or at least some of them) begin to recognize their society's closedmindedness, they may push their fellow citizens to examine alternatives. Frequently this awareness evolves as a consequence of realizing that a war is unnecessary or recognizing a missed opportunity for peace. These are situations in which people begin to acknowledge the costs they have incurred by failing to consider alternatives. Opinion leaders begin to dare to say, "This conflict is unjustified" or "Perhaps we are contributing unreasonably to the continuation of this costly conflict" or "Maybe the other side also has a reasonable case." This was the stance taken by Senator Barack Obama in the recent American presidential campaign.

Although beliefs about losses and recognition of closedmindedness sometimes emerge from enlightened reflection by a minority of a society's members, in most cases they are due to a change in the context of the conflict as perceived by most members of society. This change may be a result of fatigue (as when Prime Minister Yitzhak Rabin said, appearing with then Palestinian leader Yassar Arafat, following peace negotiations in Washington, DC,

"Enough of war"), an increase in human and property losses, continuing violence and stalemated negotiations, or an absence of effective governance. It may be a matter of a sudden, very violent outbreak of full-scale war, a dramatic peace gesture, or a change in the international context. It may come from conciliatory or trust-building actions by the rival or from a change in the rival's leadership that alters appraisals of the rival's character, goals, or intentions. The contextual change that begins an unfreezing process may not be directly related to the conflict (recession, widespread hunger or disease, the appearance on the scene of an even more threatening enemy), but it can cause people to reassess the conflict.

Sometimes a third party may change the conflict context by an intervention. That intervention can take various forms, such as mediation, bombing, sending troops, or even economic boycott. In some cases, the tide-changing event is the arrival of new leaders, a change in the relative dominance of a particular political party, or a major generational change in perspectives or values. Finally, more global geopolitical processes, such as the collapse of a superpower or a change in the global economy, can trigger reappraisals that lead to a major unfreezing of the culture of conflict. Often, the change process requires what we call a *mediating belief* about the need for change. In the next section, we discuss this important factor in the peacemaking process.

MEDIATING BELIEFS ON THE ROAD TO AN ETHOS OF PEACE

Achieving an ethos of peace may take many years. In the absence of actual peace and reconciliation, the great challenge is to lead a population to the realization that an alternative to the present unsatisfactory situation is badly needed and that previously held beliefs and expectations are invalid. This mediating stage in dissonance arousal and desire for dissonance resolution is an important step on the way to a peaceful solution to a long-standing conflict. It is quite different from the previously reigning culture of conflict, which made victory seem essential and peacemaking seem unthinkable. Once it becomes thinkable, minds are open to evaluate possible alternative strategies.

Mediating beliefs are usually stated in the form of arguments: "We absolutely must change strategy or we are going to suffer further losses;" "Some kind of change is inevitable"; "We have been going down a self-destructive path; we must alter our goals and strategies"; "The proposed change is clearly in the national interest; it is necessary for national security" (Y. Bar-Siman-Tov, 1996). These inducements open a discussion of alternatives and thereby deepen the process of unfreezing that is begun by instigating beliefs.

To be effective in moving the conflict toward resolution, the mediating beliefs must introduce new strategic possibilities around which a new consensus can be built. This process works best when it is coordinated by leaders on both sides of the conflict. They need to take successive steps to show the other side that new beliefs are emerging. This can be done by reciprocal acts of goodwill, meetings between representatives of the two groups, initiation of cooperative projects, encouraging peace education, and so on (Bar-Tal, 2008).

The full establishment of an ethos of peace and an eventual culture of peace requires complete cessation of violence, putting into place institutionalized mechanisms for resolving disagreements, investing in large-scale peace education, building cooperative relations in many domains of life (education, athletics, joint business ventures, and so on), and a continuing series of reciprocal acts of friendship that promote trust and sensitivity to both sides' needs.

CONCLUDING COMMENTS

We conclude with a brief description of the cultural repertoire that is needed to solidify peace. Achievement of reconciliation requires changes in at least five kinds of societal beliefs that were formed during the conflict (Bar-Tal, 2000b; Bar-Tal & Bennink, 2004). First, the goals of the society with respect to the conflict (societal beliefs about the group's goals) must be revised. In particular, societal beliefs about the justness of the goals that underlie the conflict must be changed (e.g., Bloomfield, Barnes, & Huyse, 2003). A new set of goals and beliefs about goals is necessary if peace is to be attained. Second, the image of the rival group (societal beliefs about the rival group) must be changed in ways that legitimize, personalize, differentiate, and equalize the rival (e.g., Bar-Tal & Teichman, 2005; Theidon, 2006). Third, the peace process needs to facilitate new beliefs about the formal relationship with the adversary (societal beliefs about the relationship with the past rival) that emphasize cooperation and friendship (e.g., Gardner Feldman, 1999). In other words, the deeply rooted zero-sum perception of the conflict has to be replaced with a mixed-motives approach, which acknowledges the possibility of win-win and loss-loss situations.

Fourth, a successful peace process requires a change in collective memories of the conflict (societal beliefs about the history of the conflict). An example is the way in which former long-standing enemies such as the British and the French or the Germans and the French can eventually have highly cooperative relations. The narratives on both sides need to be revised and integrated, a process made easier as one generation gives way to another (e.g., Borer, 2006; Nets-Zehngut, 2006; Rotberg, 2006; Salomon, 2004). Fifth, a peace process requires new beliefs about the multidimensional nature of peace (societal beliefs about peace), the conditions necessary for its achievement (e.g., negotiations, compromises), the real benefits and costs of achieving peace, the meaning of living in peace, and the conditions for building and maintaining a culture of peace.

The peace process must also include the creation of positive emotions on both sides. Fear, anger, and hatred must be largely replaced at least by hope, if not by actual optimism about the future (e.g., Averill, Catlin, & Chon, 1990; Bar-Tal, Halperin, & de Rivera, 2007; Jarymowicz & Bar-Tal, 2006). The ethos of peace requires that the fundamental needs of group members on both sides are met. People on both sides need to have confidence that their basic needs for physical and economic security are met; they also need a new positive social identity—one no longer based on stalwart opposition to the former rival. The new ethos must include a new ideology that offers more rewarding, moral, constructive beliefs than the previous ethos. As with the ethos of conflict, however, the ethos of peace may benefit from occasional fear appeals, but now these appeals should focus on the dangers inherent in sliding back toward conflict.

Obviously, making peace is not easy. Despite the strong evidence in other chapters in this volume concerning the human capacity for empathy and prosocial behavior, this capacity has been largely overridden all through human history by fear, conflict, hatred, and violence. Human good cannot flourish in a context of large-scale intergroup aggression and violence. Group behavior operates by different principles than does individual behavior, and it is easier to rally group members for conflict and war than for peace. It will take considerable insight and perseverance to build the conditions necessary for peace, but surely there is no better use of human intelligence and energy.

REFERENCES

Abbas, M. (2007, November 27). *Speech by President Mahmoud Abbas at Annapolis Conference*. Retrieved May 12, 2009, from http://imeu.net/news/article007146.shtml

Averill, J. R., Catlin, G., & Chon, K. K. (1990). *Rules of hope*. New York: Springer-Verlag.

Bandura, A. (1997). *Self-efficacy: The exercise of control*. New York: W. H. Freeman.

Bar-Siman-Tov, Y. (1996). *From war to peace: The complexity of decision-making—The Israeli case* (Research Report No. 6). Tel-Aviv, Israel: T. Steinmetz Center for Peace Research. (In Hebrew)

Bar-Siman-Tov, J. (Ed.). (2004). *From conflict resolution to reconciliation*. Oxford, England: Oxford University Press.

Bar-Tal, D. (1998). Societal beliefs in times of intractable conflict: The Israeli case. *International Journal of Conflict Management, 9*, 22–50.

Bar-Tal, D. (2000a). *Shared beliefs in a society: Social psychological analysis*. Thousand Oaks, CA: Sage.

Bar-Tal, D. (2000b). From intractable conflict through conflict resolution to reconciliation: Psychological analysis. *Political Psychology, 21*, 351–365.

Bar-Tal, D. (2001). Why does fear override hope in societies engulfed by intractable conflict, as it does in the Israeli society? *Political Psychology*, *22*, 601–627.

Bar-Tal, D. (2007a). Sociopsychological foundations of intractable conflicts. *American Behavioral Scientist*, *50*, 1430–1453.

Bar-Tal, D. (2007b). *Living with the conflict: Socio-psychological analysis of the Israeli-Jewish society*. Jerusalem: Carmel. (In Hebrew)

Bar-Tal, D. (2008). Reconciliation as a foundation of culture of peace. In J. de Rivera (Ed.), *Handbook on building cultures for peace* (363–377). New York: Springer.

Bar-Tal, D., & Bennink, G. H. (2004). The nature of reconciliation as an outcome and as a process. In Y. Bar-Siman-Tov (Ed.), *From conflict resolution to reconciliation* (pp. 11–38). Oxford, England: Oxford University Press.

Bar-Tal, D., & Halperin, E. (in press). Socio-psychological barriers to conflict resolution. In D. Bar-Tal (Ed.), *Intergroup conflicts and their resolution: Social psychological perspective*. New York: Psychology Press.

Bar-Tal, D., Halperin, E., & de Rivera, J. (2007). Collective emotions in conflict situations: Societal implications. *Journal of Social Issues*, *63*, 441–460.

Bar-Tal, D., & Salomon, G. (2006). Israeli-Jewish narratives of the Israeli-Palestinian conflict: Evolution, contents, functions, and consequences. In R. I. Rotberg (Ed.), *Israeli and Palestinian narratives of conflict: History's double helix* (pp. 19–46). Bloomington, IN: Indiana University Press.

Bar-Tal, D., & Teichman, Y. (2005). *Stereotypes and prejudice in conflict: Representation of Arabs in Israeli Jewish society*. Cambridge, England: Cambridge University Press.

Bartunek, J. M. (1993). The multiple cognitions and conflicts associated with second order organizational change. In J. K. Murnighan (Ed.), *Social psychology in organizations: Advances in theory and research* (pp. 322–349). Englewood Cliffs, NJ: Prentice Hall.

Ben, A., Landau, D., Ravid, B., & Rosner, S. (2007, November 29). Olmert to Haaretz: Two state solution, or Israel is done for. Retrieved May 4, 2009, from http://www.haaretz.com/hasen/spages/929439.html

Bloomfield, D., Barnes, T., & Huyse, L. (Eds.). (2003). *Reconciliation after violent conflict: A handbook*. Stockholm: International IDEA.

Boettcher, W. A. (2004). The prospects for prospect theory: An empirical evaluation of international relations applications of framing and loss aversion. *Political Psychology*, *25*, 331–362.

Borer, A. T. (2006). *Telling the truth: Truth telling and peace building in post conflict societies*. Notre Dame, IN: University of Notre Dame Press.

Boster, F. J., & Mongeau, P. (1984). Fear-arousing persuasive messages. In R. N. Bostrom (Ed.), *Communication yearbook* (Vol. 8, pp. 330–375). Beverly Hills, CA: Sage.

Burstein, P., & Freudenburg, W. (1978). Changing public policy: The impact of public opinion, antiwar demonstrations, and war costs on Senate voting on Vietnam War motions. *American Journal of Sociology*, 84, 99–122.

Cacioppo, J. T., & Berntson, G. G. (1994). Relationship between attitudes and evaluative space. A critical review, with emphasis on the separability of positive and negative substrates. *Psychological Bulletin, 115*, 401–423.

Cairns, E., & Roe, M. D. (Ed.). (2003). *The role of memory in ethnic conflict*. New York: Palgrave Macmillan.

de Rivera, J. (Ed.). (2008). *Handbook on building cultures for peace*. New York: Springer.

de Rivera, J., & Paez, D. (Eds.). (2007). Emotional climate, human security, and culture of peace [Entire issue]. *Journal of Social Issues, 63*(2), 233–253.

Freund, T., Kruglanski, A.W., & Shpitzajzen, A. (1985). The freezing and unfreezing of impressional primacy: Effects of the need for structure and the fear of invalidity. *Personality and Social Psychology Bulletin, 11*, 479–487.

Gardner Feldman, L. (1999). The principle and practice of "reconciliation" in German foreign policy: Relations with France, Israel, Poland, and the Czech Republic. *International Affairs, 75*, 333–356.

Gayer, C., Tal, S., Halperin, E., & Bar-Tal, D. (2008). *Overcoming psychological barriers to peaceful conflict resolution: The role of arguments about losses*. Manuscript submitted for publication.

Geva, N., & Mintz, A. (Eds.). (1997). *Decision-making on war and peace: The cognitive-rational debate*. Boulder, CO: Lynne Rienner.

Halperin, E. (2008). Group-based hatred in intractable conflict in Israel. *Journal of Conflict Resolution, 52*, 713–736.

Heath, C., Larrick, R. P., & Wu, G. (1999). Goals as reference points. *Cognitive Psychology, 38*, 79–109.

Hobfoll, S. E. (1989). Conservation of resources: A new attempt at conceptualizing stress. *American Psychologist, 44*, 513–524.

Jarymowicz, M., & Bar-Tal, D. (2006). The dominance of fear over hope in the life of individuals and collectives. *European Journal of Social Psychology, 36*, 367–392.

Kahneman, D., & Tversky, A. (1979). Prospect theory: An analysis of decision under risk. *Econometrica, 47*, 263–291.

Keinon, H., & Horovitz, D. (2008, January 1). Olmert says Israel must internalize divided Jerusalem. *Jerusalem Post*, p. 1.

Kohlberg, L. (1984). *Essays on moral development: Vol. II. The psychology of moral development*. San Francisco: Harper & Row.

Kruglanski, A. W. (1989). *Lay epistemics and human knowledge: Cognitive and motivational bases*. New York: Plenum.

Kruglanski, A. W. (2004). *The psychology of closed mindedness*. New York: Psychology Press.

Kruglanski, A. W., & Freund, T. (1983). The freezing and unfreezing of lay-inferences: Effects on impressional primacy, ethnic stereotyping, and numerical anchoring. *Journal of Experimental Social Psychology, 19*, 448–468.

Kruglanski, A. W., & Webster, D. M. (1996). Motivated closing of the mind: "Seizing" and "freezing." *Psychological Review, 103*, 263–283.

Kunda, Z. (1990). The case for motivated reasoning. *Psychological Bulletin, 108*, 480–498.

Levy, J. S. (1997). Prospect theory, rational choice, and international relations. *International Studies Quarterly, 41*, 87–112.

Lewin, K. (1947/1976). Frontiers in group dynamics. In D. Cartwright (Ed.), *Field theory in social science: Selected theoretical papers by Kurt Lewin*. Chicago: University of Chicago Press.

Mac Ginty, R., & Darby, J. (2002). *Guns and government: The management of the Northern Ireland peace process*. Hampshire, England: Palgrave.

Marcus, E. (2006). Change and conflict: Motivation, resistance, and commitment. In M. Deutsch., P, T. Coleman, & E. C. Marcus (Eds.), *The handbook of conflict resolution* (pp. 436–454). San Francisco: Jossey-Bass.

Marcus, G. E., & Mackuen, M. B. (1993). Anxiety, enthusiasm, and the vote: The emotional underpinnings of learning and involvement during presidential campaigns. *American Political Science Review, 87*, 672–685.

Mitzen, J. (2006). Ontological security in world politics: State identity and the security dilemma. *European Journal of International Relations, 12*, 341–370.

Mufson, S. (1991). South Africa 1990. *Foreign Affairs, 70*, 120–141.

Nets-Zehngut, R. (2006). Refugee tales: 1948 considered—A historical analysis of Israeli attitudes towards the creation of Palestinian refugees in 1948. *Yale Israel Journal, 10*, 12–26.

Payne, J. W., Laughhunn, D. J., & Crum, R. (1981). Further tests of aspiration level effects in risky choice. *Management Science, 27*, 953–958.

Petersen, R. G. (2002). *Understanding ethnic violence: Fear, hatred, and resentment in twentieth-century Eastern Europe*. Cambridge, England: Cambridge University Press.

Rogers, R. W. (1983). Cognitive and physiological processes in fear appeals and attitude change: A revised theory of protection motivation. In J. T. Cacioppo & R. E. Petty (Eds.), *Social psychophysiology: A sourcebook* (pp. 153–176). New York: Guilford Press.

Ross, M. H. (1998). The cultural dynamics of ethnic conflict. In D. Jacquin, A. Oros, & M. Verweij (Eds.), *Culture in world politics* (pp. 156–186). Houndmills, NJ: Macmillan.

Rotberg, R. I. (Ed.). (2006). *Israeli and Palestinian narratives of conflict: History's double helix*. Bloomington: Indiana University Press.

Salomon, G. (2004). A narrative-based view of coexistence education. *Journal of Social Issues, 60*, 273–287.

Sher, G. (2001). *Just beyond reach: The Israeli-Palestinian peace negotiations 1999-2001*. Tel Aviv, Israel: Miskal-Yediot Ahronot Books and Chemed Books. (In Hebrew)

Sisk, T. D. (1989). White politics in South-Africa: Polarization under pressure. *Africa Today: 1st Quarter, 36*, 29–39.

Small, M. (1987). Influencing the decision makers: The Vietnam experience. *Journal of Peace Research, 24*, 185–198.

Swirski, S. (2005). *The price of occupation*. Tel Aviv, Israel: MAPA. (In Hebrew)

Tetlock, P. E., Peterson, R. S., & Lerner, J. S. (1996). Revising the value pluralism model: Incorporating social content and context postulates. In C. Seligman, J. M. Olson, & M. P. Zanna (Eds.), *Values: Eighth Annual Ontario Symposium on Personality and Social Psychology*. Hillsdale, NJ: Erlbaum.

Tversky, A., & Kahneman, D. (1986). Rational choice and the framing of decisions. *Journal of Business*, 59, S251–0S278.

Valencia, J. (2008). *Emotional responses and attitudes to the peace talks with E.T.A.* Unpublished manuscript.

Wertsch, J. V. (2002). *Voices of collective remembering*. Cambridge, England: Cambridge University Press.

INDEX

ABOUT THE EDITORS

Mario Mikulincer, PhD, is professor of psychology and dean of the New School of Psychology at the Interdisciplinary Center (IDC) Herzliya, Israel. He has published three books—*Human Helplessness: A Coping Perspective; Dynamics of Romantic Love: Attachment, Caregiving, and Sex*; and *Attachment in Adulthood: Structure, Dynamics, and Change*—and over 280 scholarly journal articles and book chapters. Dr. Mikulincer's main research interests are attachment theory, terror management theory, personality processes in interpersonal relationships, coping with stress and trauma, grief-related processes, and prosocial motives and behavior. He is a member of the editorial boards of several scientific journals, including the *Journal of Personality and Social Psychology, Psychological Inquiry*, and *Personality and Social Psychology review*, and has served as associate editor of two journals, the *Journal of Personality and Social Psychology* and *Personal Relationships*. Recently, he was elected to serve as chief editor of the *Journal of Social and Personal Relationships*. He is a fellow of the Society for Personality and Social Psychology and the Association for Psychological Sciences. He received the EMET Prize in Social Science for his contributions to psychology and the Berscheid–Hatfield Award for Distinguished Mid-Career Achievement from the International Association for Relationship Research.

Phillip R. Shaver, PhD, a social and personality psychologist, is Distinguished Professor of Psychology at the University of California, Davis. Before moving there, he served on the faculties of Columbia University, New York University, University of Denver, and State University of New York at Buffalo. He has coauthored and coedited numerous books, including *In Search of Intimacy; Measures of Personality and Social Psychological Attitudes; Measures of Political Attitudes; Handbook of Attachment: Theory, Research, and Clinical Applications*, and *Attachment in Adulthood: Structure, Dynamics, and Change*, and has published over 200 scholarly journal articles and book chapters. Dr. Shaver's research focuses on attachment, human motivation and emotion, close relationships, personality development, and the effects of meditation on behavior and the brain. He is a member of the editorial boards of *Attachment and Human Development*, *Personal Relationships*, the *Journal of Personality and Social Psychology*, and *Emotion*, and has served on grant review panels for the National Institutes of Health and the National Science Foundation. He has been executive officer of the Society of Experimental Social Psychology and is a fellow of both the American Psychological Association and the Association for Psychological Science. Dr. Shaver received a Distinguished Career Award from the International Association for Relationship Research and has served as president of that organization.